Contemporary Issues in Management Accounting

Contemporary Issues in Management Accounting

Edited by

ALNOOR BHIMANI

OXFORD
UNIVERSITY PRESS

OXFORD
UNIVERSITY PRESS

Great Clarendon Street, Oxford OX2 6DP

Oxford University Press is a department of the University of Oxford.
It furthers the University's objective of excellence in research, scholarship,
and education by publishing worldwide in

Oxford New York

Auckland Cape Town Dar es Salaam Hong Kong Karachi
Kuala Lumpur Madrid Melbourne Mexico City Nairobi
New Delhi Shanghai Taipei Toronto

With offices in

Argentina Austria Brazil Chile Czech Republic France Greece
Guatemala Hungary Italy Japan Poland Portugal Singapore
South Korea Switzerland Thailand Turkey Ukraine Vietnam

Oxford is a registered trade mark of Oxford University Press
in the UK and in certain other countries

Published in the United States
by Oxford University Press Inc., New York

British Library Cataloguing in Publication Data
Data available

Library of Congress Cataloguing in Publication Data
Data available

Typeset by SPI Publisher Services, Pondicherry, India
Printed in Great Britain
on acid-free paper by
Antony Rowe Ltd., Chippenham, Wiltshire

ISBN 0–19–928335–4   978–0–19–928335–4
ISBN 0–19–928336–2 (Pbk.)   978–0–19–928336–1 (Pbk.)
1 3 5 7 9 10 8 6 4 2

◻ FOREWORD

Michael Bromwich is an exemplar of all that is good about the British tradition of academic accounting. Serious in intent, he has striven both to illuminate practice and to provide ways of improving it. Although always appealing to his economic understandings, he has been open to a wide variety of other ideas, recognizing their intellectual strengths and capabilities rather than making artificial distinctions between what is acceptable and what is not. He also has contributed widely to the accounting literature, taking forward the British tradition of economic theorizing in financial accounting as well as being a constant source of creative thinking in the management accounting field. Michael has also contributed in a number of different institutional arenas: the academic, of course, but also those of the profession and the wider public sphere. Ever helpful to regulators, the senior civil service, and international agencies, Michael Bromwich is respected for the ways in which he can combine conceptual understandings with pragmatic insights. He has been sought out to provide that extra element of conceptual clarity for the most complex of practical accounting endeavours.

No doubt such abilities reflect Michael's early grounding in both the practice of account-ing and its economic theorization, the former at Ford and the latter initially at the London School of Economics and thereafter as a lifetime endeavour. But personal though his achievements may be, they are also reflective of a wider tradition of significant involvement in the practical sphere by senior British accounting academics.

For we must remember that it was Professor Edward Stamp who was one of the first to call the British audit profession to account with his questioning of 'who shall audit the auditors?' The subsequent institutional response has most likely gained as much from the likes of Professors Harold Edey, Bryan Carsberg, Ken Peasnell, Geoffrey Whittington, and David Tweedie as it has from the *éminence grise* of the profession itself. And even in auditing, significant roles have been played by Professors Peter Bird, David Flint, and Peter Moizer amongst others. Indeed it is possible to argue that the British academic accounting profes-soriate has played an extremely important role in mediating between the profession and the state, both bringing knowledge to bear on policy issues and providing a cadre of people who can operate effectively in this policy sphere.

Michael Bromwich has certainly contributed in this way, advising accounting and com-petition regulators on complex issues and providing his own intellectual authority to the office of President of the Chartered Institute of Management Accountants.

One senses, however, that the British academic accounting community may be less able to fulfil these roles in the coming years. In part this reflects a more general decline in the academic world as falling relative salaries and status have reduced the intake of talented academic entrepreneurs. But I also think it reflects the cumulative impact of regulatory and careerist pressures in the academic world itself. With government agencies pressing for ever more standardized and conventional research and with increasingly instrumental careerist

behaviour by academics, there are fewer incentives to bridge the academic and practical spheres. No doubt this is also exaggerated by an increasingly less curious professional world. The intellectually curious Technical Partners of the past have been replaced by more market orientated purveyors of accounting solutions. Accountancy consultancies are much more interested in simple marketable solutions than more sophisticated insights into the complexity of the issues at stake.

Although there is more and more talk of the need for relevance and application, the pressures at play are more likely to push in the opposite direction. Rather than building on a strong tradition of really useful relationships between the practical and academic spheres in accounting, I sense that the two worlds have less and less to do with one another.

It is therefore ever more important to reflect on the contributions which Michael Bromwich has made. He played an important role in the diffusion of modern practices of capital investment appraisal in the United Kingdom. He has been constantly open to the insights which advances in economic theory can provide into the accounting art, in many areas pushing at the frontiers of international knowledge in his own quiet way. In the area of costing, Michael has undoubtedly deepened our understandings of both conceptual and practical issues, in recent years providing a voice of reason amidst all the consultancy excitement of seemingly new ways of costing the business world. He has played a similar role in the area of accounting standard setting, both taking forward the British tradition of the economic analysis of financial accounting and, of possibly greater significance, providing some very original analyses of the possibilities for meaningful accounting standardization. With an agenda as rich as this, it is all the more praiseworthy that Michael maintained his dialogues with both the academic and the practitioner communities. But that he did.

Those who know Michael Bromwich are not surprised by his many involvements, however. Constantly striving, always curious and ever personable, he has developed a pattern of interests, involvements, and friendships that have sustained his very effective interventions in many institutional and intellectual spheres. It is indeed fitting that so many of his friends and colleagues contribute to this volume to recognize Michael's contributions to academic accounting. I am honoured to join them.

Anthony G. Hopwood
University of Oxford
December 2005

☐ PREFACE

A multitude of forces shape management accounting. From an organizational perspective, decision-makers and other users of accounting information often perceive changes in their information needs. Consequently, providers of accounting information within organizations respond to many of these desired changes by redesigning management accounting systems and restructuring their output. The impetus for change may also originate from outside the organization. Many scholars, consultants, and commentators on management accounting are purveyors of ideas about what accounting should be. In response, users of accounting information, management accounting professionals, and system designers may seek to alter the information provided within their organizations to align with such ideals. In this sense, internal accounting changes may be driven by demand-level needs as well as supply-side influences. Moreover, forces reflecting broader changes both in structures and processes in businesses, organizations, and society and in contemporary ideas and discourses may originate from within as well as from outside the organization and reshape the nature of management accounting.

In the recent past, management accounting has not only seen changes within existing domains of the field but has also witnessed extensions outside its established realms of activity. Wider systemic transformations including changes in political regimes, novel conceptions of management controls, the impact of globalizing forces on commercial affairs, shifts in notions of effective knowledge management, governance, and ethics, and technological advances, including the rise of broadband, have all impacted management accounting endeavours. The field is today, as fast-changing as it has ever been. This book captures key facets of current thoughts, concerns, and issues in management accounting.

The book consists of eighteen chapters written by distinguished scholars in the field. The topic areas covered in some chapters reflect established management accounting topics such as budgeting and responsibility accounting, contract theory analysis, contingency frameworks, performance measurement systems, and strategic cost management, which are considered from the perspective of changing concerns facing modern organizations and present-day management thought as well as in the light of some of their historical dimensions. Other chapters deal with newly emerging concerns in management accounting, including network relations, digitization, integrated cost management systems, knowledge management pursuits, and environmental management accounting. Each chapter encompasses discussions of basic premises complemented by insights from modern-day practice, research, and thought. This approach makes the book particularly suitable for students in academic as well as executive-oriented courses in management accounting. It also provides an extensive corpus of discussions that will inform those in practice. Readers interested in gaining direct insights into specialized management accounting areas will find this book to be an especially valuable reference source.

Established fields cannot grow in the absence of committed figureheads who tirelessly contribute to their development. One individual who has contributed immensely to management accounting thought and practice over the course of more than four decades is Michael Bromwich. Bromwich, who is about to retire as CIMA Professor of Accounting and Financial Management at London School of Economics (LSE), has published over eighty papers and articles and some fifteen books and monographs. His primary contribution as a scholar has been his ability to apply economic theory to problems of accounting practice, thereby informing our understanding of the field. He wrote *The Economics of Capital Budgeting* (Penguin, 1976), one of the earliest theoretically rigorous textbooks in financial management. His co-authored books, *Management Accounting: Evolution not Revolution* (CIMA, 1989) and *Management Accounting: Pathways to Progress* (CIMA, 1994), were published during a time of dramatic change in UK management accounting practice. These textbooks contributed to the UK management accounting transformation from the costing clerk credo to strategic management proper. In 1999, he was voted the British Accounting Association Distinguished Academic. His contributions extend outside academe. Bromwich is a past president of the Chartered Institute of Management Accountants (CIMA) and has advised many commercial and public sector organizations. He is an outstanding scholar, conference sponsor, and adviser of the academy and accounting practitioners. This book is dedicated to Michael Bromwich who it is hoped will continue to provide leadership to the global management accounting community.

Alnoor Bhimani

London School of Economics
December 2005

☐ CONTENTS

⬚ CONTRIBUTORS

Thomas Ahrens is Professor of Accounting at the Warwick Business School, University of Warwick. He received his Ph.D. from the London School of Economics in 1996. His research is broadly concerned with accounting, control, and organizational process. He has also written on international comparisons and field research in accounting and is currently exploring the application of practice theory to management accounting research.

Jane Baxter, Ph.D. FCPA, is Associate Professor in the Discipline of Accounting within the University of Sydney, Australia. Jane teaches and researches in the area of management accounting. Her current research interests cover innovation/knowledge management, hybridity, and the leadership of the accounting and finance function. She has published in *Behavioral Research in Accounting*; *Journal of Management Accounting Research*; *Pacific Accounting Review*; *Australian Accounting Review*; *Accounting, Organizations and Society*; and *Management Accounting Research*, as well as contributing chapters to books. In 2002, Jane received the FMAC Articles of Merit Award from IFAC for a co-authored article appearing in the *Australian Accounting Review*.

Stanley Baiman is Ernst & Young Professor of Accounting at the Wharton School, University of Pennsylvania. He received his Ph.D. in accounting from the Graduate School of Business, Stanford University. Professor Baiman's area of research interest is the control function of managerial accounting, auditing, and organizational design. He is on the editorial board of a number of accounting journals.

Alnoor Bhimani is Reader in Accounting and Finance at the London School of Economics. He holds a B.Sc. from King's College London, an MBA from Cornell University, and a Ph.D. from the LSE. He is also a Certified Management Accountant (Canada). He has co-authored a number of books including *Management Accounting: Evolution, not Revolution* (CIMA, 1989), *Management Accounting: Pathways to Progress* (CIMA, 1994), and *Management and Cost Accounting* (Prentice Hall, 2005). Al has also edited *Management Accounting: European Perspectives* (Oxford University Press, 1996) and *Management Accounting in the Digital Economy* (Oxford University Press, 2003). He has written numerous articles in scholarly publications and serves on the editorial boards of several journals. He has undertaken management accounting-related fieldwork in a variety of global enterprises and has presented his research to corporate executives and academic audiences in Europe, Asia, and North America.

Christopher S. Chapman is head of the accounting group at the Saïd Business School, University of Oxford. He received his Ph.D. in accounting from the London School of Economics. His research focuses on the practice of management control and performance evaluation.

Robert H. Chenhall is Professor in Accounting and Finance at Monash University and Professor of Accounting at James Cook University. He holds a B.Ec. from Monash University, an M.Sc. from Southampton University, and a Ph.D. from Macquarie University. He is a Fellow of CPA, Australia. Professor Chenhall has over twenty-five years of experience in various aspects of strategic management, management information systems, and financial management from both academic and consulting perspectives. He has taught strategic change, management accounting, and financial management, and has held posts at INSEAD in France, LSE in the UK, and the Naval Postgraduate College in the USA. Professor Chenhall has assisted in the management of strategic change in a variety of major organizations and has published a wide selection of articles in professional and academic journals. He has been a member of the editorial board, or on the review panel, of most international journals that publish research in the area of management accounting.

Wai Fong Chua has been a professor at UNSW since 1994 and assumed the headship of the School of Accounting in 2000. Prior to joining UNSW in 1985, Wai Fong taught at the University of Sheffield (1981–2) and Sydney University (1983–5). She teaches and researches in the area of management accounting. Her current research projects include an examination of the role of financial and non-financial controls in the management of strategic supply relationships, knowledge management in professional service firms, and the effects of extended performance reporting on financial markets. She has published widely in international journals including *The Accounting Review*; *Accounting, Organizations and Society*; *Contemporary Accounting Research*; and *Journal of Management Accounting Research*. She is a member of the Council of UNSW and its Finance Committee.

Robin Cooper is Professor in the Practice of Management Accounting at the Goizueta Business School at Emory University. He is an expert on the design and implementation of strategic cost systems. He was a founder of the activity-based cost system movement and is an expert in Japanese cost management techniques such as target and Kaizen costing. He has authored several books, seventy articles, and fifty teaching cases. He is a frequent contributor to the *Journal of Cost Management*.

James Jianxin Gong is an assistant professor in the Department of Accountancy at the College of Business, University of Illinois at Urbana Champaign. He received his Ph.D. in accounting from the University of Southern California. His research focuses on performance measurement, evaluation, and incentives in the context of creative industries.

Lawrence A. Gordon is the Ernst & Young Alumni Professor of Managerial Accounting and Information Assurance, and the Director of the Ph.D. Program at the Robert H. Smith School of Business. He is also an Affiliate Professor in the University of Maryland Institute for Advanced Computer Studies. Dr Gordon earned his Ph.D. in Managerial Economics from Rensselaer Polytechnic Institute. His research focuses on such issues as corporate performance measures, economic aspects of information and cyber security, cost management systems, and capital investments. He is the author of more than eighty-five articles, published in such journals as *The Accounting Review*; *Journal of Computer Security*; *Journal of Financial and Quantitative Analysis*; *ACM Transactions on Information and System Security*; *Communications of the ACM*; *Accounting Organizations and Society*; *Journal of Accounting and Public Policy*; *Journal of Business Finance and Accounting*; *Computer Security Journal*; *Managerial and Decision Economics*; and *Management Accounting Research*. Dr. Gordon is also the author of several books, including *Managerial Accounting: Concepts and Empirical Evidence* and *Managing Cybersecurity Resources: A Cost-Benefit Analysis* (McGraw-Hill). In addition, he is Editor-in-Chief of *Journal of Accounting and Public Policy*, serves on the editorial boards of several other journals, and is a frequent contributor to the popular press. In two recent studies, Dr. Gordon was cited as being among the world's most influential and productive accounting researchers. An award-winning teacher, Dr Gordon has been an invited speaker at numerous universities around the world, including Harvard University, Columbia University, University of Toronto, London Business School, Carnegie Mellon University, and London School of Economics. He has also served as a consultant to several private and public organizations. Dr Gordon's former Ph.D. students are currently faculty members at such places as Stanford University, Ohio State University, McGill University, University of Southern California, College of William and Mary, Michigan State University, and National Taiwan University.

Allan Hansen is Assistant Professor at the Copenhagen Business School. His research interests cover a wide range of issues related to cost and performance management in practice, and he has been focusing on the management of new product development as well as production management and the management of interorganizational relations. Currently, he is exploring the role of constructivism as a practice-based research strategy in management accounting.

Anthony Hopwood is the Peter Moores Dean of the Saïd Business School, the American Standard Companies Professor of Operations Management, and Student of Christ Church at the University of Oxford. Educated at the London School of Economics and the University of Chicago, prior to moving to Oxford in 1995 Professor Hopwood had held professorships at the London Business School and the London School of Economics. He was also the President of the European Institute for Advanced Studies in Management, Brussels from 1995 to 2003. A prolific author, Professor Hopwood is also Editor-in-Chief of the major international research journal, *Accounting, Organizations and Society*. He has served as a consultant to commercial, governmental, and international organizations. Professor Hopwood holds honorary doctorates from universities in Denmark, Finland, Italy, Sweden, and the United Kingdom.

Keith Hoskin is Professor of Strategy and Accounting at the Warwick Business School. He has been researching and teaching across the fields of accounting, management, and strategy for a number of years, with a particular focus on the ways in which the past shapes current and future possibilities in all three. His current work with Richard Macve is a study of the genesis and growth of modern management and accounting as contemporary forms of powerful knowledge. He is also researching, on behalf of the Institute of Chartered Accountants in England and Wales, current patterns of education and training in the accountancy profession.

Liisa Kurunmäki, Ph.D., is a CIMA Lecturer of Accounting at the London School of Economics and Political Science. Her research interest is in the public sector and she has been studying the accounting aspects of New Public Management reforms in the UK and Finland. The results of her research have been published in academic journals such as *Accounting, Organizations and Society*; *European Accounting Review*; and *Management Accounting Research*.

Eva Labro is a lecturer in management accounting at the London School of Economics. She received her Ph.D. in applied economics from the University of Leuven (Belgium). Her research interests focus on the interface between management accounting and other disciplines such as purchasing, operations research, operations management, and economics. She is currently working on several projects on costing system design. She has published in leading refereed journals such as *Manufacturing & Service Operations Management*; *European Journal of Operational Research*; *Accounting and Business Research*; *European Accounting Review*; *European Journal of Purchasing and Supply Chain Management*; and *Supply Chain Management: An International Journal*. She is on the editorial review board of *Journal of Purchasing and Supply Chain Management*.

Kim Langfield-Smith is Professor of Management Accounting in the Department of Accounting and Finance at Monash University, Australia. Prior appointments were at La Trobe University, the universities of Melbourne and Tasmania, and University of Technology, Sydney. Prior to academic life, she worked as an accountant in several commercial organizations. Kim has a B.Ec. from the University of Sydney, an M.Ec. from Macquarie University, and a Ph.D. from Monash University. She is a fellow of CPA, Australia. Kim's research interests are in the area of management control systems and behavioural management accounting. She has published papers in leading referred journals including *Accounting, Organizations and Society*; *Journal of Management Accounting Research*; *Management Accounting Research*; *Behavioral Research in Accounting*; *Journal of Accounting Literature*; and *Journal of Management Studies*.

Martin P. Loeb, Ph.D., Northwestern University, is a Professor of Accounting and Information Assurance and a Deloitte & Touche Faculty Fellow at the University of Maryland's Robert H. Smith School of Business. Loeb's early research was in economic mechanism design, incentive regulation, cost allocations, and cost-based procurement contracting. His current research deals with economic aspects of information security and the interface between managerial accounting and information technology. Dr Loeb's papers span several disciplines, and have been published in leading academic journals, including *The Accounting Review*; *ACM Transactions on Information and System Security*; *American Economic Review*; *Contemporary Accounting Research*; *Journal of Accounting Research*; *Journal of Computer Security*; *Journal of Law and Economics*; *Journal of Accounting and Public Policy*; *Management Accounting Research*; and *Management Science*. Along with Lawrence A. Gordon, Dr Loeb recently authored *Managing Cybersecurity Resources: A Cost-Benefit Analysis* published by McGraw-Hill.

Richard Macve is Professor of Accounting at the London School of Economics and Political Science. He is a Fellow of the Institute of Chartered Accountants in England & Wales, and an honorary Fellow of the Institute of Actuaries. He is currently Academic Adviser to the ICAEW's Centre for Business Performance and a member of the Accounting Standards Board's Academic Panel. Formerly he was the Julian Hodge Professor of Accounting at the University of Wales, Aberystwyth, where he is now Honorary Visiting Professor of Accounting in the University's School of Management and Business. His most recent books are *A Conceptual Framework for Financial Accounting and Reporting: Vision, Tool or Threat?* (Garland, 1997) and *UK Life Insurance: Accounting for Business Performance* (with Joanne Horton) (FT Finance, 1997). He is currently working (with Dr Joanne Horton at the LSE) on a further research project on accounting for life insurance sponsored by the PD Leake Trust, and on various historical research projects including a book (with Professor Keith Hoskin of Warwick University) on the historical development of management and accounting in the USA in the nineteenth century.

Peter Miller is Professor of Management Accounting at the London School of Economics and Political Science, and a member of the Centre for Analysis of Risk and Regulation. He is Associate Editor of *Accounting, Organizations and Society*, and is also a member of the editorial board of the *Journal of Management Accounting Research*. He has published widely in accounting, management, and sociology journals. He co-edited (with Anthony Hopwood) *Accounting as Social and Institutional Practice* (Cambridge University Press, 1994). He is currently working on the roles of accounting in relation to the changing political vocabulary of public service provision in the UK, and the Payment by Results programme in particular. He is also working on the modes of mediation between science and the economy in the microprocessor industry.

Jan Mouritsen is Professor of Management Control at the Copenhagen Business School. His research is oriented towards understanding the role of Management Technologies and Management Control in various organizational and social contexts. He focuses on empirical research and attempts to develop new ways of understanding the role and effects of controls and financial information in organizations and society. He is interested in translations and interpretations of (numerical) representations (e.g. as in budgets, financial reports, non-financial indicators, and profitability analysis) through the contexts they help to illuminate. His interests include intellectual capital and knowledge management, technology management, operations management, new accounting, and management control. Mouritsen is currently editorial board member of fifteen academic journals in the area of accounting, operations management, information technology and knowledge management, and management generally, and he has published in many journals including *Accounting, Organizations and Society*; *Management Accounting Research*; *Scandinavian Journal of Management*; *Accounting, Auditing and Accountability Journal*; *Journal of Intellectual Capital*; and *Critical Perspectives on Accounting*.

David Otley is Professor of Accounting and Management at Lancaster University Management School. His research interests are centred upon the operation of management control and performance management systems in large organizations, and he has published extensively in these areas and on the behavioural aspects of management accounting. He is an editorial board member of several leading accounting journals, and was General Editor of the *British Journal of Management* for ten years. He now chairs the relevant main panel in the UK's Research Assessment Exercise.

Hanno Roberts is Professor in Management Accounting and Control at the Norwegian School of Management in Oslo. He earned his M.Sc. in Business Economics from Erasmus University in Rotterdam, his MBA from Rotterdam School of Management, and his Ph.D. from the University of Maastricht. His research and teaching interests are in the areas of intellectual capital, in accounting and control of the knowledge-based firm, and in knowledge-based value creation. He served and serves on the editorial boards of several national and international academic journals, and has held, or still holds, visiting academic positions in Germany, Spain, Sweden, Finland, and France.

Robert W. Scapens, Ph.D., MA(Econ), FCA, is Professor of Accounting at the Manchester Business School. He is also Professor of Management Accounting at the University of Groningen in the Netherlands. Together with Michael Bromwich, he was co-founder of *Management Accounting Research* and is now the Editor-in-Chief. His early work was on financial accounting, but since the early 1980s his research has primarily been in management accounting. He is now recognized as a leading international researcher in the field. He has used both quantitative and qualitative research methods in his research, and written extensively on research methodology and on methods of case research. His recent research has included major projects on management accounting change (for CIMA and ESRC) and on performance measurement systems in multinational corporations (for ICAEW).

John Shank is the Noble Foundation Professor of Management Emeritus at the Amos Tuck School of Business at Dartmouth College, and a Visiting Professor of Financial Management at the Naval Postgraduate School in Monterey, California. He also teaches at the new Rady Graduate School of Business at the University of California at San Diego, and at the F. W. Olin Graduate School of Management at Babson College, Boston. He has published twenty-one books, 109 articles, and more than 160 case studies on finance and accounting in his thirty-eight-year career. His work on strategic cost management won the Annual Excellence in Research Award of the Management Accounting Section of the American Accounting Association in 1995. The American Institute of CPAs honoured him with a Special Achievement Award in 1997 for his work in founding the Center for Excellence in Financial Management.

Regine Slagmulder is Associate Professor of Accounting and Control at INSEAD. Prior to joining INSEAD, she has been on the faculty at Tilburg University, the Netherlands, and the University of Ghent, Belgium. She has also been a visiting Research Fellow at Boston University School of Management and the P. Drucker Graduate Management School at Claremont University, USA. Regine's teaching and research activities focus on the link between performance management systems and business strategy. She has published several books and articles in both academic and practitioner journals on strategic cost and performance management, including topics such as activity-based costing, target costing, supply chain performance management, and the balanced scorecard. She often serves as invited speaker to both business and academic audiences and is a regular contributor to executive and in-company programmes.

Kazbi Soonawalla obtained her Ph.D. in Business from Stanford University. Her primary research and teaching focuses on international accounting and financial reporting issues. Within these, she is especially interested in joint ventures and associates, group accounts and consolidations, and mergers and acquisitions. Her research also examines the standard-setting process and the political and economic influences on it. This research has led her to consider corporate social responsibility and sustainable business practices and their links to management accounting issues. In particular, she looks at effects and outcomes of the interplay between financial reporting, corporate governance, corporate social responsibility, ethics, and accounting-based managerial decision-making.

John Stone is Senior Lecturer in the Department of War Studies at King's College London. He was previously a lecturer in the Department of History and Welsh History at the University of Wales, Aberystwyth. His research interests include the history of strategic thought, and technology and military affairs. He is the author of *The Tank Debate: Armour and the Anglo-American Military Tradition* (Harwood Academic, 2000) along with articles on both historical and contemporary military issues. He is presently writing a book on the influence of technology in strategic thought.

Chih-Yang Tseng is a Ph.D. student in the Department of Accounting and Information Assurance at the University of Maryland's Robert H. Smith School of Business. His current research focuses on the links between management accounting and investments in information security. He has published practical and theoretical papers in *Accounting Research Monthly* and *Contemporary Accounting* in Taiwan.

Wim A. Van der Stede is Assistant Professor at the Leventhal School of Accounting in the Marshall School of Business, University of Southern California. He received his Ph.D. in economics from the University of Ghent, Belgium. His research focuses on performance measurement, evaluation, and incentives in the context of organizational control from both an accounting and a management perspective.

S. Mark Young holds the KPMG Foundation Professorship at the Leventhal School of Accounting in the Marshall School of Business, University of Southern California. He also holds appointments in the Management and Organization Department within the Marshall School and the Annenberg School for Communication at USC. His most recent research is on control issues in the creative industries with an emphasis on developing models to predict project success, and the economics and psychology of celebrity.

1 New measures in performance management

Thomas Ahrens
Christopher S. Chapman

1.1 The problem with performance measurement

Fifty-year-old commentaries on performance measurement can have a surprisingly up-to-date feel about them:

> There is a strong tendency today to state numerically as many as possible of the variables with which management must deal.... Quantitative measures as tools are undoubtedly useful. But research shows that indiscriminate use and undue confidence and reliance in them result from insufficient knowledge of the full effects and consequences.... The cure is sometimes worse than the disease. (Ridgway 1956: 240)

Despite such long-standing and clear delineations of the limits of performance measurement, contemporary discussions of the results of performance measurement initiatives frequently conclude with a wry smile and the acknowledgement that once again this is a case where 'you get what you measure'. As with the term 'creative accounting', however, this expression reflects an ironic acknowledgement of the limits of our abilities to control behaviour through performance measurement, not of our success.

Over the decades since Ridgway wrote, questions of performance measurement and evaluation have been associated with a wide variety of issues. Frequently, discussions of the topic have addressed more general concerns with organizational management and competitiveness in the context of contemporary preoccupations. In the 1960s, the growth of conglomerates went hand in hand with an extensive discussion of misunderstandings of the role of divisionalized performance measurement (e.g. Mauriel and Anthony 1966) and, especially, the difficulties of measuring executive performance through profit measures alone (e.g. Dearden 1968). Performance measurement, control, and evaluation systems in large and small organizations were often considered alongside the impact of computers, which were, at this time, beginning to make inroads into commercial organizations, opening up possibilities for previously unimagined volumes of data processing (e.g. Dearden 1966, 1967).

Throughout the 1970s and early 1980s, there was noticeable change in the performance measurement debate, with much discussion concerning the necessity to update traditional accounting measurements to take into consideration the effects of inflation (e.g. Weston 1974; Revsine 1981). In the 1980s, as inflation receded, the performance measurement debate shifted towards the role of performance measures in competing with Japanese manufacturers (e.g. Kaplan 1983; Hiromoto 1988). Initial concerns with quality and costs as competing performance targets expanded quickly to include discussion of the support of organizational strategy through performance measurement systems. In the 1990s these concerns were expressed more generally as part of increasingly widespread calls to consider non-financial as well as financial aspects of performance (e.g. Eccles 1991; Kaplan and Norton 1992) and the packaging of performance measures as holistic models of management (e.g. Economic Value Added™ or the balanced scorecard (BSC)).

Despite these ongoing appeals to developments in performance measurement, examples of our continued failures confront us in newspapers and news reports virtually every day. Just a couple of examples taken from Neely (2003) serve to underline the point. A Channel ferry operator sought to improve customer satisfaction. Its customer complaints department was set a target of dealing with all customer complaints within five days. The department achieved this target by simply refunding many customers the cost of their tickets. A retail bank seeking to improve efficiency gave its call centre telephone operators the target to complete customer calls within 1 minute. Operators simply hung up after 59 seconds. British Telecom call centre staff were given a target for the length of time that incoming calls should be allowed to wait before being answered. The telephone operators obtained some help from engineering colleagues to route many incoming calls in a manner that bypassed the mechanism that was set up for measuring the length of time that incoming calls were waiting before being answered.

We witness such failures of performance measurement systems at a time when the technologies involved in the capture, manipulation, and distribution of information have never been better. Successive waves of information technology (IT) development have been greeted with optimistic analyses of their potential to strengthen significantly our attempts at controlling behaviour, both within and between organizations (see Chapman and Chua 2003 for a discussion). However, the advances anticipated have frequently been far more limited in scale and scope than hoped for. The following excerpt taken from the beginning of perhaps the most high-profile and detailed critique of management accounting work shares the understanding that performance management involves more than better technical systems for the quantification of, and reporting on, activity:

The computing revolution of the past two decades has so reduced information collection and processing costs that virtually all technical barriers to design and implementation of effective management accounting systems have been removed. (Johnson and Kaplan 1987: 6)

Still greater strides in technology have been made since the above was written, and management accounting and performance measurement systems can now encompass, and support speedier access to, more detailed information, on a wider range of activities than ever before. On top of data, contemporary information systems now include vast stocks of meta-data (data about data) (Gandy and Chapman 1997) designed to prevent users being completely overwhelmed.

Progress has been less dramatic, however, in our understanding of the nature of the routines and procedures through which people in organizations seek to establish links between the data available to them and everyday action. Discussing this challenge under the heading of management control systems, Simons (1990: 142) concludes his influential article by noting:

We need in fact a better language to describe management control processes. Control systems are used for multiple purposes: Monitoring, learning, signalling, constraint, surveillance, motivation, and others. Yet we use a single descriptor—management control systems—to describe these distinctly different processes.

In his subsequent writings on levers of control (Simons 1995), he argued against the traditional opposition of centralized versus decentralized modes of control, suggesting instead that contemporary management control systems must find ways to combine elements of control with elements of empowerment. He suggested that the achievement of this goal might be supported through four distinct but interrelated kinds of control systems: belief, boundary, diagnostic, and interactive.

He described *belief systems* as attempts to inspire and generate commitment by setting out ideals of achievement, providing a sense of direction to empowered staff. *Boundary systems* support empowerment by choosing to delimit certain kinds of activity, both in moral (e.g. not doing business in markets where bribery is common) and strategic (e.g. to avoid certain kinds of projects, customers, etc.) terms. *Diagnostic systems* represent the traditional mode of surveillance and control of well-understood aspects of an organization, frequently on a management by exception basis. Finally, *interactive systems* bring together senior managers and operational managers to debate and challenge assumptions and plans as a means of understanding and responding to the strategic uncertainties facing an organization.

His framework sets out a model of control in which performance measurement systems should be consciously situated in a shared context, and in which there are particular ways of working with them depending on the nature of the problem (i.e. well-understood, or strategically uncertain). In this chapter we will attempt to contribute further to the development of a more nuanced discussion of the nature and intent of performance management as a way of understanding why performance measurement continues to be seen as flawed, and how to avoid common pitfalls in its use.

1.2 Where calculation holds the answer to performance measurement

1.2.1 OPERATIONAL CONTROL SYSTEMS

In situations where there is a well-understood, stable, and measurable transformation process, performance measures in the guise of what Simons would term diagnostic control systems have a very long and successful history in controlling behaviour. An interesting example of just how long a history that is can be seen in Ezzamel (1997), who describes the calculative practices that helped to control activity in the Pharaonic bakeries and breweries of New Kingdom Egypt around 1300 BC. Detailed accounts were maintained at the level of individual bakers and brewers that numerically assessed their ratio of inputs to outputs (e.g. from measures of grain to jugs of beer). These calculations offered a performance target that took into account variances expected based on the quality of inputs (e.g. flour), allowable in-process wastage (due to various factors including evaporation), and finally adjusting for the quality of the outputs (e.g. strength of beer).

As more and more of our daily lives are mediated through computers, the potential of this particular type of control system looks set to increase in significance. In discussing an operational control system relating to the usage of food in a restaurant chain, Ahrens and Chapman (2002) discuss the phenomenon of manipulated closing inventory figures. This phenomenon was at least partly supported by the relative lack of integration of the information systems in the restaurant chain that they studied at the time of the fieldwork (1995–7). The calculation of the cost of food used was based on the reconciliation of weekly manual inventory counts with records of food purchases during the week. This left open the possibility that a food margin deficit (due to food wastage or theft) might be rendered invisible (temporarily at least) through the reporting of an artificially inflated closing inventory figure—'managers' stock' or phantom inventory.

One way to address this loophole would be available if the area manager cared to look up the number of times a closing inventory figure had been entered (presumably to check the resulting food margin reported). However, in the context of an inventory count that took place after the busiest serving session of the week, some mistakes were to be expected. Random audits of inventory were used to curtail such activity. A contemporary techno-logical solution might entail barcoding on inventory packs allowing for much more precise visibility of food usage through the detailed matching of inventories, purchases, and closing inventory. Such a solution would also reduce the chance of miscounting and allow for the automatic tracking of First-In-First-Out inventory rotation procedures to reduce wastage of fresh produce. The system would also be valuable in the context of an industry increasingly concerned with food scares by providing an audit trail of ingredient movements from suppliers to plates.

The relative success of diagnostic systems in controlling a specific set of activities is, however, heavily dependent on the simplicity of the transformation process involved. In the context of serving drinks in a bar, for example, adherence to standard portions can be built into the technology of drink delivery, and in terms of evaluating the periodic consumption of beverages, there is no room for discussing whether performance was good or bad. The numerical relationship between the actual quantities of beverage dispensed and the stand-ards allowed given the volume of sales holds the answer to the question of performance. Operational control systems for such simple transformation processes rely on a causal model of operations.

1.2.2 CAUSAL MODELLING

There has been a recent resurgence of interest in the development of causal models as a central aspect of performance management activities (e.g. Kaplan and Norton 2000). One of the few studies that has examined the extent and success of this approach suggested that causal modelling can enhance performance. In their sample of firms in the financial services industry, Ittner et al. (2003) found that whilst only a minority of firms reported that they were carrying out causal modelling, their analysis demonstrated a significant and positive relationship to stock market returns.

Organizations carry out significant amounts of measurement, and the technological advances already discussed have only increased such activity. Ittner and Larcker (2005) offered a refreshing corrective to the cynical anticipation of measurement failure by high-lighting that rather than seeing measurement as a doomed activity, there are specific technical obstacles underlying the limits of performance measurement in many cases. They suggested that many of the companies that they have been involved with have failed to approach measurement in a rigorous fashion. More difficult to correct, they also identified a number of organizational reasons for the relative scarcity of causal modelling.

Ittner and Larcker (2005) reported that measurement activity in many companies they have worked with was frequently organized as the responsibility of discrete organizational groups, with sets of measures developed piecemeal over time. Sets of measures were frequently comprehensive, covering diverse areas of performance, such as financial performance, customer satisfaction, employee skills and satisfaction, etc. However, those measures were often difficult to integrate in a systematic analysis such as causal modelling due to their technical design. For example, in one organization they worked with, different measures had mismatched time periods. One set of weekly statistics was based on a week ending on Saturday, and another ending on Sunday. In the context of a retail chain, in which a significant portion of activity took place over the weekend, this presented a significant problem when it came to statistically analysing the relationship between the two measures. Another common measurement specification problem they observed related to levels of aggregation. Some statistics were collected at the level of the branch; others were only available broken down by region, for example.

A further problem they identified related to the setting of performance targets. In many cases it seems intuitively obvious that our ambition should be to maximize aspects of performance, such as customer satisfaction for example. Ittner and Larcker (2005) presented an analysis of the relationship between reported customer satisfaction and positive and negative product recommendations for a personal computer manufacturer. The analysis showed that scoring a 5 (highest) on satisfaction had no incremental effect over scoring a 4, but that scoring a 1 or 2 had a very strong negative effect.

Acting to amplify these obstacles to strategic data analysis, they also observed that managers frequently exhibited a tendency to avoid carrying out analysis that might challenge long-held views of how things work, or that cut across different spheres of organizational responsibility, because the sharing of data would threaten organizational fiefdoms.

1.2.3 DISTRIBUTED INFORMATION PROCESSING

One further set of developments relates to the potential for information systems to provide new and more effective ways of eliciting and managing emergent data from distributed groups of individuals. Malone (2004) gave a number of provocative examples of the potential to operate internal markets that might achieve a range of objectives more efficiently than traditional management control approaches.

His first example involved an application of market trading principles to the problem, faced by British Petroleum plc (BP), of how to achieve a commitment to reducing its greenhouse gas emissions by 10 per cent. Malone acutely sketched the problems of a traditional approach to cascading such a reduction target through the hierarchy. There would be claims (both heart-felt and opportunistic) of the unfairness and unrealistic nature of the final allocation of the overall target, and bilateral negotiations would ensue. As is often the case with transfer pricing, for example, the final targets might owe much to the relative negotiation skills of those involved and little to economic or operational factors.

The actual approach adopted by BP began with the determination of business unit targets, resulting in an allocation of emission permits. The negotiation phase was carried out through an internal market mechanism, however. Individual business units were free to go to this internal market in order to buy or sell emission permits, based on the prevailing price. Thus, business units in which, for whatever reason, there were opportunities to make considerable reductions in emissions were able to sell their permits to business units in which reductions were more difficult or costly. The system was a success: BP met its emissions target nine years ahead of schedule.

A second provocative example from Malone (2004) related to the use of an internal market to generate sales forecasts in Hewlett-Packard (HP). Working with an economist from the California Institute of Technology, a system was set up that allowed HP employees (mainly from the sales force) to trade an initial endowment of shares in futures contracts representing different ranges of forecast sales. At the end of the experiment the shares each paid out $1 if actual sales turned out to be within the contract range, and nothing if not. Over sixteen experiments, the internal market produced predictions that were at least as close to actual sales as the official forecast, and that were significantly closer in all but one case.

A final example was a market set up to allocate chip-manufacturing capacity at Intel. A simulation was set up to model one product, one plant manager, and five sales representatives. The system allowed managers to buy and sell at the prevailing market price, or to place a limited order to buy (or sell) no higher (or lower) than a chosen price. The individual managers were also furnished with some private information. For example, the sales representatives knew the amount of chips their customers might wish to buy at what price in the coming period, and the plant manager knew the marginal costs of production. During the first round of the simulation, the internal market achieved 86.6 per cent of the financial returns the company might have achieved if it allocated plant capacity and sales perfectly. Over successive rounds, this rose to 99 per cent efficiency. Whilst a limited simulation, the results were sufficiently interesting for Intel to explore its application on a more realistic scale within the company.

1.3 **Where calculation is not enough**

In each of the above depictions of the potential strength of performance measurement as a tool for performance management, it is important to recognize that a crucial aspect of the problem under consideration in each case was that the right answer might be determined through a process of calculation. In the ancient bakeries, the standards were agreed (Ezzamel 1997). The absence of cause maps highlighted by Ittner and Larcker (2005) was remedied through their intervention, and calculation revealed important relationships between variables that had been previously unknown. In the companies described by Malone (2004) the problem at hand was subject to strict evaluation through calculation. In each case there was a single criterion of evaluation, and in each case that criterion was relatively simply measurable. So, for example, actual levels of emissions might be compared with target levels, the forecast sales figures might be compared with actual sales figures, and the achieved financial returns might be compared with the maximum returns theoretically possible given the profile of capacity and customer demands. In these cases, discussions of performance management might revolve around the factors that contributed or detracted from performance as understood in terms of a single measure.

A more general managerial problem, however, is how to deal with ever-increasing flows of information in situations where there is no such easy filtering mechanism available:

Looked at in the large, organisations exist to suppress data. Some data are screened in, but most are screened out. The very structure of organisation—the units, the levels, the hierarchy—is designed to reduce data to manageable and manipulable proportions. If top executives were willing and able to sift through all the booming and buzzing confusion themselves—to enjoy, like Harouun Al Rascheed, unmediated access to the primary sources—there would be no need for a 'lowerarchy', or indeed, for organisation itself. (Wildavsky 1981)

Our ability to collect and communicate ever-vaster amounts of information looks set to continue its dramatic development. As described in Section 1.2, we have a variety of approaches to mobilizing some of this information to achieve significant feats of performance management in well-understood settings. Unfortunately in considering the long-term contribution of this kind of analytical process, the prognosis is less optimistic than might be expected in the face of such potential. On its own, information processing is not generally held to provide sustainable competitive advantage (e.g. Barney et al. 2001).

The strategy literature analysing the resource-based view of the firm is clear that information communication technologies are not themselves sources of advantage since they are ultimately too easy for competitors to replicate (Barney et al. 2001). In order to understand this point in relation to performance management systems, you only need consider the packaging and mass resale of innovative analytical approaches by software and hardware vendors. So, for example, the BSC was quickly incorporated as a feature of information systems' reporting tools. However, the reproduction of specific formatting in performance reports, or, the production of calculations informed by the principles of activity-based costing (ABC), for example, do not promise sustainable competitive advantages in and of themselves. What is required for sustainable competitive advantage is an organizational capability to relate calculations to processes of management and organizational sense-making more generally.

A description of performance management as an organizational capability (Barney et al. 2001) was given by Ahrens and Chapman (2002). In the restaurant chain that they studied, performance metrics did not produce unequivocal signals for action but formed a potential basis for discussion. In their study they explored in detail the complex ways in which selective attention to different sets of performance measures formed the basis of ongoing trade-offs between various sources of legitimacy. This is not to say that management became particularly emancipatory with restaurant managers free to choose between different courses of action. In fact, highly asymmetric power relations between head office and restaurant managers prevailed. Still, in one restaurant that had opened only recently, the financial efficiency of the food preparation and delivery process was evaluated in the context of customer satisfaction in a start-up restaurant. It was agreed that in this particular case this allowed for some relaxation of percentage margin targets, given substantial cash margin growth. Senior management of this restaurant chain devoted considerable time and effort to developing a shared understanding amongst organizational members of how conversations about such trade-offs should take place (Ahrens and Chapman 2002).

Likewise, Malone's experiments (2004) with internal markets contained clues that there was more at stake than the neutral processing of information in arriving at the impressive capacity utilization reported, for example. Malone noted that through the course of repeated simulations managers 'learned to be better players'. The 'invisible hand' of market coordination was helped along by an emerging notion of cooperative competence. The software that ran the market might be easily transportable, but such cooperative competences might prove more difficult to replicate. In seeking to address Simons' call (1990) to develop a better language to describe management control processes, we might particularly consider how performance management as a skilful practical activity might represent an organizational capability.

1.3.1 ENABLING CONTROL SYSTEMS

Simons (1995), in developing his levers of control framework, emphasized that interactive control systems represented a style of use more than a discrete technical system. A detailed analysis of his discussion of the precise nature of this style by Bisbe et al. (2005) uncovers five significant dimensions of behaviour that make up an interactive control system: intensive use by senior management; intensive use by operating managers; the pervasiveness of face-to-face challenges and debates in the interactions of the two groups; a focus on strategic uncertainties; a non-invasive and facilitating involvement of senior managers in operational decision-making.

Ahrens and Chapman (2004) noted that whilst an increasing stream of work has mobilized the concept of interactive control systems, little attention has so far been given to Simons' complementary systems (1995), such as beliefs and boundaries. In their analysis Bisbe et al. (2005) noted that studies to date have tended to focus on only the first four dimensions of interactive control systems. In terms of understanding performance management as an organizational capability, however, this fifth dimension requires close attention. Ahrens and Chapman (forthcoming) drew on the framework of Adler and Borys (1996) to study this challenge of combining empowerment with control in their case company.

Drawing on the literature of human machine interfaces, Adler and Borys (1996) outlined two philosophies of bureaucratic control: coercive and enabling. Coercive control systems seek to provide a foolproof environment for action. As such they rely very little on the creative capabilities of the controlled, seeking instead tightly to coral their activity along well-understood and predetermined paths. Such systems might be appropriate in well-understood settings, and in such cases the systems provide a clear and unambiguous basis for performance evaluation such as those discussed above.

Inflexible, output-oriented budgeting systems have often been found unsuitable for environments in which activity is difficult to predict (Chapman 1997). However, a recent study of empowerment has demonstrated the potential comfort to managers from such a system, even in less stable settings (Marginson and Ogden 2005). This study showed that in an organization that sought to empower its managers, but not to engage with them in detailed discussions concerning the nature of the operations under their control, the managers felt their jobs were highly ambiguous. They dealt with this by demanding that clear performance guidelines be established in budgetary terms. In the absence of a more engaged debate with senior management about operational processes and the nature of good performance, they were uncomfortable about entering into more complex and discursive evaluations of what it meant to perform well or badly.

Adler and Borys (1996) presented an alternative to such a disengaged form of empowerment with their notion of enabling systems of control. Such systems seek to work with the intelligence of users of the systems. They do so by fostering control system design informed by four design characteristics that help to provide a structure for desirable interventions by those who are controlled by the system. These characteristics are repair, internal transparency, global transparency, and flexibility. Taken together, these four provide us with a detailed understanding of what might be at stake in a non-invasive interactive control system.

Repair is a principle in the design of control systems that reckons with the intelligence of the users. Accounting controls and performance measurement systems can be designed as foolproof systems or be amenable to the user's intervention in an unforeseen event:

Operational rules and standards are often expressed through formal control systems such as accounting. Like a locked box around a machine control panel, accounting can act to render the underlying logic of work processes unintelligible. Translated, for example, into piece rates, standard costs, or overhead allocation rules, the underlying logic may be clear to the accounting expert but irrelevant to most employees (van der Veeken and Wouters 2002). By contrast, standard cost information broken down into its constituents for each process step could more easily be used for operational problem solving. (Ahrens and Chapman 2004: 279–80)

Internal transparency in performance measurement and control systems can be achieved by integrating performance information with operational processes:

For example, budgeting processes can be integrated with operational planning activities. Variances can be calculated for operationally meaningful categories. Lookup tables can give expected cost effects of certain variations of process parameters. The key to a successful design of internal transparency lies in giving layered access to information. Targeted information requests should be met without causing information overload. (Ahrens and Chapman 2004: 280)

Global transparency seeks to make comprehensible the interdependencies between local and wider organizational processes. At the heart of global transparency often lies a clarification of the local implications of organizational strategy and, in particular, of trying to achieve customer satisfaction, for example. When processes need to be repaired, it can become important quickly to devise partial solutions. Performance measurement and control systems should help organizational members understand what the customer's priorities are and, therefore, what the colleagues working downstream require in the first instance.

Lastly, *flexibility* refers to the use of performance measurement and control systems. Pilots can use autopilot systems in different modes or turn them off altogether. Enabling performance measurement and control systems should equally be usable differently. Flexibility can take the form of customizing access to different IT systems and reports, or of customizing analysis and commentary of reports to different users:

By giving users the choice of building up different aggregations of performance information, management control systems might support highly differentiated, yet interrelated, mental maps of the organization that are specific to changing circumstances. (Ahrens and Chapman 2004: 281)

Ahrens and Chapman (2004) emphasized that they observed financial control in their study as providing a focus for the development of shared understandings of skilful practical activity. Whilst the idea of using the systems was to work with the intelligence of managers, the hierarchy remained firmly in place, and managers' prerogatives were clearly limited. As with the factory managers in Roberts (1990), it was through discussion and personal engagement that restaurant managers were encouraged to bring their creativity and ideas to bear on daily operations, despite the fact that they were subject to potentially harsh hierarchical control.

Working in this way might be understood as exactly the kind of difficult-to-replicate organizational capability suggestive of a clearer role for performance management in the generation and sustenance of competitive advantage (Barney et al. 1991).

1.3.2 A PRACTICE PERSPECTIVE ON CONTROL SYSTEMS

To summarize briefly, the concept of enabling control highlights four systemic features of controls (repair, internal transparency, global transparency, flexibility) that affect the non-invasive and facilitative potential for the exercise of control. It does so without denying that performance management frequently takes place in a hierarchical context with persistent power asymmetries. As such, the concept of enabling control holds the potential to aid in an understanding of the practical operation of performance management that combines the ambition of empowerment with the reality of individually distributed responsibilities and hierarchy.

Frequently, however, the control concepts that are written about in the academic and practitioner literatures are unable to capture the dynamics of the organizational functioning of control. They tend to give very little by way of an explanation of what makes the concept work in practice. Take the BSC as an example of a very popular overarching control concept. The catchphrase with respect to the BSC's organizational use is that it must be the 'corner-stone of a new strategic management system' (Kaplan and Norton 1996: 75). This is an important demand, which would require different specific activities in different organizations. We are not asking the BSC concept to spell out what those activities would be. That is not the task of a control concept. But we do want to know more about the nature of the BSC and the elements of organizational activity with which the BSC is supposed to interact.

For example, is the BSC a measurement tool that should monitor compliance with financial and non-financial performance targets across all management levels? If so, should it set realistic or stretch targets, is it for planning or for motivation, and what is its relationship with the budget? Or could a BSC be something that appears only occasionally on the whiteboard of the company boardroom, a tool for occasional strategic musings of senior management? Are the BSC's main qualities even technical? Or does it belong to the arsenal of ideological management tools, something to influence the language and thinking of organizational members? The BSC, like other control concepts, remains silent on those questions. This silence can be debilitating for a management concept because it leaves it to the imagination of practitioners how they might fit into a living and breathing organization and, therefore, what one can really do with them. They remain nice ideas with unspecified practical import.

In this chapter we therefore want to sketch a perspective on control that offers some insights into the relationships and interactions between performance metrics and skilful management activity. From the point of view of a practice perspective on control systems, those systems and their overall designs ('We practise responsibility accounting based on full costs') and intentions ('We want to reduce variable manufacturing costs by 12 per cent in the coming year') are too unspecific to bring about, on their own, a desirable class of day-to-day activities. The BSC as the 'cornerstone of a new strategic management process' sounds good, but how do you do it? A practice perspective turns the relationship between strategic designs and intentions and daily action on its head. Rather than emphasizing the way in which action follows design, designs and intentions might instead be considered direct outcomes of action. A design like a BSC or a set of design principles like those for enabling control systems are regarded as a loosely related array of activities, held together, mainly, by the purposes of the practitioners (Hansen and Mouritsen 2005).

This offers a distinctive way of thinking about the skilful practical activity so often observed in organizations. Practitioners work with enabling and coercive control systems in highly specific ways, ways that they find appropriate for their organization and its circumstances. For example, they seek to take account of physical work environments and technologies, established ways of working, their own plans and those of their colleagues, recent changes that may impinge on work, etc. What is it that those practitioners have in common when they work with a certain control system? What are the shared characteristics of their work? In practice, working with an enabling control system, for example, may combine general ideas about empowered working with specific physical and information-based process and output controls such that organizational members can be understood to be participating in a widely known practice (working with an enabling control system) but not be bound precisely to reproduce specific routine actions.

In the restaurant chain studied by Ahrens and Chapman, for example, the routines that made up the menu design process can be seen as an organizational practice through which key objectives were tied together and the organizational strategy was made workable. Designing a new menu involved a number of routine activities, for example, calculating the target food margin based on projections for sales mix, dish revenue, and cost. This calculative routine was more than simply a means to the implementation of strategic objectives, however. What made dish representations in the menu design spreadsheet useful for managers in the Restaurant Division was the ways in which they enabled them to think through the strategic potential of past and potential practices:

In the process of menu design abstract strategic notions such as 'We must Italianise our menu' took on concrete form through the attempt to introduce specific dishes that might contribute to achieving this end.

Routine calculations triggered a series of follow-up activity to determine the likely sales price and manufacturing cost of the new dish, its likely impact on sales mix, and resulting implications for volume (and hence cost) of other dishes. These financial considerations were bound up with nuanced discussions of 'Italian-ness' (and other marketing objectives) and the extent to which this might add to customer perceptions of the desirability of the brand and of the dish itself. Operational concerns also had to be factored into the balance, thus the 'old 2246'[1] sold sufficiently well to retain its place on the menu despite the inconvenience of its preparation. (Ahrens and Chapman forthcoming: 18)

The link between different practitioners of enabling control systems in different locations, what unites them as users of those systems, would be their purposeful engagement in what they individually think of as their shared practice. Practices are therefore not just a matter of clever design. They have a strong normative character that draws necessarily on the imagination of practitioners who need to evaluate how, in their specific organizational environments, they can draw on the principles of the practice. Practices are something that can be done well or badly, and the judgement of good or bad performances is one that is, if not always shared, then at least debated by the group of practitioners (Barnes 2001). In this way the design or intention of a control system is at least as much the outcome of action as the other way around.

What practice theorizing does for our understanding of new performance measurement systems and performance management is first and foremost to offer a new language for approaching the relationship between performance metrics and skilful practical activity. It is mindful of the intentions of organizational actors, but is not blind to the considerable variations with which performance management concepts operate in different organizations. We must take seriously the specific circumstances in which people in organizations manage performance, because performance management concepts are only going to make sense in so far as they can help people make sense of the particular circumstances of their work. Ongoing refinements and innovations in performance measurement systems and concepts are frequently brought about by practitioners' experiments and their discussions of what works, when, and how.

1.4 **The discovery of new performance measures**

At the heart of the difficulties of conceptualizing the relationships between performance management concepts and their practical use has been a false model of how practitioners use measurements and measurement theory. Much research has been seeking to guide practice either with theoretical reflections or observations of 'best practices' in exceptional organizations, as if such accounts might drive activity in other organizations. But if the actual performance management system in a real organization is better understood as arising from activity in the organization, then knowledge cannot simply be 'transferred' with the expectation that designs will soon enough work in practice.

Let us first of all look at where the performance measurement system designs come from. How are activities in organizations selected and framed so that they can be recommended as 'best practices'? In the case of the 'transfer' of best practices from organizations to the literature, a familiar tale is that of the field researcher stumbling over an innovative practice that he or she simply documents to aid its dissemination amongst practitioners and academics—'We just had to recognise a valid solution when it appeared' (Kaplan 1998: 98). Such tales are misleading in so far as they appeal to readily articulated, distinct practices 'out there in the field'. In reality, the boundaries of an innovative practice tend to be blurred. As the research on the adoption of ABC shows, even after a technique has been popularized, it can be adopted in very different ways (Gosselin 1997), and researchers are often unsure, therefore, whether what they are looking at is or is not ABC.

In light of the constant stream of field studies, reports, and surveys that document local variations, conceptual conflicts with existing techniques, and variously aborted attempts at implementation, the chances of being able to just spot a new technique functioning in practice appear minute. The pioneering practitioners themselves may not be of much help for identifying novelties if they are the outcome of incremental changes over a longer period. If the practitioners regard them as mere variants of older practices, they may not even draw attention to them with a new name. Moreover, to become visible as, specifically, accounting, management control, or performance measurement innovations, new practices need to be framed as in some way technical-numerical. New practices would remain invisible to the accounting researcher if classified as an aspect of more encompassing changes in organizational processes. Performance management innovations that are part of organizational changes may be disregarded as mere technical tweaking and their contribution to substantial organizational innovation may be overlooked.

In these scenarios the innovative performance management practices are silent. They do not advertise themselves. One important point, therefore, about the discovery of best practices is that it hinges on an articulation of performance management work that is not normally part of the actual functioning of performance management in organizations. Labelling best practices as such, whether by an academic or an 'innovation champion' inside the organization, is unusual. The articulation of innovativeness becomes part of the context in which the innovative practices function. This means that the researcher who stumbles over an innovation champion for a new practice is not just dealing with a new way of working, but with a programmatic aspiration on the part of those organizational members who felt it useful to articulate the new way of working in this manner.

Such programmatic aspirations are usually highly organization-specific. As such, they have paradoxical consequences. In principle, the packaging of the innovation assists its transfer to other organizations because it increases recognition. But the very organizational specificity that gave rise to the packaging in this particular manner impedes that transfer, especially if the innovation poses as a pure technique, uncontaminated by context, that can be 'plugged into' any organization. We would argue that underlying the spread of innovations from one organization to the next is not only the understanding of what becomes labelled as the innovation. Crucially, the success of implementation efforts depends on the wider understanding of the circumstances that gave rise to the specific promotional discourses surrounding it.

In the case of two of the most popular recent innovations 'discovered in practice', the normative, practitioner-oriented performance management literature has tended to first ignore and later schematize the organizational roles of the new techniques. The BSC was originally presented as a fairly modest technique for putting financial information in the context of different kinds of non-financial information (Kaplan and Norton 1992), brought to Robert Kaplan's attention by Arthur Schneiderman of Analog Devices (Kaplan 1998: 99). Subsequently it has been proposed as an all-encompassing management control system that should be at the heart of the strategy-making process (Kaplan and Norton 2001a, 2001b) but without giving much detail about the practical implications of this.

Whilst the tale of the lucky researcher who discovers new practices ignores the practical processes of identifying the technical aspects of the innovation and articulating its organizational roles, the tale of the thoughtful academic who peruses the literatures in economics, psychology, or sociology to develop recommendations for practice suggests that knowledge can be transferred in the opposite direction, from the academy to the organization. For example, the long-standing, unsuccessful advice to abandon full costs for decision-making usually has given little thought to organizational context. The failure to adopt has been regarded as cognitive throughout, even though the culprits changed. Initially, practitioners were regarded as not understanding the advice. More recently, academics were suspected of not conceptualizing key organizational variables—a failure some sought to remedy, for example, through the use of real options.

The deeper theoretical problem of the tales of knowledge transfer—in whichever direction—lies with the failure to think through the relationship between performance management system design and organizational activity. The 'I discovered an innovation in practice' tale pretends that it can distil a technical logic from observed practice—design represents the essence of activity. The 'I thought about it in my armchair' tale pretends that a logically argued case can change what organizational members do—design orders activity. Both versions identify design with activity. They fail to acknowledge that the ways in which designs are used is essentially practical, so much so that the links between performance management practices in different locations is mainly provided by the practitioners who think of themselves as contributing to this practice, and not by some 'essential' technical feature.

1.5 **Conclusion**

In their introduction, Ittner and Larcker (2001) stated that the most striking observation that came to them in the course of their review of the empirical management accounting literature is the extent to which research is driven by changes in practice. They note that this might mean that management accounting research has become more relevant, after having been criticized for its irrelevance in the 1980s. However, the faddish nature of management accounting research has not encouraged theoretical integration, and in some cases has meant that research topics:

tend to disappear as the next big management accounting 'innovation' appears, even though earlier 'hot topics' may not have been fully explored. (Ittner and Larcker 2001: 356)

In a similar vein, Luft and Shields (2003) raised concerns about the adoption of what they call practice-defined variables in contemporary management accounting research. The concern was that by taking developments in contemporary performance management practice directly in their own terms, researchers undermine their potential to act as little more than laggardly reporters on practice.

For many performance measurement innovations, it would appear that the apparent certainty of an acronym or label masks considerable definitional and practical uncertainty. In attempting to understand the nature of the BSC through a cross-sectional questionnaire, Ittner et al. (2003) found it to be surprisingly invisible. In their analysis of relative levels of measurement effort in different organizations (p. 734), they found no statistical differences in terms of their measurement of the drivers of long-term organizational success between those that claimed to have a BSC and those that did not. This contrasted intriguingly with the finding that those claiming to use economic value added did report significantly higher levels of customers, environmental performance, and innovation measures.

We might ask many further questions concerning the nature of the BSC. Does it involve performance-related pay and, if so, how? Is the scorecard a tool concerned with shareholders, enlightened shareholders, or is it about a wider range of stakeholders? Is the scorecard concerned to balance competing objectives, or is it a tool to support the development of causal models? Is the scorecard appropriate for use at the level of the corporation? The business unit? The individual? Is the scorecard concerned with the implementation of strategy or its development and refinement? Is the scorecard a tool for learning or control?

An appealing place to hope to find an answer to these questions is in the various writings of Kaplan and Norton. However, Kaplan (1998), in describing his approach to his work, emphasized its incremental and developmental nature, and so we should not be surprised that the concept of the BSC has been significantly transfigured through the course of successive articles and books. Even if a reliable source description of the BSC were available, however, it would be of limited use in practice. Even the idea that a BSC would comprise four families of measures has proven not to act as a definitional boundary in terms of what people will attach the label to. One of the first academic studies of the BSC was Malina and Selto (2001). They studied something that was called a BSC by those involved with it, but which operated as an interorganizational performance measurement tool between a company and its distributors, and which had five families of measures,[2] a feature that, based on anecdotal evidence, would seem quite common. Organizations naturally prioritize their own concerns over a notionally correct blueprint of what a scorecard should look like (e.g. Hansen and Mouritsen 2005).

In this chapter we have discussed various aspects of the relationship between measurement and day-to-day activity. We have emphasized the potential contribution to performance management activities of various aspects of academic knowledge. We first reviewed situations and ways in which performance management has a track record of working well. We moved on to note that unfortunately such activity on its own was unlikely to contribute to sustainable competitive advantage. Finally, informed by a practice theory perspective, we turned the problem of 'you get what you measure' on its head. Our perspective offers a particular appreciation of the role of measurement in the construction of orderly behaviour that can help to re-establish a positive link between performance measurement and skilful practical activity

☐ ACKNOWLEDGEMENTS

We would like to thank participants at the first joint workshop by the Management Control Association and the European Network for Research on Organisational and Accounting Change in Antwerp, 7–9 April 2005, for their comments on an earlier version of this chapter.

☐ NOTES

1 The 'Wings and Things' dish was a particular customer favourite, but one that was not popular with chefs since it required the synchronization of different cooking procedures for its individual ingredients.

2 The fifth category was corporate citizenship, which Malina and Selto (2001) analysed as a part of the customer value.

☐ REFERENCE

Adler, P. and Borys, B. (1996). 'Two Types of Bureaucracy: Enabling and Coercive', *Administrative Science Quarterly*, 41(1): 61–90.

Ahrens, T. and Chapman, C. S. (2002). 'The Structuration of Legitimate Performance Measures and Management: Day-to-Day Contests of Accountability in a U.K. Restaurant Chain', *Management Accounting Research*, 13(2): 1–21.

—— —— (2004). 'Accounting for Flexibility and Efficiency: A Field Study of Management Control Systems in a Restaurant Chain', *Contemporary Accounting Research*, 21(2): 271–301.

—— —— (forthcoming). 'Management Accounting as Practice'. Accounting, Organizations and Society.

Barnes, B. (2001). 'Practice as Collective Action', in T. R. Schatzki, K. Knorr Cetina, and E. von Savigny (eds.), *The Practice Turn in Contemporary Theory* (pp. 17–28). London: Routledge.

Barney, J., Wright, M., and Ketchen, D. J. (2001). 'The Resource-based View of the Firm: Ten Years after 1991', *Journal of Management*, 27: 625–41.

Bisbe, J., Batista-Foguet, J., and Chenhall, R. H. (2005). 'What Do We Really Mean by Interactive Control Systems? The Danger of Theoretical Misspecification'. Paper presented at the Global Management Accounting Research Symposium, Sydney, 16–18 June.

Chapman, C. S. (1997). 'Reflections on a Contingent View of Accounting', *Accounting, Organizations and Society*, 22(2): 189–205.

—— —— and Chua, W. F. (2003). 'Technology-driven Integration, Automation and Standardisation of Business Processes: Implications for Accounting', in A. Bhimani (ed.), *Management Accounting in the Digital Economy*. Oxford: Oxford University Press, pp. 74–94.

Dearden, J. (1966). 'Myth of Real-Time Management Information', *Harvard Business Review*, 44(3): 123–32.

—— (1967). 'Computers: No Impact on Divisional Control', *Harvard Business Review*, 45(1): 99–104.

Dearden, J. (1968). 'Appraising Profit Center Managers', *Harvard Business Review*, 46(3), 80–7.

Eccles, R. (1991). 'The Performance Measurement Manifesto', *Harvard Business Review*, Jan–Feb: 131–9.

Ezzamel, M. (1997). 'Accounting, Control and Accountability: Preliminary Evidence from Ancient Egypt', *Critical Perspectives on Accounting*, 8(6): 563–601.

Gandy, T., and Chapman, C. S. (1997). 'Data Warehousing—Unleashing the Power of Customer Information', *Chartered Banker*, 3(5): 10–42.

Gosselin, M. (1997). 'The Effect of Strategy and Organizational Structure on the Adoption and Implementation of Activity-based Costing', *Accounting, Organizations and Society*, 22(2): 105–22.

Hansen, A., and Mouritsen, J. (2005). 'Strategies and Organisational Problems: Constructing Corporate Value and Coherence in Balanced Scorecard Processes', in C. S. Chapman (ed.), *Controlling Strategy: Management, Accounting and Performance Measurement*. Oxford: Oxford University Press.

Hiromoto, T. (1988). 'Another Hidden Edge—Japanese Management Accounting', *Harvard Business Review*, 66(4): 22–6.

Ittner, C., and Larcker, D. (2001). 'Assessing Empirical Research in Managerial Accounting: A Value-based Management Perspective', *Journal of Accounting and Economics*, 32(1–3): 349–410.

—— —— (2005). 'Moving from Strategic Measurement to Strategic Data Analysis', in C. S. Chapman (ed.), *Controlling Strategy: Management, Accounting and Performance Measurement*. Oxford: Oxford University Press, pp. 86–105.

—— —— and Randall, T. (2003). 'Performance Implications of Strategic Performance Measurement in Financial Services Firms', *Accounting, Organizations and Society*, 28(7/8): 715–41.

Johnson, H., and Kaplan, R. (1987). *Relevance Lost: The Rise and Fall of Management Accounting*. Boston: Harvard Business School Press.

Kaplan, R. S. (1983). 'Measuring Manufacturing Performance: A New Challenge for Management Accounting Research', *Accounting Review*, 58(4): 686–705.

—— (1998). 'Innovation Action Research: Creating New Management Theory and Practice', *Journal of Management Accounting Research*, 10: 89–118.

—— and Norton, D. P. (1992). 'The Balanced Scorecard—Measures that Drive Performance', *Harvard Business Review*, January–February: 71–9.

—— —— (1996). *The Balanced Scorecard: Translating Strategy into Action*. Boston: Harvard Business School Press.

—— —— (2000). 'Having Trouble with Your Strategy? Then Map it', *Harvard Business Review*, September–October: 167–77.

—— —— (2001*a*). 'Transforming the Balanced Scorecard from Performance Measurement to Strategic Management: Part I', *Accounting Horizons*, 15(1): 87–105.

—— —— (2001*b*). 'Transforming the Balanced Scorecard from Performance Measurement to Strategic Management: Part II', *Accounting Horizons*, 15(2): 147–61.

Luft, J. and Shields, M. (2003). 'Mapping Management Accounting: Graphics and Guidelines for Theory-consistent Empirical Research', *Accounting, Organizations and Society*, 28(2/3): 169–249.

Malina, M. and Selto, F. (2001). 'Communicating and Controlling Strategy: An Empirical Study of the Balanced Scorecard', *Journal of Management Accounting Research*, 13: 47–90.

Malone, T. W. (2004). 'Bringing the Market Inside', *Harvard Business Review*, 82(4): 106–14.

Marginson, D. and Ogden, S. (2005). 'Coping with Ambiguity through the Budget: The Positive Effects of Budgetary Targets on Managers' Budgeting Behaviours', *Accounting, Organizations and Society*, 30(5): 435–56.

Mauriel, J. J. and Anthony, R. N. (1966). 'Misevaluation of Investment Center Performance', *Harvard Business Review*, 44(2): 98–107.

Neely, A. (2003). *Measuring Business Performance: Why What, How*. London: Economist Books.

Revsine, L. (1981). 'Let's Stop Eating Our Seedcorn', *Harvard Business Review*, 59(1): 128–34.

Ridgway, V. (1956). 'Dysfunctional Consequences of Performance Measurement', *Administrative Science Quarterly*, 1(2): 240–7.

Roberts, J. (1990). 'Strategy and Accounting in a U.K. Conglomerate', *Accounting, Organizations and Society*, 15: 107–26.

Simons, R. (1990). 'The Role of Management Control Systems in Creating Competitive Advantage: New Perspectives', *Accounting, Organizations and Society*, 15(1/2): 127–43.

—— (1995). *Levers of control*. Boston: Harvard Business School Press.

van der Veeken, H. and Wouters, M. (2002). 'Using Accounting Information Systems by Operations Managers in a Project Company', *Management Accounting Research*, 13(3): 345–70.

Weston, F. (1974). 'Prepare for the Financial Accounting Revolution', *Harvard Business Review*, 52(5): 6–13.

Wildavsky, A. (1981). 'Foreword', in M. Malvey, *Simple Systems, Complex Environments*. London: Sage.

2 Contract theory analysis of managerial accounting issues[1]

Stanley Baiman

2.1 Introduction

In the last two decades, contract theory has become the dominant analytical research paradigm in managerial accounting.[2] It has informed the managerial accounting literature both directly and indirectly. In the former case, formal contract theory modelling of managerial accounting issues has provided important insights into the design and role of managerial accounting systems. In the latter case, many of the hypotheses tested in recent behavioural and empirical research in managerial accounting have been derived from informal reasoning based on contract theory. Thus, any consumer of recent and likely future managerial accounting research would benefit from possessing a general understanding of contract theory. The purpose of this chapter is to provide that general understanding. The chapter begins with a non-technical explanation of the contract theory model and a demonstration of how two types of incentive problem are formulated within that framework. It then discusses three managerial accounting issues to which formal contract theory analysis has been applied. This discussion illustrates how the design of some observed managerial accounting procedures can be understood as a response to underlying incentive problems.[3]

2.2 Overview of the contracting model

Contract theory studies ways in which the efficiency of individual behaviour in multiperson or group settings can be improved. Clearly, a group such as a firm will be more efficient and productive if all members share the same objectives and cooperate rather than if they differ in objectives and act self-interestedly or non-cooperatively. People's preferences can be in conflict because they value actions and outcomes differently. For example, they may differ in terms of their effort aversion, time preferences, risk preferences, or beliefs.

Contract theory takes as given that people within a group can have preferences which are in conflict and that each group member will act in his own self-interest. It examines how the design of the group's managerial accounting system and the contracts among the group members can *influence what is in each person's self-interest*, and thereby mitigate the inefficiencies arising from the underlying incentive conflicts. For example, depending upon how a division manager's performance is measured, it can be affected in different ways by the amount of capital that corporate headquarters allocates to his or her division. Further, the division manager typically has better information than corporate management about the rate of return that any additional capital invested in that division could earn. Therefore, the division manager may have an incentive to misrepresent the information during the capital budgeting process, so as to manipulate the amount of capital allocated to the division and, thereby, manipulate his or her performance measure. This may result in an inefficient allocation of capital within the firm. Contract theory examines how the design of the capital budgeting process, managerial accounting system, and employment contracts can reduce this inefficient allocation of capital.

Relative to the prior literature, the methodological contribution of contract theory is that it provides a rigorous and consistent way to model problems in which there are potential conflicts of interests among individuals within a group (e.g. between shareholders and managers or between managers and workers).[4] The consistency underlying contract theory research arises from three basic assumptions. First, all parties are assumed to be rational and have unlimited computational ability. Each person knows their own best interest and acts so as to maximize it. Second, each person believes that all others in the group are rational and can correctly anticipate everyone else's behaviour. The fact that everyone acts rationally and anticipates that everyone else will act rationally means that contract theory only examines *equilibrium* outcomes. Therefore, there are no 'surprises'. Third, and related to rationality, only contracts that can be enforced are studied. If a person agrees to an unenforceable contract, the other contracting parties realize that the first person will feel no obligation to fulfil it. A promise is meaningless unless it is in the best interest of the one making the promise to keep it. And if it is, the promise need not be stated, for the other parties will infer that the one making the promise will take that action even without stating it. As a result only enforceable contracts are studied. This implies that a feasible contract can only be based on information that is jointly observable by the contracting parties and the legal system, which enforces compliance with the contract.[5]

Before we discuss specific managerial accounting issues to which the contract theory model has been applied, let us first see how two types of incentive conflicts are modelled within contract theory.

2.2.1 MODELLING INCENTIVE CONFLICTS

2.2.1.1 The basic hidden action model

In the basic contract theory setting the firm consists of two individuals: a principal and an agent. The principal acts as the owner of the firm while the agent acts as a worker. The principal hires the agent, provides the capital (i.e. the production function), and designs the agent's compensation or employment contract and the managerial accounting system including the monitoring systems, resource allocation procedures, and task allocation. The agent is hired to choose a personally costly action or effort, which, together with the production function, generates an outcome that the principal values. In this simplest of settings the incentive conflict or conflict of interest between the principal and the agent arises for two reasons. First, the agent incurs disutility from taking the action that he or she is being hired to take and the disutility is increasing in his or her action or effort. Therefore, all else equal, the agent would prefer to make as little effort as possible. Second, because the principal cannot observe the agent's action he or she cannot contract on it. Instead, the principal can only contract on an imperfect indicator of the agent's action choice. This is termed the 'hidden action' or 'moral hazard' problem. As noted above, the principal knows that the agent will behave in his or her own self-interest. The principal's problem is then to influence the action that is in the agent's self-interest through the design of the managerial accounting system and the agent's employment contract.

To simplify further the analysis and emphasize the basic trade-offs considered by the model, assume that the principal is risk-neutral and the agent is risk-averse. A risk-neutral person is indifferent between receiving a lottery and a payment equal to the expected value of that lottery. Thus, a risk-neutral person does not have to be compensated for bearing risk. In contrast, a risk-averse person strictly prefers to receive the expected value of the lottery to the lottery itself. A risk-averse person requires additional compensation for any risk that he or she is made to bear. For example, if a risk-averse person earns compensation of k but is paid in the form of a lottery, he or she requires that the lottery payment have an expected value that is strictly greater than k. The expected payment in excess of k is required to compensate the risk-averse person for bearing the risk and is referred to as the risk premium. Notice then that, all other things equal, with a risk-neutral principal and a risk-averse agent, it is efficient for the principal to bear all of the risk. Thus, when we later derive the agent's optimal contract, any risk imposed on the agent reduces risk-sharing efficiency and therefore must have been imposed in order to mitigate other sources of inefficiency.

To formulate the above hidden action problem, we will use the following notation:

x	=	the cash flow generated by the agent's action or effort
z	=	the performance report on which the agent compensation is based
$s(z)$	=	the agreed-upon compensation to the agent if the performance report is z
$h(x, z\|a)$	=	the joint probability that cash flow x and performance measure z occur given that the agent chose action or effort a
$a \in \{a_L, a_H\}$	=	the two possible actions or efforts from which the agent can choose where $a_L < a_H$
$V(a)$	=	the agent's disutility for choosing action a, where $V(a_L) < V(a_H)$
$U(s(z))$	=	the agent's utility from compensation $s(z)$ where $U(\bullet)$ is increasing and concave in the compensation, which is consistent with the agent being risk-averse

For simplicity, assume that the joint distribution over the cash flow and the performance report given action a are independent (i.e. $h(x, z|a) = g(x|a)f(z|a)$) Further, assume that the probability distributions over the performance report induced by the different actions are different (i.e. it is *not* the case that for all $z\,f(z|a_L)/f(z|a_H) = 1$).[6] This implies that the performance measure conveys information about the agent's action choice. Further, assume that a_H results in a greater expected cash flow to the principal and a greater expected performance report than a_L. The basic hidden action problem can then be stated as:

$$\max_{a\in\{a_L,\,a_H\},\,s(\bullet)} \int_{x,\,z} (x - s(z))g(x|a)f(z|a)dxdz \tag{1}$$

subject to

$$\int_z U(s(z))f(z|a)dz - V(a) \geq \overline{U} \tag{2}$$

$$a \in \underset{a'\in\{a_L,\,a_H\}}{\mathrm{argmax}} \int_z U(s(z))f(z|a')dx - V(a') \tag{3}$$

The objective function, equation (1), states that the principal wants to choose the compensation contract and the agent's action choice, that will maximize the principal's expected net cash flow, after compensating the agent. Note that the principal is not able freely to choose the agent's action choice. Instead the action specified in the objective function (referred to as the obedient action) must be the one that is in the agent's self-interest to choose, i.e. the one that maximizes the agent's expected utility *given the compensation contract chosen by the principal*. The only way in which the principal can influence the agent's action choice is through his or her own choice of the compensation contract, $s\,(\bullet)$. This constraint on the principal's ability to influence the agent's action choice is represented by equation (3), which is referred to as the agent's incentive compatibility constraint. It states that the agent will choose whatever action maximizes his or her expected utility, given the compensation contract he or she faces. The constraint in equation (3) captures the equilibrium underlying contract theory analysis: everyone acts rationally and anticipates that everyone else will act rationally. An additional constraint on the principal's ability to influence the agent is equation (2), which states that for the contract to be feasible it must satisfy the agent's (exogenously specified) outside opportunity utility, $\overline{U}$. That is, the contract must be such that the agent (at least weakly) prefers working for the firm and choosing the obedient action than working elsewhere and receiving expected utility of $\overline{U}$. Equation (2) is referred to as the agent's individual rationality constraint.

If the agent were not self-interested, but if hired would always take the action desired by the principal, there would be no incentive problem associated with the agent and the constraint in equation (3) could be dropped. To satisfy the remaining constraint, equation (2), it would be sufficient to pay the agent an amount s such that $U(s) = \overline{U} + V(a)$. On the other hand, if the agent is self-interested and the constraint in equation (3) cannot be dropped, the above payment scheme might not satisfy equation (3) and, therefore, might not be sufficient to motivate the agent to take the principal's desired action choice.

To better understand the trade-offs in the hidden action problem when the agent is self-interested, we will consider three cases. In case 1, assume that the principal wants to induce the agent to take action a_L, the action for which the agent incurs the least disutility. This is easily accomplished by paying the agent a constant compensation s such that $U(s) = \overline{U} + V(a_L)$, regardless of the cash flow x. Because the agent is work-averse, if he or she is paid a constant, his or her rational response is to choose the action for which he or she incurs the least disutility, a_L. Thus, the compensation induces the desired or obedient action choice, a_L, and hence satisfies equation (3). Further, the constant compensation pays the agent the least amount necessary to assure that the agent will work for the principal and therefore satisfies the individual rationality constraint, equation (2). Finally, the compensation scheme imposes no risk on the risk-averse agent, so that risk-sharing between the agent and principal is efficient. Notice that the optimal compensation scheme for case 1 is the same as when we assumed that the agent was not self-interested.

Next, consider case 2, in which we assume that the principal wants to induce the agent to take action a_H. Further assume $z = a$ so that the agent can be compensated directly on his or her observed action choice. In this case, the optimal compensation scheme is to pay the agent s such that $U(s) = \overline{U} + V(a_H)$, if the agent chooses a_H and zero otherwise. The compensation contract satisfies equation (3) and thereby induces the obedient action. It also imposes no risk on the risk-averse agent. Finally, it pays the agent the least amount necessary to assure that the agent will work for the firm, thereby satisfying the individual rationality constraint.

In both cases, 1 and 2, there are no unresolved incentive problems because: (a) the principal induces the agent to choose the obedient action choice (a_L in case 1 and a_H in case 2); (b) the agent is not made to bear any risk; and (c) the principal pays the agent the least amount necessary to assure that the agent will work for the firm. When all three of the above conditions are satisfied, we have achieved the maximum efficiency, referred to as the 'first-best'.

Finally, consider case 3, in which the performance measure is the firm's cash flow (i.e. $z = x$), and the principal wants to induce the agent to take a_H.[7] The optimal contract is then:

$$\frac{1}{U'(s(x))} = \lambda + \mu\left[1 - \frac{f(x|a_L)}{f(x|a_H)}\right] \tag{4}$$

The terms λ and μ are derived from the optimal solution to equations (1)–(3). λ is related to the constant that has to be paid to the agent to assure that the agent's individual rationality constraint, equation (2), is satisfied. μ is a measure of how costly it is to satisfy the incentive compatibility constraint (equation 3) and therefore how severe the hidden action problem is. In cases 1 and 2 it cost the principal nothing to induce the agent to take the obedient action beyond the cost of satisfying his or her outside opportunity utility, so that the constraint in equation (3) was not binding and $\mu = 0$.

Recall that in cases 1 and 2 the optimal contract paid the agent a constant regardless of the performance report z. That can only happen in equation (4) when there are no unresolved incentive problems and hence $\mu = 0$, or the cash flow is completely uninformative about the agent's action choice and hence $f(x/a_L)/f(x/a_H) = 1$ for all x. But by assumption, the latter case does not hold. Further, it can be shown that $\mu > 0$, when the principal wants to induce the agent to take a_H, but can only contract on an imperfect monitor of the agent's action choice such as the cash flow.[8] Therefore, the right-hand side of equation (4) varies in the performance report ($z = x$) and, unlike in cases 1 and 2, the agent's compensation must vary in the performance report (i.e. the left-hand side of equation (4) must vary in $z = x$). Even though the agent is risk-averse and the principal is risk-neutral, the most efficient way of inducing the agent to take the obedient action is by imposing risk on the agent. Otherwise, if the agent were assured a constant payment regardless of the cash flow, he or she would choose the non-obedient action choice, a_L. Given that the optimal compensation contract imposes risk on the risk-averse agent in case 3, the principal must pay the agent a risk premium, which he did not have to pay in cases 1 and 2. Thus, case 3 illustrates that with a non-trivial underlying incentive problem, the optimal contract sacrifices efficient risk-sharing in order to improve productive efficiency—getting the agent to take the more productive action a_H.

To further interpret the optimal contract (equation 4), continue to assume that $z = x$ and, in addition, that a higher observed cash flow indicates that it is relatively more likely that action a_H was chosen (i.e. $[f(x/a_L)/f(x/a_H)]$ is decreasing in x). This additional assumption together with the fact that the agent's utility function is increasing and concave, and that $\mu > 0$, implies that the agent's optimal compensation is increasing in the observed cash flow, x. The optimal compensation contract (equation 4) can now be interpreted as stating that the higher the observed cash flow, the more likely it is that the agent acted obediently, and the more the agent is paid.

Given the assumed rationality, the equilibrium solution, and the optimal compensation contract, the principal knows for certain that the agent has chosen a_H. However, the optimal compensation contract is such that it appears to an outsider *as if* the principal were using the observed cash flow to infer the likelihood of the agent having chosen a_H and rewarding the agent based on that inference. The problem is that the principal can contract only on what he or she can *prove*, not on what he or she *knows*.

To summarize then, if there is no unresolved incentive problem, either because the principal wants the agent to take his or her least personally costly action (case 1) or because the principal can contract on the agent's action choice (case 2), the agent's optimal compensation is a constant, the principal absorbs all of the risk associated with the uncertain cash flow, and we have efficient risk-sharing and efficient production. However, when the principal can only contract on an imperfect monitor of the agent's action choice, such as the observed cash flow, and wants to induce the agent to choose an action for which the agent incurs more than the minimum disutility (case 3), the principal must impose some of the risk of the uncertain performance report on the agent. Imposing on the agent the risk associated with his or her action makes the agent internalize some of the benefit of taking productive effort, but at the cost to the principal of inefficient risk-sharing and having to pay the agent a risk premium for bearing that risk. *Therefore, for the hidden action problem the optimal contract trades off risk-sharing and productive effort.*

Before leaving the basic model, one additional result needs to be discussed because it underlies much of the contract theory research in accounting. Managerial accounting fulfils part of its control function by supplying information on which performance evaluation judgements can be made, e.g. budgets, costs, revenues, and transfer prices. So an issue of fundamental importance to managerial accounting is the conditions under which costlessly producing and incorporating an additional piece of information for performance evaluation purposes is valuable. In our basic model, when does costlessly adding a signal y to a compensation contract already based on x result in a *strict* Pareto improvement?[9] The informativeness condition provides a surprisingly straightforward answer.[10] It states that the necessary and sufficient condition for adding signal y to the compensation contract to lead to a strict Pareto improvement is that the pair of signals (x, y) contains information about the action a not contained in x alone. This result is surprising for several reasons. First, the necessary and sufficient condition is a statistical condition. It says nothing about the utility functions of the parties, the extent of the incentive problem, the production function, or other seemingly important *economic* parameters of the problem. Second, incorporating y into the compensation contract has two countervailing effects: (*a*) because y is a random variable, incorporating it into the compensation contract imposes additional risk on the agent, causing him to demand a higher risk premium from the principal; and (*b*) y may enable the principal to better infer the agent's action, making it cheaper to induce the agent to choose the obedient action.[11] Thus it would seem that if signal y is too noisy, it would impose so much risk on the agent that it would not be worthwhile incorporating it into the compensation contract. However, the Informativeness Principle proves that, regardless of how noisy the signal y is, as long as (x, y) contains information about the action a not contained in x alone, incorporating it into the compensation contract results in a strict Pareto improvement. The reason is as follows. Assume that the optimal contract involving only x is $s(x)$. A feasible (although not necessarily optimal) contract involving (x, y) is $s(x) + \delta y$, where δ is a compensation weight chosen by the principal. For small but non-zero δ, adding δy to $s(x)$ results in a strictly positive incentive benefit, but no additional risk imposed on the agent. The reason for the latter is that the risk-averse agent is essentially risk-neutral when faced with an infinitesimally small risk.

2.2.1.2 The basic hidden information model

In the above analysis, the principal and the agent had the same information and beliefs about all the problem variables, such as the production function $(f(x|a))$, the utility function $(U(s) - V(a))$, and the agent's outside opportunity utility $(\overline{U})$. However, in many settings, it is reasonable to expect that the agent has superior information about these or other problem variables. Clearly, bottom-up budgeting is based on this premise.

When the agent has private information about a variable, knowledge of which, would affect the principal's valuation of the outcome or his or her choice of the agent's obedient action, we have a 'hidden information' or 'adverse selection' problem. In this section, we will see how contract theory deals with this additional complicating factor.

When the agent has private information, the principal no longer wants to induce an obedient action from the agent, but rather an obedient action *rule*.[12] Equivalently, the principal's problem now is to both elicit the private information from the agent and induce him to implement the obedient action consistent with that information. This greatly complicates the principal's problem because the principal now must search over the entire space of compensation contracts, including those that induce the agent to misreport his or her private information.

However, the Revelation Principle considerably simplifies the search process.[13] It proves that, given certain assumptions, the principal can restrict the search to the smaller space of *truth-inducing* compensation contracts. To see this, assume that the principal offers the agent a compensation contract such that it is optimal for the agent to misreport his or her private information in a particular way. Call this the first arrangement. Now consider a second arrangement whereby the principal offers the agent exactly the same compensation contract as under the first arrangement *and* commits to take whatever report the agent sends to the principal and 'lie to himself or herself' exactly as the agent would have lied under the first arrangement. With this commitment by the principal, under the second arrangement it is optimal for the agent honestly to reveal the information—the principal is lying to himself or herself in exactly the way the agent would have lied. In addition, the agent has the same action choice incentive and the principal and the agent receive the same expected utility under the second arrangement as under the first. Thus the second arrangement, which induces the agent to tell the truth, is completely equivalent to the first, in which the agent is induced to lie. It is important to keep in mind that the principal is not getting the agent to reveal honestly his or her private information for free. In order to see this, let us consider the following variation on the case 3 hidden action problem discussed above.

Assume that both the principal and the agent know that before they negotiate their contract, the agent will privately observe a productivity signal $\theta \in \{\theta_L, \theta_H\}$, where they agree on the prior probability distribution over the signal. The signal eliminates all uncertainty about the production function. That is, for any cash flow x and observed signal $\theta \in \{\theta_L, \theta_H\}$, the agent knows exactly how much effort he or she must expend to produce x. Represent that effort as $V(x, \theta_i)$. Further, assume that, for any cash flow x, if the agent's signal is θ_L, both the agent's effort and his or her marginal effort required to achieve cash flow x are greater than if the agent's signal is θ_H.[14] Thus, we can refer to the agent with signal θ_L as the low-productivity agent and the agent with signal θ_H as the high-productivity agent. Finally, given that the agent observes his or her productivity parameter before contracting with the principal, the agent will only accept the contract offered if it satisfies the agent's outside expected utility *given his or her privately observed productivity parameter.* Now if the principal could observe the productivity signal before contracting with the agent, the principal would tell the agent to produce a different outcome for each signal, e.g. x_L when $\theta = \theta_L$ and x_H when $\theta = \theta_H$ (where $x_L < x_H$), and in each case pay the agent a constant just large enough to make the agent indifferent between working for the principal and not, i.e. $U(s_L) = \overline{U} + V(x_L, \theta_L)$ and $U(s_H) = \overline{U} + V(x_H, \theta_H)$. This achieves first-best.

But what happens when, as we have assumed, only the agent observes the productivity signal? If the principal offers the agent the first-best contract, then, regardless of what the agent actually observed, the agent would maximize his or her utility by always claiming to be the low-productivity agent. If the agent actually observed θ_L and claimed θ_L, his or her utility would be $U(s_L) - V(x_L, \theta_L) = \overline{U} + V(x_L, \theta_L) - V(x_L, \theta_L) = \overline{U}$; while if the agent actually observed θ_H but claimed θ_L, his or her utility would be $U(s_L) - V(x_L, \theta_H) = \overline{U} + V(x_L, \theta_L) - V(x_L, \theta_H) > \overline{U}$.[15] This amount that the high-productivity agent earns in excess of $\overline{U}$ by claiming to be the low-productivity agent is referred to as the agent's information rent. The principal would clearly like to reduce this excess compensation that he or she is paying. But the only way of doing so is to distort the required production schedule away from first-best. In particular, it is optimal for the principal to keep the cash flow required of the θ_H agent at the first-best amount but to reduce the cash flow required of the θ_L agent to less than the first-best amount. This makes it less attractive for the θ_H agent to claim that he or she is θ_L, which allows the principal to reduce (but not eliminate) the θ_H agent's informational rent. *Thus, an unavoidable trade-off arising from the agent being privately informed is between production efficiency and information rent.*[16]

So two fundamental insights from contract theory are: (*a*) hidden action results in a trade-off between production efficiency and risk-sharing efficiency, while (*b*) hidden information results in a trade-off between production efficiency and informational rent.

2.3 Some examples of contract theory applied to managerial accounting issues

One of the reasons why contract theory has become such an important paradigm in managerial accounting research is that both share a strong control orientation. For example, a large part of the applied managerial accounting literature as well as managerial accounting textbooks focus on the design of performance measures (financial vs. non-financial, cost vs. profit vs. residual income measures, etc.) and control techniques (e.g. variance analysis). The remainder of this chapter discusses some examples of the successful application of contract theory-based analysis to such managerial accounting issues. The first illustration involves the familiar managerial accounting technique of variance investigation. The remaining two applications involve more general analyses of performance measures and compensation schemes.

2.3.1 VARIANCE INVESTIGATION PROCEDURES

Variance analysis is perhaps the most well-known managerial accounting technique. It also represents the clearest example of the change in perspective in managerial accounting research caused by the introduction of the contract theory model. To illustrate this change in perspective, consider a simple setting in which a process produces an output that can be either good or defective. The traditional analysis of variance investigation procedures is based on the idea that what is being investigated is a purely mechanical process. In the usual scenario, the process being investigated has two states: in-control and out-of-control, and there is some known but *exogenous* probability of the in-control process going out of control. When the process is in control, it generates defective units with a known probability, r, and when it is out of control, it generates defective units with a higher but still known probability. The process manager collects a sample of size S, observes the sample defect rate, say d, and decides whether to intervene in the process. If the process is out of control, the process manager benefits by intervening in the process and resetting it to in-control. However, it is costly to intervene in the process in terms of both lost production and out-of-pocket labour costs. Therefore the manager does not want to intervene when in fact the process is in control. The process manager's problem is then to determine the optimal variance investigation policy, i.e. the cut-off defect rate C, such that if $d - r \geq C$, he will investigate the process and reset it if necessary.[17]

Prior to the introduction of the contract theory model, the process subject to investigation was viewed as completely automated and unaffected by the chosen variance investigation policy. But modelling the output-generating process as completely automated may not be a reasonable description. If human operators tend the process, they can influence the probability that defects are generated by, for example, taking more or less care in how they set up the machine, or in how they feed parts to the machine. In this case, the chosen variance investigation policy can influence the actions taken by the operators and, therefore, the realized defect rate.

How then should a variance investigation policy be designed, when the objective is to influence the behaviour of the machine's operators and thereby influence the probability of the process generating good versus defective units? This was one of the earliest managerial accounting topics analysed using the contract theory model (see e.g. Baiman and Demski 1980; Dye 1986). To illustrate the results, consider a simple hidden action setting with a risk-neutral principal and a risk- and work-averse agent. The agent operates a machine, which produces an output. Let x represent the yield rate, the percentage of parts produced that are good. By taking an action a, the agent produces a probability distribution over the output of good parts, $f(x|a)$. The principal prefers a larger x to a smaller one. Further, assume that the greater the agent's action a, the more likely it is that x will be large. Thus, the principal would like the agent to choose a large a. But the agent is work-averse. The principal cannot observe the agent's action, but can observe the outcome x. Upon observing x, the principal can decide to, at cost K, investigate the process and receive a signal y, which is produced by, and stochastically related to, the agent's action choice. The principal's variance investigation policy specifies:

1. when the principal will investigate, i.e. those realizations of x such that the principal will incur cost K and acquire signal y;
2. the compensation to the agent, $s(x)$, if the outcome is x and no investigation is taken; and
3. the compensation to the agent, $s(x, y)$, if the outcome is x, and an investigation is undertaken and signal y is observed.

Assume that the labour market is such that the principal can only pay non-negative compensation regardless of the x or y realizations.

When will the principal choose to investigate? Given the policy specified in the three specifications given above and the fact that the agent has no private information, the principal will know for certain what action the agent is induced to take. Therefore, if the investigation decision is left to the discretion of the principal, he or she will never choose to investigate! The principal cannot learn anything about the agent's action choice from signal y that he or she does not already know. But then the agent will realize that the 'threat' to investigate is not credible, and hence will act the same as if he or she were given a contract that did not allow for variance investigation and paid only $s(x)$. Thus, there is no value to a contract that leaves the variance investigation policy to the discretion of the principal.

Therefore, in this setting, we will only observe the principal incurring the cost to investigate if he or she contractually commits to the variance investigation policy. But notice that the principal is committing to incur a cost K not to learn about the agent's action choice—he knows what it is with certainty. Instead, the principal is committing to incur the variance investigation cost in order to mitigate the hidden action problem by basing the agent's contract on an additional informative, but costly, signal y.

What does the optimal variance investigation policy for this problem look like? For a large class of problems, the optimal variance investigation policy will be either of two forms depending on the risk-aversion of the agent:

1. For a very risk-averse agent, investigate all x smaller than, or equal to, some $\hat{x}$ (i.e. lower-tail investigation), where for every outcome x in the investigation region the agent's expected utility of compensation from the investigation is less than the utility of compensation if there were no investigation (i.e. $E_y U(s(x, y)) < U(s(x))$ for all $x \leq \hat{x}$).

2. For a less risk-averse agent, investigate all x greater than or equal to some $\check{x}$ (i.e. upper-tail investigation), where for every outcome x in the investigation region the agent's expected utility of compensation from the investigation is greater than the utility of compensation if there were no investigation (i.e. $E_y U(s(x, y)) > U(s(x))$ for all $x \geq \check{x}$).

Notice that the optimality of one-tail variance investigation policies is certainly consistent with policies observed in practice. To understand the logic of the result, let us first consider a very risk-averse agent. Recall that the signal y is stochastically related to the agent's action choice. The agent strongly prefers to not generate an x in the investigation region for two reasons. First, it subjects the agent to a lottery in the form of an investigation and, being very risk-averse, he or she derives a lot of disutility from bearing the compensation risk associated with the lottery. Second, the investigation is an unfavourable lottery (i.e. $E_y U(s(x, y)) < U(s(x))\ \forall x \leq \hat{x}$). Given that the agent is facing a lower-tailed investigation, the agent can only reduce the probability of being investigated by increasing his or her action choice, which is exactly what the principal desires. Thus, the principal can most efficiently induce the very risk-averse agent to take a higher action by making the investigation region low-tailed and making the agent's compensation from the investigation an unfavourable lottery.

Next, consider what happens if the agent is less risk-averse. For a less risk-averse agent, the threat of being subjected to a lottery provides less of an incentive to avoid the variance investigation region and, therefore, less motivation to the agent to increase his or her action. To strengthen the agent's motivation to choose a higher action the principal has to either increase the probability of investigating (by increasing the set of xs, which trigger the investigation) or make the lottery associated with the investigation more unfavourable (i.e. by lowering the agent's expected utility of $s(x, y)$ relative to $s(x)$). But the former is costly because every investigation costs K, and the latter is restricted by the fact that the principal must pay the agent a non-negative amount. Therefore, if the agent is sufficiently risk-tolerant, it becomes more efficient to motivate the agent by choosing an upper-tail investigation region and a *favourable* lottery (i.e. $E_y U(s(x, y)) > U(s(x)) \forall x \geq \breve{x}$). In this case the principal is motivating the agent by rewarding the latter for producing outcomes that do result in an investigation.

2.3.2 DESIGN OF PERFORMANCE MEASURES AND COMPENSATION SYSTEMS

In the last two decades there has been a substantial increase in interest in new ways of measuring firm and managerial performance and new ways of compensating managers for that performance. This can be seen in the discussion of the relative merits of accounting income versus variants of residual income for performance measurement; the use of financial versus non-financial measures of performance; and the different ways of combining financial and non-financial measures for performance measurement (e.g. the balanced scorecard (BSC)). A large body of contract theory-based research has examined these issues and has provided some useful insights. I will now discuss two lines of that research.

2.3.2.1 The use of stock price for performance evaluation and compensation

The efficient market hypothesis asserts (and much evidence suggests) that stock price is an unbiased estimate of firm value. Therefore, it seems reasonable that the best way of assessing the performance of management is by reference to the performance of the firm's stock price. This was certainly the logic that motivated the explosion of the use of stock-based compensation such as stock, stock option, phantom stock, etc. awards in the USA in the last two decades. Of course, there are several arguments against the assertion that stock-based performance evaluation and compensation is always optimal. First, except for top management, a manager's action is only tangentially related to stock price both because the latter is affected by the actions of many different managers and because it is affected by information not necessarily relevant to evaluating a manager. Second, stock price excludes information that is privately held by the firm that may be informative about the manager's performance. Third, as has been demonstrated in the last few years, management can influence stock price, at least in the short term, through earnings manipulations.[18] These are all important reasons to question a total reliance on stock-based performance measurement and compensation for management.

Contract theory-based analysis provides a more subtle and more general argument for why stock-based performance measurement and compensation may not be optimal. To see this, assume away all of the above reasons why stock-based performance measurement and compensation may not be optimal. In particular, assume that there is only one manager (so it is only his or her actions that affect stock price), all information available to the firm is available to the market (so stock price and performance measurement metrics are based on the same information), and management cannot manipulate the information on which stock price and performance measurement is based. Even under these conditions, stock price is not, in general, the optimal way of compensating management. The reason is that the market aggregates the underlying publicly available information (reported revenues, expenses, balance sheet account balances, etc.) for price setting differently than would the firm for performance measurement and compensation. The following simple example illustrates this difference.

Assume a one-period hidden action problem, where the firm's cash flow, x, is not observed (for then the stock price would just be the observed cash flow). Instead assume that two signals, y_1 and y_2, are publicly observed. Further assume that the signals are $y_i = a + \varepsilon_i$ and that the future unobserved cash flow is $x = a + \varepsilon_x$, where a is the manager's action choice and the εs are exogenous normally distributed noise terms with zero means. The market will aggregate the y_i signals to efficiently estimate x—by regressing x on the y_i signals. The equilibrium assumption underlying the contract theory model and the assumption that the market and the firm have the same information imply that the market will correctly infer the manager's compensation contract and therefore be able perfectly to infer the manager's action choice a and the unconditional *expected* value of x given a, i.e. $E(x|a)$. The only thing that the market learns about x from observing the y_i signals is information about the firm cash flow noise term, ε_x. The correct stock price then is $P = \alpha + \beta_1 y_1 + \beta_2 y_2$, where $\beta_i = \text{cov}(\varepsilon_x, \varepsilon_i)/\text{var}(\varepsilon_i)$ is the covariance of the cash flow noise term and the signal y_i noise term, divided by the variance of the latter. Thus, stock price is a linear aggregation of the signals, where the weight assigned to signal y_i is $\text{cov}(\varepsilon_x, \varepsilon_i)/\text{var}(\varepsilon_i)$. If the signals are uncorrelated with the cash flow (i.e. provide no information about the cash flow noise term), then the weights assigned to the signals by the market are zero and stock price is $P = E(x|a)$.

It is clear from equation (4) that, in general, the optimal aggregation of the signals for performance measurement purposes is *not* linear in the performance measures. Hence, in general, the market does not aggregate information in a manner that is optimal for performance measurement purposes. However, under certain conditions, the optimal aggregation of the signals for performance measurement purposes will be linear (see Banker and Datar 1989). But even then, the relative weight on the signals for performance measurement purposes will be different from the relative weights on those same signals for stock price estimation purposes. Hence, even in this case, stock price is not the optimal way of measuring performance.

To demonstrate this point, assume that the optimal performance measure is linear in the signals, i.e. $z(y_1, y_2) = \alpha' + \beta_1' y_1 + \beta_2' y_2$. In this case, it can be shown that the optimal relative weights on the signals are:

$$\frac{\beta_1'}{\beta_2'} = \frac{\dfrac{dE[y_1|a]}{da}}{\dfrac{dE[y_2|a]}{da}}\frac{\text{var}(\varepsilon_2)}{\text{var}(\varepsilon_1)} \neq \frac{\beta_1}{\beta_2} = \frac{\text{cov}(\varepsilon_x, \varepsilon_i)}{\text{var}(\varepsilon_1)}\frac{\text{var}(\varepsilon_2)}{\text{cov}(\varepsilon_x, \varepsilon_2)}$$

Both the market and the linear performance measure consider the variances of the signals. However, the market, given its rationality, already knows the manager's action choice is a, and hence is not interested in using the signals to estimate it. Instead, the market is interested in using the correlation structure of the model to estimate the cash flow noise terms and therefore uses cov $(\varepsilon_x, \varepsilon_1)$ to make that estimate.

On the other hand, the shareholders are interested in motivating the manager to take the obedient action. As indicated by the earlier discussion of equation (4), this means basing the performance measurement weight of the signals on their diagnostic ability with respect to estimating the agent's action. Hence, the optimal linear performance measure weights the signals based on their signal-to-noise ratios:

$$\frac{\dfrac{dE[y_i|a]}{da}}{\text{var}(\varepsilon_i)}$$

The noisier the signal, the more risk is being imposed on the agent, and the less weight will be placed on it for performance measurement purposes. However, the more the signal varies in the agent's action, the more diagnostic it is about the agent's action choice, the more weight will be placed on it for performance measurement purposes. In the extreme case, recall that if the signals are uncorrelated with the cash flow, the market assigns zero weight to the signals in estimating the cash flow and setting the stock price. But in this case, the optimal linear performance measure still assigns non-zero weights to the signals as long as their means vary in the manager's action choice.

Thus, in summary, even though it seems logical that top managers should be evaluated on the performance of their stock, contract theory-based analysis points out the fallacy in this logic. The reason for the fallacy is that the two use the information to make very different inferences and hence aggregate the information differently.

2.3.2.2 The use of subjective information for performance evaluation and compensation

In the previous analysis, it was assumed that the stock price and the manager's performance measure and compensation were based on the same information and that all of that information was contractible. Thus, if it were valuable to do so, this information could be included in an enforceable or explicit contract and the agent's compensation would vary in the information.[19] However, it is likely that the firm has some information that is not publicly available to the market. Further, while this information may be observable to all parties within the firm, it may be too costly to make it observable to a third party, such as a court, responsible for enforcing the contract.[20] Such information is often referred to as subjective or 'soft'. Examples of such information include observations by managers of agents, informal reports, and opinions. This information would, however, be valuable if it could be made contractible and incorporated into an enforceable contract.

Given that the firm has subjective information that would be of value for motivating a manager if it could be included in the manager's enforceable or explicit compensation contract, can any use be made of it? The problem with using such subjective information to mitigate the agent's hidden action problem is that it *creates* an incentive problem for the principal. For example, say we have a one-period world where the principal can observe the agent's effort, but that such observations cannot be verified by a court and therefore cannot be incorporated within an enforceable explicit contract. Further, assume that the principal observes no other information about the agent's action. Can the principal's observation of the agent's action still be put to a valuable use? The principal could *promise* that if he or she observes the agent taking the obedient action, the principal will pay the agent s_H, whereas if the principal sees the agent taking other than the obedient action, the former will pay the latter substantially less, say s_L. This is referred to as an *implicit* contract. An implicit contract is a *promise* as to how someone will behave, where the promise cannot be enforced by a third party. If the agent found the principal's promise credible, the agent would take the obedient action. However, once the principal observed the agent's action choice, the principal's best response is to pay the lower amount—the principal has nothing to gain by honouring his or her promise. Of course, being rational, the agent anticipates this happening and will expend the least personally costly feasible action. The problem is that the principal's promise is not credible.

The above analysis is hardly satisfactory because we observe that much of the economy does rely on promises that are made and kept. Therefore, we need to understand the situations in which legally unenforceable promises are kept. Further, we need to understand what managerial accounting can do to enlarge the set of situations in which such promises can be relied on and hence can improve the efficiency of contracting.

Contract theory has analysed two types of situations in which promises by the principal to reward the agent on the basis of subjective information can be made credible. One situation is where the interaction of the principal and agent is repeated over time. In this case the principal has less of an incentive to renege on his or her promise because the cost of reneging is increased, but the benefit is unchanged. The benefit of reneging remains the one-time savings in compensation (i.e. $s_H - s_L$). The cost is now increased because as long as the principal carries out his or her part of the implicit contract, the agent will continue to choose the obedient action into the future; whereas once the principal reneges, the agent will expend the least effort into the future.[21] So in the one-period case the principal's cost of reneging is the loss of one period of productive action, while in the repeated case the principal's cost is the loss of an infinite number of periods of productive actions. Notice that once the implicit contract becomes credible, to an outsider it looks as if the principal is protecting his or her reputation for treating the employee fairly, when in fact the principal is being just as self-interested as in the one-period case where the principal would not keep his or her promise.[22]

Even more subtle issues can be analysed within this repeated game scenario using the contract theory model. For example, assume that the firm discussed above has publicly traded stock. The principal and agent again observe some subjective information but the information is not observed by the financial market. Further, assume that because the information is subjective any direct disclosure of it by the firm to the financial market is not credible. Finally, assume that this information would be valuable for both contracting and stock price setting purposes if it could be made verifiable. Therefore, assume that the principal uses the subjective information as a basis for an implicit contract in the manner described in the previous example. The financial market, being rational, will anticipate the design of the implicit contract and use the observed compensation payments to the agent to (at least partially) infer the underlying subjective information. The information inferred will then be impounded into the firm's stock price. That is, by incorporating the subjective information into an implicit employment contract the principal has come up with an indirect but credible way of disclosing the information to the financial market. But this means that the design of the implicit contract now has strategic implications; it can be used not only to motivate the agent but also to leak information to the financial market and indirectly affect stock price. Hence, in designing the implicit contract the principal now has three considerations. First, the implicit contract must be designed so that, if not reneged on, it improves the agent's motivation. Second, it must be designed so that the principal has no incentive to renege on paying the promised payment to the agent merely to avoid paying the compensation. Third, it must be designed so that the principal has no incentive to pay the agent an amount other than what is promised by the implicit contract so as to manipulate the compensation that the market sees and therefore manipulate the stock price. Otherwise the principal would have an incentive to pay the agent a bonus, even when it has not been earned according to the implicit contract, so as to convince the market that the private information is better than it really is, and thus raise the stock price (see Hayes and Schaefer forthcoming, for an analysis of this situation).

A second situation in which subjective information may be useful is when the principal has multiple agents working for him or her. Assume a one-period problem in which the principal employs n agents. Further, assume that there is information that is objective and therefore can be used as a basis for writing enforceable contracts and subjective information, which cannot be used for writing enforceable contracts. Can the subjective information be used to improve the efficiency of the contract beyond what can be accomplished with just the objective information? One way in which we observe subjective information being used in this situation is with discretionary bonus pools. In a discretionary bonus pool, the principal uses the objective information to write a contract that specifies how much money the principal will irrevocably put into a bonus pool to be shared among the agents. However, how the bonus pool is divided up among the agents is left to the principal's

discretion. He may choose to allocate the bonus pool on the basis of the objective information and/or the subjective information or completely randomly. The first advantage of the
bonus pool arrangement is that it provides a mechanism whereby the principal can promise
to use the subjective information potentially to reduce the cost of motivating the agents. The
second advantage is that because the contributions to the bonus pool are irrevocable, the
principal has no incentive to not pay out the bonus pool in the way promised. The
disadvantage of a bonus pool arrangement is that paying the agents out of the bonus pool
creates externalities among them that otherwise would not exist. The bonus pool sets up a
zero-sum game between the agents with respect to the subjective information. It also
potentially results in more risk being imposed on the agents because each agent's compensation may vary not only in their own outcome but also in the outcome of all other agents.
This may be true even though each agent's outcome is completely uninformative about the
other agents' actions. It is therefore not obvious that the beneficial effects of bonus pools
outweigh the detrimental effects.

Contract theory has established a number of very strong results with respect to the design
and efficiency of bonus pool arrangements (see Baiman and Rajan 1995; Rajan and Reichelstein 2005). To illustrate the results consider a single-period hidden action problem with
two agents and one principal. Each agent i is asked to take some action, a_i, which is
unobservable to the principal and the other agent. Agent i's action produces a jointly
observable and contractible cash flow, x_i, with probability $f(x_i|a_i)$. A larger x_i implies a
larger a_i. The distribution of agent i's outcome, x_i, is independent of the other agent's action
choice. Further, agent 2's action also produces a signal, y_2, with probability $h(y_2|a_2)$. As with
the distribution of x_2, a larger y_2 implies a larger a_2 and the distribution of y_2 is independent
of agent 1's action choice. Unlike the x_i outcomes, y_2 is subjective information that is only
observed by the principal. Therefore, the agents' explicit contracts can only be written on
(x_1, x_2). Note that (x_2, y_2) is informative about agent 2, but contains no information about
agent 1. Thus, the optimal *explicit* contracts for the agents would compensate agent 1 solely
on x_1 and agent 2 solely on x_2. Further, if y_2 *were* contractible, the optimal explicit contracts
for the agents would compensate agent 1 again solely on x_1 but agent 2 on (x_2, y_2). Agent 1
would not be compensated on (x_2, y_2), because the latter contains no information about a_1
and would just impose unnecessary risk on agent 1.

The issue of interest is whether, given that the y_2 signal cannot be used in an explicit
contract, there is any way it can be used in an implicit contract to improve the contracting
efficiency of the firm. To see how it can be so used, let the principal and agents agree on
an explicit contract that specifies that the principal will make an irrevocable donation
of $B(x_1, x_2)$ into a bonus pool, given outcome (x_1, x_2). The principal then *promises* that
he or she will pay agent 1 $s_1(x_1, x_2, y_2)$ and agent 2 $s_2(x_1, x_2, y_2)$ where $s_1(x_1, x_2, y_2)+
s_2(x_1, x_2, y_2) = B(x_1, x_2)$ for all (x_1, x_2, y_2) realizations. Thus, the principal always pays
out the entire bonus pool.

Using a contract theory analysis it has been shown that the use of the subjective signal y_2
within the bonus pool arrangement described above results in a strict Pareto improvement
over the optimal explicit contract based solely on the objective information, (x_1, x_2). But

recall that the disadvantage of the bonus pool arrangement is that it creates a zero-sum game among the agents for the bonus payments. How is this manifested in the promised payment schedules $s_1(x_1, x_2, y_2)$ and $s_2(x_1, x_2, y_2)$? That is, what are the behaviours of $s_1(x_1, x_2, y_2)$, $s_2(x_1, x_2, y_2)$, and $B(x_1, x_2)$? It has been shown that the bonus pool increases in both x_1 and x_2, and that agent i's compensation increases in his own outcome, x_i. Both properties are intuitive, consistent with observed bonus pool arrangements and consistent with our earlier discussion of equation (4). Further, agent 2's compensation increases in y_2. The reason for the latter is that a larger y_2 implies a larger a_2. This again is intuitive. However, this implies that, for a fixed bonus pool, agent 1's compensation is *decreasing* in y_2, even though y_2 contains no information about agent 1's action choice. Finally, it has been shown that agent 1's (or 2's) compensation varies in the other agent's outcome $x_2(x_1)$, again, even though the latter contains no information about the affected agent. So notice that while a bonus pool arrangement provides a way in which subjective information can be used to mitigate hidden action problems among two or more agents, it results in distorted compensation and incentives relative to what we would observe if the subjective information were objective and contractible. However, these distortions are consistent with observed group payment plans, in particular with observed Relative Performance Evaluation plans among divisional managers.

Given the distortions described above, an immediate question is how large the efficiency improvement from incorporating the subjective measures within an optimal bonus pool arrangement is. Numerical analysis indicates that the improvement is surprisingly substantial. Further, in a slightly more restrictive model but one in which each agent produces their own subjective signal, the difference in efficiency from using the subjective information in the optimal bonus pool arrangement versus in the optimal explicit contract (assuming the information were objective), on a per agent basis, decreases very quickly in the number of agents. Thus, with a large number of agents there is little efficiency lost as a result of the subjective signals not being objective and contractible.

In the bonus pool arrangement described above, we have a contract with both implicit and explicit parts. Hence, the principal must design the two parts to be mutually reinforcing. Recall that the problem with using subjective information is that the implicit contract cannot put too much compensation weight on it, for then the principal has an incentive to renege on the promised payment to the agent. Incorporating objective information into the contract allows the principal to reduce the compensation weight on the subjective information, thereby reducing the principal's incentive to renege on the implicit part of the contract. Explicit contracts based on objective information can therefore make implicit contracts more efficient. Likewise, implicit contracts based on subjective information can make explicit contracts more efficient. For example, say that the agent is responsible for two tasks but that the principal can only objectively measure the results of the second of these tasks. Any compensation weight on the objective measure will distort the agent's attention away from the unmeasured first task to the measured second task. If the principal could incorporate a subjective measure of the first task into an implicit contract, he or she could reduce the distortionary effect of the explicit contract and improve the efficiency of the agent's actions.

2.4 **Conclusion**

In this chapter I have given a brief explanation of the contract theory model and a few examples of how it has been applied to managerial accounting issues. The examples indicate that contract theory analysis is well suited to analysing managerial accounting issues. The fit comes from the fact that contract theory analysis is predicated on the existence of incentive conflicts between individuals in groups and analyses ways of mitigating those conflicts. Likewise, the control function of managerial accounting systems has long been recognized as an important tool for aligning the divergent interests of individuals within the firm (see e.g. Anthony et al. 1984; Simons 2000). The examples discussed here illustrate that contract theory analysis can provide a compelling explanation for why certain managerial accounting procedures and measures (e.g. variance analysis) as well as compensation methods (e.g. bonus pools) are designed the way they are. It can also provide a rigorous counter-argument to received wisdom (e.g. the claim that stock-based compensation is the best way of aligning top management's interests to those of the shareholders).

One of the strengths of the contract theory model is its rigorous approach to analysing incentive issues. This is reflected in its insistence on examining only equilibrium outcomes. All parties are fully rational and have unlimited computational abilities. This allows them to not only compute their own optimal strategies but also take into consideration the optimal strategies of all the other parties. It is this assumption—that everyone correctly anticipates how everyone else will behave—that results in the equilibrium nature of the analysis.

However, there are a number of weaknesses in contract theory analysis, especially as it relates to analysing managerial accounting issues. First and foremost is its insistence on complete rationality and restricting the analysis to equilibrium outcomes. This results in the optimal solutions often being very complicated and sensitive to the assumed problem parameters. In fact, many of the optimal performance measures, information aggregation procedures, and compensation contracts derived from contract theory analyses are arguably more complicated than those observed in practice. Interestingly, this complexity may be mitigated somewhat by enriching the underlying incentive problem. With a relatively simple incentive problem, the optimal solution is subject to few restrictions resulting in solutions that are complicated and very sensitive to the underlying parameters. Increasing the complexity of the incentive problem, for example by increasing the number of tasks assigned to the agent, increases the number of decisions that the contract is designed to influence. This can result in fewer degrees of freedom available in the design of the contract, and hence reduced contract complexity (see e.g. Holmstrom and Milgrom 1987).

Another weakness is that the cost of communication and cost of contracting are typically not incorporated in contracting models. Clearly, designing and maintaining managerial accounting systems is not free. Some of their features are probably better explained by cost issues than incentive issues. Although there is nothing preventing the inclusion of such costs in the contract theory model, there are few papers that have done so. The major reason is that we do not understand what those cost functions look like. The closest we have come to including such costs is in the incomplete contracting literature that posits the *effect* of such costs rather than the cost themselves. That is, rather than assuming a cost of contracting and deriving the optimal contract, this literature assumes that (usually unspecified) contracting costs will result in certain restrictions on the feasible set of contracts. For example, it has been assumed that, because of unspecified contracting costs, only single-period contracts can be negotiated even though the parties are playing a multiperiod game, or that only linear contracts can be negotiated. In the extreme case, it has been assumed that because of unspecified contracting costs, no contracts can be written. In this latter case, incentives are controlled by the one who owns the assets (see e.g. Hart and Moore 1999). Clearly, all of these assumptions result in simpler, more robust contracts that may be more consistent with what is observed. But the cost of this approach is that the analysis and the results are based on unmotivated assumptions.

To date, contract theory has clearly aided us in understanding the role of managerial accounting in the firm. I believe that this method of analysis will be even more useful in the future for three reasons. First, our technical ability to pose and analyse such problems has shown a steady improvement in the past and that should continue into the future. Second, there is increasing interest in more formally modelling situations that give rise to incomplete contracts. This will improve our understanding of contracts observed in practice. Third, with the growth in the importance of 'knowledge workers' in the economy, we will increasingly need to design managerial accounting systems to deal with workers whose 'actions' or 'efforts' cannot be directly observed and contracted on. For such workers, even the timely measurement of the quality of their output is difficult to achieve. This will make it increasingly important to incorporate a clear understanding of the incentives of such workers within managerial accounting systems.

☐ NOTES

1 This chapter was greatly improved as a result of the comments of James M. Patton and Madhav V. Rajan.

2 I include within the general heading of contract theory: agency theory, incomplete contracting theory, transactions cost economics, and mechanism design. While there are important differences among these, for our purposes there is no need to distinguish between them. As a result, I will merely use the all-inclusive term, contract theory.

3 This chapter is not intended as a comprehensive review of the literature. For recent, more technical and comprehensive surveys, see e.g. Baiman and Rajan (2002) and Lambert (2001).

4 As a comparison, neither the Stewardship Model (see Ijiri 1975) nor Team Theory (see Marschak and Radner 1972) allow for conflicts of interest between the interested parties.

5 In addition, it is usually assumed that the legal system is such that enforcement of any agreed-upon feasible contract is perfect and costless.

6 An additional technical assumption is that the set of all feasible z is the same for both actions and that for every feasible z, $f(z|a_H) > 0$ and $f(z|a_L) > 0$. Thus any feasible performance report can be produced by either action choice.

7 The assumption that $z = x$ is for simplicity only. All we need is that z is an imperfect measure of the agent's action choice, in the sense that it is not possible to infer unambiguously the action choice from z.

8 The cash flow is an imperfect monitor of the agent's action choice because, as assumed earlier, any feasible $z = x$ could be produced by either action choice.

9 A strict Pareto improvement makes at least one party *strictly* better off without making any of the other parties worse off.

10 This result is due to Holmstrom (1979).

11 In the extreme case of $y = a$, we are back to case 2, in which the principal can induce the agent to take any action at the minimum cost and achieve 'first-best'.

12 That is, the obedient action will vary in the agent's private information.

13 For a fuller discussion of the Revelation Principle, see e.g. Kreps (1990).

14 More formally, $V(x, \theta_L) > V(x, \theta_H)$ and $[\partial V(x, \theta_L)/\partial x] > [\partial V(x, \theta_H)/\partial x] \forall x$.

15 The strict inequality follows from the assumption that the effort to achieve any cash flow is greater when $\theta = \theta_L$ than when $\theta = \theta_H$.

16 This result holds even if both the principal and agent are risk-neutral.

17 That is, how big does the variance, $d - r$, have to be before it triggers an investigation of the process.

18 See, for example, the scandals involving Sunbeam, Enron, Parmalat, and WorldCom, among others.

19 An explicit contract is one that is legally enforceable. Up to this point, all of the contracts we have discussed have been explicit. We use the modifying term, explicit, now because we will be considering contracts that are not enforceable. These are referred to as implicit contracts.

20 It may be too costly for either strategic or out-of-pocket cost reasons. In the former case, making the information available to a court might inadvertently leak it to competitors who could gain a competitive advantage from its knowlege. In the latter case, an additional verification cost may have to be incurred in order to satisfy the requirements of the court.

21 The agent uses a 'trigger' strategy. The agent will continue to act obediently as long as the principal acts consistently with his or her promise or implicit contract.

22 The most prominent examples of these implicit contracts leading to corporate reputations are the implicit 'no lay-off' policies of Hewlett-Packard and many Japanese firms. However, in the past few years these policies have been reneged on. This indicates that, in each case, the environment changed, reducing the value to the employer of continuing to honour its implicit contract.

☐ REFERENCES

Anthony, R., Dearden, J., and Bedford, N. (1984). *Management Control Systems*, 5th edn. Homewood, IL: Richard D. Irwin.

Baiman, S. and Demski, J. (1980). 'Economically Optimal Performance Evaluation and Control Systems', *Journal of Accounting Research*, 18: 184–220.

—— and Rajan, M. (1995). 'The Informational Advantage of Discretionary Bonues Schemes', *Accounting Review*, 70: 557–80.

—— and Rajan, M. V. (2002). 'The Role of Information and Opportunism in the Choice of Buyer-Supplier Relationships', *Journal of Accounting Research* 40(2): 247–78.

Banker, R. and Datar, S. (1989). 'Sensitivity, Precision and Linear Aggregation of Signals for Performance Evaluation', *Journal of Accounting Research*, 27: 21–39.

Dye, R. A. (1986). 'Optimal Monitoring Policies in Agencies', *RAND Journal of Economics*, 17: 339–50.

Hart, O. and Moore, J. (1999). 'Foundations of Incomplete Contracts', *Review of Economic Studies*, 66: 115–38.

Hayes, R. and Schaefer, S. (forthcoming). 'Bonus and Non-Public Information in Publicly Traded Firms', *Review of Accounting Studies.*

Holmstrom, B. (1979). 'Moral Hazard and Observability', *Bell Journal of Economics,* 10(1): 74–91.

—— and Milgrom, P. (1987). 'Aggregation and Linearity in the Provision of Intertemporal Incentives', *Econometrica,* 55: 303–28.

Ijiri, Y. (1967). *The Foundations of Accounting Measurement: Mathematical, Economic, and Behavioral Inquiry,* Englewood Cliffs, NJ: Prentice Hall.

Kreps, D. (1990). A Course in Microeconomic Theory, Princeton, NJ: Princeton University Press.

Lambert, R. A. (2001). 'Contracting Theory and Accounting', *Journal of Accounting and Economics,* 32(1–3): 3–87.

Marschak, J. and Radner, R. (1972). Economic Theory of Teams, Yale University Press, New Haven, CT.

Rajan, M. and Reichelstein, S. (2005). 'Subjective Performance Indicators and Discretionary Bonus Pools', Stanford University.

Simons, R. (2000). *Performance Measurement & Control Systems for Implementing Strategy.* Upper Saddle River, NJ: Prentice Hall.

3 Reframing management accounting practice: a diversity of perspectives

Jane Baxter
Wai Fong Chua

3.1 Introduction

Learning about basic management accounting technologies, such as budgeting and costing systems, is a fundamental rite of passage for practising accountants. Indeed, this experience is shared by graduates from many tertiary programmes (students of health administration, engineering, building, etc.) who are required to possess some elementary competence in financial management. Underpinning these educational experiences is a belief that understanding management accounting enables participation in activities directed at achieving organizational planning and control. In a recent edition of Horngren et al. (2003: 6), it is stated:

Planning comprises (a) selecting organization goals, predicting results under various alternative ways of achieving those goals, deciding how to attain the desired goals and (b) communicating the goals and how to attain them to the entire organization.

Control comprises (a) taking actions that implement the planning decisions and (b) deciding how to evaluate performance and what feedback to provide that will help future decision making.

Set against this requirement for planning and control, management accounting is framed as providing an important element in the inscription and efficient realization of goals embedded in an organization's strategy.

Indeed, much of the contemporary debate about management accounting revolves around a need to maintain its 'relevance' in guiding an organization towards the achievement of its overarching mission in a resource-conscious fashion (Johnson and Kaplan 1987). Spurred by this debate, much has been written about the need for management accountants to embrace more 'strategic' forms of cost analysis (Shank and Govindarajan 1989)—locating planning and control within the context of a firm's value chain, encompassing customer- and supplier-related adjacencies as well as internal activities and processes. Likewise, recent debate advocating the abandonment of traditional budgeting (Hope and Fraser 2003) has been countered by arguments for its rejuvenation through the adoption of rolling budgets and continuous forecasting and performance evaluation regimes (Howell 2004; Haka and Krishnan 2005). In short, there is a persistent belief that management accounting is instrumental in the 'steering' of an organization (Czarniawska-Joerges 1988).

Yet there is the occasional suggestion within the professional literature and tertiary curriculum that predominantly technocratic constructions of management accounting may be insufficient to capture its lived experience and possibilities. For example, in a letter to the *Harvard Business Review* from Students of the Executive MBA Class (2003), the writers argue that budgets achieve more than control in organizations. They state that budgets are also important because they facilitate creativity, a common language, and ongoing conversations within an organization.

A growing number of accounting researchers too have sensed that there is more to management accounting and its accomplishment. Correspondingly, one of the emergent roles of accounting research is the characterization of different constructions of the experience of management accounting, with some research extending this to explore how management accounting affects power relations and resource allocations in organizations and societies. We argue that some of the most interesting and challenging insights into management accounting have arisen from the work of researchers mobilizing more 'critical' frames that do not necessarily characterize management accounting as an invariable quest for efficiency and effectiveness.

The purpose of this chapter is to consider the different ways in which researchers have attempted to construct, narrate, and critique the practice of management accounting, providing illustrations from seminal studies. In doing so, we introduce readers to seven ways of (re)framing practice, each drawing on different theories from the broader social sciences. In particular, this chapter introduces readers to (*a*) a non-rational design frame; (*b*) a naturalistic frame; (*c*) a radical frame; (*d*) an institutional frame; (*e*) a structurationist frame; (*f*) a Foucauldian frame; and (*g*) a Latourian frame (see Baxter and Chua 2003). Each (re)framing of management accounting is discussed in turn in the subsequent sections of this chapter.

3.2 **Non-rational frame**

Some researchers are sceptical about claims contained in economically rational accounts of the design and operation of management accounting systems (MASs), contesting the role of these in helping organizations make sensible, considered, and goal-directed decisions about the best use of organizational resources. Such scepticism assumes a number of forms and is articulated in the work of Cooper et al. (1981), for example. These researchers argue the unlikelihood that organizational goals will be translated into a stable and transitive set of preferences, which are then used to rank decision alternatives with a view to making the 'best' or highest ranking decision. Rather, what they have observed and experienced within organizations fails to conform to this type of choice process underlying conventional rhetoric about the contribution of MASs to organizational efficiency and effectiveness.

Instead, researchers working within a non-rational frame challenge a 'unitary' view of management accounting and the organizational context in which it operates. This unitary view is summarized by Banbury and Nahapiet (1979: 168):

The form and content of organizational goals are regarded as unproblematic and their decomposition to various parts of the organization is perceived as a relatively simple matter to be achieved via hierarchy and complemented by the set of information systems.

In short, Banbury and Nahapiet highlight a need to problematize the context in which MASs operate. This is reinforced by observations made by others. For example, Hedberg and Jönsson (1978: 56) are critical of the almost decontextualized rendering of management accounting technologies, stating that 'Traditional accounting systems are small wonders of logic and consistency... described by two essential variables: price and quantity'. Cooper et al. (1981: 176) embellish upon this claim by emphasizing that traditional depictions of management accounting are assumed to occur in situations in which goals are well known, as are the causal connections between various alternatives and these goals.

In comparison, a non-rational design frame conceives of a far more 'pluralistic' (see Banbury and Nahapiet 1979: 168) context in which to configure the practice of management accounting. Such a frame brings greater complexity to the construction of management accounting's context, typifying the pluralism that may exist because of disagreements between organizational participants in relation to the nature and relative importance of organizational goals and/or the connection between alternatives and their ability to satisfy stated objectives. Stemming from this, in addition to a more traditional computational role that is argued to be characteristic of very clearly defined and well-agreed-upon situations, wherein budgets and costing systems, for example, are used to identify courses of actions leading to higher levels of profitability, management accounting technologies may become attached to organizational processes that do not necessarily conform to a priori expectations of rationally constituted, efficient, and effective organizational choices (see Hedberg and Jönsson 1978; Banbury and Nahapiet 1979; Cooper et al. 1981).

Researchers working within this frame alert us to the possibility that management accounting may become embedded in situations in which there is little clarity about causation (the connection between actions taken and goals desired to be achieved), even though there may be broad agreement about the strategy and goals of an organization. In such situations, computation cedes to more bounded forms of rationality in which management accounting information facilitates learning and exploration through incrementalism and adjustment, supporting the development and implementation of organizational participants' judgement and heuristic decision rules. Indeed, it is argued that this is an important function of management accounting information systems that needs to be actively promoted, rather than ignored, denied, and considered 'sub-optimal' and requiring 'improvement'. As Hedberg and Jönsson (1978: 49) put it, good MASs should 'tickle curiosity in organizations', helping to destabilize and question routinized ways of doing things. The predictability of computational routines needs to be balanced by a frame that embraces experimentation and flexibility in the practice of management accounting, enabling environmental responsiveness.

In other situations, the context of management accounting may be fractured by fundamental disagreements about organizational goals and the corralling of management accounting technologies to serve the local goals of various political coalitions within organizations. From this vantage point, management accounting is framed in terms of the exercise of power: management accounting becomes connected to processes through which various battles over scarce resources are fought and won, and individuals' reputations are preserved or tarnished. But this is the politicization of management accounting in its most manifest form.

Researchers working within a non-rational frame have contributed significantly also to our reframing of supposedly benign and bland management accounting technologies, highlighting the values on which their accomplishment rests. Banbury and Nahapiet (1981) argue that the values of those who design MASs are embedded within, and perpetuated by, the operation of these systems. Such values (emanating from cultural, professional, and positional predispositions, for example) influence the trajectory of management accounting practice by shaping, amongst other things, the extent to which various situations are viewed as programmable and capable of delegation and resolution in terms of routinized, calculative solutions.

'Non-rational' researchers have pointed also to the possibility that management accounting may operate in highly ambiguous situations in which there is little understanding of, and only very loosely coupled relationships between, actions and goals. Such settings (described as 'organized anarchies' and 'garbage cans' by Cohen et al. 1972) represent the antithesis of the presumably well-understood situations in which technocratic constructions of management accounting prevail. Rather, management accounting is argued to provide a retrospective form of rationality—sometimes referred to as 'the technology of foolishness' (see Cooper et al. 1981: 178) in these contexts. Using budgeting as an example, Cooper et al. 1981: 181 state):

Rather, as part of the rationalization process of retrospective goal discovery, it appears that by performing the budget process—forecasting, developing standards and evaluating results—an organization may be discovering its goals.

In these circumstances a quest for efficiency is replaced by a quest for meaning. Management accounting inscriptions emerge as a way of making sense of organizational functioning—providing justifications to legitimate that which has taken place, creating memories of the past, thereby diminishing uncertainty, and developing routines to be imitated, and to shape future interactions within organizations (Cooper et al. 1981). Within this highly ambiguous organizational context, emergent management accounting routines for action and sensemaking can help to stabilize organizations. Given this, management accounting can be construed as a way of 'dramatizing' rather than facilitating efficiency (see Cooper et al. 1981: 181); 'building' (Boland 1979: 270) organizational functioning rather than reflecting it.

Research conducted within a non-rational design frame contributes also to our appreciation of 'rationality' by distinguishing between its more 'local' and 'global' constitutions. Whereas textbooks expose students to the role of management accounting in submitting to the attainment of overarching and 'grand' organizational objectives and strategies (see Boland 1981), expressing the desires and aspirations of an organization's elite, more critical research, such as that discussed above, has sensitized researchers to the possibilities of local forms of rationality connected to the particular agendas and highly embedded and decentred (management accounting) practices of dispersed and loosely coupled organizational participants.

Based on the work of pioneering researchers in constructing a non-rational frame for management accounting practice, it is now generally acknowledged that whilst management accounting technologies may have an important instrumental purpose to serve in assisting organizations confront their futures and uncertainties, this is frequently achieved in ways that do not conform to images of economic rationality. Management accounting technologies become embedded in processes that enable organizations to explore future possibilities in routinized, experimental, contested, and/or even slightly anarchic ways. Moreover, management accounting helps to construct and make sense of such processes, sometimes providing retrospective accountings of organizational functioning. These are important insights and legacies that continue to resonate in contemporary management accounting research.

3.3 **Naturalistic frame**

Researchers who attempt to study accounting in the context in which it occurs often claim to be undertaking 'naturalistic' research (see e.g. Tomkins and Groves 1983; Covaleski and Dirsmith 1986; Czarniawska-Joerges 1988). In short, naturalistic researchers are united in their concern for studying management accounting in its 'everyday' or ordinary context (see Tomkins and Groves 1983). Given this, the naturalistic frame is characterized by its *approach* to the research act, mobilizing particular philosophies about research and methods for its conduct, which sets it apart from 'more conventional'/'scientific' approaches to research. In many respects, it is not an exaggeration to state that a naturalistic framing of management accounting research was motivated initially as a reaction to the prevailing conventions of accounting research during the 1960s and 1970s.

Prior to a groundswell of breakaway support for a naturalistic approach to management accounting research in the 1980s, accounting research was characterized by its conformance to a model of 'conventional science'. This approach is described by Tomkins and Groves (1983: 362) as follows:

First, they [researchers] start with a theory formulated in terms of relationships between categories more often than not based on ideas emanating from previous academic literature; then the theory is used to establish a research problem which is transformed into hypotheses and thence into dependent and independent variables representing the categories involved. This is then followed by precise and highly structured or pre-determined procedures for data collection (nearly always in numerical form) which is followed, in turn, by subjecting the data to mathematical or statistical techniques leading to an almost exclusively quantitative validation of the hypotheses tested.

More generally, conventional accounting research was (and is) marked by its commitment to a philosophy of knowledge known as positivism (see Burrell and Morgan 1979; Chua 1986). When viewed from a positivist perspective, management accounting practice is considered to be an objective and measurable phenomenon that exists independently of the researcher: the wonders of accounting practice are there to be 'discovered' by researchers, with the role of the researcher being to convey his or her findings, based on observations of practice, as lawlike generalizations (e.g. if these conditions prevail, we predict the following accounting outcomes to occur). The pathway to such 'discovery' is moderated primarily by research methods assuming the form of laboratory experiments or cross-sectional surveys of management accounting practice. But, as Tomkins and Groves (and many naturalistic researchers after them) have argued, this style of research requires little first-hand knowledge of the phenomenon being studied—the 'research model becomes a substitute for intimate knowledge of the field being studied' (1983: 363).

In comparison, naturalistic researchers argue that the field of management accounting practice is a socially constructed one. It is through interactions embedded in ongoing organizational processes that highly situated and local meanings are attributed to management accounting technologies by those social actors connected to them. This approach stems from an 'interpretive' philosophy of the production of knowledge and does not ascribe to the objective nature of reality as postulated by a positivist perspective. Moreover, the meanings attached to management accounting technologies and their affects and effects can vary (often quite dramatically) within and between organizations.

To illustrate this contention regarding the diversity of meaning that may be found to attend the practice of management accounting, the research of Mouritsen (1999) will be considered. Using a naturalistic research frame, Mouritsen demonstrated how 'flexibility', 'productivity', and 'innovation' were constructed quite differently by the chief executive officer (CEO) and chief financing officer (CFO), as compared to the production manager, of a Danish firm. For example, the CEO and CFO both viewed flexibility in the production process as a cost-increasing activity—one that should be controlled. These two actors viewed productivity as a facet of organizational functioning that could be improved via outsourcing and innovation as a need for new products, which should then be 'stabilized' through the organization's planning system. The production manager (who was connected much more intimately with the factory floor and the conversion process), in comparison, considered flexibility to be a necessary way of satisfying customer needs. He also viewed productivity as requiring the installation of advanced technology equipment permitting reduced production set-up times. (He did not see outsourcing as the solution.) The production manager also constructed innovation as an unstable process, wherein new products emerged to satisfy customized rather than predictable needs that could be anticipated through planning (see Mouritsen 1999: Table 1). As a result of these interpretive differences, management control and the extent and nature of engagement with the MAS was enacted quite differently by these key organizational participants. On the one hand, the CEO and CFO attempted to institute a 'paper system' of management control, wherein control was exerted 'from a distance' by the CEO and CFO reacting to deviations from organizational plans. On the other hand, the production manager constructed control through the 'hands-on' management of labour and the encouragement of improvisation and local solutions to production problems.

But how was Mouritsen able to detect these nuanced and contested meanings in relation to key business terms that are used quite unproblematically in much of the mainstream professional and research literature? He was able to do so because of the research methods he employed. Mouritsen used field research methods (see Ahrens and Dent 1998; Baxter and Chua 1998; Kaplan 1998). Field research methods are a hallmark of a naturalistic framing of management accounting research, enabling an 'intimate knowledge' (Tomkins and Groves 1983: 363) of an area of management accounting practice, by requiring the researcher to collect data through his or her co-presence in an organization. By being located *in situ*, the researcher is able to observe organizational processes as they emerge (e.g. by attending meetings), consult with various proprietary forms of organizational documentation (manuals, staff intranet, reports, files, etc), and speak to organizational participants, either informally (e.g. during meal breaks) or formally (in pre-arranged interviews of which some record is made, such as a typed transcript from an audio recording), about how they understand management accounting.

As naturalistic researchers aim to achieve some degree of 'depth' in their insights about management accounting practice, this engagement with the field can become quite time-consuming and extensive. For example, Preston's ambition (1986) to conduct naturalistic research saw him spending four days of each week for one year in his target research organization. It should be added that naturalistic research may also take researchers into unusual situations, which are often a far cry from the comfort of an academic's office. Berry et al. (1985), for instance, were required to go down coal pits in the UK so that they could better understand the workings of management accounting in the National Coal Board.

So where has this adventurous form of research taken us in terms of expanding our knowledge about management accounting practice? There have been many interesting studies conducted in this vein that both complement and challenge our appreciation of management accounting. Naturalistic studies have sensitized us to the connection between management accounting and culture. For instance, Czarniawska-Joerges and Jacobsson's research (1989) on budgeting in a number of Swedish organizations illustrates the connection between the enactment of the budgeting process and national cultural values. Overt conflict was avoided in the budgeting processes considered (through incrementalism and a focus on the numbers only), reflecting a Swedish predisposition towards consensus. This led the researchers to argue that budgeting may be more usefully thought of as a way of expressing values rather than allocating scarce resources. Dent's field study (1991) of a British rail organization shows that rather than reflecting culture, management accounting can be used actively to transform organizational culture. An increasing emphasis on financial performance reporting was used to shift a once dominant engineering-based organizational culture towards a commercially oriented one. Similar conclusions are drawn by Llewellyn (1998), who narrates how an increased emphasis on financial accountability was used to reshape the work culture of caring professions.

Other naturalistic studies have been able to document the political aspects of budgetary processes, showing how organizational participants often put more emphasis on learning how better to 'play the budgetary game' rather than improve underlying resource allocation techniques (Jönsson 1982; Boland and Pondy 1983; Covaleski and Dirsmith 1986). Some field studies have emphasized the importance of interactive verbal communication (or 'talk') and tacit forms of knowledge in both resisting and facilitating the operation of MASs (Preston 1986; Ahrens 1997; Vaivio 1999). Even the fundamental emphasis that we place on the importance of management accounting in assisting decision-making in organizations has been questioned by field research. Berry et al. (1985) found that financial control was not dominant in the internal functioning of the National Control Board. Instead, MASs seemed to fulfil external pressures to appear efficient, thereby legitimating rather than instrumentally supporting resource allocations. Ezzamel and Bourn (1990), who studied a university experiencing a financial crisis, found that the MAS was unable either to detect or to provide useful answers to the problems faced by this institution.

By examining what actually takes place in the name of management accounting (rather than making presumptions to this effect), naturalistic research has helped to further a more critical research agenda by providing counterpoints to conventionally received wisdom concerning the instrumental role of management accounting in planning and control. The upshot of this is that naturalistic research has produced many 'astonished researchers' (Czarniawska-Joerges and Jacobsson 1989: 38) when confronted with these differences between the practice of management accounting and constructions of the academy! Arguably, a naturalistic framing of research enriches both practitioners' and academics' comprehension of management accounting and its variegated realizations.

3.4 Radical frame

A radical frame encompasses a number of loosely related theories, drawing on the writings of Marx (see Atkinson 1972; Keat and Urry 1982), the Frankfurt school (see Habermas 1968, 1976), and those working within the labour process paradigm (see Braverman 1974). Research conducted under this banner is united by, and distinguished from, other reframings of management accounting by its affiliation with, and commitment to, the 'politics of emancipation' (Giddens 1998: 41). This commitment aims to connect management accounting research to 'major social struggles and conflicts' (Tinker et al. 1982: 167). Such struggles and conflicts are argued to emanate from an unequal distribution of resources and life chances within society (creating the 'haves' and 'have-nots'), and the overt and latent dissatisfactions stemming from this. Radical researchers aim to show the partisan nature of accounting and its role in sustaining and perpetuating this schism. As such, radical researchers hope that their research will assist broad-scale transformation and enlightenment, enabling the formation of more just and fair organizations and societies (Laughlin 1987). This transformative mandate creates distinctive accounts of management accounting practice, marked by a preparedness to highlight, rather than marginalize, issues of power in the enactment and construction of management accounting (see Hopper et al. 1987).

The connectedness between management accounting and historically and culturally contingent values was highlighted by Tinker et al. (1982), for example. They argue that conventional forms of (management) accounting assume the existence of capital markets, privileging their role in the allocation of scarce resources, and placing them beyond the scrutiny of most contemporary research endeavours. This naturalizes a need to control and coordinate the assumed atomistic behaviour of organizational participants using accounting disciplinary mechanisms. Correspondingly, Tinker et al. (1982: 191) argue that management accounting is implicated in the perpetuation of a 'neoconservative ideological bias', playing an increasingly important role in the allocation of resources throughout society. These writers are particularly critical of a lack of overt awareness of the social and political forms of power enmeshed in, and garnered by, this approach to organizational and societal functioning. Instead, Tinker et al. question the possibilities resident in accounting: should accountants continue to align their social contribution with the enactment of 'value economics'? What other accountings may be possible by forming new alignments with different ideologies and approaches to practice?

Armstrong's (1987) research considers the role of management accounting with respect to 'the global functions of capital' (p. 417). He argues that management accounting has a key role to play in the 'extraction' and 'realization' of surplus value (see pp. 417–18) because costing systems and management controls are designed to ensure that, first, workers maximize their productivity and efficiency and, second, the resulting productive output is converted into a monetary form. In addition to this, Armstrong argues that accounting has constituted a relative monopoly in the 'allocation' of surplus value by facilitating the recognition and assignment of revenues between and within organizations. More generally, Armstrong argues that management accounting has flourished because of its compatibility with the interests of 'laisser-faire [Sic] capitalism' (p. 415).

As Neimark and Tinker (1986: 379–80) point out, this seemingly inevitable assembly of management accounting and global capitalism creates and sustains conflicts revolving around the division of the surplus generated from the production of goods and services:

Individual firms and factions of the business community compete for the resources required for production and over the distribution of social surplus that is produced. Thus, domestic capital vies with multinational capital, financial capital vies with industrial capital, small and regional businesses compete with national and multinational enterprises for access to and control over natural resources, labour, manufactured parts and components, capital equipment, government subsidies, and favourable legislation and regulation. Individual workers and factions of the workforce (e.g. organized and unorganized labour, racial and ethnic groups, men and women, domestic and foreign workers) compete for employment, wages, benefits, and social welfare programs. Nations compete for access to raw materials and markets. In addition to these various forms of intraclass conflict, there is interclass conflict as well, as capitalists and workers compete over both the size and distribution of the social surplus, over the quality of work life, and over the methods of production.

Neimark and Tinker illustrate the above conflicts in terms of a case study of General Motors' internationalization strategy (from 1916 to 1976). Under pressure to manage costs, General Motors began to locate its production in less expensive countries, as well as engage in the global sourcing of components for automotive assembly. They argue that the resultant focus on the growth in profitability of General Motors obscured social conflicts underlying its internationalization strategy. The power that General Motors exercised in managing its costs by moving its resources from one geographic location to another, for example, challenged and destabilized the interests of unions, suppliers, and even sovereign nation states.

Situated within this radical frame, the accomplishment of management accounting involves mediating conflict within and beyond organizations—and such conflict is more complex than the mere opposition of labour and management. This has been highlighted in a reinterpretation of the National Coal Board study (see Berry et al. 1985) in which Hopper et al. (1986: 11) found evidence of 'class-related behaviour by management'. Managerial staff with more 'ambiguous' relationships towards their position (such as managers drawn from the ranks of miners) subverted MASs in the same way as workers. They manipulated data and resisted their operation.

So how does management accounting get done under such conditions of conflict? Hopper et al. (1986) argue that the accomplishment of management accounting is possible in these situations when management accounting practices are 'loosely coupled' (p. 121). In the case of the National Coal Board, this involved the detachment of production and engineering functions (core activities) from support activities, such as accounting, marketing, industrial relations, and so on (see p. 118). This allowed conflict to be contained at a local level whilst building sufficient accountability and rationality to satisfy external stakeholders (p. 122).

In general, from such research we begin to appreciate the almost contradictory role of management accounting in contemporary organizations—providing a set of technologies to stabilize and manage local conflict, whilst promoting underlying differences that sustain enduring societal conflicts. Radical research, moreover, creates the possibility of considering the operation of management accounting in situations characterized by instability, disorder, and disintegration, rather than conventionally assumed conditions of equilibrium, tidiness, and ongoing order (see Cooper 1983).

3.5 Institutional frame

An institutional frame critiques the conventional idea that organizations are bounded, relatively autonomous, rational actors that exercise strategic choice in the design of managerial accounting and control systems. Contingency theorists, for example, seek to understand how particular environmental imperatives need to be 'matched' with particular organizational characteristics in order to achieve high levels of performance. By contrast, institutional theorists argue that the visible structures, control practices, and routines that make up organizations are the consequences of legitimated templates that are established (or institutionalized) within the larger environment. University, school, hospital, or firm accounting systems are thus not so much strategically chosen by organizational actors as environmentally imprinted to conform to socialized notions of rational, 'objective', accountable corporate action. Meyer and Rowan (1977), for example, referred to the school budgeting systems that they studied as 'rationalized myths'. They were adopted or emerged in conformity with cultural requirements for 'rational', 'objective' resource allocation procedures in schools. But they are 'myths' because, in practice, these systems are but loosely integrated with the day-to-day operations of the firm. Because local functional requirements are not the primary source of these accounting procedures (external legitimacy is), they end up being 'decoupled' from operational activity, and hence the connection between technique and efficient task accomplishment is loosened. DiMaggio and Powell (1991: 147) write of this 'decoupling' thesis as follows:

[S]tructural change in organizations seems less and less driven by competition or by the need for efficiency. Instead,...bureaucratization and other forms of organizational change (such as the implementation of budgeting systems) occur as the result of processes that make organizations more similar without necessarily making them more efficient.

There is some empirical support for these arguments. In an early exploration of the merit of institutional theory, Covaleski and Dirsmith (1988) studied the budget negotiations between a major state university and its state government in the early 1980s. They concluded that the budget was more of a social invention that was complicit in the construction of a legitimate social reality than a 'rational' reflection of a technical reality. Essentially, the budget enabled the state to transform politicized allocations into decisions grounded in technique. Furthermore, when the university sought to change the original quantitative budget allocation formula by recasting its budget using new qualitatively expressed categories, the state government objected. The final budget outcome was arrived at through a process of political bargaining and symbolic manipulation. In a later piece of research, Gupta et al. (1994) studied a sample of ninety-six government audits in the United States General Accounting Office. They used both a contingency theory as well as an institutional theory perspective. They found that the more institutionalized the environment was, the more the organization relied on bureaucratic procedures. They also contend that greater use of the bureaucratic mode of control is not associated with variation in the efficiency of the audit. That is, procedures were adopted primarily to conform to societal expectations of 'rational behaviour' and such adoption appeared uncorrelated with the efficient conduct of the audits.

How does environmental 'imprinting' occur? The processes by which formal organizations come to take on more and more of the rationalized aspects of their environments and thereby become more similar to one another is said to be influenced by three features of contemporary society. First, the growth of organized occupational groups and professional associations promulgate not only standardized techniques but also common norms about what constitutes 'professional behaviour' or 'ethical practice'. That is, cultural schemes and value systems are being standardized in addition to technical routines through this process of *normative isomorphism*. Second, the acts of governments and regulatory agencies at both national and extranational levels become a form of *coercive isomorphism*. They standardize accounting practice particularly in the areas of external financial reporting, as well as audit and internal risk management. Consider how the Sarbanes–Oxley regulations have influenced the internal control systems of organizations not only in the USA but also globally. More recently, Llewellyn and Northcott (2005) have shown that government efforts to benchmark hospital performance can lead to organizations converging on mean measures of performance. If the average is emphasized, it indeed may be achieved within an organizational field. Third, contemporary society is characterized by rapid change, high levels of interconnectedness between social, economic, technological, and political regimes, and high levels of complexity and ambiguity. Given this, organizations tend to copy one another— whether in the adoption of balanced scorecards (BSCs), hospital costing systems (see Abernethy and Chua 1996), or diagnosis-related group reimbursement systems (see Covaleski et al. 1993). This form of *mimetic isomorphism* can lead to the rapid diffusion of particular practices.

Since the earlier work of institutional theorists in the late 1980s and mid-1990s, recent research has begun to focus on three particular issues. First, there has been disquiet that institutional theory has overemphasized the influence of environmental models and underemphasized the strategic options available to organizational actors. Baum and Oliver (1991), for example, point out that firms may decide not to comply with environmental demands and outlines a variety of responses other than strong compliance—from active resistance to subversion to acquiescence. In addition, decoupling may not occur and systems may not be rationalized myths. Abernethy and Chua (1996), for example, detail the case of a public hospital which was forced by its state government to fundamentally alter its governance structure and organizational culture. They argue that this hospital did not seek to decouple new systems and routines from day-to-day operations. Indeed, the CEO ensured that the hospital went further in its reforms than that required by governmental edict. Second, a desire to downplay the agency of actors has led to a neglect of how influential actors may significantly affect how organizations respond in the face of cultural demands. Third, there has been concern that not enough is known about the process of institutionalization as well as deinstitutionalization. Abernethy and Chua (1996) seek partially to address some of these issues with their longitudinal field study, although they too do not detail how social and cultural expectations may be changed in the face of organizational resistance.

Future research mobilizing an institutional frame could usefully consider how environmental models of 'best practice' and isomorphic movements interact with the agency of organizational actors in the design and operation of accounting control systems. This would avoid the present problems of either environmental or organizational determinism in extant management accounting research of this nature.

3.6 **Structurationist frame**

Reflecting a preparedness to conduct studies of accounting by undertaking 'more basic conceptual work' (Roberts and Scapens 1985: 444), a number of researchers utilize the work of Anthony Giddens, an eminent sociologist from the UK, to frame their understandings of management accounting. Giddens' work grapples with some of the 'central problems' in social theory, in particular the relationship between macro/structural and micro/interactionist constructions of day-to-day life (see Giddens 1976, 1979, 1982, 1984). The particular approach that Giddens advocates to bridge these dualisms is known as a theory of 'structuration'. This theory has established its appeal by arguing instead for the *duality* or interpenetration of structure and action, each informing and requiring the other. Structures provide recursive rules and resources, which shape and inform human interaction in terms of its signification (or meaning), legitimation (or morality), and domination (or power relations). Human agency, in turn, perpetuates and changes these structures. Such changes may result from either conscious choices to act differently or the unintended consequences of behaviour. In short, Giddens' work has inspired researchers to integrate theoretically the technical and human aspects of the functioning of MASs (Robert and Scapens 1985; Granlund 2001).

Paving the way for this research agenda was the seminal paper by Roberts and Scapens (1985). Roberts and Scapens draw a parallel between the structures discussed by Giddens and MASs. These authors argue that accounting systems comprise rules and resources that routinize organizational functioning. Such routinization is argued to occur through a '"binding" of organizational time and space' (p. 448), created and sustained by the dominance of entrenched accounting cycles, accounting concepts and categories, and accounting reporting formats and processes, for example. Roberts and Scapens argue that this binding of organizational time and space constitutes a structure because management accounting rules and resources shape the relevance of, and meanings ascribed to, organizational events; comprise a moral order by embedding reciprocal obligations in an accounting system (i.e. who is responsible for whom and who is responsible for what); and inform power relations through the overt control and coordination of organizational actors and processes. More generally, they argue that this tripartite structure comprises a system of accountability within organizations, enabling reasons for behaviour to be given and demanded. Roberts and Scapens then use structuration theory to consider the operation of two different systems of organizational accountability: one involving the co-presence of actors and the other involving accountability between remote actors. When actors are co-present, face-to-face interactions are used to negotiate the significance of financial results (e.g. establishing underperformance), the rights and obligations which attend this (e.g. withholding a bonus in the event of underperformance), and accompanying power relations (e.g. a subordinate may not contest a manager's performance evaluation because of fear of recrimination). When accountability is exercised over a distance, Roberts and Scapens argue that the importance of management accounting inscriptions increases, acting as a substitute for mutual knowledge. In these remote settings, accountability becomes more closely aligned to the interests of production and profitability, resulting in less interpersonal trust and more anxiety affecting the accomplishment and interpretation of accounting practices.

A further exploration of more remote forms of accountability and their structuration may be found in a subsequent case study by Roberts (1990). In this case study Roberts examines a financially oriented model of corporate strategy in which the holding company operated in a relatively 'detached' (p. 113) fashion, allowing the business units to pursue strategies with relative independence. With the holding company focusing its attention on the return on capital employed (ROCE) from the group, Roberts argues that there was, in fact, a high degree of attachment between the centre and the business unit that he studied. The holding company's preoccupation with financial returns highlighted the importance of economic performance and its central role in the mediation of the meanings, ties, and interests prevailing within the group. Moreover, the financial routines and resources of the holding company (the budgeting cycle, the system of capital appropriation, the calculation of financially driven bonuses) created a system of accountability that connected and subsumed the interests of remote actors to those of the holding company and its managerial elite. Given that the business unit forming the basis of this case study was recently acquired by the holding company, Roberts' research also highlights the potential for changes to occur in relation to organizational systems of accountability. Prior to its acquisition by the holding company, the business unit being studied was dominated by a production culture and an emphasis on volume. After its acquisition and the institution of a financially oriented style of corporate strategy, the rules and resources structuring action within the business unit changed dramatically. Financial literacy reigned: formal reporting and conferencing around these reports dominated interactions within the business unit. Interestingly, Roberts reported very little resistance to such dramatic changes in the signification, legitimation, and domination of organizational functioning in the acquired business unit.

In comparison, the enduring and difficult-to-change nature of MASs has formed the central thrust of Granlund's research (2001). Granlund conducted field research over a period of six years in a Finnish food-manufacturing company. During the period of Granlund's research, the company experienced financial difficulties for half a decade. Motivated to improve the financial performance of the organization, a team of both external consultants and internal experts began investigating how the MAS could provide more relevant information—given that more accurate overhead allocation processes, process improvements, and changed product mix decisions were deemed to be required by this team of experts. In particular, recommendations were made regarding the need for activity-based costing (ABC) and an integrated information system. Yet there was little support for these changes within the organization (from either managers or the management account-ants), despite declining financial performance. Granlund argued that this was so because MASs provide the routines, interpretive schemes, values, and norms that *stabilize* organiza-tions and facilitate processes of legitimation and accountability. Granlund argued that these go to the very core of the ontological security of organizational participants, making MASs very difficult to change as a consequence.

Granlund's arguments are reinforced and illustrated by Jack (2005). Jack examined the persistence of an agricultural gross margin calculation (measuring the contribution towards fixed costs) within this industry in the UK since the Second World War. Spurred by attempts to develop a self-sufficient agricultural industry and government attempts to assess and report on the viability of this important sector, the gross margin calculation emerged during the late 1950s. Enshrined in government statistical publications, farm handbooks, and textbooks on agricultural accounting, this calculation has proved to be robust in the face of significant changes within the industry (such as the positioning of primary producers within business supply chains). Like Granlund, Jack argues that the calculation has become highly routinized, even trivialized, and thereby difficult to change—despite shifting circumstances suggesting the possibility of calculative change.

Ahrens and Chapman (2002) also adopted structuration theory to study the role of performance measures in micro processes of accountability in a UK restaurant chain. Based on fieldwork conducted in fifteen restaurants, Ahrens and Chapman concluded that technically similar systems of performance measurement can lead to quite dissimilar and diverse forms of organizational functioning. Expectations conveyed by the restaurant's global system of performance measurement were localized, contested, and changed continually by specific actions occurring within each restaurant. Local values (e.g. customer service is more important than the food margin) and power relations (e.g. it is acceptable for managers to exercise their discretion and use some of their cash surplus to employ extra specialist staff) interacted to reshape and contextualize the meanings attributed to the range of performance measures used to assess the chain of restaurants. As a result, the relative importance of performance measures varied across the restaurant chain, 'depending on competing notions of legitimate action and on different power constellations' (p. 164). Thus, according to Ahrens and Chapman, the micro processes of accountability were inextricably linked to contests of meaning and the use of the performance measurement systems to legitimate various restaurant managers' points of view. In comparison to Roberts' case study in which organizational participants were connected almost effortlessly to the values, meanings, and power relations desired by the centre, Ahrens and Chapman's research highlights the often self-conscious and uncomfortable couplings that characterize the duality of action and structure in some systems of accountability.

As such, management accounting research mobilizing Giddens' theory of structuration has challenged us to think about the ways in which micro-accounting practices are linked to more enduring institutional structures, whilst conveying the interpretive, moral, and political dimensions of systems of management planning and control. Yet this research is not without its critics. Boland (1996), for example, argues that extant management accounting interpretations of structuration theory have got it wrong. In particular, Boland argues that structuration theory is presented as a theory of action (rather than agency) by management accounting researchers, with action being incorrectly portrayed as the internalization of institutional values, meanings, and power relations. With respect to this, Boland argues that this style of research has not connected the micro processes of accountability studied with institutionally located patterns, such as the division of labour, globalization, etc. Nonetheless, at a more general level, Boland is in agreement with management accounting researchers employing the sociology of Giddens. He too argues that such theoretical reframings of management accounting practice highlight that systems of planning and control are contingent, continuously reflexive, and adaptive accomplishments, challenging technically neutral and socially disconnected accounts of this aspect of organizational functioning.

3.7 **Foucauldian frame**

During the 1980s, a discernible stream of management accounting research began to mobilize the work of the late, influential, French postmodernist thinker, Michel Foucault. The imprint of Foucault's work has been far-reaching, affecting disciplines as diverse as sociology, history, philosophy, literature, cultural studies, management, and law, in addition to our appreciation of management accounting. Whilst Foucault's work is broad in its scope, covering issues ranging from sexuality to discourse, his work has concentrated on issues related to the construction of knowledge, power relations (spanning governmentality by the state of its citizenry to the micro politics of the functioning of our bodies), and the constitution of the subject when considered in relation to structures such as culture (Danaher et al. 2000). Management accounting researchers who have drawn upon the work of Foucault, likewise, are concerned with these issues, producing a number of seminal papers problematizing the ways in which management accounting 'truths' have emerged, as well as critical and provocative examinations of the power relations embedded in the operation of systems of management control.

Foucauldian research concerned with the emergence of various management accounting 'truths' has focused the research gaze onto an examination of the various conditions that have made possible particular management accounting technologies, enabling them to become part of our professional discourse and taken-for-granted 'tool kit' of practices. Rather than treating management accounting technologies as objective, atemporal, and apolitical, researchers utilizing the writings of Foucault frame such technologies as historically and culturally contingent phenomena, emphasizing their ephemeral and fragile, rather than essential and indelible, nature.

Such insights have emerged as a result of a number of key historical studies of management accounting practice during the twentieth century. These histories, sometimes referred to as 'new histories', have drawn upon Foucault's historical method and are concerned with outlining the 'archaeology' and 'genealogy' of particular aspects of management accounting (see Foucault 1972; Hopwood 1987). Archaeology refers to the way in which management accounting researchers use archival material to map the relationships between discourses and events surrounding and facilitating the emergence of various forms of management accounting. Genealogy is a term reflecting the 'new historian's' concern for portraying the discontinuities in practices and ideas about management accounting. In relation to this, Foucault (1972: 146) stated:

One can see the emergence therefore of a number of disconnexions and articulations. One can no longer say that a discovery, the formulation of a general principle, or the definition of a project, inaugurates, in a massive way, a new phase in the history of discourse. One no longer has to seek that point of absolute origin or total revolution on the basis of which everything is organized, everything becomes possible and necessary, everything is effaced in order to begin again. One is dealing with events of different types and levels, caught up in distinct historical webs; the establishment of an enunciative homogeneity in no way implies that, for decades or centuries to come, men will say and think the same thing; nor does it imply the definition, explicit or not, of a number of principles from which everything else would flow, as inevitable consequences.

Such ideas have infused the new histories of management accounting undertaken by Burchell et al. (1985), Loft (1986), and Preston (1992), for example.

Burchell et al. (1985) adopted a Foucauldian frame to examine the emergence of value-added reporting in the UK during the 1970s. Value-added accounting is a way of measuring the 'market value' or 'wealth' created through ostensible cooperation between shareholders, employees, creditors, and other stakeholders (see pp. 387–90). According to Burchell et al., value-added reporting was characterized by great 'calculative diversity' and many presentational formats (p. 387). It was the overriding purpose of these researchers, however, to account for value-added accounting in such a way that demonstrated 'an accounting-society interpenetration' (p. 385), i.e. they wished to narrate how value-added accounting was informed by the social, but also capable of informing it in return.

In fulfilling this purpose, these authors articulated how value-added accounting was made possible by a web of social conditions. One element of this web constructed by Burchell et al. singles out the role of the accounting profession and, in particular, its interest in acknowledging a range of stakeholders in the corporate reporting process, as well as a desire to standardize such reporting to increase the reliability of the underlying information. A second strand of their web focuses on government discourse about macroeconomic management and a concern for productivity and efficiency. The changing nature of industrial relations discourse, and its growing emphasis on industrial democracy and profit sharing, comprises the third strand of their argument.

Burchell et al. refer to this web as an 'accounting constellation' or 'network of intersecting practices' (p. 400). Whilst shifts in industrial relations and macroeconomic policy were imprinted on a changed awareness of the accounting profession in terms of a need for alternative forms of reporting, it was the practice of management accounting that enabled the concerns of the state about efficiency to become connected to a seemingly disparate debate about democracy in the workforce. It was these conditions that enabled value-added accounting to flourish in the UK during the 1970s. The important point these researchers make is that this accounting constellation was 'unintended' (p. 401): value-added accounting was not the product of a conscious exercise in design; nor was it the outcome of a seamless evolution and progression of accounting practice. Value-added accounting is framed as having emerged from a confluence of highly situated discourses that both sustained and were sustained by it.

Similarly, Loft (1986) argues that cost accounting was made possible in the UK during the early years of the twentieth century by unintended consequences arising from the First World War. Wartime investigations to prevent profiteering on government contracts created an emphasis on costs, which was heightened by a need for the post-war British economy to grow efficiently. This heightened cost consciousness was institutionalized also by the creation of a professional body, Institute of Cost and Works Accountants (ICWA), specializing in this form of capability, as well as an increasing emphasis on costing in the examinations of the Institute of Chartered Accountants in England & Wales (ICAEW). Preston (1992), likewise, frames the emergence of a particular form of clinical costing developed in US hospitals, called diagnosis-related groups, within various but ultimately intermingling forms of discourse. Preston (1992: 96) stated:

> We may observe that the emergence of DRG prospective payment in American hospitals operating within the Medicare system was not merely the invention of a new accounting technology, but rather was the outcome of a complex of medical, social, economic and political discourses.... They are constituted within, and are constitutive of, a politics of health which was shaped by government regulation, the practices of such institutional bodies as the AMA, the AHA and the private medical insurance companies and changing public attitudes towards the rights to and in medical care.

Miller and O'Leary employ a Foucauldian frame to study the impact of distant discursive webs on practices within organizations. In their 1987 study, addressing the history of standard costing and budgeting in the early decades of the twentieth century, Miller and O'Leary argue that these management accounting technologies were made possible by shifts in discourses concerning the 'administration of social life' (1987: 239), focusing on national efficiency and scientific management, for instance. Located within this web of ideas and debates concerning the normalization of behaviour, Miller and O'Leary contend that standard costing and budgeting are calculative practices that act as a form of disciplinary power. Standard costs and budgets render the behaviour of individuals visible, making them responsible for the extent of their wastefulness and inefficiency.

In a subsequent and more micro-level study examining the shift in Caterpillar's Decatur plant towards 'world-class manufacturing', Miller and O'Leary (1994) narrate the connection between the spatial and temporal reordering of the plant (achieved by the institution of semi-autonomous production cells) and ideals of advanced manufacturing (encompassing flexibility, quality, and cost management, for example) with the governmentality of economic life, expressed in the form of debates about 'New Economic Citizenship' (see p. 17). Miller and O'Leary argue that costs were made visible in this production environment by the flow and spatial arrangement of the production processes, constructing costs in terms of new calculable spaces called 'investment bundles'. They argue that this has constituted a 'governable process', as opposed to the 'governable person' in more traditional manufacturing contexts (see p. 41).

Knights and Collinson (1987) utilized a Foucauldian frame to outline the micro power apparent in the ability of management accounting inscriptions to constitute docile organizational participants. In studying management control of the shop floor in a heavy motor vehicle manufacturer, Knights and Collinson found that workers resisted attempts at psychological control through the dissemination of in-house newsletters—regarding such material as 'a load of Yankee hypnosis on paper' (p. 461). Yet no resistance was offered by these workers to constructions of the production process, and its apparent inefficiency, when portrayed by financial reports. Knights and Collinson (1987) argue that workers on the shop floor were subjugated by the apparent 'concreteness' (p. 472) of the financial accounts and were unable to grasp or contest their symbolic and tentative character.

Knights and Collinson argue that the insights offered by a Foucauldian framing of management accounting practice, and its connections to power, create important responsibilities for those capable of conducting and promulgating the findings of more critical forms of management accounting research. They state:

Still we remain uneasy in as much as this study of an acquiescent labour force is not significantly more liberating for those involved than would be a conventional report on the specific accounting strategies and procedures at [case organisation]. Its only potential then must lie with the audience of academic accountants who, in recognising the enormous disciplinary power of accounting knowledge, may give more attention to the moral and political consequences of their practice. (p. 475)

This summation of the often overlooked or underestimated coercive dimension of management accounting, embodied in the working and day-to-day lives of individuals, resonates in the comments by Boland (1987: 272) on this particular genre of management accounting research:

It should shatter the feelings of innocence and neutrality we all prize so deeply. Most of all, it should help us ask: what are we doing when we do cost accounting?

3.8 Latourian frame

Interesting constructions of management accounting practice have also been provided by researchers mobilizing the theoretical frame of Bruno Latour and his followers (see Latour 1987, 1993, 1996). Latour has been a key figure in literatures addressing the sociology of technologies and their making in terms of 'actor networks'—or 'action nets' as they are becoming known. The key insight of a Latourian frame of practice is that management accounting technologies are not diffused into various organizations as 'ready-made', stable, and immutable objects of representation. In comparison, management accounting technologies are constructed and become 'factlike' as a result of being embedded in hybrid networks of human and non-human actants (such as software, computer hardware, production processes, plant, and equipment), connecting and corralling various and shifting interests through ties of differing intensity and scope.

As such, researchers adopting a Latourian frame are motivated to study management accounting technologies as they are being made, constructed, or 'fabricated' (Chua 1995). Basically Latour, and his followers, argue that once an accounting technology becomes stabilized and is treated as a 'factlike' aspect of organizational functioning—ceasing to be problematic and controversial (at least temporarily)—it attains the status of a 'black box' (Preston et al. 1992). Having attained this status, the opportunity to study the processual functioning of the fact-building networks, fortifying extant management accounting practices, is lost. Consequently, research conducted within this frame concentrates on emergent 'innovations' (Miller 1991) in management accounting, encompassing, for example, reforms to budgeting and costing practices in clinical settings (Pinch et al. 1989; Preston et al. 1992; Chua 1995), the adoption of discounted cash flows (DCFs) in investment analysis in the UK (Miller 1991), and shifts to activity based costing (ABC) (Briers and Chua 2001).

Central to such Latourian accounts of technology in the making is the concept of 'translation.' 'Translation' is a concept that highlights the 'deformation' (Latour, cited in Jones et al. 2004: 726) attending the passage of 'global' (management accounting) technologies as they struggle to become 'matters of fact' within particular networks (Preston et al. 1992: 566). The fate of new technologies, such as ABC, is characterized, therefore, as residing in the interests of those actors connected to local networks, and the deformations that the exercise of such interests imposes on the construction and interpretation of technologies.

These translations or deformations shaping a technology in the making are mediated by processes of 'experimentation' that occur within a particular network. Actors experiment with technologies, trying different ways of producing 'factlike' accounting inscriptions. Pinch et al., for example, describe/dramatize the experimentation that occurred in relation to the introduction of clinical budgeting within part of the British National Health Service. Various iterations and improvisations of clinical budgeting were trialled in an attempt to form a network of computers, software, ideas about health economics, and clinical practices that both improved patient care and brought about a greater awareness of costs and efficiency within the health system. Similarly, Briers and Chua (2001) describe the experimentation through which various forms of ABC were constructed in an effort to destabilize and discredit an extant standard costing system.

Such experiments are described as 'trials' (Briers and Chua 2001: 245) in which the 'strength' of a technology, and the accounting inscriptions it produces, are manufactured and assessed by a network. The stability of the network and the factlike status (or otherwise) of the accounting inscriptions being produced hinges on the ability of actors to convert 'weak possibilities' (ABC will lead to improved product profitability decisions in this organization—see Briers and Chua 2001) into 'convincing arguments' (ABC has demonstrated the undercosting of the aluminium plate product and we should therefore discontinue its production—see Briers and Chua 2001) that withstand various experiments and challenges from rival trials and anti-programmes.

Latour argues that advocates of various technologies have recourse to a variety of fact-building strategies, such as 'fortification' (making arguments seemingly more objective through increasing technical detail), 'stacking' (convincing others through the provision of supporting facts and figures), 'staging and framing' (constructing the controversy and agenda for debate), and 'captation' (managing objections by commencing with statements that are difficult to contest) (see Preston et al. 1992: 574–5). For example, in Chua's paper (1995) narrating attempts to trial diagnosis-related costing groups (a type of clinical standard costing) in a pilot group of Australian public hospitals, she reproduces a sample of the accounting inscriptions that translated weak arguments about the need for an efficient, quality universal health care system in Australia into a detailed set of costings that objectified the comparative financial performance of the pilot hospitals in terms of 470 clinical products.

However, as extant research demonstrates, it is often quite difficult for accounting inscriptions to attain a factlike status, despite prolonged and/or multiple experiments aimed at achieving such an outcome. Rational demonstrations of the costs and benefits of a proposed new accounting technology are not enough to bind an actor network (Pinch et al. 1989). Latourian researchers argue that fact-builders must mobilize 'interessement' devices or objects that 'tie together' (Chua 1995: 123) different interests within a network and are thereby beginning to explore the role of 'boundary objects' (Briers and Chua 2001) in this context. Boundary objects are described as 'plastic' enough to accommodate different actors' interests. Briers and Chua's study of the fabrication of an ABC system highlights the key role played by 'visionary' boundary objects—'conceptual objects that have high levels of legitimacy within a particular community' (Briers and Chua 2001: 242)—in the construction of accounting inscriptions. In their research, ideals such as 'world best practice' and 'better costing technologies' served to connect locals and cosmopolitans aspiring to accounting change within the network being studied (see p. 265). But these boundary objects were insufficient to make the ties durable in the case study described by Briers and Chua; the network began to decompose as the attention of the fact-builders shifted elsewhere within the organization.

Indeed, the *fragility* of accounting inscriptions—the instability and relative transience of the 'assemblage' of factors implicated in their fabrication (Miller 1991: 736)—is highlighted by Latourian research. Preston et al. remark on the 'difficulty' that actors confront in making management accounting technologies 'appear as unexceptional facts of organizational life' (1992: 589). In short, many management accounting experiments are not 'successful', failing to implement new and enduring calculative visibilities (Preston et al. 1992; Briers and Chua 2001). There are only weak consequences that linger from the process of experimentation and fact-building. For example, in relation to the British clinical budgeting trial narrated by Pinch et al., it was argued that actors involved in the experiment, such as nurses, emerged as more capable organizational participants—even though health care statistics may not have improved.

Nonetheless, some management accounting technologies become securely embedded in their organizational context. In Miller's account (1991) of the eventual adoption during the 1960s of a DCF methodology for capital investment appraisal in the UK, he outlines the connections that were forged between this accounting technology and a more general economic discourse. Strong, long, durable ties emerged from this actor network with government level concerns about the rate of economic growth and quality of investment providing a programmatic (idealized) context, which became coupled to, and translated into, organizational routines supporting the use of DCF.

Whilst this study by Miller specifically shows the ways in which the interests of actors 'beyond the boundaries of the enterprise' (p. 735) become connected to local calculative practices, it more generally illustrates the Latourian concept of 'action at a distance'. Long ties may enable and sustain the influence of distant actors, such as the British government in Miller's research (1991), over other parts of the network without direct intervention (see p. 738). In Latourian terms, durable ties within a network allow the 'centre' to exert its continuing and surreptitious influence over the 'periphery'. Moreover, accounting technologies are particularly effective in this regard. Accounting technologies, such as DCF, generate inscriptions that are 'mobile' (they can be transported to the centre in the form of accounting reports produced by the periphery), 'stable' (the numbers are not affected by time and space), and 'combinable' (the centre can consolidate, segment, and benchmark performance based on accounting inscriptions available).

Despite this potential for accounting inscriptions to travel within networks and across organizational boundaries, Latourian research also highlights practical impediments to this. Recalcitrant actors can limit the circulation of accounting inscriptions within a network and such recalcitrant actors are not only human actors with differing priorities and shifting interests; Latourian research also emphasizes the role of non-human actors in the fact-building process. Incompatible and poorly maintained computing systems, as well as a lack of general understanding about underlying programming protocols, have all been associated with blockages in the circulation of accounting inscriptions within actor networks, despite temporarily stabilized interests (Chua 1995; Briers and Chua 2001).

In conclusion, Latourian accounts of management accounting practice have raised a number of significant philosophical issues in relation to management accounting research. By connecting the intentions of both human and non-human actants within networks, a Latourian frame constitutes human–technological hybrids as its object of study. Technologies and artefacts that are often considered to constitute context in relation to other research perspectives are brought to the fore, creating interesting debates about the reification (or otherwise) of inanimate objects in action nets and the possibility of abandoning a nature–society dualism in social science research. Similarly, the crafting of long ties, connecting programmatic debates with local interests, actors, and activities points the way to a potential dissolution of 'macro' and 'micro' levels of analysis, offering instead 'flat' surfaces in which to constitute and consider the fabrication of management accounting practices.

3.9 **Conclusion**

This chapter has attempted to overview the diversity of research perspectives which have been used to (re)frame management accounting. These different perspectives are united by their sustained critique of economically rational constructions of organizational functioning in which management accounting is implicated primarily in the efficient and effective realization of organizational strategies and operational goals. Researchers mobilizing a non-rational design frame emphasize the contribution of management accounting to processes of experimentation that help organizations discover and learn about their goals. A naturalistic frame constitutes management accounting as a diverse accomplishment, highlighting the local rationalities embedding global management accounting technologies in different organizational contexts. A radical frame highlights connections between the practice of management accounting and the interests of global capitalism. The imprinting of socially 'legitimated templates' informing the myth of rationality in management accounting is configured by an institutional frame. Structurationist accounts highlight the moral, political, and interpretive dimensions of apparently neutral management accounting technologies. The bland and benign nature of management accounting is also challenged by Foucauldian framings of the coercive power of calculative regimes. Finally, a Latourian frame configures management accounting practices as action nets, rendered temporarily sensible by the translation and interessement of various human and non-human interests. In short, these more critical forms of management accounting research have fostered rich, diverse, and provocative theorizations of management accounting practice.

Overall, it is our hope that readers will be challenged by the possibilities offered by these various (re)framings of management accounting. Whilst this chapter has sought to characterize the general contours of these perspectives and some of the seminal papers that have helped to form them, readers are encouraged to explore the literary traces of this foundational research and to pursue personal research agendas sustaining and rejuvenating the trajectory of these iconoclastic characterizations.

☐ REFERENCES

Abernethy, M. and Chua, W. F. (1996). 'A Field Study of Control System "Redesign": The Impact of Institutional Processes on Strategic Choice', *Contemporary Accounting Research*, 13: 569–607.

Ahrens, T. (1997). 'Talking Accounting: An Ethnography of Management Knowledge in British and German Brewers', *Accounting, Organizations and Society*, 22: 617–37.

—— and Chapman, C. (2002). 'The Structuration of Legitimate Performance Measures and Management: Day-to-Day Contests of Accountability in a U.K. Restaurant', *Management Accounting Research*, 13: 151–71.

—— and Dent, J. (1998). 'Accounting and Organizations: Realizing the Richness of Field Research', *Journal of Management Accounting Research*, 10: 1–40.

Armstrong, P. (1987). 'The Rise of Accounting Controls in British Capitalist Enterprises', *Accounting, Organizations and Society*, 12: 415–36.

Atkinson, D. (1972). *Orthodox Consensus and Radical Alternative*. London: Heinemann Educational.

Banbury, J. and Nahapiet, J. E. (1979). 'Towards a Framework for the Study of the Antecedents and Consequences of Information Systems in Organizations', *Accounting, Organizations and Society*, 4: 163–77.

Baum, J. and Oliver, C. (1991). 'Institutional Linkages and Organizational Mortality', *Administrative Science Quarterly*, 36:187–218.

Baxter, J. A. and Chua, W. F. (1998). 'Doing Field Research: Meta-Theory and Practice in Counter-point', *Journal of Management Accounting Research*, 10: 69–88.

—— —— (2003). 'Alternative Management Accounting Research: Whence and Whither', *Accounting, Organizations and Society*, 28: 97–126.

Berry, A. J., Capps, T., Cooper, D., Ferguson, P., Hopper, T., and Lowe, E. A. (1985). 'Management Control in an Area of the NCB: Rationales of Accounting Practices in a Public Enterprise', *Accounting, Organizations and Society*, 10: 3–28.

Boland, R. J. (1979). 'Control, Causality and Information System Requirements', *Accounting, Organizations and Society*, 4: 259–72.

—— (1981). 'A Study in System Design: C. West Churchman and Chris Argyris', *Accounting, Organizations and Society*, 6: 109–18.

—— (1987). 'Discussion of "Accounting and the Construction of the Governable Person"', *Accounting, Organizations and Society*, 12: 267–72.

—— (1996). 'Why Shared Meanings Have no Place in Structuration Theory: A Reply to Scapens and Macintosh', *Accounting, Organizations and Society*, 21: 691–7.

—— and Pondy, L. R. (1983). 'Accounting in Organizations: A Union of Natural and Rational Perspectives', *Accounting, Organizations and Society*, 8: 223–34.

Braverman, H. (1974). *Labor and Monopoly Capital*. New York: Monthly Review Press.

Briers, M. and Chua, W. F. (2001). 'The Role of Actor-Networks and Boundary Objects in Management Accounting Change: A Field Study of Activity-Based Costing', *Accounting, Organizations and Society*, 26: 237–69.

Burchell, S., Club, C., and Hopwood, A. (1985). 'Accounting in Its Social Context: Towards a History of Value Added in the United Kingdom', *Accounting, Organizations and Society*, 10: 381–413.

Burrell, G. and Morgan, G. (1979). *Sociological Paradigms and Organisational Analysis*. London: Heinemann Educational.

Chua, W. F. (1986). 'Radical Developments in Accounting Thought', *Accounting Review*, LXI (4): 601–32.

—— (1995). 'Experts, Networks and Inscriptions in the Fabrication of Accounting Images: A Story of the Representation of Three Public Hospitals', *Accounting, Organizations and Society*, 20: 111–45.

Cohen, M., March, J., and Olsen, J. (1972). 'A Garbage Can Model of Organizational Choice', *Administrative Science Quarterly* (March): 1–25.

Cooper, D. (1983). 'Tidiness, Muddle and Things: Commonalities and Divergencies in Two Approaches to Management Accounting Research', *Accounting, Organizations and Society*, 8: 269–86.

Cooper, D. J., Hayes, D., and Wolf, F. (1981). 'Accounting in Organized Anarchies: Understanding and Designing Accounting Systems in Ambiguous Situations', *Accounting, Organizations and Society*, 6: 175–91.

Covaleski, M. A. and Dirsmith, M. W. (1986). 'The Budgetary Process of Power and Politics', *Accounting, Organizations and Society*, 11: 193–214.

—— —— (1988). 'The Use of Budgetary Symbols in the Political Arena: An Historically Informed Field Study', *Accounting, Organizations and Society*, 13: 1–24.

—— —— and Michelman, J. E. (1993). 'An Institutional Theory Perspective on the DRG Framework, Case-mix Accounting Systems and Health-care Organizations', *Accounting, Organizations and Society*, 18: 65–80.

Czarniawska-Joerges, B. (1988). 'Dynamics of Organizational Control: The Case of Berol Kemi AB', *Accounting, Organizations and Society*, 13: 415–30.

—— and Jacobsson, B. (1989). 'Budget in a Cold Climate', *Accounting, Organizations and Society*, 14: 29–39.

Danaher, G., Schirato, T., and Webb, J. (2000). *Understanding Foucault*. St Leonards: Allen and Unwin.

Dent, J. F. (1991). 'Accounting and Organizational Cultures: A Field Study of the Emergence of a New Organizational Reality', *Accounting, Organizations and Society*, 16: 705–32.

DiMaggio, W. and Powell, P. (1991). 'Introduction', in W. DiMaggio, and P. Powell (eds.). *The New Institutionalism in Organizational Analysis*. Chicago: University of Chicago Press.

Ezzamel, M. and Bourn, M. (1990). 'The Roles of Accounting Information Systems in an Organization Experiencing Financial Crisis', *Accounting, Organizations and Society*, 15: 399–424.

Foucault, M. (1972). *The Archaeology of Knowledge*. London: Tavistock.

Giddens, A. (1976). *New Rules of Sociological Method*. London: Hutchinson.

—— (1979). *Central Problems in Social Theory: Action, Structure and Contradiction in Social Analysis*. London: Macmillan Press.

—— (1982). *Sociology: A Brief but Critical Introduction*. London: Macmillan Press.

—— (1984). *The Constitution of Society*. Cambridge: Polity Press.

—— (1998). *The Third Way*. Cambridge: Polity Press.

Granlund, M. (2001). 'Towards Explaining Stability in and Around Management Accounting Systems', *Management Accounting Research*, 12: 141–66.

Gupta, P., Dirsmith, M., Fogarty, T., and Timothy, J. (1994). 'Coordination and Control in a Government Agency: Contingency and Institutional Theory Perspectives on GAO Audits', *Administrative Science Quarterly*, 39: 264–85.

Habermas, J. (1968). *Toward a Rational Society*. London: Heinemann Educational.

—— (1976). *Communication and the Evolution of Society*. London: Heinemann Educational.

Haka, S. and Krishnan, R. (2005). 'Budget Type and Performance—The Moderating Effect of Uncertainty', *Australian Review*, 15: 3–13.

Hedberg, B. and Jönsson, S. (1978). 'Designing Semi-confusing Information Systems for Organizations in Changing Environments', *Accounting, Organizations and Society*, 3: 47–64.

Hope, J. and Fraser, R. (2003). 'Who Needs Budgets?', *Harvard Business Review* (February): 108–15.

Hopper, T., Cooper, D., Lowe, T., Capps, T., and Mouritsen, J. (1986). 'Management Control and Worker Resistance in the National Coal Board', in H. Willmott and D. Knights (eds.), *Managing the Labour Process*. Aldershot: Gower, pp. 109–41.

—— Storey, J., and Willmott, H. (1987). 'Accounting for Accounting: Towards the Development of a Dialectical View', *Accounting, Organizations and Society,* 12: 437–56.

Hopwood, A. G. (1987). 'The Archaeology of Accounting Systems', *Accounting, Organizations and Society,* 12: 207–34.

Horngren, C., Datar, S., and Foster, G. (2003). *Cost Accounting: A Managerial Emphasis,* 11th edn. Englewood Cliffs, NJ: Prentice Hall.

Howell, R. (2004). 'Turn Your Budget Process Upside Down', *Harvard Business Review* (July–August): 21–2.

Jack, L. (2005). 'Stocks of Knowledge, Simplification and Unintended Consequences: The Persistence of Post-war Accounting Practices in UK Agriculture', *Management Accounting Research,* 16: 59–79.

Johnson, H. T., and Kaplan, R. S. (1987). *Relevance Lost: The Rise and Fall of Management Accounting,* Boston: Harvard Business School Press.

Jones, G., McLean, C., and Quattrone, P. (2004). 'Spacing and Timing', *Organization,* 11: 723–41.

Jönsson, S. (1982). 'Budgeting Behavior in Local Government—A Case Study Over 3 Years', *Accounting, Organizations and Society,* 3: 287–304.

Kaplan, R. (1998). 'Innovation Action Research: Creating New Management Theory and Practice', *Journal of Management Accounting Research,* 10: 89–118.

Keat, R. and Urry, J. (1982). *Social Theory as Science.* London: Routledge and Kegan Paul.

Knights, D. and Collinson, D. (1987). 'Disciplining the Shop Floor: A Comparison of the Disciplinary Effects of Managerial Psychology and Financial Accounting', *Accounting, Organizations and Society,* 12: 457–77.

Latour, B. (1987). *Science in action.* Cambridge, MA: Harvard University Press.

—— (1993). *We Have Never Been Modern.* Harlow: Prentice Hall.

—— (1996). *Aramis, or the Love of Technology.* Cambridge, MA: Harvard University Press.

Laughlin, R. C. (1987). 'Accounting Systems in Organisational Contexts: A Case for Critical Theory', *Accounting, Organizations and Society,* 12: 479–502.

Llewellyn, S. (1998). 'Boundary Work: Costing and Caring in the Social Services', *Accounting, Organizations and Society,* 23: 23–47.

—— and Northcott, D. (2005). 'The Average Hospital', *Accounting, Organizations and Society,* 30: 555–83.

Loft, A. (1986). 'Towards a Critical Understanding of Accounting: The Case of Cost Accounting in the U.K., 1914–1925', *Accounting, Organizations and Society,* 11: 137–69.

Meyer, J. and Rowan, B. (1977). 'Institutional Organizations: Formal Structure as Myth and Ceremony', *American Journal of Sociology,* 83: 340–63.

Miller, P. (1991). 'Accounting Innovation Beyond the Enterprise: Problematizing Investment Decisions and Programming Economic Growth in the U.K. in the 1960s', *Accounting, Organizations and Society,* 16: 733–62.

—— and O'Leary, T. (1987). 'Accounting and the Construction of the Governable Person', *Accounting, Organizations and Society,* 12: 235–65.

—— —— (1994). 'Accounting, "Economic Citizenship" and the Spatial Recording of Manufacture', *Accounting, Organizations and Society,* 19: 15–43.

Mouritsen, J. (1999). 'The Flexible Firm: Strategies for a Subcontractor's Management Control', *Accounting, Organizations and Society*, 24: 31–55.

Neimark, M. and Tinker, T. (1986). 'The Social Construction of Management Control Systems', *Accounting, Organizations and Society*, 11: 369–95.

Pinch, T., Mulkay, M., and Ashmore, M. (1989). 'Clinical Budgeting: Experimentation in the Social Sciences—A drama in Five Acts', *Accounting, Organizations and Society*, 14: 271–301.

Preston, A. (1986). 'Interactions and Arrangements in the Process of Informing', *Accounting, Organizations and Society*, 11: 521–40.

—— (1992). 'The Birth of Clinical Accounting: A Study of the Emergence and Transformations of Disclosures on Costs and Practices of Accounting in U.S. Hospitals', *Accounting, Organizations and Society*, 17: 63–100.

—— Cooper, D., and Coombs, R. (1992). 'Fabricating Budgets: A Study of the Production of Management Budgeting in the National Health Service', *Accounting, Organizations and Society*, 17: 561–93.

Roberts, J. (1990). 'Strategy and Accounting in a U.K. Conglomerate', *Accounting, Organizations and Society*, 15: 107–26.

—— and Scapens, R. (1985). 'Accounting Systems and Systems of Accountability—Understanding Accounting Practices in their Organisational Contexts', *Accounting, Organizations and Society*, 10: 443–56.

Shank, J. and Govindarajan, V. (1989). *Strategic Cost Analysis: The Evolution from Managerial to Strategic Accounting*. Homewood, IL: Richard D. Irwin.

Students of the Executive MBA Class of 2003: Hankamer School of Business, Baylor University (2003). 'Who Needs Budgets?', *Harvard Business Review* (June): 131.

Tinker, A. M., Merino, B. D., and Neimark, M. D. (1982). 'The Normative Origins of Positive Theories: Ideology and Accounting Thought', *Accounting, Organizations and Society*, 7: 167–200.

Tomkins, C. and Groves, R. (1983). 'The Everyday Accountant and Researching His Reality', *Accounting, Organizations and Society*, 8: 361–74.

Vaivio, J. (1999). 'Examining "the Quantified Customer"', *Accounting, Organizations and Society*, 24: 689–715.

4 Management accounting and digitization

Alnoor Bhimani

4.1 Digitization and economic 'newness'

It is well accepted that technology's influence extends well beyond just the particular function of products. In the nineteenth century, railroads altered not just shipping options and the economics of transportation, but transformed what could be produced, how, where, and by whom. Railroads also revamped the retail industry landscape. Department stores in city centres expanded rapidly as railroads enabled consumers to travel into towns from suburbs. The growth of the car industry likewise changed the structure of the workforce from the 1920s and further enhanced consumer mobility. Shopping centres on the outskirts of towns grew as more individuals gained access to motorized transportation. Similarly, the development of electric lifts allowed the construction of high-rise buildings bringing thousands of individuals closer to one another and enabling, as a consequence, people–organization interfaces on an unprecedented scale. These and other technological advances have had diverse attendant effects on industrial activities, enterprise productivity, and economic output.

Today, the advent of digital technologies continues to mobilize far-reaching social and economic effects. Organizational strategies for growth and the structuring of entire industries are predicated on technological changes in many areas of business and across different economic platforms. But technological change can produce varying magnitudes of effects. One impact of significance, which is not common to all new technologies, is the creation of network effects. Computer-operating systems, applications, and standards offer inherent value to users. But this value grows also with the number of users deploying the digitized technology. This is because standards that achieve widespread acceptance expand the potential deployability of the digitized technologies adopting the standards in question. Of relevance also to understanding the effects and the impact of digital technology usage is that knowledge creation, transfer, and processing take place faster today than has been possible with past technology usage. According to some management commentators, the speed of knowledge growth and exchange is representative of economic newness. This, it has been claimed, will bring about further major alterations:

The new economy...favours intangible things—ideas, information and relationships. The world of the soft—the world of intangibles, of media, of software, and of services—will soon command the world of the hard—the world of reality, of atoms, of objects, of steel and oil. (Kelly 1998: 6)

Digitization is core to what many regard as the new economy. The term 'new economy' is controversial. Some pontificate on its impact (Tapscott 2001) whilst others cast doubt on whether traditional economics has lost relevance (Shapiro and Varian 1999). Some consider that it is the multiple meanings of the term that have allowed obsessions about its implications being regarded as natural (De Cock et al. 2005). Whether or not a new economy exists is inconsequential. What matters is that beliefs mobilize change. Those who believe in the existence of a new economy act on their beliefs and do things differently. Those who refute its existence take actions that influence enterprise activities in some other ways. Ultimately, organizations change, institutions change, and management decisions change as a result of beliefs. When we think about financial controls and management accounting, there is a parallel. Beliefs that lead managers to alter costs, prices, incentive schemes, quality controls, financial monitors, etc. also extensively reorder many other organizational processes. Connections that are made between the potential of digitization and management accounting practices and concerns exist because, when an enterprise implements a new strategy based on altered economic reasoning, financial controls and cost management priorities also change. Transformations in management accounting are particularly pronounced when an enterprise adopts innovative business models and novel management control philosophies viewed as being tied to access to emerging digital technologies. This chapter draws out some links between digitized technology deployment and management accounting implications.

4.2 The economics of change

A number of management thinkers believe that during the mid-eighteenth to mid-nineteenth centuries, many societies underwent a transformation from an agricultural economy where land and labour mattered most to an industrial era where capital and labour mattered most. More recently, yet another transformation has occurred whereby we have entered an economic age where information and intellectual capital now play a major role. The term new economy has been ascribed to this shift, signalling perhaps our inability to conceptually grapple with the pace of change. It is representative of a search for a new paradigm as the gap between the world and our understanding of it grows wider.

During the late 1990s, signs of an emerging economic order were viewed as being factored into rising share prices of technology-linked organizations. The stock price collapse of April 2000 signalled to many that the concept of a changed economy was bogus or at least very short-lived. But some thinkers suggest that many signs remain that at least some altered aspects of the economy are unprecedented. For instance, Tapscott (2001) believes that the following factors characterize the modern commercial environment across different parts of the globe:

- New infrastructure for wealth creation—organizational networks and the Internet in particular are becoming the basis for economic activity and progress;
- New business models—new ways of achieving viable architectures within firms and across industrial structures are emerging. This has resulted in altered ways of bringing together different constituent elements of products;
- New sources of value—knowledge in particular continues to be infused within products and services. Ultimately its creation and processing has to be managed, monitored, and evaluated.

The role of management accounting within such a perspective faces potential change. Management accounting is, in most contexts, concerned with the capture of economic data gleaned from organizational activities and the conversion of such data into information that conforms to conceptions of what is deemed to be managerially useful (Chapman 2005). Managers and information users ground the output of formal information systems into their knowledge production practices to guide their decisions and actions. Notional changes in knowledge creation and management processes can thus be expected to affect management accounting activities and priorities.

The argument has also been made that markets are witnessing globalization on a mass scale—this is not simply a matter of a new layer of economic activity being placed on top of existing production and business processes. Rather, there is a fundamental restructuring of all economic activities based on emerging advanced information technologies. Such globalization, which is information technology-driven, brings accounting practices closer together and juxtaposes diverse modes of decision-making. Management accounting systems (MASs) as a consequence face pressures to change to accommodate globalizing forces.

Information technologies evolve following a distinctively different pattern compared to previous technologies. They exhibit an 'informational mode of development' (Castells 2001: 87), which is flexible, pervasive, and integrated. This is easy to understand if we consider the fact that the ultimate product of many pure e-business enterprises is of a digital form and thus no different, in essence, from the raw material inputs. Consequently, the process of innovation and production is speeded up. For financial management, the digitized means of representation themselves equate with the raw material and the product. There is similitude in both the digital modes of reporting on economic activity and the digital nature of products being transacted and about which the finance and accounting function seeks to report. Thus operations and information to manage operations are premised upon the same basic platform. Technologies of representation do not fundamentally differ from what is being represented, so accounting information evolves altered links to the management of operations.

The present economy is extensively powered by information technology and is dependent on intelligence organized around computer networks. This implies that organizational innovation is more and more a function, not just of highly skilled labour, but also of 'the existence of knowledge-creating organizations' (Castells 2001: 99). Knowledge creation within enterprises lends itself to novel ways of organizing and to alternative business models. Managerial innovations engender new financial management practices.

Other signs of change in the global digital economy have been identified: Burton-Jones (1999) notes that one can compress symbols, break them up, and reassemble them without altering their value. This enhances the velocity of information exchanges. The speed with which data can be aggregated into information and restructured and formatted is ever growing. Real-time accounting information provision via the deployment of digitized technologies presents opportunities not just for fast information access but also for the rapid restructuring of information structures. Additionally, within traditional economies, factors of production had to be physically co-located, thereby generating a need for physical concentration. But where economic activities have come to depend on the transfer of explicit knowledge, it becomes possible to disperse the factors of production. Such dispersal of physical assets necessitates decision-making about what to pool for information reporting purposes. If consolidating activities in economic terms is essential, should the geographical context of activities be a decisive factor in information report structuring?

The increasingly 'boundaryless' enterprise has been the focus of some management writers' thinking about emerging enterprise structures. Boundaries between economic activities have eroded across firms, industries, and nations just as the means of carrying out economic activities have undergone extensive change. Movement away from task-oriented production to process-based activities, which stress more cross-functionality and modularization of production, permits more material and information exchanges and permutations. Boundaries between not just enterprise departments but also across firms and industries are being loosened. For example, banking and insurance services are increasingly coupled. Convergence of form and function is also being witnessed across publishing, entertainment, and media services, which operate more and more on merged digital platforms. Breaking down traditional boundaries has been made possible by new technologies and is actively being pursued by many organizations. Consider Intel, the world's largest semi-conductor manufacturer, whose Chief Operating Officer expects that: 'At Intel, computing and communications will be indistinguishable. We will be a true convergence company' (Paul Otellini, cited in *Business 2.0*, May 2003: 48).

One might regard the notion of a 'new' economy as being tied to whether newness is sufficiently radical rather than minimally incremental, and demonstrably transformational rather than evolutionary. In considering 'newness' one needs to ask how distinct something must be from the familiar to be categorized as new and how new it must be to really be new. This is an important question because advocates of changes in financial controls and management accounting have in the past tended to voice their exhortations with an amplitude matching the perceived degree of newness or disruption. For the purposes of this chapter, no arguments are presented to either support or negate the existence of a new economy. Rather, the discussion recognizes that economic change is prevalent throughout geographical and institutional spaces but that its impact differs across organizational platforms. The recent fast rate of economic change in many enterprise contexts has differing implications for management accounting. This concern guides the discussion that follows regarding financial and management accounting issues arising in the face of digitization and economic changes.

4.3 Levels of digital impact on economic activities

Novel products and new services emerge at a pace that closely matches the rate of technological advances. The use of digital technologies hastens the rate of innovation and the speed at which new product offerings evolve. The advent of digitization has given rise to information goods such as e-books, digital music recordings, and mobile messaging platforms among others. Information-intensive services such as web-based airline bookings and car-rental reservation systems and Internet-based courier-tracking facilities are now commonplace. They provide benefits to consumers (value-takers) who guide the activities of firms (value-makers), which, in turn, seek to benefit commercially from these innovations. For many industries, digitization as part of technological offerings and processes underpin the extent of value creation and the basis of exchange. Management accounting information can be useful in value creation monitoring and reporting and to align changes in the types of costs incurred with revenues generated within increasingly digitized contexts. There are three broad dimensions of concern: managerial issues, organizational concerns, and wider macro-level systemic forces of change.

At a managerial level, firms will seek to analyse strategic issues, pricing approaches, quality factors, and an array of other financial implications affecting the enterprise's economic viability and success. Aside from managerial concerns, digitized economic activities entail many areas of organizational concern. Traditionally, management accountants have sought to design systems of control that are compatible with the structure of the organization and with the premise upon which organizational activities take place such as the degree of centralization, the riskiness of business unit activities, and the culture of the firm. Notionally, it has been assumed that structural contingencies exist between organizational factors and effectiveness and that, ultimately, organizational output is dependent on the design and particular practices of financial functions and how they attempt to aid other enterprise management activities. The emergence of web-enabled business operations has altered many traditional organizational relationships and technical contingencies assumed to exist within firms. Balancing organizational controls and processes is now being addressed in different ways across many enterprises. The implications for management accounting are not negligible.

At a wider level, macro-level forces of change affect how financial managers and management accountants operate within digitized organizations. The manner in which firms create alliances with one another is changing. This is because the economics thought to traditionally underpin value chains are seen to have altered. In some cases, the structuring of whole industries is being transformed with important effects on systems of financial control. Moreover, financial management precepts conditioned by conventional notions of trust in business relationships and organizational affairs are undergoing revisions. This mobilizes further financial control and management accounting changes. Management accounting considerations relating to managerial issues, organizational concerns, and wider macro-level implications are addressed below.

4.4 **Management and digitization**

4.4.1 STRATEGY

Management thinkers have generally tended to regard decision-making activities and managerial actions as occurring sequentially. The notion that some individuals are meant to think whilst others engage in action became a characteristic feature of industrial management at the turn of the last century with the rise of Taylorism. Conceiving ways of doing things is still often seen as an activity that is distinct from the actual execution of desired activities. This notion is embedded across virtually every prescribed approach to enterprise management including management accounting. Often, however, managers think of strategic processes and organizational activities as being closely intertwined. Mark Hurd, the CEO of Hewlett-Packard, notes in this respect: 'I have a hard time separating strategy from operations because they all have to flow together' (cited in *Fortune*, 8 August 2005: 19). Financial managers and accountants are today exhorted to be more strategic, and given the fervour with which professional management accountancy bodies are embracing a more strategic posture for the field, strategic thinking in the practice of financial and cost management is an increasingly important issue. But the traditional staff rather than line role played by accountants in organizations makes it difficult for strategic thinking not to be dissociated from operational action. Writings concerned with strategic aspects of management accounting suggest that practitioners 'should reposition their role within organizations to have a strategic focus' (Nyamori et al. 2001: 65). Many emerging cost management approaches, including activity-based management (ABM), product life cycle costing (LCC), target cost management, customer profitability analyses, and strategic investment appraisal among others have been predicated on the idea that strategic thinking should guide managerial actions, including those concerning technological investments (See Horngren et al. 2005). In other words, conceptions of intent should be formulated prior to the implementation of decisions.

Within extensively web-enabled enterprises, the notion that strategic decisions should precede technological choices may be misguided. Some commentators have argued that in 'the New Economy, strategic decisions...are co-mingled with technological decisions' (Rayport and Jaworski 2002: 5). The claim has been made that 'business strategy that ignores how technology is changing markets, competition and processes is a process for the old economy not the new economy' (Earl 2000: 6). This means that digital businesses cannot extract technological choices from their strategic decision-making processes.

The meshing of strategic and technological decisions suggests that there is a need to reformulate management accounting precepts across at least some areas whereby reported management accounting information intended for strategic decision-making must now be infused with an understanding of technological possibilities and issues.

In the past, an enterprise may have been able to predefine a strategy to modernize production processes. Decision-makers would then have been presented with technological improvement investment options. Supporting accounting and financial information on the likely economic implications would subsequently have been collated and supplied to the decision-makers so that managerial action would rest on financial analyses of possible technological options stemming from the strategy being pursued. The sequence of analysis might have been as follows:

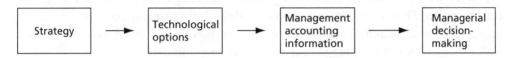

But the co-mingling of strategic and technological decisions within modern organizations implies that managerially useful information can no longer be purely financial- and account-based, whereby strategic intent and technological options are regarded as distinct elements that are separable from one another and that follow a sequential path. What constitutes relevant information and the sequence of its deployment vis-à-vis management accounting action in a digitized networked world has to be rethought.

Consequently, management accounting is to be increasingly concerned about the effective representation of strategic and technological interdependencies so as to enable managerial decisions that align with present-day organizational realities. This may be depicted as follows:

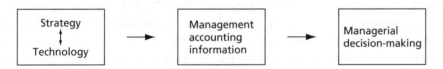

Thus, in some situations, the marriage of strategy and technology is joined by management accounting as a third partner. Consider a company like Intel. One of the co-founders, Gordon Moore, suggested in the mid-1960s that chipmakers should be able to double the number of transistors and electronic components that can be etched on a chip about every year (later revised to eighteen months). When Intel began operations in 1968, Moore's 'law' was not articulated as part of the corporate mission intent. But in the early 1980s, this notional function became part of the strategy. Technology was to expand in line with Moore's prediction, which in turn led to analyses of its economic consequences:

Intel has since enforced Moore's law with a budget recently in excess of $2 billion. The company's senior vice-president and co-general manager of the Technology and Manufacturing Group prior to his retirement saw Moore's law as 'a philosophy as well as a strategy' (Sunlin Chou, cited in Schlender 2002: 41). Commenting on Chou's contributions, the company's CEO noted: 'Under his leadership, Intel's process development teams have made Moore's Law a reality' (Craig Barrett, 3 August 2005, http://www.intel.com/employee/ retiree/circuit/chour-etire.htm). Intel engages in looking at technological investments such that when a state-of-the-art chip plant is opened, the cost of producing a chip falls by literally one-third overnight. Effectively, Intel integrates strategy, technology, and cost reduction priorities so that 'the idea with each new generation is to move a new performance group of products in to be competitive, rather than lower the price to be competitive' (Moore 2002: 42).

Enterprises like Intel consider technology issues to be coupled with strategic and financial considerations. Their interrelationships make it difficult for management accounting activities to exist in a vacuum. Financial information is becoming integral to, and immanent within, assessments of technological, strategic, and cost considerations:

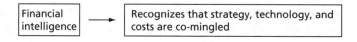

4.4.2 PRICING

Two decades ago, many financial management commentators stressed the relevance of standard costing systems in the setting of prices. Whole chapters within educational texts in the area were devoted to 'cost-based' pricing. In the late 1980s, the popular management literature began to make much of the desirability for market responsiveness and knowledge about the competition in pricing approaches. The value of standard costing systems started to be questioned. The term 'benchmarking' entered the management accounting vocabulary. Management gurus like Michael Porter wrote about 'competitive strategy' (1998) and the rationale for more intimately understanding market forces. Peters and Waterman (1982) discussed 'corporate excellence' and the need to be more customer-orientated. In 1988, Hiromoto described target costing practices within Japanese enterprises in the *Harvard Business Review* as providing a 'hidden edge'. This was followed by the publication of many articles in management journals and magazines about 'price-led' costing. The prescriptive and descriptive literature in management accounting, market analysis, and competitive strategy relating to price-based costing is now quite substantial. But there are signs that the deployment of digital technologies by enterprises is causing this thinking to be reconsidered.

Internet-based technologies have altered the possibilities of satisfying customer demand and the perceptions of what constitutes viable consumer offerings. Up to the 1970s, consumers were 'price-takers' and 'product-takers'. The customer was given little say in how the product should be designed or what should be paid for it. The seller was king.

During the 1980s and 1990s, consumers transitioned to becoming price-makers and product-takers.

Negotiations over price for given products became acceptable in the face of growing numbers of market incumbents competing against each other for more forceful customers receptive to the use of basic price-setting technology on the Web. Today, with increasing frequency, consumers are price-makers and product-makers in many industries. Moreover, both price-making and product-making are taking place at faster speeds—sometimes in real time.

At present, a small percentage of the globe's $40 trillion economy is engaged in consumer-directed product design. This is likely to expand extensively over the next decade as 'choiceboards' become more prevalent. Slywotzky (2000: 4) describes choiceboards as interactive, online systems that allow individual customers to design their own products by choosing from a menu of attributes, components, prices, and delivery options. The customer's selection sends signals to the supplier's manufacturing system that set in motion the wheel of procurement, assembly, and delivery. Choiceboards extend the potential of flexible organizational technologies and, in particular, computer-integrated manufacturing systems to platforms accessible directly to consumers (Bhimani 2005). They are enabled by Internet capabilities, which transform consumers from being 'product-takers' to 'product-makers'. Whereas consumers traditionally accepted that the firm carry out the design function, this task is being transferred to the market where viable. For instance, many online music sites allow customers to choose music tracks from different albums and to compile their own personalized albums of prior sound recordings. Here the customer becomes the product designer as well as the consumer with minimal guidance or training.

The transfer of the product design function has implications for the structure of product life cycles. It raises questions as to what defines the 'launch' of a product and how far pre-manufacturing design activities determine the extent of committed production costs and, indeed, who and what determines post-production costs and how this alters the control of Kaizen efforts. Inputs into conformance-related quality costs likewise need to be questioned. In broad terms, customers' sophistication in defining product features and price character-istics is growing in many contexts. Supporting management accounting will thus need to alter assumptions as to where price and product determination originates from, and will need to assess the forces at play in defining product costs over product life cycles.

Throughout the twentieth century, fixed pricing dominated commercial activities. Pos-sibly this was because the technology was not there for continuous price revisions. As noted, consumers today are, in many instances, price-takers and price-makers. But, in addition, pricing may be fixed or variable. Variable costing was heavily advocated in the 1960s and 1970s in financial management and management accounting books. Activity-based costing (ABC) and target costing became prominent as innovative approaches in the 1980s and 1990s. Now, given the advances made by digital technologies in reconfiguring organizational activities and the growing sophistication of markets and consumers, we are entering an era of variable pricing. So just as absorption costing gave way to variable costing, and just as fixed costs became delayered by ABC, organizations now ponder over whether fixed pricing needs to give way to variable pricing in many product contexts.

Whereas it used to be acceptable to compete on price by investing in efficiency and cost reduction, today variable pricing implies the ability to alter prices in real time depending on the situation. So accounting information systems are evolving to 'slice and dice cost data' (Pitt et al. 2001: 53) continuously. This is done in an attempt to achieve product differentiation, which may be valued by customers but which also must be rapidly altered according to changing market segment characteristics. This could contrast with extended universal costing and pricing that strategically cannot lead to the achievement of profitability over the longer term. Consequently, strategic costing information may need to feed into enabling what may be regarded as 'unsustainable' competitive advantage over short time frames in attempts to extract sustainable long-term competitiveness.

4.4.3 QUALITY

It is often said that many Western organizations in the past used to regard the provision of enhanced quality as triggering cost increases and that preventative measures to avoid quality problems led to resources having to be incurred without any evident savings or gains being achieved. But the lessons learned from Japanese businesses during the 1980s led to a rejection of such a notional trade-off. In other words, quality failures can result in costs that exceed the cost incursions associated with achieving high-quality conformance. This is pretty much the view that is espoused in contemporary writings concerning quality costing (Dale and Plunkett 1999). But there are interrelationships, entailing quality and service provision versus costing issues, which need to be effectively addressed by management accountants in the light of digitized organizational operations.

Quality has many facets. One of these concerns satisfied customers who remain loyal to a company because of the build-up of trust through effective quality of service. The service management literature has, over the past few years, suggested that customer loyalty rather than market share drives firm profits (Haskett et al. 1997). In Web-enabled firms, this has significant implications. Consider, for instance, what Internet shoppers go through in making a purchase. The first point of contact for a customer approaching a company website is negotiating navigation of the site. The consumer then advances to retrieving desired information. Next, some customer support may be sought, perhaps in the form of a telephone call, email communication, bulletin board interaction, or live chat. Finally, the company's logistics processes put into effect the sales transaction including packaging and shipping, payment processing, guarantee confirmation, and other sales back-up service. If the quality of service in the face of the price paid is deemed to be high, loyalty may also result:

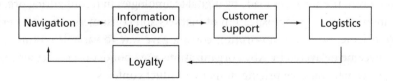

If the navigation and information collection facilities are in place through the effective development of, and appropriate investments in, technology, this will entice customers to purchase. The variable cost resource requirements to support customers at the prepurchase stages are usually very low. If logistical problems, however, occur once an order is placed in terms of, say, product availability, shipment, or delivery, extra pressure becomes placed on customer support. This tends to cascade into more extensive logistical resource problems (returns, exchanges, cancellations) and ultimately more extensive cost increases with potentially detrimental competitive consequences. Conversely, if all four aspects of logistical processes are integrated across the requisite information exchange and operational activities, a positive customer experience cycle will result. This will translate into loyalty, which has scale effects on per unit navigation and information costs (which are largely fixed) (Hallowell 2002).

The interdependencies identified in the above online purchasing and organizational processing sequence illustrates the extent to which internal and external failure costs are closely related. Traditionally, a firm separation has been seen as achievable between internal failures (those identified before delivery of the product or service) and external failures (those occurring and perceived by the customer). Internal failures can, however, be regarded more and more as external failures, as the Web lends transparency to internal organizational processes in an attempt to be more customer-oriented. Quality costs must then adopt a different classification of what is demarcated as conformance and what is seen as non-conformance. In contexts where customers engage in product design, the constitution of prevention costs may be subject to further alterations. In such instances, generalized conceptions of quality costing must give way to more realistic organization-specific understandings of the connections between financial and cost information and quality issues. Manufacturing organizations facing external failure costs whereby products need to be recalled and customers compensated must assess the measurable costs directly incurred and traceable to faulty output. This is likely to be relatively more straightforward than identifying, with any degree of accuracy, the impact on intangible cost consequences such as the loss of goodwill and curtailment of life cycle benefits that would otherwise have accrued from customer segments and future loyalty-linked sales. In considering service-based organizations, which, in most developed countries, account for at least two-thirds of national economic output, intangible failure costs are particularly high. This is because once delivered, a faulty service cannot readily be remedied or compensated for.

Both manufacturing and service sector firms face increased global competition, which transforms products that might have offered premium sources of revenues and profits at one stage into commodities. Markets can alter very rapidly when technological breakthroughs or service innovations alter the cost-benefits of consumer value propositions. Some commentators argue that few business sectors can avert intense rivalry and commoditization. Consequently, companies must create interfaces between customers and markets that are of higher perceivable quality at a lower cost per interaction. Emerging technologies enable this but rely on an understanding of what types of customer experiences should be targeted to fit in with a company's market position and brand. Rayport and Jaworsky (2005: 5) note in this respect that the concept of customer experiences should have 'everything to do with the customer's objectives' when interacting with a company. What a company does for its customers is 'inseparable' from its revenues and the margins it can potentially earn from its business.

From a management accounting perspective, this is indicative of a need to integrate an understanding of what constitutes a desirable experience for a customer to the economics of the interface between companies and customers. Consider Yahoo's objective of developing exclusive content via a strategy of both internal reorganization and the purchase of exclusive content. Until recently, Yahoo's various sites like sports, finance, news, and entertainment were semi-autonomous units and did not cooperate well. Work was being duplicated and Yahoo had difficulty dealing coherently with content suppliers, as explained by the company's CEO: 'Even though sports, news and entertainment were licensing things and doing partnerships with the same companies, we did it through five different voices and five different people' (Terry Semel, cited in *Fortune*, 8 August 2005: 43). So the company fused the different units and imposed a new layer of centralized management. Additionally, Yahoo is developing ways of delivering content exclusive to the site, based on its deep knowledge of its users. This allows the company to put content 'in front of eyeballs at moments when they are going to want to click on it—and that is a very, very valuable thing', according to Yahoo's Head of Content, Lloyd Brann. The task for management accounting in such contexts is to develop ways of understanding the interplay between organizational reallocation of resources and changes in value delivery to customers as interfaces are redefined and the quality of customer experiences enhanced.

4.5 Organizational issues

4.5.1 ORGANIZATIONAL CONTINGENCIES

An important line of research in management has been contingency theory. In the 1960s, some management researchers became interested in the idea that certain organizational forms were more suited to certain structural dimensions than others. Attempts were made to match aspects of the market, the environment, firm size, and technology deployed to organizational form. Some researchers extended this line of thinking to explore whether accounting information systems structures could also be viewed as being more aptly aligned with some organizational dimensions as opposed to others. Although the results of these investigations are seen as being inconclusive (Otley 1980; Chapman 1997; Chenhall 2003), the main thesis that structure is dependent on context along some generic economic continuum still finds appeal in financial management and accounting thought. There continues to exist a view that organizational circumstances and contextual variables need to link in to the specific configuration of accounting and financial systems.

It might be argued that enterprises operating on digital platforms, or those making extensive use of e-business technologies, or those that deal with products and services of a digital nature face more environmental uncertainty, higher decentralization, and high degrees of organizational interdependence. Consequently, digital enterprises may evidence 'a preference for more broad scope, timely, aggregated and integrated information' (Gosselin 2003). This follows directly from the logic stemming from contingency theory-based arguments that organizations exhibiting such peculiarity of structural variables also exhibit a specific alignment with form of information. This may be illustrated as follows:

If we consider strategy as an organizational dimension that affects enterprise form, we might categorize a firm as a 'differentiator' based on Porter's framework (1985) or a 'prospector' under Miles and Snow's typology (1978) in terms of the particularity of its product lines or the market it operates in. Porter (1985) identified different market strategies to enable a competitive advantage to be developed and sustained. Customers may be offered superior value through products or services that are priced lower than the competition for equivalent offerings (cost leadership), or by the provision of unique benefits that exceed the price premium charged to buyers (differentiation). A firm may also choose to adopt a narrow competitive focus within an industry. What is to be avoided is to be 'stuck in the middle' (Porter 1985: 17), as this leads to an economically unviable situation.

Ideally, a firm might seek to become a cost leader whilst also offering a highly differentiated product. This has been achieved by a number of organizations. Shoppers often show a preference for private labels beyond the impact of price differentials when compared to established manufacturer brands. Many stores have refined house brands such that they are perceived as being very price competitive and of generally high quality. Such stores include the UK's Marks and Spencer, Germany's Aldi, France's Carrefour, and the USA's Wal-Mart. The Canadian grocer, Loblaws, which launched the house brand 'President's Choice' met with so much success in creating a differentiated cost leader category of products that the label has itself become a national brand carried by a multitude of grocers across North America (Boyle 2003).

If we consider Porter's taxonomy (1985) of business-based strategies, firms seeking to design their cost management system and financial controls may do so by adhering to Porter's corporate strategy characteristics. Table 4.1 illustrates the emphasis that may be placed on selected management accounting function features and corollary strategic emphasis. Based on similar reasoning, Palmer (1992: 188) remarks that 'strategy, however it is defined, should influence the development of strategic management accounting systems'. An organization that seeks to achieve cost leadership and product differentiation should thus presumably aim to achieve 'higher' levels of emphasis on every category in Table 4.1.

Table 4.1 Cost management systems and strategic emphasis

Strategic issue	Strategic emphasis	
	Cost Leadership	Product differentiation
Importance of link between cost and price	Higher	Lower
Relevance of market competitor analysis	Higher	Lower
Importance of standard costs	Higher	Lower
Need for detailed manufacturing performance information	Higher	Lower
Need for detailed R&D design performance information	Lower	Higher

Possibly, one might conclude that since strategy and management accounting are increasingly interlinked, all firms should aspire to achieve jointness of strategic intent and MAS by design. Systems should be customized to fit strategic intent. But if one takes the view that ideally all firms should seek to be product differentiators as well as cost leaders in order to compete most effectively, such convergence of strategy among firms presupposes also convergence of MASs. If strategic excellence implies common appeal to both cost leadership and product differentiation, supporting controls must also become standard across firms. Should 'best of breed' strategy entail comprehensiveness and homogeneity of management accounting controls?

4.6 **Standardizing management accounting systems**

Some management commentators suggest that the Internet makes it difficult to 'sustain operational advantages' (Porter 2001: 71). Such a view is based on the argument that traditional avenues for differentiating value propositions to consumers through more extensive offerings of product characteristics, differences in customer service provision, or variations in packaging, shipping, modes of payment, or return policies are eroded by the Internet. This is because strategies for differentiating product offerings are readily replicated by competitors, and 'commoditization' of products ensues. This then raises the question of how far differentiated strategies are tenable on the Internet and of whether linkages and contingencies between contextual factors and management systems design can indeed prevail. One might ask: if differentiated strategies are unsustainable, should enterprises seek to achieve differentiation in the structuring of their information systems and management accounting support practices?

Other commentators note on the contrary that Internet technologies provide firms a source of novel 'sustainable operational efficiencies' (Tapscott 2001: 7). Commoditization of products and services by competing firms and the standardization of value propositions do not necessarily negate the ability of a firm to differentiate its offerings. The argument has been made that if the Internet, in some contexts, leads to the commoditization of previously differentiated products because of the ease with which it allows comparison-shopping and product/service replication, it also allows the redifferentiation of products by staging customer 'experiences', whether aesthetic, entertainment-based, educational, etc. That is, as products become more standard, organizations appeal to enhanced quality of products to attract customers as noted earlier. They may also offer a greater range of diversifying features and invest heavily in branding. But when most organizations within an industry are able to offer high perceived levels of quality, customer service can become the avenue to differentiate its value proposition to the customer. In other words, offering outstanding customer service may become the pursued means for an industry incumbent to keep customers or to draw them away from the competition. Once parity is achieved among competitors in terms of offering excellent customer service, the manner in which the customer experience is staged can become the next step to differentiation. That is, the aesthetics of the buying experience both off-line and online, including whether there is excitement or entertainment added to the purchasing process, can produce a pathway to attracting customers. Examples include, for instance, Internet merchants who encourage the customer to make price offers on products and promote haggling, or companies that provide a level of free online entertainment on their website (Pine and Gilmore 1999).

But as parity among competitors is reached in this respect, what next? Is there ultimately an increased likelihood of convergence of both product and organizational form in the long term if companies become more and more alike in their product offerings and in the way they service their customers? If so, should financial management systems in the long term seek to be standard across firms operating in the same industry as their product offerings and value propositions show a continuous tendency to converge and effectively to become commoditized?

In looking back over the last three decades, firms have become more and more alike in their attempts to offer a distinct product. Now that product differentiation is increasingly difficult to achieve (e.g. how far is a Dell laptop different from an HP laptop?), the focus is towards determining how different organizational arrangements to service the needs of similar customers desiring similar products enable a differentiation angle. In the past, as organizations became more alike, products become more distinct. Today, as products become more alike, organizations are becoming more distinct. Consider, for instance, Nike versus Adidas in the footwear industry or Zara versus Gap in the garment sector. These firms have widely different organizational arrangements and structures whilst competing in the same markets. Consider also IBM's chief strategist who makes the point as follows: 'Just spending money on IT never creates any value. It's what you do differently in terms of business processes that matters' (Bruce Harreld, cited in Kirkpatrick 2003*a*: 26). Whether IT can help an organization differentiate remains a moot issue presently (Carr 2003).

Possibly, the route to organizational excellence is to seek continuous change across both differentiated value propositions in the face of replication by the competition as well as across differentiated internal processes and organizational controls. These trends may be represented as follows:

In the past:

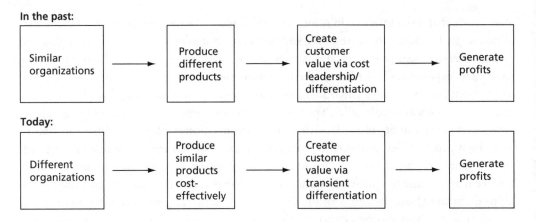

Today:

Seeking to redefine organizational structure to enable product market specificity is a necessary strategy for enterprises. This arises because organizational specificity has become a means of delivering a product that rapidly shifts from being differentiated to becoming replicated in standard form. Consequently, one might expect that MASs will continue to be designed with a high degree of organizational customization. But the implications for accounting information and financial management systems design are generally even more extensive. As products become more alike, it is not the end product that becomes the cost object but the means through which a value proposition to the customer is produced. The routings of organizational processes affect and direct cost management activities. Accounting configurations and standard financial management practices can no longer be guided by common structures producing differentiated products. Rather, differentiated enterprise structuring needs to be reflected in the management of firms producing initially different, but ultimately standard, products over short time spaces. This suggests that whereas the contingency argument presupposed the existence of ideal organizational forms and therefore of particularity of MASs that sought to match form to environment and other contingent variables, many modern-day firms now adopt strategies regarding both products and organizational structuring and technological resources that are deeply intertwined and highly enterprise-specific. It is likely that management accounting practices will need to adapt to this emerging interdependency.

4.7 Macro-level forces of change: information, knowledge, and trust

The costs of using the market to carry out an economic activity has long been regarded as an important determinant of whether firms engage in purchasing from other firms, or whether they internalize the activity. If the costs of carrying out activities in-house are lower than incurring market-based prices for having activities undertaken by an outside party, companies have an incentive to vertically integrate. Lucking-Reily and Spulber (2001: 45), however, note:

As market transaction costs fall with the maturation of business-to-business commerce, outsourcing and vertical disintegration will occur resulting in more independent entities along the supply chain.

According to Adler (2002: 26):

There is a progressive swelling of the zone between hierarchy and market. Whilst the former relies on the price mechanism and the latter on authority, the 'swelling middle' may adopt a community form that relies on trust.

This trend may lead to 'value-added communities' whereby organizations outsource many non-core functions and make more use of suppliers. They also make greater investments in brand recognition and human capital building and less in physical and working capital (Means and Schneider 2000). Firms with unique capabilities can join forces to create products that cannot readily be replicated by competitors. Such alliances take different forms including joint ventures, strategic partnerships, and extended collaborative relationships, which 'populate the vast middle ground of hybrids that lie between markets and hierarchies' (Anderson and Sedatole 2003: 36). In such organizations, the ability to manage knowledge, rather than simply to coordinate physical resources, will become more and more important. Questions regarding the effective management of knowledge necessitate an understanding of what is regarded as knowledge (Bhimani and Roberts 2004).

From ancient times through to the start of the industrial revolution, power has been associated with ownership of physical resources. The industrial organization has regarded capital and access to it as the principal source of power. But in the closing decades of the twentieth century, information started to be equated with power across different industrial sectors. Some now believe that 'future wealth and power will be derived mainly from intangible, intellectual resources: knowledge capital' (Burton-Jones 1999: 3). Writers on the emergence and significance of a new economic order based on the management of knowledge assets differentiate data from information and regard both as distinct from knowledge. Data may simply be seen as new numbers and facts. Information is viewed as data interpreted into a meaningful framework. Knowledge becomes information that has been authenticated and thought to be true. Information is consequently processed data and knowledge is information that is made actionable. Boisot (1999: 12) captures this notion by regarding knowledge as a 'property of agents', and information as residing in things that 'activates an agent'. It is knowledge and its proper management that is viewed as a source of power within enterprises, and ultimately as enabling enhanced organizational effectiveness.

To the extent that management accounting information relates to quantitative and qualitative signals that are made intelligible to users of the information, a clear role for the internal accounting function is in the collection, aggregation, and reporting of such information. In terms of knowledge management, a management accounting role has to dwell on the build-up of information and the consequent generation of capacities and competencies once the information has been communicated to the information user. At this stage, accounting executives capture and relay the qualitative and judgemental essence of raw data and bring this to bear on managerial decisions. If management accounting practices are to contribute to knowledge management activities, they must assume an understanding of the components of intellectual capital and the process by which knowledge is created and deployed.

Much research suggests that information transfer is crucial to knowledge management (Schmid 2001; Lapré and Van Wassenhove 2002). The basis of transfer is important to understand because knowledge production for an enterprise relies on knowledge transfer. If the knowledge production process slows down or stops, the organization becomes 'poorer' since it accumulates experience more slowly (Roberts 2003). There are different ways of considering knowledge transfers within organizations. Nonaka and Takeuchi (1995) suggest that formal information systems have concentrated on tacit to explicit and explicit to explicit transfers. In effect, some things are not said because if they are made articulable, a cost must be incurred. Passing from tacit to explicitly codified knowledge comprehensible by others is not costless. Information systems can help convert tacit knowledge into explicit knowledge to a degree. More usually, they enable explicit to explicit transfers. But clearly, formal information systems require resource investments. Nonaka and Takeuchi (1995) note that organizations make very little formal investment into enabling explicit to tacit and tacit to tacit knowledge exchanges.

Boisot (1999) regards the analysis of knowledge assets using a three-dimensional concept of 'information space'. He suggests that knowledge assets are to be viewed as accumulations that yield a stream of useful services over time, while economizing on the consumption of physical resources. This is achieved by codification, which creates categories to facilitate the classification of phenomena and abstraction to reduce the numbers of attributes that need to be codified. In other words, codification lends data categories to make it intelligible, and abstraction affords higher level patterns to enable this intelligibility to be applied across different spaces and thereby to give generality to the knowledge.

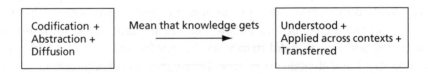

As Boisot (1999: 14) notes, 'codification and abstraction lower the cost of converting potentially usable knowledge into knowledge assets'. Additionally, diffusability establishes the availability of data to those who want to use it. It is reflective of the proportion of a given population of data-processing agents (firms, industries, countries) that can be reached with information operating at different degrees of codification and abstraction.

Such a notion of knowledge transfer conforms with the management accounting task. Essentially, accounting measures enable different organizational activities to be classified uniformly and allow these activities to be reduced so that they become economically and managerially accessible. The diffusion of data then permits the reach of action to be broadened.

In practical terms, management accounting is becoming an immanent part of knowledge management practices. From data capture to information reporting to knowledge production, key financial management capabilities become implicated. Digitized enterprises can codify, abstract, and diffuse information across different intra- and extra-organizational platforms in continuously adaptive ways. Hybrid organizational forms can thus be dynamically reconfigured. Adeptness in processing managerially useful information in such contexts can determine the effectiveness of MASs. Organizations that understand the value of managing knowledge assets can benefit from recognizing accounting as part of their asset base and of viewing management accounting practices as principal drivers of knowledge-based action.

4.8 **In search of transparency**

The management accounting malaise written about in the 1980s was, in part, the result of a perceived schism between economic representations of organizational activities and the operational nature of resource flows. Commentators wrote about accounting lags, distorted costs, and obsolescent management accounting controls in a world where financial professionals had failed to invest in an understanding of organizational realities (Kaplan 1983; Johnson and Kaplan1987). For this reason, the transparency between resource usage and accounting numbers was lacking, and confidence could not be had in accounting information, which was more reflective of anachronistic accounting calculations than of actual resource flows. In part, accounting was to blame for serving the needs of external parties rather than of managers and for not recognizing the altered logistics of industrial production. It was largely believed that enterprise management had become more complex, and internal financial reporting and cost management practices had not kept pace. The changes proposed in management accounting debates dwelt on how actual resource consumption could more closely align with financial reports of resource consumption. Costing had to be about physically following the resources and tracking organizational processes. Ultimately, the management accounting function was exhorted to look at resource flows so as to make more transparent the links between physical movement and cost accumulation, and to observe and report upon the creation of value in action. It had to confront more directly physical production flows before seeking to report on their financial consequences (Bhimani 2003).

In digitized organizations where physicality is limited to electron flows and where processes are manifested as instantaneous blips, management approaches resting on physical observability, visual transparency, and trust in spatial changes have to be reconsidered. How is the management accounting function to deal with ephemeral digital transactions, each with economic consequences that may be almost negligible but that become very significant with volume? This presents a significant challenge for managing costs. Possibly, a step forward may be not just in the procedures of data capture or in the style of information reporting but also in the professional representation of the information produced. It may be that for the work of management accountants to continue to count, it will be increasingly important to show a knowledge of digital products, digital processes, and digital conse-quences using information about enterprise activities that itself is digitally generated.

In contexts where scalability is a relevant economic issue, some important considerations are to be heeded. A decade ago, financial managers deliberated accounting problems that arose where flexible organizational technologies such as computer-integrated manufacturing systems were being implemented. But scalable operations have costing implications of a magnitude that is different to the operationalization of flexible organizational technologies (Bhimani 2005). If an investment entails participation in a network that can act locally or globally and where expansion or retrenchment can be adjusted dynamically to the business strategy without altering physical or virtual capacity, management accounting issues become more complex. Important questions relating to costing, pricing, operational control, plan-ning, and performance measurement, as well as incentives and rewards, emerge. The impact that individual digitized transactions have at an economic level may be almost negligible. But where the business model relies on driving a very large volume of such transactions, they need effective accounting input. The challenge becomes significant for managing costs.

Where an organization's architecture alters and adjusts around projects and services it engages in, in conjunction with other networked partners, the underlying accounting activities have to become equally malleable so as to report on differing elements of the dynamic production configuration. The possibly high capital costs that enable capacity to be reconfigured around projects or products have to find some basis for being managed. These are questions that the management accounting function within enterprises will increasingly address in the very near future.

It is widely accepted that habits and premises tend to structure the activities and percep-tions of organizational actors and that enterprises are not necessarily the product of deliberate design, but rather result from the persistence of practices. In other words, the worthwhileness of everyday practices are taken for granted and reproduced, whereby particular modes of operating and structuring activities are continuously replicated. The legitimacy of particular organizational structures and procedures are then not entirely predicated on conceptions of rational adaptation to constraints and opportunities facing enterprises, but become insti-tutionalized through law, custom, professional ideologies, or doctrines of effective man-agement. This is perhaps one reason why many management accounting practices like budgeting, variance analysis, and overhead cost allocations are carried out within enterprises. The present replicates the past because the past represents what is legitimate. But much of this changed a few years ago, at least in some sectors of the global economy.

The rise of e-businesses and Internet 'pure plays' was predicated on the negation of traditional views of effective enterprise management. Rather than seeking to derive legitim-acy by appealing to standard organizational structures and managerial procedures, what was taken for granted was the promise of returns to be had from denying standardization and traditional modes of configuration (Abramson 2005). In other words, departure from the norm became the norm in communicating managerial rationality, which itself had to be distinct, differentiated, and context-bound. Variety and uniqueness in organizational practices was sought. Particularity of management style and differentiated enterprise design with minimal structure was espoused.

But in the aftermath of the 'dot com' crash and the economic collapse of equity markets, much criticism of the rejection of the traditionally established virtues of robust financial management was voiced. Web-based companies that performed well, it turned out, held tight financial reins and engaged in a 'management by numbers' style of internal control. A case in point is the entrepreneur Stelios Haji-Ioannou and his Easy Group executives who have been said to 'obsess about managing yield' (Kirkpatrick 2003*b*: 76) and to consider the maximization of asset utilization and returns as 'a never-ending battle of fine-tuning' (Haji-Ioannou, cited in Kirkpatrick 2003*b*). The CEO of eBay, one of the fastest growing companies in the world with over $1 billion profits on revenues of $3.2 billion in 2004, believes that 'if you can't measure it, you can't control it' (Meg Whitman, cited in *Fortune*, 9 January 2003: 52). Amazon's founder and CEO, Jeff Bezos, also evidences a penchant for numbers that is legendary:

With most decisions you can do the maths and figure out the right answer. Math-based decisions always trump opinion and judgement. (Bezos, cited in *Fortune*, 25 May 2003: 24)

What is clear is that economic numbers continue to play a significant role in influencing managerial decisions and organizational activities. Managerial endeavours are thought through in terms of the magnitude and pace of change an enterprise faces. But industry leaders tend always to make decisions and take managerial action supported in part by knowledge that qualitatively embeds an understanding of what they regard as essential to organizational functioning. Altering management accounting practices requires an understanding of the type and extent of shifts that are ongoing and determining the desirable speed of response such change demands. Management accounting has increasingly sought to do so by quantitatively and qualitatively reporting on much more than simply the economics of enterprise activities. Whether the field can sustain its significance within digital enterprises is now a challenge it must address.

☐ REFERENCES

Abramson, B. (2005). *Digital Phoenix: Why the Information Economy Collapsed and How it will Rise Again*. Boston: MIT Press.

Adler, P. S. (2002). 'Markets, Hierarchy and Trust: The Knowledge Economy and the Future of Capitalism', in C. W. Choo and N. Bontis (eds.), *The Strategic Management of Intellectual Capital*. Oxford: Oxford University Press, pp. 23–46.

Anderson, S. W. and Sedatole, K. L. (2003). 'Management Accounting for the Extended Enterprise', in A. Bhimani (ed.), *Management Accounting in the Digital Economy*. Oxford: Oxford University Press, pp. 36–73.

Bhimani, A. (ed.) (2003). *Management Accounting in the Digital Economy*. Oxford: Oxford University Press.

—— (2005). *Strategic Finance and Cost Management*. London: Management Press.

—— and Roberts, H. (2004). 'Management Accounting and Knowledge Management: In Search of Intelligibility', *Management Accounting Research*, 15 (1): 1–5.

Boisot, M. (1999). *Knowledge Assets*. Oxford: Oxford University Press.

Boyle, M. (2003) 'Brand Killers', *Fortune* (11 August): pp. 48–52.

Burton-Jones, A. (1999). *Knowledge Capitalism.* Oxford: Oxford University Press.

Carr, N. G. (2003). 'IT Doesn't Matter', *Harvard Business Review,* 81(5): 41–9.

Castells, M. (2001). *The Internet Galaxy: Reflections on the Internet, Business and Society.* Oxford: Oxford University Press.

Chapman, C. (1997). 'Reflections on a Contingency View of Accounting', *Accounting, Organizations and Society* 22(2): 189–205.

—— (2005) Not because they are new: Developing the contribution of ERP systems to management control research *Accounting, Organizations and Society,* 30(7/8): 685–689.

Chenhall, R. H. (2003). 'Management Control Systems Design within its Organizational Context: Findings from Contingency-based Research and Directions for the Future', *Accounting, Organizations and Society,* 28: 127–68.

Dale, B. G. and Plunkett, J. J. (1999). *Quality Costing.* London: Gower.

De Cock, C., Fitchett, J., and Volkmann, C. (2005). 'Constructing the New Economy: A Discursive Perspective', *British Journal of Management,* 16: 37–49.

Earl, M. (2000). 'IT Strategy in the New Economy', *Mastering Management.* London: FT/Prentice Hall.

Gosselin, M. (2003). Management Control and E-Logistics in A. Bhimani (ed) *Management Accounting in the Digital Economy,* Oxford: Oxford University Press pp. 205–217.

Hallowell, R. (2002). *Service on the Internet: The Effects of Physical Service on Scalability.* Harvard Business School Note 5-802-168.

Heskett, J. L., Sasser, W. E., and Schlesinger, L. A. (1997). *The Service Profit Chain.* New York: Free Press.

Hiromoto, T. (1988). 'Another Hidden Edge: Japanese Management Accounting', *Harvard Business Review* (July/August): 22–6.

Horngren, C., Bhimani, A., Datar, S. and Foster, G. (2005). *Management and Cost Accounting.* London: FT/Prentice Hall.

Johnson, H. T. and Kaplan, R. S. (1987). *Relevance Lost: The Rise and Fall of Management Accounting.* Boston, Mass.: Harvard Business School Press.

Kaplan, R. S. (1983). 'Measuring Manufacturing Performance: A New Challenge for Managerial Accounting Research', *The Accounting Review,* 58: 686–705.

Kelly, K. (1998). *New Rules for the New Economy.* New York: Viking.

Kirkpatrick, D. (2003*a*). 'Tech: Where the Action Is', *Fortune* (12 May): 24–9.

—— (2003*b*). 'How to Erase the Middleman in one Easy Lesson', *Fortune* (17 March): 76.

Lapré, A. and Van Wassenhove, N. L. (2002). 'Learning across Lines: The Secret to More Efficient Factories', *Harvard Business Review* (October): 107–11.

Lucking-Reily, D. and Spulber, D. (2001). 'Business to Business E-Commerce', *Journal of Economic Perspectives,* 15(1): 55–68.

Means, D. and Schneider, D. (2000). *Meta-capitalism: The E-Business Revolution and the Design of the 21st Century Companies and Markets.* New York: John Wiley and Sons.

Miles, R. E. and Snow, C. C. (1978). *Organizational Strategy, Structure and Process.* New York: McGraw-Hill.

Moore, G. (2002). 'How Intel took Moore's Law From Idea to Ideology Interview', *Fortune* (11 November): 42.

Nonaka, I. and Takeuchi, H. (1995). *The Knowledge-Creating Company. How Japanese Companies Create the Dynamics of Innovation.* New York: Oxford University Press.

Nyamori, R. O., Perera, M. and Lawrence, S. (2001). 'The concept of strategic change for management accounting research', *Journal of Accounting Literature,* 20: 62–83.

Otley, D. T. (1980). 'The Contingency Theory of Management Accounting: Achievement and Prognosis', *Accounting, Organizations and Society,* 5: 413–28.

Peters, T. and Waterman, R. H. (1982). *In Search of Excellence,* NY: Harper Collins.

Pine, B. J. and Gilmore, J. (1999). *Experience Economy: Work is Theatre and Every Business a Stage.* Boston, Mass.: Harvard Business School.

Pitt, L., Berthon, P., Watson, R. and Ewing, M. (2001). 'Pricing Strategy and the Net', *Business Horizon* (March/April): pp. 45–54.

Porter, M (1985). *Competitive Advantage.* New York: Free Press.

—— (1995). *Competitive Advantage.* New York: Free Press.

—— (2001). 'Strategy and the Internet', *Harvard Business Review,* 79(1): 62–78.

Rayport, J. F. and Jaworski, B. J. (2002). *E-Commerce.* Boston: McGraw-Hill.

—— —— (2005). *Best Faces Forward.* Boston: Harvard Business School Press.

Roberts, H. (2003). 'Management Accounting and the Knowledge Production Process', in A. Bhimani (ed.), *Management Accounting in the Digital Economy.* Oxford: Oxford University Press.

Schlender, B. (2002). 'Intel's $10 Billion Gamble', *Fortune* (11 November): 36–41.

Schmid, B. F. (2001). 'What is new about the Digital Economy', *Electronic Markets,* 11(1): 44–51.

Shapiro, C. and Varian, H. R. (1999). *Information Rules: A Strategic Guide to the New Economy.* Boston: Harvard Business School.

Slywotzky, A. J. (2000). 'The Age of the Choiceboard', *Harvard Business Review* (January/February): 4–5.

Tapscott, D. (2001). 'Rethinking Strategy in a Networked World', *Strategy and Business,* 24(8): 2–8.

5 The contingent design of performance measures

Robert H. Chenhall

5.1 Introduction

Performance measurement is at the heart of organizational control. Performance measures can articulate organizational purpose and strategy. Potentially, they identify key aspects of the organization's value chain that direct business towards achieving strategy and goals. In addition to measuring the effectiveness and efficiency of processes, they measure the performance of those individuals carrying out these processes and may provide the criteria for their compensation. The measures can be targeted on individuals, groups, or structural units and as such can be supportive of the intent of the organization's structure.

Traditionally, management accounting performance measures have been derived from financial relationships within income statements and balance sheets, such as return on investment. An innovation in financial measures has been economic value measures. At a more detailed level, budgetary control provides financial measures related to sales, production, materials, labour, selling and administration, and cash management. While these measures appear to be employed widely there has been increasing criticism concerning their lack of timeliness, their aggregation, and the static nature of performance expectations. Many management accountants have argued for more specific measures that incorporate non-financial items, and measurement systems that attempt to provide an integrated suite of measures that relate to business planning models, such as balanced scorecards (BSCs). In recent years these 'improved' performance measures have become popular, with many organizations adopting them. Research has shown that certain types of measures, such as non-financial measures, are associated with organizations that have employed advanced manufacturing processes, such as total quality management (TQM), or with those that have pursued different types of business strategies. However, the evidence is unclear as to whether innovations in performance measurement improve organizational performance. Possible reasons for the failure of performance measurement innovations to provide benefits include poor technical systems or inadequate implementation. However, even given technically superior innovations and careful implementation, positive outcomes may still not eventuate if the innovations are inappropriate for the context within which the organization operates. In this chapter, it is argued that enhanced performance outcomes will depend on how different types of measurement systems best suit, or fit, with an organization's specific context. Drawing on ideas and research employing contingency frameworks, the chapter will review the most recent developments in performance measurement and examine the context within which they may best assist managers to enhance organizational performance. Specifically, the chapter will consider the role of the external environment and strategy, technology, structure, and size.

5.2 Why study context?

Contingency thinking has been an important approach to the study of organizations and of the role of management accounting within organizations (Chenhall 2003). In essence, contingency approaches are based on the view that organizational effectiveness results from fitting administrative practices, such as performance measurement, to the contingencies within which the organization operates. Contingency approaches provide insights into how organizations adapt to changing situations. As the context of an organization changes it will invariably move to a situation where the existing performance measures are no longer suitable for the new circumstances. To avoid a decline in performance caused by this misfit the organization will adopt new performance measures that fit the new contingencies. This may involve adopting established performance measures that are already used by other organizations facing the new situation, or if these are not available, experimentation with novel methods to find suitable practices. Thus, contingency approaches see organizations changing their performance measures over time to fit their changing circumstances in an attempt to maintain effective operations (Donaldson 2001). It is also possible, at least in the short term, for organizations to use their strategies to change the context within which they operate, thereby bringing context into fit with existing performance measures. Such an approach is unlikely to be viable in the long term, as most organizations have to engage with the changing external situation to remain competitive.

There are various approaches to studying the way aspects of performance measures may 'fit' with their contingencies (Donaldson 2001; Luft and Shields 2003; Gerdin and Greeve 2004). Selection studies examine the way contextual factors are related to aspects of performance measures with no attempt to assess whether this association is linked to performance. For example, it may be that a reliance on accounting performance measures is found in situations that are relatively stable and certain. Selection studies assume that 'survival of the fittest' means that only organizations with effective combinations of context and performance measures are observed. It is therefore pointless to try and identify which combinations of context and performance measures lead to improved performance, as any inappropriate combination will not survive. However, this form of 'Darwinism' ignores the processes whereby organizations attempt to move towards the optimal combination of context and performance measures. At any point in time there are likely to be some organizations that face changing contextual situations and are in the process of readjusting their performance measures to suit the new context (Milgrom and Roberts 1992). Thus, there will be variations between firms as they seek optimal choices.

The congruence perspective aims to identify connections between contextual variables and particular performance measures that lead to enhanced performance. This approach suggests that we can observe certain combinations of context and performance measures that will be more effective than other combinations. Thus, it may be proposed that a combination of high levels of uncertainty and a more flexible use of budgets will perform better than a combination of high levels of uncertainty and less flexible budget use. Similarly, low levels of uncertainty and less flexible budgets will have better performance than low levels of uncertainty and more flexible budget use. The idea is that certain combinations of context and performance measures will result in better performance than other combinations between the same contextual and performance measurement variables.

While most selection and congruence approaches consider how performance measures are related to only one or two contextual variables, there is a view that these approaches are overly molecular and that performance measurement design should be considered in terms of the many contextual variables that describe the operating situation. Examining how performance measures should best be designed becomes more than considering the sum of the effect of each contextual variable or their combinations. Considering performance measures and multiple contextual variables provides a systems form of fit. The exact consequences of multiple contingencies may be difficult to predict. In combination, one contextual variable may suit a performance measure, while another may have an opposite effect. Alternatively, one contextual variable may act synergistically with other variables, intensifying the effects of context on a requisite aspect of performance measurement. Nevertheless, it is the complexity generated from multiple elements of context that eventually compels the organization to adopt a particular type of performance measurement.

Many proponents of performance measures attempt to identify universalistic effects of different performance measures. It is important to the continued diffusion of performance measurement innovations to demonstrate that they have positive outcomes. For example, the designers of BSCs often use selected case examples to show how these systems help provide a strategic focus and improve performance (Kaplan and Norton 1996, 2000, 2001, 2004). However, as the practices become more widely adopted, evidence becomes available to test for universalistic effects, and if context has an affect in helping explain variation in the effectiveness of the practices. Generally, in management accounting research, several contingencies have been found to be important in studying the effectiveness of the practices. These include environmental uncertainty, strategy, technology, organizational structure, and size. Theories to understand the importance of these variables were first identified by organizational theorists and have been adapted to relate to management accounting (Chenhall 2003). In Section 5.3 each element of context is considered. This is followed by an examination of different performance measurement innovations and how their implementation may be affected by context.

5.3 **Contextual variables**

5.3.1 THE EXTERNAL ENVIRONMENT

The external environment is a powerful contextual variable that is at the foundation of contingency-based research (Burns and Stalker 1961; Lawrence and Lorsch 1967; Perrow 1970; Galbraith 1973) and has been examined extensively in management accounting (Chapman 1997; Hartmann 2000; Chenhall 2003). Uncertainty presents the organization with difficulties in planning the future as events cannot be identified or the impact of events on operations is unknown. Evaluating performance becomes difficult as managers' performance will depend on events over which they have little control.

In addition to uncertainty, the environment presents difficulties due to its turbulence (risky, unpredictable, fluctuating, ambiguous), hostility (stressful, dominating, restrictive), diversity (variety in products, inputs, customers), and complexity (rapidly developing technologies) (Khandwalla 1977); its complexity and dynamism (Duncan 1972), the extent to which events are controllable and uncontrollable (Ewusi-Mensah 1981), and the level of ambiguity (Ouchi 1979) or equivocality (Daft and Macintosh 1981). These aspects, while predictable, present managers with threats and opportunities to develop strategies and potential difficulties in implementing these strategies. When evaluating employees, the way they manage these factors will likely have an important impact on their performance.

5.3.2 STRATEGY

There are clear links between strategy and uncertainty. On the basis of an organization's strategy it will select its markets, product, and technologies. These may be subject to varying levels of uncertainty and difficulty. If the current product range is too uncertain, reformulating product strategy into a market that is more predictable may reduce the difficulty in adapting to the environment. Notwithstanding the strategic direction selected by the organization, contingency-based research predicts that certain types of performance measures will be more suited to particular strategies (Langfield-Smith 1997).

The meaning of strategy has been articulated by different researchers as involving an entrepreneurial or conservative approach (Miller and Friesen 1982); as prospecting-analysing-defending (Miles and Snow 1978); building-holding-harvesting (Gupta and Govindarajan 1984); and as either product differentiation or cost leadership (Porter 1980). Evidence from the strategy–organizational design research suggests that strategies characterized by a conservative orientation, defending, harvesting, and cost leadership present managers with less uncertain environments, technologies that are less complex, and structures that involve centralized authority, specialized and formalized work, and simple coordination mechanisms (Miles and Snow 1978; Porter 1980; Miller and Friesen 1982). Strategies characterized by an entrepreneurial orientation, prospecting, building, and product differentiation are linked to more uncertain and complex environments, technologies that involve more task uncertainty, and more flexible structures and processes.

5.3.3 TECHNOLOGY

Technology refers to how the organization's work processes operate (the way tasks transform inputs into outputs) and includes hardware (such as machines and tools), materials, people, software, and knowledge. Technologies present important contingencies for organizations as they generate work situations that are complex, and involve task uncertainty and interdependence. Complexity derives from standardization of work, with large-batch and mass production (e.g. highly automated factories), process and small-batch unit technologies representing increasing levels of complexity (Woodward 1965). Task uncertainty refers to variability in tasks and the analysability of methods of performing the tasks with high variability and unanalysable tasks inducing control difficulties (Perrow 1970). Task uncertainty is also caused by lack of knowledge of transformation processes and unpredictability in measuring outputs (Ouchi 1979). Interdependence increases the level of coordination difficulties, and has implications for control systems, as the interdependencies move from pooled (no direct relationship between adjacent processes), to sequential (one-way interdependencies), to reciprocal (two-way interdependencies) (Thompson 1967). These contingencies present challenges for the design of performance measures.

Technological complexity, uncertainty, and interdependence can be combined to describe two idealized technological contingencies. First, organizations producing highly specialized, non-standard, differentiated products are likely to employ complex unit/batch technologies. These will tend to involve processes that have low analysability of processes and many exceptions. Also, managers are likely to have imperfect knowledge of processes and low ability to measure outputs. A need for flexible responses to specific customers increases interdependencies across the value chain involving reciprocal interactions with customers, suppliers, and functional units such as marketing, production, purchasing, and research and development. It might be expected that these types of technologies would require flexible responses, high levels of open communication within the workforce, and systems to manage the interdependencies. The design of performance measures should be sensitive to these organizational characteristics. It seems that highly formalized financial performance measures would be unlikely to be satisfactory; rather more open, flexible, and organic controls would be more suitable.

Second, organizations that produce standard, undifferentiated products employing capital-intensive, automated processes are likely to employ mass production and process technologies. These will involve highly analysable processes and few exceptions. Knowledge of processes and measures of output will be more readily available. Interdependencies are moderate being sequential. This technology requires standardized, administrative controls such as traditional, formal financial performance measures. A variant of this technology is where there are non-standard products but the processes are well understood. Interdependencies with customers are likely to be reciprocal. This technology is typical of an organization producing customized products but employing reasonably automated processes. Performance measures will be required that are flexible and that are consistent with managing interdependencies.

Over the past twenty years management control systems research has recognized the importance of advanced technologies such as just in time (JIT), total quality management (TQM), and flexible manufacturing (FM) as dimensions of context. Understanding the appropriate fit between performance measures and advanced technologies is assisted by reflecting on the basic, generic notions of technology addressed above. JIT, TQM, and FM generate potential control problems by developing close linkages across the value chain that can cause variability (task uncertainty due to many exceptions) and interdependence between elements of production processes. It can be argued that advanced technologies are best suited to performance measurement systems that have a wide diversity and are used flexibly. These measures can best manage the close linkages or coupling within advanced technologies that can cause variability and interdependence. In situations of advanced technologies there is a need for flexible responses to customers, which involves coordinating reciprocal interdependencies across the value chain. Also, advanced manufacturing practices implies continuous improvement and a commitment to change (Kalagnanam and Lindsay 1999).

5.3.4 ORGANIZATIONAL STRUCTURE

Organizational structure is about the formal specification of different roles for organizational members, or tasks for groups, to ensure that the activities of the organization are carried out. Structural arrangements influence the efficiency of work, the motivation of individuals, information flows, and control systems and can help shape the future of the organization. Most commonly, in management accounting research, structure is considered in terms of the extent to which decentralization of authority leads to differentiating activities around profit centres, typically focused on geographic areas or products. More recently, in some organizations, authority has been delegated down through the organization with the final decision-making responsibility residing with self-empowered work teams. In addition to differentiation, structure concerns mechanisms used to ensure there is effective integration between the activities of differentiated sub-units, and between sub-units' activities and corporate goals, strategies, and policies. These notions of structure have important implications for the design of performance measures. To evaluate the performance of individuals, measures should reflect the work that they do, whether they have responsibility for this work, and whether actions elsewhere in the organization affect their performance or, alternatively, if their actions have effects elsewhere in the organization. Similarly, performance measures should be sensitive to the need for sub-unit managers' efforts to be consistent with corporate and other sub-unit goals. The aim to ensure that performance measures reflect the effective integration of highly decentralized sub-units may conflict with measuring the effectiveness of the sub-unit manager. To achieve the latter it is necessary that the performance measures be sensitive to the decision-making autonomy of divisional managers, while the former may involve the intrusion of centralized management, by way of specific performance measures, to ensure effective integration.

5.3.5 SIZE

Size is an important contingency variable as it has an influence on other aspects of context. Large organizations tend to have more power in controlling their operating environment, and when employing large-scale, mass production techniques have relatively lower levels of task uncertainty. However, as organizations become larger, the need for managers to handle greater quantities of information increases to a point where the organization has to change structures by decentralizing authority and introducing controls to achieve integration, such as rules, documentation, specialization of roles, and functions (Child and Mansfield 1972). Contemporary large organizations often develop close associations with suppliers and customers, which blurs the boundaries between organizations, thereby increasing further the size of the entity. Size has also provided organizations with the resources to expand into global operations, sometimes by way of mergers, takeovers, licensing, or other collaborative arrangements. These developments create additional challenges for designers of performance measurement systems due to increased levels of complexity within the production processes and with managing interdependencies with global partners.

Figure 5.1 provides an illustration of the contextual variables examined in this chapter. It should be noted that the specific nature of the causal relationships between performance measures, context, and outcomes is not specified; rather, the connecting arrows merely show links between context to the association between performance measures and outcomes.

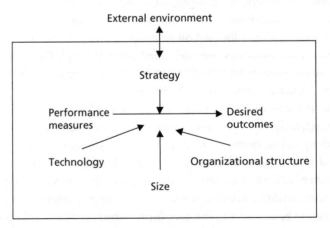

Figure 5.1 Performance measures and contextual variables

5.4 **Performance measurement innovations**

Over the last ten years there has been a series of trends that have initiated innovations in performance measures. First, there has been an interest in developing metrics that reflect the way the organization is adding value to shareholders. Measures that attempt to show how cash from activities provide returns in excess of an organization's cost of capital have been developed—notable economic value measures. Second, an awareness of how performance measures have been developed in operations management, marketing, and human resource management has provided the impetus to provide non-financial measures as part of the organization's formal performance measurement system, to reflect better the performance outcomes in these areas. Third, the growth in importance of a strategic approach to managing organizations has seen management accountants develop integrative performance measures that reflect business models, which connect activities across the value chain with the strategy of the organization. The remainder of this chapter examines each of these innovations and reviews evidence on their effectiveness. It is concluded from this evidence that these innovations in performance measures have not provided universal benefits. It is proposed that a contingency approach can shed light on situations within which the different performance measures may be best suited.

5.4.1 FINANCIAL MEASURES AND ECONOMIC VALUE MEASURES

In management accounting, performance measures were developed originally to evaluate the internal operations of the organization, employing information that was couched in terms of financial accounting. Performance measures derived from financial statements, such as income and return on investment (ROI), are used to evaluate divisional and managerial performance. Budgetary control is often used as a financial model of the organization's operations. Sales budgets identify revenues derived from sales. Production, materials, labour, and overhead budgets distinguish the key resources required and used in producing the organization's goods or services. Cash budgets recognize that the financial accounting numbers differ from cash receipts or expenditures and will depend, in part, on managing working capital. These tools have been among the most widely employed management accounting practices for decades.

A belief that reliance on traditional financial measures causes sub-optimal decisions led to the development of economic value measures (Rappaport 1986). These measures are based on the idea that deducting the cost of capital from income to derive a performance measure helps ensure that managers take decisions to make sure that income, recomputed as cash flows, will exceed the cost of capital, therefore enhancing economic value. A variety of methods have been developed ranging from early suggestions to calculate shareholder value as the present value of cash flows (Rappaport 1986); economic value added (EVA) developed by Stern Stewart & Co (Stewart 1991); and cash flow return (Snyder 1995). The differences in these approaches are in how the cost of capital is included and in the adjustments made to financial accounting reports to ensure they reflect cash flows and economic profit.

An important issue is whether measures of economic value are superior performance measures. Research as to the advantages of economic value is limited and the results are equivocal. Biddle et al. (1998) found that economic value measures were not superior to earnings when the measures were associated with stock returns. Wallace (1998) found that economic value measures (residual income method) changed managers' behaviour in utilizing assets more intensively, decreased new investments, and increased payout to shareholders through share repurchases. There was weak evidence that the share market responded positively to companies adopting economic value measures. An important consideration in economic value measures is the use of the measures for compensation. This is seen to encourage use of the measures as the cornerstone of financial management. It seems likely that a minority of organizations use economic value measures for compensation. This has prompted Stewart (1995) to claim that poor results from economic value measures are due to their lack of inclusion in compensation schemes. In summary, it appears that the association between economic value measures and enhanced performance is not clear.

5.4.2 CONTINGENCY EFFECTS AND ECONOMIC VALUE MEASURES

The lack of evidence on the superiority of economic value measures raises the issue as to whether economic value measures are best suited to different contextual settings. As yet there is little direct evidence on contingency effects related to economic value measures. However, certain characteristics of contextual variables provide indications as to the potential suitability of economic value measures to different situations.

Firms pursuing more entrepreneurial strategies, where they are building markets and prospecting for opportunities by way of product differentiation, tend to position themselves in relatively complex environments, which have high degrees of unpredictability. Economic value measures can attempt to build in uncertainty by way of the cost of capital; however, the projection of cash flows from managers' decisions may mean that cash flows become little more than guesswork. If economic value measures are continually revised as events unfold, they may lose their significance as a way of moving planning away from the short-term to longer-term economic value. If they are not revised, they may reflect events that bear little relationship to managers' actual performance. Managers may benefit or be penalized due to events beyond their control when actual economic value is higher or lower than expected. Ittner and Larcker (1998a: 214) note that in cyclical industries economic value measures may regularly be negative, even when managers have taken appropriate actions.

Motivation for managers to maximize economic value measures may work to discourage investment in innovation where such innovations take a relatively long period to generate positive cash flows. It is also likely that it is difficult to identify the drivers of innovation and build these into economic value measures, particularly drivers related to employees and customers. Thus, it may be that economic value measures are more appropriate in organizations following conservative strategies where the environment is relatively certain and cash flows more stable and predictable.

The technology of the organization may influence the suitability of economic value measures. In more complex technologies the causal connections between strategic priorities and operations can be quite complex. Moreover, tasks will tend to have high variability and be low in the analysability of methods used to perform the tasks. A key to effective economic value measures is the identification of key drivers of future performance. This is a highly structured, mechanistic approach and implies that the causal connections between strategy and operations and the tasks themselves are well understood. If this were not the case, developing economic value measures that can drill down to examine the economic value of operations would seem to be difficult. Theories from organizational behaviour have stressed the inappropriateness of mechanistic controls in situations of high task complexity and uncertainty (Perrow 1970).

An alternate view is that only a single, aggregate economic value measure should be used to evaluate managers. These aggregate measures do not identify the links between operations and value for purposes of performance evaluation. Rather, managers have the responsibility to ensure that the causal links between operations and economic value are managed effectively. It is managers' responsibility to manage task uncertainty, and as this may be done in many different ways, it is only the final result related to economic value that is pertinent for evaluation. This assumes that managers have responsibility for decisions affecting economic value and that economic value is used merely to assess managesrs' performance and not as a tool to understand and plan how operations relate to value. The issue of the effect of structure on the suitability of economic value is discussed next.

Organizational structure is likely to influence the extent to which economic value measures can be used effectively throughout the organization. If economic value measures are to be used at the level of operational managers, those managers will require authority over decisions related to the value-drivers that enhance the organization's economic value. Even if managers do have the authority to take decisions to improve economic value, it has been claimed that employees outside corporate headquarters do not understand how their actions affect economic value measures, despite extensive training (Ittner and Larcker 1998a: 215). Proponents of economic value measures claim that to be successful, these measures must become a way of life in the organization, be linked to compensation, have the commitment of the chief executive, and be supported by appropriate training (Stern et al. 1995). There are two issues that are relevant to these suggestions. First, it will be necessary that the culture of the organization be compatible with a highly formalized, quantitative approach to management. Some organizations tend to be run by the numbers, whereas others are not. Differences often depend on the ease with which operations can be measured with accuracy by quantitative performance measures. Also, managerial orientation and cognitive preferences often explain a predilection for a more numeric orientation. Second, as the adoption of economic value measures usually involves considerable change, it may be expected that there will be the potential for resistance to change. In organizations where there is a high risk of failure, resistance to change may be less and economic value measures may be accepted more readily. This is likely to be the case where a new Chief Executive Officer sees that survival will depend on the use of economic value measures, changing the culture to one more attuned to considering, explicitly, the economic value of decisions.

Finally, the size of the organization is likely to be implicated in the role of economic value measures. Economic value measures may best suit larger organizations. This will follow if large size is associated with a higher degree of control over the external environment, an organizational structure where managers have a high level of autonomy over value-creating decisions, and technologies that are more highly automated with low task uncertainty. Also, large organizations may have the resources to experiment with economic value measures and learn how to implement and adapt the systems to their needs.

5.4.3 NON-FINANCIAL PERFORMANCE MEASURES

Non-financial performance measures have been proposed to overcome the perceived limitations of traditional accounting measures. There is a view that financial measures do not capture the potential long-term outcomes of managers' decisions and that non-financial measures incorporate information, not available in financial measures, that is informative in evaluating managers (Feltham and Xie 1994; Hemmer 1996). Initiatives in functions such as manufacturing, marketing, and human resource management have motivated management accountants to develop more specific measures related to the specific processes of the function. Measures may involve the ad hoc use of specific metrics from marketing such as customer satisfaction or product returns, from operations management such as production rejects or throughput time, and from human resource management such as intellectual capital or 360-degree performance ratings. These measures have been used for many years by functional managers, quite often separate from their organization's main performance measurement system.

Theoretical reasons as to why non-financial measures may enhance managers' performance can be derived from goal and feedback theories (Ilgren et al. 1979; Locke et al. 1981). Feedback provides the basis for learning. Goal theory suggests that feedback is most effective when related to specific goals. Such feedback clarifies preferred outcomes and expectations, reduces task ambiguity, which enhances concern and commitment to strategic priorities. Individuals focus on activities that are related to particular goals and ignore others. The effectiveness of feedback from performance measures is seen to have a greater impact when the measures are used to evaluate a manager's performance (Briers and Hirst 1990; Bruns and McKinnon 1992).

Given the interest in non-financial measures, it may be expected that they would be adopted widely by organizations and lead to enhanced performance. A series of studies has examined the association between non-financial measures and organizational performance.

These have examined non-financial measures related to manufacturing and to marketing. Studies related to manufacturing measures have produced equivocal results (Chenhall 2003). However, several studies examining the effectiveness of customer satisfaction measures have found positive associations with performance, although the findings are industry-specific. For example, performance was related to customer satisfaction measures in hotels (Banker et al. 1998), for non-service, but not service, organizations in Sweden (Anderson et al. 1994). Banker et al. (1996) identified that sales personnel increased sales over time in response to financial rewards associated with sales-based bonuses evaluated by determining the quality of sales greater than a sales goal. Customer satisfaction measures were linked to growth in customers and revenue, accounting performance, and current market values, with variation depending on industry (Ittner and Larcker 1998b). However, Foster and Gupta (1997) found that positive effects of customer satisfaction measures depended on the type of measure. In summary, there appear to be links between customer satisfaction measures and performance, but they likely depend on the type of measure and the industry.

5.4.4 CONTINGENCY EFFECTS AND NON-FINANCIAL PERFORMANCE MEASURES

There appears to be strong organizational interest in non-financial measures with widespread adoption. However, from existing research, direct links to performance are not apparent. This signifies that an examination of the context within which these measures are applied is warranted. There is evidence that the organization's strategy and consequent positioning within the external environment may be important in assessing the suitability of non-financial measures, particularly more subjective measures. Govindarajan and Gupta (1985), Gupta (1987), Simons (1987), and Govindarajan (1988) suggest that objective performance evaluation and reward systems support defender strategies, whereas for prospector strategies more subjective performance evaluation is suitable. This may be explained by the nature of these strategies and links to environmental uncertainty. Prospector strategies involve building strategy by seeking out new products, while defending involves competing within existing product lines. The search for new products inherent in prospector-type strategies is usually associated with high levels of environmental uncertainty, with a consequence that it may be difficult to set targets accurately and to measure managerial performance objectively. Additional evidence from Govindarajan and Gupta (1985) showed that a greater reliance on long-term, subjective, non-financial measures provided enhanced performance benefits in build rather than harvest strategies. There are indications that customer service measures are likely to be important, but this may depend on their implementation within service industries (Anderson et al. 1994) such as hospitality (Banker et al. 1998).

It seems clear that initiatives within operations management have had an important role in raising the profile of manufacturing non-financial measures within management accounting. Of interest is whether non-financial measures suit particular manufacturing settings. Most of the empirical evidence considers the usefulness of non-financial measures for technologies that employ advanced manufacturing. There appears to be consensus that non-financial measures are more widely adopted in JIT, TQM, and FM settings. However, links to improved performance are mixed. There are several studies suggesting that non-financial measures enhance performance in advanced manufacturing settings. Symons and Jacobs (1995) reported that TQM-based reward systems were linked to higher production output, lower scrap, and reduced product variability (the study did not consider overall profitability). Chenhall (1997) found that performance in TQM settings was enhanced when there was a reliance on manufacturing performance measures systems. Abernethy and Lillis (1995) found that performance in organizations following FM was enhanced by the use of informal liaison mechanisms (non-financial). Several studies have failed to find associations between non-financial measures and performance. For example, Perera et al. (1997) found that performance was not enhanced in organizations following customer-focused and TQM programmes and the use of non-financial measures. Ittner and Larcker (1995) found that in situations of low to medium TQM, non-financial measures enhanced performance. However, this was not the case in organizations with more advanced TQM. Certainly, this result contradicts the proposition that non-traditional measures assist in enhancing performance in advanced TQM settings. However, it may be that non-financial systems assist companies that are at the early stages of implementing TQM programmes in ways that enhance performance. As the programmes become more successful the measures become less important to sustain effort. Highly developed TQM programmes may achieve feedback on effectiveness by more informal (non-financial) means or the feedback may become part of the process (process controls).

Another stream of studies has examined the provision of non-financial measures at the shop floor level. Young and Selto (1993) found little evidence that providing non-financial operational measures to workers in JIT facilities improved manufacturing performance. Banker et al. (1993) did not find positive performance effects in the provision of non-financial measures to online workers. These studies suggest that provision of non-financial measures to operational workers does not appear to enhance performance. However, it is possible that contingencies associated with the shop floor may generate situations that are more or less suitable to employing non-financial measures. A key is whether the information provided by non-financial measures is valuable to shop floor workers and whether they have incentives to use that information. The relative certainty of the tasks is likely to indicate how well the non-financial measures capture the technological cause–effect relationships. The extent to which the shop floor workers are accountable for their work and the extent to which the measures are linked to this accountability would appear to be important.

Consideration of studies that examine the performance effects of non-financial measures within advanced manufacturing raises the issue of how best to examine the role of non-financial measures. Is it sufficient to establish the importance of the non-financial measures, or will the effects of non-financial measures depend on how they are used? This may be important to studying linkages with performance. For example, consider the findings of Chenhall (1997) and Perera et al. (1997), which, on the face of it, appear to be contradictory. Chenhall (1997) found that performance was enhanced by the application of non-financial measures in firms employing TQM, whereas Perera et al. (1997) did not. It is important to note how performance measures systems were examined. In Chenhall (1997), after establishing that the organization used manufacturing measures, the instrument evaluated how they are used by asking managers to rate a series of questions on the type of use of non-financial measures such as the extent to which quantitative measures of the manufacturing process are used to evaluate performance; performance evaluation by comparisons of specific targets set for quantitative measures of the manufacturing process with actual performance; the use of targets for quantitative measures of manufacturing that are subjected to revision based on a need to improve continuously; quantitative measures of the manufacturing process formally included in the determination of remuneration; promotion prospects determined by formal consideration of quantitative measures of the manufacturing process. This may be contrasted with the way Perera et al. (1997) measured non-financial measures. This was the relative importance of eleven non-financial items and four financial measures with respect to the extent of their use in the performance measurement systems. The Perera et al. (1997) instrument refers to the overall use of the measures in performance measurement systems. It is unclear if these are used as part of remuneration or promotions. If, as argued above, feedback from performance measures will be more effective when used to reward managers, indicating that measures are important may not tap into this aspect of performance measurement. Evidence suggests that performance measures are more effective when they are part of the managers' reward systems (Larcker 1983; Sim and Killough 1998; Banker et al. 2000).

Organizational structure establishes the levels of decision authority throughout the organization. There has been considerable attention to the type of performance measures that best suit different structures. This topic was of great interest to early management accountants who grappled with the issue of matching the most appropriate measure of profit with divisionalized structures. An issue of concern was establishing a profit measure that reflected the activities over which the managers had control, with many textbooks recommending the deduction of only traceable but controllable items to determine 'controllable profit'. This was to be used for managerial evaluation and was distinguished from overall profit to be used to evaluate the economic viability of the division. Despite the textbook recommendations to evaluate managers on controllable profit, studies have shown that many organizations hold managers accountable for uncontrollable items (Merchant 1987). This motivated closer examination of the meaning of controllability.

Initially, the meaning of a controllable measure was of a metric that reflected whether a manager had decision authority over the activities being measured or not. More recently, the meaning of a controllability metric has been refined to mean the probability that a manager's actions affect the potential evaluation measure, suggesting that controllability is a matter of degree (Banker and Datar 1989; Demski 1994; Feltham and Xie 1994). More specifically, controllability is seen to depend on the sensitivity of the measure (changes in the mean value of the measure in response to the manager's actions, adjusted for the correlation with other measures that may also change) and precision (lack of noise or variability in the measure due to uncertain events that are independent of the manager's action) (Banker and Datar 1989).

Merchant (1987) provides reasons why organizations include 'uncontrollable' events in a manager's performance evaluation. Performance measures that include uncontrollable events induce subordinates to share risks with superiors; it informs managers of how their decision affects areas outside their control or provides information on unidentified events (assuming a positive association between identified and unidentified events); it provides a relative performance evaluation that enables comparison of a manager's performance with others who face the same environment.

Notwithstanding this precise meaning of controllability, it can be argued that non-financial measures are more controllable than financial measures (Ittner and Larcker 2000). This follows as financial measures are too aggregated and may not provide information about the details of managerial performance. Thus, if performance measures are to assess the performance of managers, non-financial measures provide information that can relate more precisely to controllable events. However, to evaluate divisional economic performance, financial measures are required (Schiff and Hoffman 1996; Ghosh 2005: 59).

An alternative view to the suitability of non-financial measures to evaluate divisional managers is that summary financial measures are more appropriate. This view stresses that the use of non-financial measures transfers authority from division to corporate managers. Non-financial measures reduce the authority of managers to make trade-offs among the measured activities necessary to optimize divisional profit (Abernethy et al. 2004). However, if the non-financial measures are constructed in terms of the contemporary controllability principle, their inclusion in the manager's performance evaluation would seem consistent with decentralized authority. That is, the performance assessment would assess the mean value of the measure as it responds to the manager's decentralized actions, adjusted for other measures that may also change.

An important element of contemporary structures is teams. As yet there are few studies that have considered the role of performance measures within team-based structures. Scott and Tiessen (1999) reported that team-based structures were associated with high task complexity and that team performance was associated with the use of comprehensive performance measures (financial and non-financial), formulated participatively and used for compensation. In an experimental study, Drake et al. (1999) found that in team structures the interaction between activity-based costing (ABC) (cf. volume-based accounting) and rewards based on group incentives (cf. assessment of individuals compared to other workers) was associated with cooperative innovations, lower costs, and higher profits. Often teams are implemented as a way of encouraging workers to develop a commitment to the organization and to develop trusting behaviour. In these situations the use of formal controls may be inappropriate and more informal personal controls of a non-financial nature, which are consistent with developing trust and commitment, may be suitable (Chenhall and Langfield-Smith 2003).

5.4.5 INTEGRATED PERFORMANCE MEASURES

Recently, management accountants have sought to broaden the measurement base of performance measures to provide an integrated set of measures that establishes a business model of the organization. This approach has been developed in France as the 'tableau de bord' (Lebas 1994), and elsewhere as performance hierarchies (Lynch and Cross 1995); the performance prism (Neely et al. 2002); the Skandia navigator (Edvinsson 1997); and most popularly as the BSC (Kaplan and Norton 1996, 2000, 2001, 2004). These approaches have moved performance measurement from a simple diversity of both financial and non-financial measures to more complex frameworks based on a balanced suite of measures that explicitly link those measures to strategy. These often take the form of causal maps, which aim to show the operational implications of different strategies. The BSC is said to provide a powerful tool for communicating strategic intent and motivating performance towards strategic goals (Ittner and Larcker 1998a). Kaplan and Norton's (1996) approach includes measurement related to a financial perspective and then to customers, processes, and a learning and growth orientation. Neely et al. (2002) provide an approach that includes five facets. It has a central concern with stakeholder satisfaction and stakeholder contribution, with these being served by strategies, processes, and capabilities. The Skandia navigator (Edvinsson 1997, 2002) has a five-dimensional balanced performance measurement system that relates key dimensions of human resource management practices to the history of the organization, a financial focus, today's operations measured in terms of customer and process dimensions, and future considerations identified as renewal and development

The BSC has been well documented and praised in a range of professional journals. By providing explicit links between strategy, goals, performance measures, and outcomes, the BSC is presented as the key to achieving high-level performance (Kaplan and Norton 1996, 2000, 2001, 2004). However, despite the high profile and apparent high levels of acceptance of BSCs in practice, there has been only limited research testing the claimed outcomes of BSC and the processes involved in using them for their intended purposes. Hoque and James (2000) found that overall usage of BSCs was significantly correlated with organizational performance. In a study of banks, Davis and Albright (2004) identified that a group of branches that used BSCs outperformed a group that did not use BSCs on common composite financial measures. Chenhall and Langfield-Smith (1998) reported that BSCs were part of the 'best practices' of high-performance firms. Also, they were evident in poorly performing firms that had less well-developed management techniques. Further support for the importance of BSCs is provided by Banker et al. (2004) in their experimental study of the judgement effects of performance measures and strategy. They found that the evaluations of business unit managers were influenced more by measures linked to strategy than those not linked to strategy, but only when managers are informed of the details of the business unit strategies. Banker et al. (2001) and Sandt et al. (2001) provide evidence that the provision of systematic linkages between measures enhances satisfaction with the systems. Malina and Selto (2001) presented a case study that focused on the effectiveness of the BSCs as a management control to communicate strategy.

Other evidence is not as supportive of the positive benefits of BSCs. Ittner et al. (2003) found that finance firms using a BSC to reward managers had the potential to counter many of the criticisms of short-term accounting-based reward systems. However, the varying subjective weighting given by managers to performance measures allowed supervisors to ignore many of the performance measures when undertaking evaluations and awarding bonuses, even when some of those measures were leading indicators of the bank's strategic objectives of financial performance and customer growth. Concerning the extent to which BSCs helped clarify strategy, Ittner and Larcker (1998a) report that scorecards assisted only a minority of managers in understanding goals and strategies or in relating their jobs to business objectives. Ittner et al. (2003) found that techniques such as BSCs, economic value, and business modelling were associated with increased measurement systems satisfaction but not with economic performance. Also, Ittner and Larcker (2003) established that managers made little attempt to link non-financial performance measures to advance their chosen strategies. Moreover, only 23 per cent of these managers were able to show that they built causal models and most did not validate the causal links. Firms that did build cause–effect linkages had higher return on assets (ROA) and return on equity (ROE) than those that did not. In an experimental study, Lipe and Salterio (2000) demonstrated that managers had cognitive difficulties working with measures to evaluate performance that were specific to a situation (unique measures) and preferred measures that were the same for different situations (common measures). Ittner et al. (2003) also found that firms in the financial services sector that had more coherent performance measurement systems were associated with enhanced satisfaction with performance measures. However, their results indicated that these systems were not associated with improved economic performance. Chenhall (2005) reported only a weak association between firms with BSCs and the extent to which their performance measurement systems provided information that integrated operations with strategy and provided links across the value chain.

5.4.6 CONTINGENCY EFFECTS AND INTEGRATED PERFORMANCE

Evidence to support the claims of proponents of BSCs that they enhance organizational performance is limited. As with other performance measurement innovations examined in this chapter there are strong reasons to suggest that the effectiveness of integrated performance measures may depend on the context within which they are implemented. One difficulty in studying BSCs is that the precise nature of an organization's scorecard is often not identified. While there is some support for growing BSC implementation (Chenhall and Langfield-Smith 1998; Ittner and Larcker 1998a; Silk 1998; Hoque and James 2000), the characteristics or information dimensions of the systems are not examined in these studies. It seems clear that there is wide variation in the nature of BSCs, ranging from combinations of financial and non-financial measures to more comprehensive systems linking operations to various perspectives and to strategy (Ittner and Larcker 1998a; Hoque and James 2000; Ittner and Larcker 2003; Ittner et al. 2003).

If integrated performance measures, such as BSCs, are intended to be used as tools to assist in strategic management, it is implied that they are built into some form of business model. These models attempt to show the cause–effect relationships between strategy and the operations required to achieve those strategies. Contingency ideas suggest that highly structured approaches to planning and control are unlikely to be effective in situations of high uncertainty. That is, highly detailed and comprehensive business modelling and the associated performance measures will be ineffective if the conditions affecting the models are changing in unpredictable ways. Similarly, if organizations pursuing entrepreneurial strategies to build market share and those employing high levels of differentiation find themselves in uncertain and diverse environments, integrated performance measures may not produce promised benefits. Moreover, it may be that the mechanistic nature of integrated performance measures restricts innovation and flexibility, which may inhibit effective performance, particulary in those organizations where innovation is an important part of survival (Quinn 1980; Mintzberg 1987). There is little empirical evidence on the role of environment and strategy on the effectiveness of integrative performance measures. However, in a study of banks, Nager (1998) found that non-financial drivers of future accounting performance varied depending on the bank's competitive strategy. Chenhall and Langfield-Smith (1998) showed that the use of combinations of performance measures including BSCs differed depending on the type of product differentiation. Chenhall (2005) found that various dimensions of integrated performance measures, reflecting links between operations and strategy, assisted organizations in achieving a variety of product differentiation and cost-based strategies.

The organization's technology presents varying degrees of complexity. Less complex technologies have routine processes and well-understood tasks, while more complex situations involve tasks that are less routine, less well understood, and possibly having high levels of interdependencies across the value chain. This complexity can result in more complex business modelling with a large number of causal connections between strategy and operations. Attempts to build in performance measures to mirror these models can result in a wide diversity of measures. It is possible that this could cause information overload where attempts to manage performance against the measures exceed the information-processing capabilities of managers, which at the extreme could result in a decline in performance. With a highly diverse set of measures, managers must decide how they will spread their efforts over the different areas. Ideally, a balanced set of measures will indicate which decision areas should receive priority as the causal connections between performance areas will be clear. If the technology is complex and uncertain, mangers will need to make judgements on these trade-offs. It is unlikely that an unambiguous, balanced approach will be achievable in complex settings. Finally, it is possible that performance in complex and uncertain technologies will be harder to measure than in more routine situations. Holstrom and Milgrom (1991) showed that the advantages of adding more measures to an incentive contract decrease with the difficulty of measuring activities that make competing demands on managers' efforts.

It is possible in situations of technological complexity, uncertainty, and interdependence to use probabilistic and subjective measures. However, some research has shown that these softer measures tend to be manipulated by senior management. Also, it is possible that the range of measurement will be compressed, which may lead to less differentiation in assessing employees' performance and an overall perception of unfairness (Prendegast and Topel 1993; Moers 2005).

The extent to which organizational structure is relevant to the effectiveness of integrative performance measures depends on the use of the performance measure. If the performance measures are to be used as a tool for evaluating managerial performance, there is an implication that the different measures within the system will match the controllability principles, as discussed above. Clearly, with a wide diversity of measures, determining the level of controllability of individual measures becomes increasingly difficult and it is likely that the incremental value of the information will decrease with additional measures. An additional benefit of BSCs is that they can be used as an effective communication channel to communicate strategy throughout the structure of the organization. Malina and Selto (2001) provide evidence that BSCs were successful in communicating strategy. However, Ittner and Larcker (1998a: 228) report that more than a third of respondents to a survey by the consulting firm, Towers Perrin, found it difficult to decompose BSCs for lower levels in the organization. More complex hierarchical structures may contribute to the difficulty of identifying how the implied business model translates across the organization's structure. Finally, integrated performance measures would seem to be particularly suitable used as an interactive control (Simons 1995, 2000). The interactive use of integrated performance measures involves processes whereby the measures are used to generate an information network within the organization that scans and reports on change. In this way events critical to achieving strategy, including emerging ideas, can be identified throughout the organization. To be effective in this role, the organization requires structures that are sufficiently open and flexible to ensure that employees are empowered to search out alternatives to respond to strategic uncertainties and that these are discussed regularly in face-to-face meetings (Simons 1995, 2000).

Given that integrated performance measures are costly to design and implement, it might be expected that size would indicate the extent to which the organization might have resources to experiment with the systems. As with other performance measures, size may also act as a surrogate for a more benign and less uncertain environment, less complex technologies, and more hierarchical structures. Inasmuch as these provide important contingencies, we might expect to see more effective integrated performance measures in large organizations.

5.5 **Conclusion**

The purpose of this chapter has been to examine recent innovations in performance measurement systems and identify if evidence supports their effectiveness in assisting managers improve the performance of their organizations. These innovations were economic value measures, non-financial measures, and integrated performance measures. Drawing on contingency thinking, a basic proposition is that it is unlikely that these innovations will be appropriate for all organizations. It was concluded from existing findings that positive benefits are not universalistic. Using existing findings from contingency studies in organizational theory and management accounting, this chapter argued that different innovative performance measures may best suit particular contexts. While existing research into the effects of contingencies on performance measure is limited, there are sufficient clues to suggest that the external environment and strategy, technology, structure, and size are likely to be important when considering the suitability of different performance measures.

In most studies to date, contingency relationships have explored the extent to which a single aspect of context can indicate the relative suitability of a performance measure. This approach is somewhat molecular and does not account for the fact that the context of an organization acts as a system. Much can be learned by considering the role of innovative performance measures within the context of broader patterns of organizational relationships. Early examples that identified configurations of context and associated control systems were Bruns and Waterhouse (1975) and Merchant (1981). More recently, Chenhall and Langfield-Smith (1998) examined how a selection of management accounting practices, including innovative performance measure, 'fitted' with configurations involving organizations' strategies and a variety of management practices.

Finally, given the lack of positive universalistic outcomes, it may be suggested that innovations in performance measures are the result of 'fads and fashions'. The practices are adopted because organizations mimic each other and wish to appear to be contemporary with little concern as to whether the practices lead to economic benefits. This conclusion would be premature without examining if the practices do indeed lead to positive performance effects in certain contextual settings. As part of this investigation it is also important to study the dynamics of contingencies. Specifically, how do organizations adapt their performance measures as their contextual setting changes (Donaldson 2001)?

☐ ACKNOWLEDGEMENT

This chapter is dedicated to the memory of Professor Bill Birkett who was an inspiration for many researchers in management accounting.

☐ REFERENCES

Abernethy, M. A. and Lillis, A. M. (1995). 'The Impact of Manufacturing Flexibility on Management Control Systems Design', *Accounting, Organizations and Society*, 20(4): 241–58.

—— Bouwens, J., and van Lent, L. (2004). 'Determinants of Control Systems Design in Divisionalized Firms', *Accounting Review*, 79(3): 545–70.

Anderson, E. W., Fornell, C., and Lehmann, D. R. (1994). 'Customer Satisfaction, Market Research and Profitability: Findings from Sweden', *Journal of Marketing Research*, 58 (July): 53–66.

Banker, R. and Datar, S. (1989). 'Sensitivity, Precision and Linear Aggregation of Signals for Perform-ance Evaluation', *Journal of Accounting Research*, 27: 21–39

—— Chang, H. and Pizzini, M. (2004). The balanced scorecard: judgmental effects and performance measures linked to strategy. *Accounting Review*, 79(1): 1–23.

—— and Srinivasan, D. (1998). 'An Empirical Investigation of an Incentive Plan Based on Non-financial Performance Measures', Working Paper, University of Texas at Dallas, Cornell University, and University of Pittsburgh.

—— Potter, G., and Schroeder, R. G. (1993). 'Reporting Manufacturing Performance Measures Systems to Workers: an Empirical Study', *Journal of Management Accounting Research*, 5 (Fall): 33–55.

—— Lee, S., and Potter, G. (1996). 'A Field Study of the Impact of a Performance-Based Incentive Plan', *Journal of Accounting and Economics*, 21: 195–226.

—— Potter, G., and Srinivasan, D. (2000). 'An Empirical Investigation of an Incentive Plan that Includes Nonfinancial Performance Measures Systems', *Accounting Review*, 75(1): 65–92.

—— Janakiraman, S. N., Konstans, C., and Pizzini, M. J. (2001). 'Determinants of Chief Financial Officer's Satisfaction with Systems for Performance Measurement', Working Paper, University of Dallas.

Biddle, G. C., Bowen, R. M., and Wallace, J. S. (1998). 'Does EVA Beat Earnings? Evidence on the Association With Stock Returns and Financial Values', *Journal of Accounting and Economics*, 24: 301–36.

Briers, M. and Hirst, M. (1990). 'The Role of Budgetary Information in Performance Evaluation', *Accounting, Organizations and Society*, 15(4): 373–98.

Bruns, W. J. and McKinnon, S. M. (1992). 'Performance Evaluation and Manager's Descriptions of Tasks and Activities', in W. J. Bruns, *Performance Measurement, Evaluation and Incentives*. Cambridge, MA: Harvard University Press.

—— and Waterhouse, J. H. (1975). 'Budgetary Control and Organizational Structure', *Journal of Accounting Research* (Autumn): 177–203.

Burns, T. and Stalker, G. (1961). *The Management of Innovation*. London: Tavistock.

Chapman, C. S. (1997). 'Reflections on a Contingent View of Accounting', *Accounting, Organizations and Society*, 22: 189–205.

Chenhall, R. H. (1997). 'Reliance on Manufacturing Performance Measures Systems, Total Quality Management and Organizational Performance', *Management Accounting Research*, 8: 187–206.

—— (2003). 'Management Accounting Within its Organizational Context: Findings from Contin-gency Modelling and Directions for Future Research', *Accounting, Organizations and Society*, 28: 127–68.

—— (2005). 'Integrative Strategic Performance Measurement Systems, Strategic Alignment of Manu-facturing, Learning and Strategic Outcomes: An Exploratory Study', *Accounting, Organizations and Society*, 30: 395–422.

—— and Langfield-Smith, K. (1998). 'The Relationship Between Strategic Priorities, Management Techniques and Management Accounting: An Empirical Investigation Using a Systems Approach', *Accounting, Organizations and Society*, 23(3): 243–64.

—— —— (2003). 'The Role of Employee Pay in Sustaining Organisational Change', *Journal of Management Accounting Research*, 15: 117–43.

Child, J. and Mansfield, R. (1972). 'Technology, Size and Organizational Structure', *Sociology*, 6: 369–93.

Copeland, T., Koller, T., and Murrin, J. (1996). *Valuation: Measuring and Managing the Value of Companies*. New York: John Wiley and Sons.

Daft, R. L. and Macintosh, N. J. (1981). 'A Tentative Exploration into the Amount and Equivocality of Information Processing in Organisational Work Units', *Administrative Science Quarterly*, 26: 207–44.

Davis, S. and Albright, T. (2004). 'An Investigation of the Effect of Balanced Scorecard Implementation on Financial Performance', *Management Accounting Research*, 15 (2): 135–53.

Demski, J. (1994). *Managerial Uses of Accounting Information*. Norwell, MA: Kluwer Academic.

Donaldson, L. (2001). *The Contingency Theory of Organizations*. Foundations for Organizational Science. Thousands Oaks, CA: Sage.

Drake, A. R., Haka, S. F., and Ravenscroft, S. P. (1999). 'Cost System and Incentive Structure Effects on Innovation, Efficiency and Profitability in Teams', *Accounting Review*, 74(3): 323–45.

Duncan, R. (1972). 'Characteristics of Organizational Environments and Perceived Environmental Uncertainty', *Administrative Science Quarterly* (September): 313–27.

Edvinsson, L. (1997). 'Developing Intellectual Capital at Skandia', *Long Range Planning*, 30(3): 320–31.

—— (2002). *Corporate Longitude: What You Need to Know to Navigate The Knowledge Economy*. London: Brookhouse.

Ewusi-Mensah, K. (1981). 'The External Organizational Environment and its Impact on Managerial Information Systems', *Accounting, Organizations and Society*, 6(4): 310–16.

Feltham, G. and Xie, J. (1994). 'Performance Measure Congruity and Diversity in Multi-task Principal/Agent Relations', *Accounting Review*, 69: 429–53.

Foster, G. and Gupta, M. (1997). 'The Customer Profitability Implications of Customer Satisfaction', Working Paper, Stanford and Washington Universities.

Galbraith, J. (1973). *Designing Complex Organizations*. Reading, MA: Addison-Wesley.

Gerdin, J. and Greve, J. (2004). 'Forms of Contingency Fit in Managerial Accounting Research—a Critical Review', *Accounting, Organizations and Society*, 29(3–4): 303–26.

Ghosh, D. (2005). 'Alternative Measures of Managers' Performance, Controllability, and the Outcome Effect', *Behavioral Research in Accounting*, 17: 55–70.

Govindarajan, V. (1988). 'A Contingency Approach to Strategy Implementation at the Business-Unit Level: Integrating Administrative Mechanisms with Strategy', *Academy of Management Journal*, 41: 828–53.

—— and Gupta, A. K. (1985). 'Linking Control Systems to Business Unit Strategy: Impact on Performance', *Accounting, Organizations and Society*, 10(1): 51–66.

Gupta, A. K. (1987). 'SBU Strategies, Corporate-SBU, and SBU Effectiveness in Strategy Implementation', *Academy of Management Journal*, 20: 477–500.

—— and Govindarajan, V. (1984). 'Business Unit Strategy, Managerial Characteristics, and Business Unit Effectiveness at Strategy Implementation', *Academy of Management Journal*, 27(1): 25–41.

Hemmer, T. (1996). 'On the Design and Choice of "Modern" Management Accounting Measures', *Journal of Management Accounting*, 8: 87–116.

Hartmann, F. (2000). 'The Appropriateness of RAPM: Towards the Further Development of Theory', *Accounting, Organizations and Society*, 25(4–5): 451–82.

Holstrom, B. and Milgrom, P. (1991). 'Multi-task Principal-agent Analysis: Incentive Contracts, Asset Ownership, and Job Design', *Journal of Law, Economics and Organization*, 7: 24–52.

Hoque, Z. and James, W. (2000). 'Linking Balanced Scorecard Measures to Size and Market Factors: Impact on Organizational Performance', *Journal of Management Accounting Research*, 12: 1–17.

Ilgren, N. B., Fisher, C. D., and Taylor, M. S. (1979). 'Consequences of Individual Feedback on Behaviour in Organizations', *Journal of Applied Psychology*, 64: 383–84.

Ittner, C., Larcker, D. and Randell, T. (2003). Performance implications of strategic performance measurement in financial services firms. *Accounting, Organizations and Society*, 28(7–8): 715–41.

Ittner, C. D. and Larcker, D. F. (1995). Total Quality Management and the Choice of Information and Reward Systems, *Journal of Accounting Research*, 33 (Suppl.): 1–34.

—— —— (1997). 'Quality Strategy, Strategic Control Systems, and Organizational Performance', *Accounting, Organizations and Society*, 22: 293–314.

—— —— (1998*a*). 'Innovations in Performance Measurement, Trends and Research Implications', *Journal of Management Accounting Research*, 10: 205–38.

—— —— (1998*b*). 'Are Non-financial Measures Leading Indicators of Financial Performance? An Analysis of Customer Satisfaction', *Journal of Accounting Research*, 26 (Suppl.): 1–34.

—— —— (2000). 'Determinants of Performance Measure Choices in Worker Incentive Plans', Sidney G. Winter Lecture in Accounting, University of Iowa, November.

—— —— (2003). Coming up short on nonfinancial performance measurement, *Harvard Business Review, November*, 88–95.

—— —— Nagar, V., and Rajan, M. V. (1999). 'Supplier Selection, Monitoring Practices and Firm Performance', *Journal of Accounting and Public Policy*, 18 (3): 253–81.

Kalagnanam, S. S and Lindsay. R. M. (1999). 'The Use of Organic Models of Control in JIT Firms: Generalizing Woodward's Findings to Modern Manufacturing Practices', *Accounting, Organizations and Society*, 24(1): 1–30.

Kaplan, R. S. and Norton, D. P. (1996). *The Balanced Scorecard: Translating Strategy into Action*. Boston: Harvard Business School Press.

—— —— (2001). *The Strategy-Focused Organization: How Balanced Scorecard Companies Thrive in the New Business Environment*. Boston: Harvard Business School Press.

—— —— (2004). *Strategy Maps—Converting Intangible Assets into Tangible Outcomes*. Boston: Harvard Business School Press.

Khandwalla, P. (1977). *Design of Organizations*. New York: Harcourt Brace Jovanovich.

Langfield-Smith, K. (1997). 'Management Control Systems and Strategy: a Critical Review', *Accounting, Organizations and Society*, 22(2): 207–32.

Larcker, D. F. (1983). 'The Association Between Performance Plan Adoption and Corporate Capital Investment', *Journal of Accounting and Economics*, 5: 3–30.

Lawrence, P. and Lorsch, J. (1967). *Organization and Environment*. Homewood, IL: Irwin.

Lebas, M. (1994). 'Managerial Accounting in France: Overview of Past Tradition and Current Practice', *European Accounting Review*, 3: 471–87.

Lipe, M. and Salterio, S. (2000). 'The Balanced Scorecard: Judgemental Effects of Common and Unique Performance Measures', *Accounting Review*, 74(3): 283–99.

Locke, E. A., Shaw, K. N., Saari, L. M., and Latham, G. P. (1981). 'Goal Setting and Task Performance', *Psychological Bulletin*, 90: 125–52.

Luft, J. L. and Shields, M. D. (2003). 'Mapping Management Accounting: Making Structural Models From Theory-based Empirical Research', *Accounting, Organizations and Society*, 28(2–3): 169–249.

Lynch, R. L., and Cross, K. F. (1995). *Measure Up! Yardsticks for Continuous Improvement.* Cambridge, MA: Basil Blackwell.

Malina, M. A., and Selto, F. H. (2001). 'Communicating and Controlling Strategy: An Empirical Study of the Effectiveness of the Balanced Scorecard', *Journal of Management Accounting Research*, 13: 47–90.

Merchant, K. (1981). 'The Design of the Corporate Budgeting System: Influences on Managerial Behavior and Performance', *Accounting Review*, 4: 813–29.

—— (1987). 'How and Why Firms Disregard the Controllability Principle', in W. J. Bruns and R. S. Kaplan (ed.), *Accounting and Management: Field Study Perspectives.* Boston: Harvard Business School Press, pp. 316–38.

Mia, L and Chenhall, R. H. (1994). 'The Usefulness of Management Accounting Systems, Functional Differentiation and Managerial Effectiveness', *Accounting, Organizations and Society*, 19(1): 1–13.

Miles, R. W. and Snow, C. C. (1978). *Organizational Strategy, Structure and Process.* New York: McGraw-Hill.

Milgrom, P. and Roberts, J. (1992). *Economics, Organization and Management.* Englewood Cliffs, NJ: Prentice Hall.

Miller, D. and Friesen, P. H. (1982). 'Innovation in Conservative and Entrepreneurial Firms: Two Models of Strategic Momentum', *Strategic Management Journal*, 3(1): 1–25.

Mintzberg, H. (1987). 'Crafting Strategy', *Harvard Business Review*, 65(4): 66–75.

Moers, F. (2005). 'Discretion and Bias in Performance Evaluation: the Impact of Diversity and Subjectivity', *Accounting, Organizations and Society*, 30(1): 67–80.

Nager, V. (1998). 'The Information Content of Balanced Scorecard Measures; Evidence from the Retail Banking Industry', Working Paper, University of Michigan.

Neely, A., Adams, C., and Kennerley, K. (2002). *The Performance Prism: The Scorecard for Measuring and Managing Business Success.* London: *Financial Times*–Prentice Hall.

Ouchi, W. (1979). 'A Conceptual Framework for the Design of Organizational Control Mechanisms', *Management Science*, 25(9): 833–48.

Perera, S., Harrison, G., and Poole, M. (1997). 'Customer-focused Manufacturing Strategy and the Use of Operations-based Non-financial Performance Measures Systems: A Research Note', *Accounting, Organizations and Society*, 22(6): 557–72.

Perrow, C. (1970). *Organizational Analysis: a Sociological View.* Belmont, CA: Wadsworth.

Prendegast, C. and Topel, R. (1993). 'Discretion and Bias in Performance Evaluation', *European Economic Review*, 37: 355–65.

Porter, M. (1980). *Competitive Strategy.* New York: Free Press.

Quinn, J. B. (1980). *Strategies for Change: Logical Incrementalism*. Homewood, IL: Richard D. Irwin.

Rappaport, A. (1986). *Creating Shareholder Value*. New York: Free Press.

Rimmer, M., Macneil, J., Chenhall, R.H., Langfield-Smith, K., and Watts, L. (1996). *Reinventing Competitiveness: Achieving Best Practice in Australia*. Melbourne: Pitman.

Sandt, J., Schaeffer, U., and Weber. J. (2001). 'Balanced Performance Measurement Systems and Manager Satisfaction—Empirical Evidence from a German Study', Working Paper, WHU-Otto Beisheim Graduate School of Management.

Schiff, A. D. and Hoffman, L. R. (1996). 'An Exploration of the Use of Financial and Nonfinancial Measures of Performance in a Service Organization', *Behavioral Research in Accounting*, 8: 134–53.

Scott, T. W. and Tiessen, P. (1999). 'Performance Measurement and Managerial Teams', *Accounting, Organizations and Society*, 24(3): 107–25.

Silk, S. (1998). 'Automating the Balanced Scorecard', *Management Accounting*, 78(11): 38–42.

Sim, K. L. and Killough, L. N. (1998). 'The Performance Effects of Complementarities between Manufacturing Practices and Management Accounting Systems', *Journal of Management Accounting Research*, 10: 325–46.

Simons, R. (1987). 'Accounting Control Systems and Business Strategy: An Empirical Analysis', *Accounting, Organizations and Society*, 12: 357–74.

—— (1995). *Levers of Control: How Managers use Innovative Controls Systems to Drive Strategic Renewal*. Boston: Harvard University Press.

—— (2000). *Performance Measurement & Control Systems for Implementing Strategy*. Upper Saddle River, NJ: Prentice Hall.

Snyder, A. V. (1995). *Value-based Management: Highlighting the Resource Allocation Challenge*. Boston: Braxton Associates.

Stern, J. M., Stewart, G. B., III, and Chew, D. H. Jr. (1995). 'The EVA Financial Management System', *Journal of Applied Corporate Finance*, 8: 32–46.

Stewart, G. B. III. (1991). *The Quest for Value: A Guide for Senior Managers*. New York: Harper Business.

—— (1995). 'EVA works—But Not if You Make These Mistakes', *Fortune*, 131(8): 117–18.

Symons, R. T. and Jacobs, R. A. (1995). 'A Total Quality Management-based Incentive System Supporting Total Quality Management Implementation', *Production and Operations Management*, 4(3): 228–41.

Thompson, J. D. (1967). *Organizations in Action*. New York: McGraw-Hill.

Wallace, J. S. (1998). 'Adopting Residual Income-based Compensation Plans: Do You Get What You Paid For?', *Journal of Accounting and Economics*, 24: 275–300.

Woodward, J. (1965). *Industrial Organization: Theory and Practice*. Oxford: Oxford University Press.

Young, S. M. and Selto, F. H. (1993). 'Explaining Cross-sectional Workgroup Performance Differences in a JIT Facility: a Critical Appraisal of a Field-based Study', *Journal of Management Accounting Research* (Fall): 300–26.

6 Integrated cost management

Robin Cooper
Regine Slagmulder

6.1 Overview

Cost management techniques form part of an integrated cost management programme when the output of one technique becomes the input for another technique and the techniques mutually reinforce each other. The advantage of integrated cost management programmes over the use of single techniques is the additional cost reductions that can be achieved. In this chapter we describe two forms of integrated cost management programmes, internal and external. Internal integrated cost management programmes operate within a single entity and typically create cost reduction pressures across the entire product life cycle. External integrated cost management programmes operate interorganizationally by linking the cost management programmes of buyers and suppliers, and by supporting joint buyer–supplier efforts to reduce costs.

6.2 Internal integrated cost management programmes[1]

6.2.1 INTRODUCTION

For many firms the ability to manufacture products at low cost is critical to their success. When particularly aggressive cost management is required, it is sometimes insufficient to use independent cost management techniques to create the desired cost reduction pressures. Instead, multiple techniques are required that operate in an integrated manner to reduce costs.

In this section of the chapter, we describe the internal integrated cost management programme at Olympus Optical Company. This programme consists of five distinct cost management techniques that together create aggressive cost reduction pressures across the entire product life cycle.

6.2.2 THE COMPANY

We studied the cost management practices of the Consumer Products division of Olympus Optical Company. We adopted an in-depth field research approach because a detailed understanding of the firm's entire product cost management programme was required adequately to explore the ways in which the firm applies cost management techniques across the product life cycle. We chose this research site for four reasons. First, Olympus Optical was known operate to in a highly competitive environment that demanded aggressive cost management. A highly competitive environment was chosen to ensure that the cost management systems documented were a critical aspect of firm survival (Khandwalla 1972). Second, the Consumer Products division was part of a company that had a reputation for having a mature and sophisticated cost management programme (Cooper 1995). Third, the division was known to operate as a lean enterprise. The adoption of lean design and production principles increases the effectiveness of cost management both during the product development process, such as through the application of target costing, and during manufacturing (Womack and Jones 1996).

The specific product development project used as the basis for the research, the new Stylus Zoom camera, was selected based upon two criteria. These two selection criteria were designed to ensure that we could observe and document the full spectrum of Olympus Optical's cost management practices in action. First, Olympus Optical management viewed the project as creating significant technical and cost reduction challenges for their product engineers. The new Stylus Zoom camera was the first 'mother' camera, i.e. it contained components that were going to be used both across the members of a family of cameras and for several generations of that family. Previously, camera components were typically only used in a single model. Second, the new Stylus Zoom camera was being developed during a period of yen appreciation that was placing considerable pressure on Olympus Optical to reduce costs even more aggressively than usual. The effective worldwide selling prices of the division's products, when specified in yen, were dropping. This price reduction caused the target costs of new products to fall and the firm was having trouble meeting them for some products, including the Stylus Zoom.

6.2.3 FIVE INTERNAL COST MANAGEMENT TECHNIQUES

The observations at Olympus Optical revealed the use of five major techniques for internal cost management: target costing, product-specific Kaizen costing, general Kaizen costing, functional group management, and standard costing. Each of these techniques is discussed in depth in this section.

6.2.3.1 Target costing[2]

At Olympus Optical, target costing was applied as a feed-forward cost reduction technique during the design stage for all new products. The first step in setting target costs at Olympus Optical was to identify the price point at which a new camera model would sell. Once the price point was identified, the free on board (FOB) price was calculated by subtracting the appropriate margin of the dealers and the US subsidiary plus any import costs, such as freight and import duty. Target costs were established by subtracting the product's desired target profit margin from its FOB price. To achieve the target cost reduction objective, established by comparing the product's target cost to its current estimated cost, Olympus Optical product engineers tried to find creative ways to realize the desired level of functionality and quality at the target costs. Aggressive cost reduction was achieved at Olympus Optical by applying value engineering in three different areas. First, the number of parts in each unit was targeted for reduction. Second, expensive, labour-intensive, and mechanical adjustment processes were eliminated wherever possible. Third, metal and glass components were replaced with less expensive plastic ones where appropriate. In addition, pressure was mounted on the firm's suppliers (both internal and external) more aggressively to reduce costs.

Approximately 20 per cent of the time the current estimated cost was equal to, or less than, the target cost, and the product design was immediately released to the production group at Tatsuno, the firm's initial camera production plant. The other 80 per cent of the time, however, further analysis by the research and development (R&D) group was required. First, marketing was asked if the price point could be increased sufficiently so that the target cost was equal to the estimated cost. If the price could be increased by an appropriate amount, the product was released to the production group. If the market price could not be increased sufficiently, the effect of reducing the functionality of the product was explored. Reducing the product's functionality decreased its estimated cost to manufacture. If these reductions were sufficient and did not cause the target selling price to fall, the product was released to production. If it was not possible to increase the price or decrease the production cost sufficiently to reduce the estimated cost below the target cost, a life cycle profitability analysis was performed. In this analysis, the effect of potential cost reductions over the production life of the product was included in the financial analysis of the product's profitability. The product was released if these life cycle savings were sufficient to make the product's overall profitability acceptable. If, even with these additional cost savings included, the estimated costs were still too high, the project was abandoned unless some strategic reason for keeping the product could be identified.

Target costing was considered of particular importance by Olympus Optical's senior management because the manufacturing phase of the life cycle of modern point-and-shoot compact cameras was short, with the typical compact camera only being on the market for between twelve and eighteen months. This short manufacturing phase made it difficult for Olympus Optical's product engineers to correct any design problems that led to high manufacturing costs, after the product had entered production. Thus, the short life cycle encouraged the firm to solve any cost problems during the design, as opposed to the manufacturing, phase.

6.2.3.2 Product-specific Kaizen costing

The existence of product-specific Kaizen costing highlighted the importance that Olympus's management attached to achieving the cost reduction objective established by the target costing system. Like target costing, the unit of analysis for product-specific Kaizen costing was the product, and its objective was specified in financial terms. However, product-specific Kaizen costing activities were initiated to correct any cost overruns incurred during the manufacturing phase that were caused by design issues. Thus, it extended the product development process into the early stages of manufacturing. At Olympus Optical, product-specific Kaizen costing was only applied to strategic products that had significant cost overruns in the earliest stages of the manufacturing phase.

The unwillingness of Olympus Optical management to launch products that had not attained their target costs reflects management's belief that the discipline of target costing would be lost if too many products were launched that exceeded their target costs. In particular, they were concerned that the workforce would begin to accept that it did not matter if target costs were not achieved, since they could be achieved later during the manufacturing phase. However, for strategic products the cost of not launching was considered higher than the cost associated with any loss of discipline in the target costing process. Thus, the existence of product-specific Kaizen costing and the way it is used at Olympus Optical indicates a sophisticated cost–benefit trade-off with respect to cost management across the life of the firm's products.

The product-specific Kaizen costing process was initiated when one of Olympus Optical's new products failed to meet its target cost. Such products were quickly redesigned during the early stages of the manufacturing phase to bring their costs in line with their target costs. The willingness of the firm to take such corrective actions was dependent upon three factors. First, the magnitude of the expected volume of product sales: the higher the sales volume, the more willing the firm was to take corrective actions. Second, the anticipated magnitude of the investment required to reduce costs: as the magnitude of the investment increased, the firm was less likely to approve the cost reduction project. Third, the potential savings had to be sufficient to justify undertaking a special cost reduction programme.

The practice of product-specific Kaizen costing at Olympus Optical was observed during the new Stylus Zoom camera project. Problems with the cost of the new product surfaced during trial production when its costs were found to be about 10 per cent above target. Furthermore, when the product entered mass production at Tatsuno, its costs were found to be even higher and did not fall as much as expected. Overall, the production costs were 5 per cent higher than the trial production costs, leading to a total cost overrun of 15 per cent. Under normal conditions, the 10 per cent cost overrun at the trial production stage would have led to the postponement of the launch of the new Stylus or complete cancellation of the product. However, not only was the new Stylus viewed as a 'flagship' product but it was also the first of a new family of products designed to increase parts commonality. Delaying the launch of the new Stylus would have meant that the evaluation of the parts commonality programme would have to be postponed. Given the strategic importance attached to this new product and the parts commonality programme, postponement or cancellation were considered unacceptable.

The window of opportunity for cost reduction for the new Stylus was shorter than might first be anticipated for such a high-volume product with a multiyear manufacturing life. Olympus Optical management believed that the product-specific Kaizen window closed eleven months after product launch. The cost of the new Stylus was reduced in four primary ways: (*a*) to reduce the number of parts in the product; (*b*) to replace more expensive materials with less expensive ones; (*c*) to manage supplier costs; and (*d*) to transfer production overseas where overall costs were lower. The primary rule applied to post-launch cost reduction was that the product's functionality and quality were not allowed to change. From the customer's perspective, the last Stylus Zoom off the production line would be identical to the first one.

6.2.3.3 General Kaizen costing

General Kaizen costing, or production cost control and reduction as it was called at Olympus Optical, was applied during the manufacturing stage of the product's life. Unlike target costing and product-specific Kaizen costing, the design of the product was treated as given and the cost reduction process focused on the way the product was manufactured. Thus, the unit of analysis for general Kaizen costing was the production process, not the product per se. Reducing the cost of production processes was an effective way to save costs because many production processes were used across several generations of products. Therefore, savings achieved during the manufacturing cycle of a particular product could continue to be replicated long after that product had been withdrawn or replaced.

General Kaizen costing consisted of setting cost reduction targets for production processes and empowering the workforce to find ways to achieve them. Olympus Optical's production cost control and reduction approach focused primarily on removing material, labour, and some overhead costs from products; for example, selling, general, and administrative costs associated with the control and procurement departments were included in the cost reduction objectives. The general Kaizen costing system at Olympus Optical was mature and had been widely applied for many years. At Tatsuno, individual cost reduction objectives were set for each assembly line and, thus, each internally produced component. These objectives were designed to be challenging, but attainable.

6.2.3.4 Functional group management

Functional group management focused on making Olympus Optical's production processes more efficient. Like general Kaizen costing, the design of the firm's products was assumed to be given and it was the efficiency and yield of the production processes that were the focus of improvement. However, the primary difference between general Kaizen costing and functional group management was the ability to reduce costs through increased output as well as through increased efficiency of manufacturing. Like general Kaizen costing, the savings were non-design in nature. All production processes at Olympus Optical were systematically subjected to functional group management. The emergence of this new cost management technique focused on the manufacturing phase indicated that Olympus Optical management perceived that there were further savings that could be achieved in that phase of the product life cycle.

Functional group management consisted of breaking the production process at Tatsuno into ten autonomous groups and treating them as profit centres instead of cost centres.[3] Functional group management was introduced at Olympus Optical for two reasons. First, the switch to profit as opposed to cost centres enabled the production groups to include ways to increase the throughput of the production processes under their control into their improvement activities. In addition, the functional group management system supported actions that increased both costs and profits by increasing revenues, whereas these actions were not supported by the general Kaizen system, which focused solely on reducing costs. The second motivation for the functional group management system was the change in mindset that it induced. Converting the production lines to profit centres allowed the groups to understand better their contribution to the firm's overall profitability. The motivation for inducing this mindset change was primarily driven by the observation that general Kaizen costing systems tended to lose their effectiveness over time. By switching from a cost to a profit perspective and by operating in a bottom-up as opposed to a top-down manner, the functional group management system helped revitalize Olympus Optical's general Kaizen costing system.

By finding ways to increase their output levels, the groups increased their ability to generate 'revenues' and hence profit. As the groups increased their revenues, the capacity of the factory also increased, leading to real performance improvements. For example, in the first three years of functional group management, approximately 80 per cent of the profit improvements were from changes that increased output; the remaining 20 per cent of improvements were from cost reduction initiatives, such as increased use of unmanned processing and improvements in shortening processing time.

6.2.3.5 Standard costing

Olympus Optical used its standard cost system primarily to achieve cost containment. The standard cost system helped identify cost problems, which were subsequently addressed by the other cost management techniques. Product costs, as reported by the standard costing system, were mainly used for three purposes. The first was to determine if three months into production, new products were indeed being manufactured at their target costs. Three months was used as the cut-off because experience had shown that a product's manufacturing processes tended to mature over that time frame; therefore, changes in reported costs were typically much less significant after three months. There was little use of the reported product costs for strategic decision-making purposes as the target costing process primarily helped determine the firm's product mix and profitability. Second, reported product costs were used to ensure that production processes were operating at the expected level of efficiency. Actual performance was compared to standard performance and the variances computed. These variances were used to create cost containment pressures on the work groups. Third, standard product costs were used to identify ways to make unprofitable products profitable. If an existing product became unprofitable, Olympus Optical had three options. First, it could do nothing and wait until a new model replaced the existing one.

Second, it could accelerate the replacement of the product. Finally, it could establish a more aggressive general Kaizen costing objective.

6.2.4 KEY CHARACTERISTICS OF THE FIVE INTERNAL COST MANAGEMENT TECHNIQUES

Based upon statements made by Olympus management and from our own field observations, the total amount of resources dedicated to cost management at Olympus Optical was high, as anticipated for a firm in an intensely competitive environment (Khandwalla 1972). The five cost management techniques differed in four key aspects: the stage in the product life cycle at which they were applied; their objective of achieving either cost reduction or cost containment; their focus on either product design or production process; and, finally, their application on an ad hoc, as opposed to systematic, basis (Table 6.1).

6.2.4.1 Stage in the product life cycle

At Olympus Optical, cost management techniques are applied from the early stages of product development until the product is discontinued. Our observations showed that while only one cost management technique was applied during the product design phase (target costing), four distinct techniques were applied during the manufacturing phase (product-specific Kaizen costing, general Kaizen costing, functional group management, and standard costing).

6.2.4.2 Cost reduction versus cost containment

Of the five cost management techniques observed, four were utilized for cost reduction and one for cost containment. Cost reduction sets out actively to lower costs to pre-established levels, while cost containment is more passive and consists of ensuring that previously

Table 6.1 Key Characteristics of the five cost management techniques

Cost management technique	Phase in product life cycle	Objective	Focus	Application
Target costing	Product design	Cost reduction	Product design	Systematic
Product-specific Kaizen costing	Manufacturing	Cost reduction	Product design	Ad hoc
General Kaizen costing	Manufacturing	Cost reduction	Production process	Systematic
Functional group management	Manufacturing	Cost reduction	Production process	Systematic
Standard costing	Manufacturing	Cost containment	Production process	Systematic

achieved cost reduction objectives are sustained. Target costing was used in the design phase as a cost reduction technique with the explicit objective of reducing the anticipated manufacturing cost of a product to a pre-established level—the target cost. Of the four techniques applied during the manufacturing phase, three—product-specific Kaizen costing, general Kaizen costing, and functional group management—were used as cost reduction techniques, while standard costing was used as a cost containment technique.

The costs reported by the standard cost system reflected actual performance and this technique was used to ensure that the costs did not increase during the manufacturing phase. If the reported cost of a product did increase to unacceptable levels, for example due to increases in component purchase prices, then the product was subjected to general Kaizen costing until its cost was brought back in line with previously established cost reduction objectives. This limited role for standard costing might seem surprising given the attention paid to activity-based cost (ABC) management in recent years, but it reflects the way that Olympus Optical had designed its cost management programme (Kaplan and Cooper 1999).

The dominance of techniques devoted to cost reduction as opposed to cost containment is in line with their individual purposes. Cost containment has a monitoring role designed to ensure that previously achieved cost reduction objectives are maintained; therefore, it would be surprising if the firm dedicated multiple techniques and the associated resources to such a passive activity. In contrast, cost reduction, which is a more open-ended, active objective, is more likely to require multiple techniques if significant cost savings are available.

6.2.4.3 Product design versus process improvement

Cost management during the design phase consisted solely of the cost reduction technique target costing, which necessarily focused on improving the product design. In contrast, cost management in the manufacturing phase consisted of three cost reduction techniques: product-specific Kaizen costing, general Kaizen costing, and functional group management. Of these three techniques only one, product-specific Kaizen costing, focused on product redesign. The purpose of the other two techniques was to render the production processes more efficient. These two techniques played different but reinforcing roles. General Kaizen costing focused on reducing the cost of performing production processes, while functional group management focused on increasing the output of the production processes either by speeding them up or by increasing their yields. It also motivated individuals in the workforce to make trade-offs between increased output and increased costs.

6.2.4.4 Ad hoc versus systematic application

Of the five techniques observed at Olympus Optical, only one—product-specific Kaizen costing—was applied in an ad hoc manner. Olympus Optical management stated that product-specific Kaizen costing was only used for those products that failed to achieve their target costs, but were launched for strategic reasons. Thus, the purpose of product-specific Kaizen costing was to access design-related savings that might have been missed during the design phase due to competitive time pressure. Management viewed target costing and product-specific Kaizen costing as part of a continuous process with the objective of achieving the target cost through innovative product design.

Management's rationale in applying product-specific Kaizen costing in an ad hoc manner was that changing a product's design and hence the associated production processes during the manufacturing phase was highly disruptive, and, in most cases, the savings anticipated for products that had achieved their target costs were not sufficient to justify the effort. Consequently, the technique was only used for high-volume products launched above their target costs. Furthermore, it was applied immediately after the product was launched and only in the early stages of manufacturing to ensure that an adequate number of units were sold after the intervention to justify the upfront investment. One possible interpretation of the way that product-specific Kaizen costing was applied is that Olympus Optical management might believe that there is a limit to the level of cost reduction that can be achieved via product design and that the firm's target costs are close to that level. Consequently, they might consider it is not worth trying to achieve additional savings when a product is launched at its target cost. In contrast, the benefits were believed to outweigh the costs when a product was launched above its target cost, as was the case with the new Stylus Zoom camera. All of the other cost management techniques were applied systematically to all of the firm's products, including those subjected to product-specific Kaizen costing (although their application was delayed to some extent).

Our observations also suggest that Olympus Optical management had spent a lot of time thinking through the design of its cost management programme. For example, the way that product-specific Kaizen costing was applied demonstrates how carefully they managed the cost–benefit trade-offs, with cost management techniques only being applied in those instances where the benefits were believed to outweigh the costs. Similarly, the recent development of functional group management in the manufacturing phase with the aim of revitalizing the general Kaizen costing programme indicates that management was still actively improving the programme. Furthermore, it suggests that management believed that significant savings via production process improvement were possible even if a general Kaizen costing system was in place.

6.2.5 INTEGRATION OF THE FIVE INTERNAL COST MANAGEMENT TECHNIQUES

The cost management programme at Olympus Optical consisted of more than just five independent cost management techniques; it was an integrated programme with the outcomes from some of the techniques being inputs into the application of other techniques. Cost system integration started with the target costing system whose outputs acted as inputs to the product-specific and general Kaizen techniques and the standard costing system. The interaction of the target costing system and the general Kaizen system was reinforced by the product-specific Kaizen costing system; both of these systems ensured that no excessive pressure was placed on the general Kaizen system to reduce costs during the manufacturing phase. Integration continued with the new functional group management system expanding the scope and reinforcing the effectiveness of the general Kaizen costing system. It ended with the interaction between the standard costing system and the general Kaizen costing system.

The integration between target costing and product-specific Kaizen costing was seamless with continual redesign of the product. Target costing also reinforced the effectiveness of the product-specific Kaizen costing system by identifying products that had cost overrun problems before they entered production. Thus, the target costing system provided an early warning of the need to initiate a product-specific Kaizen costing intervention. The only real difference between the design activities under the two techniques was the ability to change product functionality in target costing and not in product-specific Kaizen costing, because management had decreed that the functionality of the first product off the production line had to be the same as the last one. The other impact of launching the product was to freeze the design for the first few months of production until the workforce was efficiently producing the new product. During this hiatus, the engineers were still busy identifying ways to reduce the cost of the new product through redesign.

Target costing was also used to reinforce the application of general Kaizen costing because it helped identify the savings that should be achieved during the manufacturing phase and isolated them from the cost reductions that could reasonably be anticipated during the product development phase. If the target costs of new products were appropriately established, only achievable cost reduction objectives would be set for the general Kaizen and functional group management systems. Thus, an effective, well-designed target costing system through its life cycle profitability analyses helps ensure that excessive cost reduction pressures are neither required nor applied during the manufacturing phase. This interaction is important because general Kaizen costing (and for that matter any cost reduction technique) is most effective when the cost reduction objectives are considered achievable by the workforce even if they require considerable effort.

The product-specific Kaizen costing system played a similar role in ensuring that the general Kaizen costing system was not subjected to excessive pressure to reduce costs in the manufacturing phase. It achieves this objective by continuing to reduce costs through product redesign in the manufacturing phase. If the product's costs can be reduced to their target levels (or as close as possible), the pressure on the general Kaizen costing system will be kept at acceptable levels.

The anticipated savings from general Kaizen costing typically were not included in the target costing analysis. However, if the life cycle profitability analysis indicated that the product would not achieve its target profit margin objectives, the anticipated general Kaizen savings were imputed into the analysis. If these savings were sufficient to allow the product to achieve its target margin, the product development process continued. If the savings were insufficient and the product was not considered strategic, the development project was cancelled. The decision to exclude the anticipated general Kaizen savings from the target costing analysis reflects a conservative approach on the part of management.

The interaction between target costing and standard costing was subtler. In firms that do not have sophisticated target costing systems, the role of the standard cost system includes determining whether new products (as well as existing ones) are profitable. By reducing the importance of the product costing role through the use of target costing and of operational control through Kaizen costing and functional group management, Olympus Optical management enabled the standard cost system to be focused solely on cost containment (Monden 1995; Kaplan and Atkinson 1998). Thus, the standard cost system is not seen as a source of cost savings at Olympus Optical; its primary role is to support the other systems and ensure that cost savings achieved by those programmes are maintained.

General Kaizen costing and functional group management were also integrated. The role of the functional group management system was to enhance the general Kaizen system by giving the workforce a new way to think about cost reduction. In particular, it shifted the task from cost reduction to profit enhancement. This shift expanded the type of activities that the workforce could consider to include ways to increase throughput (these actions were captured by increases in 'revenue') and trade-offs between enhanced revenue and increased costs (these actions were captured by increases in 'profits'). In addition, Olympus Optical management believed that the shift to profit enhancement from cost reduction led to greater employee motivation to achieve cost reduction.

The standard costing system was modified with the introduction of functional group management. The cost pools were conformed to match the functional groups and certain reporting processes were adapted to supply the information required by the new technique. These modifications enabled the standard costing system to provide the functional group management system with the cost information it needed to generate profit and loss statements for the groups.

The general Kaizen system was thus subsumed into the functional group management system. However, the general Kaizen system kept its separate identity because it was used in tandem with the standard costing system to contain costs. When reported standard costs climbed above previously achieved levels, new cost reduction targets were established for the general Kaizen system to bring reported costs back in line. It did not matter what caused the increase in reported costs, loss of efficiency, or increased input prices levels; the objective was to keep costs at previously achieved levels so that budgeted profits would be sustained.

In summary, our field observations show that Olympus Optical actively uses the outputs of some of its cost management techniques as inputs to other techniques. The target costing system integrates with the product-specific Kaizen costing system to bring product costs down to target levels where possible and with the general Kaizen and functional group management system to help ensure that life cycle profitability is adequate. Functional group management reinforces the general Kaizen costing system by expanding the range of actions considered and the nature of the motivation utilized to achieve the cost management objectives in the manufacturing phase. Finally, the standard costing system is used to trigger extra cost reduction activities by the workforce via establishing new objectives for the general Kaizen costing system when the reported cost of a product increases to unacceptable levels. The integration of the various techniques is illustrated in Figure 6.1.

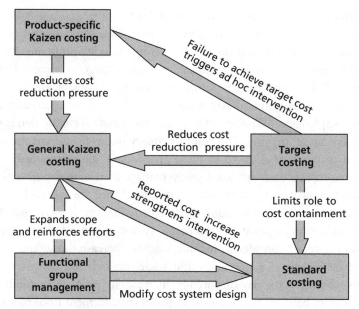

Figure 6.1 Distribution of cost management techniques across the product life cycle

6.2.6 THE BENEFITS OF INTERNAL INTEGRATION

Olympus management argued that integration of the various cost management techniques was necessary if the firm was to achieve its profit objectives. They clearly believed that integration provided additional savings above and beyond those associated with the individual techniques. They associated three benefits with the integrated programme compared to simply relying upon a standard costing system to manage costs. First, they claimed that it led to overall lower costs throughout the product life cycle. Not only did products cost less at launch (an outcome of target costing), but also the ongoing cost reduction activities ensured that they cost less—and by an increasing amount—all the way through to discontinuance (see Figure 6.2). Second, Olympus' experience showed that products were launched on time more frequently. Without the programme and, in particular, the discipline of both target costing and product-specific Kaizen costing, more product launches would have to be delayed to bring their costs into line with their selling prices. Third, Olympus Optical management believed that the number of new product introduction projects that were cancelled because the product costs were too high was reduced. The tight discipline of target costing with its emphasis on target prices forced the design process to be cost-sensitive from the very beginning.

6.2.7 IMPLICATIONS TO PRACTICE

Senior management in firms that compete aggressively on cost should consider adopting a cost management programme like the one at Olympus Optical. Such a programme will necessary rely upon multiple cost management techniques that are applied in an integrated manner to different phases of the product life cycle. These multiple techniques will have

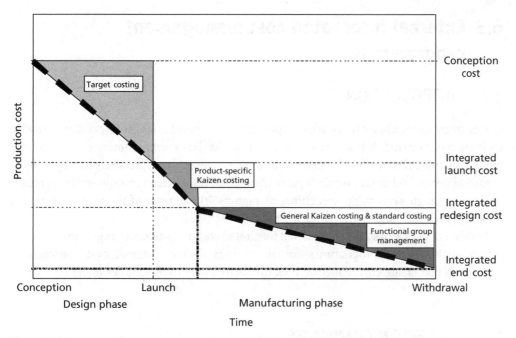

Figure 6.2 Integrated cost management programme at Olympus Optical

different objectives (cost reduction vs. cost containment) and a different focus (product design vs. production processes). Furthermore, some of the techniques might be applied systematically to all products while others might be applied in an ad hoc manner on products that require special attention. Integrating the various techniques that make up a cost management programme can lead to superior overall performance as measured by on-time launches of profitable products.

The exact nature of the programme that is adopted, the techniques that are applied, and the way that they are both applied and integrated will probably differ; for example, Olympus Optical does not use ABC. Two reasons for the non-adoption of ABC at Olympus Optical suggest themselves. First, Olympus may not need an ABC system to obtain accurate product costs because all of its products are produced in high volumes. Consequently, its traditional unit-based cost system reports accurate costs because the batch and product sustaining costs are simply not large enough to create significant distortions in reported costs. Second, Olympus may not require the cost reduction insights provided by ABC because of its use of general Kaizen costing and functional group management. These techniques might substitute, at least to some extent, for the insights provided by an activity analysis of the firm's production process. However, other firms, especially those that have high levels of diversity in both production volume and product complexity, might want to include an activity-based system in their integrated cost management programme. Some firms might not want to adopt target costing because of high levels of innovation in their products. Target costing works best in environments where the cost information about previous generations of products is highly predictive of the costs of future generations. Finally, other firms might want to integrate the six sigma efforts into their cost management programme.

6.3 **External integrated cost management programmes**[4]

6.3.1 INTRODUCTION

For many firms the ability to source components and subassemblies at low cost is critical to their success. For such firms, it is not sufficient to just be experts at internal cost management; they must also be skilled at external cost management, i.e. aggressively managing costs across their supply chain. This skill is particularly important in lean enterprises that typically outsource a high percentage, sometimes as high as 70 per cent, of the manufacture and design of the total value added of their products.

In this section, we describe the external integrated cost management programmes in three supply chains. These programmes contain various distinct external cost management techniques that create cost reduction pressures across the buyer–supplier interface.

6.3.2 THE SEVEN COMPANIES

We studied the external cost management programmes at seven Japanese manufacturing companies, belonging to three different supply chains (see the Appendix for a short description of each company). Komatsu was selected because of its reputation for effectively managing costs across its supply chain. Toyo Radiator was chosen because it had a particularly rich and effective relationship with Komatsu. Isuzu was chosen because of its reputation as one of Japan's best practitioners of value engineering and cost management during the product development phase. Jidosha Kiki Company (JKC) was identified as a highly effective supplier by Isuzu management. Tokyo Motors was selected for its reputation for undertaking thorough customer requirements analyses that were tied to its target costing system. Its first-tier supplier, Yokohama Corporation, and its second-tier supplier, Kamakura Iron Works, were chosen since they formed a three-tier supply chain that Tokyo Motors' management considered particularly successful at practising external integrated cost management.

6.3.3 THREE EXTERNAL COST MANAGEMENT TECHNIQUES

Our observations at the seven companies revealed the use of three major external cost management techniques: functionality-price-quality (FPQ) trade-offs, interorganizational cost investigations, and concurrent cost management. At the heart of each technique was a set of chained target costing systems. Target costing systems are said to be chained when the output of the buyer's target costing system—the target cost of an outsourced item—

becomes the target selling price of the supplier's target costing system. Thus, each of the three external cost management techniques observed are already integrated via the buyer's and supplier's target costing systems. Consequently, they are considered interorganizational cost management (IOCM) techniques. Each of these IOCM techniques is discussed in depth in this section.

6.3.3.1 Functionality-price-quality trade-offs

An FPQ trade-off is initiated when the supplier determines that the manufacturing cost of the outsourced item is expected to exceed its target cost and that the only way to reduce its costs to the target level is by relaxing the functionality and/or quality specifications of the outsourced item in ways that are acceptable to the buyer. Once such relaxations are identified, the supplier requests a meeting to obtain buyer approval. Successfully identifying such opportunities helps the supplier ensure that it earns an adequate return.

Typically, an FPQ trade-off is an outcome of a target costing analysis. It can be initiated at any time in the design process up to the release of the item into mass production. Particularly successful FPQs were observed between Tokyo Motors and Yokohama. Yokohama's success at initiating these interventions relies upon the in-depth knowledge that its engineers have developed about the way that Tokyo Motors uses its products. This knowledge allows their engineers to identify where and to what extent relaxations in the specifications of the outsourced item are likely to be acceptable to Tokyo Motors buyers. Examples of changes in specifications that result from FPQ trade-offs include requesting that the colour of a part be limited to black or silver instead of matching the colour of the end product; requesting that surface tolerances be relaxed when they are not visible to the end-user; reducing the number of strengthening bars; and reducing the material content without reducing the strength of the part.

6.3.3.2 Interorganizational cost investigations

An interorganizational cost investigation is initiated whenever a firm in the supply chain determines that it is unable to manufacture a part at its target cost and that an FPQ trade-off will not produce sufficient cost reductions to resolve the problem. The major difference between an FPQ trade-off and an interorganizational cost investigation is the ability to include design engineers from more than two firms in the supply chain.

There are two ways in which costs can be reduced through interorganizational cost investigations. First, the need to perform activities can be reduced or avoided by redesigning the product and the components it contains to take full advantage of the manufacturing skills located throughout the supply chain. Second, the location of where activities are undertaken can be changed so that they are performed more efficiently. For example, Tokyo Motors' target costing system specified the purchase price of an internal part and transmitted it, along with the functionality and quality specifications, to Yokohama. The purchase price that was subsequently set by Yokohama for the part supplied by Kamakura, however, was too tight to enable

Kamakura to generate an adequate profit. The problem was that the specifications for the part established by Tokyo Motors required that Kamakura forge, as opposed to cast, the blank—a more demanding process. Kamakura requested an interorganizational cost investigation involving engineers from all three firms to identify a technical solution that satisfied the end-user's demands and was financially viable for all three firms because it started with a casting.

6.3.3.3 Concurrent cost management

Concurrent cost management is initiated whenever the cost challenge faced by the buyer and supplier is so severe that only sustained and coordinated cost reduction actions by both design teams can reduce costs to an adequate extent. Concurrent cost management interventions can be triggered by either firm, though it is often the buyer who identifies the need for the intervention at the same time that it communicates the specifications for the outsourced item to the supplier. Thus, typically the need for action is identified much earlier in the design process than for interorganizational cost investigations or FPQ trade-offs.

The cost reduction actions envisioned for a concurrent cost management intervention are often so significant that design changes to both the outsourced item and the end product itself are required to ensure that adequate cost reduction is achieved. For example, one of the events that triggered concurrent cost management at Komatsu was the requirement that Toyo Radiator produce an engine-cooling system for the A20 and A21 power shovels with 40 per cent more capacity at only 18 per cent higher cost. Komatsu engineers realized that only heroic efforts on both sides would enable them to achieve that objective. The redesign of Toyo Radiator's engine-cooling systems required major modifications to both the engine and the cooling system.

We observed two fundamental approaches to concurrent cost management: parallel and simultaneous. In the parallel approach the engineering teams at the buyer and supplier firms operate essentially independently, whereas in the simultaneous approach they work together to co-design the end product and the outsourced major function. The choice between parallel and simultaneous cost management is driven by the perceived benefits that can be derived from close interactions between the buyer and supplier design teams. If the value of such interactions is considered high, the firms use simultaneous engineering; otherwise, parallel engineering is utilized.

6.3.4 CLUSTERS OF EXTERNAL COST MANAGEMENT TECHNIQUES

The three external techniques are associated with different magnitudes in the design changes of the items being produced by the interacting firms. FPQ trade-offs are associated with relatively minor design changes that can be accommodated by a single firm in the supply chain with the permission of at least one other firm (it is this need for permission that renders the technique interorganizational). Interorganizational cost investigations are associated with more significant changes that require modifications to the design or production processes of the items produced by more than one firm in the supply chain. These design changes are interrelated, but they can be accomplished independently of each other with relatively low levels of communication between the design teams. These changes also have minimal impact on the buyer's product. Finally, concurrent cost management is associated with the most significant changes. Frequently, these changes are so substantial that the designs of both the buyer and supplier's products have to be altered, and these alterations have to be co-determined.

Although the scope and magnitude of the changes to the design of the products constitute a continuum, ranging from small changes that are almost imperceptible to large changes that are obvious to the customer, the observed IOCM practices consist of three discrete clusters of external cost management techniques. Each of these clusters represents a different external integrated cost management programme.

The first cluster captures the external integrated cost management programmes for firms that were capable of performing all three IOCM techniques. For example, one of the product development projects studied was subjected to both a concurrent cost management intervention and an interorganizational cost investigation. In the second cluster, the firms were able to perform interorganizational cost investigations and FPQ trade-offs, but could not undertake concurrent cost management. The third cluster captures the firms that have the lowest ability to perform IOCM. Here only FPQ trade-offs were observed. Managers at the three end-buyer firms in the sample confirmed that these patterns of IOCM capability were replicated throughout their supplier networks. The three clusters and related external cost management techniques are illustrated in Table 6.2.

6.3.5 KEY CHARACTERISTICS OF ASSOCIATED RELATIONAL CONTEXTS

Each of the three different cost management programmes required a different relational context to support it. Komatsu called the three relational contexts within which its suppliers operated family members, major suppliers, and subcontractors. Family members can support all three external cost management techniques, while major suppliers can support all but concurrent cost management, and subcontractors can only support FPQ trade-offs.

Five attributes appear to be of particular importance when determining the appropriate relational context to support undertaking each of the three external integrated cost man-

Table 6.2 Clusters of IOCM techniques practised

Cluster	Magnitude of design changes	Concurrent cost management	Interorganizational cost investigations	FPQ Trade-offs
1	High	Observed	Observed	Observed
2	Medium	Not observed	Observed	Observed
3	Low	Not observed	Not observed	Observed

agement techniques. Four of these attributes—design dependence, resource sharing, supplier participation, and bilateral commitment—relate to the interaction characteristics of the buyer–supplier relationship. The fifth relates to the choices surrounding the governance structure of the buyer–supplier relationship, in particular the mechanism adopted to provide incentives for the firms to cooperate and protection against opportunistic behaviour on the part of one or more of the firms in the supply chain.

6.3.5.1 Design dependence

Design dependence is created when the buyer and supplier split responsibility for establishing the specifications of the outsourced item and/or for designing it (Asanuma 1989). The highest level of design dependence—family membership—occurs when the supplier and buyer jointly establish specifications and jointly take responsibility for product design. Under these conditions, the two firms must actively integrate their product development processes.

The next level of design dependence—major supplier—occurs when the supplier accepts responsibility for design and manufacture, but the buyer retains sole responsibility for establishing high-level specifications. Here the level of integration between the buyer and supplier design teams is lower than under family membership, but still demanding, since the two firms must ensure that the end product and the outsourced item are compatible.

The final level of design dependence—subcontractor—occurs when the buyer both establishes the specifications and takes responsibility for design while the supplier only accepts responsibility for manufacture. Here the buyer must ensure that the outsourced components are designed in a way that enables the supplier to manufacture them for a reasonable cost. The supplier has few additional responsibilities other than ensuring that the parts are delivered on time and on specification. Consequently, the level of design dependence is low. The relationship between the level of design dependence—determined by the responsibility for establishing specifications and product design—and the relational context is illustrated in Table 6.3.

6.3.5.2 Resource sharing

The various relational contexts observed enabled the buyer and supplier to share different proportions of their design-related resources. The objective of any increased sharing was

Table 6.3 Design dependence and relational context

Relational context	Level of design dependence	Primary responsibility for specifications	Primary responsibility for design
Family member	High	Joint	Joint
Major supplier	Medium	Buyer	Supplier
Subcontractor	Low	Buyer	Buyer

to enable more sophisticated interactions between the two design teams. The resource sharing took two major forms: increased asset specificity and increased sharing of strategic information.

Asset specificity. Asset specificity relates to the degree to which an asset can be redeployed to alternative uses without sacrificing productive value (Williamson 1979). It was only when the suppliers were considered major suppliers or family members that significant levels of design-related asset specificity were observed. As an illustration, Isuzu provided considerable design support to its major supplier, JKC, as did Komatsu to its family member, Toyo. However, none of the firms dedicated any significant design-related assets to subcontractors.

Two types of increased asset specificity were observed: physical and human. Examples of increased physical asset specificity between Komatsu and Toyo include the development of proprietary software to model engine cooling and the sharing of prototyping assets. Examples of increased human asset specificity include the large number of individuals involved in the joint product development process and the guest engineers adding cost considerations to their design activities.

Strategic information sharing. Achieving cooperative buyer–supplier relationships requires intensive bilateral communication and information sharing to engender appropriate levels of learning and trust (Lamming 1993; Carr and Ng 1995; Dyer and Singh 1998). The level of strategic information sharing varied across the three relational contexts observed at the sample firms. Under family membership, Komatsu and Toyo share an extensive range of strategic information with each other, despite being separate firms. The objective of this information sharing is to allow Komatsu to find new ways to reduce costs. While still sharing a considerable amount of information with their major suppliers, the buyers did not share as much strategic information as they did with their family members. When the suppliers were considered subcontractors, little strategic information sharing was considered necessary since design responsibility resided at the buyer while the supplier was only asked to manufacture the part.

6.3.5.3 Supplier participation

Supplier participation across the three relational contexts varied systematically in two ways: (*a*) in the nature of the outsourced item; and (*b*) in the timing of the supplier's involvement.

Outsourcing more substantive items. The value and complexity of the outsourced items varied by relational context. For subcontractors, the items that were typically outsourced were simple components, such as radiator fan blades. In contrast, for major suppliers, they were group components, for example radiators. Finally, for family members, the outsourced items were typically major functions, such as engine-cooling systems.

The need to outsource large value items such as major functions typically leads to a concentration of the design work with a single supplier because it allows the supplier to make more fundamental changes to the design than would be possible if the major function were sourced from multiple suppliers. For example, Toyo Radiator redesigned the engine and oil-cooling systems of its A20 and A21 power shovels by placing the oil condenser in front of the radiator and thus reducing the need for two fan units (one to cool the condenser and the other to cool the radiator). Such a modification would not have been possible if responsibility for the design of the engine-cooling system and the oil-cooling system had resided at two different firms.

Timing of supplier involvement. For family members, the interaction between the design teams began earlier than would have been the case for a major supplier; for example, for Komatsu and Toyo Radiator the interaction began a full twelve months earlier. The aim of involving the supplier early in the design process is to provide that firm with more time to undertake fundamental redesigns of the major function. Major suppliers were typically brought in after product conceptualization had been completed and the design of the product was nearly finalized. For subcontractors, the involvement occurred even later, typically after the parts list had been generated.

6.3.5.4 Bilateral commitment

The increased resource sharing and reliance upon the supplier's product development skills associated with some of the observed relational contexts required that the buyer and supplier strengthen their bilateral commitment. They achieved this objective by increasing the stability of their relationship and the degree of collaboration between the two design teams.

Stability. Increased stability is important because it takes considerable time for the buyer and supplier to develop the in-depth knowledge of each other that is required for effective co-design under family membership. This knowledge includes joint technical expertise, mature personal relationships, and extensive prior experience. For example, over time, Toyo engineers had developed considerable expertise that was specific to Komatsu. While other engine-cooling suppliers existed, they did not have this Komatsu-specific know-how and technology. It would take considerable time and resources on the part of Komatsu to bring them up to the same level of capabilities as Toyo Radiator.

At the major supplier level, the relationships were still quite stable. Only if a major supplier consistently failed to be competitive would it cease to remain in that supplier group. In contrast, at the subcontractor level, the buyer firms were willing to take back in-house certain items that were previously outsourced if there was not enough work to keep their own workforce occupied.

Collaboration. Collaboration between buyers and suppliers is considered a necessary condition for effective buyer–supplier interactions that go beyond pure arm's-length contractual relationships (Heide and John 1990; Dyer 1996; Gietzmann 1996). The conversion of the relationship of Komatsu and Toyo from major supplier to family member was accompanied by an increase in the level of collaboration. For example, the simultaneous redesign of both the engine and the engine-cooling system required considerable coordination between the two engineering teams since the product development process was highly iterative. The aim of these periodic meetings was to integrate the R & D efforts of the two groups, allow suppliers to provide greater input earlier in the development process, and help ensure that cost reduction negotiations were more substantive.

The magnitude and intensity of the collaboration varied with the relational context. It was highest for family members, followed by major suppliers, and then subcontractors. For example, since subcontractors were not responsible for any of the design aspects of the parts they manufactured, the help they received was limited to the manufacturing process. In addition, the buyer did not look to the subcontractors for any significant help, as there was little additional value that they could provide to the buyer in terms of design support.

6.3.5.5 Governance structure

To reap the full benefits from enhanced buyer–supplier relationships, consideration has to be given to any necessary shifts in governance structure (Gietzmann and Larsen 1998). Governance structure refers to the mechanisms that create both incentives (i.e. reward and coercion mechanisms) for the buyer and supplier to interact, and safeguards that protect each transactor against the risk of opportunistic behaviour on the part of the other (Williamson 1985, 1991).

Incentive mechanisms. The nature and importance of the incentive mechanisms utilized varied across the observed relational contexts. For family members, the primary incentive mechanism was trust-based and took the form of mutual benefit (Nooteboom et al. 1997). Family members actively worked together to increase the joint economic benefit from their cooperative product design efforts.

At the major supplier level, the principle of mutual benefit was still operative, but it was less important. For major suppliers such as Toyo (before it became a family member), JKC, and Yokohama, the primary incentive mechanism was the volume of business that the buyer awarded to the supplier. For example, Isuzu used direct competition between its major suppliers to ensure that the suppliers were as innovative as possible. When a supplier failed to remain competitive, Isuzu punished that firm by awarding it slightly less volume than in previous years. Similarly, it rewarded innovative suppliers with slightly more volume than in previous years. To help the poorly performing suppliers become competitive, Isuzu provided them with additional engineering support.

For subcontractors, the primary incentive appeared to be continued business. While severing relationships was rare because most subcontractors had achieved a high level of performance, it was understood that suppliers would only be retained if they maintained adequate performance levels. At the subcontractor level, the principle of mutual benefit was still in operation, but played a relatively minor role. It was enacted primarily by the firms sharing engineering expertise where beneficial. For example, the buyer might provide the supplier with engineering support to resolve particularly difficult manufacturing problems associated with its outsourced items so as to help ensure that the supplier's target costs were achieved.

Protection mechanisms. To mitigate the risk of opportunistic behaviour by their trading partners, the sample firms relied upon a number of protection mechanisms, which varied with the relational context. In trust-based relationships the dominant risk is unilateral defection (Granovetter 1985). One way that firms can signal a low risk of defection is to structure the relationship so that the commitment of both sides is clearly observable (Parkhe 1998). In the case of family members, trust was maintained by ensuring that both parties were visibly mutually interdependent. For example, Komatsu openly relied upon Toyo Radiator for its expertise in engine-cooling systems, and Toyo Radiator openly relied upon Komatsu for a significant portion of its business and for engineering support to develop new technologies. This high level of mutual interdependence led to barriers to unilateral defection and created an additional safeguard against opportunistic behaviour. More specifically, Toyo had access to Komatsu's future product plans, which was highly valuable information for Komatsu's competitors. However, Komatsu in turn had access to highly proprietary information about Toyo, and if Toyo defected, Komatsu could retaliate by sharing that information with Toyo's competitors.

For major suppliers, mutual interdependence was still a major protection mechanism, but less so than for family members. The sequential nature of the design process across the interorganizational boundary between buyers and major suppliers coupled to the existence of multiple competing suppliers reduced the dependence of the buyer upon the supplier. However, major suppliers still had extensive and specialized knowledge of the needs of their customers. It was therefore not feasible for the buyer simply to switch from an existing major supplier to a new one from outside their supplier base. Furthermore, the small number of firms in the supplier base that could make a given family of products made it virtually impossible for the remaining major suppliers to expand production immediately to offset the loss of capacity. Thus, the buyer had visibly rendered itself dependent upon each of its major suppliers for a reasonable period into the future. The major suppliers, in turn, had rendered themselves similarly dependent on their customers because they only transacted with a limited number of customers in this type of relationship. Therefore, they would suffer considerable economic hardship by the loss of a customer to whom they were a major supplier. Since it was difficult to create new major supplier relationships in the short term, the suppliers were equally committed for a reasonable period into the future. Thus, major suppliers and their customers were mutually interdependent, but not to the same extent as family members and their customers.

For subcontractors, the level of mutual interdependence was much lower than for family members and major suppliers. The buyer typically dealt with multiple subcontractors and could relatively easily compensate for the defection of a subcontractor. Furthermore, if business dropped, it was not unusual for the buyer to take some of the outsourced work in-house to keep its employees busy. In this type of buyer–supplier relational context, the subcontractor was somewhat left to fend for itself.

6.3.6 EXTERNAL INTEGRATED COST MANAGEMENT PROGRAMMES AND RELATIONAL CONTEXTS

Each of the three observed external cost management programmes was associated with a distinct hybrid relational context. The motivation behind the linkage appears to be the level of interorganizational coordination required by the various IOCM techniques on the one hand, and the level of cooperation supported by the relational contexts on the other. The more demanding the techniques contained in the cost management programme, the further the relational context is removed from that of a pure arm's-length market. First, for all relational context attributes studied (i.e. those related to design dependence, resource sharing, supplier participation, bilateral commitment, and governance structure), the subcontractor relational context is the closest of the three to a common supplier, followed by the major supplier, with the family members being the furthest removed from the classical market form. Thus, a systematic monotonic relationship was observed in the attributes associated with each relational context. Second, our observations suggest that the IOCM techniques practised by buyers and suppliers are linked to their relational context, with each external integrated cost management programme being associated with a particular relational context and vice versa, i.e. we observed a one-to-one relationship between cost management programme and relational context.

The observed sets of pairing between cost management programme and relational context can now be interpreted (see Table 6.4). The higher the level of design changes envisioned in the programme, the more buyers and suppliers are required to interact in a rich and varied manner. Thus, a programme that supports concurrent cost management, which involves the largest design changes, is associated with a family member context as this context enables the richest interactions between the design teams of the two firms. It is important to observe that family membership and concurrent cost management evolved simultaneously at Komatsu and Toyo Radiator and that senior management perceived them as essentially a single outcome. Cost management programmes that only support FPQ trade-offs, which involve the smallest design changes, are associated with a subcontractor relational context,

Table 6.4 Relational context and IOCM techniques utilized

Relational context	Level of design change supported	Predominant IOCM technique utilized
Family member	High	Concurrent cost management
Major supplier	Medium	Interorganizational cost investigation
Subcontractor	Low	FPQ trade-off

which is the closest to pure markets of all the hybrid relational contexts observed. Finally, the middle level of design changes involved in programmes that support interorganizational cost investigations and FPQ trade-offs is associated with the intermediate relational context, major suppliers. Thus, the three observed external cost management programmes are associated with three different relational contexts.

6.3.7 THE BENEFITS OF INTERORGANIZATIONAL COST MANAGEMENT

The managers in the sample firms appear to adopt the external integrated cost management programmes and associated relational contexts because they believe that these combinations will lead to superior joint performance. It is extremely difficult to generate a priori numerical support for the contention that the application of IOCM in a hybrid relational context is more effective than conventional internal cost management. Consequently, the decision to adopt a new cost management technique can be viewed as a calculated gamble based upon the expected benefits and costs of developing the expertise necessary to undertake the IOCM technique and creating its associated relational context.

There are two ways to measure the effectiveness of a given IOCM technique. The first compares the savings to the incremental cost of an individual IOCM intervention. The second compares the total savings associated with a given IOCM technique from all affected suppliers discounted over time to the cost of creating the ability to undertake the technique and establishing the appropriate relational context.

6.3.7.1 Effectiveness of individual IOCM interventions

The economic justification of an individual IOCM intervention compares the anticipated savings against the cost of undertaking the intervention. The anticipated joint savings of a single intervention, when considered as a percentage of the overall value of the outsourced item, were considered to vary with the IOCM technique utilized. The savings from FPQ trade-offs were expected to be modest, representing only a few percentage points of the cost of the outsourced item. For interorganizational cost investigations, the savings were typically expected to be in the 5–10 per cent range. Finally, for concurrent cost management the savings were expected to be 10–15 per cent. Since the value of the outsourced item increases with the distance of the relational context from a pure market situation, so apparently do the expected cost savings (see Table 6.5).

6.3.7.2 Effectiveness of an IOCM technique

The overall effectiveness of any IOCM technique is captured by the net discounted cash flows (DCFs) associated with the savings derived from all suppliers using the technique over the time frame that they use it, minus the cost of establishing and maintaining the technique

Table 6.5 IOCM technique utilized and typical level of cost savings

IOCM technique utilized	Type of item outsourced	Relative value of item outsourced	Typical level of cost savings (%)
Concurrent cost management	Major function	High	10–15
Interorganizational cost investigation	Group component	Medium	5–10
FPQ trade-off	Component	Low	0–5

and its associated relational context. None of the firms in the sample had even attempted a formal economic justification of their external cost management programmes. Instead, they relied upon their perceptions of the economic success of the programmes. For example, Komatsu management adopted a holistic view of the make-or-buy decision and the development of concurrent cost management. They believed that the benefits from the new technique quantified as the reduction in the costs of outsourced items exceeded any additional investment and coordination and transaction costs associated with the new approach. However, they admitted that there was no easy way for them to evaluate the net benefits inherent to the new buyer–supplier relationship. The problem was that while the increased investment in specific assets could theoretically be measured, the incremental coordination and transaction costs were difficult to observe and incorporate into any formal economic evaluation of the overall process.

Most of the benefits to Komatsu from its new relationship with Toyo were from the improved design capabilities of the dyadic pair. These benefits included the lower costs and higher functionality of the end products that resulted from their joint design activities. The benefits to Toyo, however, were less obvious. While indeed the value added and the profit margin of an engine-cooling system were higher than for Komatsu-designed components, Toyo now had to invest in a more extensive research and development programme. Unfortunately, there was no way to determine if Toyo's profits from its business with Komatsu were higher under the new versus old approach because of the problem of isolating the incremental revenues and costs (in particular, the costs associated with the new relational context). Neither firm had maintained detailed records of their prior investments in each other; therefore there was no way to determine the incremental costs. Consequently, a formal incremental profit analysis was not considered feasible. However, both Komatsu and Toyo management stated that, in their opinion, the two firms were better off and they actively supported the new relationship.

6.3.8 IMPLICATIONS TO PRACTICE

Firms that outsource a significant proportion of the value added of their products need to consider aggressively managing costs across the interorganizational boundaries between themselves and their suppliers. In particular, they need to find ways to improve the coordination between the product design teams via IOCM. Three different IOCM techniques associated with different levels of design changes were observed at the research sites, FPQ trade-offs (involving the least change), interorganizational cost investigations, and concurrent cost management (involving the highest degree of change).

To manage costs across organizational boundaries required the creation of different relational contexts. For FPQ trade-offs, the relational context required was the closest to a common supplier. The degree of design dependence was the lowest, as was the level of resource sharing, supplier participation, and bilateral commitment. In addition, the governance structure relied the least on both incentive and protective mechanisms. For concurrent management, the relational context was the furthest from a common supplier and more akin to a subsidiary. The degree of design dependence was high as was the level of resource sharing, supplier participation, and bilateral commitment. Here the governance structure relied the most on both incentive and protective mechanisms. For IOCM, the relational context was between that observed for FPQ trade-offs and concurrent cost management.

Thus, to achieve IOCM requires not only developing the necessary technical skills relating to both product design and design team coordination, but also developing a relational context that supports the demands of the IOCM techniques, which the firms want to apply.

6.4 Conclusion

Integrated cost management programmes consist of a number of distinct cost management techniques that reinforce each other, with the output of one technique creating the input for another. Using field research, two different types of integrated cost management programmes were observed. The first type was the internal integrated cost management programme at Olympus Optical Company. This programme consisted of five distinct internal cost management techniques that created aggressive cost reduction pressures across the life cycle of the product. These techniques focused on both product design and production processes.

The second type was the external integrated cost management programmes at Komatsu, Isuzu, and Tokyo Motors, and their respective suppliers, Toyo Radiator (Komatsu), JKC (Isuzu), and Yokohama Corporation and Komatsu Iron Works (Tokyo Motors). These programmes consisted of three distinct cost management techniques that created aggressive cost reduction pressures across the organizational boundaries between buyer and supplier. They focused in particular on interorganizational product design.

All of these sample firms competed in environments where they faced competitors with equivalent strategic capabilities requiring them to be highly cost-efficient in both their product design and manufacturing capabilities. Clearly, the level of cost reduction that could be achieved through the use of independent cost management techniques was not sufficient for these firms. Instead, they developed aggressive integrated cost management programmes that relied upon multiple cost management techniques, which reinforced each other to achieve even more intense levels of cost reduction. Olympus, which only outsourced simple parts, developed an internally oriented integrated cost management programme that focused on reducing costs across the entire product life cycle. The other firms, which outsourced more substantive components that required significant design skills at the supplier, developed external integrated cost systems that focused on designing products which could be manufactured at low cost, in addition to their internal cost management programmes.

☐ NOTES

1 This section relies heavily on Cooper and Slagmulder (2004*a*).

2 For a thorough description of target costing, see Cooper and Slagmulder (1997).

3 Other firms have introduced similar systems for the same reason. For example, Kirin Breweries used its Kyoto Brewery System and Higashimaru Shoyu introduced its Price Control System to motivate cost reductions in their production processes (see Cooper 1995).

4 This section relies heavily upon Cooper and Slagmulder (2004*b*).

5 The names of the firms in italics have been disguised for reasons of confidentiality.

☐ REFERENCES

Asanuma, B. (1989). 'Manufacturer-Supplier Relationships in Japan and the Concept of Relation-Specific Skill', *Journal of the Japanese and International Economies*, 3(1): 1–30.

Carr, C. and Ng, J. (1995). 'Total Cost Control: Nissan and Its U.K. Supplier Partnerships', *Management Accounting Research*, 6: 347–65.

Cooper, R. (1995). *When Lean Enterprises Collide. Competing Through Confrontation*. Boston: Harvard Business School Press.

—— and Slagmulder, R. (1997). *Target Costing and Value Engineering*. Portland, OR: Productivity Press.

—— —— (2004*a*). 'Achieving Full-Cycle Cost Management', *Sloan Management Review*, 46(1): 45–52.

Cooper, R. (2004*b*). 'Interorganizational Cost Management and Relational Context', *Accounting, Organizations and Society*, 29(1): 1–26.

Dyer, J. H. (1996). 'Specialized Supplier Networks as a Source of Competitive Advantage: Evidence from the Auto Industry', *Strategic Management Journal*, 17(4): 271–91.

—— and Singh, H. (1998). 'The Relational View: Cooperative Strategy and Sources of Interorganizational Competitive Advantage', *Academy of Management Review*, 23(4): 660–79.

Gietzmann, M. B. (1996). 'Incomplete Contracts and the Make or Buy Decision: Governance Design and Attainable Flexibility', *Accounting, Organizations and Society*, 21(6): 611–26.

Gietzman, M. B. and Larsen, J. G. (1998). 'Motivating Subcontractors to Perform Development and Design Tasks', *Management Accounting Research*, 9: 285–309.

Granovetter, M. (1985). 'Economic Action and Social Structure: The Problem of Embeddedness', *American Journal of Sociology*, 91: 481–510.

Heide, J. B. and John, G. (1990). 'Alliances in Industrial Purchasing: The Determinants of Joint Action in Buyer-Supplier Relationships', *Journal of Marketing Research*, XXVII: 24–36.

Kaplan, R. S. and Atkinson, A. A. (1998). *Advanced Management Accounting*. Upper Saddle River, NJ: Prentice Hall.

—— and Cooper, R. (1999). *Cost and Effect*. Boston: Harvard Business School Press.

Khandwalla, P. N. (1972). 'The Effect of Different Types of Competition on the Use of Management Controls', *Journal of Accounting Research* (Autumn): 275–85.

Lamming, R. (1993). *Beyond Partnership: Strategies for Innovation and Lean Supply*. New York: Prentice Hall.

Monden, Y. (1995). *Cost Reduction Systems: Target Costing and Kaizen Costing*. Portland, OR: Productivity Press.

Nooteboom, B., Berger, H., and Noorderhaven, N. (1997). 'Effects of Trust and Governance on Relational Risk', *Academy of Management Journal*, 40(2): 308–38.

Parkhe, A. (1998). 'Building Trust in International Alliances', *Journal of World Business*, 33(4): 417–37.

Williamson, O. E. (1979). 'Transaction Cost Economics: The Governance of Contractual Relations', *Journal of Law and Economics*, 22: 233–61.

—— (1985). *The Economic Institutions of Capitalism*. New York: Free Press.

—— (1991). 'Comparative Economic Organization: The Analysis of Discrete Structural Alternatives', *Administrative Science Quarterly*, 36: 269–96.

Womack, J. P. and Jones, D. T. (1996). *Lean Thinking*. New York: Simon and Schuster.

☐ APPENDIX

The seven firms and three supply chains included in the sample are[5]:
Isuzu–Jidosha (I–J) Chain

- *Isuzu Motors, Ltd*, one of the largest automobile manufacturing companies in Japan. The firm had a specialized market strength in heavy- and light-duty trucks and in the bus market.
- *Jidosha Kiki Co., Ltd* (JKC), a first-tier supplier to the automobile industry. The company's products were related to the basic functions of a vehicle and included brakes, clutches, steering systems, and pumps.

Komatsu–Toyo (K–T) Chain

- *Komatsu, Ltd*, one of the largest heavy industrial manufacturers in Japan. It was organized in three major lines of business-construction equipment, industrial machinery, and electronic-applied products. Since 1989, the company had been aggressively diversifying and expanding globally.

- *Toyo Radiator Co., Ltd*, one of the world's largest independent manufacturers of heat-exchange equipment for use in automobiles and heavy construction and agricultural vehicles, air conditioners for home and office, and freezers. Its product lines included radiators, oil coolers, intercoolers, evaporators, and condensers.

Tokyo–Yokohama–Kamakura Chain

- *Tokyo Motors, Ltd*, one of the world's top ten automobile manufacturers. It produced vehicles at 20 plants in 15 countries and marketed them in 110 countries through 200 distributorships and over 6,000 dealerships.
- *Yokohama Corporation, Ltd*, a manufacturer of hydraulic systems for automobiles and trucks, and associated equipment. The firm was split into three corporate divisions: injection pump; air conditioning; and hydraulics and pneumatics.
- *Kamakura Iron Works Company, Ltd*, a relatively small, family-run business, which supplied automotive parts to either automobile manufacturers or suppliers to that industry.

7 Capital budgeting and informational impediments: a management accounting perspective

Lawrence A. Gordon
Martin P. Loeb
Chih-Yang Tseng

7.1 Introduction

Capital budgeting refers to the planning and control process associated with capital expenditures. Capital expenditures, often referred to as capital investments, are expenditures for projects not intended for immediate consumption. Accordingly, capital expenditures increase, or at least maintain, the capital assets of an organization. The term capital assets, as used above, refers to what economists usually call capital goods.[1] Unlike land and labour, which are factors of production not produced by the economic system, 'capital goods are produced goods which are used as factor inputs for further production' (Pearce 1991: 51). Accountants usually refer to capital assets as fixed assets.

In contrast to capital expenditures, operating expenditures relate to items that will only benefit the current operating period. Technically speaking, capital and operating expenditures are costs in that they both require the use of resources. Operating expenditures are usually thought of as an expense because the resources are consumed during the current period and the associated benefits are also assumed to be derived during the current period. Capital expenditures are treated as investments because the resources, or at least part of them, are not consumed during the current period and the benefits derived from such resources are received over more than the current period. However, the proportion of capital investments consumed (i.e. the proportion of capital consumption) during the acquisition period becomes an operating expenditure.[2]

As discussed above, the distinction between capital and operating expenditures hinges largely on the timing associated with consuming resources and generating associated benefits, where benefits are expressed in terms of the revenues and, in turn, cash flows derived from such consumption. More to the point, operating expenditures relate to the consumption of resources and the generation of associated benefits during the current operating time period (usually thought of in terms of the current fiscal year). Capital expenditures are consumed and generate benefits over several time periods. Thus, the uncertainties of future operations and the time value of money are critical concerns to decisions associated with allocating resources to capital goods.

The uncertainties related to future operations and the time value of money associated with capital expenditure decisions create informational impediments not present for decisions associated with operating expenditures. These informational impediments include the need to forecast the consumption time path of initial capital expenditures, and the need to forecast additional future costs. Future revenues, and in turn cash flows, also need to be forecasted when considering capital expenditures. In addition, there is the need to determine the appropriate cost of capital to be used in discounting future cash flows. The literature in accounting, economics, and finance addressing capital budgeting issues between the 1950s and 1980s focused on the above noted informational impediments, often in the context of the following questions: How should future cash flows (derived from future revenues and costs) be forecasted? What is the theoretical meaning of the cost of capital? What role does the Capital Asset Pricing Model (CAPM) play in determining the cost of capital? What is the relation between the use of sophisticated capital budgeting methods for selecting projects (i.e. methods based on discounted cash flows (DCFs) analysis) and firm performance?

The capital budgeting literature referred to above was premised on the basic assumption of classical economics, whereby mangers are assumed to maximize the value of the firm.[3] This assumption, however, was seriously challenged by those writing about asymmetric information and agency theory. By the mid-1980s, agency theory, with its focus on conflict of interests and asymmetric information among principals and agents, surfaced as an issue to consider in the capital budgeting arena. More to the point, by the mid-1980s, issues surrounding the conflict of interest between principals and agents, and issues associated with asymmetric information, became other informational impediments that needed to be discussed in the context of capital budgeting decisions.

During the 1980s another issue associated with informational impediments was recognized as having an important impact on capital budgeting decisions. This issue has to do with the role of real options. The informational impediments related to the uncertainty of future cash flows and the proper timing of investments are central to addressing issues related to capital budgeting in a real options environment.

During the early 1990s, it became apparent that the focus in the literature was on the planning aspects of the capital budgeting process, with particular emphasis on the models used to rank and select specific capital projects. In contrast, the control side of the capital budgeting process was not receiving much attention. Accordingly, the role of post-auditing capital investments, and the associated informational impediments, surfaced as critical issues to consider during this time period.

The 1990s also brought about the Internet revolution. The full impact of the Internet's digital economy on capital budgeting decisions is only starting to surface. However, it is clear that capital budgeting decisions face new informational impediments as a result of these developments. These new informational impediments include such issues as information overload, information and system security, and interdependencies among various organizational decisions.

This preceding brief overview of the evolution of some (although not all) of the key issues related to capital budgeting makes it clear that informational impediments is one of the fundamental themes that flows throughout much of the capital budgeting literature over the last sixty years. The first objective of this chapter is to review the literature espousing this theme in the context of the following three specific, albeit related, issues:

1. the use of the sophisticated methods for selecting capital investments;
2. asymmetric information and capital budgeting; and
3. post-auditing capital investments.

Figure 7.1 is intended to show that while these issues can be viewed separately, they clearly overlap with one another. In addition, Figure 7.1 also points out that informational impediments impact all three of these issues.

Given that management accountants are concerned with the design and use of information systems, and that capital expenditures are by their very nature a management accounting issue, the second objective of this chapter is to discuss the role that management

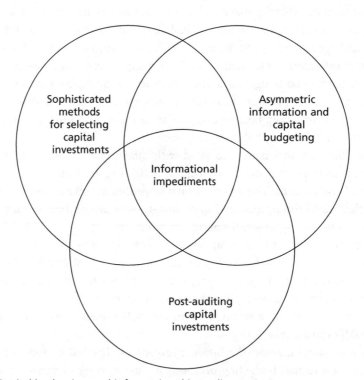

Figure 7.1 Capital budgeting and informational impediments

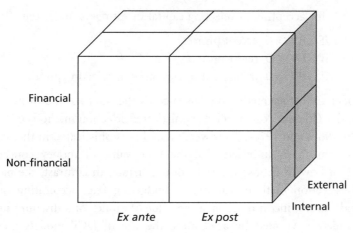

Figure 7.2 Broad-scope view of information

accounting systems (MASs) can play to help mitigate the informational impediments to capital budgeting in the context of the above noted issues.

For purposes of this second objective, we take a broad-scope view of MAS (Gordon and Miller 1976; Chenhall and Morris 1986; Mia 1993; Gordon 2004: ch. 1). In essence, this means we will consider non-financial as well as financial information, *ex ante* as well as *ex post* information, and external as well as internal information. Figure 7.2 summarizes this broad-scope view of information.

7.2 **Sophisticated methods for selecting capital investments**

By the late 1970s, the use of DCF analysis for selecting capital investments (projects) was widely advocated by academics (see e.g. Klammer 1972; Schall et al. 1978). The underlying argument for using DCF is that capital investment decisions need to be evaluated in terms of the entire life of the capital project and that means the time value of money is a critical concern. The most fundamental DCF model, and the one most commonly discussed, is the net present value (NPV) model. In its simplest form, the NPV model, and the investment decision rule, is as follows:

$$\text{NPV} = \sum_{t=1}^{n} \text{CF}_t/(1+k)^t - \text{Cost}$$

where, CF_t = net cash flow in period t, $t = 1, 2, \#, \ldots n$, n = economic life of capital investment, k = economic rate of return (usually discussed in terms of the cost of capital), Cost = the initial cost of the capital investment.

The decision rule for accepting or rejecting capital investments under the NPV model is:

> If NPV > 0, accept project
>
> If NPV < 0, reject project
>
> If NPV $= 0$, indifferent to accepting or rejecting project

The NPV model and other related models such as the internal rate of return (IRR) and profitability index (PI) were often called sophisticated selection methods of capital budgeting back in the 1960s and 1970s. They were viewed as sophisticated in that computing the DCF requires some basic knowledge of the time value of money concept and some understanding of how to choose the right discount rate. In contrast, the naive (i.e. non-sophisticated) selection methods for capital budgeting (e.g. accounting rate of return, payback period) do not incorporate the time value of money or a discount rate.

Although widely advocated by academics, the use of DCF models met with much resistance from practitioners. In fact, studies on the use of basic sophisticated capital budgeting methods for selecting capital projects showed that many firms were slow to adopt such models. Reasons for not using such models fall into several broad categories. Gordon et al. (1979) categorized these reasons into (*a*) emotional impediments; (*b*) political impediments; (*c*) technical impediments; and (*d*) informational impediments. Based on an empirical study, Gordon et al. (1979) found that the primary reason firms did not use sophisticated methods was due to informational impediments. Furthermore, they found that, even among firms that claimed to be using sophisticated capital budgeting methods, the use of such models was sporadic. In other words, these models were used only some of the time, especially when it came to strategic capital expenditures. The three issues raising the largest informational impediments, according to the Gordon et al. (1979: 73) study, were (*a*) the requisite information was absent from the firm's information system; (*b*) the information gathered was error-prone; and (*c*) the information was carried over unreliable information channels with no permanent record.

By the 1980s, most firms in industrialized countries seemed to be using, to one degree or another, the basic DCF models (Haka et al. 1985; Pike 1988). This fact notwithstanding, the informational impediments noted above are still often present and likely account for the fact that many managers tend to use basic DCF models as a 'screening device' as opposed to a final decision-making tool. Indeed, paraphrasing the words that a corporate senior manager told one of the authors of this chapter several years ago: 'I rarely make a major capital expenditure decision without conducting NPV and IRR analyses, but rarely make final decisions based on such analyses.' The executive went on to say:

There are three basic reasons why I do not make final capital expenditures based on the NPV and IRR analyses. First, the data underlying the analyses is often faulty. Second, the uncertainties of future investments are extremely difficult to quantify, and yet they clearly have a significant affect on the analyses. Third, these analyses often do not effectively incorporate the capital investment's compatibility with the firm's corporate strategy.

It is interesting to note that the second and third concerns raised by the above noted senior executive (i.e. about uncertainties and organizational strategies) are specifically addressed in the real options literature. The real options literature, which surfaced in the 1980s, became the modern-view of sophisticated methods of selecting capital investments by the 1990s (see e.g. Dixit and Pindyck 1994). The real options literature focuses on the timing of investments as well as the uncertainties of cash flows associated with such investments. In essence, this literature treats the option to make a capital investment in a manner similar to the way financial options are handled (see e.g. Brealey and Myers 2000: chs. 21 and 22). One aspect of the timing of capital investments has to do with the option to defer. According to this view, investments are no longer viewed as taking place now or never. In fact, due to the value of the option to defer an investment, it may pay to defer an investment that has a positive NPV, based on a traditional DCF analysis. In contrast, under traditional sophisticated selection methods of capital budgeting, it is assumed that projects with a positive NPV are accepted immediately.

A second aspect of the timing of capital investments in a real options environment has to do with the strategic (or flexibility) aspects of investments. In other words, there is a strategic option associated with some capital investments. The strategic option is based on the idea that a firm's strategy (i.e. the way it positions itself in the market place) often requires several intermediary steps. Thus, the strategic option could lead to a decision to invest in a capital expenditure that has a negative NPV based on a traditional DCF analysis. In essence, this investment is seen as an intermediary step. For example, a US-based firm planning a long-term strategy of positioning itself in a foreign market (e.g. in China) may initially make an intermediary investment in a negative NPV project as one way of understanding the operations of that foreign market (including customs of the people in the country). The rationale underlying such an investment is that the intermediary investment has a positive strategic option value that more than offsets the negative NPV. Under traditional sophisticated selection methods of capital budgeting, such negative NPV investments would be rejected (i.e. the value of the strategic option would be ignored).

The uncertainties associated with the cash flows are at the heart of the real options issues noted above. Indeed, there is a direct correlation between the uncertainties and the value of real options. Unfortunately, there is also a much higher level of mathematical sophistication required to apply real options analyses. In addition, the informational requirements (especially in terms of cash flow probability distributions) are significantly greater under the real options approach to capital budgeting than under the traditional DCF analysis. As a consequence, anecdotal evidence that exists on the use of such methods suggests that real option models are not in wide use in practice, despite their theoretical appeal.

7.2.1 MANAGEMENT ACCOUNTING SYSTEMS

The informational impediments to the use of sophisticated capital budgeting models (i.e. DCF models and real options models) for selecting capital investments can be grouped into three broad areas. First, there is the need to derive the requisite information related to future cash flows, discount rates, and capital consumption. Since all of these issues are directly related to the domain of accounting, MASs can, and clearly should, play a fundamental role in mitigating these informational impediments. For example, a decision support systems approach to MASs can easily incorporate forecasting models, including potential probability distributions, for future cash flows (see e.g. Gordon and Pinches 1984). In a similar manner, MASs can incorporate cost of capital information, based on the Capital Asset Pricing Model[4] (so as to facilitate the decision-maker's ability to derive the correct discount rate). Of course, since capital consumption information is what accountants call depreciation, MASs can, and should, incorporate this information. However, for capital budgeting decisions, the type of capital consumption information required should relate to economic, as well as accounting, depreciation (e.g. Gordon 1974). Economic depreciation is required because it relates to the economic life of capital assets, whereas accounting depreciation is needed in order to derive the tax implications of capital consumption.

Second, there is the need to develop valid and reliable information channels. In addition, the confidentiality of information also needs to be protected.[5] More generally, what are needed are strong internal controls on the information and information systems utilizing sophisticated capital budgeting models. Of course, the adoption and maintenance of internal controls are, and always have been, fundamental issues of concern in designing and using MASs. This need for internal controls with particular emphasis on information security is currently receiving major attention in the USA due to the Sarbanes–Oxley Act of 2002. More to the point, section 404 of the Sarbanes-Oxley Act has made internal control of financial information systems a fundamental concern of all companies listed on US stock exchanges.

Third, the implementation of sophisticated capital budgeting techniques requires better information related to uncertainties and risk management aspects of such uncertainties. The recent trend towards incorporating the concept of enterprise risk management (ERM) into internal controls (which includes MASs) is an obvious step in mitigating this informational impediment. The ERM philosophy emphasizes the fact that risk management needs to be thought of as a process, with a focus on managing the risk of the entire enterprise so as to achieve the organization's objectives (see e.g. the report by the Committee of Sponsoring Organizations of the Treadway Commission (COSO) 2004). As such, it addresses one of the important informational impediments to using sophisticated capital selection models often overlooked. That impediment has to do with the failure by most models to incorporate the interactions among the uncertainties created by various organizational decisions. For example, it is logical to argue that the uncertainties associated with capital budgeting decisions cannot be fully resolved without first resolving the uncertainties associated with pricing decisions. However, in a similar vein, the uncertainties associated with pricing decisions cannot be fully resolved without first resolving the uncertainties associated with capital budgeting decisions. Thus, there is a simultaneity concern that requires a holistic approach towards making capital budgeting and pricing decisions, as well as other decisions. Nearly all discussions of capital budget decisions ignore this interaction among various decisions. However, the ERM philosophy, coupled with enterprise resource planning (ERP) systems (i.e. software systems that integrate the various business processes), should allow MASs to go a long way in mitigating these problems.

7.3 Asymmetric information and capital budgeting

Information plays a crucial role in the allocation of resources in an economy—both in market activity and in non-market activity (including the development and functioning of firms). In the early 1970s, in recognition of the fact that information is not symmetrically distributed among all parties of a firm, economists began to incorporate information explicitly in their models of the firm (e.g. Alchian and Demsetz 1972; Marschak and Radner 1972; Ross 1973). It did not take long for the development of what has come to be called information economics to have a profound effect on research in related disciplines including accounting and finance, in general, and capital budgeting in particular.

Since asymmetric information is a key element of all information economics models, by their very nature, such models highlight informational impediment issues. An early application of information economics to the problem of capital budgeting can be seen in the papers of Loeb and Magat (1978) and Groves and Loeb (1979). These papers apply what has become known as the Vickrey–Clarke–Groves (or VCG) mechanism to the firm's problem of internally allocating capital among multiple divisions.[6] They were the first papers in the capital budgeting literature explicitly to model asymmetric information and communication.[7] In particular, these papers assume that division managers have private information about the profitability of the projects they sponsor and analyse the incentives that must be provided for them truthfully to reveal this information.

Moving into the 1980s, agency theory became the dominant information economics paradigm. While Ross (1973) is often credited with introducing formal agency theory to the literature, the papers by Jensen and Meckling (1976) and Holmstrom (1979), along with the Baiman (1982) review paper, have had a major impact in promoting the use of agency theory to examine managerial accounting issues. Two key assumptions underlie agency theory: (*a*) divergence of preferences: there is an inherent conflict of interest between principals and agents; and (*b*) asymmetric information: agents have access to information not available to principals. Whereas conflict of interest provides the motivation for agents to behave in a manner that is not in the best interest of the principals, asymmetric information allows such behaviour to go undetected unless specific mechanisms are designed to affect the situation. Although the mechanisms of Loeb and Magat (1978) and Groves and Loeb (1979) explicitly modelled asymmetric information, divergence of preferences was only implicitly acknowledged.[8]

The two components of asymmetric information usually discussed in the agency theory literature are adverse selection and moral hazard. Adverse selection refers to the agent's concealing of relevant information or misrepresenting his or her ability.[9] The agent may have certain information that the principal cannot completely verify, so *ex ante* the principal believes that the agent will make opportunistic decisions that serve the agent's interests over the interests of the principal. The used car market (the market for lemons as modelled by Akerlof 1970) is one typical example where the adverse selection problem comes into play. In the used car market, sellers possess better information than buyers about the quality of the cars being offered for sale. This leads buyers to assume that only the poorest quality cars ('lemons') are being offered, and results in higher quality cars being withdrawn from the market. Moral hazard means that agents take actions *ex post* (i.e. after contracting) that cannot be observed by the principal and are harmful to the principal. For example, after purchasing car insurance, a driver may take less safety precautions (drive recklessly), since the car insurance company will absorb (at least part of) any costs of a crash.

A seminal paper in the agency theory literature dealing with capital budgeting issues is Antle and Eppen (1985). This paper, which builds on earlier work by Harris et al. (1982), was the first to explain endogenously the phenomenon of capital rationing—the fact that firms reject projects that appear to have a positive NPV. Using a framework incorporating both asymmetric information and divergence of preferences, Antle and Eppen (1985) show that it is optimal for a firm to set a required rate of return for accepted projects above the firm's cost of capital (the rate k discussed in Section 7.2).

In the Antle and Eppen (1985) model (and most other subsequent capital budgeting agency papers), the principal–agent relationship is exemplified by the relationship between the firm's owner and manager. The manager makes a project proposal in the firm's annual capital allocation process. The manager has private information about the true productivity state (i.e. the profitability) of the project, but the owner only knows the probability distribution of the productivity. Since only the manager knows the true productivity state, a communication process is modelled in which the manager reports the productivity state to the owner. The owner (the principal) provides the capital allocation contract as a menu with pairs of allocated capital and required output for each possible productivity state. By selecting among the menu of contracts, the manager reports the productivity state and is then required to attain the level of output specified in the contract. Divergence of prefer-ences arises in this model from the manager's desire to maximize organizational slack, defined as the amount of capital allocated in excess of the capital actually used to produce the required level of output. The owner seeks to maximize the expected net present value of investment (i.e. the sum of all productivity states of the product of the owner's prior probabilities that a productivity state occurs and the difference between the discounted value of required output and the allocated capital for the given productivity state). The time line for the Antle and Eppen (1985) model is shown in Figure 7.3.[10]

In the Antle and Eppen (1985) model, the firm optimally commits to providing excess capital (i.e. capital beyond what is required to produce the given output) for the most favourable productivity states and commits to rejecting some marginally favourable invest-ments (some intermediate productivity). The excess capital provided becomes the manager's organizational slack and represents an information rent paid to the manager when the productivity state is highly favourable. This cost of the excess capital along with the

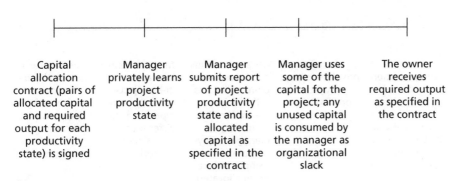

Figure 7.3 Time line for Antle and Eppen (1985) Model

opportunity cost of not investing in marginally favourable productivity states together provide the manager with incentives to reveal truthfully the manager's private information. The principal must commit to behaviour (allocating excess capital for high states and rejecting projects for marginally favourable states) that is *ex ante* optimal, but *ex post* (i.e. after receiving the manager's report of the productivity state) inefficient. Capital rationing and organizational slack are efficient (i.e. optimal) in the second best world where the costs of the asymmetric information are explicitly considered.

The asymmetries in information in the model may be viewed as the informational impediments that drive down the value of the project to the owner. The value of the optimal solution in the Antle and Eppen (1985) framework (i.e. the value of the second best solution) is less than the value when the owner has full information. There are two sources of informational asymmetries in the Antle and Eppen (1985) model, the first giving rise to the adverse selection problem and the second to the moral hazard problem. These sources of informational asymmetries are: (*a*) the manager knows the productivity state (the profitability of the investment), while the owner cannot observe the state; and (*b*) the manager knows how much of the allocated capital is applied to production and, hence, how much the manager consumes as organizational slack, while the owner cannot observe the slack.

While a number of agency papers (e.g. Antle and Fellingham 1990, 1995, 1997; Antle et al. 1999, 2001; Arya and Glover 2001; Arya et al. 1996) examine capital budgeting issues using a model directly or closely related to that of Antle and Eppen (1985), there are some substantial differences in some other models (e.g. Gordon et al. 1990; Baiman and Rajan 1995; Harris and Raviv 1996; Dutta and Reichelstein 2002; Baldenius 2003; Dutta 2003). In many of these other papers, divergence of preferences arises from other factors besides the manager's desire for organizational slack. Gordon et al. (1990), for example, following basic agency models of Holmstrom (1979) and Penno (1984), assume that the manager receives disutility from effort and that managerial effort is unobservable. Harris and Raviv (1996) and Baldenius (2003) assume that the manager receives non-pecuniary benefits from receiving a larger capital allocation and thereby managing a bigger organization. Baldenius (2003) points that this empire benefit may be derived from (*a*) the manager's perception that market reputations are enhanced by running a bigger organization; and/or (*b*) plush offices and other fringe benefits are associated with the organization's size; and (*c*) the

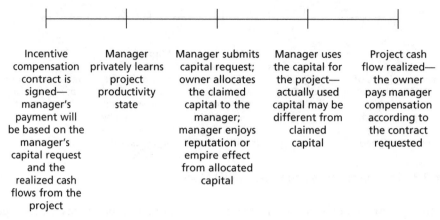

Figure 7.4 Alternative time line for capital budgeting models

enhanced feeling of power of running a larger organization. Bernardo et al. (2001) point out that an effort-averse manager would seek extra capital resources when capital can substitute for effort. Dutta (2003) notes that human capital may also be a source of divergence of preferences, when the manager has unique skills for the project, and can pursue the project inside the firm or as an outside venture on his or her own.

In Antle and Eppen (1985) and derivative models, the manager seeks to maximize the amount that allocated capital exceeds actual capital used, i.e. organizational slack. In Gordon et al. (1990), Bernardo et al. (2001), Baldenius (2003), and Dutta (2003), the manager maximizes utility that depends on direct monetary payment from the owner and one or more terms representing the disutility effect of managerial effort and/or the direct utility (the empire) effect from having capital allocated. The owner's pay-off comes from the project's net cash inflows less the allocated capital and the compensation paid to the manager. Figure 7.4 illustrates a time line that typifies the story for many of the papers (e.g. Bernardo et al. 2001; Baldenius 2003; Dutta 2003) modelling the capital budgeting problem.

A number of the more recent capital budgeting papers (Baiman and Rajan 1995; Dutta and Reichelstein 2002; Baldenius 2003; Dutta 2003) investigate the issue of whether investment decision rights should be retained by the owner or delegated to a (division) manager. When the investment decision is delegated to the manager, the papers by Dutta and Reichelstein (2002), Dutta (2003), and Baldenius (2003) investigate the use of a residual income compensation scheme and the relation between the optimal capital charge and the firm's cost of capital.

7.3.1 MANAGEMENT ACCOUNTING SYSTEMS

The agency costs (the difference between the value of the full information solution and the second best solution) are directly related to the degree of asymmetric information. Suppose a public information system (i.e. an information system whose signals could be publicly verified, so that contracts based on these signals could be enforced) were available at no cost that would reduce the asymmetries by providing the owner with better information about the actual productivity state (observed by the manager). The owner could write a new contract that would reduce the agency cost. Antle and Fellingham (1995) examine this issue in their extension of the Antle and Eppen (1985) paper. In particular, they examine the nature of the information system that the owner and the manager would each wish to have implemented. With a finer information (management accounting) system, the owner would be able to reduce *ex post* inefficiencies by investing in some lower productivity states (i.e. by lowering the hurdle rate). However, Antle and Fellingham (1995) demonstrate that while it is always in the owner's interest to implement a costless public information system, the manager sometimes loses because of the reduced information rents. Hence, while the presence of the information systems leaves the owner and manager better off (e.g. systems that provide signals separating low-productivity states from high-productivity states, but not distinguishing among high-productivity states), the manager and owner have conflicting preferences among information systems. A manager has incentives to expend resources to block any information system that would increase the owner's profits, but reduce the manager's informational rents. Antle and Fellingham (1995: 48) point out that at a minimum a manager has no incentive to find and propose such an information system to the owner. Hence, in terms of designing an MAS for capital budgeting systems, there are informational (and behavioural) impediments to reducing the informational impediments!

Gordon et al. (1990) present a capital budgeting agency model in which the manager has imperfect information about the productivity state (which proxies for estimates of future cash flows from the project). The information available to the manager, though imperfect, is superior to the information available to the owner. Whereas Antle and Fellingham (1995) investigate the value of introducing a public information system to reduce asymmetries of information, Gordon et al. (1990) investigate the value of providing the manager (the agent) with a new private information system (e.g. MAS) that provides superior information about the productivity state (cash flows).

In the Gordon et al. (1990) model, the owner determines the manager's compensation based on the manager's report on the productivity state and on the realized cash flows generated by the project. Moreover, the owner uses the communicated information to make a planning decision (i.e. whether or not to invest in the project, as well as to control for the manager's disposition to avoid expending personal effort to enhance the probability of favourable cash flow outcomes). Gordon et al. (1990) thus extend the analysis of Penno (1984) concerning the value of participative budgeting to a setting where the communication has a planning as well as control role. They show that if providing a given information system (e.g. MAS) to the manager is valuable in the setting without a planning problem, it is valuable when there is a control problem. Gordon et al. (1990) also show that some information systems that were not valuable when used in connection with only the control problem become valuable when the planning dimension is added to the owner's control problem. Moreover, they show that even when the owner uses communicated information to plan (i.e. to make the investment/no investment decision), the owner may be worse off by supplying the manager with a private predecision information system. The implication of the preceding discussion for the MAS is that providing the manager with an information system that reduces the manager's uncertainty regarding future cash flows (i.e. reducing the manager's informational impediments concerning future cash flows) is not always in the interest of the owner.

The informational impediments from a manager's private information can be at least reduced by the MAS via auditing information, although some other informational impediments are associated with post-auditing (as discussed in Section 7.4). This *ex post* MAS information of auditing is suggested by Antle and Eppen (1985: 172): '[A]uditing the manager's reports and monitoring the resources actually invested in the project are substitutes for resource rationing.' In Harris and Raviv (1996) the audit probability is a function of audit cost, but the true technology is revealed with certainty when the audit occurs. From the cost–benefit analysis perspective, if the incremental benefits from reducing agency costs exceed the incremental costs in auditing, we should invest in the auditing function in MAS to ameliorate the information impediments. Besides verifying the actual productivity state, auditing can alert the manager in advance, as Antle and Fellingham (1997: 898) describe: 'Anticipating the audit, the manager's communication alternatives are narrowed to being consistent with audit outcome.' Consequently, the optimal owner–manager contract will be modified in anticipation to the manger's response to the contract.

Besides auditing the project at the very end of it, MAS can provide interim auditing information that allows the owner to delay the capital investment decision until receiving updated information about the productivity state. Arya and Glover (2001) show the option value of delaying the project approval decision since the owner's information is improved and so the manager's information rents are reduced. If the benefits from the deferment option can justify the costs of interim auditing, we should invest in an interim auditing function as part of the MAS.

The informational impediments in a manager's preferences can also be resolved by providing a better performance evaluation scheme in the MAS. As shown in Holmstrom (1979) and discussed in the context of the issue of controllability in responsibility accounting by Antle and Demski (1988), a MAS can reduce the informational impediments giving rise to agency costs by including imperfect signals of non-observable private information (such as the manager's effort or the amount of the allocated capital consumed directly by the manager) as long as these signals provide information about the private information, conditional on the other information available. Arya et al. (1996) show how using the information communicated about the productivity state by one manager can reduce agency costs associated with capital budgeting with another manager. Even though the productivity state of one manager is not controllable by the other manager, as long as the productivity states (and hence reports) are correlated the signal has information content and is valuable.

Finally, there are some informational impediments to capital budgeting that are implicit in all (or nearly all) the information economic models. First, these models assume that realized cash flow is observable. In the context of a one-period model and a single project this assumption is reasonable. However, when there are many projects undertaken over several periods, observing actual cash flow associated with any single project is near impossible. Decoupling the cash flows for individual projects is a formidable task, but a task that should receive the attention of designers of MASs. Second, the information economics models assume that both the manager and the owner are able costlessly to compute complicated optimal strategies. While a few models restrict analysis to linear models using bounded rationality as justification, the informational impediments related to bounded rationality associated with deriving complicated optimal strategies are only addressed in an ad hoc fashion. In a similar fashion, the informational impediments related to informational overload are only addressed in an ad hoc fashion. Thus, there is an important role for MASs to play in terms of identifying and reducing such constraints as bounded rationality and information overload.[11]

7.4 **Post-auditing captial investments**

As noted in the introduction, capital budgeting refers to the planning and control process associated with capital expenditures. The planning side of this process consists of the following three basic phases: (*a*) setting organizational objectives; (*b*) identifying opportunities and/or problems associated with those objectives; and (*c*) using capital budgeting models to rank and select specific capital projects. Until the 1990s most of the discussions of capital budgeting focused on the ranking and selection phases of capital budgeting. Some noted exceptions to this claim do exist. For example, the importance of, and difficulty in, collecting information related to setting organizational objectives and identifying opportunities and/or problems were explicitly discussed in the context of capital budgeting by Gordon et al. (1978), Larcker (1981), and Gordon and Pinches (1984).[12]

Although some papers discussed the control side of capital budgeting as a by-product of the selection phase (e.g. as noted earlier, Antle and Eppen (1985) did discuss the role of auditing and/or monitoring related to capital investments), it was not until the 1990s that the control side of capital investments received prominent attention by researchers. This latter literature, often discussed under the heading of post-auditing capital investments, focused on the process of comparing the actual results with anticipated results. The objectives of this comparison were often presented in terms of financial control, improving future capital investment decisions, and overcoming psychological and political problems (see e.g. Gordon 2004: ch. 13). Implicit in this literature was the notion that post-auditing also helped address the informational impediments associated with asymmetric information between the principals and agents (i.e. the issue of asymmetric information discussed in Section 7.3).

In one of the earlier papers on this topic, Myers et al. (1991) provided a rational explanation, plus empirical evidence, for the mixed findings by researchers concerning the relation between sophisticated methods for selecting projects and firm performance (see Pike 1984, 1988; Haka et al. 1985). The basic argument provided by Myers et al. (1991) was that the effectiveness of sophisticated selection techniques is premised on the assumption that compatible control techniques are used to weed out poorly performing projects. In other words, if a firm used DCF techniques to select capital projects, they should be controlling such projects based on actual cash flows over the life of the project. Unfortunately, a large number of firms are controlling the very same projects based on a one-time review of accounting profits or accounting rates of return (what Myers et al. (1991) refer to as naive post-auditing techniques). For a group of firms using sophisticated models for selecting capital projects, Myers et al. (1991) empirically confirmed the argument that firms which use sophisticated post-auditing techniques for controlling capital investments based on DCF techniques (i.e. firms that compare actual cash flows to expected cash flows at periodic and regular intervals) are likely to show improved firm performance relative to those firms using naive post-auditing techniques. These findings were statistically significant, based on Tobin's q as the measure of firm performance. The work by Myers et al. (1991) was confirmed by the empirical research conducted by Gordon et al. (1994), where firm performance was gauged in terms of accounting rates of return.

Of course, the fact that the findings regarding the use of sophisticated post-auditing techniques were statistically significant does not mean that the divergence in sophistication between the way capital investments are initially selected and ultimately controlled was true for all firms (i.e. statistical significance is an averaging process). In an effort to examine the contingency nature of benefits derived from sophisticated post-auditing, taking explicit account of the emerging literature in the 1980s on asymmetric information, Gordon and Smith (1992) examined the role of asymmetric information in driving the benefits of sophisticated post-auditing techniques for capital budgeting. The basic argument advanced by Gordon and Smith was that the greater the degree of asymmetric information between senior level managers responsible for approving capital expenditures decisions and lower level managers requesting such fund, the greater the value derived from post-auditing. Based on an admittedly crude measure of asymmetric information, Gordon and Smith (1992) empirically confirmed their argument. In other words, they found that firm performance indeed related to the appropriate match between post-audit sophistication and the degree of asymmetric information between senior managers responsible for allocating capital expenditures funds and lower level managers requesting such funds.

Whereas most corporations use, to one degree or another, sophisticated capital budgeting models for selecting projects, the same is apparently not true for the use of sophisticated post-auditing methods. In fact, less than half of the firms included in several empirical studies were using these methods (see e.g. Myers et al. 1991; Gordon and Smith 1992). The primary impediment to using such techniques relates to gathering the requisite information. In other words, to conduct sophisticated post-auditing, it is necessary to compare (on a periodic basis) actual cash flows with expected cash flows. Unfortunately, the actual cash flows derived from individual capital projects are rarely gathered by an organization's information system. It is, however, possible for MASs to help alleviate this impediment.

7.4.1 MANAGEMENT ACCOUNTING SYSTEMS

As the preceding discussion detailed, control can play an important role in facilitating firm performance. However, to accomplish this role information is required to conduct what has been referred to as sophisticated post-auditing. The primary informational impediment to conducting sophisticated post-auditing relates to the lack of periodic cash flow data on the actual performance of capital projects. There are two key reasons for the absence of such data. First, firms collect data through their normal accrual system of accounting. This system records revenues when earned and expenses when incurred. The timing of the actual cash flows and, in turn, the time value of money, is not explicitly considered. However, to be consistent with DCF selection techniques, the cash flows are required. In other words, the actual cash flows need to be compared to expected cash flows. Thus, it is incumbent upon the designers of MASs to incorporate cash flow conversion models (i.e. models that convert actual revenues and expenses into cash flows) for individual capital projects.

Attempting to convert actual revenue and expenses into cash flow data for individual capital projects raises the second reason why such data are rarely available. The reason is that individual capital projects are often selected as if they operate in isolation to other organization projects. In reality, however, projects interact with one another and separating the actual cash flows received from one project versus another is next to impossible in many, if not most, situations. Of course, to the extent that such separation is possible, it is up to the MAS to provide the necessary cash flow allocations for individual projects. In addition, wherever possible, cash flows could be derived for 'bundles' of projects. The cash flows derived for these bundles of projects could then be compared to the sum of the expected cash flows for the individual projects.

In addition to cash flow data on individual projects, information on the actual productivity states associated with projects is also needed for the control side of capital investments. Here again, a well-designed MAS can play an important role in mitigating this informational impediment.

7.5 **Concluding comments**

Capital budgeting has always been an integral part of management accounting. However, over time, management accounting researchers have slowly relinquished at least part of their claim to this field. Developments related to such issues as the CAPM model and real options have been in large part responsible for this situation. Nevertheless, a fundamental issue still affecting the area of capital investments relates to informational impediments. A key objective of this chapter has been to emphasize that management accounting, and more specifically MASs, should play an important role in rectifying informational impediments to capital investments. Indeed, in our opinion, it is time for management accounting as a discipline to reclaim its rightful role in the field of capital budgeting.

☐ NOTES

1 Although beyond the scope of this chapter, there is a large body of macroeconomics literature that links capital formation (i.e. the accumulation of capital goods through capital investments) with the gross domestic product of a country.

2 In accounting, an expense is often referred to as an expired cost (Gordon 2004: ch. 3).

3 Much of the early literature on capital budgeting is examined in Bromwich (1976).

4 The Capital Asset Pricing Model, known widely as simply CAPM, was developed in the early 1960s. See e.g. Sharpe (1964).

5 See Gordon and Loeb (2002, 2005) for extensive discussions of confidentiality and other aspects of information security within the context of internal capital allocation.

6 The essential elements of the VCG mechanism along with its historical development are explored in Loeb (1977). The primary references are Vickrey (1961), Clarke (1971) and Groves (1973). The Demand Revealing Process, the pivot mechanism, and the Groves scheme are among the other names used to refer to the VCG mechanism.

7 Ronen and McKinney (1970) model communication and incentives within the firm in the context of the transfer pricing problem. The mechanism proposed by Ronen and Mckinney (1970) is a slightly modified version of the VCG mechanism (see Groves and Loeb 1976).

8 As pointed out by Harris et al. (1982), when divergence of preferences is absent, incentive problems vanish, as the principal can pay a constant wage and agents will have no incentives to distort their privately held information. Cohen and Loeb (1984) showed that the VCG model can easily be reinterpreted in such a way that it easily handles divergent preferences for the division managers' effort. However, such a reinterpretation does not consider the inherent conflict that the principal wishes to maximize pay-off net of incentive payments to the agents.

9 The term *adverse selection* does not always convey the same exact meaning in the literature. In some contexts adverse selection is used only to refer to a situation in which the agent has private information before the agent enters into a contact with the principal (i.e. private precontract information).

10 Figures 7.3 and 7.4 indicate that the manager receives private information concerning the productivity state subsequent to contracting with the owner. If one assumes, as do Antle and Eppen (1985), that the manager must be guaranteed the reservation utility level for each possible productivity state (e.g. limited liability), then it is inconsequential whether the manager receives private information before or after contracting.

11 See Miller and Gordon (1975) for a discussion concerning information overload and designing the MAS.

12 The control, or post-auditing, of capital investments has several objectives.

☐ REFERENCES

Akerlof, G. (1970). 'The Market for Lemons: Quality Uncertainty and the Market Mechanism', *Quarterly Journal of Economics*, 84: 488–500.

Alchian, A. and Demsetz, H. (1972). 'Production, Information Costs, and Economic Organization', *American Economic Review*, 62: 777–95.

Antle, R. and Demski, J. (1988). 'The Controllability Principle in Responsibility Accounting', *Accounting Review*, 63: 700–18.

—— and Eppen, G. (1985). 'Capital Rationing and Organizational Slack in Capital Budgeting', *Management Science* (February): 163–74.

—— and Fellingham, J. (1990). 'Resource Rationing and Organizational Slack in a Two-Period Model', *Journal of Accounting Research*, 28: 1–24.

—— —— (1995). 'Information Rents and Preferences among Information Systems in a Model of Resource Allocation', *Journal of Accounting Research*, 33: 41–58.

—— —— (1997). 'Models of Capital Investments with Private Information and Incentives: A Selective Review', *Journal of Business Finance and Accounting*, 7/8: 887–908.

Antle, R., Bogetoft, P., and Stark, A. (1999). 'Selection from Many Investments with Managerial Private Information', *Contemporary Accounting Research*, 16: 397–418.

—— —— —— (2001). 'Information Systems, Incentives and the Timing of Investments', *Journal of Accounting and Public Policy*, 20: 267–94.

Arya, A. and Glover, J. (2001). 'Option Value to Waiting Created by a Control Problem', *Journal of Accounting Research*, 39: 405–16.

—— —— and Young, R. (1996). 'Capital Budgeting in a Multidivisonal Firm', *Journal of Accounting, Auditing, and Finance*, 11: 519–33.

Baiman, S. (1982). 'Agency Research in Managerial Accounting: A Survey', *Journal of Accounting Literature*, 1: 154–213.

—— and Rajan, M. (1995). 'Centralization, Delegation, and Shared Responsibility of Capital Investment Decision Rights', *Journal of Accounting Research*, 33: 135–64.

Baldenius, T. (2003). 'Delegated Investment Decisions and Private Benefits of Control', *Accounting Review*, 78: 909–30.

Bernardo, A. E., Cai, H., and Luo, J. (2001). 'Capital Budgeting and Compensation with Asymmetric Information and Moral Hazard', *Journal of Financial Economics*, 61: 311–44.

Brealey, R. and Myers, S. (2000). *Principles of Corporate Finance*. New York: Irwin/McGraw-Hill.

Bromwich, M. (1976). *The Economics of Capital Budgeting*. London: Penguin.

Chenhall, R. and Morris, D. (1986). 'The Impact of Structure, Environment, and Interdependence on the Perceived Usefulness of Management Accounting Systems', *Accounting Review*, 61: 16–35.

Clarke, E.H. (1971). 'Multipart Pricing of Public Goods', *Public Choice*, 11: 17–33

Cohen, S. and Loeb, M. (1984). 'The Groves Scheme, Profit Sharing, and Moral Hazard', *Management Science*, 30: 20–4.

Committee of Sponsoring Organizations of the Treadway Commission (2004). 'Enterprise Risk Management-Integrated Framework: Executive Summary' (September). Available at http://www.coso.org/publications.htm.

Dixit, A. and Pindyck, R. (1994). *Investment Under Uncertainty*. Princeton, NJ: Princeton University Press.

Dutta, S. (2003). 'Capital Budgeting and Managerial Compensation: Incentive and Retention Effects', *Accounting Review*, 78: 71–93.

Dutta, S. and Reichelstein, S. (2002). 'Controlling Investment Decisions: Depreciation and Capital Charges', *Review of Accounting Studies*, 7: 253–81.

Gordon, L. A. (1974). 'Accounting Rate of Return vs. Economic Rate of Return', *Journal of Business Finance and Accounting*, 1: 343–56.

—— (2004). *Managerial Accounting: Concepts and Empirical Evidence*. New York, McGraw-Hill.

—— and Loeb, M. P. (2002). 'The Economics of Information Security Investment', *ACM Transactions on Information and System Security*, 5: 438–57.

—— —— (2005). *Managing Cybersecurity Resources: A Cost-Benefit Analysis*. New York: McGraw-Hill.

—— and Miller, D. (1976). 'A Contingency Framework for the Design of Accounting Information Systems', *Accounting, Organizations and Society*, 1: 59–69.

—— and Pinches, G. (1984). *Improving Capital Budgeting: A Decision Support System Approach*. Boston: Addison-Wesley.

—— and Smith, K. (1992). 'Postauditing Capital Expenditures and Firm Performance: The Rose of Asymmetric Information', *Accounting, Organizations and Society*, 17: 741–57.

—— Larcker, D. F., and Tuggle, F. (1978). 'Strategic Decision Processes and the Design of Accounting Information Systems: Conceptual Linkages', *Accounting, Organizations and Society*, 3: 203–13.

—— —— —— (1979). 'Informational Impediments to the Use of Sophisticated Capital Budgeting Models', *Omega*, 7: 67–74.

—— Loeb, M. P., and Myers, M. (1994). 'A Note on Postauditing and Firm Performance', *Managerial and Decision Economics*, 15: 177–81.

—— Loeb, M. P. and Stark, A. W. (1990). 'Capital Budgeting and the Value of Information', *Management Accounting Research*, 1: 21–35.

Groves, T. (1973).'Incentives in Teams', *Econometrica*, 41: 617–31

—— and Loeb, M. (1976). 'Reflections on Social Costs and Benefits and the Transfer Pricing Problem', *Journal of Public Economics*, 5: 353–9.

—— —— (1979). 'Incentives in a Divisionalized Firm', *Management Science*, 25: 221–30.

Haka, S., Gordon, L. A., and Pinches, G. (1985). 'Sophisticated Capital Budgeting Selection Techniques and Firm Performance', *Accounting Review*, 60: 651–69.

Harris, M. and Raviv, A. (1996). 'The Capital Budgeting Process: Incentives and Information', *Journal of Finance*, 51: 1139–74.

—— Kriebel, C., and Raviv, A.(1982). 'Asymmetric Information, Incentives, and Intrafirm Resource Allocation', *Management Science*, 28: 404–620.

Holmstrom, B. (1979). 'Moral Hazard and Observability', *Bell Journal of Economics*, 10: 74–91.

Jensen, M. and Meckling, W. (1976). 'Theory of the firm: Managerial Behavior, Agency Costs and Ownership Structure', *Journal of Financial Economics*, 3: 303–60.

Klammer, T. (1972). 'Empirical Evidence of the Adoption of Sophisticated Capital Budgeting Techniques', *Journal of Business*, 45: 387–97

Larcker, D. F. (1981). 'The Perceived Importance of Selected Information Characteristics for Strategic Capital Budgeting Decisions', *Accounting Review*, 56: 519–38.

Loeb, M. (1977). 'Alternative Versions of the Demand-Revealing Process', *Public Choice*, 29: 15–26.

—— and Magat, W. (1978). 'Soviet Success Indicators and the Evaluation of Divisional Management', *Journal of Accounting Research*, 16: 103–21.

Marschak, J. and Radner, R. (1972). *Economic Theory of Teams*. New Haven, CT: Yale University Press.

Mia, L. (1993). 'The Role of MAS Information in Organisations: An Empirical Study', *British Accounting Review*, 25: 269–85.

Miller, D. and Gordon, L. A. (1975). 'Conceptual Levels and the Design of Accounting Information Systems', *Decision Sciences*, 6: 259–69.

Myers, M., Gordon, L., and Hamer, M. (1991). 'Postauditing Capital Assets and Firm Performance: An Empirical Investigation', *Managerial and Decision Economics*, 12: 317–27.

Pearce, D. (1991). *The MIT Dictionary of Modern Economics*, 3rd edn. Cambridge, MA: MIT Press.

Penno, M. (1984). 'Asymmetry of Pre-decision Information and Managerial Accounting', *Journal of Accounting Research*, 22: 177–91.

Pike, R. H. (1984). 'Sophisticated Capital Budgeting and Their Assocation with Corporate performance', *Managerial and Decision Economics*, 5: 91–7

Pike, R. (1988). 'An Empirical Study of the Adoption of Sophisticated Capital Budgeting Practices and Decision-Making Effectiveness', *Accounting and Business Research*, 18: 341–51.

Ronen, J. and McKinney, J. (1970). 'Transfer Pricing for Divisional Autonomy', *Journal of Accounting Research*, 8: 99–113.

Ross, S. (1973). 'The Economic Theory of Agency: The Principal's Problem', *American Economic Review*, 63: 134–9.

Sarbanes-Oxley Act of 2002 (PL 107–204, 30 July 2002). Available at http://news.findlaw.com/hdocs/docs/gwbush/sarbanesoxley072302.pdf.

Schall, L., Sundem, R. L., and Geijsbeek, W.R. Jr. (1978). 'Survey and Analysis of Capital Budgeting Methods', *Journal of Finance*, 33: 281–7.

Sharpe, W. F. (1964). 'Capital Asset Prices: A Theory of Market Equilibrium Under Conditions of Risk', *Journal of Finance*, 19(3): 425–42.

Vickrey, W. (1961). 'Counterspeculation, Auctions, and Competitive Sealed Tenders', *Journal of Finance*, 16: 8–37.

8 Accounting and strategy: towards understanding the historical genesis of modern business and military strategy

Keith Hoskin
Richard Macve
John Stone

8.1 Introduction

A working definition of strategic management accounting is: the provision and analysis of financial information on the firm's product market and competitors' costs and cost structures and the monitoring of the enterprise's strategies and those of its competitors in these markets over a number of periods. (Bromwich 1990: 28)

Bromwich's analysis (1990) of the information requirements for cost and management accounting, to meet the challenges of modern economic analyses of the conditions for competitive success in both input and sales markets, emphasizes the need 'to release management accounting from the factory floor' and focus externally (on both customers and competitors) and over the long-term horizon (Bromwich and Bhimani 1989: 95–6). In a later extension of this 'strategic management accounting' (SMA), Bromwich has argued that further attention is needed to the revenue side of the strategic profit-maximization function: 'revenue management might profit from adopting the technical and detailed approach of accounting' (2000: 46). He has also emphasized there (e.g. p. 46) the importance of other quantitative as well as qualitative information on performance factors in complementing the more traditional cost-focused approaches.

In summary, in looking at accounting's role in relation to strategy, Bromwich's approach to SMA exhorts the firm and its management accountants to look beyond the firm itself and its cost structures to competitor firms and customer demand, not only in the immediate environment but, in principle, including all potential competitors and potential customers over the long-term decision horizon. The immediate 'traditional' battle to fight to control costs internally must, of course, not be lost sight of, but managements'—and their accountants'—eyes must also be scanning the wider horizons, present and future, and collecting and processing information in a number of forms. While Bromwich (2000: 47) concludes that so far 'progress ... [has] been somewhat disappointing', he has also sketched 'an argument for expecting future growth' in SMA. More recently, he has linked SMA to the new statutory requirements on UK-listed companies to publish an 'Operating and Financial Review' (OFR) (Bromwich 2005).

Bromwich's SMA reflects primarily the 'rational planning' form of strategy exhibited by mainstream economists as well as by strategists such as Porter (1980, 1985) or Roberts (2004). But he also recognizes 'the need to fit into the analysis other views of strategy' such as the 'resource-based' view of competitive advantage (e.g. Kay 1993) or the 'processual' characterizations (e.g. Mintzberg 1984) and other forms, which increasingly live alongside each other (e.g. Whittington 1993; Richardson and Thompson 1995: 260–8; Mintzberg et al. 2005).

In this chapter[1] we intend to address the following double question: precisely how and when did the modern practice of strategy and its theorization emerge? What is its historical and thereby present link to accounting (Roberts 1990)? It is a commonplace that the evolutions of business strategies and structures are interlinked (e.g. Chandler 1962; Roberts 2004),[2] and the linkages between the historical genesis of 'modern' accounting and the emergence of US 'big business' structures from the 1840s have been (and are continuing to be) explored (e.g. Hoskin and Macve 2000, 2005). So are the histories of strategy and accounting likewise intertwined? And if so, how? And what is the relationship, if any, to *military* strategy?

We shall first need to clarify the history of strategy itself, and here we shall show that the modern practice must be distinguished from earlier ideas of strategy. A qualitatively new practice emerged at some point after 1800. Just as the 'modern business enterprise' has no parallel in earlier business history, and just, equally, as there was nothing previously equivalent to the modern power of accounting in business, so within the business world strategy became an insistent presence where before it was a conspicuous absence. In parallel, in the military sphere also, strategic discourse was refocused away from its traditional concerns with the operational aspects of bringing armies to battle, and towards the logistical relation of means (not necessarily military) to geopolitical ends (e.g. Builder 1989: 49). We shall argue that these innovations in both the business and military arenas are intimately linked as aspects of the modern 'disciplinary' world: a world firstly where disciplinary techniques of power are widespread, but also where new disciplinary forms of knowledge arguably play an even more significant role.

We shall contend that much conventional analysis of strategy—both business and military—is misdirected because it has as yet no proper understanding of the *history* of strategy. In the conventional view, 'self-evidently' strategy first entered business from the military domain, but has then developed along some very different trajectories. It is not so. On the contrary, a new discourse of military strategy was invented *alongside* business strategy. Indeed, under our analysis it was the same people who invented both. And in doing so they also reflected the practices that were creating a new and much more powerful discourse of accounting and accountability.

Our purpose here, then, in collaborating as a team of business, accounting, and military historians and theoreticians is to enable us to use history to understand theory.

Section 8.2 briefly considers the nature of 'disciplinary' power, and what it means to say that strategy, as a form of *knowledge* as well as of power, comes to be 'disciplinary'. It stresses the need to examine the emergence of the *practices* that constitute modern strategy, and focuses on how strategy combines the practices of writing, examination, calculation, and valuation that also generate the modern 'accounting' regime.

Section 8.3 considers how these practices could have remade strategy into its modern form. It briefly reviews how recent work (e.g. Hoskin and Macve 1988, 1990, 1994*a*, 2000, 2005) has challenged Chandler's thesis (1977) of the 'irrelevance' of the military to the development of modern business organization and has suggested that the modern practices of managerialism and accounting have a joint historical genesis, not in the military sphere per se, but more crucially in the sphere of *military education.*[3] It was the revolution in the education at the US Military Academy (USMA) at West Point from 1817 that represented a new kind of 'human engineering' and transformed both business and military discourse. In the light of the revisions offered here to Chandler's historical analysis, we suggest that strategy comes not before structure but alongside it in the new organizational structure of managerialism that enters both the business and military domains in the mid nineteenth century: both are simultaneous outcomes of the new power–knowledge nexus.

Section 8.4 then takes up the possible objection that strategy has a long history stretching back into the military past (first to its Greek etymological root στρατηγία [*strat-eegia*] and then 'reinvented' after the Second World War): this objection is challenged by briefly tracing the earlier history of the practice of military strategy and demonstrating its nineteenth-century transformation. In this section we advance the thesis that von Clausewitz is not the first of the modern, but the last of the premodern, military strategists.

In Section 8.5, we address the question: why is it that modern strategy appears to show up, both in the business and military fields, in mid-nineteenth-century America? The reason, we suggest, is that in both cases it is the West Point graduates who implement it: first in business in the 1850s, then in the Civil war with the development of the Staff Office. Correspondingly, the first theorist of modern military strategy, we suggest, is not von Clausewitz, but Alfred Mahan—an American, who although not himself a graduate of West Point, was born and brought up there.

In Sections 8.6 and 8.7, we ask how this revised history of strategy is relevant to modern theory in both spheres, military and business. Did not the advent of 'nuclear technology' in the twentieth century, and subsequently the rise of international terrorism in the twenty-first, bring a far more fundamental shift in the nature of military strategic doctrine? Has not the growth of globalized business in the twentieth and twenty-first centuries fundamentally altered the nature of strategic business thinking? We suggest in both cases that the answer remains 'no'. Our history of the nineteenth-century discontinuity, albeit tentative, is indeed a history of the present.

In conclusion (Section 8.8), we therefore suggest that there are two major implications from doing this history. First, it is important to provide strategy with a history, in order to prevent false assumptions from claiming the status of truth. Second, if our account here of the why and how of strategy's emergence is valid, its growth in power and significance in business (and the development of its own academic discourse) can be seen (alongside and parallel to that of accounting) as an outcome of the prior shift in power–knowledge relations. Whatever its inherent limitations (some of which are far from trivial), 'strategy'—inconceivable before the disciplinary shift—becomes inevitable once it has taken place. Business cannot now distance itself from the military discourse of strategy by externalizing it as a post-Second World War import: rather, both business and war have become the 'war of the accountants' (van Creveld 1977: 202). Accounting calculation and accountability relations are now central, albeit now so 'natural' that they are often invisible. From this perspective, SMA itself may be seen as a contemporary articulation and re-identification of what is in essence a genetic symbiosis.

8.2 **The nature of 'disciplinary power'**

'Disciplinary power' (e.g. Foucault 1977)[4] is the key form of power that makes the modern world run; but 'disciplinary power' is a term much misunderstood. It is not enough to talk of the power effects of disciplining; what is equally involved is the rise of sustained cognitive growth.

Writing, examination, grading (calculation of relative value): these are the practices that constitute 'disciplinary power'. From small, unobserved beginnings in a tiny elite world (medieval European universities; the nineteenth-century USMA (Hoskin and Macve 1994b)), there emerged a new 'human success system': this set of practices, turning things into writing, constant examination, and numerical grading of performance, constituted an as-yet-unparalleled way of (a) forming human subjects and (b) running human organizations.

We have suggested that these new practices embody two new interacting principles; new dynamics that come to drive the power–knowledge interaction. The first is 'grammatocentrism', as power and knowledge become increasingly exercised through writing. As individuals and organizations we are 'grammatocentric', i.e. centred on writing, in a world where the written takes priority: we operate via texts, handbooks, plans, data, models, memos, evaluations, budgets, accounts, analyses; and then at a meta-level we construct accounts of the accounts, meta-narratives, meta-analyses, new models, critical theories, and so on. The second is the principle of subjecting everything (including all this new writing) to constant examination and grading. This is the principle of 'calculability'. The mark is the invisible technology that lies beneath this. It does not just put a number on performance; it puts a value on the person. It provides for the first time in history what can be perceived as an objective measure of human success, and failure.[5]

From 1817 onwards, and initially at West Point, a generation in the USA 'learned how to learn' in a historically new way. Later, as adults, they came to construct power systems that stressed examination, grading, and the centrality of writing. Among these were the first modern systems of managerialism and accounting in both the business and military spheres. And this same generation also came to construct knowledge systems that stressed the same three practices. Thus emerged the modern academic discipline form in which our own research work is still carried on,[6] as did key practices through which one now becomes a successful player in the modern corporate or military managerial world. This complementarity, we are suggesting, is no coincidence.

8.3 The disciplinary genesis of the 'modern business enterprise': Alfred Chandler re-examined

Recent work (e.g. Hoskin and Macve 1990, 1994b, 2005) has applied this general insight to re-evaluate the emergence of the 'modern business enterprise' in the USA. This is described by Chandler (1962, 1977) as simply a necessary and rational *response* to prior economic and technological change. Specifically:

Modern business enterprise is the institutional response to the rapid pace of technological innovation and increasing consumer demand in the United States during the second half of the 19th century. (Chandler 1977: 12)

However, Chandler himself concedes that there is something strange here. His 'pioneers of modern management'

were a new type of businessman. It is worth emphasizing again that they were salaried employees with little or no financial interest in the companies they served. Moreover most had had specialized training... [as] civil engineers. (1977: 95)

In fact, when one looks closer at the first key changes, at the Springfield Armory (single-unit factory management) and on the Western Railroad (multi-unit enterprise), the two pioneers, Daniel Tyler and George W. Whistler, are even stranger. Neither ever ran a business in their lives; the one thing they have in common is that they had gone through the *same* specialized training, as cadets at the USMA at West Point. The two were in fact classmates, graduating together in the Class of 1819.

Therefore we have argued that historians of modern business have generally been looking at the wrong technological stimulus, for they should have been looking at the development of the *invisible* technologies: writing, examination, and grading. The primary reason why the USA (then only a marginal player on a world economic scene dominated by Britain) invented the 'modern business enterprise' around 1840 is to be found at West Point before 1820.

From 1817, West Point became perhaps the most 'disciplinary' institution anywhere. Its fourth Superintendent, Sylvanus Thayer, having gone to Paris to ascertain what was taught at the *Ecole Polytechnique* and how it was taught, brought the deployment of writing, examination, and grading to a new pitch. On the French model he used numerical marks to grade all aspects of academic performance: but in addition he created files for all aspects of behaviour and began to run the institution like a modern chief executive officer (CEO). He is perhaps the first modern 'human engineer', with West Point as his little human laboratory.

In an institution of only some 200 cadets he introduced his own line-and-staff system. From 1817, he divided the Academy into two 'divisions', creating in each a line management system (involving both officers and cadets). Daily, weekly, and monthly reports were required, all in writing. There were continual relays of written communication and command, going from the bottom to the top of each line, before being consolidated and passed to the central 'Staff Office', which consisted of Thayer, a personal clerk, and two hand-picked cadets. One of these two cadets was George Whistler.

It was a truly modern 'grammatocentric' organization. Everything was centred on the use of *writing* to run the organization. Thayer even discarded the traditional leader's role of direct, visible command. He left this to his Number Two, the Commandant. He kept himself in the Staff Office, ruling his world indirectly by the power of writing, and hardly ever being seen in person. And combined with writing was the ubiquitous practice of examination, so that Thayer equally deployed 'calculability' at every turn. Daily, weekly, termly, and annually, all grades were entered, weighted, summed, and averaged. Every cadet was precisely ranked and known by his or her performance from the day of entry to the day of graduation: and assignment to favoured Corps was strictly by order of merit. These cadets were the first to live under what is commonplace today: a constant system of objective accountability.

What, though, does all this have to do with 'strategy'? Our argument is this. 'Administrative coordination' is a power–knowledge invention, not a response to prior economic or technological stimuli. Reversing the presumed direction of change, this new disciplinary practice is what makes possible the new economic order that Chandler identifies, where the 'visible hand' overwhelms market forces, bringing in its train 'imperfect competition and misallocation of resources' (1977: 4). Thayer's West Point revolution was fundamental. A second generation of 'Thayer' graduates succeeded the likes of Tyler and Whistler, and it was one of these, Herman Haupt (Ward 1971), Superintendent of the Pennsylvania Railroad (PRR), who introduced there, from 1849 onwards, a structural and strategic reorganization, grounded in the collection and analysis of operating statistics, costs, and revenues, including comparison with other railroads, and leading to strategic analyses of the advantages and costs of organic growth, of potential alliances and/or takeovers, and of what should be the State of Pennsylvania's tax policy on rail freight, given the competition with New York and its Erie Canal. He thereby laid the foundations for the development of what was to become the largest railroad in the USA, later known as the 'Penn Central' (Hoskin and Macve 2005).

Managerialism in all its aspects is an expression of this historic reversal. It is always about 'action at a distance', effected primarily through multiple forms of writing (i.e. 'grammatocentric'), and only secondarily through speech. But it is also action through constant examination and grading of accounting data, personnel evaluations, norms and variances, targets and outcomes, projections, and post-mortems.

Thus managerialism institutes a certain way of constructing space–time relations. Its orientation to time is—like that of modern accountability—towards the future, a future it strives to know by drawing on the medium of 'objectively' measured past performance. To this end it rewrites time. It is not just that clock-time replaced body-time; clock-time is then rewritten (e.g. as the 'machine-hour') to produce a new quality of time-control and time-knowledge. Concerning space, its reach is similarly extensive and intensive. By extension of the simple originating practices in administrative coordination managerialism can know and control the furthest reaches of organizational space, and actively construct new scales of organizational complexity and size (e.g. divisionalization, matrix structures); at the same time, it penetrates intensively down into every tiny corner of the organization. It is a kind of 'panopticism' (Foucault 1977).[7] But specifically it is a grammatocentric panopticism. Moreover, it extends beyond the walls of the 'organization' to its environment—including its customers and competitors (actual and potential, present and future)—and its positioning in its whole economic, social, political, and technological milieu.

Thus, inevitably, managerialism invents strategy, for strategy is simply one more manifestation of this desire for, and enactment of, grammatocentrism and calculability (cf. Smith 2003).[8] Like management accounting, it takes and examines past data to produce a way of seeing the future. Like the line-and-staff structure within which it first emerges, it actively promotes the intensification of the principles that underlie its existence. Clearly Chandler is right here: there is a constant reciprocal movement between strategy and structure. Also strategy is unthinkable without structure. Historically, it comes into existence only in the first instance in organizations where we find the staff office above and beyond the operational lines. However, does it therefore *precede* structure? It must at least be feasible, if the analysis we advance here has any validity, that in that first instance it comes into existence *alongside* it. Following the moment of discontinuity when a new 'disciplinary' relation between power and knowledge begins to take shape, modern business strategy and structure—and indeed modern management accounting—can emerge as complementary aspects of the new power–knowledge apparatus. And apparatus must be just the word. For business hereafter becomes an apparatus of uninterrupted 'objective' examination and constant grammatocentric activity.

8.4 **Towards a re-analysis of the history of strategy**

How does this explanation square with the history of strategy, as generally understood? The first point to make is that it does not entirely dismantle Chandler's thesis. It does not attack his history of the subsequent evolution of the 'modern business enterprise'; nor does it necessarily attack him on the question of where strategy comes from. But then he does not ever explicitly raise this question. He offers definitions, whereby the strategic is differentiated from the tactical:

Strategic decisions are concerned with the long-term health of the enterprise. Tactical decisions deal more with the day-to-day activities necessary for efficient and smooth operations. (1962: 11)

Strategy is then slightly redefined in the conclusion (1962: 383), as 'the plan for the allocation of resources to anticipated demand' (while structure is 'the design for integrating the enterprise's existing resources to current demand').

We gather that strategy is concerned with forward planning and analysis, and implicitly must take into account, dependent on the level of the executives involved, different levels of 'business horizons and interests'. At a normative level, Chandler is clear that in any large segmented or divisionalized business organization strategy *should* emerge. Where it does not, and where

entrepreneurs... concentrate on short-term activities to the exclusion... of long-range planning, appraisal and coordination, they have failed to carry out effectively their role in the economy as well as in their enterprise. (1962: 12)

However, in the end, the answer that he comes up with to the question of 'why and how strategy?' only reiterates the view outlined above:

Strategic growth resulted from an awareness of the opportunities and needs—created by changing population, income and technology—to employ existing or expanding resources more profitably. (1962: 15)

In our view, for the reasons set out above, this 'pragmatic' explanation is to acknowledge discontinuity, but to fail to explain it.

However, the major alternative histories do not even do that. They accept what we would describe as 'surface manifestations' of strategy at face value. Of these the most dominant is the old presumption that 'strategy' is a unitary concept with a continuous history that leads back eventually to either a Greek or other military precedent (e.g. Cummings 1993). Alternatively, we get the presentist view, that nothing counts as strategy until there is a modern academic discourse of that name.

In one of the very few studies that considers the history of strategic management head-on,[9] Bracker (1980) combines both of these tendencies. First, he refers us to strategy's distant origins, right back to its 'first mention in the Old Testament', but concentrating mainly on its Greek etymology. He is very bullish on this, suggesting that the verb στρατηγέω [*strateegeo*] means to 'plan the destruction of one's enemies through the effective use of resources' (1980: 219). (More usually it is taken just to mean 'to lead an army' (Liddell and Scott 1871).) He even contends that

the underlying principles of strategy were discussed by Homer, Euripides and many other early writers.

This might come as a surprise to Homer and Euripides. Homer (an oral poet who never wrote) sings of the confrontations and machinations of fighting heroes. Euripides, the playwright, unfolds stories where complex motives and excessive ambition, desire, and lust lead inevitably to tragedy, nemesis, and, too late, recognition of the folly of men's ways: hardly the 'principles of strategy', if sometimes the fate of unwary strategists.

Bracker then shifts to the other extreme. The strategic viewpoint, after briefly flourishing in ancient Greece (particularly, he adds, in the ideas of Socrates)

was then lost, for all practical purposes, with the fall of the Greek city-states and was not to rise again until after the Industrial Revolution. (1980: 219)

Even then, it only really emerged after the Second World War, as business 'moved from a relatively stable environment to a more rapidly changing and competitive environment' as a result of '(1) the marked acceleration in the rate of change within firms and (2) the accelerated application of science and technology to the process of management.'[10] The founding fathers of strategy switch from being Homer and Socrates (and jumping a whole series of famous ancient, medieval, and modern practitioners)[11] to being Von Neumann and Morgenstern.[12] Thus, either strategy has always been there or it has been called forth by the needs of high-tech, knowledge-intensive modernity.

What, though, if we do go behind these two supposed histories? First, if we return to the Greeks, it is true that they did develop an intellectual and reflective discourse on what was to become known as 'the art of war'. But that phrase itself should alert us to one central aspect of strategy's ancient history. War, like philosophy, rhetoric, and kingship, was an Art, in Greek a τέχνη [technee]. It comprised two dimensions: technical skill and ethical goodness.

As such it is a discourse foreign to modern concerns.[13] Two big-picture issues that would be taken for granted today simply fail to enter the frame of intellectual reference. First, there is no focused concern with logistics, with the economics of campaigning, none even with systematic planning. The focus is above all on conflict in its immediate aspects. Second, the structural difference that particularly stands out in ancient warfare is the absence of any staff structure. In a famous phrase, 'the general is the strategy'.[14] Furthermore, this appears to remain the case into the nineteenth century. We have to wait till then, and what has been christened the 'first modern, industrial war'—the American Civil War—for the appearance of a central Staff Office whose concerns transcend the battlefield to encompass a broader set of factors including operational and logistical planning.[15]

If we revert to the terms we used previously, there is in the ancient world no set of practices that promotes the viewing of the military situation globally, by turning all aspects of it into writing and subjecting them individually and in combination to examination: there is no calculus of decision-making. No amount of hero worship for Alexander or Caesar changes that. Although the Greeks had a word for it—στρατηγία [strat-eegia]—we cannot take it for granted that they also had the modern conceptual framework within which we locate 'strategy'. Even the primary meaning of στρατηγία is not 'strategy', but the office, or period, of command (Liddell and Scott 1871).[16]

The subsequent history of strategy down to the nineteenth century is equally full of pitfalls for the unwary.[17] There is certainly no coordinated holistic vision. Military art encompasses the tasks of drilling and training the army, educating young aristocrats to be officers in military academies, and beyond this the direction of campaigns. But still 'the general is the plan'. The horizon of strategy remains set by (*a*) the skill of that one individual and (*b*) the expression of that skill in terms of the ability to manoeuvre forces in the theatre of operations, and to conduct them in battle.[18]

The development of military thought during the nineteenth century was marked by a heavy emphasis on battle, a fact that was largely attributable to a preoccupation with the exploits of Napoleon. Military officers during this period possessed at least a passing acquaintance with the history of the Napoleonic wars, and also came into contact with the works of von Clausewitz and Jomini, whose attempts to distil the essence of Napoleonic warfare proved highly influential.

A central feature of the Napoleonic wars was the swift, decisive battle that resulted in the destruction of one or other of the armies engaged. Napoleon made his reputation in the wake of the French Revolution, when the rising power of nationalism was dramatically changing the character of warfare. Limited wars of manoeuvre, in the eighteenth-century mould, were giving way to a more unrestrained type of conflict. The strength of national sentiment meant that wars were prosecuted with greater alacrity than was previously the case and that victory could be achieved only by dealing a truly shattering blow against an adversary. It was in this context that Napoleon made a reputation for himself by seeking to engage his enemy in a decisive battle that would cripple his opponent's army and thereby destroy his will to continue fighting:

I see only one thing, namely the enemy's main body. I try to crush it, confident that secondary matters will then settle themselves.[19]

The decisive battle is in fact one of the most spectacular aspects of the Napoleonic wars, and its position in nineteenth-century theories of war was correspondingly important. Significantly, Napoleon still does not have a central staff function overseeing his generals. Indeed he sees the best way of controlling them as letting them have their heads, so that each aspires to outdo the others.

In Europe, the corresponding concept of war that emerged was largely based on the writings of the Prussian military theorist Carl von Clausewitz (1780–1831). Indeed, von Clausewitz—like his Swiss contemporary Jomini—exercised a profound impact on successive generations of military thinkers, and even today is widely held to be the first great military theorist of modern times.

von Clausewitz defined strategy as the 'use of engagements for the object of the war'. As Howard (1983) has noted, in producing such a narrow—even simplistic—definition of strategy, von Clausewitz was effectively clearing the air prior to embarking on an investigation of the particular aspect of strategy that most interested him—which was still the conduct of direct military operations. Within this limited purview he is rightly honoured for the extensions that he brought to the premodern discourse, having analysed a wide range of factors bearing on military success, including the psychological and the contingent. Nevertheless, strategy still revolves around the traditional notion of annihilating the opposition on the field of battle.[20]

Thus:

Destruction of the enemy forces is the overriding principle of war, and, so far as positive action is concerned, the principal way to achieve our object.

And:

Destruction of the enemy's forces is generally accomplished by means of great battles and their results; and, the primary object of great battles must be the destruction of the enemy's forces. (von Clausewitz 1976: 258)

It is true that von Clausewitz's views on this matter were undergoing a profound change towards the end of his life. However, he died before fully revising his key work (*On War*, first published in 1832), and this, combined with his metaphysical style of writing, tended to obscure his emerging doubts about the destruction of one's enemy being the sole legitimate course of strategic action. Moreover, the dramatic Prussian victories during the second half of the nineteenth century lent the writings of von Clausewitz a Europe-wide popularity amongst readers who were seeking ready formulae for victory and who treated his incomplete ideas as a practical prescription for strategic success. Nowhere is this tendency more pronounced than in the case of the French general, Ferdinand Foch, whose writings upheld the destruction of the enemy by means of the decisive battle to be the sole method of victory. According to Foch:

[I]t is to the theory of *decision by arms* that war is now wholly returning; one can now apply no other. Instead of condemning Bonaparte's battles as acts less civilised than those of his predecessors, this theory considers them as the only efficient means; it seeks to repeat them by seeking the same sources of action as he had. (Foch 1918: 42)

Likewise, the British Army's *Field Service Regulations* (1909) stated that the 'destruction of the enemy's main force on the battlefield' was the 'ultimate objective' of operations.[21]

It was not until 1873 that Colonel J. J. Graham provided an English translation of von Clausewitz.[22] Thus, it was Jomini's *Art of War* (1836/1971) that provided a route through which Napoleon's methods influenced American strategic theory during the years before the Civil War (Weigley 1973: 77–91). The central feature of Jominian strategy was the requirement to generate numerical superiority at a decisive point in the theatre of operations via a carefully conceived scheme of manoeuvre (Jomini 1971: 70–1). Weigley has observed that Jomini's interest in manoeuvre lent his work an eighteenth-century flavour, but that he was nevertheless cognizant of the emphasis placed by Napoleon on destroying the enemy's armed forces. And, indeed, Jomini clearly stated that Napoleon focused on '*the destruction or disorganization of the enemy's forces, without giving attention to geographical points of any kind*' (Jomini 1971: 330). Jomini's influence, moreover, was supplemented with that of the popular military imagination, which upheld the Napoleonic battle as a practical guide to conduct in the field of war (Weigley 1973: 83, 89). At the outbreak of the Civil War, therefore, decisive battle was an important concept in American strategy.

Thus, our review of the history of military strategy offers no clear basis for translation from the military past into the business present.[23] The ancient past of strategy is another country, and the dominant nineteenth-century military discourse (focused on the Napoleonic battle of annihilation) also offers no easy line of descent. So why do we contend that a definitive discontinuity occurs in the mid-nineteenth century in both the military and business spheres? The answer, we suggest, lies in the emergence of the new disciplinary practices, which fundamentally shift the focus of both business and military strategy and are to lead, by the end of the century, to a fundamental reformulation of the military strategic discourse, and thence, in the twentieth century, to its suitability for adoption and adaptation as the discourse of modern business.

8.5 The genesis of modern business and military strategy

Intensified competition and increasing traffic brought two further significant structural developments in the organization of the large railroad during the years following the Civil War. One was the building of a separate Traffic Department to administer the getting and processing of freight and passengers. The other was the creation of a central office manned by general executives... (who) concentrated less on day-to-day operation and more on long-term problems of cost determination, competitive rate setting and strategic expansion. In both these developments the Pennsylvania made the largest contribution. (Chandler 1965: 37–40)

Discovering the invention of *modern* strategy, we suggest, requires re-examining the history told by Chandler. The focus here though has to be not only post-Civil War but also earlier, on the period after 1850; for this is the period when the PRR, whose role Chandler rightly highlights here, gets established. The 'prime mover' in the reorganization of the railroad is its superintendent, the West Point graduate, Herman Haupt, who, despite having no previous business experience (except in running a school (Ward 1971)), introduced there, from 1849 onwards, a strategic reorganization, grounded in the collection and analysis of operating statistics and costs, and laid the foundations for the development of the largest railroad in the USA (e.g. Hoskin and Macve 1993, 1994b, 2005). The PRR is the organization where modern business practice takes shape; so once again the conclusion must surely be that strategy does not precede structure. Rather, they are indissolubly linked, as soon as 'disciplinary' practices are finally and definitively put in place.

Now we can explain our contention that it is the same people who invent modern business *and* military strategy. The key link is the American Civil War (1861–5), which was essentially the first 'industrial' war, the first war in which the logistical element of strategy ultimately became as conspicuous as its operational counterpart (Howard 1983: 102–3). Likewise, and for this reason, it was the first war in which a general staff (remote from the day-to-day distractions of the battlefield) ultimately controlled the direction of events. But this change did not happen immediately, or easily. Indeed, before the new disciplinary way intervened, the Union Army was to lose the opening (Napoleonic-style) battles in the face of operationally superior Confederate generalship.

Indeed, initial operations during the American Civil War were dominated on both sides by the desire to destroy the enemy in a decisive battle of annihilation. Weigley has shown that even the war's most capable soldiers were motivated to this end. Confederate General Robert E. Lee's operational brilliance enabled the South to hold out in the face of the Union's preponderance in manpower and material resources, although his aim in each case was to bring the Union army to battle under conditions in which he could deal it a knock-out blow. This, too, was the intent of the majority of Union generals until the offensives of General Ulysses S. Grant ushered in a new approach to the conduct of the war (Weigley 1973: 92–152).

Grant succeeded in crushing the Confederacy where his predecessors had failed by dint of developing a new systematic application for the operational deployment of the superior Union numbers. No slouch himself in operational terms, he considered that the separate Union armies had, in the past, 'acted independently and without concert, like a balky team, no two ever pulling together'.[24] He subsequently prevented the Confederate armies from manoeuvring and offering mutual support, by coordinating the advance of his forces on several fronts, with the overall intent of bringing Lee into open combat where Union numbers and firepower would prove decisive (McPherson 1988: 722). But his campaign of 1865 relied equally heavily on the General Staff's unprecedented success in mobilizing the Union's superior manpower and industrial strength. Logistical planning, as much as operational virtuosity, proved vital to the Union victory in the first industrial war.[25]

The American Civil War has been much studied, but one aspect that is still deeply unsatisfactory concerns the precise emergence of this Staff Office. Perhaps that is the result of the great liability exposed here—namely because it has been seen as a military innovation. Perhaps historians have been looking in the wrong place. What they should be considering is not the fact of the General Staff as such (since we know that early general staffs emerged in Napoleonic Europe), but how a *successful* system of operating a General Staff was put into place.[26] The two top 'staff men' in the new regime were the Secretary of War, Stanton, and the General in Chief, Henry Halleck, who, known as 'Old Brains', had graduated from West Point in the mid-1830s.

Here, in the field of military organizational reform, we come to the crucial role of the railroads, and their managers. The Union side quickly marshalled a considerable roll-call of such talent. Haupt's former subordinate on the PRR, Thomas Scott, was made Assistant Secretary of War. Chandler's great hero (1965), Daniel McCallum of the New York and Erie Railroad, was appointed 'Superintendent of Railroads',[27] and finally Haupt himself. As a sign of his distaste for the military, he stipulated that he should not be required to wear uniform and should draw no pay beyond expenses: on those conditions he became Chief of Construction and Transportation, a role wherein he gained the personal admiration of Lincoln (Ward 1973). Ironically he and McCallum ended up working with (when they were not working against) each other. Given this confluence of men who knew how to operate disciplinary systems, a new organizational culture began to take over the running of the war.

Perhaps all one can draw attention to at present is the contingency and the emergence of the 'conditions of possibility': perhaps it has to do with the assembly of a 'critical mass' of West Point veterans (another figure who shows up, now as a General, is Daniel Tyler, who—after instigating the reforms at the Springfield Armory (Hoskin and Macve 1994*a*)—had quit the army in 1834). Certainly, previous historical accounts, which have tried to paint either Stanton or Halleck as the primary cause for the new way of warfare, have failed to convince. At least we now have a plausible alternative. For we are faced with a problem like that of the early PRR. Out of the most unpromising of outlooks somehow came a new successful mode of operations. We have some of the same people involved. Occam's Razor suggests it makes sense to consider their contribution to have been crucial.

And what of the business arena after the Civil War?[28] There is one particular disciplinary pay-off produced by the managerial innovation on the PRR that cannot be ignored. This is the Andrew Carnegie story. Carnegie is the first great industrial robber-baron cum captain of industry. He perfects the art of running an industrial organization by the numbers; in a Foucauldian-style phrase repeated by Chandler (1977: 268):

[T]he men felt and often remarked that the eyes of the company were always on them through the books.

Yet Carnegie seems to be, in Social Darwinian terms, the 'missing link'. He was just seventeen when he was hired by Thomas Scott in 1853, on the western division of the PRR.[29] He learned well and quickly. He became Scott's special protégé; indeed Scott bankrolled him for his first major investment. But most of all, he was there at the birth of Haupt's grammato-centric, calculable system for running a business (he called Haupt 'the first "great man" I ever knew'—Ward 1971: 80). He then did well out of the Civil War, by investing in that most necessary commodity for a transport-hungry army, iron rail manufacture. But he did not stop at that. He drew, like the men who ran the PRR, on both sides of the power–knowledge equation. By the 1870s he had a double competitive advantage over his rivals in iron and steel. First, he knew, to a degree that they apparently did not, the operating costs of his production. He scrutinized, just like Haupt (Ward 1971), 'the minutest details of cost of materials and labor in every department . . . day to day and week to week' (Chandler 1977: 267). And he extended this knowledge to a strategic understanding of the cost structures of his competitors, such that in good times he tolerated his competitors and allowed them to provide extra capacity to the industry, relying on the knowledge that in bad times their inferior cost structures would mean that they would be the first to exit, leaving Carnegie's own capacity largely intact. But equally he invested constantly in disciplinary knowledge. He sent for the best experts in metallurgy and furnace construction from Europe; he paid them accordingly. Truly we can say of him that as a young man he had seen the future. In his maturity he made sure it worked (see e.g. Livesay 1975).

However, it is in the military sphere that a new *discourse* of strategy emerges. It is Alfred Mahan—a navy man—whom we now claim as the first *theorist* of modern strategy (and by first we mean first in the business or the military fields). He is the first man to articulate the nature of modern strategy: that it is something that must stretch indefinitely over time and space, continuous, ubiquitous, and constantly under appraisal. Where the European de-votees of von Clausewitz (Moltke, Schlieffen, Foch) were still obsessed with battle, Mahan switches the frame of reference. It is true that he himself placed great emphasis on the decisive naval battle as a means of gaining victory *in* war, but he also perceived how the practice of strategy should transcend the confines of war itself.

It was while studying the course of the second Punic War (218–202 BC) that Mahan apparently first gained his insight into the broader significance of sea power. Having noted the significant advantages that command of the sea conferred on the Romans vis-à-vis Hannibal, their Carthaginian opponent, he was struck

> by the enormous impact which Roman sea power exerted simply by its existence. He wondered if perhaps sea power had an influence on historical events far beyond the immediate impact of battles lost or won. (Till 1982: 30)

His subsequent major works, *The Influence of Sea Power upon History, 1660–1783* (1890) and *The Influence of Sea Power upon the French Revolution and Empire, 1793–1812* (1892), are testament to the significance of this initial insight. Looking beyond conflict as such, they advance the proposition that what matters is pre-emptive control, restriction through dominance of the range of possible enemy actions. The lessons of history revealed that the first naval necessity was to control sea *approaches*, not to operate from shore bases on one-off sorties. Moreover, since sea and land power interlock, his ideas carried broader implications for strategy as a whole. For Mahan, the horizons of strategy transcended 'immediate' operational concerns associated with the annihilation of the enemy, to extend continuously into an indefinite future, and extensively over all conceivable space. Thus the only strategic position became constant vigilance, 'looking outward' from a clearly defined territory which must extend into the ocean. Actual geographical boundaries had now become irrelevant and dangerous; boundaries were instead what were written by the imposition of power.

With Mahan, strategy *begins* from logistics. Success comes not on the battlefield but by dominating whole geopolitical areas (which can then be subdivided into 'theatres of war' if the worst-case scenario unfolds). However, the key is dominance, to be achieved via trading wealth and control of economic resources—an approach with a more than contemporary resonance today now that the 'space' to be dominated has been extended from land and sea to both air and extraterrestrial space.

Mahan restructures the discourse of strategy, in a way that rapidly affects military thinking. In Britain, Germany, and the USA his books became a theoretical justification for an orgy of naval building. The strategy of engagement in the First World War and even more in the Second is affected by Mahan's thinking (remember Pearl Harbor). Moreover, this kind of globalizing approach is also that which will come to frame business thinking in the new global multidivisional corporations that are beginning to take shape during the very period in which he is writing.

Who was Mahan? Alfred *Thayer* Mahan was born and raised at West Point.[30] Born in 1840, he lived the first fourteen years of his life in the world of grammatocentrism and calculability:

> His father was Dennis Hart Mahan, whose classes on the art of war and military engineering were known to an entire generation of West Point cadets. Even though Mahan caused his father some disgruntlement by choosing to attend the Naval Academy at Annapolis rather than West Point the elder Mahan nevertheless influenced his son's historical and intellectual methodology. The father's interest in the strategic thinking of Henri Jomini impressed the younger Mahan with the importance of fitting things into an orderly system. (Till 1982: 30)[31]

We have suggested how the disciplinary practices at Thayer's West Point engendered a new power–knowledge regime, which would invent strategy and structure for the complexity of modern business and military development. Certainly in the military sphere, for whatever reason, the important lesson of the Civil War was that industrial war had made logistics into a vital component of strategy. From the mid-nineteenth century onwards, only under exceptional circumstances could operational virtuosity alone produce victory. Subsequent history confirmed this.

The conduct of the two World Wars would demonstrate how important the new strategic discourse had become in an age when conflicts were increasingly global and resource-intensive in character. Both World Wars were ultimately attritional conflicts in which victory went to the side that won the 'battle of production'. In both instances, strategy proceeded from logistics, and in both instances German operational virtuosity proved to be no substitute for a sound human and material resource base (Stone 2004: 411–12).

But the conventional histories of business strategy focus on the transfer of discourse after 1945. And by 1945, had not military strategy itself been transformed yet again by the quantum leap in destructive capacity inherent in nuclear weapons? Even if our research has clarified the history of strategy up till then, how can it be a history of the present and of relevance to the modern theory of strategy?

8.6 The history of the present: military strategy after 1945, pre- and post-1991

The dawn of the nuclear age in 1945 gave military minds a host of new problems to confront, but at the same time it gave rise to the civilian strategist. The sheer destructive effect of nuclear weapons ultimately undermined attempts to integrate them into traditional military force structures and planning concepts which aimed at achieving complete victory over the enemy. Instead, the civilianization of nuclear strategy emphasized war-avoidance and limitation through deterrence, rather than unrestrained war-fighting in pursuit of what could only be a pyrrhic victory (Stone 2004: 415–16).

Even under these new conditions, however, the strategic discourse articulated by Mahan retained its relevance. The first reason for this was the continuing presence of conflict at 'subnuclear' levels. The proliferation of nuclear weapons after 1945 was a symptom of the emergence of a new world order, dominated by two power blocs whose uneasy relationship was characterized by mutual suspicion and, on occasion, outright antagonism. And yet, while nuclear weapons may have deterred another world war, nevertheless, as some of the first 'nuclear' strategists (Brodie and Brodie 1973: 282) observed, beneath the nuclear umbrella there was still scope for conflict in all its traditional forms. Beyond Europe a global struggle for influence and access to strategic resources ensued that encompassed all means including military action, which itself often became highly attritional (and thereby resource-intensive) in character as, for example, in Korea and Vietnam. Closer to home, 'fighting' the cold war demanded much more than the creation and maintenance of large standing forces. Truman's policy of 'containing' the Communist threat was initially articulated in political and economic terms. It took on a pronounced military dimension with the outbreak of the Korean War in 1950 but, after the crash rearmament programme that ensued, maintaining the long-term economic health of the new transnational Atlantic economy was once more viewed as a priority. Ultimately, therefore, cold war strategy was predicated as much on logistical factors as it had been during the two World Wars. Indeed, it was in this context that Defense Secretary Robert McNamara (brought into government from Ford Motors) made a reputation for himself by exploiting the techniques of systems analysis to quantify and rationalize the application of finite resources to strategic missions.[32]

The second important reason why Mahan's modern discourse retained its relevance lies in its 'future orientation'. This same orientation underlies the deterrence regime that dominated after 1945. As the proliferation of early-warning systems during this period suggests, peace was now understood to rest on a constant state of watchful alert. In this sense, the practice of strategy was no longer predicated on the destruction of the enemy, but on maintaining the ability to predict and deter aggression over the long term. Limited advantages might be sought and achieved, but the battle of annihilation had become a recipe for global catastrophe. Thus, the advent of the nuclear age by no means undermined the modernity of the strategic discourse which was articulated at the end of the nineteenth century, the emphasis remaining on logistics and on a future orientation.

Moreover, much the same can be said for the character of strategy since the collapse of the Soviet Union in 1991. The new threats posed by international terrorism and 'weapons of mass destruction' have recently prompted responses of a kind that would have been understood by Mahan. 'The National Security Strategy of the United States of America' (2002) is predicated on the idea of restricting, forestalling, and pre-empting aggressors by linking US military and economic power to a global coalition of like-minded nations whose own contributions to the project will, in turn, be subject to close surveillance:

In building a balance of power that favors freedom, the United States is guided by the conviction that all nations have important responsibilities. Nations that enjoy freedom must actively fight terror. Nations that depend on international stability must help prevent the spread of weapons of mass destruction. Nations that seek international aid must govern themselves wisely, so that aid is well spent. For freedom to thrive, *accountability* must be expected and required. [emphasis added]

Thus, the nature of the threat may have changed but the fundamental character of the strategy required to defeat it remains rather more constant. Its concerns extend forward into a distant future and outward across distant space. This is a point echoed by President George W. Bush in his preamble to the National Security Strategy, for whom: 'The war against terrorists of global reach is a global enterprise of uncertain duration.'

Moreover, a prerequisite for joining the global alliance against terror is now 'accountability' for democratic freedoms: it is the individual citizens of democracies who are now continuously in the front line and military strategy takes its place among the constellation of modern systems—practices, discourses, and organizations—that 'quietly order us about' (Foucault, quoted in Megill 1979: 493).

8.7 **The history of the present: implications for the theory of business strategy today**

Returning to our starting point—locating SMA—the primary concern of this chapter has been not simply with rewriting the history of strategy, but with rethinking strategy as it is and exists today, as 'disciplinary power' with accounting at its core. Clearly we confront here a discourse of great power and status in both the business and the military fields—a power–knowledge regime creating both new truth effects and new power relations—and yet the linkages between these two arenas of discourse have more often been simply assumed or left to one side, as if they were relatively or indeed fundamentally autonomous. That, we hope, is something that has now been put under serious question. For, if our analysis is correct, there is no such simple relationship, but instead one that is both complex in its past and important in the present.

Our history suggests that strategy, as it was developed in the mid-nineteenth century, is something significantly new and different from strategy as exercised and discussed before the shift into modernity, or rather into a 'disciplinary' world, dominated by the expertise of disciplinary knowledge as much as by any disciplining, even self-disciplining, of action and behaviour. What existed previously was without doubt a form of power, and one dependent on expert knowledge, but both the power and the knowledge exercised were different in their concerns and effects. Both the practice and the discourse concerned with the $\sigma\tau\rho\alpha\tau\eta\gamma\acute{o}\varsigma$ (the 'general') were not focused on the concerns of today's strategy: the logistical, the coordinative, the big temporal and spatial picture, the integrated and coordinated 'organization' of time, space, objects, and persons, establishing a position within a measured, calculated, and totalized space and time. There was an absence of the practices of writing, examining, and grading, constantly deployed, and so of a practice of strategy across entities, controlled at a higher level than the $\sigma\tau\rho\alpha\tau\eta\gamma\acute{o}\varsigma$, or for purposes beyond the immediate battle, siege, or campaign.

But, secondly, this is more than just a claim that the genesis of these practices, in some unspecified way, as if by osmosis, made strategy possible. What our historical reconstruction suggests is that these practices, as new modes of communicating, of learning, and of valuing, were internalized by specific individuals, and were then translated by them into particular versions of this new formation of 'strategy', but all discontinuous with the old. Therefore, even though there is a historical significance in tracing such personal and coincidental histories (which are therefore manifestly not purely coincidental), that is not all that is significant historically, for the two fields are not linked purely at the level of the dramatis personae but much more profoundly, from the outset and still today, through their shared practices and discourses.

Certain cherished assumptions therefore fall. For instance, the idea that business strategy comes from military strategy in some wholly derivative way (e.g. as in Bracker (1980) where it only begins after the Second World War); or alternatively that it is something essentially autonomous—a view that has been shared by most modern approaches to strategy (whether in the rationalist form in which it appears in Chandler (1962), Williamson (1985), Ansoff (1969), and Porter (1980), or in the more nuanced, context-sensitive processual form of Mintzberg et al. (2005), and Pettigrew (1985)). This view has even affected radical critiques of modern business strategy. Thus, Knights and Morgan (1991: 255), in wishing to capture the limitations of this discursive field, argue that 'it is possible to identify a discourse of strategy that has a specific relation to corporate business. This discourse has its own historical conditions of possibility... it has particular truth effects which are disciplinary on subjects and organizations.'[33] But their insights are, for us, compromised by their decision to mark business strategy off from its military sibling, as well as by their analysis of the role of strategic knowledge solely as mystification.

Our conclusion is that all these ways of seeing strategy, including this type of critical meta-analysis, are trapped in a historical (and therefore, in this case, theoretical) cul-de-sac. For in every case a fundamental separation is maintained between the business and military fields, so that the integral relation is always held at arm's length. There is therefore a kind of general historical amnesia, which produces, in different ways, a shared ahistoricism.[34] In our view, this now needs to be transcended, for the relation between business and military discourses needs to be thought through, in a way that is both more nuanced and more historically reflective about the interplays between the discourses.

We can here only begin the attempt to develop such a theoretical approach. We would focus initially on three major elements: strategy and structure; the 'totalizing' nature of strategic discourse; and the paradox that its success is best demonstrated where it is most redundant. And here we may note that, given their common genesis, we should not be surprised to find that these features also reflect the problematic nature of modern accounting, which has been likewise subject, from its beginnings, to sustained critiques of its limited rationality and, more recently, of its legitimation of power relations reflecting vested interests, but yet is now also an inseparable constituent of the nature of the modern organization (e.g. Hoskin and Macve 1990, 2000).

First, given our history, we can abandon the presumption that either strategy or structure in some sense comes first, in favour of a recognition of both as aspects of the same disciplinary breakthrough, a transformation at a prior level of the practices through which people as individuals (such as Haupt at West Point) learned to learn, and through which simultaneously the formal and social organization of their learning was restructured. At which point, one can instead see, within both the military and the business fields, a reconstitution of ways of seeing and acting. Through knowing what had happened, in writing, via accounting and examining, men like Haupt on the PRR began to extrapolate to what could happen: the future could be made in the image of the past and the world beyond the organization could begin to be made subject to the organization by being remade in its image—a process hastened and extended almost exponentially once his railroad began to prove successful through this 'strategic' vision, and so became copied by others. Then indeed the world outside the organization did become remade in its image, as it has continued to be down to the present.

From this new vantage point, looking now at both the military and business discourses, and so seeing a joint significance in the structural changes engineered on the PRR and in the Union Army Staff Office, we may suggest that what is of most significance is that structure itself is *formalized*, and written as a location of expert knowledge and power relations—and that it thereby can become the object of discourse—not that a *particular form* of structure is invented. So the focus on the accounting-driven, line-and-staff theme does not require us to see the 'M-form' as its apotheosis or ideal type. The divisionalized structure—ultimately the 'M-form'—is rather its first elaborated version, and for that reason a powerful one, but once managerial structure is written, its precise version will vary in relation to local, cultural, and contextual factors.[35] Such a conclusion is consistent with recent comparative research that looks beyond the USA (e.g. Whittington 1993; Whitley 1994). In which case, there will be a continuing range of possible such forms, as evidenced by the limits to the 'success' of the M-form over such alternatives as the holding company within Europe during the past three decades (Whittington and Mayer 1997, 2000).

Second, one may begin to see what distinctive features are shared between the two discourses, business and military, and so get a better sense of what strategy invokes, and where its *inherent* limitations as mode of truth lie. From its nineteenth-century invention, it is a totalizing discourse, turning not just space and time into a shared grid, but turning objects, events, and activities into calculated accountable nodes in that grid. It is a high-powered writing, examining, and grading machine. If one looks from this perspective at the first extended literary discourse in the new strategic genre, Mahan's 1890 *Influence of Sea Power Upon History* (surely an unpromising title for 'Management Book of the Month'), its particular and wider significances become much more apparent.[36]

Thus, we should not be surprised if, since their common genesis in the mid-nineteenth century, there has been continual interpenetration and transformation between these two worlds. Here the conventional view that the discourse of business strategy derived from the military discourse after 1945, and was 'discovered' then, still reflects an important aspect—but only one aspect—of the story. For the internal development of the logic of such a totalizing discourse has enabled military and business strategy in their modern forms to say versions of the same thing. The outcome of the attempts, begun by Mahan, at totalizing strategy, the knowing through rewriting of all relevant space and time, was the vision of total war—which experience then showed not to be total and definitive. The First World War proved not to be the 'war to end all wars', and the end of the Second proved only that there was now a possibility of a totalizing, which would, for humans, end time and space as we knew them. Now we have a global 'war on terror', which may never reach an end. So, both under pressure of empirical data and from within the discourse of military strategy itself, 'totalizing' was at this point reconstituted, not by abandoning it and relapsing into pure localization, but by developing a new range of levels of the possible within strategy: the global scenario, the regional, the limited, and the 'individual' war.

It was, historically, in this context that business began to adopt and adapt the military discourse to 'discover' its own articulate discourse of strategy (that which the business academic tradition has so far taken as being the discovery of strategy as such). But the overlap must be seen as a more subtle one. Thus, some pioneers of business strategic discourse pick up on the dynamics of the first form of 'totalizing' military discourse, becoming the first 'big strategists' (e.g. Ansoff 1965, 1969). But then we also get those who take up, unconsciously no doubt, the newly revised version. In Porter (1980, 1985), for instance, we still have the same commitment to total writing, examining, and grading of corporate possibilities, but now two possible major outcomes: either the dominance outcome, in terms of price or product leadership, or the regional, limited one within the 'niche' market. Other versions have followed (e.g. Mintzberg et al. 2005).

We conclude with our third, and perhaps most significant, point for the *future* of strategy and strategic discourse—the paradox of its 'redundancy'. This is again a feature it shares with accounting.

8.8 Conclusion

Seeing how the practices and discourses of military and business strategy have always been linked, even given the chronological priority of the *articulation* of the military discourse, may help us to see how business strategy is always trapped and limited in precisely the way, structurally, that military strategy is, by the practices through which it is exercised. So we discover the same internal evolution of discursive possibilities, only within a shorter time span, and, equally, the same structural range of positively reasoned conclusions and recommendations. Of course, we are not the first in here proposing a critique or meta-analysis of business strategy's supposed rationality, there being now many meta-analyses of 'big strategy' discourse.[37]

We only suggest that the kind of historical critique we can now offer of both discourses has an implication not readily visible before. If there is the commitment to totalizing, in a simple or more elaborate contextualized form, at the heart of all discourses of strategy, we need to recognize the double paradox which emerges out of the fact that strategy's great success (like structure's and accounting's) lies in its ability to turn both the world and time into a space for writing, examining, and grading. The paradox is the same in both cases. First, concerning time, strategy will (like accounting—e.g. Yamey 1964) be most successful where the future is like the past (since what it writes is the past rewritten, however sophisticated its rewriting), but that is when it is most unnecessary; meanwhile, it will be most necessary when the future is different from the past, which is when it will be most useless. Second, it also confronts a spatial complement of this temporal paradox—i.e. that in terms of controlling organizational space, it will always be, through its deployment of disciplinary practices and its alliance with structure, most apt at dealing with the 'space in here'; and it is therefore not surprising that strategy as practice (military or business) devotes most of its real-time effort to controlling that space (through the various mixes of strategic centralization and operational decentralization). However, strategic *success* actually needs control of the 'space out there', where the enemy and/or competition lies (as in SMA—Bromwich 1990, 2000); but that is where strategy proves so easily disproven and overturned, whether by counter-strategy or simply by events.

So, in conclusion, we have sketched (in this and the preceding section) three major theoretical issues (concerning strategy and structure; the 'totalizing' nature of strategic discourse; and the paradox of its success through redundancy) that we see emerging from our interpretation of the historical genesis of both business and military strategy, and their subsequent interpenetration. In so doing, we are perhaps opening a space for a new level of discursive possibility, which in time may not be occupied solely by radical meta-analysis but also by more historically and theoretically aware formulations of strategy as such. Dent (1990) concluded his study of research at the interface between accounting and strategy with the following caveat: that while

[s]trategy research, of both the normative and descriptive variety, had made valuable contributions to the organizational literature...it is not a field with uniformly strong empirical research traditions.[38]

We have argued here that lack of strong empirical grounding is certainly the case where its history is concerned. At the same time, we have suggested that from the empirical re-examination of its history there emerges a consequent need for theoretical reformulation as well, if we are to understand both its inherent limitations and its inescapable disciplinary power.

To return to the start of this chapter, there have been calls for accounting to become more 'strategic'. SMA focuses attention away from 'the shop floor' to the external environment of customers and competitors (actual and potential), to the longer-term horizon, and to other sources and types of information to supplement the accounts. We have explored 'what is strategy'? Our historical framework positions 'strategy' as a power–knowledge regime—comprising both disciplinary power relations and disciplinary expert knowledge, and constituted through practices and discourse—that is inherent in modern military and business organizations. It is through strategy—and within its inherent limitations—that they both now inevitably utilize formalized internal structures and meticulous accounting of their past to evaluate ends and means and thereby strive to objectify and rationally control—so far as is feasible—what lies externally and in the future. Accounting and accountability provide the central, albeit increasingly invisible, enabling technology: and from this perspective, SMA itself may be seen as a contemporary articulation and re-identification[39] of what is in essence a genetic symbiosis.

◻ **NOTES**

1 We are appreciative of the constructive comments of John Roberts and others on an earlier version of part of this chapter. Financial Assistance from the ESRC (ref: 0023 2405) is gratefully acknowledged for funding some of the archival research on which this study is based.

2 Bromwich also recognizes that the strategic focuses on external cost information and economies of scope imply organizational restructurings, including the relationship of the accounting and finance function to marketing management: 'This makes the organizational structure of enterprises of crucial significance and links accounting very strongly with organizational matters' (1990: 35, 41). As Miller (1992: 79) puts it: 'Ways of organizing and ways of calculating have developed hand in hand.' We also concur with Bromwich's concern (1990: 27) that the reforms urged by Kaplan and his collaborators remain focused within the firm (see further Ezzamel et al. 1990). Further insights into SMA may be found in Bromwich (1992), Bromwich and Bhimani (1994), and Tomkins and Carr (1996).

3 The theory that suggests that the genesis of US management is to be found in army innovations themselves (e.g. O'Connell 1985; Smith 1985) is not discussed in detail here (cf. Hoskin and Macve 2005) but it does not fit the historical data as effectively as our thesis, that this genesis is rather to be found in the domain of military *education*. (Cummings (2002: 82, 90) mistakenly attributes the 'military importation' thesis to Chandler himself.)

4 For further discussion of the relevance of Foucault to management accounting research, see e.g. Bhimani (1999); Hoskin and Macve (2000); cf. Cummings (2002: 3–7).

5 For contemporaneous 'objectifications' in other US scientific, social, economic, and political spheres, see e.g. Porter (1995).

6 Consider its central practices. Aspirants can only enter this specialist world by succeeding in written, graded examinations; they then become successful, disciplinary experts only by constant examination of specialist problems, and then writing up the results of their analysis and passing the critical examination of their peers (in the UK, for example, now 'graded' in the Research Assessment Exercise: http://www.rae.ac.uk/). It is no coincidence that these are also key practices through which one now becomes a successful player in the modern corporate or military managerial world. This is particularly apparent in the US Army, where promotion currently requires demonstrable familiarity with an officially approved series of texts (including works of strategy and military history and biography).

7 Anthony Hopwood and Dick Fleischman have kindly drawn our attention to the fact that Foucault was planning a project on 'the history of the factory' in the early 1980s just before his death (Gandal and Kotkin 1985).

8 Smith argues for the centrality of the profit numbers—largely overlooked in strategic theorizing—in actual strategic management practice, citing the enthusiasm since the 1990s for 'shareholder value' and EVA®, which have enabled companies to throw off the image of being 'accountancy-driven'. However, he does not recognize the antecedents of these popular ideas in the academic accounting literature that long antedate Rappaport (1981) (e.g. those cited in Bromwich 1974). Moreover, while recognizing the behavioural implications of 'politicization' of the control and presentation of the numbers (Smith 2003: 379), he does not address the technical difficulties that have long been explored in 'financial and management accounting theory'. Cummings (2002: 240, 281) commends the simple strategy model of 'C + M = SP' and 'M*V = Π' without considering the underlying problematics (either behavioural or technical) of cost, revenue, and profit calculation, both of which the academic accounting literature addresses extensively.

9 Cummings (2002: 329–30) gives a list of works covering the history of management, organization, and strategy more generally.

10 He is here citing Ansoff (1969: 7).

11 Such as Alexander, Aeneas Tacticus, Julius Caesar, Onosander, Aelian, Frontinus, Machiavelli, Maurice of Nassau, Frederick the Great, Napoleon, von Clausewitz, Bismarck, Moltke, Mahan, and so on. This leap also ignores the important developments from the twelfth century AD in the textual array of geometrical order and visibility (e.g. in describing the layouts of military camps, of drill, and of plans for crossfire and rotation of firing). Examples include, *inter alia*, Cataneo's *Libro Nuovo di Fortificare, Offender et Difendere* (Brescia 1567); Leonard and Thomas Digges' (father and son) *An Arithemticall Militare Treatise named Stratioticos* (1579, 1590); du Bellay's *Instructions for the Warres* (1589). See further Hale (1988); McNeill (1982/1983). These textual advances parallel (and so reflect) those that have also been argued to have been important for accounting's own development (e.g. Hoskin and Macve 1986).

12 He cites Von Neumann and Morgenstern's text (1947) as the first 'to relate the concept of strategy to business'.

13 Cummings (e.g. 1995, 2002) argues for a reformulation of strategy by reference to 'premodern' Greek ideas and examples of generalship and political leadership such as that of Pericles of Athens in the fifth century BC. However, the very argument that this premodern dimension has been lost itself demonstrates that his approach does not provide the history of the actual development of the prevailing modern discourses of military and business strategy. Moreover, Cummings himself tends to conflate στρατηγός [*strat-eegos*—'the general'] with 'the strategist' and 'strategy'—terms that have inescapably modern significances.

14 For example, Xenephon in *Memorabilia*, Book III, Chapter 1 [3] (Bonnette 1994) has Socrates say: 'For, since the whole city entrusts itself to the general in the risks of war, it is plausible that if he acts correctly great good things will come to pass, and if he acts incorrectly great bad things will come to pass'. Such generalship could be 'in the blood': in Chapter 5 [22] Socrates says to Pericles' illegitimate, but adopted, son (also named Pericles): 'Indeed I think that you have inherited and preserve many things from your father's store of generalship.' For Aristotle's formulation of the primary importance of the general see Cummings (2002: 105).

15 One clarification: we are not suggesting that successful armies managed to succeed without considering logistics. Modern scholarship has shown the importance of the logistics dimension to premodern generals. Engels (1978) does it for Alexander the Great (cf. Lane Fox 2004; Cartledge 2005); Parker (1972) does it for the Spanish versus Maurice of Nassau. Our point is that there is no premodern discourse that factors this necessary dimension systematically and in a theorized way into the analysis and practice of strategy.

16 Clearly there can be no link in classical antiquity between military and 'business' strategy, not least because, whereas the military sphere defined 'nobility', *visible* managerial activity in the economic sphere was generally conducted by those on the margins of society, such as women, foreigners, or slaves (e.g. Macve 2002). (However, while the Athenian situation seems clear, some have identified increasing evidence of greater involvement in 'respectable' business activity in the Roman era (e.g. Moore and Lewis 1999).) Interestingly Xenophon (Bonnette 1994) in *Memorabilia*, Book III, Chapter 4 [2], after Socrates has commented that a general has to be 'competent to procure provisions for the soldiers' and Nicomachides has expostulated that 'Merchants too are competent to gather wealth but they wouldn't, on this account, have the capacity to be generals as well', has

Socrates go on later [6–12] to compare the skills of 'household management' favourably with those of generals. ('Household management' is οἰκονομία [*œco-nomia*], from which we ultimately derive 'economics'.)

17 For an excellent review of eighteenth-century European military theory see Gat (2001: book 1).

18 Chen (1994) considers the importance, in the eyes of modern Asian businesses, of the famous fourth-century BC Chinese writings of Sun Tzu on war and military strategy. As Chen explains it, while Sun Tzu does look beyond war itself to a preference for political outcomes, the main focus, in addition to explaining the advantages of various practical stratagems, is on the personal qualities of the general, including the need to balance predetermined plans against flexibility in the face of unpredictable circumstances. Here we see the 'Periclean' qualities as emphasized by Cummings (1995, 2002).

19 Quoted by Chandler (1966: 141).

20 It is true, of course, that von Clausewitz considered war too important to be left to the generals and that government should exercise overall control, but he provided no mediating organizational mechanism for enabling and ensuring this: a general staff is still lacking. Thus, there is still not that necessary modern concern with the whole field of operations, where preparedness must continue indefinitely into an infinite future. Even in his dictum that war is but 'the continuation of politics with the admixture of other means' von Clausewitz remains fixated on the theatre of operations *per se*.

21 General Staff, War Office (1909/1914: 133).

22 For a recent reprint see von Clausewitz (2004), *On War*, trans. Col. J. J. Graham. New York: Barnes and Noble.

23 Except in so far as macho fantasies in business find their self-justification through identifying the CEO with 'Alexander the Great' (e.g. Mintzberg et al. 2005: 44–5; 134).

24 Quoted in McPherson (1988: 722).

25 It is true that Jomini (1971: 252–68) systematically considers the problems of logistics, and provides an analysis of how to coordinate the ordering, transportation, and storage of supplies. Yet it is only a glimpse: Jomini does not confront the question of strategic integration and coordination, but only coordination and planning of logistics at the tactical and operational levels. Thus, he does not fit the profile of a Chandler 'pioneer', although he articulates the importance of the functions undertaken by a central administrative staff in any modern army.

It is therefore interesting to note that in the same decade men in the US Army, particularly the Ordnance Department, begin to tackle the same kind of problems. Interesting because Jomini is one of those products of the reformed French *Grandes Ecoles*, to which Sylvanus Thayer looked when designing his own ultra-disciplinary system for West Point. And, as it transpires, the Americans who produce the first successful nuts-and-bolts army reforms—again they do not effect change system-wide—are all from the post-Thayer generation of West Point graduates. (Important innovators include George Talcott, Chief of Ordnance from 1842, the 'soldier-tech-nologist' Alfred Mordecai, and Daniel Tyler.)

26 The creation of the Prussian 'Great General Staff' between 1803 and 1809 provides a case in point. As McNeill notes, this new organization provided an 'intellectual stronghold within the Prussian army for intellectually vigorous officers'. In accordance with reforms instituted by the Hanoverian, Gerhard Johann David von Scharnhorst, from 1808 Prussian officers were appointed and pro-

moted on the basis of their performance in professional examinations. Appointment to the General Staff likewise required a period of study and examination at a special school for officers aspiring to higher commands. Since the seventeenth century, Prussian civil officials had been recruited from German universities, and after 1770 they had to sit an examination. Thus, after 1808 the system of Prussian officer recruiting fell in line with methods already extant within the civilian state (McNeill 1983: 216–17). For a discussion on the development of the German university see Clark (1989). The relationship between such European developments and their transformation in the US context calls for our further research.

27 For a critical re-evaluation of McCallum's achievements on the New York and Erie Railroad, see Hoskin and Macve (2005).

28 Cummings (2002: 128–9) cites with approval the 'alternative curriculum' proposed by General Robert E. Lee (himself a West Point graduate) in 1869 when he favoured the establishment of a business school at Washington College (now Washington and Lee University) where he was President, but which was not implemented following his death in 1870.

29 Scott became General Superintendent of the PRR in 1858 and later succeeded J. Edgar Thomson to the PRR's Presidency on Thomson's death in 1874 (Hoskin and Macve 2005).

30 His father, Dennis Mahan, graduated head of the West Point Class of 1824, and from 1832 to 1871 lived and worked there as Professor of Military Engineering.

31 Before transferring to the Naval Academy at Annapolis, Maryland (where he graduated second in his class in 1859), he had spent two years at Columbia University: http://www.answers.com/topic/ alfred-thayer-mahan (consulted August 2005).

32 McNamara has famously now publicly recanted his support for the Vietnam War (McNamara 1995).

33 We acknowledge the dynamic of the argument that informs their analysis, and their concern with how strategy is not purely neutral but an exercise of power, not just over organizational members, or in relation to other companies, but also on behalf of strategists themselves, who 'secure their sense of meaning, identity and reality through participation in the discourses and practices of strategy' (Knights and Morgan 1991: 269). There is a real importance in seeing this power as positive, in relation to the powerful as well as those subject to it, something that may be missed, not only by the rationalists but also by the processualists, who 'in reporting the political machinations surrounding strategy, may merely encourage a more reflective and efficient approach to its implementation'. The case of military strategy is discussed by Knights and Morgan, but is now relegated to being prior and separate. Ironically, given their Foucauldian persuasion, they therefore see it (1991: 258–9) as having emerged in itself for purely internalist military reasons: 'notions of strategy had been central to military discourse from the late 18th century' (discussed at greater length in Knights and Morgan 1990). Even more ironically, given their inherent critique of demand–response technorationalist theories of business strategy, they see military strategy's development after the Second World War as a response to technorationalist change when 'advances in communications technology facilitated the use of military information and surveillance techniques as strategic devices which could break down temporal and spatial distances' (1991: 258).

34 Here the ahistoricism to be overcome is similar to that found until recently in the mainstream discourse on management accounting. A leading US scholar such as Robert Anthony could concede that he had no knowledge of the early history of cost accounting until he read about it in Chandler's

work, by which time he had been a professor for almost two decades (Anthony 1989). He did not know about books like Knight's *Risk, Uncertainty, and Profit* (1921) until he was in graduate school; 'nor did I know about the early history of management accounting until I read Al Chandler's *Strategy and Structure* and *The Visible Hand,* which were published even later' (1989: 1).

35 In any writing of structural form, accounting is fundamentally implicated. For the M-form organization, accounting's ROI is the way in which performance is written, examined, and graded (e.g. Ezzamel et al. 1990), whether in its 'basic' or 'residual income' formulation (e.g. Bromwich 1974).

36 If we just take Mahan's opening sentence, we find already writ large a commitment to turning a totality of relevant space and time into a written, examined text: 'The definite object proposed in this work is an examination of the general history of Europe and America with particular reference to the effect of sea power upon the course of that history' (Preface, p. iii). It even sounds like an examination question, but of the most ordered and totalized kind. And within this text (as we then read on in the book), the field of analysis is now articulately remade as a totalized entity, where space is already coordinated or available for coordination, through being made subject to the examination of the grammatocentric gaze and where time is already being most meticulously measured in terms of timely planning, constant readiness, and instant capability of response. What has been added to this, in terms of practices, is essentially the articulation of refinements on the basics: why be reactive when (having made time and space into writing) one can be proactive, and one can plan contingent possibilities, when readiness can be internalized and disseminated across all available space, when the old strategic concerns with intelligence (with knowing the enemy's 'truth') can be served and extended in so many high-tech ways, bugging, decoding, recoding, using spy satellites, etc. (none of these high-tech ways is of course restricted to either the military or the business worlds).

37 It has been critiqued not only in processual terms concerning the limits to which such rationality applies within the organization, given contingent, individual, and sociological factors (e.g. Pettigrew 1985; Mintzberg 1994), but also, for example, by signalling the theoretical inadequacy of the approach, in terms of its failure to see the logical limits of planning, and the necessity of recognizing that system always has to work through human, contingent interactions, so that analysis should begin from recognizing the centrality of that interplay (Zan 1987, 1995). For recent attempts to relate to the example of Pericles and 'premodern' Greek ideas the concept of a necessity to 'oscillate' (or 'surf') between formal, *ex ante* rational plans and extemporization as the 'chaotic' situation unfolds, see Cummings (1995, 2002) and Cummings and Wilson (2003). A twentieth-century military or political example might be the anecdotes about Churchill's 'strategy of muddling through' (albeit underpinned by Alanbrooke's careful, systematic strategic analyses) in the Second World War (e.g. http://www.lbdb.com/TMDisplayLeader.cfm?PID=6009, consulted August 2005). The symbolic idea is the 'learning organization' (cf. Legge 2003: 92–4). The classic treatment in the accounting literature of how organizations approach the construction and interpretation of accounting reports in differing ways and under differing circumstances is given in Hopwood (1973, 1974).

38 Thomas Kirchmaier has emphasized to us in conversation his view of the importance of improved use of empirical evidence (in his view primarily statistical) for measuring performance over the long term, in the future direction of business strategy research (see e.g. Kirchmaier 2003). (In following this path, it will, in our view, be important to identify how far empirical research can

deal successfully with the logical—and fundamental—question in an uncertain world of the difference between (*a*) what is envisageable *ex ante*, and appears quantifiable as an expectation over a range of anticipated risks, when strategy is formulated and (*b*) what then occurs in actual time and space—in each case a singular and inherently non-commensurable 'event' outcome— and how far statistical aggregation across a sample of such outcomes, over companies and over time (itself subject to biases and/or noise from the vagaries of accounting procedures), can overcome this categorical difference in interpreting what has been 'successful' (cf. Gould's discussion (1974: 103–4) of Thirlby's 'The Ruler').

39 SMA may also be seen as now having a complement in the financial accounting and reporting arena, the 'Operating and Financial Review' (OFR), which will be mandatory for UK-listed companies (e.g. Bromwich 2005).

□ REFERENCES

Ansoff, H. J. (1965). *Corporate Strategy.* New York: McGraw-Hill.

—— (1969). *Business Strategy: Selected Readings.* London: Penguin.

Anthony, R. (1989). 'Reminiscences about Management Accounting', *Journal of Management Accounting Research*, 1: 1–20.

Bhimani, A. (1999), 'Mapping Methodological Frontiers in Cross-national Management Control Research', *Accounting, Organizations and Society*, 24 (5/6): 413–40.

Bonnette, A. L. (1994), *Xenephon, Memorabilia* (translated and annotated). Ithaca, NY: Cornell University Press.

Bracker, J. (1980). 'The Historical Development of the Strategic Management Concept', *Academy of Management Review*, 5: 219–24.

Brodie, B. and Brodie, F. M. (1973). *From Crossbow to H-Bomb*, rev. edn. Bloomington: Indiana University Press.

Bromwich, M. (1974). 'Measurement of Divisional Performance in the Long Run', in H. Edey and B. S. Yamey (eds.), *Debits, Credits, Finance and Profits*. London: Sweet and Maxwell, pp. 15–20.

—— (1990), 'The Case for Strategic Management Accounting: The Role of Accounting Information for Strategy in Competitive Markets', *Accounting, Organizations and Society*, 15(1/2): 27–46.

—— (1992). 'Strategic Management Accounting', in C. Drury (ed.), *Management Accounting Handbook*. London: CIMA, pp. 128–53.

—— (2000). 'Thoughts on Management Accounting and Strategy', *Pacific Accounting Review* (Millennium Edition), 11(2): 41–8.

—— (2005), 'The OFR and Intangibles'. Paper presented at MARG, LSE, 14 April.

—— and Bhimani, A. (1989). *Management Accounting: Evolution not Revolution*. London: CIMA.

—— —— (1994). *Management Accounting: Pathways to Progress*. London: CIMA.

Builder, C. H. (1989). *The Masks of War: American Military Styles in Strategy and Analysis*. London: Johns Hopkins University Press.

Cartledge, P. (2005). *Alexander the Great: The Hunt for a New Past*. London: Pan Macmillan.

Chandler, A. (1962). *Strategy and Structure: Chapters in the History of American Enterprise*. Cambridge, MA: MIT Press.

—— (1965). 'The Railroads: Pioneers in Modern Corporate Management', *Business History Review*, 39(1): 16–40.

—— (1977). *The Visible Hand: the Managerial Revolution in American Business*. Cambridge, MA: Harvard University Press.

Chandler, D. G. (1966). *The Campaigns of Napoleon*. London: Weidenfeld and Nicolson.

Chen, Min (1994). 'Sun Tzu's Strategic Thinking and Contemporary Business', *Business Horizons*, 37(2): 42–8.

Clark, W. (1989). 'On the Dialectical Origins of the Research Seminar', *History of Science*, 27: 111–54.

Cummings, S. (1993). 'Brief Case: The First Strategists', *Long Range Planning*, 26(3): 133–6.

—— (1995). 'Pericles of Athens—Drawing from the Essence of Strategic Leadership', *Business Horizons*, 38(1): 22–7.

—— (2002). *ReCreating Strategy*. London: Sage.

—— and Wilson, D. (2003). 'Images of Strategy', in S. Cummings, and D. Wilson (eds.), *Images of Strategy*. Oxford: Blackwell.

Dent, J. (1990). 'Strategy, Organization and Control: Some Possibilities for Accounting Research', *Accounting, Organizations and Society*, 15: 3–26.

Engels, D. (1978). *Alexander the Great and the Logistics of the Macedonian Army*. Berkeley: University of California Press.

Ezzamel, M., Hoskin, K., and Macve, R. (1990). 'Managing It All by Numbers: A review of Johnson and Kaplan's *Relevance Lost*', *Accounting and Business Research*, 78: 153–66.

Foch, F. (1918). *The Principles of War*, translated by Hilaire Belloc. London: Chapman and Hall.

Foucault, M. (1977). *Discipline and Punish*. London: Allen Lane.

Gandal, K. and Kotkin, S. (1985). 'Governing Work & Social Life in the USA and the USSR', *History of the Present* (Department of Anthropology, University of California, Berkeley), 1: 4–14.

Gat, A. (2001). *A History of Military Thought: From the Enlightenment to the Cold War*. Oxford: Oxford University Press.

General Staff, War Office (1909). *Field Service Regulations*, Part I, *Operations*. London: HMSO. Reprinted with Amendments, 1914.

Gould, J. R. (1974). 'Opportunity Cost; The London Tradition', in H. Edey and B. S. Yamey (eds.), *Debits, Credits, Finance and Profits*. London: Sweet and Maxwell, pp.91–107.

Hale, J. R. (1988). 'A Humanistic Visual Aid. The Military Diagram in the Renaissance', *Renaissance Studies*, 2(2): 280–98.

Hopwood, A. G. (1973), *An Accounting System and Managerial Behaviour*. Lexington, MA: Saxon House.

—— (1974), *Accounting and Human Behaviour*. Exeter: Accountancy Age Books.

Hoskin, K. and Macve, R. (1986). 'Accounting and the Examination: A Genealogy of Disciplinary Power', *Accounting, Organizations and Society* 11(2): 105–36.

—— —— (1988). 'The Genesis of Accountability: The West Point Connections', *Accounting, Organizations and Society* 131(1): 37–73.

—— —— (1990). 'Understanding Modern Management', *University of Wales Business & Economics Review*, 5: 17–22.

—— —— (1993). 'Accounting as Discipline: The Overlooked Supplement', in E. Messer-Davidow, D. R. Shumway, and D. J. Sylvan (eds.) *Knowledges: Historical and Critical Studies in Disciplinarity.* Charlottesville: University Press of Virginia, pp. 25–53.

—— —— (1994*a*). 'Reappraising the Genesis of Managerialism: A Re-Examination of the Role of Accounting at the Springfield Armory, 1815–45', *Accounting, Auditing and Accountability Journal*, 7(2): 4–29.

—— —— (1994*b*). 'Writing, Examining, Disciplining: The Genesis of Accounting's Modern Power', in A. Hopwood and P. Miller (eds.), *Accounting as Social and Institutional Practice.* Cambridge: Cambridge University Press, pp. 67–97.

—— —— (2000). 'Knowing More as Knowing Less? Alternative Histories of Cost and Management Accounting in the U.S. and the U.K.', *Accounting Historians Journal*, 27(1): 91–149.

—— —— (2005). 'The Pennsylvania Railroad, 1849 and the "Invention of Management"', LSE/WBS Working Paper

Howard, M. (1983) *The Causes of War and Other Essays.* London: Temple, Smith.

Jomini, Baron de (1836/1979). *Précis de l'Art de la Geurre* (reprinting of English translation, *The Art of War*. Westport, CT: Greenwood, 1971). Also available at http://www.gutenberg.org/etext/13549.

Kay, J. (1993). *Foundations of Corporate Success.* Oxford: Oxford University Press.

Kirchmaier, T. (2003). 'Corporate Restructuring of British and German Non-Financial Firms in the Late 1990s', *European Management Journal*, 21(4): 409–20.

Knights, D. and Morgan, G. (1990). 'The Concept of Strategy in Sociology: A Note of Dissent', *Sociology*, 24(3): 475–83.

—— —— (1991). 'Corporate Strategy, Organizations and Subjectivity: A Critique', *Organization Studies*, 12(2): 251–73.

Lane Fox, R. (2004). *Alexander the Great* [1st edn., Allen Lane, 1973; reissued with updates, 2004]. London: Penguin.

Legge, K. (2003). 'Strategy as Organizing', in S. Cummings and D. Wilson (eds.), *Images of Strategy.* Oxford: Blackwell.

Liddell and Scott's *Greek-English Lexicon* (abridged edn.). Oxford: Oxford University Press, 1871.

Livesay, H. C. (1975). *Andrew Carnegie and the Rise of Big Business.* Boston: Little, Brown.

Macve, R. H. (2002). 'Insights to be Gained from the Study of Ancient Accounting History: Some Reflections on the New Edition of Finley's *The Ancient Economy*', *European Accounting Review*, 11(2): 453–72.

Mahan, A. T. (1890). *The Influence of Seapower Upon History 1660–1783.* London: Sampson Low, Marston, Searle & Rivington. Available at http://www.gutenberg.org/etext/13529.

—— (1892). *The Influence of Sea Power upon the French Revolution and Empire, 1793–1812.* Boston: Little, Brown.

McNamara, R. S. (with VanDeMark, B.) (1995). *In Retrospect: The Tragedy and Lessons of Vietnam.* New York: Random House.

McNeill, W. (1982/1983). *The Pursuit of Power.* Chicago: University of Chicago Press, 1982; Oxford: Blackwell, 1983.

McPherson, J. M. (1988). *Battle Cry of Freedom: The Civil War Era.* Oxford: Oxford University Press.

Megill, A. (1979). 'Foucault, Structuralism and the Ends of History', *Journal of Modern History,* 51(3): 451–503.

Miller, P. B. (1992). 'Accounting and Objectivity: The Invention of Calculable Selves and Calculable Spaces', *Annals of Scholarship,* 9(1/2): 61–86.

Mintzberg, H. (1984). *The Rise and Fall of Strategic Planning.* Englewood Cliffs, NJ: Prentice Hall.

—— Ahlstrand, B., and Lampel, J. (2005). *Strategy Bites Back.* Harlow: *Financial Times*/Prentice Hall.

Moore, K and Lewis, D. (1999). *Birth of the Multinational: 2000 Years of Ancient Business History, from Ashur to Augustus.* Copenhagen: Copenhagen Business School Press.

'The National Security Strategy of the United States of America' (17 September 2002), http://www.whitehouse.gov/nsc/nssall.html, sourced July 2005.

Neumann, J. von and Morgenstern, O. (1947). *Theory of Games and Economic Behaviour,* 2nd edn. Princeton, NJ: Princeton University Press.

O'Connell, C. (1985). 'The Corps of Engineers and the Rise of Modern Management, 1827–1856', in M. R. Smith (ed.), *Military Enterprise and Technological Change: Perspectives on the American Experience.* Cambridge, MA: MIT Press, pp. 87–116.

Parker, G. (1972). *The Army of Flanders and the Spanish Road, 1567–1659: The Logistics of Spanish Victory and Defeat in the Low Countries Wars.* Cambridge: Cambridge University Press.

Pettigrew, A. (1985). *The Awakening Giant.* Oxford: Blackwell.

Porter, M. (1980). *Competitive Strategy.* New York: Free Press.

—— (1985). *Competitive Advantage.* London: Collier Macmillan.

Porter, T.M. (1995). *Trust in Numbers: The Pursuit of Objectivity in Science and Public Life.* Princeton, NJ: Princeton University Press.

Rappaport, A. (1981). 'Selecting Strategies that Create Shareholder Value', *Harvard Business Review,* 59(3): 139–49.

Richardson, B. and Thompson, J. (1995). 'Strategic Evaluation: a Multi-Competency Approach', in J. L. Thompson (ed.), *The CIMA Handbook of Strategic Management* London: Butterworth-Heinemann, pp. 248–70.

Roberts, J. (1990). 'Strategy and Accounting in a UK Conglomerate', *Accounting, Organizations and Society,* 15: 107–26.

Roberts, D. J. (2004). *The Modern Firm: Organizational Design for Performance and Growth.* Oxford: Oxford University Press.

Smith, C. (2003). 'Strategy as Numbers', in S. Cummings and D. Wilson (eds.), *Images of Strategy.* Oxford: Blackwell.

Smith, M. R. (1985). 'Army Ordnance and the "American System" of Manufacturing, 1815–1861', in M. R. Smith (ed.), *Military Enterprise and Technological Change: Perspectives on the American Experience.* Cambridge, MA: MIT Press, pp. 39–86.

Stone, J. (2004). 'Politics, Technology and the Revolution in Military Affairs', *Journal of Strategic Studies,* 27(3): 408–27.

Till, G. (1982). *Maritime Strategy and the Nuclear Age.* London: Macmillan.

Tomkins, C. and Carr, C. (1996), 'Strategic Management Accounting', *Management Accounting Research*, Special issue (June): 165–80.

van Creveld, M. (1977). *Supplying War: Logistics from Wallenstein to Patton*. New York: Cambridge University Press.

von Clausewitz, K. (1976). *On War*, eds. and trans. M. Howard and P. Paret. Princeton, NJ: Princeton University Press. Also available at http://www.gutenberg.org/etext/1946.

Ward, J. (1971). 'Herman Haupt and the Development of the Pennsylvania Railroad', *Pennsylvania Magazine of History*, 95: 73–97.

—— (1973). *That Man Haupt: A Biography of Herman Haupt*. Baton Rouge: Louisiana State University Press.

Weigley, R. F. (1973). *The American Way of War: A History of United States Military Strategy and Policy*. London: Collier Macmillan.

Whitley, R. (1994). 'Dominant Forms of Economic Organization in Market Economies', *Organization Studies*, 15(2): 153–82.

Whittington, R. (1993). *What is Strategy? And Does It Matter?* London: Routledge.

—— and Mayer, M. (1997). 'Beyond or Behind the M-form? The Structures of European Business', in D. O'Neal and H. Thomas, *Strategy, Structure and Styles*. New York: John Wiley and Sons.

—— —— (2000). *The European Corporation: Strategy, Structure and Social Science*. Oxford: Oxford University Press.

Williamson, O. E. (1985). *The Economic Institutions of Capitalism: Firms, Markets, Relational Contracting*. New York: Free Press.

Yamey, B. S. (1964). 'Accounting and the Rise of Capitalism: Further Notes on a Theme by Sombart', *Journal of Accounting Research*, 2(2). Reprinted in Yamey, B. S. (1978), *Essays on the History of Accounting*. New York: Arno Press.

Zan, L. (1987). 'What's Left for Formal Planning?', *Economia Aziendale*, VI(2): 187–204.

—— (1995). 'Interactionism and Systemic View in the Strategic Approach', *Advances in Strategic Management*, 12A: 261–83.

9 Modernizing government: the calculating self, hybridization, and performance measurement[1]

Liisa Kurunmäki
Peter Miller

9.1 Introduction

How can we assess the performance of others? This apparently simple question has been at the heart of management and cost accounting for a century or so. The calculating self is central to this aspiration to evaluate and act upon the actions of others (Miller 1994). The individual endowed with the ability to compare and calculate the costliness of his or her actions, and that of others, owes much to the battery of devices that management accounting has developed. Standard costing and budgeting, return on investment (ROI), discounted cash flow (DCF), break-even analysis, activity-based costing (ABC), the balanced scorecard (BSC), and much more all share this aspiration to create and shape the capacity of individuals to calculate and to measure the performance of themselves and others. The 'modernizing government' agenda in the UK, as it has developed in the last decade or so, poses a particular challenge for this desire to measure performance. For the aspiration to create calculating selves, which has extended from the private sector to the public sector since the mid-1980s, comes into contact here with a separate process: the hybridization of expertise and organizational forms that the modernizing government agenda requires and inspires (Miller et al. 2006). In the process of seeking to make public service providers accountable, a diverse range of experts and professionals have become hybridized in varying degrees. Medical professionals, nurses, physiotherapists, teachers, police officers, and others are being encouraged to learn increasing amounts of management accounting, resulting in hybrid forms of expertise (Kurunmäki 2004). In parallel, organizational forms and processes are being transformed and hybridized as organizational boundaries are increasingly blurred and modes of performance assessment draw explicitly on principles and practices normally found separately (Miller et al. 2006).

The 'modernizing government' programme thus exemplifies two distinct and potentially contradictory pressures: the drive to calculate the activities of various professionals in terms of the single financial figure, and the drive to reform public services by various types of cooperative working. A variety of slogans such as 'joined-up working', 'partnership working', and 'cooperative working' articulate the aims and aspirations of the 'modernizing government' agenda. Intense and innovative cooperative working among public, private, and voluntary providers is promoted as a way of replacing the existing fragmented and dispersed service provision. The ideal has long been to break down the 'Berlin Wall' between health and social services. Curing and caring, which have very separate histories and professional identities yet intersect and overlap at so many points, are henceforth to be viewed as conjoint processes with shared governance and performance assessment systems.

The 'flexibilities' identified in Section 31 of the Health Act 1999 are a particularly clear example of such ambitions, and the issues they raise for performance measurement. In this chapter, we draw upon our study of those flexibilities to illustrate how the calculating self and the hybridization of expertises and organizational forms are emerging out of contemporary policy developments in the public sector. Three mechanisms were specified in the 1999 Health Act: the pooling of budgets, the delegating of commissioning responsibilities to a lead organization, and the integrating of health and social service provider functions (Kurunmäki et al. 2003). The use of these new flexibilities requires the partners to make a formal 'notification' to the Department of Health (DOH), in which the intended aims, objectives, and targets of the partnership project, as well as its governance arrangements, are specified. Central to this formal notification is the requirement to establish systems for governance and performance measurement that provide 'an account of the improved performance in respect of the outcomes of the arrangement' (DoH 2000*a*). As stated in the Guidance on the Health Act Section 31 Partnership Arrangements (Health and Social Care Joint Unit 2000):

All those who introduce the new partnership arrangements must monitor their effectiveness, and use measures of performance to develop their work. There needs to be a range of performance measures which can capture a balanced view of progress, cover the interest of all stakeholders, and reflect the business activity as a whole.

It is through such obligations to put in place formalized systems of governance and performance assessment that the process of hybridizing expertise is encouraged, and the calculating self becomes a more prevalent character across public sector management. And it is through these processes that performance assessment systems compatible with the modernizing government agenda are to be made operable. This interaction between the new political vocabulary of modernization, cooperation, and partnership, on the one hand, and the various practices of performance assessment and governance, on the other, exemplifies the interaction between programmes and technologies of government (Miller and Rose 1990; Rose and Miller 1992). Programmes of government, Miller and Rose argue, are more or less systematic discursive frameworks within which policies are defined and the objects and objectives of government specified. Programmes of government seek to link the mundane worlds of service delivery with those of much broader ethical and political objectives. Programmes of government are both analytic and prescriptive, and seek to establish the legitimacy of particular ways of delivering services and organizing social life. But programmes of government do not work by themselves. They require 'technologies' if they are to be made operable (Miller and Rose 1990). Technologies defined in this sense refer to the routine and often humble mechanisms and devices through which the activity of government is conducted. In Hacking's terms (1983), they are devices for 'intervening'. They can include techniques of notation, computation, and calculation, procedures of examination and assessment, and much else besides.

Understood in this sense, the Health Act flexibilities and related performance assessment systems can be viewed as part of the technologies through which the modernizing government programme is articulated and made operable. We seek to build on and extend the work of Miller and Rose (1990) by examining how the interaction between programmes and technologies occurs in a relatively localized setting, yet within the contours of much wider transformations in political vocabulary and ideals. Whereas the work of Miller and Rose largely addresses programmes and rationalities of government at a relatively abstract or macro level, our concern here is with what happens when the dreams and schemes of neoliberalism, 'marketization', cooperation, and so forth come into contact with specific policy domains and objectives, the activities and aspirations of those providing services and the self-identify of the different bodies of expertise that are involved.

The example of health care, and its recent interactions with social care at the policy level, pose very clearly the problems that arise when such encounters occur. For, as Rose and Miller (1992) have argued, experts have the capacity to generate *enclosures*, relatively bounded locales, or types of judgement within which their power and authority is concentrated, intensified, and defended. Even if such enclosures are only provisional and subject to contestation, they can nonetheless make it difficult for the 'centre', whether this be the cabinet office or the DoH, to act *as* a centre in full knowledge of both costs and performance. This has been an issue ever since the formation of the welfare state: how to assess and regulate the performance of those who claim discretionary power because of their professional expertise? How to make administrable and comparable the multitude of individual decisions by physicians, consultants, general practitioners, nurses, physiotherapists, and others? The history of the welfare state in the UK has been a history of attempts to transform the activities of healers into figures that would make medicine calculable. The 'modernizing government' agenda, and the appeals to partnership working and joined-up working, together represent yet another stage in this process, albeit framed in the language of cooperation rather than the harsh language of markets and market forces.

The performance assessment and governance dimensions of the 'modernizing government' agenda are fundamental to these long-standing issues. And, when considering the possible outcomes of these reform processes, we need to bear in mind variation across countries which shows that in some contexts hybridization can result in significant transformations in the set of capacities possessed by medical professionals, whereas in other contexts professional enclosures can be much more resistant to change (Kurunmäki 2004). In so far as government is a congenitally failing activity, but also an eternally optimistic one, which presumes that social life and the networks through which it is enacted can be made governable, we can only ever expect temporary stabilizations of networks of power and influence (Rose and Miller 1992).

The chapter is structured as follows. We start by describing in more detail the modernizing government agenda and the Health Act 1999 flexibilities. We analyse the aspirations of the reformers, and how they sought to link pragmatic issues of service delivery with broader political objectives. On the basis of fieldwork conducted in five sites, we then explore how the modernizing government agenda and the injunctions to cooperate have been articulated and made operable in a range of locales.[2] We address these issues under three sections. The first, 'Measurement of outcomes versus formal commitments' (Section 9.3.1), starts from the premise that what is counted usually counts, and that performance measurement systems impact on the capacities and characteristics of the calculating self. The second, 'Multiple performance measures and organizational boundaries' (Section 9.3.2), considers the multiple and overlapping performance measures that currently exist, and the ways in which they tend to respect organizational boundaries and limit the possibilities for hybridization. And the third, 'Curing versus caring: the interprofessional dimensions of modernizing government' (Section 9.3.3), considers the ways in which professional boundaries and self-identities impact on the modernizing government agenda. We conclude by discussing the broader implications of these issues for management accounting research.

9.2 **Modernizing government and flexibilities**

The 'modernizing government' programme, originally outlined in the White Paper *Modern Public Services for Britain: Investing in Reform* (HMSO 1998), and later presented in more detail in the *Modernising Government* White Paper (Cabinet Office 1999), holds out the promise of improving public services by promoting innovative joined-up working between agencies and experts that provide complementary services to citizens. The impetus to erode the boundaries between health and social care, and to build services 'around the needs of those who use them' (DoH 1998*a*: 5), was reflected similarly in two White Papers: *New NHS: Modern, Dependable* (DoH 1997), and *Modernising Social Services: Promoting Independence, Improving Protection, Raising Standards* (DoH 1998*b*). Innovative, cross-sectoral working has since been encouraged in the National Audit Office and Audit Commission reports (see e.g. National Audit Office 2001 and Audit Commission 2002), and through a range of initiatives including health improvement programmes (HImPs), joint investment plans (JIPs), health action zones (HAZs), and partnership grants. Partnerships have been encouraged at multiple levels: between service users, their carers, and service providers; between service provider organizations and government departments; and between the public sector, voluntary organizations, and private providers (DoH 2000*b*). In a separate, yet complementary, stream of policy developments, a number of initiatives over the last few decades have sought to introduce private sector provision into both health and social care. Public–private partnerships have been promoted by the Labour government, and the Private Finance Initiative, inherited from the Conservatives, is now an established part of the political landscape, as the government drives towards a mixed economy of service provision (Midwinter 2001).

Sections 26 to 32 of the Health Act 1999 implemented measures to strengthen formal partnership working, both within the National Health Service (NHS) and between the NHS and local authorities. They created a new duty of cooperation within the NHS, and extended the duty of cooperation between NHS bodies and local authorities; they provided a new statutory mechanism for strategic planning to improve health and health care services; and they provided for NHS bodies and local authorities to make payments to one another, and make use of new operational flexibilities to improve the way health and health-related functions are exercised (see HMSO 1999).

More specifically, the partnership arrangements set out in Section 31 of the Health Act introduced measures to strengthen existing partnership working between 'health' and 'social care', and to encourage innovative, cross-sectoral working. The key operational tools introduced in this section were *pooled funds*, and the delegation of functions through either *lead commissioning* or *integrated provision*. These partnership arrangements gave NHS bodies and local authorities the flexibility to improve services by building on existing joined-up working, or by developing new user-focused services between health and social care, as well as with other local government services and the independent sector. *Pooled budgets* allowed health and social services to bring together resources, in a discrete fund, to pay for the services that are an agreed part of the pooled fund arrangement for a given client group. Instead of users being inconvenienced by disputes about the respective responsibilities of health and local authorities, organizations would agree at the outset the full range of services to be purchased and provided from the fund. The distinctive flexibility allowed for within pooled budgets is that they would be based on the principle that expenditure should depend on the needs of the users, and not on the level of contribution from each partner. *Lead commissioning*, in contrast, allowed one authority—either health care or social services—to take responsibility for commissioning a range of services for a client group on behalf of the other from a single point. Improved coordination arising through the work of the Lead Commissioner would, it was hoped, result in improved services for users. Finally, *integrated provision* was designed to allow local authorities, Primary Care Trusts, and NHS Trusts to provide services under a single management structure, thus offering integrated services from one provider rather than many. The advantages of joining up services under a single management structure were seen to lie in a more fully coordinated approach, resulting ultimately in a seamless service for users (Health and Social Care Joint Unit 2000).

The declared aims of these flexibilities were to improve services, to avoid wasteful duplication and gaps in service provision, and to ensure public funds are used more efficiently and effectively (DoH 1998*a*: 7). To achieve these results, joined-up working would have to operate at all levels of organizational hierarchies, from strategic planning to service delivery, but it would also have to extend beyond the boundaries of the collaborating organizations. Cooperation and joined-up working would be required, for example, between management and auditors, and among public auditors themselves. In discharging their specific remits, public auditors should seek to cooperate with other auditors and use each other's work, with a view to minimizing any overlap of audit examinations, for example by exchanging evidence or by joint audits (National Audit Office 1999: 5; Public Audit Forum 1999: 10; Ling 2002).

The NHS Plan, published in summer 2000 by the DoH, reinforced the overall programmatic importance of partnership arrangements and the significance of 'breaking down the Berlin Wall' between health and social care. It also introduced a new organizational form, 'Care Trusts', for partnership working. Care Trusts could be used to form legal bodies to commission and take responsibility for all local health and social care. The result, it was declared, would be 'a new relationship between health and social care' and a 'radical redesign of the whole care system' (DoH 2000*b*: 71).

Such were the aspirations of the reformers. 'Modernizing government' would link long-standing concerns about fragmented service provision with a political vocabulary inherited and yet adapted from the more extreme versions of neoliberalism articulated under the previous Conservative government. Notions of 'the customer' would be retained, along with the critique of unresponsive bureaucracies, but these were now to be framed in terms of a more mellow concept of 'cooperation' and 'partnership' as embodied in 'third way' politics. In turn, these aspirations were to be aligned with the specific policy objectives as set out in the Health Act 1999: to achieve formal partnership working across organizational and professional boundaries, and to do so in such a way that performance improvements could be clearly demonstrated. It is to these issues that we now turn.

9.3 Performance measurement across organizational and professional boundaries

If assessing the performance of others is itself a difficult task, doing so across organizational and professional boundaries is even more daunting. And doing so while transforming at the same time organizational forms, local working relationships, and professional boundaries, as well as reporting and governance mechanisms, is perhaps to ask management accounting practices to deliver more than they were designed for. Nonetheless, these are the demands that management accounting in the public sector has faced increasingly across the last two decades (Hopwood 1984). In seeking to align notions of 'modernization' and 'cooperation' with the 'flexibilities' introduced in the Health Act 1999, accounting practices are once again linked up to much wider objectives and aspirations. Changes are made in the name of accounting when they have little connection with accounting practices. Equally, accounting is called upon to deliver at the operational and organizational level things that have little to do with its calculative practices.

The gap between the general and the specific can be a very large one. The modernizing government programme provided a broad discursive framework within which individual policies could be developed. 'Cooperative working' became established within the modernizing government programme as a desirable sociopolitical objective, and as a means of seeking to improve services. In turn, the flexibilities introduced in the 1999 Health Act offered a set of technologies that were consistent with the overall aim of joined-up working. Pooled budgets, lead commissioning, and integrated provision provided ways of linking these broad objectives with the pragmatic world of service delivery in a range of areas. Accounting and performance assessment thus became enmeshed in a much wider set of social and institutional processes. And these all had to be worked out at local levels through a multiplicity of individual service providers who were called upon to rethink, redescribe, and reorganize their work processes so as to align them with the wider political ideals.

As the noble and abstract aspirations of cooperation and joined-up working intersected with the specifics of existing administrative, professional, and service delivery frameworks, the gap between the general and the specific became increasingly apparent. For the NHS and social services in the UK have distinct budgetary, legal, and cultural histories (Hudson 1998; Bridgen and Lewis 1999). Different governance arrangements for service provision—with social services falling under the auspices of local government and health care under that of central government—have resulted in differential treatments for such apparently mundane issues as terms and conditions of employment, value-added tax (VAT) and charging, dispute resolution procedures, and the treatment of inflation in budgets.

The performance measurement dimensions of the Health Act flexibilities illustrate very clearly the gap between the general and the specific. The formal 'notifications' of partnership agreements required that systems for governance and performance measurement be put in place to demonstrate improvements in performance resulting from the new arrangements.[3] These would include arrangements for addressing issues regarding decision-making processes, monitoring, and accountability, as well as ensuring that these offered appropriate mechanisms for external scrutiny. The performance measurement of jointly provided services was regarded as particularly challenging, given the difficulties of aligning such diverse practices and cultures in a relatively short period of time. The new arrangements had to come into contact with existing ways of working and existing performance measurement systems. They had to be seen to measure appropriate activities and processes, and they had to try and satisfy different stakeholder groups internally and externally. The new performance measurement systems were expected to incorporate and align existing systems within a broader framework that demonstrates and measures the benefits of cooperative working, as well as the contribution of individual providers.

9.3.1 MEASUREMENT OF OUTCOMES VERSUS FORMAL COMMITMENTS

If what is counted usually counts, defining the objects and objectives of performance measurement systems is paramount (Burchell et al. 1980; Miller 1992). In both the public and private sectors, traditional accounting measures have increasingly been supplemented by non-financial measures (Model 2004). A system that incorporates multiple financial and non-financial performance measures creates a problem of trade-offs, however. Although 'balance' may require a manager to perform well on multiple dimensions, actions taken to improve measurable performance on one scale may lead to a short-term decline on another scale. A key question becomes how to retain 'balance' in managerial actions and perform-ance evaluations in the presence of these trade-offs (Ittner and Larcker 1998).

In the context of the newly available flexibilities, and the felt imperatives to demonstrate that innovation was occurring, one obvious option for planners was to include indicators that simply measure progress in implementing formal partnerships. Consistent with this view, one health authority representative expected service providers 'each year to be judged on how they are doing in terms of the partnership agenda'. According to this interviewee:

One of the measures will be what are you doing about joint commissioning, what are you doing about pooled budgets, and what are the benefits arising from that, and are you measuring them, are you still achieving those benefits and if so, what are the future benefits? (Health Authority CEO)

As one would expect, the importance of measuring performance and progress was not contested. But the issue of what to measure and how to 'capture a balanced view of progress' that would 'cover the interests of all stakeholders' and 'reflect the business activity as a whole' (Health and Social Care Joint Unit 2000) was seen as deeply problematic. It was considered important to appreciate the inherent complexity of choosing the appropriate measures, as well as interpreting their results (Glendinning 2002). But there was a difference of opinion concerning the extent to which monitoring should focus on the use of formal partnership arrangements, compared with a focus on the outputs and outcomes of the new types of cooperative working. While service providers realized the importance of demonstrating to central government that progress was being achieved at the level of broad policies, a number of those interviewed argued strongly that any measures should focus on the outcomes and the benefits to users, rather than simply the formal adoption of the flexibilities. According to one interviewee, a Partnership Manager: 'It's not about how we use the mechanisms, it's about what we do for service users in the future that actually improves services for them.'

The aims, objectives, and targets set out in the formal 'notification' to the DoH in one of the sites studied were consistent with this view. A 'lead commissioning' arrangement was proposed in this site to commence in April 2000. Its stated aim was 'to maximise commis-sioning efficiency by creating a unified seamless service for the provision of continuing care in institutional care establishments or equipment and care packages in the community by using the social services existing contract management infrastructure'. Targets set for the end of March 2001 included improved price control and quality assurance, a reduction in the percentage of delayed discharges, and a reduction in the number of cases being presented for arbitration. Targets also included a positive evaluation with respect to budget management and commitments, as well as the achievement of a developed model for collaborative working among Primary Care Groups across the country.

The chief executive officer (CEO) of a hospital trust specializing in learning disabilities strongly supported measurement of the outcomes of joined-up working for users, particularly where these sought to facilitate the move from institutional care to community-based care:

We can give you numbers of people moving from institutional care into more independent living. We can do surveys of satisfaction from families and they can say, yeah, things are better than they were, or no, they're not. We can talk to GPs and do surveys of GPs that say yeah we get a more responsive service, or no we don't. We can do all that stuff. (Hospital Trust CEO)

Similarly, a social services representative gave examples of user-focused measures of the impacts of partnership working:

We've still got a long way to go in setting sufficiently tight performance targets to say what difference is this [partnership working] making, and to quantify it. . . . They might be things like waiting times, to show we've reduced waiting times. . . . It will be user surveys and that sort of thing in terms of whether there's greater satisfaction in terms of what they're getting; whether they feel they can understand the system; whether they feel they know where to go; whether they get a quicker response service; whether they know that the assessment has finished and they're now getting treatment; whether they feel that they've been told what the assessment was. (Head of Children's Services)

It was seen as important by this interviewee that measurement should focus on outcomes for users, even though it was recognized that this could prove difficult in practice:

Some of the outcomes will be about improved attendance and attainment, fewer children in the care system . . . fewer children on child protection registers . . . all those overall indicators. But that actually is too broad really because there are so many variables that will be impacting on that. (Head of Children's Services)

The formal 'notification' document for this interviewee's site set out a large number of targets that included the above items, together with other outcomes such as reducing the rate of hospital readmission, reducing the numbers of children who attempt suicide or self-harm, or who kill themselves, and improvements in user satisfaction.

The issue of what was being measured, and whether this included outcomes for users, was considered important in terms of engaging the service providers. According to one interviewee:

Most health and social care professionals would be fairly sympathetic about performance measurements about outcomes, less responsive to performance measurements about the technical process by which you get to that outcome. (Partnership Manager)

A Community Care Manager in one of the sites commented as follows:

We've spent quite a lot of time in the last 18 months trying to look at our processes of measurement to make sure that we do start to evaluate outcomes. (Community Care Manager)

This had meant, he continued:

Trying to get our systems to produce [for] us the information that can make us more analytical about our activity . . . evaluating those, not just in how much money did we spend but in the quality of what we're delivering . . . and getting the loop back on the consumer view back on the quality of the services and (a) the sorts of services we buy, and (b) are they what people want, and (c) are they creating better outcomes for people. (Community Care Manager)

Irrespective of the specific performance measures proposed, it was clear that there was a general preference on the part of service providers for emphasizing outcomes, defined as benefits to users. But while this might seem relatively unproblematic in the abstract, it was to prove far from straightforward in the context of developing joined-up performance measures across organizational boundaries. It is these issues we turn to in Section 9.3.2.

9.3.2 MULTIPLE PERFORMANCE MEASURES AND ORGANIZATIONAL BOUNDARIES

When performance measurement is addressed in the academic literature, the focus is typically on the private sector (Ittner and Larcker 1998). There is, however, a long tradition of performance assessment in both health care and local government (Bowerman et al. 2000, 2001). Recent decades have witnessed an avalanche of performance indicators, performance reviews, audits, and inspections in the UK public sector (Pollitt 1986; Lapsley and Mitchell 1996; Power 1997; Bowerman et al., 2000; Chow et al. 2005). These include National Service Frameworks (for cancer, paediatric intensive care, mental health, coronary heart disease, older people, diabetes, etc.), local government Best Value Performance Indicators, Best Value Performance Plans, and Best Value Reviews, Audit Commission Quality of Life Indicators, Comprehensive Performance Assessment framework for local authorities, NHS Reference Costing, as well as NHS and Social Services Performance (star) Ratings. The employment and implications of these performance measures have been a focus of much academic research, as have attempts to combine various measures through such devices as the BSC (Pollitt et al. 1999; Bowerman et al. 2000, 2001; Model 2004).

The rhetoric of modernizing government promotes 'local solutions' and innovation (Cabinet Office 1999), yet combines this with a centralizing agenda that increases the capacity of the centre to monitor and control local service provision. Performance measurement is one of the key aspects of this centralizing dimension. Multiple and sometimes overlapping systems of performance reporting combine with multiple regulatory bodies to create an 'audit society' (Power 1997). Regulatory control and reviews are increasingly conducted on behalf of central government by third-party inspectorates such as the Health Care Commission, the Commission for Social Care Inspection, and the Audit Commission. The declared aim of many of the more recent performance measurement systems and performance ratings and reviews has been to give increased autonomy, greater resources, and less inspection for those who succeed or can demonstrate good progress on one or more dimensions. Providers of failing services, on the contrary, are told that they will face more direct and intense centralist control. Regulators and inspectors have been given powers to 'trigger' intervention in local services where the service provider is perceived as failing either to discharge its functions adequately or to meet its statutory obligations (Brooks 2000; DoH

2002). At the limit, 'reserve powers' can mean that local management is wholly replaced by nominees from central government.

Centralism and localism thus go hand in hand in a performance measurement culture, which has one notable characteristic in the context of the modernizing government agenda—the imperative to develop *joined-up performance measurement* to complement *joined-up working*. The tension between encouraging local autonomy, while demonstrating tangible improvements for central control purposes, requires national and local targets and standards that cross organizational boundaries. In some areas, the government had already set the targets in such a way that their achievement required cooperation among different agencies. According to one social services interviewee, joined-up working was encouraged by joined-up performance measurement in many areas of children's services:

We have never been more dependent on one another to deliver our individual performance indicators. So education [providers] have got to improve attendance and attainment; they need health facilities and social services to help them with that. We [social services] have got to deliver improved outcomes for children in a looked-after system, and we need the help of education for that. Health [providers] have got to deliver things like reduced pregnancy rates and other kinds of agendas which they need us to help do it. (Head of Children's Services)

Mental health services was regarded as another area where national targets had been set in a way that they cut across organization and institutional boundaries. According to one health services representative:

The NSF [national service framework] for Mental Health Services...establishes the standards and performance targets that Mental Health Services should be attaining, and we built that into the accountability structures and mechanisms....Now that actually crosses health and social care, because the targets cross the boundaries. (Health Authority CEO)

Despite a small number of contrasting examples, national targets were still largely regarded as functionally focused. Most of them were seen as ultimately designed to lead to performance ratings of individual organizations such as a particular hospital or school. Or, like Comprehensive Performance Assessment, they were seen as resulting in the comparative rating of local authorities on the basis of combining ratings of individual organizations or services. Despite the requirements of the formal 'notifications' for partnership working under the Section 31 provisions, there were still very few indicators that set targets or measures for the outcomes of joined-up working. This is ironic in the context of the modernizing government programme, for the modernizing government programme depends heavily on interorganizational cooperation and the sharing of resources and outcomes. By focusing on particular functional services, rather than taking a cross-cutting or client-focused approach, and by sharpening the focus on failing services, central government has been viewed as discouraging service providers from changing the ways services are organized to deliver long-term benefits. Success on one register could mean failure on another. By following a cooperative agenda, and by encouraging innovative ways of working, an organization might in the short term jeopardize its ability to meet its own statutory targets, or the requirements of national audit and inspection regimes. These standards and inspection regimes, or at least the way in which they have been implemented, have been viewed as hindering innovation by inducing a greater sense of vulnerability among senior staff (Martin 2000; Newman et al. 2001).

There was considerable concern among those interviewed that local and voluntary performance measurement systems should be developed that would recognize and reward cooperative working. A representative from social services commented on the efforts in one site to develop such systems as follows:

What we've done is we've involved colleagues from Health in our annual assessment meetings. So we've really begun to get them engaged.... And the other element is the Health Authority, in developing its performance management role for the Primary Care Trust. So again, I've written to the Health Authority saying can we all sit down together and actually... you're performance managing the PCT, a lot of it is actually jointly provided with local government, so if you're going to develop a performance management framework and tool, you really need to be engaging us with that as well. (Corporate Director of Social Services)

Developments were slow, however. Most interviewees commented that they were awaiting the provision by national government of formal and centralized systems. According to one interviewee from health services:

I gather we are expecting an NSF in Learning Disability Services, but that might not happen until next year. If that happens, then that will help enormously, because if you put some national framework around that... which we would then find easy to adopt, I guess. (Health Authority CEO)

A representative from social services commented on his expectations regarding the role of central government in issuing performance measurement systems as follows:

As yet we haven't seen it... but there will be some performance measurement of partnership work which is new and I think that will be a bit of a wake-up call for some people, but obviously it depends what lead we get about performance management. (Partnership Manager)

If the multiple performance measurement systems already in place tended to respect organizational boundaries, and if it was more or less self-evident that this needed to be rectified in the context of joined-up working, there remained the issue of how to devise joined-up performance measures that satisfy various stakeholders with different professional and organizational backgrounds. It is to that issue we now turn.

9.3.3 CURING VERSUS CARING: THE INTERPROFESSIONAL DIMENSIONS OF MODERNIZING GOVERNMENT

The providers of health and social care have long been criticized for their poor coordination of services.[4] The separation of service providers into different units, and the rigid boundaries between them, have been held to result in fragmented provision, uncoordinated service delivery, inefficiency, complication, and confusion (Cabinet Office 1999: 23). This is especially the case in areas where the division of tasks and responsibilities between different service providers and professionals is vague. In the realms of health care and social services, the issue of performance measurement brings the interprofessional boundaries into sharp relief, and makes visible and measurable the contrast between curing and caring.

The provision of services for people with learning difficulties provides an example of an area where the definition of tasks and responsibilities between different providers is not clear-cut. When asked how the responsibility between social services and health care is determined in the case of people with learning disabilities, a CEO of a specialist health care trust for people with learning difficulties replied:

You tell me . . . I've no idea. . . . It's completely arbitrary . . . and relates very much to the tradition of care in any particular geographical area. (Hospital Trust CEO)

According to this CEO, the concept of 'learning disability' is itself a category that is difficult to define. He explained:

Learning disability is . . . a constellation of factors usually measured according to functional perform-ance along lines of intellectual functioning, social functioning, habilitation functioning, two or three others as well. . . . There are no set tests for those levels of functioning. It's very much in the eye of the beholder. . . . It's very, very difficult to identify what learning disability is. (Hospital Trust CEO)

A number of distinct professional groups are involved in the care of people with learning disabilities. Health care and social services professionals often disagree not only on the diagnosis but also on the appropriate form of care:

It's quite often the case that there will be an argument between a social worker and a doctor, and one of our psychiatrists about whether someone really has a learning disability or not. The psychiatrist will argue on the grounds of IQ, the social worker on the grounds of functioning, and it's very much in the eye of the beholder and based on the experience of those professionals. And I think that's one of the things that creates quite difficult circumstances of working together, because there's no shared sense of who has a learning disability, who doesn't, what constitutes a learning disability. (Hospital Trust CEO)

In these circumstances, defining the relative responsibilities of social services and health care is a difficult exercise. According to the same CEO:

There are some indicators but they have no credibility. . . . That's the thing. They have no credibility when you get to practitioner level, they have no credibility because they're not reliable in terms of actually identifying administrative responsibility for care. They're reasonably good at indicating the level of dysfunctioning. When it comes to indicating who should be responsible for paying for care, they're not reliable. (Hospital Trust CEO)

There are many other areas where the administrative responsibilities of health and social care providers overlap or are difficult to define, and where professional boundaries are ill-defined. Continuing care for the elderly or the disabled, as well as services for children with mental or behavioural problems, are further examples. All too often, it has been claimed, good quality services are sacrificed for sterile arguments about boundaries when people have complex needs spanning both health and social care (DoH 1998a: 3). Curing and caring are not distinct and opposed activities, argue those who seek to reform service provision, but are complementary and in need of improved coordination.

But, while the notion of joined-up working celebrates the breaking down of such boundaries, it typically does not demonstrate how this might be achieved in detail, and how appropriate joined-up performance measures might be designed. Systems of performance measurement have to satisfy a number of stakeholders and audiences. For example, accountability to the public for the use of resources needs to be demonstrated via traditional local authority mechanisms (Bowerman et al. 2001). This was a concern to a head of Learning Disability Services, who also acted as a Lead Commissioner:

Some people if they just survive living in a house and being able to look after themselves is a significant improvement to what they were doing in a more confined ward in a hospital. You see it's relative. (Lead Commissioner of Learning Disability Services)

The problem, according to this interviewee, is as follows:

How can we demonstrate the investment is actually giving you a return and how can we satisfy the community at large that their investment is well spent? (Lead Commissioner of Learning Disability Services)

As discussed earlier, there was tension between policy-makers and service providers regarding the extent to which the formal adoption of flexibilities, as distinct from their outcomes for users, should be measured. However, tension was also felt between social services staff and health care representatives about the appropriate use of resources and the means of reporting outcomes. The Lead Commissioner of Learning Disability Services spoke of the difficulties in explaining to colleagues in the health service some of the expenditure incurred by social services. Different expectations on the part of health and social services with respect to desired outcomes were considered to cause problems. He explained:

Profound people [those with profound learning disability] are funded on a joint formula, 60% Social Services, 40% Health. There is a feeling at times that health will say what is the outcome of this because they don't get better. ... We're not growing a percentage of hip operations, we're not reducing the number of heart attacks, we're not going to reduce the number of people with a learning disability. (Lead Commissioner of Learning Disability Services)

A social services representative at one of the sites commented on the way in which the multiprofessional nature of the programme had influenced the progress of the reforms:

The speed at which we've been able to go is slower than we would have anticipated in spite of our enthusiasm and commitment, because of our individual agendas, understanding different priorities of our individual agencies, language, the different disciplines we come from, the different ethos and philosophies. (Head of Children's Services)

While the principle of joined-up working was endorsed by both health care and social service providers, developing the technologies of performance assessment that would enable progress to be made visible and measurable proved problematic. A long tradition of distinct and sometimes competing professional agendas had resulted in a situation where, in the words of one Head of Commissioning and Performance Management, 'we don't speak the same language'. Outcomes that one group would see as progress would, in such a situation, be much less valued and recognized by the other. A contrast between curing and caring seemed to be a significant obstacle to the development of joined-up performance measurement.

9.4 **Conclusion**

The battle cry of 'modernizing government' is as reassuring to reformers as it is incontestable to those who have to make it work. The same applies to all the slogans that accompany it, whether these be 'joined-up working', 'partnership working', or much broader appeals to 'cooperative working'. But, as we have argued, the gap between the general and the specific, between programmes and technologies, is often considerable. This is exacerbated to the extent that the broad political objectives of the modernizing government agenda bring together the aspiration to create and shape calculating selves, and the hybridization of expertise. To create a centre from which one can calculate and compare the performance of the multitude of daily decisions of medical and social care professionals is a large enough task in itself. To achieve this while redefining organizational forms and interprofessional relations is a considerably larger task. The enclosures formed over many decades within the framework of the welfare state by professionals and experts of varying kinds are at the heart of this project, and breaching such enclosures is fundamental to the task of performance measurement.

We have examined one particular instance of this phenomenon here, and one dimension of the 'modernizing government' agenda in the UK, namely the flexibilities defined in Section 31 of the Health Act 1999: pooled budgets, lead commissioning, and integrated provision. We have sketched, albeit briefly, the aspirations of the reformers and how they have sought to link broad political objectives with the specifics of service delivery. We have considered the performance measurement and governance requirements associated with these flexibilities, and the obligations these impose for the monitoring of the new partnership arrangements so as to provide a 'balanced' view of progress that 'reflects the business activity as a whole'. On the basis of fieldwork conducted in five sites, we have contrasted the measurement of outcomes in terms of benefits to users with the measurement of formal commitments to partnership working. We have considered the multiple and overlapping performance measures that currently exist, and how these are typically tied to existing organizational boundaries. And we have examined the interprofessional dimensions of the modernizing government agenda, how these bring into sharp relief the differences between the curative and caring aspirations of health care and social care respectively, and how these impact on the design of appropriate mechanisms of performance measurement.

The Health Act 1999 flexibilities represent one episode in the long history of attempts to encourage cooperation between health and social services. If anything, the pursuit of interagency collaboration has become even more insistent in recent years (Hudson 1998). It is unsurprising, then, that our research on the early experiments with the Health Act flexibilities found a positive yet relatively cautious approach to the issue of formal partnership working, and little tangible steps to develop joined-up performance measurement. As one might expect, existing performance indicators developed for different organizations persisted, albeit in combined forms. Existing national frameworks, such as for mental health care, tended to survive while other areas such as learning disability services eagerly awaited their own national frameworks. Local innovation focused largely on individual functions, rather than the overall benefits of cooperative projects, in view of the difficulty of making visible and measurable such dimensions. And the assessment of demonstrable benefits to users, as distinct from progress in adopting the formal flexibilities, remained elusive, at least at an early stage of the reforms.

We have argued elsewhere that the hybridization of expertise, and of organizational forms and processes, is increasingly prevalent (Kurunmäki 2004; Miller et al. 2006). The extent to which this emerges is an empirical issue, and appears to be dependent on the dynamics of interprofessional encounters between such groups as medics and accountants in specific national and organizational contexts, as well as more general political trends such as the marketization of the public sector. The role of management accounting practices in such developments is curious. For, in so far as societies record and monitor the activities and entities they value most, one might expect the performance measurement of hybrid forms to be further developed than it currently is. The undeveloped state of performance assessment for hybrids may be explained, at least in part and somewhat perversely, by the relative success that accounting has had in creating 'calculating selves'. If accounting gives selective visibility to organizational actions and outcomes, and if it tends to give more attention to the economic than the social, it may be that the hybrid forms of expertise and organizational forms that we encounter increasingly continue to escape from the somewhat restricted and incessant calculative routines that have tended to dominate management accounting. If the 'real' management of risk escapes the formalized and compliance-dominated frameworks of risk management (Miller et al. 2006), it is equally possible that 'real' cooperative frameworks and working patterns are similarly intractable for management accounting and performance assessment systems.

▢ NOTES

1 A version of this chapter appeared in *Financial Accountability and Management* (2006), vol. 22, No. 1, pp. 65–84. This study would not have been possible without the willing cooperation provided by staff at the organizations studied. The authors gratefully acknowledge their input. The support of the Economic and Social Research Council (ESRC) is gratefully acknowledged. The work was part of the programme of the ESRC Centre for Analysis of Risk and Regulation, London School of Economics and Political Science. For more information visit: www.lse.ac.uk/depts/carr. The researchers wish to acknowledge also the funding provided by the PD Leake Trust (a charity associated with the ICAEW), the King's Fund, and the Suntory and Toyota International Centres for Economics and Related Disciplines. We are grateful for comments on an earlier version of this

chapter received at the Chartered Institute of Management Accountants (CIMA) Workshop on New Public Management at the University of Edinburgh, September 2003. The authors would like to thank Iida Keto and Debbie Ranger for their research and administrative support.

2 We studied the early experimentation with the Health Act 'flexibilities' in five sites. The research on which we draw here commenced in summer 2000, and most of the fieldwork was conducted during the following eighteen months. The selection of the research sites was based primarily on the following three criteria: (*a*) to cover a range of client groups (e.g. the elderly, children's services, and physical and learning disabilities); (*b*) to provide a reasonable geographical spread (i.e. to include a mix of metropolitan boroughs and shire counties); and (*c*) to include a mix of large and small budgets. In these different sites, we were able to observe how the Health Act 'flexibilities' were used formally to develop 'cooperative working' in the provision of care for those with learning disabilities, to help create support for multiagency cooperation in the care of children with behavioural problems, and to develop and speed up processes of care home placements for the elderly. In one site, we also observed how plans emerged to experiment with the Health Act 'flexibilities' to develop partnership working further in the care of people with mental health problems. Finally, in one site, where the formal processes of the Health Act 'flexibilities' were not yet being used, we were able to study how various actors were developing plans for partnership working in a number of service areas. Research data were collected primarily through thirteen semi-structured interviews with a variety of stakeholders involved in the financing and delivery of services, as well as through observation of three 'Section 31' meetings in two research sites. Those interviewed included a mixture of managers responsible for overall organizational strategy and commitment (e.g. Health Authority Chief Executives) and those responsible managerially for developing and designing partnership arrangements and governance mechanisms (e.g. Service and Purchasing Managers). A standardized set of questions was developed at an early stage, and this was used as the basis for conducting the interviews and their analysis. All interviews were tape-recorded and transcribed. Further documentary material related to partnership working, including confidential internal documents, was collected from the study sites to complement material collected by interviews.

3 The signatories to a formal 'notification' of a proposed partnership arrangement are asked to be satisfied that there exist robust arrangements for governance, reviews of the partnership arrangements, terms, conditions, and policies for human resources, information-sharing practices, identification of functions included in the partnership arrangement, eligibility criteria and assessment processes, complaints procedures, financial issues (such as charging), dispute-resolving mechanisms, and plans for exit strategies (Source: Application form for Section 31 Partnership Arrangements by the Department of Health).

4 See e.g. Audit Commission reports 1997, 1999, and 2000 regarding coordination of services for the elderly.

☐ REFERENCES

Audit Commission (1997). *The Coming of Age: Improving Care Services for Older People*. London: Audit Commission.

—— (1999). *Forget Me Not: Mental Health Services for Older People*. London: Audit Commission.

Audit Commission (2000). *The Way to Go Home: Rehabilitation and Remedial Services for Older People.* London: Audit Commission.

—— (2002). *Integrated Services for Older People: Building a Whole System Approach in England.* London: Audit Commission.

Bowerman, M., Raby, H., and Humphrey, C. (2000). 'In Search of Audit Society: Some Evidence from Health Care, Police and Schools', *International Journal of Auditing*, 4: 71–100.

—— Ball, A., and Graham, F. (2001). 'Benchmarking as a Tool for the Modernisation of Local Government', *Financial Accountability & Management.* 17: 321–9.

Bridgen, P. and Lewis, J. (1999). *Elderly People and the Boundary between Health and Social Care 1946–1991: Whose Responsibility?* London: Nuffield Trust.

Brooks, J. (2000). 'Labour's Modernization of Local Government', *Public Administration*, 78: 593–612.

Burchell, S., Clubb, C., Hopwood, A. G., and Hughes, J. (1980). 'The Roles of Accounting in Organizations and Society', *Accounting, Organizations and Society*, 5: 5–27.

Cabinet Office (1999). *Modernising Government.* London: HMSO, Cm 4310.

Chow, D. S. L., Humphrey, C. G. and Miller, P. (2005). 'Financial Management in the UK Public Sector: Historical Development, Current Issues and Controversies', in J. Guthrie, C. Humphrey, L. R. Jones, and O. Olson (eds.), *International Public Financial Management Reform.* (Greenwich, CT: Information Age).

DOH (Department of Health) (1997). *The New NHS: Modern, Dependable.* London: HMSO, Cm 3807.

—— (1998*a*). *Partnership in Action: New Opportunities for Joint Working between Health and Social Services, A Discussion Document.* London: Department of Health.

—— (1998*b*). *Modernising Social Services: Promoting Independence, Improving Protection, Raising Standards.* London: HMSO, Cm 4169.

—— (2000*a*). *Implementation of Health Act Partnership Arrangements.* London: HSC, 2000/101.

—— (2000*b*). *The NHS Plan: A Plan for Investment, a Plan for Reform.* London: HMSO, Cm 4818–I.

—— (2002). *Delivering the NHS Plan: Next Steps on Investment, Next Steps on Reform.* London: HMSO, Cm 5503.

Glendinning, C. (2002). 'Partnerships between Health and Social Services: Developing a Framework for Evaluation', *Policy Press*, 30: 115–27.

Hacking, I. (1983). *Representing and Intervening.* Cambridge: Cambridge University Press.

Health and Social Care Joint Unit (2000). *Guidance on the Health Act Section 31 Partnership Arrangements.* www.doh.gov.uk/jointunit/pship1.htm.

HMSO (1998). *Modern Public Services for Britain: Investing in Reform Comprehensive Spending Review: New Public Spending Plans 1999–2002.* Cm 4011.

—— (1999). *Health Act 1999 Explanatory Notes* (chapter 8).

Hopwood, A. G. (1984). 'Accounting and Pursuit of Efficiency', in A. G. Hopwood and C. Tomkins (eds.), *Issues in Public Sector Accounting.* Deddington: Philip Allan.

Hudson, B. (1998). 'Circumstances Change Cases: Local Government and the NHS', *Social Policy and Administration*, 32: 71–86.

Ittner, C. D. and Larcker, D. F. (1998). 'Innovations in Performance Measurement: Trends and Research Implications', *Journal of Management Accounting Research*, 10: 205–38.

Kurunmäki, L. (2004). 'A Hybrid Profession: The Acquisition of Management Accounting Expertise by Medical Professionals', *Accounting, Organizations and Society*, 29: 327–48.

—— Miller, P., and Keen, J. (2003). *Health Act Flexibilities: Partnerships in Health and Social Care.* London: ICAEW.

Lapsley, I. and Mitchell, F. (eds.) (1996). *Accounting and Performance Measurement. Issues in the Private and Public Sectors.* London: Paul Chapman.

Ling, T. (2002). 'Delivering Joined-Up Government in the UK: Dimensions, Issues and Problems', *Public Administration*, 80: 615–42.

Martin, S. (2000). 'Implementing "Best Value": Local Public Services in Transition', *Public Administration*, 78: 209–27.

Midwinter, A. (2001). 'New Labour and the Modernisation of British Local Government: A Critique', *Financial Accountability & Management*, 17: 311–20.

Miller, P. B. (1992). 'Accounting and Objectivity: The Invention of Calculating Selves and Calculable Spaces', *Annals of Scholarship*, 9: 61–86.

—— (1994). 'Accounting and Objectivity: The Invention of Calculating Selves and Calculable Spaces', in A. Megil (ed.), *Rethinking Objectivity.* London: Duke University Press.

—— and Rose, N. (1990). 'Governing Economic Life', *Economy and Society*, 19: 1–31.

—— Kurunmäki, L., and O'Leary, T. (2006). 'Accounting Hybrids and the Management of Risk', *Journal of Management Studies*, 43(5): 65–84.

Model, S. (2004). 'Performance Measurement Myths in the Public Sector: A Research Note', *Financial Accountability & Management*, 20: 39–55.

National Audit Office (1999). *Modernising Government—The NAO Response.* London: National Audit Office.

—— (2001). *Joining up to Improve Public Services.* London: Stationery Office, HC 383.

Newman, J., Raine, J., and Skelcher, C. (2001). 'Transforming Local Government: Innovation and Modernization', *Public Money and Management*, 21: 61–8.

Pollitt, C. (1986). 'Beyond the Managerial Model: The Case for Broadening Performance Assessment in Government and the Public Services', *Financial Accountability and Management*, 2: 155–70.

—— Girre, X., Lonsdale, J. , Mul, R., Summa, H., and Waerness, M. (eds.) (1999). *Performance or Compliance? Performance Audit and Public Management in Five Countries.* Oxford: Oxford University Press.

Power. M. (1997). *The Audit Society.* Oxford: Oxford University Press.

Public Audit Forum (1999). *Implications for Audit of the Modernising Government Agenda.* London: Public Audit Forum.

Rose, N. and Miller, P. (1992). 'Political Power beyond the State: Problematics of Government', *British Journal of Sociology*, 43: 173–205.

10 Analytics of costing system design

Eva Labro

10.1 Costing as an approximation exercise

In most organizations costing systems serve many different needs such as product costing, pricing, product line decisions, capacity planning and allocation, performance measurement and control, project scheduling, project selection, and benchmarking, among other uses. In order to assess the cost implications of their short- and long-term planning and control functions, managers try to understand how costs behave and how cost objects consume resources by means of cost functions. A cost function is a mathematical description of how cost changes with changes in volume or in the level of an activity or process relating to that cost. Costing is therefore in essence an estimation or approximation exercise: within a relevant range, management accountants seek to derive a linear function that approximates the underlying true cost behaviour (which may not be linear, as discussed below). Traditional costing methods estimate cost as a linear function of volume, whereas more sophisticated costing methods such as activity-based costing (ABC), which will be discussed in more detail later, view cost as a function of changes in level of activity.

Looking at costing as an approximation exercise, this chapter discusses the research literature in this area, identifying where there is sufficient knowledge to guide practitioners and where further advances are sought in both costing research and practice. The focus here is mainly on analytical and empirical work based on theoretical constructs. Although of clear relevance to costing system design, behavioural and organizational issues are only minimally considered. Section 10.2 briefly discusses what costing systems should seek to approximate, while Section 10.3 looks at 'how' system objectives are pursued. The subsequent section provides an overview of where approximations can go wrong. Section 10.5 discusses how we can choose among alternative costing system approximations. Section 10.6 then concludes with some avenues to advance costing system design research and practice. Some sections that have relevance to this chapter have been kept succinct as they are more directly covered by other chapters in this volume (such as agency theory, which is discussed in more detail in Chapter 2).

10.2 What to approximate: the marginal versus full costing debate

According to economic theory, decisions (e.g. pricing) are made such as to have marginal revenues equate with marginal costs. The costing system therefore should focus on finding the marginal cost for each decision. This cost is termed the relevant cost as it differs between alternatives in a particular decision. Given that some costs are not changed by the decision, they are not relevant. Likewise sunk costs should not be regarded as relevant. Fixed costs fall into this category. In practice, however, we observe the extensive use of full costing, whereby fixed costs get allocated (Drury and Tayles 1994; Brierley et al. 2001). The accounting literature has tried to reconcile the use of full costing in practice with economic theory via a variety of routes. First, the ABC advocates have argued that in the long-term all costs are variable and that (at least for long-term decisions) all costs (i.e. full costs) should be included in the decision-making process (Cooper and Kaplan 1992). Second, others argue that full cost-based pricing and capacity planning are used as heuristics where the cost allocations are valuable because they approximate the opportunity cost of the resource based on expected use at the time of resource acquisition. Balakrishnan and Sivaramakrishnan (2002) provide an excellent overview of the research literature in this area.[1] Third, in an agency context, others have written about the incentive effects of cost allocations (Zimmerman 1979). Fourth, the behavioural literature has indicated other factors that may result in the inclusion of sunk cost for decision-making purposes, such as reputation of the decision-maker and loss aversion (see e.g. Buchheit 2004).

10.3 How to approximate: activity-based costing versus traditional costing

Johnson and Kaplan (1987), Cooper and Kaplan (1987), and others have claimed that the traditional costing methods used before the birth of ABC were systematically distorting product costs, leading to wrong decisions being taken on the basis of these costs. Traditional costing overcosts high volume/low complexity products and undercosts low volume/high complexity products.[2] Misallocations under traditional costing favour low volume specialty products. They critiqued the exaggerated use of direct labour hours as an allocation base in a 'new' production environment where fewer hours of direct labour were used. Also, a bigger share of the costs in this 'new' production environment was indirect and therefore had to be allocated using some allocation base. Picking the wrong allocation base in this setting made for disastrous consequences. ABC was then posed as a more accurate costing method whereby allocation bases are chosen better to reflect the cause-and-effect relationships in resource consumption patterns. Where the traditional costing methods estimate cost as a

Panel A: in traditional costing   *Panel B: in activity-based costing*

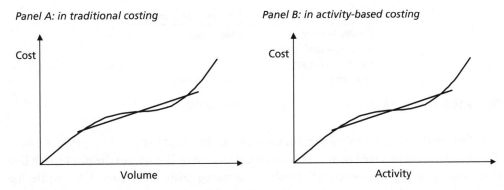

Figure 10.1 Costing as an approximation exercise

linear function of volume, Figure 10.1 shows how ABC estimates changes in cost as a function of changes in level of activity. New cost drivers, other than volume-based drivers such as direct labour hours and direct machine hours, were now used. Examples are number of set-ups, number of purchasing orders, number of machine insertions, number of inspections, and number of different components. Another novel feature of ABC at the time was that the focus of the costing system was no longer solely on product costing, but that anything could be a 'cost object': products, services, clients, distribution channels, suppliers, etc. Figure 10.2 contrasts the two approaches.

Where traditional costing only distinguished between costs that were either fixed or variable with volume (number of units),[3] ABC introduces a hierarchy with various levels at which costs become variable. The most commonly used hierarchy includes four levels: facility, product-sustaining, batch, and unit level. The hierarchical level at which a particular cost is classified indicates when this cost becomes variable. Costs at the unit level are the

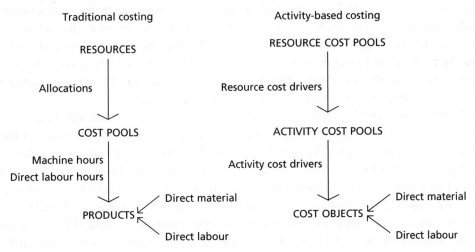

Figure 10.2 Traditional costing versus ABC

ABC	Traditional costing
Facility level costs	Fixed costs
Product-sustaining costs	
Batch level costs	
Unit level costs	Variable costs

Figure 10.3 Cost hierarchies in ABC versus traditional costing

costs that are traditionally called variable costs and are incurred per unit (e.g. price). Costs at the batch level are incurred each time a batch is delivered or brought to the production line (e.g. inspection and set-up costs). Product-sustaining costs are incurred to enable the production and sale of a particular product (e.g. product design and product advertising). Facility sustaining costs are costs that are fixed in the short term. They only become variable when the facility is closed down or reduced in size.[4]

Within each hierarchical level, several activities are performed. The cost of these activities is determined by multiplying their cost-rate with their cost-driver use. For example, the total set-up cost on batch level is calculated by multiplying the set-up cost-rate (the cost of one set-up in terms of its consumption of resources such as engineer's time) with the number of set-ups needed (i.e. the cost-driver use).[5] Figure 10.3 compares the ABC hierarchy with the traditional costing 'hierarchy'. Under traditional costing, costs were often wrongly assumed fixed, although they were variable with a level in the hierarchy, other than unit level. Product advertising, as an example of a product sustaining cost, would typically be lumped together with all other advertising costs that were considered fixed. However, these product-specific advertising costs are no longer incurred if one chooses to stop producing and selling the particular product. Traditional cost systems view the expenses of resources performing batch-level activities also as fixed, because they are independent of the number of units processed in a batch activity (Kaplan and Atkinson 1998a). But, as more batch-level activities are demanded (such as set-ups, material handling, purchasing, handling production orders), the organization must supply additional resources to perform these activities.[6] Traditional costing therefore loses some opportunities to work on costs that are variable with cost drivers on other levels in the ABC hierarchy, such as batch and product level, by treating these as fixed (and thus only avoidable by ceasing production). Recognizing that these costs are variable, albeit not with volume,[7] allows decision-makers to reduce cost rates, reduce cost-driver use, and eliminate non-value adding activities.

The following example of the workings of ABC and traditional costing will illustrate how products are costed differently by the two approximation methods. A firm produces three products, imaginatively labelled product A, product B, and product C. Panel A in Table 10.1 provides some data for this example: units of each product, sold, direct material cost for a unit of each product, direct labour cost for a unit of each product, and labour hours per unit. We have £135,000,000 in indirect costs to allocate to the three products. Panel B provides the calculations for a traditional costing system where direct labour hours are used as the overhead allocation base. In total we have 90,000 direct labour hours,[8] which means we have an overhead rate of £135,000,000/90,000 = £1,500 per direct labour hour. Applying this overhead rate to the number of labour hours used by each product, we obtain the cost figures as calculated in Panel C. Before we can calculate ABC for our products, we first need to collect a lot more data. The remaining part of Panel A shows data on the consumption of the cost drivers by the products. These cost drivers were chosen by the costing system designer to reflect better the cause-and-effect relationship in the resource consumption patterns. They are machine hours per unit of a product (to allocate automatic assembly costs), production batches for a product (to allocate set-up costs), sales orders for a product (to allocate wrapping costs), and purchase orders for a product (to allocate reception costs). Also more information on the detailed use of overheads by the various activities is needed, as in Panel C.[9]

Panel D provides the calculations for the activity-based product costs. Each time the total costs for an activity is divided by the total use of the activity driver to come up with a cost rate for that activity. Subsequently, this rate is then applied to the number of cost driver units consumed by a particular product and then divided over the total volume of that product.[10] Panel E compares the product costs derived under the two alternative approximation methods. Products A and B are both slightly cheaper under ABC (respectively 20 per cent and 13 per cent). Product C, the cheapest product under the traditional costing system, becomes the most expensive one under the ABC system, increasing in cost by 212 per cent. This is due to the fact that the low volume Product C consumes very few direct labour hours and therefore gets only a small part of overhead costs allocated under the traditional costing system. However, the ABC analysis shows that Product C is a complex product that consumes a lot of the activities that generate overhead costs: reception, set-up, assembly, and wrapping.

As a consequence of traditional costing systems favouring low volume products, we tend to see similar effects when firms move from a traditional to an ABC system. As the example illustrates, high volume (low complexity) products tend to drop slightly in costs, whereas low volume (high complexity) products increase dramatically in costs (see also Cooper and Kaplan 1987). This is due to the decrease in cost for the high volume products having to be spread out over lots of products, whereas the increase in costs for low volume products has to be borne by a few products only. Cooper and Kaplan (1987: 220) report on the Schrader Bellows case where the change in reported product costs ranged from about minus 10 per cent to plus 1,000 per cent[11]. In the John Deere Component Works (JDCW) case (Kaplan and March 1998a, 1998b) this effect would have killed their bidding for business. The JDCW A case (Kaplan and March 1998) shows one of the classical symptoms of cost system failure: the division is winning orders for the parts that it is least well configured to produce (the low volume parts) and losing bids on parts where it should have a competitive advantage (the high volume parts). Their traditional costing system indeed favours these low volume products. The JDCW B case (Kaplan and March 1990) then shows how a new ABC system was developed as a result of this diagnosis. Combining both cases and recalculating the bid prices in the A case as if they were calculated under the new ABC system, however, shows that ABC brings the large volume products down in cost, but only to a limited extent, given that the cost decrease has to be spread out over many units. On the other hand, ABC brings

Table 10.1 A costing example

Panel A: Data for example

	Product A	Product B	Product C	Total
Units sold	20,000	15,000	5,000	
Direct material cost (£)	2,500	2,300	2,000	
Direct labour cost (£)	1,400	2,100	700	
Labour hours per unit	2	3	1	90,000
Machine hours per unit	1	2	5	75,000
Production batches	2	4	6	12
Sales orders	10	18	20	48
Purchase orders	20	15	25	60

Indirect costs:	
indirect wages (£)	33,000,000
depreciation (£)	85,000,000
material and tools (£)	17,000,000
Total:	135,000,000

Panel B: Traditional costing with direct labour hours as allocation base

	Product A	Product B	Product C
Direct material cost (£)	2,500	2,300	2,000
Direct labour cost (£)	1,400	2,100	700
Indirect cost (£)	3,000	4,500	1,500
Total	6,900	8,900	4,200

Panel C: Activity-Based Costing: additional information on indirect costs needed

Activity	Activity driver	Indirect wages (£)	Depreciation (£)	Material and tools (£)	Total (£)
Automatic Assembly	Machine Hours	12,000,000	58,000,000	5,000,000	75,000,000
Reception	Purchase orders	9,000,000	2,000,000	1,000,000	12,000,000
Set-up Machines	Production batches	6,000,000	15,000,000	3,000,000	24,000,000
Wrapping	Sales orders	6,000,000	10,000,000	8,000,000	24,000,000
Total		33,000,000	85,000,000	17,000,000	135,000,000

Panel D: Activity-based product costs (£)

	Product A	Product B	Product C
Direct material cost	2,500	2,300	2,000
Direct labour cost	1,400	2,100	700
Assembly	1,000	2,000	5,000
Reception costs	200	200	1,000
Set-up costs	200	533	2,400
Wrapping	250	600	2,000
Total	5,550	7,733	13,100

(Contd.)

Table 10.1 (*Contd.*)

Panel E: Comparison of ABC and traditional product costs (£)

	Product A	Product B	Product C
Traditional	6,900	8,900	4,200
ABC	5,550	7,733	13,100
% difference	−20	−13	+212

the small volume products up in cost and this to a large extent. Since JDCW tended to win bids on the small volume products and since some of their costs on these now increase dramatically, they would lose some of these bids under ABC. Most of the cost decreases under ABC turn out to be on the negative contribution margin parts that are not cost-competitive. Some are on the positive contribution margin parts that had too high a full cost under the old costing system to win the bid. The small decreases in costs brought by ABC to these products, however, still do not make them sufficiently competitive.

The implicit assumption of the advocates of ABC is that multiple cost pools and multiple cost drivers better reflect the cause-and-effect relation between overhead resource consumption and cost objects. They believe that refinement in the costing system will lead to improved accuracy of product cost numbers and thus to better decisions. The example developed in the previous section effectively has only shown that ABC costs are different from traditional (pre-ABC) costs. But being different is not enough to make the case for ABC costs being superior! In effect, it is not normally possible to prove that ABC figures are more accurate than the traditional costing figures. ABC is implemented as an approximation method only when the firm does not know their true product costs.[12] Whether or not a particular approximation method leads to more accurate product costs can only be defined in comparison to these true benchmark costs, which are usually not available. In my view, this unobservable true benchmark system requirement which is necessary to define how accurate an approximation method is, has been a major obstacle in the research literature on costing system design, where only a limited number of academic studies have been published in the last decade. This obstacle has also limited the advice academics have been able to give to practitioners to improve their costing system design. Section 10.6 will indicate some ways in which recent academic literature has sought to overcome or work with this need for a true costing benchmark, which has opened up possibilities to further our knowledge in this area.

10.4 **Where can our approximation go wrong?**

The analytical accounting literature (e.g. Noreen 1991; Datar and Gupta 1994; Bromwich 1997; Christensen and Demski 1997) has established that conditions under which cost accounting systems in general and ABC in particular provide accurate costs are very stringent. As a consequence, accounting systems are hardly ever error-free. Noreen (1991) and Datar and Gupta (1993) complement each other in establishing where exactly our costing approximations can go wrong.

Noreen (1991) shows the stringent conditions that have to hold for ABC[13] to provide accurate costs. Noreen characterizes ABC as a full costing method whereby all costs are allocated: $C = \sum CP_i$ with CP_i the cost assigned to the ith cost pool.[14] In general, the cost function can be modelled as $C(a(q))$ whereby q (the vector of the firm's outputs) drives the vector of activities, a, which in turn generates costs. Nothing restricts the form of this cost function or the nature of the link between activities and output in theory. Noreen then shows the restrictive conditions that need to be placed on this cost function for ABC to provide valid avoidable product costs[15] and incremental activity costs.[16] First, total cost can be partitioned into cost pools, each of which depends solely upon one activity: separability. In mathematical notation: $C(a(q)) = \sum C_i(a_i(q))$.This rules out situations whereby a particular cost pool is a function of more than one activity driver. It is, for example, quite likely that the engineering cost pool is not just a function of the number of engineering change orders, but also of the number of unique components in the product design.[17] Second, the cost in each cost pool must be strictly proportional to the level of activity in that cost pool. In mathematical notation, $C_i(a_i(q)) = p_i a_i(q)$, whereby p_i is a constant. This means that, at the level of the cost pool, the cost in the cost pool must be a linear function (with a zero intercept) of the level of activity in that cost pool. Non-linear cost functions and even linear cost functions with a non-zero intercept[18] are ruled out. Figure 10.4 shows an example where this linearity assumption does not hold. Incremental units discounts are widely offered as purchasing quantity discounts. As a consequence, the direct materials cost pool is no longer a linear function of the units purchased. Third, activity drivers assigned to the individual products can be simply summed to arrive at total activity. When j indexes the products, this condition can be written in mathematical notation as: $a_i(q) = \sum a_{ij}(q_j)$ where, depending on whether or not product j is produced, $a_{ij}(q_j) = 0$ if $q_j = 0$ or $a_{ij}(q_j) \geq 0$ if $q_j > 0$. This means that each activity can be divided among products in such a way that the portion attributed to each product depends only upon that product. This condition rules out all dependencies between products in the production process. This precludes also joint processes whereby production costs are a non-separable function of the outputs of two or more products. Joint costs exhibit a public good characteristic (Bromwich and Bhimani 1994; Bromwich 1997): once made available for one use, joint resources can be used simultaneously for a number of other uses because the quantity of the resource is not reduced by its use.[19] Examples of joint resources are capacity in information technology, corporate advertising, and corporate credit rankings. Banker et al. (1988) provide another counterexample where Noreen's third condition does not hold in practice. They show that the addition of a product caused increased congestion and queuing delays. These delays occur not only for the newly introduced product, but also for the existing products and increase work-in-progress inventories for the whole plant, resulting in incremental inventory carrying costs.

Incremental unit discounts:
Unit 1 to 99: no discount
Unit 100 to 199: 10% discount
From unit 200: 20% discount

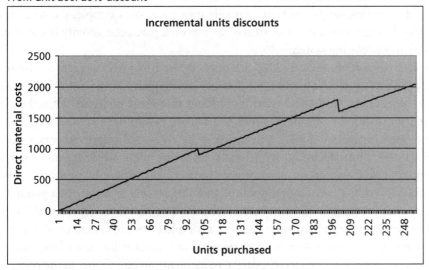

Figure 10.4 An example of non-linearity at the cost pool level

Taken together, these conditions are very stringent. Noreen (1991) warns that care should be taken when applying ABC in that it should only be used when cost behaviour conforms to these conditions.

Datar and Gupta (1994) complement Noreen (1991) in that they assume a context where there is non-jointness and linearity and subsequently study other issues that can go wrong in a costing approximation. Datar and Gupta (1994) classify errors that can occur when designing a costing system as aggregation error, specification error, and measurement error. Aggregation error of the cost pools occurs when resources are aggregated over heterogeneous activities to derive a single cost allocation rate. An example could be the pooling of set-up costs in one overall pool, instead of having one cost pool of expensive engineer-related set-up costs and a second one of cheap labourer-related set-up costs. Specification error arises when the method used to identify costs to products does not reflect the demands placed on resources by individual products. This happens when a cost driver is selected that does not exhibit a cause-and-effect relationship, such as allocating set-up costs via direct labour hours instead of via number of set-ups or set-up hours.[20] Traditional costing systems exhibit a lot of specification error in their choice of too many volume-based measures. Measurement error can occur at two different places in the costing system. First, practical difficulties in identifying costs with a particular cost pool may result in over- or undercharging cost pools. For example, when the cost of a manual labourer is by accident assigned to the secretarial staff cost pool, the latter resource cost pool will be overcharged and the manual labour cost pool will be undercharged.[21] Second, there can be measurement error on the units of allocation bases, when the specific units of resource consumed by individual products are wrongly measured. For example, the number of set-ups required or the time a member of staff spends on a particular activity is not plugged in accurately to the costing system.

New costing systems such as ABC are often devised to increase accuracy by reducing specification and aggregation error (e.g. Cooper and Kaplan 1988). Cost drivers are chosen better to reflect cause-and-effect relationships and more cost pools are defined to increase homogeneity within a cost pool. Cooper and Kaplan (1988) have argued that this costing system refinement can be done gradually, focusing on partial improvements. Cooper and Kaplan (1998) stress focusing refinements on areas with large expenses in indirect and support resources and on areas where there is high variety in products, customers, and processes. From a behavioural point of view, arguments in favour of a gradual refinement are clear: reduction in resistance to change, less resources are needed for a small costing system improvement project than for a complete costing system overhaul, redesigning the complete costing system is often regarded as infeasible because of the extent of the measurement exercise, and focus of a partial refinement can be on parts in the company that are most inclined to be cooperative (Cooper et al. 1992).

The economics-based accounting literature, in contrast, has indicated that gradual refinement may not lead to more accurate costing. Datar and Gupta (1994) find two reasons for this. First, using a few simple examples,[22] they show that partially improving on specification of cost drivers and disaggregating cost pools can actually increase the total error in the costing system in cases where (some of the) errors in the old costing system were (partially) offsetting (some leading to overcosting, others leading to undercosting). Gupta (1993)[23] finds that such negative covariations in errors in costs allocated to cost objects across processes are often found where the manufacturing process uses both labour and machine intensive technologies. Second, reducing aggregation and specification error may increase measurement errors and therefore result in lower accuracy of cost objects. This happens when the firm measures overheads and units of allocation base at the aggregate cost pool fairly accurately, but significant error is introduced in measuring overhead and units of allocation base at the disaggregate cost pools. Information on the exact cost or the nature of resource usage at less aggregate cost pools is often difficult to obtain (Datar and Gupta 1994). Christensen and Demski (1995) make the related point that the use of multiple cost pools (less aggregation) may not necessarily lead to more accurate product costs, as measurement error may increase. Cardinaels and Labro (2005) indeed find empirical support for the hypothesis that the use of allocation base is measured more accurately at aggregate cost pool level than at disaggregate cost pool level in a laboratory experiment that focuses on the use of time estimates as cost drivers. As a result, Datar and Gupta (1994) caution against gradual refinement of costing systems as the resulting error may increase.[24]

10.5 **How to choose a particular costing system approximation**

After having shown that costing systems can go wrong in multiple ways and therefore may provide poor approximations of the underlying true cost benchmark, it is time to ask the question of how to choose which costing system to use. Let us assume that the best costing system is the one that most accurately approximates the underlying true cost benchmark in its product cost calculations. We will come back to this assumption later in this section. Can we now rank alternative costing systems on the basis of overall accuracy from very accurate to highly inaccurate? As this section will show, ABC presents us with a problem here. The traditional costing method basically pools all overhead in one overhead cost pool to allocate these to product volume on the basis of one allocation base, usually direct labour hours. Regressing the dependent variable (overhead costs) on the independent variable (some volume-based cost driver, in this example direct labour hours) shows the average amount of change in overhead cost that is associated with a unit change in the amount of the volume-based driver. Adding more of these volume-based drivers (such as direct machine hours, direct material, and volume itself) to this regression analysis will increase its goodness of fit (as measured by R^2) as more and more of the variability in overhead costs will be explained by the cost drivers. We could therefore rank a costing system with more volume-based drivers as being more accurate than one with just one volume-based driver.[25] The problem that ABC poses that prevents it from finding its place in a costing system ranking is that it explicitly incorporates non-volume-based drivers, such as the numbers of set-ups. Whilst on the input side resources in the set-up cost pool can be viewed as linear with the number of set-ups, this driver is not linear with volume on the output side (Christensen and Demski 1995). Theoretically, an ABC hierarchy can be extended so that for each cost pool an activity level in the hierarchy can be defined that can be considered linear with the cost pool (on the input side).[26] The problem lies on the output side, where many of the chosen drivers for these activities will be non-linear with volume.[27] The cost of a product i is then calculated as $TC_i = \sum cr_j \times cdu_{ij}$ whereby the activities performed in the firm are indexed by j, cr_j stands for the cost rate of activity j, and cdu_{ij} represents the cost driver use product i makes of activity j. Since ABC adds non-volume-based drivers,[28] either next to volume-based drivers or as a replacement, it cannot easily be ranked in comparison with other available costing systems.[29] Since we cannot make an absolute ranking, the choice of the costing system will become the subject of a cost–benefit trade-off, which is difficult fully to specify (Christensen and Demski 1995).

Such a cost–benefit trade-off can only be made in the context of a particular use of the costing data. Possible uses of accounting information range wider than the traditional dichotomy between decision-making and control–performance measurement. In most organizations costing systems serve many different needs such as product costing, pricing, product line decisions, capacity planning, capacity allocation, control, performance measurement, benchmarking, project selection, and project scheduling. This variety in the range of possible objectives for which to collect costing data makes it very difficult to say anything in general about which costing system would best suit which firm. When choosing the optimal level of accuracy of the costing system, Kaplan and Atkinson (1998) typically weigh cost of errors (which decreases with the level of accuracy) against the cost of measurement (which increases with the level of accuracy). The cost of measurement plays both in the initial development but also in the ongoing maintenance of the costing system.[30] Behavioural reasons will also play an important role in this decision. For example, humans constrained by bounded rationality[31] will find it difficult to deal with very complex systems. It is, however, very difficult to quantify the cost of errors in the costing system. Additionally, given that we cannot come up with an absolute ranking of costing systems, the cost of errors in the costing system can only be assessed in relation to a particular context. The answers to the questions of what kind of errors would be easier to tolerate, where in the product space to tolerate errors (Christensen and Demski 1997), and whether an error-free costing system would indeed be preferable, necessarily depend on the specific circumstances faced by an organization.

The literature in this area has used a variety of costing system accuracy measures. One class of measures compares the cost approximation by the costing system with the true benchmark cost that they assume to be available (e.g. Babad and Balachandran 1993; Hwang et al. 1993; Datar and Gupta 1994; Christensen and Demski 1997; Homburg 2001). This 'true' benchmark cost is not easily obtainable in a practical context, however, and this has limited their practical relevance. These studies have, on the other hand, put forward many new insights in this research area. Because total resources are typically assumed observable without error, errors in product cost cancel out: overcosting some products will have to be compensated by undercosting some other products by an equal amount. The measures used cannot therefore just sum the errors across all products, as that will lead to a zero resulting error. Datar and Gupta (1994) use the mean squared error of the costing system as their accuracy measure:[32]

$$MSE = \frac{1}{CO} \sum_{k=1}^{co} \left(tc_k - fc_k \right)^2$$

They motivate (p. 579) their choice of a symmetric quadratic error metric as a measure of the expected loss due to errors in product costs with reference to the economics-based literature where it has been shown that this loss function is valid for pricing in monopolistic and oligopolistic markets (Vives 1990; Banker and Potter 1993; Alles and Datar 1998). Hwang et al. (1993)[33] focus their squared error measure at the cost pool level rather than the cost object level, and multiply this with a parameter that reflects the degree of competition in the product market.[34] Babad and Balachandran (1993) and Homburg (2001) use the square root of a symmetric quadratic error measure:

$$EUCD = \sqrt{\sum_{k=1}^{co} \left(tc_k - fc_k \right)^2}$$

to get results that are interpretable in dollar terms.[35] Christensen and Demski (1997) take average percent errors by product and mean squared percent error for the whole costing system:

$$MPE = \frac{1}{CO} \sum_{k=1}^{co} \frac{|tc_k - fc_k|}{tc_k}$$

as their dependent variables.[36] In some contexts, management may be more interested in these relative measures since a £10 cost difference on a £10 product has different implications to such a difference on a £1,000 product. The 'materiality' perspective provides a second way of looking at costing system accuracy. Dopuch (1993) argues that a necessary condition for potential improvements in managerial decisions from new accounting systems is that the new system generates accounting numbers that are materially different from those obtained from the existing system. Earlier in this section it was pointed out, however, that 'different' does not necessarily mean 'more accurate'. But we can also use a materiality perspective in comparison to the true benchmark cost, e.g. if products are costed within a 10 per cent accuracy range, our costing system is providing us with 'accurate enough' figures. This seems to be the perspective taken by Kaplan and Atkinson (1998: 111) who coined 10 per cent as an accuracy target.

As mentioned earlier, relevant measures of accuracy and accuracy targets are very context specific. Let us turn to the classical dichotomy in management accounting between decision-making and control or performance measurement objectives to illustrate this.

First, the basic intuition in a single *decision*-maker[37] context is that more and more accurate information is always valuable, as long as it comes free. When information (or incremental accuracy) comes at a cost, it will depend on the decision-maker's preferences and the decision problem at hand whether or not the decision-maker will be prepared to pay the price for the information.[38] We can therefore see that when information or incremental accuracy comes at a cost, it *may not always be desired*. But even without considering a transaction cost of implementing a new costing system, measurement cost of maintaining the system, or a boundedly rational human who cannot deal with very complex costing systems, more accuracy may *not always be needed*. There are two reasons for this.

The first reason can be explained through the information economics concept of fineness. In information economics, information is looked at in terms of how it refines our knowledge on the occurrence of states of the environment.[39] An information source reveals a signal from a possible set of signals. These signals form a partition of the set of events $S = \{s_1, s_2, \ldots, s_n\}$. Perfect information tells us exactly which state is going to occur as it associates a unique and precise signal on a one for one basis with every state. The partition created by the information system is one with all singletons: $\Delta = \{\{s_1\}, \{s_2\}, \ldots, \{s_n\}\}$. Null information, on the other hand, tells us nothing about which state is going to occur, as it does not distinguish between states. The partition is just the full set of events: $\Delta = \{s_1, s_2, \ldots, s_n\}$. Imperfect information lacks completeness in its partitioning, as signals may be associated with the occurrence of more than one state and there is no unique and specific signal associated with each state. An example could be $\Delta = \{\{s_1\}, \{s_2, s_3\}, \{s_4, s_5\}\}$. The Blackwell theorem then suggests that a finer system (with a finer partitioning) will always be preferred in a costless setting by an individual.[40],[41]

But the finest perfect information system may not always be needed. Pay-off adequate information systems allow the same decisions to be made as would a perfect and complete information system. Access to a pay-off adequate information system allows the decision-maker to select the *ex post* optimal action. Bromwich (1992) uses the example of traffic lights to illustrate this point. If we think about the possible states of the driving conditions at a crossing, we could define three: 'safe' state, 'proceed with care' state, and 'dangerous' state. A perfect traffic light system could signal each of these states with, for example, a green, yellow, and red light respectively. If I am a careful driver who would stop both in the 'dangerous' as well as in the 'proceed with care state', a traffic light system that signals red for 'dangerous' or 'proceed with care' and green for 'safe' state is pay-off adequate for me. Adding finer information is not necessary to allow me to implement my optimal decision. If I am, however, a busy driver who is more concerned with not wasting time than with safety, a pay-off adequate traffic light system that signals red for the 'dangerous' state and green for the 'safe' and 'proceed with care' states would allow me to implement my optimal decision.[42] A pay-off adequate system can additionally be characterized as pay-off relevant if there is not a coarser classification of the underlying states that is pay-off adequate. Coming back to a costing example, pricing decisions could be viewed as an objective for which high accuracy[43] is needed; to support decision making on whether or not an additional plant should be build a lower accuracy is possible. As Figure 10.5 illustrates, the sensitivity of optimal decisions to cost parameters can be very different. Some decisions (for example a pricing decision represented by the dotted line) may only be optimal for a very narrow range of cost parameters and therefore high accuracy is required, whereas in other decision contexts a decision will remain optimal over a large range of cost parameters (as for the additional plant decision represented by the full line).

The second reason why incremental accuracy, even if free, may not always be needed in a decision-making context is that other information (that is not fully reflected in the cost reports) may be available and that decision-makers can make effective use of heuristics to include this non-costing information (Gupta and King 1997). An example could be a rule of thumb as was reportedly used in Rockford (Cooper and Kaplan 1987). Management in the

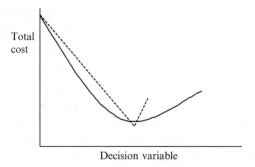

Figure 10.5 Sensitivity to cost parameters

firm realized that their traditional costing favoured low volume products and therefore required a profit margin that was three times as high as that for the high volume products.

Second, in a control context, more accuracy may *not always be desired*. The role of additional (cost) information in a control setting is to give a better indication to the principal of the action(s) taken by his or her agent(s) (see Chapter 2 for a more elaborate development of agency theory). With good quality information, the principal will be able to write more efficient contracts with the agent (who is effort averse) so that getting the agent to exert the desired effort (which is unobservable by the principal) becomes less costly. Holmström (1979) has established what constitutes useful information in a basic agency model. Often we can do better when including additional information that is at our disposal. The only time we would not make use of an additional performance measure is when it satisfies the so-called 'sufficient statistic condition' (Holmström 1979). Using both performance measures (or source of information) x and y (instead of x alone) will lead to a Pareto improvement in contracting if and only if it is *not* the case that $p(x,y|a) = p(y|x) * p(x|a)$ whereby a is the effort level provided by the agent. If this condition holds, observing y does not provide the principal with any new information about the effort level the agent put in that was not already available by observing x.[44] Without seeking to elaborate excessively, agency theory has demonstrated in a variety of ways that it is not desirable to have additional information where it increases the cost of contracting. The value of information, even if provided free, is negative in these cases. The basic reason for this is usually that a multiperson setting is assumed where, if information is available, we cannot choose to ignore it, even if we would be better off without it in terms of contracting efficiency.[45] Also, the strategic role of cost information may affect the demand for the accuracy of the costing system.[46]

As a conclusion, it is important not to strive for accuracy for the sake of accuracy, but to carefully consider context specific issues in making the decision on the level of accuracy required. Because we cannot generally rank costing systems with respect to accuracy and we have to make cost–benefit trade-offs when developing costing systems, it is very important to learn more about the sensitivity (or robustness) of costing system designs to the variety of errors, about the bias introduced by different costing approaches (as, for example, the bias in favour of low volume products in traditional volume based allocation systems as discussed in Section 10.3), and the variance in the errors resulting from alternative systems (e.g. Christensen and Demski 1997).

10.6 **How to move research and practice in costing system design forward**

I see three important areas for future research in the costing system design area.

First, after the previous section's plea not to strive for accuracy just for accuracy's sake, it is important that future research links the design of the costing system to its objective. There is an extensive theoretical literature looking at the role of precision of information that is or can be disclosed in valuation or contracting settings[47] (see Verrecchia (2001) for an overview of the disclosure literature)[48]. The theoretical literature on costs for decision-making centres more on the full costing versus marginal costing debate (as briefly discussed in Section 10.2) and does not usually discuss accuracy as such. Empirical papers (mostly experimental), on the other hand, seem to focus on the decision-making objective and again focus on how accuracy in product costs impacts cost-based judgement and decision performance (e.g. Briers et al. 1997; Gupta and King 1997; Callahan and Gabriel 1998; Dearman and Shields 2001). Some articles have focused on the use of volume versus non-volume drivers (volume-based costing (VBC) versus ABC) (e.g. Drake et al. 1999). Other more specific costing system design parameters (separability, linearity, interdependence) have been left relatively unexplored. To my knowledge, there exists little empirical research on costing system design in a perform-ance evaluation context. However, it is important to learn how better to design costing systems, what biases and types of errors are tolerable, and which are not *for particular contexts*.

Second, we have to find ways to overcome or work with the requirement for a true benchmark costing system that is not normally observable in practice. This requirement has plagued many research papers (Kaplan and Thompson 1971; Babad and Balachandran 1993; Gupta 1993; Datar and Gupta 1994; Homburg 2001). Although these papers have generated many interesting insights, we now have come to a point where we have to overcome this difficulty in order to be able to give better advice to practitioners, both to those designing the costing systems as well as those using the costing figures. A first example of a study that overcomes the true benchmark requirement problem is the simulation study by Labro and Vanhoucke (2005). For each hypothesis, they simulate 500 true benchmark systems and, for each of those, over 1000 error-ridden costing system approximations. In doing so, they are able to generalize[49] their results on trade-offs between aggregation, specification, and measurement error. Cardinaels and Labro (2005) focus on the measurement error on duration drivers in an experimental set-up that allows them to observe the accurate true benchmark.[50] Finally, Datar et al. (2004) develop a costing system refinement indicator that is based on more aggregate information that is typically easier to obtain and observe in practice than the detailed information of the true benchmark case. This refinement indica-tor shows in which situations better specification and less aggregation are likely to increase costing system accuracy (in contrast to reducing it) and therefore provides practical guidance to costing system developers.

Third, information economics and agency theory related concepts, such as fineness and sufficiency, have been studied in great detail, resulting in a vast literature. Attempts to translate these concepts and incorporate their results into a practical costing system design context should be further pursued.[51]

☐ NOTES

1 See also Noreen and Burgstahler (1997).

2 The example later in this section will illustrate this point.

3 In order to define which costs are 'variable' or 'fixed', accountants technically first have to define the time period they are using. Nearly all costs could be considered fixed in the very short term and become variable in the very long term. Note that economists approach this issue in the opposite sequence: they define 'long term' as the time period by which all costs become variable.

4 It will depend on the position taken in the marginal costing versus full costing debate as to whether or not these facility sustaining costs should be allocated to cost objects.

5 Research has shown that the costing hierarchy is case specific and therefore the four-level hierarchy example just discussed will not fit every case context (Ittner et al. 1997). Degraeve et al. (2005) use hierarchies ranging from three to five levels for their different case studies, costing out a firm's purchasing policy. Labro (2004) uses another ABC hierarchy (supplier, component, order, batch, and unit level) to check on the cost effects of varying levels of component commonality in product design.

6 Interestingly, the operations management (OM) literature often makes the mistake of considering set-up costs (a cost accountants would typically classify as variable at batch level) to be variable *at unit level*. Classical examples in OM textbooks divide set-up costs over units. Set-up cost actually only occurs with each batch for which the production equipment has to be set up. Whether there are 10 or 10,000 units in the batch is not impacting on the set-up cost. Although it is often done in practice, set-up costs should not be averaged out over all units to support any form of decision-making!

7 Foster and Gupta (1990) have, however, shown that a major part of overhead costs are volume driven anyway. Others document that other cost drivers, next to volume, are important in explaining manufacturing overhead (e.g. operations-based drivers in Banker and Johnston 1993; product mix heterogeneity in Anderson 1995; manufacturing transactions in Banker et al. 1995).

8 $2 * 20,000 + 3 * 15,000 + 1 * 5,000 = 90,000$

9 ABC, as a more complex costing system, requires a lot of extra measurements on the additional cost drivers and cost pools defined. Kaplan and Atkinson (1998) recommend for the costing system designer to balance the cost of errors made from inaccurate estimates (by the use of simplified systems) with the cost of measurement (of increasingly complex systems) when determining the optimal accuracy of the costing system.

10 An example to clarify: the total cost of the reception activity is £12,000,000. In total, 60 purchase orders (the cost driver chosen to allocate reception costs) are used. Therefore the cost rate per purchase order is £200,000. Product A consumes 20 purchase orders and will therefore be allocated $20 \times £200,000 = £4,000,000$. This results in a reception cost per unit of product A of $£4,000,000/20,000 = £200$.

11 Some extremely low volume items' product costs even increased several thousand per cent.

12 This is (virtually) always the case (other than in a one product firm where all resources are devoted to the production and sale of that one product). If firms were able to observe their true product cost, cost accountants would be out of business!

13 Given that traditional costing systems are merely simplified special cases of ABC, the results in Noreen's paper (1991) apply equally to traditional costing systems. It is Noreen's intention (and my intention in this section also) to contrast any two-stage costing system with the underlying true benchmark costing system, rather than contrast ABC with traditional costing systems.

Although the ABC terminology is used in this section, the results can be easily translated to a traditional costing system context.

14 He acknowledges later in the paper (p. 165) that ABC systems need not necessarily be full costing systems. Indeed, at the time of this publication, Cooper and Kaplan advocated that facility level costs should not be allocated down to the product level.

15 Avoidable product cost is defined as the change in total cost if the product were dropped, keeping the volumes of all other products the same.

16 The incremental cost of changing the level of an activity is defined as the change in total cost that would be incurred.

17 A special case of non-separability happens when drivers across cost pools are correlated. For example, Datar et al. (1993) find that drivers across the supervision and the scrap cost pools are correlated: if supervision of employees is increased, the amount of scrap the employees generate is reduced.

18 If the relationship is approximately linear, but there is a non-zero intercept, the ABC system will generate estimates of product and activity costs that are biased upwards. Moving the non-zero intercept to the facility level cost category and not allocating this category down to products can circumvent this problem.

19 That is, up to a certain capacity constraint. Maher and Marais (1998) report on a field study that shows the limitations of ABC in a joint cost situation.

20 It may become less obvious in the choice between the latter two that a specification error is being made!

21 Datar and Gupta (1994: 583) assume that the sum of the measurement errors over all cost pools adds to zero. This is a reasonable assumption as a firm can be expected to know its total costs. This means that overcharging and undercharging will cancel out over all resource cost pools.

22 A summary of some of Datar and Gupta's (1994) examples that illustrate this point can be found in the Appendix.

23 Gupta (1993) is a very interesting field study that focuses on how heterogeneity in products' resource usage across activities, between cost allocation measures at different levels of aggregation, and in products relate to the distortions in cost numbers generated by an aggregated costing system.

24 Note that both Noreen (1991) and Datar and Gupta (1994) focus on the second stage of the cost allocation process. When they use the term 'cost pools' they have 'activity cost pools' in mind. They implicitly assume a one-to-one relationship between 'resource cost pools' and 'activity cost pools'. Based on the pioneering work of Datar and Gupta (1994), Labro and Vanhoucke (2005) elaborate on a classification of errors that explicitly takes the two-stage nature of the cost allocation process into account. As is shown in Figure 10.6, they define aggregation error both on resource cost pool and activity cost pool level and split measurement error of units of allocation bases up into measurement error on the resource drivers (first stage) and measurement error on the activity drivers (second stage).

25 Note that the measure used here is a statistical goodness of fit measure that shows that there is correlation between the dependent and independent variables. This measure does not speak at all to causality, something that is stressed by the ABC advocates (e.g. Kaplan and Cooper 1998). Therefore, most management accounting textbooks stress the use of an 'economic plausibility check' when applying regression analysis, as without this it is unlikely that a high level of

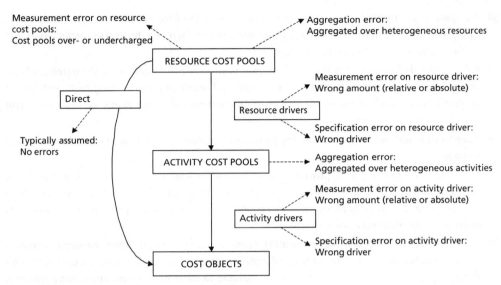

Figure 10.6 Errors in costing system design
(*Source*: Labro and Vanhoucke 2005)

correlation observed in one set of data will be found in other similar sets of data (e.g. Horngren et al. 2005: 290).

26 In practice we will need to find a compromise between the complexity of the costing system in terms of the number of hierarchical levels and the loss in accuracy resulting from the approximation of linear relationships.

27 Especially those that have been termed 'non-volume' drivers!

28 In their comparison of 'modern' costing with classical (economics-based) theory of costing, Christensen and Demski (1995) make the interesting point that some non-volume based drivers, such as complexity drivers, enter the 'modern' costing system to proxy for an inappropriate grouping of some products and suppressing of other product groups in the cost function identification. In contrast, the classical school speaks to the cost of the entire time indexed vector of products.

29 Note that ABC not only considers product volume as cost object. Other cost objects can include customers, distribution channels, suppliers, etc. The same problem is, however, likely to occur in these cases as activity drivers will not be linear with volume (number) of customers, etc.

30 Cost driver rates and cost drivers use have to be recalculated at regular time intervals.

31 All of us!

32 The following notation is used in this section:
CO number of cost objects, indexed k: $1 \ldots co$
tc_k true cost allocated to cost object k by the benchmark system
fc_k (false) cost allocated to cost object k by the costing system approximation.

33 Hwang et al. (1993) shows how the extent of EUCD is a function of the heterogeneity of the production technology, the unit input costs, and the product mix. The second part of their paper develops and evaluates algorithms to choose the best allocation base at each cost pool.

34 This parameter ranges from zero for a monopoly situation to 1 for a perfectly competitive market. This is consistent with the notion that greater competition increases the firm's potential loss from costing inaccuracies (Cooper and Kaplan 1988).

35 Babad and Balachandran (1993) present an optimization model to determine the number of cost drivers and the representative cost drivers, trading off information processing costs with loss of accuracy. They include the possibility to assign different weights to errors in costs of different cost objects in their error measure.

36 They focus mainly on how well a costing procedure can deal with various underlying production technologies.

37 Merchant and Shields (1993) provide several reasons for less accuracy in costing in a multiple decision-maker context: upwardly biased costs to prevent salesmen from shaving down margins to true cost level, downwardly biased costs in a target costing setting, lower precision than possible in order to create focus on a few cost drivers only.

38 Note that, even in a decision-making context where information or incremental accuracy comes at a cost, it will become impossible to rank information systems when multiple decision-makers with different preferences use it. This situation is common to most firms where one costing system is developed to serve all decision-makers (and possibly even all decision problems).

39 The occurrence of states of the environment is what we are uncertain about in a state/strategy/ outcome set-up.

40 Now we can rank information systems in terms of fineness. If one information system is as fine as the other, then and only then is the first system at least as valuable for all preferences and beliefs. Note however that, often, imperfect information systems would require consideration of preferences in order to rank them. The following example illustrates this. Three different information systems provide three different partitions of the state space, S.

Information system	State classification	
η_1	$\{S_1\}$	$\{S_2, S_3\}$
η_2	$\{S_1, S_3\}$	$\{S_2\}$
η_3	$\{S_1, S_2\}$	$\{S_3\}$

41 Moving from a discrete to a random set-up, the notion of better information transforms to the condition that one random variable W is more informative than another random variable Z with respect to some random variable B if there exists a random variable ε which is independent of B and has $E[\varepsilon] = 0$ such that $Z = W + \varepsilon$. The random variable Z is equal to the random variable W plus a noise term that is totally unrelated to the variable of interest B (Christensen and Demski 2003).

42 Note that the actual colour of the signal does not matter, only the partitioning.

43 The theoretical results on fineness do not translate in a very practical way to accuracy in costing system design. In a discrete setting, we could think of an exhaustive set of events in a pricing example as being all possible costs for a product, but we are uncertain as to which one is the true cost. For each cost we can optimally decide what our price should be. The costing system gives us information in that it signals a cost approximation. If, for example, the costing system signals the cost of product X to be £10, we could translate this in several ways: (*a*) the state 'true cost is £10' will occur; (*b*) realizing our costing approximation is not fully accurate, the subset of states 'true cost £9, £10, or £11' will occur; (*c*) realizing our costing approximation is not fully accurate, but

having a view on the bias and variance it creates, 'true cost of £9 will occur with 25% probability', 'true cost of £10 will occur with 50% probability', 'true cost of £11 will occur with 15% probability', and 'true cost of £12 will occur with 10% probability'; or (*d*) interpret this as noisy information that lacks precision (only a probability that a given state or set of states will occur following the receipt of a specific signal), 'true cost of £10 may occur with 50% probability'. Alternatively, and probably more realistically, we could lose the discrete setting and describe true cost by a random variable, e.g. one that is normally distributed with mean μ and variance σ^2. The costing system can then report, instead of an element from the partition Δ, just a specific number x. Whether or not our costing system is pay-off adequate will depend on whether or not our pricing decision would be the same for all the potential costs of product X that are signalled. When extending to multiple products and therefore overall accuracy of the costing system, the interpretation of the concept of fineness becomes even more cumbersome.

44 Again, it is difficult to translate the concept of sufficient statistic into practical guidance with respect to costing system design, even if the purpose of the costing system was exclusively performance evaluation oriented. The value of information in such a control setting can only be evaluated with respect to all other information that is already out there, so we cannot look at the costing system in isolation. See Antle and Demski (1988) for some numerical examples.

45 Christensen and Demski (2003: ch. 12) provide a good start for the reader who wants to learn about this in more detail.

46 For example, Alles and Datar (1998) find that, in a transfer-pricing context where the choice of the costing system is an endogenous and strategic variable, firms may choose to cross-subsidize their products in order to maximize their ability to raise prices in the strategic environment.

47 Precision is usually modelled as the reciprocal of the variance of a signal (see Verrecchia 2001), with notable exceptions (e.g. Gigler and Hemmer 1998).

48 Aggregation and bias (e.g. as in conservatism) have also been explored as themes, but mainly in a financial reporting context.

49 This is in contrast to the papers mentioned earlier that have assumed one particular true cost benchmark system.

50 They study the impact of several costing system design parameters and the underlying job design on the accuracy of time estimates.

51 A nice example here is Hemmer (1996).

52 Note that Datar and Gupta (1994) define aggregation error as occurring over activity cost pools, i.e. when the same activity type cost pools are lumped together across departments. Labro and Vanhoucke (2005) explicitly define aggregation error at two different levels in the costing system: (*a*) at activity cost pool level (as do Datar and Gupta 1994); and (*b*) at resource cost pool level.

53 The calculations for product B are no longer summarized here, but note that, because we are working in a two product setting, they are always leading to the same size of error as for product A, but with the opposite sign. If one product is overcosted, the other will be undercosted for the same amount since total costs remain constant.

☐ REFERENCES

Alles, M. and Datar, S. (1998). 'Strategic Transfer Pricing', *Management Science*, 44(4): 451–61.

Anderson, S. W. (1995). 'Measuring the Impact of Product Mix Heterogeneity on Manufacturing Overhead Cost', *Accounting Review*, 70(3), 363–87.

Antle, R. and Demski, J. (1988). 'The Controllability Principle in Responsibility Accounting', *Accounting Review*, 63(4): 700–18.

Babad, Y. M. and Balachandran, B. V. (1993). 'Cost Driver Optimization in Activity-Based Costing', *Accounting Review*, 68(3): 563–75.

Balakrishnan, R. and Sivaramakrishnan, K. (2002). 'A Critical Overview of the Use of Full Cost Data for Planning and Pricing', *Journal of Management Accounting Research*, 14: 3–31.

Banker, R. and Johnston, H. (1993). 'An Empirical Study of Cost Drivers in the U.S. Airline Industry', *Accounting Review*, 68(3): 576.

—— Datar, S. and Kekre, S. (1988). 'Relevant Costs, Congestion and stochasticity in Production Environments', *Journal of Accounting and Economics*, 10: 171–97.

Banker, R. D. and Potter, G. (1993). 'Economic Implications of Single Cost Driver Systems', *Journal of Management Accounting Research* 5: 15–33.

—— —— and Schroeder, R. G. (1995). 'An Empirical Analysis of Manufacturing Overhead Cost Drivers', *Journal of Accounting & Economics*, 19(1): 115.

Brierly, J. A., Cowton, C. J., and Drury, C. (2001). 'Research into Product Costing Practice: A European Perspective', *European Accounting Review*, 10(2): 215–56.

Briers, M., Luckett, P., and Chow, C. (1997). 'Data Fixation and the Use of Traditional Versus Activity-Based Costing Systems', *Abacus*, 33(1): 49–68.

Bromwich, M. (1992). *Financial Reporting, Information and Capital Markets*. London: Pitman.

—— (1997). 'Accounting for Overheads: Critique and Reforms, Acta Universitatis Upsaliensis', *Studia Oeconomiae Negotiorum*, 1–41.

—— and Bhimani, A. (1994). *Management Accounting: Pathways to Progress*. London: CIMA.

Buchheit, S. (2004). 'Fixed Cost Magnitude, Fixed Cost Reporting Format, and Competitive Pricing Decisions: Some Experimental Evidence', *Contemporary Accounting Research*, 21(1): 1–24.

Callahan, C. M. and Gabriel, A. E. (1998). 'The Differential Impact of Accurate Product Cost Information in Imperfectly Competitive Markets: A Theoretical and Empirical Investigation', *Contemporary Accounting Research*, 15(Winter): 419–55.

Cardinaels, E. and Labro, E. (2005). 'Measurement Error in Costing Systems: Time Estimates as Cost Drivers'. Working paper, London School of Economics.

Christensen, J. and Demski, J. S. (1995). 'The Classical Foundations of "Modern" Costing', *Management Accounting Research*, 6(1): 13–32.

—— —— (1997). 'Product Costing in the Presence of Endogenous Subcost Functions', *Review of Accounting Studies*, 2 (1): 65–87.

—— —— (2003). *Accounting Theory: An Information Content Perspective*. New York: McGraw-Hill.

Cooper, R. and Kaplan, R. S. (1987). 'How Cost Accounting Systematically Distorts Product Cost', in W. J. Bruns and R. S. Kaplan (eds.), *Accounting and Management: Field Study Perspectives*. Cambridge, MA: Harvard Business School Press.

—— —— (1988). 'Measure Costs Right: Make the Right Decisions', *Harvard Business Review*, 66(5): 96–103.

—— —— (1992). 'Activity-Based Systems: Measuring the Cost of Resource Usage', *Accounting Horizons*, 6(3): 1–13.

—— —— (1998). *Design of Cost Management Systems*, 2nd edn. Englewood Cliffs, NJ: Prentice Hall.

—— —— Maisel, L. S., Morrissey, E., and Oehm, R. M. (1992). *Implementing Activity-Based Cost Management: Moving from Analysis to Action*. Montvale, NJ: Institute of Management Accountants.

Datar, S. and Gupta, M. (1994). 'Aggregation, Specification and Measurement Errors in Product Costing', *Accounting Review*, 69(4): 567–91.

—— —— and Alles, M. (2004). 'When Does ABC Improve Product Costing? Developing Indicators for Accuracy Increasing Cost System Refinements'. Working paper, Washington University at Saint Louis.

—— Kekre, S., Mukhopadhyay, T., and Srinivasan, K. (1993). 'Simultaneous Estimation of Cost Drivers', *Accounting Review*, 68(3): 602–14.

Dearman, D. T. and Shields, M. (2001). 'Cost Knowledge and Cost-Based Judgment Performance', *Journal of Management Accounting Research*, 13: 1–18.

Degraeve, Z., Labro, E., and Roodhooft, F. (2005). 'Constructing a Total Cost of Ownership Supplier Selection Methodology based on Activity-Based Costing and Mathematical Programming', *Accounting and Business Research*, 35(1): 3–27.

Dopuch, N. (1993). 'A Perspective on Cost Drivers', *Accounting Review*, 68(3): 615–20.

Drake, A. R., Haka, S., and Ravenscroft, S. P. (1999). 'Cost System and Incentive Structure Effects on Innovation, Efficiency and Profitability in Teams', *Accounting Review*, 74(3): 323–45.

Drury, C. and Tayles, M. E. (1994). 'Product Costing in UK Manufacturing Organisations', *European Accounting Review*, 3(3): 443–69.

Foster, G. and Gupta, M. (1990). 'Manufacturing Overhead Cost Driver Analysis', *Journal of Accounting & Economics*, 12(1–3): 309–37.

Gigler, F. and Hemmer, T. (1998). 'On the Frequency, Quality, and Informational Role of Mandatory Financial Reports', *Journal of Accounting Research*, 36 (Suppl.): 117–47.

Gupta, M. (1993). 'Heterogeneity Issues in Aggregated Costing Systems', *Journal of Management Accounting Research*, 5 (Fall): 181–212.

—— and King, R. (1997). 'An Experimental Investigation of the Effect of Cost Information and Feedback on Product Cost Decisions', *Contemporary Accounting Research*, 14(1): 99–127.

Hemmer, T. (1996). 'Allocations of Sunk Capacity Costs and Joint Costs in a Linear Principal-Agent Model', *Accounting Review*, 71(3): 419–32.

Holmström, B. (1979). 'Moral Hazard and Observability', *Bell Journal of Economics* (Spring): 74–91.

Homburg, C. (2001). 'A Note on Optimal Cost Driver Selection in ABC', *Management Accounting Research*, 12: 197–205.

Horngren, C., Bhimani, A., Datar, S., and Foster, G. (2005). *Management and Cost Accounting*. Hemel Hempstead: Prentice Hall.

Hwang, Y., Evans J. H., III, and Hegde, V. G. (1993). 'Product Cost Bias and Selection of an Allocation base', *Journal of Management Accounting Research*, 5 (Fall): 213–42.

Ittner, C., Larcker, D., and Randall, T. (1997). 'The Activity-Based Cost Hierarchy, Production Policies and Firm Profitability', *Journal of Management Accounting Research*, 9: 143–62.

Johnson, H. T. and Kaplan, R. S. (1987). *Relevance Lost—The Rise and Fall of Management Accounting*. Boston: Harvard Business School Press.

Kaplan, R. S. and Atkinson, A. (1998). *Advanced Management Accounting*. Englewood Cliffs, NJ: Prentice Hall.

—— and Cooper, R. (1998). *Cost and Effect: Using Integrated Cost Systems to Drive Profitability and Performance*. Boston: Harvard Business School Press.

—— and March, A. (1998*a*). 'John Deere Component Works (A)'. Harvard Business School, Case 9-187-107.

—— —— (1998*b*). 'John Deere Component Works (B)'. Harvard Business School, Case 9-187-108.

—— and Thompson, G. L. (1971). 'Overhead allocation via mathematical programming models'. *Accounting Review* (April): 352–64.

Labro, E. (2004). 'The Cost Effects of Component Commonality: A Literature Review Through a Management Accounting Lens', *Manufacturing & Service Operations Management*, 6(4): 358–67.

—— and Vanhoucke, M. (2005). 'A Simulation Analysis of Interactions between Errors in Costing System Design'. Working paper, Ghent University.

Maher, M. W. and Marais, M. L. (1998). 'A Field Study on the Limitations of Activity-Based Costing when Resources are Provided on a Joint and Indivisible Basis', *Journal of Accounting Research*, 36(1): 129–42.

Merchant, K. and Shields, M. D. (1993). 'When and Why to Measure Cost Less Accurately to Improve Decision-Making', *Accounting Horizons* 7(2): 76–81.

Noreen, E. (1991). 'Conditions Under Which Activity-Based Costing Systems Provide Relevant Costs', *Journal of Management Accounting Research*, 3: 59–168.

—— and Burgstahler, D. (1997). 'Full-cost Pricing and the Illusion of Satisficing' *Journal of Management Accounting Research*, 9: 239–63.

Verrecchia, R. (2001). 'Essays on Disclosure', *Journal of Accounting and Economics*, 32: 97–180.

Vives, X. (1990). 'Trade Association Disclosure Rules, Incentives to Share Information, and Welfare', *RAND Journal of Economics*, 21: 409–30.

Zimmerman, J. (1979). 'The Cost and Benefits of Cost Allocations', *Accounting Review*, 54(3): 504–21.

☐ APPENDIX: A SUMMARY OF DATAR AND GUPTA'S (1994) EXAMPLE

The example considers a manufacturing firm with two departments that produces two products, A and B. The firm performs two activities: set-up and machining. Datar and Gupta (1994) assume that the 'true' cost drivers in both departments are set-up hours for the set-up activity and machine hours for the machining activity. Table 10.A.1 provides the data for the example in panel A and the calculations for the true benchmark case in panel B. The true product cost of A is $8,500; that of B is $6,500.

They then study an approximation of this true benchmark by a first costing system (costing system 1). This costing system has two cost pools. All set-up costs are aggregated in one cost pool; all machining costs are aggregated in another cost pool. As the allocation basis for set-up costs the number of set-ups is used. To allocate machining costs direct labour hours is used. Under costing system 1, the total cost allocated to products A and B respectively are:

Table 10.A.1 Datar and Gupta (1994) example

Panel A: Data for the example

| Products | Department 1 | | Department 2 | | |
	Set-up	Machining	Set-up	Machining	Total
Number of set-ups					
A	7		3		10
B	13		2		15
Total	20		5		25
Set-up hours					
A	15		6		21
B	15		4		19
Total	30		10		40
Direct labour hours					
A		32		34	66
B		18		16	34
Total		50		50	100
Machine hours					
A		115		120	235
B		85		80	165
Total		200		200	400

Panel B: Costs in the true benchmark case ($)

| | Department 1 | | Department 2 | | |
	Set-up	Machining	Set-up	Machining	Total
Total process cost	3,000	8,000	2,000	2,000	15,000
Cost drivers	Set-up hours	Machine hours	Set-up hours	Machine hours	
Cost rates	100/hour	40/hour	200/hour	10/hour	
Allocations					
A	1,500	4,600	1,200	1,200	8,500
B	1,500	3,400	800	800	6,500
Total	3,000	8,000	2,000	2,000	15,000

$$TC1_A = \left(\$5,000 * \frac{10}{25} \right) + \left(\$10,000 * \frac{66}{100} \right) = \$8,600 > \$8,500$$

$$TC1_B = \left(\$5,000 * \frac{15}{25} \right) + \left(\$10,000 * \frac{34}{100} \right) = \$6,400 < \$6,500$$

Costing system 1 overcosts product A and undercosts product B. In order to find which part of this total costing error to attribute to specification error and which part is due to aggregation error, costing system 1′ is introduced. This costing system 1′ has no aggregation of the activity cost pools across departments[52], but keeps the wrong specification. Under costing system 1′, the total cost allocated to products A and B respectively are:

$$TC1'_A = \left(\$3{,}000 * \frac{7}{20}\right) + \left(\$2{,}000 * \frac{3}{5}\right) + \left(\$8{,}000 * \frac{32}{50}\right) + \left(\$2{,}000 * \frac{34}{50}\right) = \$8{,}730$$

$$TC1'_B = \left(\$3{,}000 * \frac{13}{20}\right) + \left(\$2{,}000 * \frac{2}{5}\right) + \left(\$8{,}000 * \frac{18}{50}\right) + \left(\$2{,}000 * \frac{16}{50}\right) = \$6{,}270$$

For product A, we can then calculate the specification error (SE) and aggregation error (AE), introduced by costing system 1 as follows:

$$SE_A(CS1) = TCtrue_A - TC1'_A = \$8{,}500 - \$8{,}730 = -\$230$$

$$AE_A(CS1) = TC1'_A - TC1_A = \$8{,}730 - \$8{,}600 \quad = \$130.$$

Specification error in costing system 1 undercosts product A, where aggregation error overcosts product A. Note that, because of the sign difference, specification and aggregation errors for product A partially cancel each other out. Because we work in a simple two-product environment, the SE and AE for product B are exactly of the opposite sign.

Costing system 2 is adopted to improve on costing system 1 by introducing a better specification. Machine hours will now be used as the cost driver for machining costs instead of labour hours. The total cost of product A under costing system 2 can be calculated:

$$TC2_A = \left(\$5{,}000 * \frac{10}{25}\right) + \left(\$10{,}000 * \frac{235}{400}\right) = \$7{,}875$$

Total costing error for product A now becomes = $8,500 − $7,875 = $625. This is a lot higher than the costing error for product A in costing system 1, which was only $100. So improving on specification leads to a higher costing error in this case![53]

Datar and Gupta (1994) then introduce a further improvement to the costing system. They disaggregate the machining cost pool into two departmental machining cost pools, thereby reducing aggregation as they move from a system with two cost pools to one with three. The total cost of product A under costing system 3 can be calculated:

$$TC3_A = \left(\$5{,}000 * \frac{10}{25}\right) + \left(\$8{,}000 * \frac{115}{200}\right) + \left(\$2{,}000 * \frac{120}{200}\right) = \$7{,}800$$

Total costing error for product A now becomes = $8,500 − $7,800 = $700. This is a lot higher than the costing error for product A in costing system 1 and even higher than the costing error in costing system 2. In this case, less aggregation leads to a higher total costing error!

These examples indeed lead Datar and Gupta (1994) to conclude that specification error does not always decrease with improved cost allocation bases at aggregate cost pools and that aggregation error does not always decrease with an increase in the number of cost pools. As a consequence, stepwise refinement of a costing system is not necessarily a good thing to do!

11 Understanding management control systems and strategy

Kim Langfield-Smith

11.1 Introduction

Over the last twenty years, the relationship between management control systems (MCS) and strategy has become a popular theme of many empirical research papers. There is some ambiguity as to what constitutes an organizational control or MCS, and many writers have defined it very broadly (Fisher 1995). For example, MCS have been described as the processes by which managers ensure that resources are obtained and used effectively and efficiently to accomplish the organization's objectives (Anthony 1965), actions, or activities taken to influence the probability that managers and employees will behave in ways that lead to the attainment of organizational objectives (Flamholtz 1983), and formal, information-based routines, and procedures managers use to maintain or alter patterns of organizational activities (Simons 1995: 5). MCS may encompass a range of formal and informal controls, including performance measurement systems, employee and managerial incentive systems, budgeting systems, procedures and policies, physical controls over assets, personnel controls, and cultural and social controls.

Thus, MCS provide a means for supporting the strategic orientation of an organization, by directing, thinking, and encouraging efforts that are consistent with the achievement of organizational strategies and goals (Ouchi 1979; Flamholtz 1983). Over the last two decades, the means by which MCS can provide this support, or relate to strategy has been the focus of many research studies. The relationship between MCS and strategy has been studied from several different research perspectives and underlying assumptions about the nature of the relationship have changed over time.

The purpose of this chapter is to explain the relationship between MCS and strategy, and how this research area has developed over the last two decades. Examples of empirical studies that utilize various theoretical frameworks and research methods will be presented to indicate the breadth of the research area and the multifarious ways that researchers have studied the field.

Section 11.2 defines different perspectives of strategy that have emerged and explains how they have been used in MCS research. Section 11.3 tracks the development of MCS from its origins as a static cybernetic process, through to its focus as a strategic tool. The remainder of the chapter contains detailed examples of empirical research in the MCS–strategy area that illustrates the major types of research that have influenced our thinking of the MCS–strategy relationship.

11.2 **The MCS–strategy nexus**

The field of organizational strategy (or business policy) emerged as a formal area of study in the 1950s among researchers at Harvard Business School (see Andrews 1980 and Chandler 1962 for early views of strategy). Chandler (1962: 13) was influential in shaping the early thinking about strategy, which he defined as 'the determination of the basic long-term goals and objectives of the enterprise and the adoption of courses of action and the allocation of resources necessary for carrying out these goals'. Initially, strategy was envisaged as a discrete activity which resulted from the deliberate decisions of senior management. Strategy formulation was a formal systematic process and strategy implementation involved introducing changes in products, structures, activities, systems, and processes to deliver that strategy. Strategies were formulated to constrain and focus managerial thinking and activities, and MCS were put in place to support the strategic orientation.

In the 1970s, strategy came to be seen as sometimes less formalized or explicit. Mintzberg (1978) viewed strategy as an ongoing pattern of decisions, which could be deliberate or unintended. Strategy could emerge in response to opportunities that arose within the organization or marketplace and there may be no formal written strategies or strategic formulation processes. Strategies may result from interactions between managers, employees, and the external environment, from experimentations to find out what worked best, and from spontaneous decisions (Mintzberg 1987; Merchant and van der Stede 2003).

Also, in some situations there may be inconsistencies between an intended strategy and the actual strategy that is enacted by managers in their decisions and activities. This may occur when formal strategies are seen as obsolete by managers and employees, or if there is a slippage between the strategy and the focus of the MCS. The MCS may be designed inappropriately and may focus on encouraging behaviour that is not consistent with the intended strategy. When strategy is implicit or lacking in formalization, it becomes more difficult to identify and to design an appropriate MCS.

11.2.1 CORPORATE STRATEGY

Strategies occur at various levels of an organization. Corporate strategy relates to the organization as a whole and encompasses decisions about the types of businesses to operate in, what businesses to acquire or divest, how best to structure and finance the organization, and how resources should be allocated between different businesses (de Wit and Meyer 2004; Hax and Majluf 1996). Corporate strategy is concerned with the way resources are focused to convert distinct competences into competitive advantage (Andrews 1980: 18–19). These corporate strategy choices have implications for the design of MCS. For example, a firm may decide to structure into strategic business units (SBUs) that reflect different markets or regions. SBU managers may be assigned high or low decision-making autonomy and there may be different degrees of interdependencies between those business units. As an organization increases in size and SBUs become more remote and independent, so MCS need to provide assurance to head office management that operations are under control. However, MCS also need to encourage SBU managers and employees to follow the 'correct' behaviours. The MCS needs to encompass vertical and horizontal information flows and reporting structures, consider the degree of formalization of planning and communication processes, and include the design of managerial performance reporting and incentive systems.

One of the early debates in the strategy literature surrounded the link between strategy and structure, with Chandler (1962) arguing that choice of strategy preceded the choice about structure. Thompson (1967), Lawrence and Lorsch (1967), and Perrow (1967) built on this work to develop frameworks to explain how structure and processes were chosen to match the chosen strategy and the environment. Cyert and March (1963) presented arguments for the development of processes and systems to support strategy. They argued that managers are parochial in their perceptions and responsibilities and tend not to search beyond familiar territory to find solutions to problems. So structure and systems can constrain managers in their search for the best solution.

There has been relatively limited research that has studied the relationship between corporate strategy choices and MCS. Van der Stede (2000) studied the effect of the corporate diversification decision and business strategy on two aspects of MCS: budgetary slack and incentives. He found that the greater the corporate diversification (the number of distinct businesses managed by the organization), the more likely was budgetary slack in SBU budgets. Bushman et al. (1995) found that the extent to which the incentive compensation of SBU managers was based on the aggregate performance criteria of the organization, rather than business level criteria, increased with the degree of SBU interdependencies. Most MCS–strategy research has focused on business strategies.

11.2.2 BUSINESS STRATEGY

Business strategies relate to each of the SBUs of the organization. However, some writers distinguish between the strategic mission and the competitive strategy of an SBU (Merchant and van der Stede 2003). The strategic mission of an SBU has been defined as the stages of build, hold, harvest, and divest, which change across the life cycle of an organization (Gupta and Govindarajan 1984). The choice of strategic mission signifies the organization's intended trade-off between market share growth and maximizing short-term earnings. A build strategy focuses on improving market share and competitive position, even if this decreases short-term earnings or cash flow. Under a harvest strategy a firm aims at maximizing short-term profit and cash flow rather than increasing market share. A hold mission is used to maintain market share while obtaining a reasonable return on investment, thus protecting market share and competitive position, while a divest strategy occurs when a business plans to cease operations. This perspective of business strategy has been used by only a few MCS researchers (see Govindarajan and Gupta 1985; Gupta 1987; Fisher and Govindarajan 1993).

Competitive strategies focus on how individual SBUs compete within their particular industries and position themselves in relation to competitors. Within an SBU, operational strategies may relate to marketing or production functions, and address how the various functions of the organization contribute to the business strategy and competitiveness of the organization. Various typologies have developed to classify the specific competitive stance of an SBU, and have been adopted by many MCS researchers to facilitate the analysis of the relationship between business strategy and MCS. Two widely used typologies are those of Miles and Snow (1978) and Porter (1980, 1985).

Miles and Snow (1978) developed a framework that characterized four strategy types as prospector, defender, reactor, and analyser. This was elaborated in a book of detailed case studies, and was one of the first publications to consider how control systems choice, including the focus of performance measures, costing information, and reporting styles, may vary depending on the nature of the specific business strategy. This typology analysed strategy in terms of the rate of change in products or markets relative to competitors.

Defenders have narrow product-market domains and there is limited product or market development. Managers become experts within their domain and seldom search for new opportunities. The focus is on improving the efficiency of existing operations and there is rarely the need to make major adjustments to technology, structure, or systems. The finance, production, and engineering functions are considered critical for success and there is limited emphasis on marketing or research and development. The functional organizational structure reflects the specialization of products, markets, and technology. Performance measurement systems focus on financial or efficiency-based measures. Information flows are vertical and senior managers are responsible for decision-making.

Prospectors are continually searching for market opportunities. They create change and uncertainty in a market, to which their competitors must respond. Product and market innovation are the focus, not efficiency. Prospectors use decentralization and short-looped horizontal information systems to enable quick local responses to problems. The marketing and research and development (R&D) functions dominate finance and production, so efficiency and profit performance are not as important as maintaining industry leadership in product innovation. There is a lack of formality in systems and these organizations are results-oriented. Performance measures focus on effectiveness, rather than on efficiency, and are likely to be assessed in relation to competitors. Analysers fall between defenders and prospectors and combine the strongest characteristics of both, while reactors are not considered successful strategic types.

The Miles and Snow typology is significant as it was one of the first frameworks adopted by accounting researchers to operationalize and measure business strategy, and to study the fit between strategy and MCS. Key papers in this area include Simons (1987), Collins et al. (1997), Abernethy and Brownell (1999), and Abernethy and Lillis (2001).

Porter (1980, 1985) was influential in introducing the idea of strategic positioning. He defined three sources of sustainable competitive advantage: cost leadership, differentiation, and focus. Each of these strategies defines the context for actions in each functional area of the organization. As with the Miles and Snow typology, the successful implementation of each strategy involves different resources and skills, supportive organizational arrangements, and control systems.

A cost leader aims to become the lowest cost producer in its industry. The source of competitive advantage may arise from factors such as economies of scale, access to favourable raw material prices, and superior technology. Differentiators focus on providing unique products attributes, which may be in the area of quality or dependability of the product, after-sales service, wide product availability, and product flexibility. In a focus strategy, a company directs its activities to a specific segment of the market and bases its competitive advantage on either cost leadership or differentiation.

Porter's categorization of business strategy has been the most widely used approach to conceptualizing strategy in the MCS–strategy literature. Studies that have used the classifications of cost leadership and differentiation include Govindarajan and Fisher (1990), Fisher and Govindarajan (1993), Chenhall and Langfield-Smith (1998), and Baines and Langfield-Smith (2003). In recent years there has been a tendency to focus on the relationship between MCS and specific types of differentiation strategies. For example, Ittner and Larcker (1997) and Daniel and Reitsberger (1994) focused on quality strategies, Abernethy and Lillis (1995) studied manufacturing flexibility, Perera et al. (1997) researched customer focus strategies, Ittner et al. (2003) studied innovation and flexibility, and Davila (2000) focused on product innovation strategies. Chenhall and Langfield-Smith (1998) studied a range of component differentiation and cost leadership combinations and Mouritsen et al. (2001) focused on technological innovation, flexibility, and productivity.

11.3 Different frameworks for studying the MCS–strategy relationship

Despite the intense interest in business strategy in the academic and practitioner literatures, up to the mid-1990s there were relatively few empirical papers published in the area of strategy and MCS. This was highlighted by Langfield-Smith (1997), who provided a review and critique of empirical research in the area emphasizing a range of deficiencies and areas for future research.[1] This review concluded that research published up to that time was fragmentary, and the approach taken and research findings were sometimes conflicting. Most studies were cross-sectional surveys that followed a contingency framework.

However, over the past decade there have been changes in the way that researchers have viewed the MCS–strategy relationship. Papers that continue to use a contingency approach have come to adopt more complex conceptualizations, and there is a large increase in the number of studies that adopt qualitative methods and sociological theories to draw on 'alternative' theoretical frameworks.[2] Some of these approaches are summarized in Table 11.1

11.3.1 THE CONTINGENCY APPROACH TO MCS–STRATEGY

The origin of the contingency approach to MCS design lies in organizational theory, and in the work of Burns and Stalker (1961), Perrow (1970), Thompson (1967), and Lawrence and Lorsch (1967) (Chenhall 2003). It is assumed that MCS are adopted to achieve planned organizational outcomes and the design of MCS will be influenced by contextual variables, including the environment, structure, technology, and strategy. In this approach, an objective reality is assumed, which allows the dominant research method to be surveys that can measure these MCS and contextual variables, and assess fit.

In the 1960s, MCS were viewed as situated between operational controls and strategic controls (Anthony 1965). MCS itself did not have a strategic orientation but was seen as a means for allowing managers to coordinate and control operations. Formal control systems were associated with stable environments and mechanistic organizations (Burns and Stalker 1961). The design of control systems followed a cybernetic model, consisting of a self-regulating systems and feedback loops (Ashby 1960). Controls such as standard costing and budgeting systems are examples of the type of formal controls systems that reinforced this view. Appropriately designed MCS were seen as allowing organizations to adapt and respond to environmental uncertainties to ensure the correct strategic response.

The strategic focus of MCS research emerged in the 1980s, and most research adopted a contingency perspective (Langfield-Smith 1997). In these contingency approaches, it was assumed that strategy is static and the MCS should be designed to support that strategy. Strategy formulation was as a rational process of formulation and then implementation. Much of the initial MCS–strategy research focused on business strategy, and the focus was on the fit between business strategy, some aspects of MCS, other contextual variables, and sometimes organizational effectiveness. A contingency approach argues that the design of MCS is influenced by elements of an organization's context, such as the environment, technology, structure, and strategy. Strategy is not a contingent variable in the strict sense, as it is not an element of context (Chenhall 2003). Rather, managers have 'strategic choice'. They can select a strategic direction that will position their organization in a particular external environment or market. Under a contingency perspective, certain styles of MCS are said to suit certain types of strategies.

Table 11.1 Frameworks for studying MCS–strategy

Framework	Source	Orientation	Method
Contingency frameworks	Organizational theory: Burns and Stalker (1961), Perrow (1970), Thompson (1967), and Lawrence and Lorsch (1967)	• MCS are adopted to achieve planned organizational outcomes • The design of MCS will be influenced by contextual variables, including the environment, structure technology, and strategy • MCS are an outcome of a rational design choice • An objective reality is assumed	Surveys Statistical analysis to determine 'fit' between MCS, strategy, and other contextual variables
Positivist case studies	May draw on organizational theories, economics, organizational behaviour, sociology	• The focus may be on the processes and the complex organizational interactions that influence the design, use, or role of MCS • MCS are usually assumed to be a result of rational choice • An objective reality more often assumed than subjectivity	Case studies that utilize qualitative and quantitative data
Structuration theory	Sociological theory: Giddens (1976, 1979)	• Focus on processes of accountability • MCS are social structures that provide a way of regularizing organizational functioning over time and space • Structuration is where actors draw on structures (MCS) and effect changes • Reality is subjective	Case studies that utilize qualitative data
Institutional theory	Sociological theory: DiMaggio and Powell (1983), Meyer and Rowan (1977)	• An organization operates in various institutional environments • The design of an MCS influenced by interactions between, and expectations of, the various environments • Reality is subjective	Case studies that utilize qualitative data
Actor-network theory	Sociological theory: La Tour (1987, 1993)	• Reality is structured through the interactions of networks of human and non-human actors • MCS may be constructed and control achieved through processes that are performed by one actor on another • Reality is subjective	Case studies that utilize qualitative data

In the MCS literature of the 1990s that adopted a contingency approach, business strategy was characterized using various typologies: prospector–defender, differentiation–cost leadership, and build–harvest. These studies focused primarily on questionnaire surveys, which took a snapshot of the status of the business strategy and various aspects of MCS at a point in time. However, this limited the breadth of the MCS that could be studied and did not provide insights into the dynamics of the relationship between MCS and strategy. Some detailed examples of survey-based studies that use a contingency framework are outlined in the following section. A shortcoming in many of the quantitative papers in this area was the lack of consistency in the way that both strategy and MCS were conceptualized and measured (Langfield-Smith 1997).

In the later 1990s, research tended to focus more on component business strategies. These include quality strategies (Ittner and Larcker 1997; Daniel and Reitsberger 1994; Carr, Mak, and Needham 1997), manufacturing flexibility (Abernethy and Lillis 1995), and new product development strategies (Davila 2000). Studies in the early 1990s adopted a dichotomous view of strategy as either cost leadership or differentiation, or prospector or defender. However, more recently it is acknowledged that organizations may pursue business strategies characterized by several aspects of differentiation or cost leadership. For example, Chenhall and Langfield-Smith (1998) found that firms adopted a mix of cost leadership and specific differentiation strategies, with varying degrees of emphasis. Reitsberger et al. (1993) found that firms may follow different combinations of cost and quality strategies, with varying intensities.

Recently, the view that the firm's MCS should be in alignment with the firm's specific business strategy, has come under question. This 'alignment hypothesis' (Ittner et al. 2003) is supported by a range of contingency studies (see review by Fisher 1995) as well as economic theories that argue that the orientation of information systems and reward systems should align with the specific business strategy (Brickley et al. 1997; Milgrom and Roberts 1992). However, the alignment hypothesis may be too simplistic, and the relationship between MCS and strategy may be more complex (Ittner et al. 2003). Alternative approaches to studying the MCS–strategy relation have opened the way for studying the complexity and dynamics of the interaction.

To illustrate contingency approaches to the study of MCS and strategy, three examples will be outlined. Simons (1987) is one of the first examples of a 'conventional' survey of MCS and strategy. Ittner and Larcker (1997) studied the fit between quality controls and a quality strategy. Finally, Bisbe and Otley (2004) focused on innovation strategy and the contemporary constructs of interactive control systems and the BSC.

11.3.1.1 A survey of control systems and strategy—Simons (1987)

Simons (1987) is an example of one of the early contingency studies that investigated the relationship between MCS and strategy. Simons conducted a postal survey of Canadian manufacturing firms across thirty-eight industries, which he developed following a series of interviews with managers in twelve firms. The survey focused on ten control system attributes, tight budget controls, external scanning, results monitoring, cost control, forecast data, goals related to output effectiveness, reporting frequency, formula-based bonus remuneration, tailored control systems, and control systems changeability.[3] The focus was on formal accounting controls, which reflects the era in which the research was undertaken. Broader conceptions of controls were to emerge in later empirical studies. The contextual variables were industry dynamism and strategy, defined as prospector or defender.

Simons (1987) found that high performing prospectors placed importance on controls, such as forecasting data, tight budget goals, and the careful monitoring of outputs, but gave little attention to cost control. Also, large high-performing prospectors emphasized frequent reporting and the use of uniform control systems, which are modified when necessary. Simons (1987) also found that control systems were used less intensively by defenders, particularly large defenders, compared with prospectors. In large defenders, high financial performance was negatively correlated with tight budget goals and the use of output monitoring. It was only in small defenders that tight budget goals were positively correlated with high performance. While these findings are not consistent with Miles and Snow (1978) and Porter (1980), who argued that prospectors/differentiators rely less on tight formal accounting controls compared to defenders, Simons offered limited insights into possible causes.

There are two aspects about Simons' results that are intriguing (Langfield-Smith 1997). First, certain aspects of formal control systems were important to prospectors, but not to defenders, particularly large defenders. Second, small defenders found tight budget goals important, but large defenders did not. Dent (1990) proposed possible explanations. First, control systems may balance the innovative excess encouraged by prospectors' organizational arrangements (Miller and Freisen 1982). Second, prospectors may rely on performance monitoring to encourage organizational learning in the face of high task or environmental uncertainty. Finally, financial controls may be the only way that the wide scope of a prospector's activities can be captured. Also, defenders, being more stable organizations, may not require intense cost control, but may achieve greater efficiency using non-financial measures (Dent 1990).

This paper appears to be the only quantitative contingency paper published by Robert Simons, who went on to publish a series of qualitative studies (Simons, 1990, 1991, 1994) leading to his 'levers of control' framework of diagnostic and interactive controls (Simons 1995). This framework has had a major influence on contemporary MCS research (see Bisbe and Otley 2004 in Section 11.3.1.3).

11.3.1.2 Quality strategy and strategic control practices—Ittner and Larcker (1997)

Ittner and Larcker (1997) is a survey of automotive and computer companies and some of their suppliers, across Canada, Japan, Germany, and the USA. The analysis used survey data that had been collected by a consulting firm. The strategy focus was on quality, which is one form of differentiation.

The results indicated that organizations following a quality-oriented strategy made greater use of strategic control practices, consistent with the quality orientation. The strategic control practices focused on strategic implementation practices (action plans, project controls, and management rewards), internal monitoring practices (feedback mechanisms, meetings, and board reviews), and external monitoring practices (benchmarking, market research, and strategic audits of products and processes). Compared with Simons (1987), the control systems investigated here were more encompassing of a broader control system. They were not limited to formal accounting controls and included externally focused controls to monitor comparative performance with competitors and to assess customer and market perspectives.

The extent of the relationship between strategy and control practices varied by country. The results indicated that in the American and German organizations there was a very strong relation; while in Japan extensive use was made of quality-related control systems, regardless of the strategic orientation. Interestingly, the alignment of quality strategies and strategic control practices was not always associated with high organizational performance, and this varied by industry. For some control practices there was a negative performance effect, suggesting that formal control systems might sometimes reduce performance. Despite expectations, there was no evidence that Japanese companies closely aligned their control practices with their competitive strategy of quality, compared to the other countries.

11.3.1.3 Interactive control systems, the balanced scorecard, and strategy—Bisbe and Otley (2004)

Bisbe and Otley's is a comprehensive paper that integrates the concepts of interactive controls and the BSC in a survey of Spanish manufacturing firms that followed a product innovation strategy.

Simons (1990, 1991, 1994) levers of control framework outlines how senior managers use controls to implement and develop business strategy. Simons argued that the focus of control systems design should not be on the types of controls that are needed to suit the organization's strategy, but the distribution of management attention among controls. Managers use controls 'interactively' to signal the strategic uncertainties and assist in managing those uncertainties. Controls are used diagnostically on 'automatic pilot' to monitor outcomes and correct deviations from preset goals. Simons broadened the role of MCS as impacting on strategy formulation, implementation, and change. Empirical papers that have used Simons' interactive/diagnostic controls include Abernethy and Brownell (1999), de Haas and Kleingold (1999), Bisbe and Otley (2004), Tuomela (2006), and Henri (2006).

One of the variables in Bisbe and Otley (2004) is the interactive use of the BSC. Kaplan and Norton (1996) presented their BSC in the early 1990s, and this has become a popular framework for combining financial and non-financial performance measures, with explicit links to strategy and organizational objectives. The BSC provides a way for communicating strategic intent and motivating performance towards achieving strategic goals (Ittner and

Larcker 1998). Recent papers that have studied the BSC include Hoque and James (2000), Malina and Selto (2001), and Ittner et al. (2003).

Bisbe and Otley (2004) tested whether the interactive use of controls leads companies to develop and launch new products, and whether it contributes to the impact of the new innovative products on organizational performance. The control systems that were studied were the budgeting system, the BSC, and project management systems, and the focus was on the interactive use of these controls. However, in the quantitative analysis, a single 'interactive MCS' measure was constructed which, in most cases, makes it difficult to determine the specific relations between the individual controls, strategy, and performance. Overall, the results indicated that in low innovating firms, the use of an interactive control system may lead to greater innovation, by providing guidance for the search, triggering, and stimulus of initiatives and through providing legitimacy for autonomous initiatives. However, in high innovating firms, interactive use of controls seemed to reduce innovation. This was thought to be caused by the filtering out of initiatives that result from the sharing and exposure of ideas. Another finding was that the interactive use of controls moderated the impact of innovation on organizational performance. This was thought to be a result of the direction, integration, and fine-tuning that is provided by those interactive control systems. Thus, support was found for the positive impact of formal MCS on innovation and long-term performance. In terms of the interactive use of the specific controls, the interactive use of budgeting was found to moderate the impact of an innovation strategy on performance. However, the interactive use of the BSC and of project management did not moderate the relationship. No reasons were advanced as to why the results may have held for the budgeting, but not for the other two forms of controls that were investigated. This opens the way for new research on why some interactive controls have different implications for strategy and performance.

Simons' levers of control framework is significant as it may contribute to our understanding of the contradictory evidence of the role of formal MCS in organizations that follow on prospector strategies. (See Langfield-Smith 1997 and the discussion of Simons 1987 in an earlier section of this chapter.) Bisbe and Otley (2004) provide some empirical evidence of the role of interactive controls in promoting a successful innovation strategy.

11.3.2 NATURALISTIC AND OTHER ALTERNATIVE APPROACHES

Naturalistic approaches to management accounting research focus on investigating phenomena in their 'everyday setting' (Hopper et al. 1987; Baxter and Chua 2003). These studies tend to utilize case studies that rely on quantitative data, rather than statistical analysis of data-sets, and draw on various sociological theories. They do not emphasize 'fit' or means–end causality that are features of contingency-based studies, and they focus on processes and multifarious interactions between phenomena over time. They allow for the possibility of studying the complex dynamics between strategy and MCS that cannot be uncovered in cross-sectional survey-based contingency approaches.

A disadvantage of these naturalistic studies is that it can be difficult to integrate findings across studies, as the focus of each one tends to be unique and the underlying theories and assumptions may differ. Many of these studies draw on different theories to explain their findings, including actor-network theory, structuration theory, and institutional theory, which can hinder comparisons and integration of findings. Depending on the theoretical framework that is adopted, these approaches may focus on the differing interpretations that organizational participants place on strategy, control systems, and other phenomena, and the different roles that MCS can play in an organization. Contingency studies are positivist approaches that emphasize the rational and assume an objective reality. Alternative approaches assume that reality is subjective, and it is individuals' interpretations that are important in understanding the interplay between strategy and control systems and other organizational and environmental phenomena. Naturalistic studies do not always identify strategy as a variable for examination, and may not utilize the strategic typologies outlined in an earlier section of the paper. Strategy may be explicit or implicit and may blur with other organizational phenomena to become the way that people think, act, make decisions, and interact with those inside and outside of the organization.

To illustrate alternative approaches in the areas of MCS-strategy, three studies will be outlined. Mouritsen et al. (2001) draw on actor-network theory to present two case studies of strategy and control in outsourcing. Roberts (1990) replies on structuration theory to explain how accounting controls may need to be balanced with non-accounting controls to avoid dysfunctional consequences for strategy development. Euske and Riccaboni (1999) use institutional theory to explain the influences on, and the roles of, MCS in managing internal and external interdependencies.

11.3.2.1 MCS in outsourcing—Mouritsen et al. (2001)

Mouritsen et al. (2001) provide two case studies of outsourcing situations (NewTech and LeanTech) which highlight the interdependencies between strategy and control systems of both partners. As an important determinant of success in interorganizational relationships is a supportive cooperative relationship based on trust (Langfield-Smith and Smith 2003; van der Meer-Kooistra and Vosselman 2000), careful consideration is needed in designing the control system to manage the relationship. In both case studies, outsourcing was regarded as part of the strategy of the firms and was needed to maintain competitiveness. However, the introduction of outsourcing left a gap in the control system of both firms and new controls were introduced to reinstall control and to retain a sense of involvement in the outsourced activities.

This paper draws on actor-network theory (ANT) to explain the role of MCS in effecting strategic change. ANT derives from the work of the sociologists Latour (1987, 1993) and Callon (1986), and can focus on understanding how reality can be structured through the interactions of networks of human and non-human actors (Briers and Chua 2001; Baxter and Chua 2003). In the study of MCS, these non-human actors may include reports, systems, data, and other objects. MCS may be constructed and control achieved through 'translations'. A translation is simply the process that is performed by one actor on another, throughout a network (Latour 1987). In accounting research, case studies have examined how accounting numbers can be used to accommodate and persuade diverse interests within an organization (Baxter and Chua 2003). In recent years a number of papers have utilized ANT. These include Mouritsen (1999) and Mouritsen and Thrane (2006).

The strategy of NewTech focused on rapid technological development and technological innovation was considered key to maintaining competitiveness. However, this was the function that was outsourced. Functional analysis, an aspect of target costing, was introduced to regain control over the product development function and became a way to improve the suppliers' understanding of the technology, strategy, and organization and to direct and control the suppliers' development activities. As a result of these changes, New-Tech developed a new identity as a technology coordinator and manager.

LeanTech found that as customer demand changed, the strategy of flexibility towards individual customers started to move towards productivity. This led to the outsourcing of production, but also to a lack of control over those outsourced processes. Open book accounting was introduced to provide logistics management with access to time and cost information about production processes, which assisted the company to coordinate supplier activities and improved production flexibility. However, open book accounting also led to new conceptions of competitive strategy with LeanTech and a reinterpretation of what a technological edge and customization meant for the firm.

In both of these case studies, the new controls that were introduced to gain control over the outsourced activities let to changes in company perception of what were the core competencies of the two firms and new conceptualizations of the nature of their strategy and competitive edge. The approach taken in this research differs markedly to that of contingency approach. In this paper, perceptions of strategy were seen to evolve and emerge as a result of reinterpretations of competitive strengths. New MCS were adopted to manage the outsourced functions and this in turn served to stimulate thinking of core strengths and the role of each of the two focal companies in these new structural relationships. Rather than focusing on the appropriateness of the fit between MCS and strategy, the focus is on the dynamics of the relationships between systems, structures, and other actors.

11.3.2.2 Formal and informal controls—Roberts (1990)

Giddens (1976, 1979) structuration theory has been used by some management accounting researchers to focus on processes of accountability. Structuration theory distinguishes between structures and structuration. Structures are static and consist of practices. Structuration is the process where actors draw on structures and effect change (Ahrens and Chapman 2002). Roberts and Scapens (1985) described accounting systems as an example of social structures that provide a way of regularizing organizational functioning across time and space. MCS can be viewed in a similar manner. An understanding of structuration facilitates the study of the social processes that can lead to change in control structures. There are only a few papers that have drawn on structuration theory to explain the

MCS–strategy relation. These include Roberts (1990), Knight and Wilmott (1993), and Ahrens and Chapman (2002).

Roberts (1990) studied strategic change in a large decentralized company. The high level of decentralization encouraged competition between profit centre managers, and distanced the head office managers from the changes in market conditions that affected those profit centres. Accounting information was a powerful influence in shaping managers' activities and relationships, and created an external image of success. However, it also concealed potentially damaging strategic consequences. Roberts' study emphasized how accounting controls can create a climate that can act against successful strategy formation and implementation processes. The accounting controls emphasized individuality, instrumentality, autonomy, and dependence. However, they encouraged conformity and distorted communications that conflicted with the requirements for successful formulation and implementation of strategy. Management meetings played an important integrative function to help resolve conflict between accounting controls and strategy, through providing managers with a means for developing strategy, encouraging interdependence and reciprocity among the profit centre managers and enabling a sharing of market knowledge. They also helped create a set of shared meanings around which actions could be mobilized. This study is valuable as an example of how accounting controls, which for some organizations may have dysfunctional implications for strategy development, can be balanced by non-accounting controls (in this case, management meetings).

While there are several unresolved issues and some debate as to how structuration theory has been applied in accounting research (Macintosh and Scapens 1990; Scapens and Macintosh 1996; Boland 1996), structuration theory does provides a way of recognizing how MCS may be implicated in the creation of social order within organizations. Rather than focusing on what tools and techniques are included as part of an MCS, it allows us to focus on how MCS can be used to produce and reproduce meaning, morality, and power within organizations (Macintosh and Scapens 1990).

11.3.2.3 Managing interdependencies—Euske and Riccaboni (1999)

Institutional theory is focused on the rules, norms, and ideologies that confer social legitimacy on organizations and their participants (DiMaggio and Powell 1983; Meyer and Rowan 1977). Thus, an organization not only has an internal 'technical' environment, it has various institutional environments, which may include legal, professional, and regulatory environments (Baxter and Chua 2003). The design of an MCS will be influenced by the complex interactions between, and the expectations of, those various environments.

Euske and Riccaboni (1999) draw on the work of Fligstein (1991) and Fligstein and Freeland (1995) to interpret their case study of an Italian bank. Fligstein proposes that the senior manager in an organization is responsible for maintaining control of internal and external interdependencies, managing resources, and initiating change. The manager's view provides the conduit through which events and environments are interpreted. Thus, the design of the MCS is an outcome of the manager's interpretations of the demands of the institutional environment, which leads to an awareness of what events need to be controlled and how they should be controlled.

Credito Italiano was a large Italian bank, and the case study focused on the role of the MCS during the privatization process. While the privatization led to changes in the external and internal independencies, at the same time the state was redefining the parameters of the banking and financial markets. The researchers interviewed senior managers over a two-year period to track the changes in the bank, its management, and the activities of the state and other institutional environments over thirty years. For example, in the early 1990s, the state made many changes to the Italian banking environment, making it more market oriented and enhancing competitiveness. This moved the criteria for success for the bank to that of 'managing risk to produce a profit'. The CEO of more than twenty years instituted a series of changes in the MCS, implementing new budgeting systems, costing systems, compensation systems, and reporting systems, which provided a MCS consistent with the expectations of the new banking environment. Up to that time the MCS had played a symbolic role, but now the MCS consisted of tools that were necessary in the new efficiency-based environment. The move towards privatization created a new focus on bottom-line results and efficiency, and there was a greater need for accurate service costing information. Structures and systems were created to support that new focus. The new budgeting system emphasized the increased levels of autonomy granted to area managers and a new profit-based strategy. The CEO provided the direction for change within the bank through his interpretations of the external interdependencies and what needed to be done to retain legitimacy in the eyes of the banking regulators and the market.

An institutional interpretation of the MCS–strategy relation provides quite a different perspective to that of the other theoretical frameworks that have been discussed. There is recognition of the influence of a range of interdependent environments, particularly those external to the organization, and systems may be implemented and change made not always for rational reasons, but sometimes driven for the need to maintain legitimacy in the eyes of external players. To date there have been few studies of MSC–strategy studies that have utilized institutional theory.

11.3.3 POSITIVIST CASE STUDIES AND MIXED METHOD STUDIES

While MCS–strategy research can be delineated as following a contingency framework or an 'alternative' sociological theory, there are other 'middle ground' approaches that have been taken. These studies tend to follow a positivist perspective, in that they assume a more objective than subjective reality. They often draw on literature from organizational theory, economics, and organizational behaviour, among others, and sometimes combine quantitative and qualitative analysis within fieldwork-based case studies. For example, Simons' paper (1990) of two case studies focuses on how managers used controls under different strategic and environmental situations. Abernethy and Lillis (1995) conducted interviews to collect quantitative and qualitative data from a range of companies to understand the design of MCS and flexibility strategies. Davila (2000) presented four case studies to explore the diversity of practices in product development projects and the design of MCS, and followed this up with a mail survey to study product innovation strategies as a driver of MCS design. Slagmulder (1997) conducted ten case studies focused on the adaptation of MCS for strategic investment decisions. Chenhall and Langfield-Smith (2003) was a single case study that explored the match and mismatch between business strategy and performance measurement and reward systems over fifteen years. Malina and Selto (2001) conducted an extensive interview survey to explore the effectiveness of the BSC as a strategy communication and management control device. Marginson (2002) provided a single case study of the nature and extent of the MCS–strategy relationship at middle- and lower-management levels, and the effects that the design and use of three groups of MCS had on the development of new ideas and initiatives. Three of these studies will be explained in more detail.

11.3.3.1 Theory building from two contrasting case studies—Simons (1990)

Simons (1990) reports two case studies which illustrate the relation between strategic position and senior managers' use of management controls. Company A was a defender, a cost leader, and adaptive, while Company B was a prospector, followed a differentiation strategy (based on product innovation and quality), and was entrepreneurial. Company A operated in a relatively stable environment and many aspects that were important for sustainable competitive advantage were highly controllable, and therefore were treated as diagnostic controls. Interactive control focused on the strategic uncertainties of product or technological change that could undermine the company's low-cost position. Company B used budgeting systems and planning systems interactively to set agendas to debate strategy and action plans in the face of rapidly changing environmental conditions. Simons found that subjective reward systems motivate organizational learning in rapidly changing environments where rewarding team effort is important.

This paper laid the foundation for Simons' levers of control framework that distinguishes between diagnostic and interactive controls (Simons 1995), which was developed further in subsequent papers and books.

11.3.3.2 Fieldwork combining quantitative and qualitative data—Abernethy and Lillis (1995)

Abernethy and Lillis (1995) interviewed managers of forty-two manufacturing business to study the impact of a manufacturing flexibility strategy on the design of two aspects of MCS: performance measurement systems and structural arrangements required to coordinate activities (integrative devices). The interviews provided the opportunity to make both quantitative assessment (using established measurement scales) and qualitative assessments of each of the variables. Flexibility was defined as technological difficulty in making product changes, strategic commitment to flexibility, and turnaround time to meet customer demands. Integrative liaison devices included the use of teams, task forces, meetings, and spontaneous contacts. Performance measures were focused on the use and relative importance of efficiency-based performance measures. As predicted they found a positive relation between a flexibility strategy and the use of integrative liaison devices. These devices supported the functional interdependencies that were needed to achieve flexibility effectively. Irrespective of the degree of focus on flexibility, there was a positive relation between the use of integrative liaison devices and firm performance. However, there was a negative relation between the use of efficiency-based performance measures for the evaluation of manufacturing performance and the commitment to flexibility, and in only firms that were 'not flexible' did the use of efficiency-based performance measures correlate with higher firm performance.

This study is unusual as the method was effectively a survey. However, it was administered face-to-face, which allowed for more detailed investigation and provided more insights than a postal survey as it allowed both quantitative and qualitative data to be collected.

11.3.3.3 Model building in a single case study—Malina and Selto (2001)

Malina and Selto (2001) studied the effectiveness of the BSC as a strategy communication and management control device. They conducted telephone interviews with many managers across a division of a large manufacturing company. The interviews were analysed using complex coding procedures, based on theoretical constructs, and derived causal relations between constructs. The level of detail disclosed about the coding and analysis process is extensive and contributes to their desire to enhance the reliability and credibility of their analysis and conclusions.

In the case study, managers reorganized their resources and activities to achieve the required performance targets, which they perceived as improving the overall performance of the company. However, difficulties in the design and implementation of the BSC affected its credibility among managers, resulting in conflict and tension and an inability of the BSC to meet its stated outcomes. Problems included the development of inaccurate or subjective measures, a top-down rather than participatory communication process, and the use of inappropriate benchmarks for performance evaluation. These problems have been found in other studies of performance measurement systems (Simons 2000; Merchant 1989; Ittner et al. 2003). The paper provided evidence that the BSC may provide opportunities for the development and communication of strategy, and a means for controlling strategy.

11.4 **Summary and conclusion**

The purpose of this chapter was to explain the various approaches that have been taken in research that has addressed the relationships between strategy and MCS. This stream of research only emerged in the 1980s, and there have been many developments in the ways that the research has been conceptualized and operationalized.

The majority of papers up to the mid-1990s adopted a conventional positivist approach, informed by a contingency perspective. While this could have provided the opportunity for building up a body of research findings about how strategy and MCS relate, which could be generalized across many different types of organizational situations, this did not eventuate due to differences in the way that variables were defined and measured, differences in the focus of the control systems, and the consequent conflicting findings (Langfield-Smith 1997). There is also a limitation to the potential insights that can be developed from cross-sectional, arm's-length surveys.

The more innovative quantitative and qualitative approaches that have followed have adopted different theoretical perspectives and utilize methods, which allow the dynamics of the MCS and strategy relation to be studied. At times strategy is not a formalized discrete variable. Rather, it may be implicit, emerging through interactions and processes. This can make it difficult to study and to understand. However, case studies utilizing qualitative data may provide depth and insights into how MCS and strategy may interact, which is a perspective not available in cross-sectional survey-based contingency studies. However, as with contingency studies, it is difficult to integrate findings across qualitative studies as they often focus on different aspects of controls and strategies and draw on various interpretative frameworks which have differing areas of focus. However, these alternative approaches are still in their infancy and there is potential for knowledge to accumulate.

There have been interesting conceptual developments which may inform future studies, including the levers of control and the BSC. These models provide possibilities for more complex conceptions of MCS and strategy, and we have only just started to see research studies that have utilized these ideas. In critiquing this area we need to remember that it has only been two decades since formal research into the MCS–strategy relation commenced.

☐ NOTES

1 Langfield-Smith (1997) provided a review of survey research to 1992 and case study research up to 1995.
2 Baxter and Chua (2003) use the term 'alternative management accounting research' to characterize seven non-positivist approaches.
3 These were an outcome of the factor analysis of thirty-three individual controls, which themselves were derived from an analysis of interviews with managers.

☐ REFERENCES

Abernethy, M. A. and Brownell, P. (1999). 'The Role of Budgets in Organizations Facing Strategic Change: An Exploratory Study', *Accounting, Organizations and Society*, 24: 189–204.
—— and Lillis, A. M. (1995). 'The Impact of Manufacturing Flexibility on Management Control System Design', *Accounting, Organizations and Society*, 20(4): 241–58.

Abernethy, M. A. and Brownell, P. (2001). 'Interdependencies in Organization Design: A Test in Hospitals', *Management Accounting Research*, 13: 107–29.

Ahrens, T. and Chapman, C. (2002). 'The Structuration of Legitimate Performance Measures and Management: Day-to-day Contests of Accountability in a U.K. Restaurant Chain', *Management Accounting Research*, 13(2): 1–21.

Andrews, K. R. (1980). *The Concept of Corporate Strategy*. Homewood, IL: Richard D. Irwin.

Anthony, R. N. (1965). *Planning and Control Systems: A Framework for Analysis*. Boston: Harvard University Press.

Ashby, W. R. (1960). *Design for a Brain, the Origin of Adaptive Behavior*. New York: John Wiley and Sons.

Baines, A. and Langfield-Smith, K. (2003). 'Antecedents to Management Accounting Change: A Structural Equation Approach', *Accounting, Organizations and Society*, 28: 675–98.

Baxter, J. and Chua, W. F. (2003). 'Alternative Management Accounting Research—Whence and Whither', *Accounting, Organizations and Society*, 28: 97–126.

Bisbe, J. and Otley, D. (2004). 'The Effects of the Interactive Use of Management Control Systems on Product Innovation', *Accounting, Organizations and Society*, 29: 709–37.

Boland, R. J., Jr. (1996). 'Why Shared Meanings Have no Place in Structuration Theory: A Reply to Scapens and Macintosh', *Accounting, Organizations and Society*, 21(7/8): 691–7.

Brickley, J., Smith, C., and Zimmerman, J. (1997). *Managerial Economics and Organizational Architecture*. Burr Ridge, IL: Richard D. Irwin.

Briers, M. and Chua, W. F. (2001). 'The Role of Actor-Networks and Boundary Objects in Management Accounting Change: A Field Study of an Implementation of Activity-Based Costing', *Accounting, Organizations and Society*, 26(3): 237–69.

Burns, T. and Stalker, G. M. (1961). *The Management of Innovation*. London: Tavistock.

Bushman, R. M., Indjejikian, R. J., and Smith, A. (1995). 'Aggregate Performance Measures in Business Unit Manager Compensation: The Role of Intrafirm Interdependencies', *Journal of Accounting Research*, 33: 101–28.

Callon, M. (1986). 'Some Elements of a Sociology of Translation: Domestication of the Scallops and the Fishermen of St. Brieuc Bay', in J. Law (ed.), *Power, Action and Belief: A New Sociology of Knowledge?* Sociological Review Monograph: 32. London: Routledge and Kegan Paul, pp. 196–233.

Carr, S., Mak, Y. T, and Needham, J. E. (1997). 'Differences in Strategy, Quality Management Practices and Performance Reporting Systems between ISO-Accredited and non-ISO-Accredited Companies', *Management Accounting Research*, 8: 383–403.

Chandler, A. (1962). *Strategy and Structure*. Boston: MIT Press.

Chenhall, R. H. (2003). 'Management Control Systems Design within its Organizational Context: Findings from Contingency-Based Research and Directions for the Future', *Accounting Organizations and Society*, 28(2/3): 127–68.

—— and Langfield-Smith, K. (1998). 'The Relationship between Strategic Priorities, Management Techniques and Management Accounting: An Empirical Investigation Using a Systems Approach', *Accounting, Organizations and Society*, 23(3): 243–64.

—— —— (2003). 'The Role of Employee Pay in Sustaining Organisational Change', *Journal of Management Accounting Research*, 15: 117–43.

Collins, F., Holtzmann, O., and Mendoza, R. (1997). 'Strategy, Budgeting, and Crisis in Latin America', *Accounting, Organizations and Society*, 7: 669–89.

Cyert, R. M. and March, J. G. (1963). *A Behavioral Theory of the Firm*. Englewood Cliffs, NJ: Prentice Hall.

Daniel, S. J. and Reitsperger, W. D. (1994). 'Strategic Control Systems for Quality: An Empirical Comparison of the Japanese and U.S. Electronics Industry', *Journal of International Business Studies*, 25(2): 275–94.

Davila, T. (2000). 'An Empirical Study on the Drivers of Management Control Systems design in New Product Development', *Accounting, Organizations and Society*, 25: 383–409.

de Haas, M. and Kleingeld, A. (1999). 'Multilevel Design of Performance Measurement Systems: Enhancing Strategic Dialogue Throughout the Organization', *Management Accounting Research*, 10: 233–361.

de Wit, B. and Meyer, R. (2004). *Strategy: Process, Content, Context*. London: Thompson.

Dent, J. F. (1990). 'Strategy, Organization and Control: Some Possibilities for Accounting Research', *Accounting, Organizations and Society*, 15: 3–25.

DiMaggio, P. J. and Powell, W. W. (1983). 'The Iron Cage Revisited: Institutional Isomorphism and Collective Rationality in Organizational Fields', *American Sociological Review*, 48: 147–60.

Euske, K. J. and Riccaboni, A. (1999). 'Stability to Profitability: Managing Interdependencies to Meet a New Environment', *Accounting, Organizations and Society*, 24: 463–81.

Fisher, J. (1995). 'Contingency-based Research on Management Control Systems: Categorization by Level of Complexity', *Journal of Accounting Literature*, 14: 24–53.

—— and Govindarajan, V. (1993). 'Incentive Compensation Design, Strategic Business Unit Mission, and Competitive Strategy', *Journal of Management Accounting Research*, 5: 129–44.

Flamholtz, E. G. (1983). 'Accounting, Budgeting and Control Systems in Their Organizational Context: Theoretical and Empirical Perspectives', *Accounting, Organizations and Society*, 8: 153–74.

Fligstein, N. (1991). 'The Structural Transformation of American Industry: An Institutional Account of the Causes of Diversification in the Largest Firms, 1919–1979', in W. W. Powell and P. J. DiMaggio (eds.), *The New Institutionalism in Organizational Analysis*. Chicago: University of Chicago Press, pp. 311–36.

—— and Freeland, R. (1995). 'Theoretical and Comparative Perspectives on Corporate Organization', *Annual Review of Sociology*, 21: 21–43.

Giddens, A. (1976). *New Rules of Sociological Method: A Positive Critique of Interpretive Sociologies*. London: Hutchinson.

—— (1979). *Central Problems in Social Theory: Action, Structure and Contradiction in Social Analysis*. London: Macmillan Press.

Govindarajan, V. and Fisher, J. (1990). 'Strategy, Control Systems, and Resource Sharing: Effects on Business-Unit Performance', *Academy of Management Journal*, 33(2): 259–85.

—— and Gupta, A. K. (1985). 'Linking Control Systems to Business Unit Strategy: Impact on Performance', *Accounting, Organizations and Society*, 20: 51–66.

Gupta, A. K. (1987). 'SBU Strategies, Corporate-SBU, and SBU Effectiveness in Strategy Implementation', *Academy of Management Journal* 20: 477–500.

—— and Govindarajan, V. (1984). 'Business Unit Strategy, Managerial Characteristics, and Business Unit Effectiveness at Strategy Implementation', *Academy of Management Journal,* 27: 25–42.

Hax, A. C. and Maljuf, N. S. (1996). *The Strategy Concept and Process: A Pragmatic Approach.* Upper Saddle River, NJ: Prentice Hall.

Henri, J. F. (2006). 'Management Control Systems and Strategy: A Resource-Based Perspective', *Accounting, Organizations and Society,* forthcoming.

Hopper, T., Storey, J., and Willmott, H. (1987). 'Accounting for Accounting: Towards the Development of a Dialectical View', *Accounting, Organizations and Society,* 12: 437–56.

Hoque, Z. and James, W. (2000). 'Linking Balanced Scorecard Measures to Size and Market Factors: Impact on Organizational Performance', *Journal of Management Accounting Research,* 12: 1–17.

Ittner, C. D. and Larcker, D. F. (1997). 'Quality Strategy, Strategic Control Systems, and Organizational Performance', *Accounting, Organizations and Society,* 22(3/4): 295–314.

—— —— (1998). 'Are Non-Financial Measures Leading Indicators of Financial Performance? An Analysis of Customer Satisfaction', *Journal of Accounting Research,* 36 (Suppl.): 1–35.

—— —— and Meyer, M. W. (2003). 'Subjectivity and the Weighting of Performance Measures: Evidence from a Balanced Scorecard', *Accounting Review,* 78(3): 725–58.

—— —— and Randall, T. (2003). 'Performance Implications of Strategic Performance Measurement in Financial Services Firms', *Accounting, Organizations and Society,* 28: 715–41.

Kaplan, R. S. and Norton, D. P. (1996). *The Balanced Scorecard—Translating Strategy into Action.* Boston: Harvard Business School Press.

Knight, D. and Wilmot, H. (1993). 'It's a Very Foreign Discipline: The Genesis of Expenses Control in a Mutual Life Insurance Company', *British Journal of Management,* 4(1): 1–18.

Langfield-Smith, K. (1997). 'Management Control Systems and Strategy: A Critical Review', *Accounting, Organizations and Society,* 22: 207–32.

—— and Smith, D. (2003). 'Management Control and Trust in Outsourcing Relationships', *Management Accounting Research,* 14(3): 281–307.

Latour, B. (1987). *Science in Action.* Cambridge, MA: Harvard University Press.

—— (1993). *We Have Never Been Modern.* Harlow: Prentice Hall.

Lawrence, P. and Lorsch, J. (1967). *Organization and its Environment.* Boston: Harvard University Press.

Macintosh, N. B. and Scapens, R. W. (1990). 'Structuration Theory in Management Accounting', *Accounting, Organizations and Society,* 15: 455–77.

Malina, M. A. and Selto, F. H. (2001). 'Communicating and Controlling Strategy: An Empirical Study of the Effectiveness of the Balanced Scorecard', *Journal of Management Accounting Research,* 13: 47–90.

Marginson, D. E. W. (2002). 'Management Control Systems and Their Effects on Strategy Formation at Middle-Management Levels: Evidence from a U.K. Organization', *Strategic Management Journal,* 23: 1019–31.

Merchant, K. A. and van der Stede, W. A. (2003). *Management Control Systems: Performance Measurement, Evaluation and Incentives.* Harlow: Pearson Education.

Meyer, J. and Rowan, B. (1977). 'Institutional Organizations: Formal Structure as Myth and Ceremony', *American Journal of Sociology,* 83: 340–63.

Miles, R. W. and Snow, C. C., *Organizational Strategy, Structure and Process*. New York: McGraw-Hill.

Milgrom, P. and Roberts, J. (1992). *Economics, Organizations and Management*. Englewood Cliffs, NJ: Prentice Hall.

Miller, D. and Friesen, P. H. (1982). 'Innovation in Conservative and Entrepreneurial Firms: Two Models of Strategic Momentum', *Strategic Management Journal*, 3(1): 1–25.

Mintzberg H. (1978). 'Patterns in Strategy Formation', *Management Science*, XXIV: 934–48.

—— (1987). 'Crafting Strategy', *Harvard Business Review*, 65(4): 66–75.

Mouritsen, J. (1999). 'The Flexible Firm: Strategies for a Subcontractor's Management Control', *Accounting, Organizations and Society*, 24(1): 31–56.

—— and Thrane, S. (2005). 'Accounting, Network Complementarities and the Development of Interorganisational Relations', *Accounting, Organizations and Society*.

—— Hansen, A., and Hansen, C. O. (2001). 'Interorganization Controls and Organizational Competencies: Episodes Around Target Cost Management/Functional Analysis and Open Book Accounting', *Management Accounting Research*, 12: 221–44.

Ouchi, W. G. (1979). 'A Conceptual Framework for the Design of Organizational Control Mechanisms', *Management Science*, 25: 833–49.

Perera, S., Harrison, G., and Poole, M. (1997). 'Customer-focused Manufacturing Strategy and the Use of Operations-based Non-financial Performance Measures: A Research Note', *Accounting, Organizations and Society*, 22: 557–72.

Perrow, C. (1967). 'A Framework for the Comparative Analysis of Organizations', *American Sociological Review*, 32: 194–208.

Porter, M. E. (1980). *Competitive Strategy: Techniques of Analyzing Industries and Competitors*. New York: Free Press.

—— (1985). *Competitive Advantage: Creating and Sustaining Superior Performance*. New York: Free Press.

Reitsberger, W. D., Daniel, S. J., Tallman, S. B., and Chismar, W. G. (1993). 'Product Quality and Cost Leadership: Compatible Strategies?', *Management International Review*, 33(1): 7–21.

Roberts, J. (1990). 'Strategy and Accounting in a U.K. Conglomerate', *Accounting, Organizations and Society*, 15(1/2): 107–26.

—— and Scapens, R. (1985). 'Accounting Systems and Systems of Accountability—Understanding Accounting Practices in Their Organizational Contexts', *Accounting, Organizations and Society*, 10: 443–56.

Scapens, R. W. and Macintosh, N. B. (1996). 'Structure and Agency in Management Accounting Research: A Response to Boland's Interpretive Act', *Accounting, Organizations and Society*, 21(7/8): 675–90.

Simons, R. (1987). 'Accounting Control Systems and Business Strategy: An Empirical Analysis', *Accounting, Organizations and Society*, 12: 357–74.

—— (1990). 'The Role of Management Control Systems in Creating Competitive Advantage: New Perspectives', *Accounting, Organizations and Society*, 15: 127–43.

—— (1991). 'Strategic Orientation and Top Management Attention to Control Systems', *Strategic Management Journal*, 12(1): 49–62.

Simons, R. (1994). 'How New Top Managers Use Control Systems as Levels of Strategic Renewal', *Strategic Management Journal*, 15(3): 169–89.

—— (1995). *Levers of Control*. Boston: Harvard University Press.

Slagmulder, R. (1997). 'Using Management Control Systems to Achieve Alignment Between Strategic Investment Decisions and Strategy', *Management Accounting Research*, 8: 103–39.

Thompson, J. D. (1967). *Organizations in Action*. New York: McGraw-Hill.

Tuomela, T. S. (2006). 'The Interplay of Different Levers of Control: A Case Study of Introducing a New Performance Measurement System', *Management Accounting Research*, 16(3): 293–320.

van der Meer-Kooistra, J. and Vosselman, E. (2000). 'Management Control of Inter-firm Transactional Relationships: The Case of Industrial Renovation and Maintenance', *Accounting, Organizations and Society*, 25(1): 51–77.

van der Stede, W. A. (2000). 'The Relationship Between Two Consequences of Budgetary Controls: Budgetary Slack Creation and Managerial Short-term Orientation', *Accounting, Organizations and Society*, 25(6): 609–22.

12 Management accounting, operations, and network relations: debating the lateral dimension

Jan Mouritsen
Allan Hansen

12.1 Introduction

In *Evolution Not Revolution* (1989) and *Pathways to Progress* (1994), Bromwich and Bhimani analyse significant developments in management accounting practices across the world. One of the themes of their work is the question of how accounting extends itself and takes into further consideration new objects such as strategy, manufacturing processes, technology, and markets. They clearly point out that accounting research and practice is at a crossroads where the fundamental identity of management accounting and control are at stake. In Bromwich and Bhimani's words (1994: vii):

> The external and manufacturing environments in many countries ... are undergoing a large variety of rapid changes in an increasingly competitive context. Many firms are adopting innovative production systems, advanced manufacturing technology and many new organisational and managerial techniques. Some commentators believe that management accounting is experiencing a prolonged 'crisis' because it has lagged behind these changes.

Here, Bromwich and Bhimani suggest that management accounting has an identity crisis where its relevance is challenged by changes in other disciplines such as manufacturing or operations management, and perhaps operations management may prove not only to alter management accounting but also to be a possible alternative to management accounting when managing value creation in modern firms. Both management accounting and operations management are concerned with the coordination of organizational and interorganizational spaces, but while the management accounting emphasis may be the hierarchical relation to target setting, motivation, incentives, and rewards, operations management is more concerned with the lateral flows between production places or stations; while the management accounting focus may be with people in an organizational scheme, operations management is more concerned with the flow of products and services through the factory or the firm. These emphases should not be taken too literally but they suffice to indicate that management accounting and operations management have some things to say about the objects that are interesting for the management of the firm.

But what will management accounting and operations management have to say to each other? How may operations be an interesting agenda for management accounting research and practice? Such broad concerns are behind our investigation, which can be narrowed to a question of how management accounting responds to the challenges that operations management poses for itself in research and practice today. In this sense, through analysis of appropriate literature, we ask how management accounting practices are made sense of in operations management research and management accounting research in relation to the central proposition made in the operations management literature, namely the introduction of modern manufacturing systems typically under the auspices of *lean manufacturing*. The lean enterprise images the firm and its entities as 'no islands' but connected relations, a network. This has also energized some management accounting research and therefore there are connections and challenges in the interrelationships between operations and management accounting, some of which are clearly visible in the literature, as we will show in the remainder of the chapter.

First, we focus on what operations management and management accounting say about the sources of performance and then we look at their interchanges on interorganizational control. Through these two debates it is possible, thirdly, to develop a new appreciation of the possibilities of control in modern manufacturing environments: informational and physical/technological carriers of control can form a trading zone where they can stand in for each other.

12.2 Managing operations: lean manufacturing and management accounting

Lean manufacturing is best practice operations management.[1] Karlsson and Åhlström (1996) describe lean manufacturing as a set of thoughts that integrate a firm's development, procurement, manufacturing, and distribution, and it suggests that the firm can best be conceptualized in lateral terms. As illustrated by Figure 12.1, lean manufacturing develops a series of concerns so that the best practice firm can emerge as a form. It is interesting to note that lean manufacturing consists of many different areas of practice and that a priori it is not possible to make a strong demarcation of what is inside and what is outside. In different firms the configuration of the different elements will be assembled differently and, therefore, even if it builds on generally, perhaps universally, best practices, these have to be prioritized in each situation.

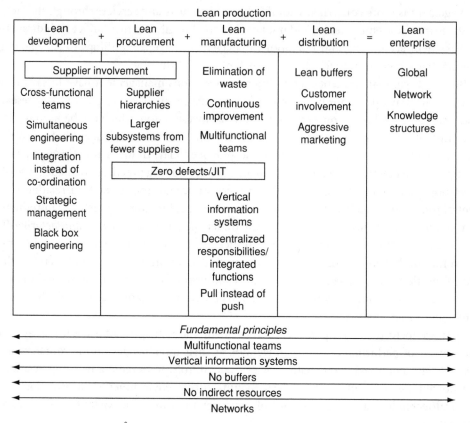

Lean production

| Lean development | + | Lean procurement | + | Lean manufacturing | + | Lean distribution | = | Lean enterprise |

Figure 12.1 Karlsson and Åhlström's conceptualization of lean manufacturing (1996: 26)

Table 12.1 also suggests that lean management is tied neither only to the production space nor to an individual firm. There is a clear lateral orientation of the firm where the principle of assembling and moving a product or a service into, through, and beyond the firm is fundamental to an understanding of how value is created. Lean manufacturing is radical here, even to the point that there is a reluctance to regard management as a value-adding activity, and to the extent possible, shop floor workers should coordinate activities rather than management cadres. The ambition is to minimize the number of management layers in the firm: it is not the hierarchical but the lateral orientation that is advocated. Hierarchical activities are non-value added.

This is a big agenda. Lind (2001) demonstrates that lean manufacturing (or world-class manufacturing) is different from traditional manufacturing in a series of respects (see Table 12.1). The table shows two extreme versions of the organization of manufacturing operations. While lean or world-class manufacturing are fast, flow-orientated, responsive, decentralized, and customer-orientated, traditional manufacturing is slow, hierarchical, bureaucratic, centralized, and production-oriented. There is little doubt about which one is preferred: lean or world-class manufacturing is a benchmark best practice that is relevant,

Table 12.1 Lind's conceptualization (2001) of the differences between lean manufacturing or world-class manufacturing and traditional manufacturing

Aspect	World-class manufacturing	Traditional manufacturing
Technology Product structure		
Customization	High degree of product differentiation and fast response to customer demand.	Low degree of product differentiation and slow response to customer demand.
New products	New products are a significant part of the total volume of production. Time to market is important.	New products are not a significant part of the volume of production. Time to market is not so important.
Production technology		
Automation of equipment —Machinery automation —Administrative automation —Number of operations	High degree of automation in both machinery and administrative routines. Few operations and few set-ups, a short set-up time, and flexible machine centres.	Low degree of automation in both machinery and administrative routines. Many operations and multiple set-ups, a long set-up time, and many discrete machines.
Sequence of operations in terms of workflow rigidity	Variable.	Variable.
Specificity of evaluation of operations	High degree of quality control in the machines.	Low degree of quality control in the machines.
Continuity of the units of throughput —Batch size	No change in the production system. Small batch sizes.	No change in the production system. Large batch sizes.
Production layout		
Physical grouping of the machines	Flow-based layout. Short throughput time.	Functional layout. Long throughput time.
Organization structure **Company level**		
Differentiation-integration	Less need of integration functions such as production planning.	Several functions such as production planning integrate the company.
Centralization	Responsibility and authority are delegated within the company.	Responsibility and authority are concentrated to the senior managers.
Specialization	Less need of specialization functions.	Several functions are specialized within a particular area.
Hierarchy	There are few organizational levels and few managers.	There are several organizational levels and several managers.
Work level		
Differentiation-integration	Activities are combined into complex tasks. Work group organization. The wage system is group based.	Activities are combined into simple tasks. Individual piecework organization. The wage system is individual piece rate.

(contd.)

Table 12.1 (*contd.*)

Aspect	World-class manufacturing	Traditional manufacturing
Centralization	Delegation of responsibility and authority. For example, the workers are responsible for the quality.	Concentration of responsibility and authority. For example, specialized workers responsible for inspection of the quality.
Specialization	Mastery of multiple skills through training.	Labour is semi-skilled and specialized.
Hierarchy	Coordination and advice.	Instructions.

while the traditional form is merely boring. Lean manufacturing is more than a practice; it is an aspiration that is formulated in positive terms, in terms claiming that all organizational ills can be resolved by the one and same remedy. There is no hesitance in lean manufacturing; there is no doubt. The preferred model is in place; now it is for practice to follow suit. There is no serious alternative and therefore there are no 'pros and cons'—only 'pros'. If they do not work in individual situations, it is a matter of mistaken implementation.

Looking at Figure 12.1 and Table 12.1, it is clear that there is little room for management accounting in lean manufacturing. There is no mention of accounting calculation; nor is there any mention of the precise form in which management control is supposed to happen. It just happens: if the structural conditions are in place, lean manufacturing will work. Accounting, it appears, has no input to operations management activities. This is noteworthy because in operations management texts there is no shortage of ambitions to reduce cost. Cost is a common performance criterion in operations management but cost accounting is frowned on. There is therefore an interesting paradox—costs are important but the techniques that produce them are not. To get a bit closer to how management accounting and operations management deal with cost and performance, the rest of this section considers management accounting and operations management research on issues of performance.

12.2.1 COST ACCOUNTING AS A PROBLEM FOR OPERATIONS

The field of operations management is generally hostile to control devised by cost accounting. Schoenberger (1990: 188) is vivid about this:

Controlling what causes costs is logical, direct, and effective. It replaces the ineffective conventional approach to cost control, which is the carrot and the stick: a limp carrot and a thin stick. The cost-variance report was the stick. It said, Cut your costs, or else. But it offered no specific hints as to how. The limp was the pay and reward systems—again not tied much that was specific and clearly worthy of reward.

And he continues (Schoenberger 1996: 113):

Don't try to pin down all costs.... Instead, drive costs down and quality, response time, and flexibility up by plotting quality, cycle time, set up time, etc. on large visible screens on the wall. This is the cost-effective way there is for upper managers and line employees alike to size up results and take pride in accomplishments.

In both places, Schoenberger ridicules accounting for its ambiguities and lack of answers to what to do. Cost accounting, it appears, is presented as unable to provide answers that are understandable and guide a future. The 'non-monetary process data are the lifeblood of improvement projects.... [They] tell what needs to be done and, to a very large extent, prioritize those needs. Cost data are not part of that improvement methodology' (1996: 104). Cost accounting is—from the perspective of operations—a problem rather than a solution. It brings the carrot and the stick but no remedy to solve problems. It mystifies organizational arrangements because through allocation mechanisms nobody understands what goes on. Even 'modern' cost accounting such as activity-based costing (ABC) is a problem. It may be that attention to activities and causation is fine, but the bureaucracy associated with the production and use of this information is unbearable; and still it is too cursory:

One reason is the ABC paradox. If the method employs few cost drivers, the cost data may be too imprecise to be useful at the level of an improvement project.... Cost analysis will want to employ many cost drivers for greater precision. Then, however, the ABC methods become too complex to be understood, believed in, and willingly and confidently used by the improvement team. (Schoenberger 1996: 105–6)

Cost accounting—even it its most 'modern' form—is a misspecification, and 'we can agree at least that the conventional accounting system with its overhead allocation does not tell a straight story. What does, at the operational level, are process data' (1996: 106). Process data are better not only because they are clearer but also because they engage a more interesting theory of business behaviour through total quality management (TQM):

TQM clarifies objectives and restates them as universal principles of good business practice. Less rework, flow distance, set-up time, throughput time, process variation—the common stuff of continuous improvement—*always* are cost-beneficial. (Schoenberger 1996: 104)

The critique of accounting is monumental and fundamental: accounting misrepresents and distorts; it creates carrots and sticks but no specific indication of how things can be improved; and it develops bureaucracy. Operations, on the other hand, develop 'universal principles of good business practice' and develop actions that are always preferable through process-oriented information and actions. Accounting delays important improvement activities.

12.2.2 PERFORMANCE IN LEAN PRINCIPLES

The problem of accounting has not always been as critical as it is now. Transformation of manufacturing systems from traditional to world-class manufacturing or lean production systems has developed a lateral orientation in contrast to hierarchical orientation in the conception of what has to be managed. There are five principles:

[S]pecify value by specific product, identify the value stream for each product, make value flow without interruptions, let customer pull value from the producer and pursue perfection. (Womack and Jones 2003: 10)

The lean firm is one where the product rather than the organization is central to understanding the firm. Production technologies are developed around the product, and the value stream constitutes the flow so that functions and entities perform services to the product. The flow is a perspective on the firm but it is also a performance criterion: everything that can halt the flow is non-value added, and therefore time and waste are central concerns. Waste can have many forms. Superfluous materials, time, idle equipment, and inventory are examples, and it is claimed that many companies waste 70–90 per cent of their available resources. Lean manufacturing attempts to get rid of waste through a bundle of separate techniques such as cellular manufacturing, pull scheduling/just in time (JIT; Kanban), six sigma/TQM, rapid set-up, and team development. Cellular manufacturing is an example of directed attention to the flow of the product between production locations. To allow this to happen fast, stumbling blocks have to be erased through attention to waste and failure. To develop productivity and cost consideration, the firm has to be flexible; and to be flexible, it has to be dependable, which requires speed, and in turn this requires quality to be in place. Or: quality → speed → dependability → flexibility → cost reduction (e.g. Slack et al. 1998: 680).

This is a line of transformation where to reach cost objectives—which appear to be central to operations management—the firm (or management) has to be sure that quality is in order, which will allow speed to be in place; with speed, dependability can be assured, which again is a condition for flexibility; flexibility is the precondition for cost reduction. Cost is the general lagging indicator while a series of non-financial information constitutes a sequence of leading indicators beginning with quality and ending with flexibility.

12.3 Financial and non-financial information

Operations management has a fairly clear sequence of leading and lagging indicators, and non-financial—i.e. operational—data and information are important here. The literature crossing accounting and operations is clear on this and a significant survey-based literature exists that tests this proposition, and it generally finds that conventional accounting information is relatively absent in lean manufacturing environments and that instead non-financial information takes precedence.

Research suggests that with lean production (JIT production systems, quality management emphasis, and teamwork), there is more attention to non-financial, quality, and productivity measures in the factory (Foster and Horngren 1988; Banker et al. 1993; Carr et al. 1997; Daniel et al. 1995; Mia 2000; Hoque et al. 2001), and for the strategic purposes (Chenhall 1997; Mia 2000). Flexibility and customer orientation correlate with increased emphasis on non-financial information (Abernathy and Lillis 1995; Perrera et al. 1997; Baines and Langfield-Smith 2003). Also non-financial information is sometimes a leading indicator for financial performance (Nagar and Rajan 2001).

More specifically, TQM programmes are often seen as central to modern manufacturing (Daniel and Reitsperger 1991; 1992), and TQM, external benchmarking, and the integration of quality and strategic information are important (Ittner and Larcker 1995). Quality programmes and a series of strategic controls are related (Ittner and Larcker 1997), and there is higher customer and quality performance in TQM and JIT situations than in traditional situations (Sim and Killough 1998).

This survey-based research largely confirms one central thesis produced by lean manufacturing, namely that financial accounting information is of less value in managing advanced manufacturing environments than is non-financial information. The management of the firm goes along other routes, and accounting calculation, if at all, is a lagging indicator that per se leads nowhere. It is the final performance measure, but when it is realized it is too late and too ambiguous to be of help and value in the forward-looking management of the firm.

However, looking at the case-based—rather than survey-based—research about the roles of accounting calculation in manufacturing settings the evidence is different, and accounting calculations turn out to be of much higher significance in developing and operating the manufacturing space, as will be shown below. Here, though, accounting calculation takes on surprising roles.

12.4 Structural and executional cost drivers

The challenge proposed by operations management to management accounting and the responses made by some parts of the academic accounting community as stipulated above are, however, not the only possible way to think about the role of management accounting and accounting calculation. One interesting distinction is made by Shank and Govindarajan (1993) who identify structural and executional cost drivers. Structural cost drivers are concerned with the economics of structure, technology, and the boundaries of the firm (e.g. outsourcing), and executional cost drivers are concerned with continuous improvement such as quality, productivity, speed, and punctuality. Structural cost drivers are always considered in the context of trade-offs between configurations of things, e.g. between costs and benefits of a centralized versus a decentralized firm or a modern versus conventional manufacturing paradigm—this type of cost driver can be understood as always involved in 'pros and cons'. Shank and Govindarajan suggest that even issues such as modern manufacturing cannot be taken for granted because, at least in principle, modern manufacturing could be a disadvantage if, for example, unique products were produced. Structural cost drivers concern the economics of a configuration of things—the configuration of complementarities (Milgrom and Roberts 1995). Traditional production has one configuration and lean production has another configuration and each may be, at least in principle, advantageous in different situations.

In contrast, each of the executional cost drivers are not related to trade-offs—there are only 'pros'. They are one-dimensional and 'more is always better': better quality, faster cycle times, more productivity, less waste, etc. are always preferred. This does not mean that it is easy to determine the range of executional cost drivers to be in place, but a given set of executional cost drivers maintains that management decisions are 'easy' because decision-makers focus on immediately understandable, operational, non-financial information. Such information is seen as objective and has a common-sense interpretation that can be felt on the body of the decision-maker; such information is said to be concrete in the sense that most have a common sense of their qualities and all can act on it—e.g. time:

Time's major advantage as a management tool is that it forces analysis down to a physical level.... This physical way of looking at the business gives managers more insight and power in looking for ways to improve results than cost analysis typically can.... Once a manager sees a layout of where time goes, he or she can start to translate it into cost reduction opportunities. But looking at cost analyses first doesn't often tell anyone where to save time. (Stalk and Hout 1990: 192–3)

Time is 'concrete' because all have a watch; quality is 'concrete' because all have experienced malfunctioning products; waste is 'concrete' because all know that it is expensive; and so on. Executional cost drivers are thus tightly connected to human experience. Executional cost drivers are therefore practical. They are near to direct translations of ordinary human experience and the irritations that accompany lack of foresight and engagement. They make the management of the firm akin to the self-management of ordinary lives. And, by implication, the management of the firm can be delegated to all.

It is easy to see that lean management is often explained around executional cost drivers and evades attention to questions regarding structural cost drivers. In the operations management literature this is witnessed by a clear preference for *best practice* solutions so that the development of advisable forms of production is generally across all situations, and this is why the principle of lean production is generally favoured to traditional production philosophy. Lean is simply a generally accepted production form and, consequently, in operations management there is but little attention to the structural problem of choosing a production regime—there is no decision to be made about structural cost drivers in operations management.

There is a relationship between structural and executional cost drivers, however. In their discussion of time-based management in a production firm, Mouritsen and Bekke (1997) show how the executional cost driver 'time' as speed and punctuality cannot exist without the construction of a space through structural cost drivers, which configure the production space so that time can be the primary managerial lever. Time, whether lead time, throughput time, speed, or punctuality, is a one-dimensional performance indicator. It evades decision-making situations where different types of managerial issues are compared such as productivity versus flexibility or inventory versus capacity utilization. Time has to be reduced (speed) and adhered to (punctuality).

These imperatives are only sound when other measures are already in place. Certain mechanisms to simplify production are crafted structurally prior to production and make time a possible management lever. One mechanism is to develop a group of mobile workers who go to the place in the factory where there is a bottleneck. Rather than making complex decisions about how to use scarce capacity, which would require more than time information to execute, new capacity is added. Another mechanism is to situate component inventories with suppliers until paid for even if used by the firm, which seemingly effaces the 'waste' that inventories constitute. A third mechanism is to turn finished goods into marketing devices in sales companies, which removes finished goods from the factory and makes them the responsibility of others; again the 'waste' of inventories has been erased. These three mechanisms are structural conditions that take certain decisions out of the production space, which is emptied of decisions that require 'conflicting' objectives to be in place. All three mechanisms mediate between productivity and flexibility, or between inventories and capacity utilization. They all help produce the situation where time can be allowed to be a primary decision parameter.

The distinction between structural and executional cost drivers develops a new relation between management accounting and operations management. Operations management is concerned with a space that is amenable to management through executional cost drivers where one-dimensional information can reign. This is where the complexities of trade-offs are put beyond the scope of management interventions because the structural concerns of a production arrangement have been managed in a different place. This is the effect of operations management's critique of management accounting, which is seen as irrelevant because it mystifies the firm through its calculations. But this is perhaps what is necessary to make decisions about structural cost drivers that are always related to questions about what would happen if the production space were organized differently. There are accounting calculations around lean manufacturing!

12.5 Accounting in lean manufacturing

Is there also accounting in lean manufacturing? Ezzamel and Willmott (1998), Lind (2001), and Jazayeri and Hopper (1999) each in their way suggest that even if lean management does pay heightened attention to the primacy of management at the production face and does elevate the shop floor into the management of the firm, the financial sphere is hardly decoupled form the factory. In Ezzamel and Willmott's case, it is clear that superiors' quest for visibility creates a new layer of control at a distance on top of the information produced at, and for, the shop floor. In Lind's case, factory management is given increased responsibility for standard costs with the introduction of lean manufacturing. And in

Jazayeri and Hooper's case, the accounting department's role remains intact after the implementation of world-class manufacturing, but via a manufacturing resource planning (MRP II) system, traditional cost control is strengthened at the shop floor.

All three examples suggest that with the advent of lean manufacturing there is a substantial transformation of the production space and there is an introduction of new decentralizing principles of management and an increased use of non-financial information on the shop floor. However, they also find that accounting information may increase in importance. This does not mean that the accounting department's role necessarily changes a lot or that complex new forms of accounting are installed. Rather, this research suggests that accounting perpetuates its role in servicing top management with information about the affairs of the firm with a view to, for example, supervision and accountability. The hierarchical gaze would still be intact and the three studies suggest that the often implicit assumption in lean manufacturing that the factory can run the firm by itself is problematical. Top managers want to be in control and accounting helps here. While non-financial measures and local financial considerations may be workable locally (Jönsson 1996), top managers also want control and they cannot accept the array of loosely coupled mechanisms of information typically found in lean manufacturing.

In a sense, Munro and Hatherly's 'New Commercial Agenda' (1993) provides a discourse of this interpretation of lean manufacturing. According to Munro and Hatherly, modern firms organize themselves laterally vis-à-vis the customer and suppliers and this task is performed by middle managers; but modern firms also have to perform hierarchically because of the importance of capital markets, and this is where top managers' role is constituted. There are tensions between those two dimensions of the firm's management. The lateral perspective developed by middle managers in cooperation with suppliers and customers and the hierarchical perspective developed by top managers do different things. It may be that the lateral can be managed by the information and practices, which stand in direct relation to the conversion of supplies into products and services, but this may not be good enough for the management of the firm that sees suppliers, employees, and customers not only as ends (as in supplier, employee, and customer satisfaction) but also as means to other ends (such as profitability and market value). These tensions arise from the modern firm having to respond to various 'stakeholders' not always sharing interests.

Miller and O'Leary (1993, 1994) extend the analysis of the place of modern—or lean—manufacturing. In their analysis of the introduction of modern manufacturing they identify a series of relations between accounting and operations, both in the place of actual advanced production programmes and in the space for the development of aspirations for such advanced production programmes. Accounting is here seen as both a problem and a solution. In a situation of change, accounting cannot be assumed to be one thing, and in their research Miller and O'Leary show that the development of linkages between accounting calculation, the product, manufacturing systems, the person, and national aspirations form productivity. Specifically, among other things, they show how various kinds of strategic and competitor accounting, capacity cost analyses, and investment bundles were introduced to debate the form that manufacturing can have. This shows how accounting attaches and informs debates about competitiveness including speculation on how various types of manufacturing systems would be able to cope with the problems of operations as they develop over time. In various ways accounting calculations are integral to our understanding of what problems manufacturing systems have. And in a transformed factory, the development of accounting calculations is juxtaposed with modelling of the factory layout, which motivates accounting to develop a lateral rather than a hierarchical view of the government of the factory. The relation between manufacturing and accounting is a multifaceted one where accounting calculations are both input and output—even if the structure of accounting calculations changes when they help make the object they attempt to describe amenable to intervention.

Case-based accounting studies of lean manufacturing add a corrective to operations management. They add that accounting calculation has to be seen as a much more pervasive force to understand the transformation of manufacturing practices than presented in the operations literature. They point out, however, that the precise way in which accounting asserts itself can be a variable: it can be a hierarchical mode of power (Ezzamel and Willmott 1998), a strengthening of the production function's responsibility for standard costs (Lind 2001), a problematizing device, which engages the development of the specific form that the lateral flow will have in the development of calculative spaces and lateral accountabilities (Miller and O'Leary 1993, 1994). The lateral space is thus made a managerial object, and accounting, rather than being ousted by lean management, gets new forms and effects under such conditions. This case-based research suggests, in contrast to the survey-based research, that accounting calculation engages lean manufacturing in forceful ways even if accounting departments may not necessarily be involved in this.

An emphasis on lateral flows in the factory is heightened as a research concern when management accounting and operations management research meet. This perspective can be extended beyond the enterprise into the interorganizational space particularly through supply chain management and network-based firms.

12.6 **Managing flows beyond the firm**

Supply chains and networks are part of new version and visions of lean manufacturing where the lateral flow is so strong that it extends the space of operations. Womack and Jones (2003: 20) write:

[L]ean thinking must go beyond the firm . . . to look at the whole: the entire set of activities entailed in creating and sustaining a specific product, from concept through design to actual availability, from the initial sale through order entry and production scheduling to delivery, and from raw materials produced far away and out of sight right into the hands of the customer.

The product is here 'larger' than the firm, but the firm's management has to contemplate, justified again by waste reduction, how the firm can develop a value chain that adds quality and cost reduction to the product. The extended firm is one where the supply and demand chains are crucial objects of decision-making; where the product or service requires collaboration between several firms. To make this collaboration work, increased transparency between the parties is required, lean manufacturing suggests, and Womack et al. (1990: 149) say that information-sharing is pivotal here:

Obviously, for the lean approach to work, the supplier must share a substantial part of its proprietary information about costs and production techniques.

The space between the firm and the supplier is information-rich; otherwise it would not be possible to make the relationship work. This is also the conclusion made in much accounting research on supply and demand chains and on networks' management control systems. However, looking at the two literatures, it appears that accounting research sees the relation as more problematical than operations management research, and often accounting research seeks to find the conditions that make such an arrangement possible whilst the operations management literature simply stresses that information-sharing is important, and to allow this to happen, 'supplier development means making suppliers like a family' (Schoenberger 1986: 156), or a 'chain of customers' has to be installed (Schoenberger 1990). This is an aspiration to make interorganizational relations into a win-win game.

12.6.1 THE SUPPLY CHAIN AND THE ROLE OF ACCOUNTING CALCULATIONS

Operations management claims that information exchange is important, but there is some resistance towards actually analysing how this is to take place. Even if Lamming (1993) and Womack and Jones (2003) cautiously advocate the use of open-book arrangements and target costing, their achievability is analysed more in management accounting research.

There is interest in management accounting research about the possibilities of informing the interorganizational space. Accounting calculations are involved in supply chain relations (Frances and Garnsey 1996; Seal et al. 1999; Seal and Cullen 2004), cost saving and product development across firms (Mouritsen et al. 2001; Cooper and Slagmulder 2004; Kajüter and Kulmala 2005; Wouters et al. 2005), and outsourcing arrangements (Gietzman 1996; Mahama and Chua 2002; Langfield-Smith and Smith 2003). More generally, the design of interorganizational management accounting has been theorized in relation to bureaucracy and markets (Dekker 2004; Håkansson and Lind 2004). Management accounting is intertwined with other forms of governance explained by transaction frequency and uncertainty (Meer-Kooistra and Vosselman 2000; Dekker 2004) and is related to trust and fairness (Seal and Vincent-Jones 1997; Tomkins 2001).

In many respects, the accounting literature echoes some of the central tenets of operations management here. There is a relationship between information and trust: either information creates trust or trust creates information or some combination of this. The exact ways in which trust and information are related is difficult to unravel, but there are relationships. So, in a sense, the management accounting literature accepts that in order for a relationship to exist it has to have informational and social dimensions; to a certain degree the relationship has to be one resembling 'family'.

However, this thesis only goes some way because it assumes that the relationship is 'outside' the firms that make it up, but this is a problem because, in principle, in operations management the product is considered a flow *through* firms and not only between them. Otherwise they would not add to the product or service and thus not add quality or cost reduction to it. Somehow, operations management and most management accounting research accept that interorganizational concerns are on the outside of the firm since they hardly consider how a strategy to develop interorganizational spaces impacts on the firm itself.

A possible alternative can be found in Mouritsen et al. (2001) who analyse the effects of the introduction of interorganizational controls such as target costing and open-book accounting on two focal firms. In both cases the mobilization of new interorganizational controls leads to unexpected results; when outsourcing happens, a new urge to get informed is generated and the new accounting calculations create new types of visibility that can be used reflexively in altering the relationships between the firms. This also requires the focal firm to change: if technology development is outsourced, the focal firms need to reduce 'development' expertise and insource 'coordination' expertise between different technology suppliers. And when open books are created, the focal firm may wish to establish itself as a meta-organizer that takes responsibility for the management of the whole supply chain, thus changing from a singular producer to a supply chain-wide planner. In addition this means that others in the supply chain will have to accept that planning and to a certain degree management activities get outsourced from them when they insource production tasks. This requires new competencies again. The information generated by the new interorganizational accounting calculations can then act on the parties involved in the exchange and continually alter their relationships and dependencies. This also means, however, that each of the parties' position in the supply chain continuously changes and thus there is a movement of strategic capability.

Likewise, Mouritsen and Dechow (2001) illustrate how finding out what the supply chain consists of and how it can be controlled or accounted for is a huge endeavour. Multiple actors promote various kinds of accounting controls and calculations (such as life cycle costing (LCC) and open books) in relation to their preferred version of the supply chain often through the vision of the capabilities possessed by certain groups of actors more than a 'corporate'-wide analysis of core competencies. Organizational actors identify possible interorganizational relations and equip them with accounting calculations to suggest how a configuration of relations and controls can function. There is not only one supply chain; and there is not only one accounting calculation and control mechanism. There are multiple supply chains and controls, at least at the crucial point where really the supply chain is not there but a set of possible and fragile promises that could make sense if made the preferred solution of the firm.

A parallel conclusion can be learned from Mouritsen's study (1999) of the adoption of a manufacturing system because at stake is the question of how far in space an integrated manufacturing system should travel. Staging a debate between an operations management approach that uses ABC and an extensive knowledge of factory operations, one proposition was to make the firm flexible around ability to deliver by maintaining control over all aspects of the production space. Another possibility was voiced, however, which was justified by a contribution accounting argument that if all production activities were outsourced, the firm would have developed flexibility by having outsourced all investments and transformed fixed costs into variable costs. Investments would have been exported and a complex manufacturing operation could be supplanted by extensive interorganizational relations based on substantive outsourcing. Both justified by the foggy concept of flexibility, the two manufacturing strategies were motivated in part by the visibility constructed by accounting calculations and the ease by which actors could attach to these techniques for guidance about appropriate managerial responses. Clearly, these proposals were attached to management competencies; those who could understand the politics of a factory operation preferred insourcing, whilst those comfortable with economic analysis preferred the outsourcing alternative. But also, clearly, the two possible manufacturing systems draw the boundaries around the manufacturing systems differently: the operations management approach is inclusive of the activities to be performed in the firm, while the management accounting approach prefers heavy outsourcing. The place of the boundaries between firm and environment is at stake between these approaches to manufacturing strategy.

These comments suggests that the role of accounting in establishing the supply chain may be more complex than suggested both by operations management and large parts of accounting research. Accounting is hardly one technique that can arbiter various possible supply chains because each of them requires a unique control system to stabilize the relationships between not only the firms involved in the exchange but also the kinds of expertise inside the individual firm, whose power will be affected by the outsourcing activity. This should, however, be no surprise. If accounting calculations were powerful, we should expect them to change things. These things involve, primarily, the reconfiguration of competencies within the firm—the interorganizational relations change the firm involved through the insights provided by accounting calculations.

12.6.2 THE NETWORK ENTERPRISE

The supply chain perspective on interorganizational control clearly stipulates that the firms engaging in cooperation exist before the development of the relations and therefore there is the question about how to develop a (set of) dyadic relationship(s) as discussed above. However, networks of firms may constitute another challenge, as Håkansson and Lind (2004) and Kajüter and Kulmala (2005) point out. Several firms are dependent on each other and have to share information to predict consequences beyond the dyadic relation from, for example, technological advances. Both Håkansson and Lind, and Kajüter and Kulmala suggest that the problem of coordination increases dramatically and that therefore firms engage even more coordinating practices such as ongoing work in cross-functional, cross-company teams and technical support free of charge. In a sense, however, this is not really surprising even if it extends quantatively the concerns raised by research on dyadic relations.

Perhaps more radical is Mouritsen and Thrane's (forthcoming) proposal that network enterprises *are* their system of accounting calculations and controls. They suggest, based on a study of horizontal networks, that accounting calculations and control such as transfer prices, fees to the centre, intellectual capital statements, competency accounts, peer review of actors before they can enter the network, and geographical segmentation, all contribute to creating the boundaries of the network—or creating who is inside and who is outside the network—not only by passively registering network partners but by inscribing them in relation to each other. Through these mechanisms, partner firms' relations to each other are already regulated through accounting calculations and these are the criteria that allow potential partners to enter and failing partners to leave. Mouritsen and Thrane suggest that interorganizational cooperation has to pass the obligatory passage of accounting calculation, which manages, develops, and executes network activities either through self-regulating mechanism, where accounting makes interaction between partner firms easy, or through orchestration mechanisms, where accounting is involved in structuring the partner firms vis-à-vis each other. The accounting calculations reach out and make it possible to connect more spaces than would have been possible by mere attention to the sociality of local places.

In a network—rather than in a proper supply chain where positions among participating firms are fixed—participating firms have to find each other on a project basis and therefore the interorganizational relations are constituted anew all the time. In such a flux, where configurations of partners are found in each project (in principle), the network enterprise controls the rules of interaction through various mechanisms of which accounting calculations are a principal set. The network is more than its owners, who can be expelled if they violate the rules; the network enterprise is stronger than its partners—who are also its owners—who can be expelled if not playing by accounting's rules. The network enterprise is exactly an enterprise because of the accounting.

This will sound strange from an operations management (and probably also from most accounting research) perspective(s). Here, accounting is a possible addendum to a relation between two firms that are already constituted, and if the two (or more) firms give up, there is no relationship. This is not the case in a network.

12.7 Accounting calculations, management control, and the operations environment: debating the lateral dimension

In some sense, management control is in conflict with operations management. According to operations management, management control as performed through accounting calculations mystifies value creation, and various other mechanisms have to be put in place that all are situated much closer to 'practices' than to 'representations'. Yet, the analysis conducted above suggests that accounting research in many ways endorses this view through a series of survey-based research findings, but management accounting through some case-based research also extends it in many ways, turns it on its head, and comes out with a much more profound role for accounting calculations in developing and operating operations within and beyond the enterprise.

Operations management introduces the lateral dimension to a theory of what a firm is and what it does. It makes the product or service a more important management object than people in organizational positions. As such, operations management advances the claim that the lateral dimension be prioritized relative to the hierarchical dimension. To make the lateral work, operations management argues against hierarchy; all that could strengthen hierarchy is ridiculed, and accounting calculations are accused of being more a servant of hierarchy rather than of the flow of products, and thus unable to develop satisfactorily and improve the functioning of the firm. Accounting calculations are enemies of the development of quality, flexibility, and even cost because they mystify the affairs of the firm. In the place of financial numbers, non-financial operating data are more relevant because they help point out what has to be done to improve the business, operations management argues.

Our analysis of this challenge is supportive in many respects and much accounting research has been conducted that confirms many of its central tenets. Accounting research has responded to the challenge of manufacturing by analysing the claims about the relevance of non-financial information, and largely this relevance is confirmed. It is true that, in lean manufacturing environments, attention to non-financial data is higher than in traditional manufacturing, and survey-based research confirms that conventional accounting has less to do in lean environments than in traditional manufacturing environments. However, accounting research also challenges some of the claims made by lean thinking—particularly through case-study research, roles of accounting have been identified that add not only to the operations management literature but also significantly to the body of management accounting knowledge.

12.7.1 ACCOUNTING CALCULATIONS AND INFORMATIONAL CONTROL

Accounting research on lean manufacturing has identified roles of accounting that may be invisible to research on operations management because accounting calculations are prior to the factory. Accounting calculations can have many forms and they are often present when issues involving 'pros and cons' are manifested. They help illuminate and analyse the factory before it is there (Miller and O'Leary 1994) just as they help illuminate the functioning and effects of interorganizational relations before they are there (Mouritsen and Dechow 2001). Accounting calculations are here prior to the factory and the supply chain and they are strongly involved in devising what the factory and the supply chain can be. Here, accounting calculations are rarely conventional accounting techniques such as overheads allocation but more advanced analyses such as customer profitability analysis, life cycle accounting, target costing, and investment bundle analysis. Such movements are often invisible to operations management research because, even if cost is a primary concern, there is little interest in the calculation of cost, which, however, is interesting to operations management practice. Here, accounting calculations are involved in realizing a set of virtual spaces—they are involved in understanding the production space or the interorganizational space before they are set up. They craft spaces of possibility; reversibility and alternative worlds are in place.

Accounting calculations can also be invisible to operations management because they are prior to the operations of operations management. They can delimit the space within which it is possible to govern an operation by one-dimensional, non-financial criteria. As suggested, modern lean manufacturing is a best practice that orientates itself towards the elimination of waste, but for this to be functional, the decision-making in the factory space has to be designed so that questions about trade-offs never enter this space. Accounting calculations that push such decision-making activities out of the factory space helps lean manufacturing. Such accounting calculations and modes of organizing resources can concern the treatment of supplier costs, inventory costs, and capacity constraints, all of which may reduce the need for complex decisions such as flexibility versus productivity, etc. This is where accounting calculations can be involved: they are invisible because they control the boundaries of the factory space from outside—they are not visible to the inside because trade-offs have been exported from this space.

Last, ironically, it is not always clear that increasing attention to non-financial information will necessarily reduce the conventional functions of accounting. It is often seen in case studies that new local information creates better insight not only for the shop floor and its local decision-making; it may also develop new forms of hierarchical visibility when this new information is appropriated and enters new cycles of control and decision-making. Local, operating, non-financial data are not only useful locally but can also be transformed and made part of wider systems of accountability. Likewise, it can be demonstrated that the introduction of lean principles can be accompanied by a stronger conventional cost management focus on production managers, who then are charged with increasing conventional accounting. A paradox this may be, but clearly the hope that cost is to be seen as an effect of the sequence of other non-financial information may be a hypothesis, but it is an uncertain relationship also for lean firms.

12.7.2 NON-FINANCIAL INFORMATION AND THE PROBLEM OF THE REAL

Non-financial information may be more 'real' as operations management points out, and this proposition is also made by numerous survey-based studies. They are operational and therefore real. However, as mentioned earlier, this does not prevent lean manufacturing companies from having cost accounting systems and overhead allocation. So, what does it mean that non-financial information is more real? One question is, obviously, whether it is really true that the common-sense understanding of quality, speed, flexibility, etc. are as unproblematic as operations management assumes. For example, the concept of quality—does it have a clear and robust commons-sense status?

In *Zen and the Art of Motorcycle Maintenance*, Pirsig (1974) presents quality as largely incomprehensible; as an ambition that can never be controlled particularly when it is individualized. There are so many potential 'facts' to look for when addressing quality that it is impossible to know whether two persons direct attention to the same phenomenon when discussing quality. The concept of quality (and dependability, speed, flexibility, etc.) is a personal experience, and therefore it may be difficult to have as much confidence in the common sense that individuals attach to it given that a lean manufacturing factory is a social space. There is therefore uncertainty about the claim that non-financial data are obvious—they may develop misconceptions of the state of affairs or at least disagreements about how to understand what quality is (Wilkinson and Willmott 1995; Mouritsen 1997); what flexibility may mean (Mouritsen 1999); or what customer value is (Vaivio 1999). There is the question of just how far the non-financial data tell a straight story. This may be why there is still a wish to get cost data.

Another reason for the demand for cost data may be that the sequence of non-financial leading indicators to the lagging cost indicator is a highly complex assumption and so many things can go wrong in the translations from quality to dependability to speed to flexibility to cost reduction. Each translation is a problem because it entails the possibility that things could go wrong and therefore the sequence may not be stable. It is, at least, a huge bet and even if often this set of transplantations could be found to exist statistically, the explanatory power of this relation is far from 100 per cent. Therefore, breakdown will be expected rather than the exception, and suddenly non-financial data will not reflect pure story—they will not necessarily lead to cost reduction automatically (Mouritsen 2005). They could go out of their role and create costs—after all it is possible that high quality means high concern and careful production and checking, which could mean expensive production processes. Is a Ferrari of a higher quality than a Fiat?

Non-financial data may not be easier to understand than financial ones. At least they carry ambiguity and, like financial information, have to be interpreted. They are hardly common sense even if said so by operations management and indeed also by a series of management accounting propositions. Even if they carry predictive ability, however, non-financial data are also ambiguous, and the statistical tests made of their predictability explain 10–20 per cent of the variation (R^3). Not a lot to bet a firm on, and therefore financial data are still in demand.

12.7.3 LAYOUT AND CONTROL

The dilemmas between financial and non-financial information about the factory space also have another coordinate, namely the shop floor and its technologies themselves. In Miller and O'Leary's analysis (1994) of lean manufacturing, the working of advanced manufacturing methods is as much cast in concrete as in information—actual concrete; the product or service cast in concrete and technology! The factory space is a layout of machines, equipment, devices, and technologies that transform materials into products. The factory layout pushes the progress of the product through its design of the factory floor: where machinery is situated, where people work, where inventories are, how the transportation of parts, products, and services is accomplished, and how production technology defines the rhythm of the factory. Layout and technology rather than the individual efforts of people push the product or the service, and the person, rather than being a manufacturing worker, becomes a technician—an appendix to machinery where he or she is an overhead to control and manage the machine.

Here, technology secures the rhythm of the factory rather than individuals' efforts and productivity. Surely, people matter but they are pushed by machinery and the factory is less a *manu*facturing system than a *machino*facturing system where the hand of the worker is increasingly absent. In a sense, such a system does not have quality, speed, or productivity problems because they are all inscribed in technology. The performance required by operations management—quality $\rightarrow$ dependability $\rightarrow$ speed $\rightarrow$ flexibility—is not really so important any more. Surely, the operator has to supervise the machine but increasingly it will mind its own quality, etc. Control is already in the machinery, and there is a new set of concerns about the role of the operator. Is he or she actually able to act on information, non-financial or financial? Is the technology already equipped with performance in its design? Does information matter?

In such operations environments that allow completely 'lights out' production processes, the extreme of a technologically determined process may be in place, but this is probably the exception rather than the rule. However, the flow of the product across the factory floor is an interesting idea of control where performance is an input rather than an output; where performance is a design rather than an ongoing monitoring of people's efforts. In Miller and O'Leary's case (1994), the factory layout—the 'assembly highway'—involved a sequencing of flows and materials supervised by logistics information. It is interesting to note that the 'serious' types of accounting calculations performed in this case were prior to the choice of the 'assembly highway'—accounting in the manufacturing process is not given much weight in the case analysis.

Accounting calculations for Miller and O'Leary (1994) and Mouritsen and Bekke (1997) are prior to manufacturing, and to a certain extent the economics of the factory—the structural cost drivers—are forceful in the construction of the factory layout and its principles of operation.

12.8 **Conclusion**

So, what can management accounting and operations management say to each other? Probably they have a lot to say to each other because, as Bromwich and Bhimani (1994) note, a lot of the challenges facing modern management accounting come from an operations environment. Our analysis corroborates this view, but it also shows that it is possible to look at management accounting in new ways from the experiences emerging from its interactions with operations management. Surely, a series of concerns and conclusions are similar across management accounting and operations management: e.g. the importance of non-financial information in modern manufacturing environments such as lean manufacturing. However, our analysis also allows new insights to be noted that, in addition, may be important not only in the operations environment but more generally. These are:

1. Management accounting—the provision and use of accounting calculations—is no fixed entity. When we refer to management accounting systems (MASs), we refer to a set of stabilized calculations, but as the analysis above shows, when management accounting makes a differences, it is also in place in forms that are clearly beyond expectations.

2. In production environments where we would expect management accounting to be absent, it is still there. This may be because there is not complete trust in the messages uttered by non-financial information. They are effective leading indicators only in rare situations. They are too much of a bet in the development of manufacturing operations. Therefore, there are still some things to be concerned about to unravel a 'causal' mechanism that accounts for the sequence of non-financial information.

3. The absence of accounting in manufacturing environments advocated by operations management is to look away from actual accounting calculations. Accounting calculations help to develop and also seal the production space since they render the trade-offs between scope and scale, and stability and variability, visible. In many situations, accounting calculations create the operations space that can be governed by non-financial, one-dimensional information.

These propositions make accounting calculation interesting. This does not necessarily mean that present routinized accounting systems are important from the perspective of actors, and it does not mean that the accounting department is necessarily very important in the management of operations. However, accounting calculations are important because they help develop the spaces and processes that are pivotal in the running of modern manufacture. Operations management research can learn from this; but then so can accounting research and practice. This, we suspect, is also what Bromwich and Bhimani (1994: 248) hint at when they say:

What is essential is for management accounting to continue its self-inspection, and to do so by heeding transformations external to its field....Within a context of dynamic change, management accounting cannot afford to be inward oriented. Its continued development must rest on its rich history side by side with an appreciation of pressures, constraints and opportunities that enable it to maintain a proactive edge.

It is possible that management accounting and operations management can start to communicate with each other fruitfully. They could help each other see opportunities in the lateral dimension with a view to conceptualizing and controlling value creation in companies. Management accounting not only constitutes a space for operations (investment calculus, account for intangibles) but is also defined and mobilized through operations (through-put accounting, ABC, non-financial performance measurement). Operations within the company are often formed by network relations beyond the company, e.g. JIT regimes, and they are brought beyond it through network relations (e.g. product development subcontracting, production suppliers). Network relations have also formed new calculations (e.g. value chain costing, open-book accounting) formed and phrased by accounting. Management accounting and operations management meet in the lateral space and provide different—sometimes complementary—explanations of how value creation occurs.

▢ NOTES

1 Lean manufacturing is a best practice for most managerial perspectives on operations management. In other disciplines such as sociology, lean management is criticized for pushing rationalization and employment relations too far (Berggren 1992; Moody 1997; Reinehart et al. 1997; Smith 2000), and for its inability to acknowledge differences in logics of factory regimes across the world (Lash and Urry 1994: 60ff).

▢ BIBLIOGRAPHY

Abernethy, M. A. and Lillis, A. M. (1995). 'The Impact of Manufacturing Flexibility on Management Control System Design', *Accounting, Organizations and Society*, 20(4): 241–58.

Baines, A. and Langfield-Smith, K. (2003). 'Antecedents to Management Accounting Change: A Structural Equation Approach', *Accounting, Organizations and Society*, 28(7/8): 675–98.

Banker, R. D., Potter, G., and Schroeder, R. G. (1993). 'Reporting Manufacturing Performance Measures to Workers: An Empirical Investigation', *Journal of Management Accounting Research*, 3: 34–55.

Berggren, C. (1992). *Alternatives to Lean Production*. New York: ILR Press.

Bromwich, M. and Bhimani, A. (1989) *Management Accounting: Evolution not Revolution*. London: CIMA.

—— —— (1994). *Management Accounting: Pathways to Progress*. London: CIMA.

Carr, S., Mak, Y. T., and Needham, J. E. (1997). 'Differences in Strategy, Quality Management Practices and Performance Reporting Systems between ISO accredited and non-ISO accredited Companies', *Management Accounting Research*, 8(4): 383–403.

Chenhall, R. H. (1997). 'Reliance on Manufacturing Performance Measures, Total Quality Management and Organizational Performance', *Management Accounting Research*, 8: 187–206.

Cooper, R. and Slagmulder, R. (2004). 'Interorganisational Cost Management and Relational Context', *Accounting, Organizations and Society*, 29(1): 1–26.

Daniel, S. J. and Reitsperger, W. D. (1991). 'Linking Quality Strategy with Management Control Systems: Empirical Evidence from Japanese Industry', *Accounting, Organizations and Society*, 16(7): 601–18.

—— —— (1992). 'Management Control Systems for Quality: an Empirical Comparison of the U.S. and Japanese Electronics Industries', *Journal of Management Accounting Research*, 4 (Fall): 64–78.

Daniel, S. J. and Gregson, T. (1995). 'Quality Consciousness in Japanese and U.S. Electronics Manufacturers: An Examination of the Impact of Quality Strategy and Management Control Systems on Perceptions of the Importance of Quality to Expected Management Rewards', *Management Accounting Research*, 6: 367–82.

Dekker, H. C. (2004). 'Control of Inter-Organizational Relationships: Evidence on Appropriation Concerns and Coordination Requirements', *Accounting, Organizations and Society*, 29(1): 27–49.

Ezzamel, M. and Willmott, H. (1998). 'Accounting for Teamwork: a Critical Study of Groupbased Systems of Organizational Control', *Administrative Science Quarterly*, 43: 358–96.

Foster, G. and Horngren, C. (1988). 'Flexible Manufacturing Systems: Cost Management and Cost Accounting Implications', *Journal of Cost Management* (Fall): 16–24.

Frances, J. and Garnsey, E. (1996). 'Supermarkets and Suppliers in the United Kingdom: System Integration, Information and Control', *Accounting, Organizations and Society*, 21(6): 591–610.

Gietzman, M. (1996). 'Incomplete Contracts and the Make or Buy Decision: Governance Design and Attainable Flexibility', *Accounting, Organizations and Society*, 21(6): 611–26.

Hoque, Z., Mia, L., and Alam, M. (2001). 'Market Competition, Computer-Aided Manufacturing and the Use of Multiple Performance Measures: An Empirical Study', *British Accounting Review*, 33: 23–45.

Håkansson, H. and Lind, J. (2004). 'Accounting and Network Coordination', *Accounting, Organizations and Society*, 29(1): 51–72.

Ittner, C. D. and Larcker, D. F. (1995). 'Total Quality Management and the Choice of Information and Reward Systems', *Journal of Accounting Research* 33 (Suppl.): 1–34.

—— —— (1997). 'Quality Strategy, Strategic Control Systems, and Organizational Performance', *Accounting, Organizations and Society* 22(3/4): 295–314.

Jazayeri, M. and Hopper, T. (1999). 'Management Accounting within World Class Manufacturing: A Case Study', *Management Accounting Research*, 10(3): 263–301.

Jönsson, S. (1996). *Accounting for Improvement*. Oxford: Pergamon.

Kajüter, P. and Kulmala, H. I. (2005). 'Open-Book Accounting in Networks: Potential Achievements and Reasons for Failures', *Management Accounting Research*, 16(2): 179–204.

Karlsson, C. and Åhlström, P. (1996). 'Assessing Change towards Lean Production', *International Journal of Operations and Production Management*, 16(2): 24–41.

Lamming, R. (1993) *Beyond Partnership. Strategies for Innovation and Lean Supply*. New York: Prentice Hall.

Langfield-Smith, K. and Smith, D. (2003). 'Management Control Systems and Trust in Outsourcing Relationships', *Management Accounting Research*, 14(3): 281–307.

Lash, S. and Urry, J. (1994). *Economies of Sign and Space*. London: Sage.

Lind, J. (2001) 'Control in World Class Manufacturing: a Longitudinal Case Study', *Management Accounting Research*, 12(1): 41–74.

Mahama, H. and Chua, W. F. (2002). 'Accounting Inscriptions and Framing Devices: A field Study of the Placing and Timing of Financial and Non-financial Measures in the Framing of "Collaborative" Supply Relations'. Presented at the European Accounting Association Conference, Copenhagen.

Meer-Kooistra, J. van d. and Vosselman, E. G. J. (2000). 'Management Control of Interfirm Transactional Relationships: The Case of Industrial Renovation and Maintenance', *Accounting, Organizations and Society*, 25(1): 51–77.

Mia, L. (2000). 'Just-In-Time Manufacturing, Management Accounting Systems and Profitability', *Accounting and Business Research*, 30(2): 137–51.

Milgrom, P. and Roberts, J. (1995). 'Complementarities and Fit: Strategy, Structure, and Organizational Change in Manufacturing', *Journal of Accounting and Economics*, 19(2/3): 179–208.

Miller, P. and O'Leary, T. (1993). 'Accounting Expertise and the Politics of the Product: Economic Citizenship and modes of Corporate Governance', *Accounting, Organizations and Society*, 18 (2/3): 187–206.

—— —— (1994). 'Accounting, "Economic Citizenship" and the Spatial Reordering of Manufacture', *Accounting, Organizations and Society*, 19(1): 15–43.

Mouritsen, J. (1997). 'Marginalising the Customer: Quality, Customer-Orientation and Accounting Performance', *Scandinavian Journal of Management*, 13(1): 5–18.

—— (1999). 'The Flexible Firm: Strategies for a Subcontractor's Management Control', *Accounting, Organizations and Society* 24(1): 31–55.

—— (2005). 'Beyond Accounting Change: Design and Mobilisation of Management Control Systems', *Journal of Contemporary Accounting and Organizational Change* 1(1): 97–113.

Mouritsen, J. and Bekke, A. (1999). 'A Space for Time: Accounting and Time-Based Management in a High-Tech Company', *Management Accounting Research*, 10(2): 159–80.

—— and Dechow, N. (2001). 'Strategies, Controls and Technologies of Managing: Translations between Strategy and Procedure in Organisational Transformation', in Karnøe, P. and Rahgu, R. (eds.), *Path Creation and Path Dependence*. London: Lawrence Erlbaum, pp. 355–80.

—— Hansen, A., and Hansen. C.Ø. (2001). 'Inter-organizational Controls and Organizational Competencies: Episodes Around Target Cost Management/Functional Analysis and Open Book Accounting', *Management Accounting Research*, 12(2): 221–44.

—— and Thrane, S. (forthcoming). 'Accounting, Network Complementarities and the Development of Inter-organisational Relations', *Accounting, Organizations and Society*.

Munro, R. J. B. and Hatherly, D. J. (1993). 'Accountability and the New Commercial Agenda', *Critical Perspectives on Accounting*, 4 (4): 369–95.

Nagar, V. and Rajan, M. V. (2001). 'The Revenue Implications of Financial and Operational Measures of Product Quality', *Accounting Review*, 76(4): 495–513.

Perera, S., Harrison, G., and Poole, M. (1997). 'Customer-Focused Manufacturing Strategy and the Use of Operations-Based Non-Financial Performance Measures: A Research Note', *Accounting, Organizations and Society*, 22(6): 557–72.

Pirsig R. M. (1974). *Zen and the Art of Motorcycle Maintenance*. New York: Bantam New Age Books.

Reinehart, J., Huxley, C., and Robertson, D. (1997). *Just another Car Factory? Lean Production and its Discontents*. New York: ILR Press.

Schoenberger, R. J. (1986). *World Class Manufacturing*. New York: Free Press.

—— (1990). *Building a Chain of Customers: Linking Business Functions to Create the World Class Company*. New York: Hutchinson Business Books.

Schoenberger, R. J. (1996). *World Class Manufacturing: The Next Decade. Building Power, Strength and Value.* New York: Free Press.

Seal, W., and Vincent-Jones, P. (1997). 'Accounting and Trust in the Enabling of Long-Term Relations', *Accounting, Auditing and Accountability Journal*, 10/3: 406–31.

—— Cullen, J., Dunlop, A., Berry, T., and Ahmed, M. (1999). 'Enacting a European Supply Chain: A Case Study of the Role of Management Accounting', *Management Accounting Research*, 10(3): 303–22.

—— Berry, A., and Cullen, J. (2004). 'Disembedding the Supply Chain: Institutionalized Reflexivity and Inter-Firm Accounting', *Accounting, Organizations and Society*, 29(1): 73–92.

Shank, J. K. and Govindarajan, V. (1993). *Strategic Cost Management.* New York: Free Press.

Sim, K. L. and Killough, L. N. (1998). 'The Performance Effects of Complementarities between Manufacturing Practices and Management Accounting Systems', *Journal of Management Accounting Research*, 10: 325–46.

Slack, N., Chamber, S., Harland, C., Harrison, A., and Johnston, R. (1998). *Operations Management.* London: Financial Times/Pitman.

Smith, T. (2000). *Technology and Capital in the Age of Lean Production.* New York: State University of New York Press.

Stalk, G. and Hout, T. M. (1990). *Competing Against Time.* New York: Free Press.

Tomkins, C. (2001). 'Interdependencies, Trust and Information in Relationships, Alliances and Networks', *Accounting, Organizations and Society*, 26(2): 161–91.

Vaivio, J. (1999). 'Examining "The Quantified Customer"', *Accounting, Organizations and Society*, 24(8): 689–715.

Wilkinson, A. and Willmott, H. (eds.) (1995). *Making Quality Critical: New Perspectives on Organizational Change.* London: Routledge.

Womack, J. P. and Jones, D. T. (2003). *Lean Thinking: Banish Waste and Create Wealth in Your Corporation.* London: Free Press Business.

—— —— and Roos, D. (1990). *The Machine that Changed the World.* New York: Rawson Associates/Macmillan.

Wouters, M., Anderson, J. C., and Wynstra, F. (2005). 'The Adoption of Total Cost of Ownership for Sourcing Decisions—A Structural Equations Analysis', *Accounting, Organizations and Society* 30(2): 167–91.

13 Trends in budgetary control and responsibility accounting

David Otley

13.1 Introduction

Budgetary control and responsibility accounting have been the foundation of management control systems design and use in most business (and other) organizations for many years. But whereas in the 1960s and 1970s such systems were almost exclusively based on management accounting information, more recently we have seen a recognition that a wider set of tools are required involving both the use of a range of non-financial performance measures and alternative concepts of accountability such as value chain management. Nevertheless, the focus remains on accountability arrangements within and outside organizations, and on taking a broad, holistic approach to the management of organizational performance.

This chapter begins by reviewing the roles that budgetary control systems take in helping managers assure organizational performance and by considering some of the growing body of criticisms of their efficacy that have been made in recent years. Two distinct views have been taken about the best way to proceed in future. The first espouses incremental improvement to budgetary control processes, both in terms of linking them more closely to operational requirements and planning systems, and also coping with the issues of rapid change by more frequent budget revision and the adoption of techniques such as rolling budgets. The second is more radical and suggests the abandonment of budgetary control, replacing it with a variety of alternative techniques that will enable organizations to become more agile and adaptive. Interestingly, both these approaches suggest that greater reliance needs to be placed on non-financial measures of performance and that techniques such as the balanced scorecard (BSC) can assist in this respect.

The chapter will conclude with an outline of the main issues facing control systems designers, and attempt to indicate some ways forward for both practitioners and researchers. However, it needs to be clearly recognized that the issues involved are not just those of the technical design of planning and control systems but also those of embedding such systems in the wider framework of organizational activities and functions. In short, budgetary control and responsibility accounting are not just techniques that can be applied to organizations, but rather an essential part of the underlying fabric of organizational functioning.

13.2 **The roles of budgetary control**

Budgetary control systems play a variety of roles in organizational activity. Many lists of the functions of budgets have been suggested over the years, but the following are some of the major purposes that have been suggested (Emmanuel et al. 1990):

- A means of authorizing actions
- A focus for forecasting and planning
- A channel of communication and coordination
- A means of motivating organizational participants
- A vehicle for performance evaluation and control

However, these functions are potentially in conflict and it appears that no single system can serve all of them equally effectively. A major and fundamental conflict arises between the widespread use of such systems for performance evaluation (both of managerial performance and of the performance of organizational units) and the need for accurate forecasting to support organizational planning. This is not so much a conflict of basic functions, but more a trade-off that needs to be made between short-term performance and longer-term action. Wildavsky (1975) pithily described planning as 'future control', whereby we anticipate future circumstances and take current action to improve our likely future state. Attempting to use a budget system to give effective short-term control whilst encouraging managers to make accurate estimates of future outcomes has long been recognized as a knife-edge that managers need to walk.

A recent summary of the major issues and problems engendered by budgetary control systems has been provided by Neely et al. (2001). Drawn primarily from the practitioner literature, they maintained that the twelve most cited weaknesses of budgetary control are:

- Budgets are time-consuming and costly to put together;
- Budgets constrain responsiveness and are often a barrier to change;
- Budgets are rarely strategically focused and often contradictory;
- Budgets add little value, especially given the time required to prepare them;
- Budgets concentrate on cost reduction and not value creation;
- Budgets strengthen vertical command and control;
- Budgets do not reflect the emerging network structures that organizations are adopting;
- Budgets encourage 'gaming' and perverse behaviours;
- Budgets are developed and updated too infrequently, usually annually;
- Budgets are based on unsupported assumptions and guesswork;
- Budgets reinforce departmental barriers rather than encourage knowledge sharing;
- Budgets make people feel undervalued.

Given such an extensive and all-encompassing list, one is led to wonder why budgets continue to be so widely used! Nevertheless, it is clear that many managers and budgetary control system operators are finding the traditional mechanisms of budgetary control increasingly unwieldy and ineffective at serving their central purpose of helping guide organizational activities in appropriate ways.

13.3 **Two responses to budgetary control problems**

Two very distinct approaches have emerged from these problems. Intriguingly, both these approaches have been espoused by a single practitioner-based organization that has made a series of extensive studies of these issues, namely Consortium for Advanced Manufacturing—International (CAM-I). The US-based activity-based budgeting (ABB) group of CAM-I has taken the approach of examining how the budget system can be improved by marrying an activity-based operational model with a detailed financial model. The European-based CAM-I beyond budgeting (BB) group has taken a more radical approach, which first involves changing (or eliminating) the traditional budgetary process and replacing it with more adaptive procedures generally based on non-financial performance measures. Beyond this, it then advocates radical decentralization and the empowerment of lower-level managers and employees (see Hansen et al. 2003 for a more detailed review). Although both the ABB and BB are both practice-led developments supported by prominent organizations, they do not represent the totality of new budgetary practice developments. Nevertheless, the two distinct positions provide a valuable codification of the dilemma that the budgetary control process has found itself in, and Sections 13.3.1 and 13.3.2 describe more fully the two approaches.

13.3.1 IMPROVING BUDGETARY PROCESSES

The ABB approach concentrates primarily on improving budgetary planning. It focuses on generating a budget from an activity-based model of the organization as opposed to the traditional responsibility centre focus. The ABB group contends that the planning role of budgeting has suffered because traditional budgetary processes are too high-level and too aggregate; more detailed capacity management and process-based approaches can be used to ground it more effectively in organizational reality. The ABB approach first establishes a plan that is operationally feasible before attempting to generate a financial budget. Although this may seem to be exactly the budgetary approach recommended by accounting textbooks, in practice budgets are often constructed incrementally from budgets of the previous period, with operational detail being added later. If a feasible financial plan is not produced at the first iteration, the ABB approach allows the organization to adjust five possible elements to achieve the budget target: (*a*) activity and resource consumption rates; (*b*) resource capacity; (*c*) resource cost; (*d*) product or service demand quantity; and (*e*) product or service price. Because the traditional budget process does not collect information on activity and resource consumption rates, it offers fewer possibilities to adjust the budget.

The ABB group lists several potential benefits of their approach (Hansen and Torok 2003):

1. The detailed operational model used avoids unnecessary financial calculations being made for operationally unfeasible plans.
2. The more sophisticated operational model provides a richer set of tools for balancing capacity.
3. Lower-level managers and employees can more easily understand information expressed in operational rather than financial terms.
4. Activity-based approaches reinforce a horizontal, process-based view of the organization, in contrast to traditional budgeting's vertical orientation.

In many ways, the ABB approach can be seen as correcting one of the two deficiencies introduced by taking a purely management control (Anthony 1965) view of budgeting. Anthony separated management control from both strategic planning and operational control and, as a result, management control came to be seen as primarily driven by financial information. More recently, improvements to budgeting can be seen as restoring the connections between these other two important processes. From the strategic point of view, approaches such as the BSC (Kaplan and Norton 1992) have been concerned to restore the link between performance management and strategy. Most obviously in their book *The Strategy-Focused Organization*, Kaplan and Norton (2001) maintain that the process of strategic mapping is a necessary step in the construction of effective measures of performance within a BSC. Other authors, such as Simons (1995) in his 'levers of control' framework, have combined a focus on strategy with a wider view of the control mechanisms that can be used to implement strategy. In the contingency theory literature also, strategy has been identified as a key contingent variable for control systems design. Considerably less work in management control has focused on the second interface in Anthony's categorization, namely that with operational control. There may be several reasons for this, such as the concentration of researchers on top-level controls, the prevalence of many different control practices at lower levels, and the unfamiliarity of accounting researchers with the types of non-accounting controls (including production line layout and physical inventory controls) that have gained increased importance at first-line management levels. The ABB approach can be seen as a major contribution in this arena.

13.3.2 RADICALLY CHANGING BUDGETARY PROCESSES

The European-based BB group has taken a more radical approach in arguing that traditional budgetary control is fundamentally flawed in such a way that incremental improvement will not be effective in eliminating the major problems from which it suffers (see Hope and Fraser 2003 for a more detailed exposition of their work). The BB approach seeks to avoid what they label the *annual performance trap*. This is their shorthand for the set of dysfunctional behaviours that commonly stem from evaluating managers' performance against budgetary targets that are set without reference to credible external benchmarks and that remain fixed for the next budget year. There is no doubt that the literature on budgeting is replete with examples of dysfunctional behaviour driven by undue emphasis on meeting (possibly inappropriate) budgetary targets. These range from manipulating budgetary estimates before the year begins, through the manipulation of reported numbers during the budget year (often by exploiting timing differences) to the adoption of inappropriate management decisions (such as the postponement of maintenance expenditure); all have the objective of producing numbers that look good against budget targets whilst simultaneously destroying value. To avoid these problems, the BB group recommends replacing rigid annual budget-based performance evaluations with *performance evaluations based on relative performance contracts reviewed with hindsight.*

The first stage of the BB approach is thus to adopt more adaptive management processes freed from the rigid annual routine of budgetary control. Drawing on experience with participant firms, six principles of managing with adaptive processes were set out as follows:

- Base goals on medium-term benchmarks;
- Base evaluation and rewards on relative performance contracts *with hindsight*;
- Make resources available as required;
- Make action planning a continuous and inclusive process;
- Coordinate cross-company actions according to prevailing customer demand;
- Base performance measures on continuous reviews against medium-term goals.

The first principle is designed to remove the emphasis on preset and fixed (budget) targets, and to replace them with *benchmarked* performance standards. Thus, a common form of performance target would be a *league table*, either internally (e.g. different branches in the same company) or externally (e.g. performance in comparison with leading competitors) referenced. The first principle forms the basis implementing the second, and arguably the most important, principle. Here the objective is to remove reliance on an arbitrary performance target that is set for a fixed period (typically a year) many months in advance. It is to be replaced by a relative performance target that is continually updated in light of changing conditions. More radically, performance against such targets will be evaluated *with hindsight*, that is, fixed targets are not set at the beginning of the period, but may well be adjusted to reflect the actual operating experience and economic circumstances during the period. Rewards may be connected to performance, but typically by relying more on subjective performance evaluations with an emphasis on workgroup rather than individual rewards. The aim appears to be to attempt to engender a philosophy of doing what is best for the firm in light of current circumstances, and to encourage teamwork.

The third principle is that resources are not fully budgeted for in advance, but held in a central pool so that they can be applied at short notice to those areas that have the greatest current need for them. The other three principles are not unique to this framework, but reinforce the others. The BB group's hope is that these six principles will make forecasting more accurate and more useful again.

Although the problems with budgetary control are the centrepiece of the BB approach, Hope and Fraser (2003) go further in claiming that any fixed contract performance measurement and management technique can have the same stultifying effect as budgets. As an example, they cite the fate of the BSC in many organizations, as having consequences very similar to those of budgetary control in that they often are associated with fixed performance contracts. Thus, although using a wider range of operational and customer-focused measures is recommended as necessary when budgets are removed, it is argued that it is important that such measures be also used in a relative performance-based manner. Nevertheless, they still believe that techniques such as the BSC can be used, especially if attention is paid to seriously gaining insight into the operational factors that drive financial performance. Indeed, they suggest that organizations that do not have the *budgeting barrier* are more likely to implement a BSC successfully.

Finally, whilst abandoning budgets as the primary means of management control provides a first stage of improvement that is worthwhile in itself, it is viewed as a starting point only towards more radical decentralization and empowerment, which is seen as offering even greater potential. While this second stage of the BB approach speaks more pertinently to the failure of traditional budgetary controls to empower people to make decisions that are congruent with strategic goals, a detailed discussion of *radical decentralization* is outside the scope of this chapter. The essence, however, is that effective devolution and empowerment are argued to be virtually incompatible with the use of budgetary controls because they fail, amongst other things, to create a high performance climate based on competitive success (because a fixed target is the definitive measure of success); to make people accountable for satisfied and profitable customers (because mostly, or only, financial performance is considered); to empower people to act by providing them with resource capabilities (because resources have been committed for the budgeting period); or to implement business processes that map onto the value chain of an organization (which have a horizontal emphasis, whilst budgetary controls have a vertical emphasis). However, this second stage of BB is more controversial, perhaps because it seems to apply only to organizations that can be organized in quasi-independent 'micro' profit centres. How it can be implemented in organizations that require more internal coordination between activities is still an open issue.

A crucial element of the BB approach is that it is specifically concerned with the management of organizational activities, not just (or even) with financial control. Even under BB, it is likely that the financial planning function will continue, but primarily as a *back-office* activity. That is, financial managers may well construct budgets to serve their own financial management purposes. However, these back-office budgets (e.g. profit plans, cash flow budgets) will likely be internally constructed, with minimal involvement from line managers. More importantly, they will not be issued to line managers in order to act as standards and targets that are required to be attained. Instead, alternative performance management devices will be used for management control purposes. In other words, financial management will continue to be the responsibility of a finance department, which will use whatever forecasting, planning, and control techniques it sees fit. By contrast, management control involving line managers will use other performance measurement and management systems and will not rely on budgetary control mechanisms in the traditional way.

The place of the budget in management control will be taken by other performance management systems. These may include such mechanisms as BSC of non-financial performance measures; activity-based management (ABM) systems and other forms of business process management; benchmarking techniques for target-setting; customer relationship management models; and so on. Managers will thus be given a variety of operating performance measures by which their performance will be assessed and managed. The general assumption is that by attaining appropriate levels of performance on these variables, the desired financial performance of the enterprise will be achieved. The financial outcomes will continue to be monitored by the finance department, but the budget will not be used to measure and control the activities of line managers.

13.4 Conclusions on budgetary control

It is possible to view planning and control techniques as a spectrum. At one end is a focus on robust planning techniques where implementation is primarily a matter of ensuring that the preset plans are actually realized. At the other end is a focus on agility where planning becomes so unreliable that it is dispensed with, and the control focus is moved towards rapid response once actual operating conditions are observed. Organizations need to place themselves appropriately on this continuum. For example, in a rapidly moving and unpredictable market, it may be that control solutions based on agility are appropriate (e.g. in the fashion industry, where fashion is notoriously fickle and difficult to predict). In a more stable marketplace, and in an industry where long-term trends can be forecasted, a planning solution might still be the best (e.g. in a local school, where the number of returning children can be easily forecasted). An interesting situation arises when market conditions preclude too much reliance on planning, but production and technological capability demand long-term resource allocations decisions, especially where these involve assets of high specificity and long investment pay-off cycles. An example is a mobile telephone network provider in Europe where the third generation licences were bought at much higher prices than appears to be sustainable by current consumer behaviour. A set of research questions is suggested by this analysis. How does reliance on (accounting-based) planning and control systems differ across organizations facing different degrees of unpredictability in their operating environments? Can budgetary control be adapted to work effectively in unpredictable environments? If not, what control systems are deployed where planning-based solutions fail?

The two approaches outlined above are aimed at different parts of this problem. The ABB approach seeks to align budgeting more cogently with operational planning and control. The technological core of an organization is often protected to some extent from external uncertainties, and here improved planning and better forecasting may provide useful improvement. And if financial plans can be tied more closely to feasible operational plans, budgetary control can serve a useful purpose. However, from an overall organizational perspective, levels of complexity and uncertainty may be much higher and planning becomes as much of a problem as a solution. Methods of coping with this include decentralization and the decoupling of overall financial control from more detailed operational decision-making and adaptability. If the issue is primarily one of motivation and effective performance management, the BB approach has insights to offer. The key issue is how to combine the two approaches in a real situation.

A related question in uncertain environments is whether giving up budgeting is a necessary precondition for the performance improvements that the BB group suggests. Can firms retain budgetary control, but modify its application or reduce its importance in such environments? For example, could firms retain budgeting, but incorporate relative performance targets? Could firms periodically revise budgets and use rolling forecasts to mitigate the problems of static budgets? Some firms clearly use budgeting successfully in dynamic environments; Simons' case of Johnson & Johnson documents one such example, but clearly uses only subjective performance evaluation. This suggests that budgetary controls can be effective as part of a comprehensive management control system with features, such as subjective performance evaluation, that in combination mutually reinforce their effectiveness. But equally, the conditions under which the more radical BB approach can be usefully applied, and the type of control techniques that can be used to replace budgeting under such conditions, are also worthy of investigation.

13.5 **How budgets are used**

The above discussion has concentrated mainly on the features of budgetary control systems design and structure, although this does carry over into the ways in which the budgetary control system is used. In this section, we will consider the ways in which control systems are used by accountable managers. Remarkably, we seem to have made little progress on this issue since the work of Hopwood (1972) and others in the 1970s and 1980s. Hopwood made the distinction between a 'budget-constrained' style of use and a 'profit-conscious' style, and demonstrated the consequences of each style in his subject company. This categorization was used by Otley (1978) in a deliberately different organizational context, and his contrasting conclusions formed one of the bases of the contingency theory of management accounting, which was developed during the late 1970s and early 1980s. The theme was taken up by other researchers and became known as 'reliance on accounting performance measures' (RAPM). By 1991 it had been rather generously characterized by Brownell and Dunk (1991) as 'the only organized critical mass of empirical work in management accounting at present'. Briers and Hirst (1990) and Hartmann (2000) give excellent reviews of this body of work.

However, it has not been without its problems. The original measurement instrument developed by Hopwood has been used uncritically in very different situations where it may not apply in the same way, and different methods of measurement have been used (see Otley and Fakiolis 2000 for a review). Further, virtually none of the work has ever been replicated (Otley and Pollanen 2000). Thus we can have little confidence that any of the published results are robust, even in the settings in which they were conducted, let alone in a more modern context.

Nevertheless, the key feature that Hopwood had uncovered does seem to have an ongoing relevance in current organizational settings, and with reference to a range of control systems (not just budgetary control). He essentially distinguished between a short-term approach characterized by a rigid insistence by senior managers that targets should be attained in the current period, with a longer-term approach that might condone current failure to meet a target if it could be demonstrated that the chosen managerial actions would likely lead to better performance over the longer term. It is regrettable that this stream of research seems to have withered when it appears to be addressing an issue of fundamental importance.

The only other major characterization of control systems use that has received attention in the literature has been Simons' distinction (1995) between 'diagnostic' and 'interactive' use of organizational control systems. The concept of 'interactive' use appears to have developed over the course of Simons' ten-year research project that led to his 'levers of control' framework, and may therefore be somewhat confused. Certainly, Bisbe et al. (2005) have identified five separate sub-dimensions of the interactive use construct that may not be correlated with each other. These are (*a*) intensive use by senior managers; (*b*) intensive use by operating managers; (*c*) face-to-face challenge and debate; (*d*) focus on strategic uncertainties; and (*e*) non-invasive, facilitating, and inspirational involvement. They argue that all five conditions are required for true interactive use to occur in the full sense of Simons' construct. However, this is essentially an empirical question, as it is not clear that Simons observed all these dimensions in each of the case studies on which the construct is based. But again, this represents a promising focus for studies on the effects of different ways of using budgetary and other control systems.

Finally, it is worth mentioning one of the oldest principles of accountability and control, the so-called controllability principle. This states that managers should be held accountable only for those outcomes they can control. Although organizations do take steps to try to implement this principle, for example by designing performance measures that match organizational responsibility structures, these are designed before the measurement period starts. After it has ended, only limited devices such as variance analyses and flexible budgets tend to be used. In practice, it has been observed (Merchant 1989; Otley 1990) that managers are frequently held responsible for things they cannot control. This seems to occur for two reasons. First, it is often difficult to separate out the controllable from the uncontrollable items that have affected performance outcomes. Second, there is often an attitude that, although managers clearly cannot control some external events, it is still their responsibility to adapt organizational activities in response to them. Clearly, there is a fine line between holding a manager responsible for items over which no influence can be exerted, and

expecting an intelligent and adaptive response to new circumstances that were not anticipated when budget targets were originally set.

All of the above aspects of how budgetary and other control systems are used in practice
require further study. Control systems use has been established to be a fundamental driver of
managerial behaviour. What is less clear are both the characteristics of different 'style' of
control systems 'use' and the impact of these in different circumstances. These are very
practical and relevant issues to the effective use of control systems; they also represent a clear
conceptual challenge to academics to codify the constructs involved more cogently.

13.6 **Other control mechanisms**

A further feature of the literature on control and accountability is that a much wider set of
controls beyond financial controls are now being considered. One indication of this has been
the widespread popularity of the BSC, which primarily serves as an organizing framework
for a range of non-financial performance measures to complement traditional financial
measures. Since the first *Harvard Business Review* article in 1992, the BSC framework has
had truly amazing success, with most major companies worldwide adopting, at least for a
time, some variant of its features.

Although alternative (and generally equivalent) frameworks exist (e.g. the Business
Excellence model, itself a variant of the European Framework for Quality Management
(EFQM)), the single distinguishing feature of the BSC has been its continuing emphasis that
performance measures need to be explicitly linked to strategy. This has provided a much
needed focus in the field and, together with the insistence that there should be no more than
16–20 measures on any scorecard, has provided a discipline greatly needed in a field where
large numbers of performance measures have proliferated. Nevertheless, the BSC framework
has claimed some remarkable capabilities. Kaplan and Norton (1996) outline twelve areas in
which the BSC has the capability of making a significant contribution. These are:

1. Clarifying organizational vision
2. Gaining consensus around it
3. Communicating goals and educating employees
4. Setting goals
5. Linking rewards to performance measures
6. Setting targets
7. Aligning strategic objectives
8. Allocating resources
9. Establishing milestones
10. Articulating the shared vision
11. Supplying strategic feedback
12. Facilitating strategy review and learning

This whole process is designed to facilitate the adoption of a 'strategic framework for action'. Interestingly, it is contrasted with the same organizational processes that occur when the budget is placed at the centre of the control system, rather than the BSC. Described under the subtitle of 'barriers to strategic action', the general message is that the traditional system of budgetary control is an impediment to sensible action in contrast to the potential of the BSC.

However, what is also noticeable is that, despite the wide-ranging claims for the potential of the BSC to revitalize strategy implementation, *The Balanced Scorecard* contains virtually no guidance as to how any of the twelve areas highlighted can actually be implemented in practice. Although the book contains numerous case examples of how particular organizations have gone about developing their own BSCs, there is little or no general advice on how to do this in practice. In particular, the key processes of selecting and developing the measurement of key performance indicators is totally neglected, except by way of example. Maybe the success of the BSC framework can be partly attributed to this lack of specificity; one size can indeed be adapted to fit all! On the other hand, there is also abundant evidence that considerable benefit has been gained in many different types of organization (manufacturing and service; private and public) from attempting to go through the process of developing their own scorecards.

As the BSC process has been refined and developed in practice, Kaplan and Norton (2001) have subtly changed the objectives the scorecard is designed to serve. From being an organizing framework for performance measures, it has become a way of developing and implementing strategic intent. In *The Strategy-Focused Organization*, Kaplan and Norton (2001) develop a set of procedures for constructing 'strategy maps'. These trace the steps that are believed to be necessary to achieve certain overall strategic goals by drawing tree diagrams, which connect key sub-objectives to overall objectives, and casting these down through the organization.

In some ways, the BSC can be seen as an alternative to traditional systems of budgetary control that are totally dependent upon financial measures of performance. It has both explicitly connected these measures to organizational and departmental strategies, and also emphasized the development of key non-financial measures that related to specific activities conducted by functional managers. In so doing, it has reconnected the areas of strategic planning and operational control that were deliberately disconnected by Anthony (1965) in the construction of his concept of management control systems. This has been a much needed development, as it has become apparent that financial controls alone are insufficient to guide an organization. But it is a much more debatable position to argue that techniques such as the BSC completely replace budgetary control systems, as implied by Kaplan and Norton (1996). More probably, BSCs of non-financial performance measures (with a few key financial performance measures) provide an important complementary set of controls to add to the repertoire of budgetary control techniques that has been developed over the years. It is an important empirical issue to assess how these two different types of control can be most effectively used in combination in different circumstances.

13.7 **Performance management**

Although Kaplan and Norton (1996) provided little guidance on how to achieve their twelve desirable features of well-functioning control systems, the extensive academic study of budgetary control systems that has occurred over the last thirty years can provide some useful pointers. Many of the factors that have been identified as good practice in budgetary control systems design can easily be transferred to apply to more general management control and performance management systems, which utilize non-financial as well as financial performance measures.

One attempt to do this has been set out by Otley (1999). He took the literature on the design and operation of budgetary systems and first tried to generalize and codify it in a number of key issues; these areas were then used to analyse other types of control systems that occur in organizations. He argued that there are five main sets of issues that need to be addressed in developing a framework for managing organizational performance, and represented these as a set of questions. The questions were phrased in a normative tone, reflecting a managerial perspective, but can easily be rephrased descriptively for use as a research tool. The questions themselves appear to remain constant, but organizations need continually to develop new answers to them. This is because the context in which the organization is set is constantly changing and new strategies need to be developed to cope with new operating environments.

The questions are as follows:

1. What are the key objectives that are central to the organization's overall future success, and how does it go about evaluating its achievement for each of these objectives?

2. What strategies and plans has the organization adopted and what are the processes and activities that it has decided will be required for it to implement these successfully? How does it assess and measure the performance of these activities?

3. What level of performance does the organization need to achieve in each of the areas defined in the above two questions, and how does it go about setting appropriate performance targets for them?

4. What rewards will managers (and other employees) gain by achieving these performance targets (or, conversely, what penalties will they suffer by failing to achieve them)?

5. What are the information flows (feedback and feed-forward loops) that are necessary to enable the organization to learn from its experience, and to adapt its current behaviour in the light of that experience?

These questions relate very closely to some of the central issues of modern management and management accounting practice. The first is concerned with the definition of goals and the measurement of goal attainment, not just financially but also in terms of meeting all stakeholder aspirations. Clearly, the relative importance given to different goals may well reflect the relative power of different stakeholders. However, the issue of evaluating organizational effectiveness cannot be addressed without confronting these issues. The second is closely connected to issues of strategy formation and deployment, and with very practical issues of business process and operations management. It represents the codification of the means by which objectives are intended to be attained. The third question is more traditional and has a long pedigree of research connected with it, but remains important, as is reflected in the emphasis given to practices such as benchmarking. The fourth question has tended to be neglected by those concerned with performance measurement as being in the purview of the human resource management function. However, the interconnections between the two fields need to be better recognized to avoid the many counterproductive examples of short-termism driven by financial incentive schemes that are seen in practice. The fifth question has been considered in part by management information systems (MIS) and monitoring control and surveillance (MCS) specialists, but still needs to be better linked to issues such as the 'learning organization', employee empowerment, and emergent strategy.

Otley (1999) then showed that the experience we had gained from trying to understand the operation of budgetary control systems could be applied to other control techniques such as economic value added (EVA) and the BSC. He concluded that trying to answer the questions gave insights into the contributions that newer techniques could make. He characterized the Stern Stewart approach, which used EVA as the major performance measure required in an organization as being narrow (concentrating on a single, financial measure) but deep (considering the issues implied by each of the five questions). In contrast, the BSC was characterized as being broad (wide range of performance measures required) but shallow (few of the issues raised in the questions were considered). The two approaches taken together, however, could give guidance on how all the questions could be usefully considered for each of a wide range of types of performance measure.

In some ways, Otley's examples (1999) were a little misleading in that he applied his questions to analysing specific control techniques, whereas the intention had been to use them to understand better the whole of an organizational control system. This deficiency was more recently rectified by Otley and Ferreira (2005) when they combined the performance management framework with Simons' 'levers of control' framework to analyse four case studies of overall control systems. This has led to a more comprehensive set of questions, which both amplify and extend the original list that proved to be an effective research tool in getting to grips with many of the varied aspects of control systems design and use in practice. Although it is still a very rudimentary approach, it provides some evidence that the same approaches that have been used in studying the ways in which budgetary control systems behave in different conditions can be used to help understand how more up-to-date systems, which utilize non-financial measures, behave.

13.8 **Conclusion**

Budgetary control systems and responsibility accounting still form the backbone of the management control systems of many organizations. However, in the last decade, they have been supplemented by a wide variety of non-financial measures and controls, many of which still have to be studied in detail by academic researchers. In addition, the boundaries of management control have been extended in two ways. First, there has been a process of reintegrating the ideas of strategic planning and operational control that were separated out by Anthony (1965). It seems clear that he always intended his classification to represent a temporary simplification to enable progress to be made on an artificially narrowed front. Perhaps the time has now come to broaden the approach and include them once more in the mainstream of performance management systems design and use. Second, the boundaries of management control systems now often extend outside the legal boundaries of a single organization (see Otley 1994) and encompass control of business processes and value chains that covers chains or networks of organizations. Some aspects of control in networks of organizations are covered in other chapters of this book.

Indeed, to talk of the 'management control system' may itself be misleading. Some twenty-five years ago, in an article on the contingency theory of management accounting, Otley (1980) initially labelled one of the boxes in a diagram the 'organizational control *system*', but this was later changed it to the 'organizational control *package*' because the term 'system' seemed to imply too rational a perspective. Organizational control systems are more like packages. Different elements are added by different people at different times. Studying such systems is perhaps more akin to archaeology (see Hopwood 1987)than anything else, although we have the advantage of being able to talk to the current operatives of the 'systems'! It is therefore misleading to assume that the study of performance measurement and management methods will result in a totally coherent outline of a rational set of control mechanisms well suited to the purposes for which they have been designed. Although individual component parts of such systems may approach this degree of rationality, it is unlikely that the total package of control measures that are in place at any point in time will possess such a degree of coherence. This situation has a number of implications for research methods, the most major of which is that we need to study overall control systems (not just their parts) over extended periods of time (not just taking 'snapshots'). Given the significant changes that have taken place in management and control systems practice over the last decade or so, there is clearly scope for a great deal of important research to be undertaken.

The performance management framework therefore provides an important integrating device, both academically and practically. It goes well beyond the traditional boundaries of management accounting, and will require the skills of management accountants (who have been the traditional designers and operators of budgetary control systems) to be developed in at least three areas. First, the management accountant will need fully to understand the operational activities of the organization. This was a traditional skill of the old 'cost and works' accountant, but one that may have been neglected more recently. Attempting to design control systems without having a detailed knowledge of how the business works is likely to prove a recipe for disaster. Second, there is a need to connect control systems design with issues of strategy, both espoused and emergent. Control systems need to reflect the aims of an organization and the plans that have been developed to achieve those aims. The 'strategic management accounting' (SMA) movement has recognized this challenge, but has been more concerned to develop new techniques than to design overall control systems. Third, there is a need to focus on the external context within which the organization is set, rather than just being concerned with internal activities. Competitor analysis is clearly important, but even more central is the value that an organization is delivering to its customers. A process orientation that focuses on value chains is required to complement the vertical and hierarchical approach to control that has long dominated the literature.

Further, the developments outlined so far cannot be treated as purely technical matters that can be analysed from an economic perspective alone. The intention in using performance measures is to influence managerial behaviour, so that managers have the knowledge and motivation to act in the organization's best interests. This is an area where there are likely to be very different approaches that are dependent upon national and organizational culture. Interestingly, this is exactly the field to which that early pioneer of budgetary behaviour, Hofstede (1980), devoted much of his later career.

The conclusion is straightforward. Although individual techniques of management accounting and control have been studied individually within a restricted context, they need also to continue to be studied as parts of wider systems of organizational control. The use of management accounting and budgetary control systems can be fruitfully analysed from the framework of performance measurement and performance management. This makes it clear that management accounting and other performance measurement practices need to be evaluated not just from an economic perspective but also from a social, behavioural, and managerial perspective, within an overall organizational context. It is these social, behavioural, cross-national, and cultural aspects that make the study of control systems such a fascinating topic for academic research and such a challenge to the practitioner in a global environment.

Budgetary control is now widely regarded as an inadequate solution to the problems of organizational control and integration. But approaches aimed at both improving and complementing it have been developed and show continuing potential. Although sometimes criticized as being 'past its sell-by date', budgetary control systems still provide a unique contribution to the assessment of overall performance at an aggregate organizational level. No other approach provides the overall holistic perspective that the use of financial language offers in summarizing disparate activities in common terms. But the very simplifications inherent in devising a common unit of measurement (i.e. money) also lose much important detail and complexity, and it is not surprising that budgetary control can no longer satisfactorily meet all the demands placed upon it. However, it will continue to provide a foundation upon which other, more detailed and more extensive, control systems can rest.

☐ REFERENCES

Anthony, R. N. (1965). *Management Planning and Control Systems: A Framework for Analysis.* Boston: Harvard Business School Press.

Bisbe, J, Batista-Foguet, J. M., and Chenhall, R. (2005). 'What do we Really Mean by Interactive Control Systems: The Risks of Theoretical Misspecification'. Working paper, ESADE Business School, Barcelona.

Briers, M. and Hirst, M. (1990). 'The Role of Budgetary Information in Performance Evaluation', *Accounting, Organizations and Society,* 15(4): 373–98.

Brownell, P. and Dunk, A. (1991). 'Task Uncertainty and Its Interaction with Budgetary Participation and Budget Emphasis: Some Methodological Issues and Empirical Investigation', *Accounting, Organizations and Society* 16: 693–703.

Emmanuel, C. R., Otley, D. T., and Merchant, K. (1990). *Accounting for Management Control*, 2nd edn. London: Chapman and Hall.

Hansen, S. C. and Torok, R. (2003). *The Closed Loop: Implementing Activity-Based Planning and Budgeting*. Bedford, TX: CAM-I.

—— Otley, D. T., and Van der Stede, W. A. (2003). 'Practice Developments in Budgeting: An Overview and Research Perspective', *Journal of Management Accounting Research*, 15: 95–116.

Hartmann, G. H. (2000). 'The Appropriateness of RAPM: Toward the further Development of Theory', *Accounting, Organizations and Society*, 25: 451–82.

Hofstede, G. (1980). *Culture's Consequences: International Differences in Work-Related Values*. Beverly Hills, CA: Sage.

Hope, J. and Fraser, R. (2003). *Beyond Budgeting*. Boston: Harvard Business School Press.

Hopwood, A. G. (1972). 'An Empirical Study of the Role of Accounting Data in Performance Evaluation', *Empirical Research in Accounting (Supplement to Journal of Accounting Research)*, 10: 156–82.

—— (1987). 'The Archaeology of Accounting Systems', *Accounting, Organizations and Society*, 12(3): 207–34.

Kaplan, R. and Norton, D. (1992). 'The Balanced Scorecard: Measures that Drive Performance', *Harvard Business Review*, 70(1): 71–9.

—— —— (1996). *The Balanced Scorecard: Translating Strategy into Action*. Boston: Harvard Business School Press.

—— —— (2001). *The Strategy-Focused Organization*. Boston: Harvard Business School Press.

Merchant, K. A. (1989). *Rewarding Results: Motivating Profit Center Managers*. Boston: Harvard Business School Press.

Neely, A., Sutcliffe, M. R., and Heyns, H. R. (2001). *Driving Value Through Strategic Planning and Budgeting*. London: Accenture.

Otley, D. T. (1978). 'Budget Use and Managerial Performance', *Journal of Accounting Research*, 16: 122–49.

—— (1980). 'The Contingency Theory of Management Accounting: Achievement and Prognosis', *Accounting, Organizations and Society*, 5: 413–28.

—— (1990). 'Issues in Accountability and Control: Some Observations from a Study of Colliery Accountability in the British Coal Corporation', *Management Accounting Research*, 1: 91–165.

—— (1994). 'Management Control in Contemporary Organizations: Towards a Wider Perspective', *Management Accounting Research*, 1994, 5: 289–99.

—— (1999). 'Performance Management: A Framework for Management Control Systems Research', *Management Accounting Research*, 10(4): 363–82.

—— and Fakiolis, A. (2000). 'Reliance on Accounting Performance Measures: Dead End or New Beginning?', *Accounting, Organizations and Society*, 25(4/5): 497–510.

—— and Ferreira, A. (2005). 'The Design and Use of Management Control Systems: An Extended Framework for Analysis'. Working paper, Lancaster University Management School.

—— and Pollanen, R. (2000). 'Budgetary Criteria in Performance Evaluation: A Critical Appraisal using New Evidence', *Accounting, Organizations and Society,* 25(4/5): 483–96.

Simons, R. (1995). *Levers of Control: How Managers Use Innovative Control Systems to Drive Strategic Renewal.* Boston: Harvard Business School Press.

Wildavsky, A. (1975). *Budgeting: A Comparative Theory of Budgetary Processes.* Boston: Little, Brown.

14 Making management accounting intelligible

Hanno Roberts

14.1 Introduction

From the beginning of the debate on the relevance of management accounting over two decades ago, new challenges to the field have continued to emerge (Kaplan 1984*a*, 1984*b*, 1986; Bromwich and Bhimani 1989). In the original debate in the mid-1980s, the role of computer technology provided the major challenge. The diminishing importance of labour costs and the countervailing increase in indirect manufacturing (technology) costs triggered the development of alternative mechanisms for overhead allocation. Simultaneously, this debate made many (once again) become aware that the competitive environment and the ways that firms organize was tied in with the origins of the management accounting field.

Technological developments continue to challenge the field even though the focus may be less upon developments in computerized manufacturing technology. Rather, it is information and communication technology (ICT) that appears to have taken over as the main source of worries in management accounting. The ever-decreasing cost of ICT as well as the emergence of the Internet have made alternative forms of organization possible and enabled the emergence of electronic commerce and electronic markets. This has resulted in a revisit of the existing theories of the firm, to assess whether the emerging 'new economy' continues to fit with prior concepts and what the impact has been on accepted insights within the fields of economics, strategy, management, and accounting (Senge 1993; Shapiro and Varian 1998; Bhimani 2003).

One dimension of the emerging new economy relates to competition on the basis of the accumulated knowledge and competences of the firm in relation to the strategy-conduct-performance paradigm of classic strategic management. Concomitantly, the so-called 'knowledge-intensive firm' emerged, alerting the management field to the need to address questions about managing knowledge beyond that which is codified and stored in databases and in other formal depositories owned and accounted for by the firm. Management accounting's interest in knowledge management is, in large part, a function of the practical problems of accounting for knowledge resources: is it an asset that can be capitalized, or is it an expense relating to various knowledge processes? These questions are especially complex in that most knowledge processes are conceptually unfamiliar and invisible to the standard repertoire of management accounting's functional tools.

The consequence of the technology challenge is an organizational challenge within the management accounting field whereby each problem finds its origin in daily organizational practice. From a conceptual point of view, ICT has made it possible to reduce information asymmetries across markets and in-between economic actors, thus reducing coordination costs within and across firms. In turn, reduced coordination costs allowed for alternative forms of organization, both internally and externally. With lower coordination costs, a series of innovations in coordination activities and organization are possible. For example, coordination cost levels no longer prevent the creation of multi-unit firms, matrix organizations, and in-house outsourcing ('insourcing'). The same low coordination cost levels also allow for experimentation with different forms of organization and their accompanying administrative arrangements. For instance, the so-called 'virtual' and team-based organization consists of a number of collaborators who are loosely coupled in their work activities, use their expertise as main work input, and whose organizational memberships are defined by themselves instead of by the organization. How to manage, if not to account, for such forms of organizations with unclear and ever-changing boundaries (Birkinshaw and Hagström 2000; Brusoni et al. 2001)? Consequently, the organizational challenge to management accounting can be rephrased as an issue of how knowledge is organized, managed, and administered. Only then can the question of how to account for knowledge in its organizational context be addressed, evolving, as is presently the case, from knowledge's administrative aspects.

To start accounting for the knowledge-based firm, it becomes necessary to find a theoretical anchoring point on knowledge organizations and their workings. For the purpose of this chapter, a resource-based theory (RBT) approach is selected because it allows for a market-economics orientation, which informs traditions in accounting thought. Also, it allows alternative resource conceptions other than of financial assets to be discussed in relation to managerial and accounting implications. RBT postulates the firm as the locus of technological and organizational knowledge, and its role as an integrator of learning processes, both informal and tacit, and formal and explicit (e.g. in R&D departments). It views the firm as a depository *and* a generator of competence and knowledge (Penrose 1959; Loasby 1999; Foss and Mahnke 2000). A key idea of RBT is that the firm is primarily a mechanism for the production of knowledge. The managerial element is based on this knowledge production role—management is considered equivalent to the coordination and integration of learning processes. Management, thus, is largely procedural: it consists of the creation, maintenance, and change of coordination procedures that facilitate the accumulation of knowledge from various localized learning processes.

One key question is how the existing managerial accounting mechanisms and conceptual frameworks can be brought to bear on the coordination and integration of (accumulated and generated) knowledge. We draw upon a diverse and still emerging literature from different quarters, each at different stages of empirical maturity, to build a line of argument: the RBT of the firm, the concepts of intellectual capital and of social networks, knowledge management and knowledge transfer writings, and the innovation and learning literatures in relation to organizational capabilities.

This chapter is organized in three sections. First, the RBT and the roles of learning processes, knowledge, and the generation of organizational capabilities are briefly discussed. Second, the intellectual capital framework is introduced and the place that management accounting takes within that framework is considered. Third, the implications of the intellectual capital concept for the management accounting field are discussed, with a particular focus on the concepts of connectivity and relational networks. The chapter adopts a functionalist reference frame. It does not address questions of method or epistemology.

14.2 Resource-based theory, knowledge, and the generation of organizational capabilities[1]

The RBT with its focus on the integration of (accumulated) knowledge and the management of learning processes contrasts with alternative views of the firm as a processor of information, notably espoused in transaction-cost economics (TCE). This contrast is important to note because it relates to the distinction between information and knowledge from a theoretical point of view and because it relates to the high level of comfort that management accounting evidences with the transactional perspective. Transactions provide valid legal claims that can be registered and processed by the accounting information system and, as such, provide the 'raw material' for accounting processes and the decision-making tools using them.

The TCE perspective of the firm as a nexus of contracts is to correct the market failures of costly information processing by the market mechanism. Moreover, TCE acknowledges the existence of information asymmetries and the resultant opportunistic rent-seeking behaviour of individuals. The firm, thus, is depicted as a governance structure to solve misaligned incentives resulting from imperfect information. The hypotheses underlying TCE include the one of bounded rationality, allowing for cognitive limitations of the persons involved, and the existence of learning-by-doing. However, the cognitive capabilities of transacting individuals are taken as given, and not considered as dynamic and open for change with respect to, for example, environmental perception, attention to rule sets, or language. Similarly, TCE conceives knowledge as a stock resulting from the process of accumulation of information; this equates knowledge basically to the mere sum of information values and, consequently, implies that knowledge can be managed in the same way as information.

The contrasting RBT sees the firm as a processor of knowledge, and not of information. It specifically questions the contractual perspective of the firm and opens up for the view that 'agents' are not given in terms of their cognitive profile but, rather, are dynamically changing their cognitive stance. As a result, individuals learn continuously and build cognitive competences allowing them to keep on learning. At firm level, this implies a social perspective on how it knows how to do things, using a set of routines related to learning. This set of routines is also known under the header of 'competences' that are continuously built, changed, maintained, and protected. Hence, the dynamic element of routines turns into the management of knowledge—its acquisition, production, absorption, storage ('memorization'), transfer, and sharing. Knowledge, thus, is not considered equivalent to information; rather, it relates to a set of learning routines and procedures used to fill a dynamic stock of knowledge, sometimes also called the 'core competences' of the firm.

The above contrast has important implications for the management accounting field, primarily in terms of how coordination (i.e. the 'management' part) is achieved and, secondarily, of how knowledge is identified and visualized (i.e. the 'accounting' part).

Coordination involves (*a*) an awareness of the distributed nature of knowledge as it resides in different locations and processes of the firm; and (*b*) the creation of a commonly shared body of procedures, rules, and 'mental models' that uniformizes and homogenizes the exchange of knowledge in a given interaction. The overall purpose of coordination is to assure the integration and use of distributed, heterogeneous knowledge; this requires the creation of a common denominator, a vehicle that allows knowledge to be integrated and acted upon across the organization. Explicitly, coordination requires that knowledge circulates and flows across and between individuals and organizations, thus creating collective learning and collective knowledge that can (or cannot) be embedded in an organization structure.

In turn, the consideration of knowledge as a collective process of learning (that can be coordinated) raises the issue of how knowledge can be transferred from the individual to the organization and vice versa (see also Figure 14.1).

A central concept in the creation of collective knowledge is that of the *routine*, defined as 'an executable capability for repeated performance in some context that has been learned by an organization in response to selective pressures' (Cohen et al. 1996: 683). In organization studies, the concept of routines has a long history with an accompanying sizeable body of research; it goes beyond the purpose of this chapter to address this issue at length (see Grandori and Kogut 2002 for an overview and discussion of routines). Suffice to say that routines can be interpreted in multiple ways: e.g. as an elementary coordination scheme, as

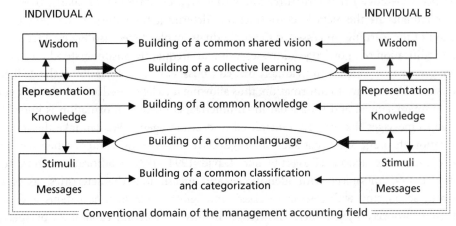

Figure 14.1 Interactions between agents in the formation of knowledge
(*Source:* Adapted from Amin and Cohendet 2004: 26)

the 'gene' in evolutionary economics, as a capability, as a cognitive device, as a reductionist mechanism in complex problem-solving, and as a building block in constructing firm-level competences. As the godfathers of the concept stated: 'the behavior of firms can be explained by the routines they employ. Knowledge of routines is at the heart of understanding behavior. Modeling the firm means modeling the routines and how they change over time' (Nelson and Winter 1982: 128). For the purpose of this chapter, we interpret routines as the building blocks in constructing firm-level competences with these competences resulting from routines in the accumulation and usage of knowledge, i.e. learning routines.

A related issue to that of collective knowledge is that it is something that individuals rather than organizations possess, as evidenced by the frequent question 'why should I share what is mine, giving away what I have?' For knowledge to become actionable and, in a sense, valuable, it needs to be placed into context—knowledge needs to become 'situated' (Lave and Wenger 1991). The circumstances of action shape even the most abstractly presented tasks, illustrating that what individuals actually 'own' is not 'the knowledge' but the practice of knowing, i.e. of putting their knowledge in context and acting upon it. The provisional nature of knowledge and its continuous unfolding in time and space indicates that the nature of knowledge does not rely on an epistemology of possession but on one of practice (Cook and Brown 1999; Carlsen et al. 2004). This has important implications, the most dominant being that the unit of analysis of knowledge is neither the individual nor the organization, but socially distributed activity systems (Engestrom 1993), such as communities, project teams, and social networks.

It is this meso-level of the group or community that forms knowledge, notably through its heterogeneity and diversity and the resulting situated exchange of what knowledge 'makes sense' and what does not. Hence, this continuous interaction between the different processes of knowledge formation is what constitutes knowledge-as-flow. Clearly, among these cognitive mechanisms there is a role set aside for practice and experience on the one hand, and beliefs and judgements on the other. It is practice that provides the 'knowing' while it is experience ('memory') that structures knowledge (representations). Similarly, beliefs and value statements are the meta-level routines that determine the nature of the rules and the direction of the learning processes of the individuals involved (see also Figure 14.2).

The codification of knowledge addresses a similar, frequently misunderstood mechanism of giving away that which is individually owned ('possessed'). Codification is the deliberate conversion of knowledge to information, thus allowing it to be treated as an economic good, ready to be exchanged and transacted in commercial contexts: 'Information is knowledge reduced to messages that can be transmitted to decision agents. We can take the standard information-theoretic view that such messages have information content when receipt of them causes some action' (Dasgupta and David 1994: 493). Codification, thus, turns knowledge into an object with identifiable and measurable characteristics, as is well known in accounting with respect to classic intangible assets such as patents and other intellectual property rights. Tacit knowledge, in this mainstream economics perspective, then, is no more than an economic residual that also can be codified, be it at higher cost as it requires more advanced forms of ICT deployment.

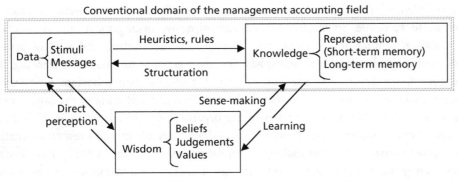

Figure 14.2 The interactive system of knowledge formation and the different processes at stake (*Source:* Adapted from Amin and Cohendet 2004: 20)

However, the process of codifying knowledge is more complex than assumed in mainstream economics: it involves creating models, creating languages, and creating messages (Cowan and Foray 1997). Each of these process stages has its own related cost. For example, the first two steps—creating models and languages—involve high fixed costs and considerable time and effort to implement standards of reference. A well-known accounting example is the (ongoing) codification process of international accounting standards that create a vocabulary of commonly understood terms and definitions, and a grammar to stabilize that language. Once this codebook is in place, only then can individuals ('agents') start to carry out knowledge operations at low marginal cost since these messages are reproducible, i.e. auditing of annual reports and other disclosed financial reporting becomes possible. As regards the harmonization of accounting standards, this can be seen as yet another wave of codification, strengthening the language on which auditing processes are based.

As can be observed from Figure 14.2, knowledge is simultaneously an input and an output, requiring knowledge to codify knowledge. This recursive dynamic implies that knowledge cannot be perceived as a mere stock (in the sense of conventional inventory accounting) resulting from the accumulation of information over time. Moreover, it also implies that knowledge cannot be separated from its context, whether in terms of ownership, or location in time or in space. Stated differently, the codification process alters the relationship between the codified and tacit forms of knowledge.[2] There are continuous contextual trade-offs in which individuals ('agents') are willing to invest in codification and in which to reinforce their tacit knowledge. In other words, the ability of the 'agent' to exploit different categories of knowledge in different contexts matters significantly (Hansen et al. 1999). For example, when the knowledge we want to use is tacit, the 'know-who' becomes important as we want to interact with the holder of that tacit knowledge. Alternatively, when it is codified knowledge we are after, the 'know-where' becomes important, as is evidenced by the popularity of search tools in ICT and on the Internet.

The above discussion of knowledge ownership and knowledge codification brings us back to the issue of coordination. The perspective of the firm as a processor of knowledge needs to be reconciled with the (familiar) issue of resource allocation. A governance challenge emerges: to reconcile organizational and administrative arrangements for transactional efficiency—a familiar topic within the 'management accounting and control systems' field—with organizational and administrative arrangements for sustained learning. This dual governance structure stresses, on one hand, rule-following behaviour necessary for decision-making and, on the other hand, the continuous challenging of the same existing rule set and its related mental models of the organization and its purposes. This duality reflects the environmental conditions of firms—does it operate in stable response situations where programmable decision-making is appropriate (i.e. does it impinge upon conventional management accounting's turf)? Or does it operate in dynamically changing environments where unprogrammable decision-making is more appropriate? Phrased differently: what are the learning strategies for management accounting (Den Hertog and Roberts 1992)?

The emerging answer to this governance duality and, consequently, to the question of coordination arises from the concept of routines; the rules, procedures, and mental models that create a common language and a common knowledge within firms (see also the mid-level elements in Figure 14.1). These routines are located in practice or, better said, in *practising* the activities of a firm, and observed at the meso-level, i.e. in between the learning at individual and at organizational level in the firm. It is this level in which individuals interact in project teams, groups, and communities, and build their collective learning. The organization facilitates that collective learning at meso-level but will need to 'harvest' it at organizational level in terms of the (re)design of higher-level coordination routines and procedures, governing both ransactions and learning. This organizational level tends to be the domain of operation of the management accounting toolbox and concepts: it codifies (financial) data into (accounting) knowledge representations on the transactional status of the firm, using a set of accounting rules and decision-making heuristics. Conversely, the (accounting) knowledge representations, such as budget reports, cost overviews, and product-line income statements, structure the acquisition and accumulation of (accounting) data.

In other words, management accounting operates in the areas of data and knowledge representation as indicated by the top boxes of Figure 14.2. Similarly, the management accounting body of knowledge itself is a well-established, textbook-diffused, and globally certified set of common knowledge, with a common financial language and using equally common classifications and categorizations (e.g. the fixed–variable and direct–indirect cost typologies, used to create cost structure insights). In terms of Figure 14.1, this means management accounting operates in the area between the bottom two boxes, making it possible for two individuals to interact and form knowledge on the financial status of the firm. However, the management accounting field falls short when it comes to building collective learning, the area between the top boxes in Figure 14.1. In a sense, the governance and related coordination demarcation line of what management accounting can provide runs horizontally between the top and the bottom two boxes in Figure 14.1. The question, thus, becomes whether and, if so, how management accounting should cross this demarcation line, and start to include heuristics, rules, and procedures that build collective learning and move towards a commonly shared vision of the firm as knowledge processor (and not only as an information processor). Here, it is regarded as desirable for management accounting to be made intelligible, and to continue to play a decisive, sense-making role.

In terms of the 'how' question, this is addressed by discussing the intellectual capital model, and how it helps in selecting management accounting concepts and procedures to create intelligibility, i.e. to build collective learning as well.

14.3 **Intellectual capital**[3]

The concept of intellectual capital has been recently developed to address the gap between the observed value of a firm in the market and its corresponding book value, postulating that the gap represents the financially invisible value of the firm (Edvinsson 1997; Stewart 1997; Bontis 1998; Lev and Zarowin 1999). Or, stated differently, that the market is able to observe the 'intelligence' of a firm that accounting representations are unable to represent and disclose. The external use of the intellectual capital concept has revolved around bridging that disclosure deficiency by providing an alternative, so-called intellectual capital report (Larsen et al. 1999; Mouritsen et al. 2001; Danish Ministry of Science, Technology and Innovation 2003). The internal use of the intellectual capital concept addresses its use as a managerial representation of the combined knowledge resource of the firm. For the purpose of this chapter, the focus is placed on the internal use of the intellectual capital concept.

Intellectual capital is commonly defined as complementary to financial capital, and comprises the accumulated knowledge of a firm, both in dynamic and in static terms (i.e. knowledge flows and knowledge stocks). Although several categorizations of intellectual capital exist, the commonly accepted one is that by Bontis (1998), separating it into the three subcategories of human, relational, and structural capital (see also Figure 14.3).

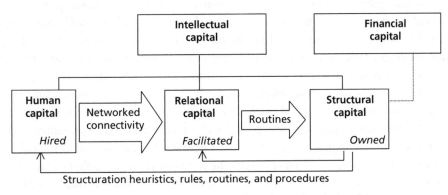

Figure 14.3 Categories of intellectual capital and their dynamic relationships

Human capital provides the basis of intellectual capital and contains the accumulated knowledge, experience, and competences of the firm's employees. This deliberately does not make a difference between the knowledge held by employees or by management, as they are all 'human capital' accessible for use by the firm. Moreover, human capital is not limited to the formal education and training of people; it also includes the accumulated work experience of people that is not formally certified by diplomas or degrees. For example, a firm that has a majority of senior employees without formal education can have a higher (experience-based) human capital than a firm staffed by people with postgraduate degrees. Human capital is not 'owned' by the firm; rather, it is hired or leased (thus including freelancers and other mobile professionals) and can be accessed by the firm. Typically, human capital is a dominant feature of so-called 'people businesses', and requires the appropriate managerial and accounting treatment (Barber and Strack 2005).

Relational capital covers the relational networks between people and groups of people inside and outside the firm; clearly, the issue of organizational boundaries matters less than the linkage or connectivity between communities of people. Where human capital addresses the individual human being, relational capital addresses the meso-level of the group. It provides the arena for exchange of the knowledge and experience held by human capital (a property market with wage prices as outcomes) while simultaneously providing the arena for sense-making and interpretation (a cognition market with reputation as outcome). It is in relational capital that the divergent opinions, experiences, formal knowledge, and professional insights are combined into new knowledge, either in terms of commercial innovations or in terms of ways of working, organizing, or administering. In a sense, the exploration of knowledge—the knowledge production process—takes place within the category of relational capital. It is the 'engine' of intellectual capital, and provides the basic source of new revenue streams and innovations. Relational capital cannot be owned or hired by the firm, but only facilitated, i.e. enabled by the appropriate organizational arrangements and systems. Its fundamental concepts are those of networks and of connectivity (Nahapiet and Ghoshal 1998; Adler and Kwon 2002).

Structural capital is the only element that the firm actually owns as proprietary knowledge, and contains the various systems of the organization, e.g. its ICT systems and its managerial accounting system. It includes elements of proprietary knowledge that are also represented by statutory accounting as its intangible assets, such as intellectual property rights (IPRs) and goodwill, indicated by the dotted line in Figure 14.3. Structural capital provides the organizational skeleton of a firm; that which remains if capital and labour are stripped away or gone home after work. It institutionalizes and 'solidifies' the organization and, as such, carries a strong resemblance to the above discussed concept of routines.

When positioning the concept of intellectual capital, one can think of it in terms of an iceberg. The part above the waterline provides the visible and well-represented financial capital of the firm, while the (much larger) part below represents the accumulated knowledge of the firm that keeps it afloat and feeds the competitive sustainability of the firm over time. Nevertheless, the use of the word 'capital' carries strong (and incorrect) connotations of ownership and hints at attempts to legitimize the appropriation of individual and network knowledge by the firm. Considering the accumulated knowledge resources as 'capital' also opens it up to a perspective of knowledge as an object, allowing its manipulation by codified managerial technologies such as accounting. Hence, the term intellectual capital can be misleading, pushing it into an epistemology of possession (see above) and stripping it of its process nature. For example, it is an obvious reflex to start representing a firm's intellectual capital by reporting on the number of people holding a formal degree (the number of 'intellectuals')—which does not say anything about how this knowledge is actually used, i.e. the contextual processes and routines that generate the firm's core competences and provide its sustainability (Chaminade and Roberts 2003).

The usefulness of the intellectual capital model is in the dynamic relationships between the various categories, i.e. the arrows between the boxes in Figure 14.3 (Roberts 2003*a*). The formation of (new) knowledge starts out from the individual knowledge held by human capital elements, either formally members of the organization or not. Individual knowledge is understood to contain both the tacit and the codified knowledge dimensions. The codified dimension, captured in spreadsheets, specifications, and computations, needs the tacit dimension to create alternative interpretations, insights, and understandings. Both types of knowledge become connected to other individuals' knowledge repertoires in the relational capital category. This connectivity is a network process, and is facilitated by search, identification, accessing, and combining processes. From an instrumental and managerial perspective, connectivity can be conceived in terms of social network analysis, identifying the 'right' expertise, locating the people, artefacts, and institutions that hold that expertise, and then bringing them together. Once connected, conventional forms of project or team management with their accompanying mechanisms and routines can be employed.

However, the novel insights and innovations that are generated by the networked connectivity in relational capital provide a massive and heterogeneous pool of opportunities and potential. Only when this pool is filtered in terms of the routines and procedures that improve learning and knowledge processes, as indicated by the thinner arrow in Figure 14.3, additional structural capital is created and knowledge value becomes available to the firm. In other words, the innovative 'explosion' occurring in relational capital creates a first knowledge value moment but it is only after 'harvesting' this innovative explosion in terms of new or improved learning (rule sets) in this second value moment that the firm actually gains intellectual capital. These new or improved rule sets are then fed back to the human capital and relational capital categories, for example by improving the procedures within human resource management (Fleming et al. 2005) or by improving the rules around internal and external collaboration (Evans and Wolf 2005; Fischer and Boynton 2005).

Obviously, 'harvesting' of innovation potential also takes place in the conventional sense of project or R&D management and their concrete outcomes and results. This can be understood in terms of Argyris and Schon's typology (1978, 1996) of single- and double-loop learning, with single-loop learning taking place within the regular project activities and second-loop learning taking place at the meta-level of improved routines for managing projects as such (Acha et al. 2005). In other words, connecting the elements of intellectual capital in the direction of the arrows in Figure 14.3 carries a strong resemblance to process

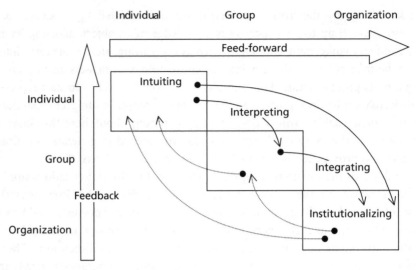

Figure 14.4 Organizational learning as a dynamic process
(*Sources*: Crossan et al. 1999: 532)

theories of organizational learning. For example, the direction of the intellectual flow ('learning') from the individual to the group (network) to the organization, and the corresponding stages of intuiting (human capital), interpreting, integrating (relational capital), and institutionalizing (structural capital) in the work of Crossan et al. (1999; see Figure 14.4), overlaps strongly with the arguments presented as part of the intellectual capital model and its related knowledge formation process.

14.4 **Management accounting implications**

The intellectual capital model holds several relevant promises for making management accounting more intelligible. These are:

- The formulation of a basis for developing management accounting tools and concepts other than as derivatives from financial accounting or from a financial capital perspective
- The concept of connectivity and networks that ties in with the unit (meso-level) of analysis that is of increasing relevance for management accounting
- The possibility to apply management accounting to the differing demands of service and people-oriented firms

The development of management accounting tools and concepts, which are crossovers, if not shared tools, with other managerial disciplines, necessitates a relaxation of the financial capital orientation, notably of the following aspects: that capital is scarce, that it operates under decreasing returns to scale, and that resource utilization and consumption are key criteria for allocation. Knowledge, in contrast, is both a (codified) object and a (tacit) interpretation simultaneously; the tacit element (a process) cannot be separated from the explicit and codified form of knowledge (a good) as both are embodied in the practice of doing and learning-by-doing (Polanyi 1967). Knowledge as such is not a scarce good; nor is knowing a scarce process. Rather, it is abundant and unlimited in size; typically, it cannot be 'used up' with a resultant zero stock as outcome. Moreover, knowledge works with rather distinct time values—either it has a very punctual value in time (e.g. a specific solution only works there and then) or it has a very stretched-out value in time (e.g. the knowledge on how to build oneself a house, which has meaning and application to multiple generations). This means, for example, that inventory accounting and asset depreciation are concepts of limited meaning. The more knowledge gets used, the more value it gains as it is combined to different circumstances in time and space; increasing returns to scale, thus, seem to be more likely. And given the combinatory nature of knowledge—it is combined with other knowledge in order to create 'more'—the calculative regime becomes one of multiplication and not one of aggregation and subtraction. This is likely to be of importance in situations where human, relational, and business resources need to be 'partnered' in teams, project groups, consortia, or other forms of business combinations. Such combinatory calculative regimes tend to play out in the top, revenue part of the income statement and far less in its cost (consumptive) part. This new calculative regime is already emerging in the area around revenue-sharing arrangements between firms and gain-sharing arrangements between individuals in a unit or group, i.e. how can the profit pool be maximized and what are the *criteria* for the claim of each party on this profit pool?

Similarly, as knowledge cannot be 'used up', resource *consumption* gives way to issues around resource *contribution*. Criteria for contribution are to go beyond the mere financial or factor inputs, and include process or relational criteria—e.g. the facilitation of access to certain groups or individuals, or the creation of knowledge-sharing incentives or a positive teamwork environment (Casciaro and Lobo 2005; Florida and Goodnight 2005). A typical management accounting area where contribution issues come above the waterline is that of pricing (Dawson 2000; Roberts 2003b). Instead of textbook-type cost-plus pricing, the price arrangement is stretched over time and composed of multiple elements, related to both cost coverage and to appropriating a share of the benefits obtained by the customer (i.e. 'success fees'). Another typical example is the use of the multiple contribution-margin income statement (Roberts and Gutschelhofer 1997). Well known in German and continental European management accounting, revenue income is presented in gradual steps, subtracting layers of types of fixed cost (e.g. marketing, R&D, management), resulting in a more transparent contribution of different organizational functions and areas to net income.

Connectivity addresses the concepts of networks and bundled or 'sticky' assets. As such, connectivity is an extension of the concept of reciprocal interdependence, putting it into a multidyadic perspective and paying particular attention to facilitating the exchange and combination of knowledge into novel ways and formats. It plays out in the relational capital sub-category of intellectual capital and, in a sense, is its creative engine (Roberts and Bjurström 2004). Without knowledge transfer or exchange, knowledge will stand still, i.e. reduce to a passive property of human capital. Moreover, when knowledge is not circulated and applied, its relevance for contributing value will diminish. Connectivity in its most elementary form consists of bringing the 'right' people (human capital) together, in order to make sure that both their tacit and their explicit knowledge is shared. The latter is particularly important as knowledge is context-specific and tends to be both embodied (in a person) and embedded (in a practice); i.e. knowledge is 'sticky' and cannot be separated and identified as a single item. Hence, the desire to create connectivity between asset bundles of people, artefacts, experiences, and competences.

From a management accounting perspective, connectivity relates to criteria for allocation, to the accumulation of costs, and to the organizational pooling of activities and procedures in responsibility centres. The conventional criteria for allocation are based on resource consumption. For example, cost allocation tends to follow the consumption pattern of a typical activity with its related cost (as in activity-based costing (ABC)), or it follows the physical consumption of space, material, or labour as assigned to it via cost centre accounting. Allocation criteria tend to be represented by cost drivers or physical cost allocation denominators. The recent advances in creating cost hierarchies of units, batches, product-line sustaining, facility-sustaining categories, and their related groupings of cost drivers provide a step towards creating connectivity—making transparent in the accounting system how activities are interdependent and drive cost.

Taking a human capital perspective, people are allocated to projects and teams following allocation criteria that tend to be based not on resource consumption, but on competence contribution. These criteria are not originating from the administration or from an activity analysis, but from a certain revenue logic, i.e. how to staff this project in order to get the best out of it? The comparison of staffing criteria (from human resource management) and cost driver hierarchies (from management accounting)—both are allocations—is likely to lead to the inclusion of more learning-oriented allocation principles, to be used in both fields.

Connectivity tends to create a group of interacting and knowledge-sharing people, a unit or a 'community'. Once connectivity is established and the unit is operational, cost can be accumulated and pooled on the basis of that network. In management accounting terms, this implies a more extensive use of project accounting (and budgeting) with each project being itemized as a separate responsibility centre. Once again, responsibility centres and projects tend to have a reflection in human capital—project participation provides an experience build-up and value increase of the knowledge of the individual, i.e. there is more 'sticking to him or her'. Accumulation and pooling of project costs, and the registration in competence profiles, are two sides of the same coin (of building collective learning).

Connectivity conceived as a network of relationships is also receiving increasing attention in terms of its interventionist and measurement properties. A technique called social network analysis (SNA) exists that plots and visualizes how people actually relate to each other and work and/or communicate in collaborative units. Typically, SNA graphs show the 'hidden' organization of work and can substantially deviate from the declared and formalized work organization pictured in organization charts and responsibility designs. The value of SNA is located in visualizing human collaboration—which is the reason why SNA provides a key tool for the relational capital sub-category of intellectual capital. SNA literally shows that information does not flow unchanged through organizations but that network participants enrich it in its passing, add meaning, interpretation, and context. These 'add-ons' are what turn information into knowledge, and build collective learning. Empirical research has shown that networks have a substantial impact on performance, learning, and innovation (i.e. the sustained renewal of revenue streams). Examples include intrafirm collaboration (Uzzi 1996; Tsai and Ghoshal 1998; Hansen 1999), interfirm networks such as joint ventures (Gulati 1995; Uzzi 1997), and communication patterns that support learning within the firm (Gabbay and Leenders 2001; Lin et al. 2001; Chaminade and Roberts 2002). In short, SNA is a relational tool for identifying, visualizing, and directing collaborative efforts of many sorts (Cross and Parker 2004).

From a management accounting perspective, SNA has an immediate impact on issues relating to management control, notably in assigning budget and decision-making responsibilities. Once the collaborative network of a particular unit has been visualized and fed back to it, proposals for improvement in communication, information flow, and responsibility distribution start flowing. A less immediate but perhaps stronger management accounting impact of using SNA is the impact it has on internal reporting, suggesting several changes in both *what* is reported to *whom* and, more importantly, *why* certain information categories deserve to be reported and are stored and transmitted through the formal management accounting system (MAS). The discussion on 'rich information', i.e. the tacit component that adds contextual meaning and localizes information to where knowledge actually is deployed (Roberts 1999; Westin and Roberts 2005), is closely linked to the ongoing debate on changes in management accounting and control systems (Burns and Scapens 2000). The use of accounting systems for permanent improvement efforts and for deliberate and specific interventions (Jönsson 1996) will benefit from a visual tool such as SNA. Similarly, the recent developments in performance measurement tools, also with respect to measuring the performance of intangible activities and the 'hidden factory' of fixed costs (Miller and Vollmann 1985), is likely to benefit from the relational mapping of work interdependences.

Finally, the different demands that service and 'people businesses' place on MAS have put an emphasis on steering the intangibles of an organization. Typically, these businesses have low capital intensity with their productive assets mostly located in the human resource and in their market reputation or branding. These are 'assets' that are not represented in (management) accounting systems, requiring these types of firms to experiment with alternative organization formats and administrative arrangements. Thus far, the attempts are to define the organizational formats that work best, and subsequently use their properties and characteristics to develop administrative and coordination arrangements, making do with whatever management accounting can offer to support them.

This implies two things for the management accounting field: first, that challenges as well as management accounting innovations are most likely to emerge in these types of businesses, turning them into prime areas for research; and second, that attention to organizational format is warranted, before discussing management accounting change of any sort. An example of the latter is the recent discussion on the so-called 'community of practice' format of organizing in the field of organization science (Brown and Duguid 1991; Wenger 1998; Wenger et al. 2002); a bottom-up and highly autonomous form of work organization, the community of practice provides alternative mechanisms of coordination (consensus-oriented and distributive in its participation) and of control (reputation and interaction-based, located primarily in the human resource category). This implies a thorough reconsideration of management accounting concepts, putting communication and relations before production and transactions, and of management accounting tools, placing emphasis on time(liness) over money as its currency of choice. Taken together, both management accounting implications suggest a strong role for practice-based research and praxis-oriented development of theory—the way things are being done 'out there' is to feed into new ways of looking at management accounting and its constituent parts. In itself, it implies a strong(er) emphasis on field research methodologies and their accompanying rigour in development and execution (Lukka 2000).

14.5 **Conclusion**

Making management accounting intelligible requires a multidisciplinary perspective in attempting to 'take the best of both worlds'. Knowledge as a bundled and 'sticky' resource is hard to reconcile with the transactional orientation underlying management accounting. The visibility of financial resources and their manipulation by the management accounting toolbox requires finding common ground with creating visibility for the knowledge resources and learning processes that constitute it. However, some things do not differ across disciplines, such as the need for coordination, for organization, and for innovation. Interdependencies arising from work or relations need to be coordinated and arranged in communal formats that allow connectivity in order to renew and innovate resource contributions.

It is most certainly possible for management accounting to 'think out of the box' and evolve further; hence the message is a positive one. It can be done. But it requires careful selection of the 'boxes' from which to pick and of the 'boxes' in which to put. Summing up the above discussion, this chapter suggests RBT, knowledge management, and intellectual capital as the 'boxes' to pick from. Equally, it suggests various management accounting concepts and instrumental areas as the 'boxes' for putting the new ideas into.

A common element is that 'thinking out of the box' requires a return to the basics of theory: what are the key elements we need to reconsider?—and of research: what are the key questions and methodologies we need to employ? Answers are likely to differ; which is a positive signal—it is diversity that drives intelligibility. However, this chapter has argued that theorizing and research might benefit heeding the calls from several business sectors and forces that act as 'canaries in the mine', whistling to management accounting that action is needed to respond to an upcoming challenge. These 'canaries' point to areas where collaborative and multidisciplinary research and thought will likely prove beneficial:

- Professional service firms—consisting almost entirely of intangible assets and intangible processes, these 'knowledge-based firms' require a concurrent rethinking of organizational

General and Industrial Management	
Management functions ➡	**Principles of management**
1. <u>Planning:</u>study the future and arrange the means for dealing with it— fore casting, goal setting, determine actions.	1. *Division of work—specialization of labour.*
	2. *Authority—the right to give orders must accompany responsibility.*
2. <u>Organizing:</u>design a structure to assist in goal accomplishment and that effectively combines human and non-human resources to the tasks of the enterprise.	3. *Discipline—obedience and respect help an organization run smoothly.*
	4. *Unity of command—each employee should receive orders from only one superior.*
3. <u>Coordinating:</u> uniting all activities that take place within the organization, so that elements are given proper resources and means to accomplish goals.	5. *Unity of direction—the efforts of everyone should be coordinated and focused.*
	6. *Subordination of individual interests to the general interest.*
4. <u>Directing:</u> engaging in those activities that ensure effective operation, including leadership and motivation of employee action towards goals.	7. *Remuneration—employees should be paid fairly in accordance with their contribution.*
5. <u>Controlling:</u> ensuring that everything is carried out according to plan.	8. *Centralization—the relationship between centralization and decentralization is a matter of proportion.*
	9. *Scalar chain—subordinates should observe the formal chain of command, unless expressly authorized by their respective superiors to communicate with each other.*
	10. *Order—both material things and people should be in their proper places.*
	11. *Equity—fairness that results from a combination of kindliness and justice will lead to devoted and loyal service.*
	12. *Stability and tenure of personnel— people need time to learn their jobs.*
	13. *Initiative—one of the greatest satisfactions is formulating and carrying out a plan.*
	14. *Esprit de corps—harmonious effort among individuals is the key to organizational success.*

Figure 14.5 The historical functions of management and its administrative principles

format, production processes, coordination and administration arrangements, and accounting tooling. The related research fields are a combination of service marketing, organization science (communities and networks), sociology (social capital), and innovation management.

- Project management—a focal point of productive efforts in a limited time and space, the temporary organization of a project requires the coordination of multiple resources, not allowing one single discipline to overshadow others. The platform for further thinking provided by project management offers a rich arena for multidisciplinary exploration. Related research fields include project and innovation management, organization science (teams and communities), and cognitive psychology (group learning).

- Transfer of 'best practices'—lessons learned at specific locations provide embedded and embodied knowledge bundles. Management accounting as a common repertoire of rules is continuously challenged at the level of this repertoire to include new routines 'from elsewhere'. Firm-level inventions on how to transfer and implement internally the knowledge gained from within diverse organizations is reflective of how local knowledge can be linked to larger structures of accountability, responsibility, and governance. The related research fields include management control, strategic management (dynamic capabilities), sociology (social capital), knowledge management (tacit knowledge), and the economics of governance.

In conclusion, a historical point bears significance for the considerations noted above. The management functions and principles of management advanced by Henri Fayol in 1916 (see Figure 14.5) gave rise to thinking in terms of planning, decision-making, and controlling—all reflective of management accounting concerns today.

The technological and organizational challenges to the management accounting field suggests a further reconsideration of what management is, what functions it fulfils, and what principles it continues to fit. Immense change has been witnessed since 1916 and research fields have evolved just as organizations have learned and practised what they know. Fields that retain value are the ones that invest in understanding their body of knowledge and how they may learn from others.

☐ NOTES

1 This section draws heavily on the work by Amin and Cohendet (2004), notably its chapters on the firm (ch. 3) and its governance (ch. 4).
2 For a typology of the different sorts of knowledge and their relationship to different types of learning in a firm, see Blackler (2002).
3 This section draws on earlier work by Roberts (2003).

⬚ REFERENCES

Acha, V., Gann, D. M., and Salter, A. J. (2005). 'Episodic Innovation: R&D Strategies for Project-based Environments', *Industry and Innovation*, 12(2): 255–81.

Adler, P. S. and Kwon, S.-W. (2002). 'Social Capital: Prospects for a New Concept', *Academy of Management Review*, 27(1): 17–40.

Amin, A. and Cohendet, P. (2004). *Architectures of Knowledge: Firms, Capabilities, and Communities*. Oxford: Oxford University Press.

Argyris, C. and Schön, D. (1978). *Organizational Learning: A Theory of Action Perspective*. Reading, MA: Addison-Wesley.

—— —— (1996). *Learning Organizations II*. Reading, MA: Addison-Wesley.

Barber, F. and Strack, R. (2005). 'The Surprising Economics of "People Business"', *Harvard Business Review* (June): 80–90.

Bhimani, A. (ed.) (2003). *Management Accounting in the Digital Economy*. Oxford: Oxford University Press.

Birkinshaw, J. and Hagström, P. (eds.) (2000). *The Flexible Firm: Capability Management in Network Organizations*. New York: Oxford University Press.

Blackler, F. (2002). 'Knowledge, Knowledge Work, and Organizations', in C. W. Choo and N. Bontis (eds.), *The Strategic Management of Intellectual Capital and Organisational Knowledge*. New York: Oxford University Press, pp. 47–62.

Bontis, N. (1998). 'Intellectual Capital: An Exploratory Study that Develops Measures and Models', *Management Decision*, 36(2): 63–76.

Bromwich, M. and Bhimani, A. (1989). *Management Accounting: Evolution, not Revolution*. London: CIMA.

Brown, J. S. and Duguid, P. (1991). 'Organizational Learning and Communities of Practice: Towards a Unified View of Working, Learning and Innovation', *Organization Science*, 2(1): 40–57.

Brusoni, S., Prencipe, A. and Pavitt, K. (2001). 'Knowledge Specialization, Organizational Coupling and the Boundaries of the Firm: Why Do Firms Know More Than They Make?', *Administrative Science Quarterly*, 46(4): 597–621.

Burns, J. and Scapens, R. W. (2000). 'Conceptualising Management Accounting Change: An Institutional Framework', *Management Accounting Research*, 11(1): 3–25.

Carlsen, A., Klev, R., and von Krogh, G. (2004). *Living Knowledge: The Dynamics of Professional Service Work*. London: Palgrave Macmillan.

Casciaro, T. and Lobo, M. G. (2005). 'Competent Jerks, Lovable Fools and the Formation of Social Networks', *Harvard Business Review* (June): 92–9.

Chaminade, C. and Roberts, H. (2002). 'Social Capital as Mechanism'. Paper presented at the Third European Conference on Organizational Knowledge, Learning, and Capabilities, Athens.

—— —— (2003). 'What it Means is What it Does: A Comparative Analysis of Implementing Intellectual Capital in Norway and Spain', *European Accounting Review*, 12(4): 733–51.

Cohen, M. D., Burkhart, R., Dosi, G., Edigi, M., Marengo, L., Warglien, M., and Winter, S. (1996). 'Routines and Other Recurring Action Patterns of Organizations: Contemporary Research Issues', *Industrial and Corporate Change*, 5(3): 653–98.

Cook, S. D. N. and Brown, J. S. (1999). 'Bridging Epistemologies: The Generative Dance Between Organizational Knowledge and Organizational Knowing', *Organization Science*, 10(4): 381–400.

Cowan, R. and Foray, D. (1997). 'The Economics of Codification and the Diffusion of Knowledge', *Industrial and Corporate Change*, 9(2): 211–53.

Cross, R. and Parker, A. (2004). *The Hidden Power of Social Networks: Understanding How Work Really Gets Done in Organizations*. Boston: Harvard Business School Press.

Crossan, M. M., Lane, H. W., and White, R. E. (1999). 'An Organizational Learning Framework: From Intuition to Institution', *Academy of Management Review*, 24(3): 522–37.

Danish Ministry of Science, Technology and Innovation (2003). 'Intellectual Capital Statements'. Available at: http://www.videnskabsministeriet.dk/cgi-bin/theme-list.cgi?theme_id=100650&_lang=uk.

Dasgupta, P. and David, P. A. (1994). 'Towards a New Economics of Science', *Research Policy*, 23: 487–521.

Dawson, R. (2000). *Developing Knowledge-based Client Relationships: The Future of Professional Services*. Boston: Butterworth-Heinemann.

Den Hertog, J. F. and Roberts, H. (1992). 'Learning Strategies for Management Accounting in Unprogrammable Contexts', *Accounting, Management and Information Technology*, 2(3): 165–82.

Edvinsson, L. (1997). 'Developing Intellectual Capital at Skandia', *Long Range Planning*, 30(3): 366–73.

Engestrom, Y. (1993). 'Work as a Testbed of Activity Theory', in S. Chaiklin and J. Lave (eds.), *Understanding Practice: Perspectives on Activity and Context*. Cambridge: Cambridge University Press, pp. 65–103.

Evans, P. and Wolf, B. (2005). 'Collaboration Rules', *Harvard Business Review* (July–August): 96–104.

Fischer, B. and Boynton, A. (2005). 'Virtuoso Teams', *Harvard Business Review* (June): 117–23.

Fleming, J. H., Coffman, C., and Harter, J. K. (2005). 'Manage Your Human Sigma', *Harvard Business Review* (July–August): 107–14.

Florida, R. and Goodnight, J. (2005). 'Managing for Creativity', *Harvard Business Review* (July–August): 124–31.

Foss, N. and Mahnke, V. (eds.) (2000). *Competence Governance and Entrepreneurship: Advances in Economic Strategy Research*. Oxford: Oxford University Press.

Gabbay, S. and Leenders, R. (2001). *Social Capital in Organizations*. Stanford, CA: JAI Press.

Grandori, A. and Kogut, B. (2002). 'Dialogue on Organization and Knowledge', *Organization Science*, 13(3): 224–31.

Gulati, R. (1995). 'Social Structure and Alliance Formation Patterns: A Longitudinal Analysis', *Administrative Science Quarterly*, 40: 619–52.

Hansen, M. T. (1999). 'The Search-Transfer Problem: The Role of Weak Ties in Sharing Knowledge Across Organization Subunits', *Administrative Science Quarterly*, 44: 82–111.

—— Nohria, N., and Tierney, T. (1999). 'What is Your Strategy for Managing Knowledge?', *Harvard Business Review* (March–April): 106–16.

Jönsson, S. (1996). *Accounting for Improvement*. Oxford: Pergamon Press.

Kaplan, R. S. (1984a). 'The Evolution of Management Accounting', *Accounting Review*, 59(3): 690–718.

—— (1984*b*). 'Yesterday's Accounting Undermines Production', *Harvard Business Review* (July–August): 95–101.

—— (1986). 'Accounting Lag: The Obsolescence of Cost Accounting Systems', *California Management Review*, 28(2): 174–99.

Larsen, H. T., Mouritsen, J., and Bukh, P. N. D. (1999). 'Intellectual Capital Statements and Knowledge Management: Measuring, Reporting and Acting', *Australian Accounting Review*, 9(3): 15–26.

Lave, J. and Wenger, E. (1991). *Situated Learning: Legitimate Peripheral Participation*. New York: Cambridge University Press.

Lev, B. and Zarowin, P. (1999). 'The Boundaries of Financial Reporting and How to Extend Them', *Journal of Accounting Research*, 37(2): 353–85.

Lin, N., Cook, S., and Burt, R. S. (2001). *Social Capital: Theory and Research*. New York: Aldine de Gruyter.

Loasby, B. J. (1999). *Knowledge Institutions and Evolution in Economics*. London: Routledge.

Lukka, K. (2000). 'The Key Issues of Applying the Constructive Approach to Field Research', in T. Reponen (ed.), *Management Expertise for the New Millennium*. Turku: Publications of the Turku School of Economics and Business Administration, Sarja/Series A-1:2000, 113–28.

Miller, J. G. and Vollmann, T. E. (1985). 'The Hidden Factory', *Harvard Business Review* (September–October): 142–50.

Mouritsen, J., Larsen, H. T., and Bukh, P. N. D. (2001). 'Intellectual Capital and the "Capable Firm": Narrating, Visualising and Numbering for Managing Knowledge', *Accounting, Organizations and Society*, 26(7/8): 735–62.

Nahapiet, J. and Ghoshal, S. (1998). 'Social Capital, Intellectual Capital and the Organizational Advantage', *Academy of Management Review*, 23(2): 242–66.

Nelson, R. R. and Winter, S. (1982). *An Evolutionary View of Economic Change*, Cambridge, MA: Belknap Press.

Penrose, E. T. (1959), *The Theory of the Growth of the Firm*. Oxford: Basil Blackwell.

Polanyi, M. (1967). *The Tacit Dimension*. New York: Doubleday.

Roberts, H. (1999). 'The Control of Intangibles in the Knowledge-Intensive Firm'. Paper presented at the 22nd Annual Congress of the European Accounting Association, Bordeaux.

—— (2003*a*). 'Management Accounting and the Knowledge Production Process', in A. Bhimani (ed.), *Management Accounting in the Digital Economy*. Oxford: Oxford University Press, pp. 260–83.

—— (2003*b*). 'Knowledge Pricing: Adding up Intangibles or Producing Knowledge?' Paper presented at the 26th Annual Congress of the European Accounting Association, Seville.

—— and Bjurström, E. (2004). 'The Principle of Connectivity: Networked Assets, Strategic Capabilities and Bundled Outcomes'. Paper presented at the 27th Annual Congress of the European Accounting Association, Prague.

—— and Gutschelhofer, A. (1997). 'Anglo-Saxon and German Life-Cycle Costing', *International Journal of Accounting*, 32(1): 23–44.

Senge, P. M. (1993). *The Fifth Discipline: The Art and Practice of the Learning Organization*. London: Century Business.

Shapiro, C. and Varian, H. (1998). *Information Rules: A Strategic Guide to the Network Economy*. Boston: Harvard Business School Press.

Stewart, T. A. (1997). *Intellectual Capital: The New Wealth of Organizations*. New York: Doubleday.

Tsai, W. and Ghoshal, S. (1998). 'Social Capital and Value Creation: The Role of Intrafirm Networks'. *Academy of Management Journal*, 41(4): 464–76.

Uzzi, B. (1996). 'The Sources and Consequences of Embeddedness for the Economic Performance of Organisations: The Network Effect', *American Sociological Review*, 61: 674–98.

—— (1997). 'Social Structure and Competition in Interfirm Networks: The Paradox of Embeddedness', *Administrative Science Quarterly*, 42: 35–67.

Wenger, E. (1998). *Communities of Practice: Learning, Meaning and Identity*. Cambridge: Cambridge University Press.

—— McDermott, W., and Snyder, M. (2002). *Cultivating Communities of Practice*. Boston: Harvard Business School Press.

Westin, O. and Roberts, H. (2005). 'Accounting for Working Knowledge—The Role of Local Information Systems in Knowledge Management'. Paper presented at the 28th Annual Congress of the European Accounting Association, Gothenburg.

15 Changing times: management accounting research and practice from a UK perspective

Robert W. Scapens

15.1 Introduction

Recent years have witnessed significant changes in both management accounting research and practice. For both management accounting researchers and management accounting practitioners these are changing times. This chapter discusses the changes that have been taking place in recent years, and also suggests the challenge for the future. The focus is primarily on management accounting research and practice in the UK, but broader international developments are also considered. Developments in the UK, particularly in management accounting research, are reflected elsewhere, although there are some differences in the approach to management accounting research in the UK and the USA. In addition, there seem to be similar trends in management accounting practices in many countries, even though there are differences in the professional organization of management accountants in the UK and in some other European countries.

In order to put the more recent developments into their historical context, this chapter begins with a brief history of management accounting thought over the last thirty-five years. Personally, I believe that historical analysis is very important: *in order to understand where we are today, we need to understand where we have come from.* So I will start with a brief overview of how we have got to where we are in UK management accounting research. This will enable me to place the more recent and continuing changes in their longer historical context. After this brief history, in Section 15.3, I will discuss some of the UK responses to Johnson and Kaplan's claim (1987) about management accounting's lost relevance. In Section 15.4, I will describe the changing nature of management accounting practices in the UK over the subsequent years. This will be followed by a discussion of recent trends in management accounting research in Section 15.5. In Section 15.6, I will outline some current issues in management accounting that I personally find interesting. The chapter will finish with some comments on the nature of UK management accounting research and directions for the future.

15.2 **A brief history**

This section briefly reviews developments in management accounting research over the last thirty-five years, i.e. beginning in the early 1970s. To some extent this reflects my own personal journey as a management accounting researcher. I began my academic career at the beginning of the 1970s and have witnessed various changes in both management accounting research and practice over the years. When I first became an academic, management accounting research was primarily concerned with sophisticated quantitative models for management decision-making—especially decision-making under uncertainly (see Scapens et al. 1984 for a review). These decision models provided normative solutions to management accounting problems. Mathematical techniques such as sensitivity analysis, linear programming, and statistical decision theory were all applied to management accounting problems. For example, researchers explored probabilistic budgeting (Ferrara and Hayya 1970), cost-volume-profit analysis under uncertainty (Magee 1975), and cost-variance investigation models (Kaplan 1975). These models were intended to provide solutions to the problems that the researchers believed were faced by management accounting practitioners and business decision-makers. However, the research was not based on a detailed understanding of practice; rather, it was grounded on the assumptions of neoclassical economic decision models (see Arnold and Scapens 1986). This research was largely done by US researchers. At that time, there was only a quite small group of UK accounting researchers. It was only in the 1970s that accounting started to become an established field of study in UK universities. During that decade, there was considerable expansion in the number of universities in the UK teaching and researching in accounting, and the emerging group of UK accounting scholars tended to look to the USA as a source of guidance and inspiration.

UK management accounting researchers shared the beliefs of their US counterparts that if 'optimal' decision models could be developed, practitioners would use them. However, it was recognized that practitioners, in general, did not use the techniques of marginal economic analysis, which were advocated in the management accounting textbooks of the time, and which underpinned the research into optimal decision models. Instead, practitioners used full costing techniques. But this was thought to be due to the practitioners' lack of understanding, and that the researchers had an educational role in communicating the optimal techniques, such as marginal costing and the emerging economic decision models, to those practitioners.

It was at the beginning of the 1980s that UK management accounting researchers started taking a serious interest in what management accounting practice is actually like, and recognized that there was a gap between the theory and practice of management accounting. This followed an Accounting Research Initiative launched by the Social Science Research

Council (SSRC) in 1976. As part of this initiative Michael Bromwich was charged with the responsibility for setting up a network of management accounting researchers, and for commissioning literature surveys.[1] In December 1979 a conference was organized by Bromwich and Hopwood at the London Graduate School of Business at which various papers were presented reviewing the state of 'British Accounting Research' (see Bromwich and Hopwood 1981). A year later, in December 1980, another conference, this time focusing on management accounting research, was held at the Manchester Business School.[2]

Several of the papers presented at that Manchester conference reviewed various aspects of both management accounting research and practice (see Cooper et al. 1983). Despite a general awareness of the apparent gap between theory and practice, participants at the conference clearly recognized that researchers' knowledge of management accounting practice was severely limited and based largely on anecdotal evidence. Few researchers had much current knowledge of management accounting practice, either from doing research in organizations or from personal practical experience. Furthermore, where researchers did have some practical experience, it was rather dated and very limited in scope. Generally, it was recognized that academic researchers lacked detailed knowledge of prevailing management accounting practices, and it was agreed that they needed to know more. It was from about that time that researchers in the UK began to undertake research, first to describe, and later to explain, the nature of management accounting practice. Initially, researchers conducted questionnaire surveys, next they undertook fieldwork, interviewing both managers and management accountants, and then subsequently and more recently they started using in-depth longitudinal case studies.

Alongside these descriptive studies of management accounting practice, the 1980s and 1990s also saw the emergence of alternative research perspectives, which questioned the traditional mainstream economic approaches to management accounting research. These alternative perspectives emphasized the need to study management accounting within its broader social, political, and organizational contexts. The journal *Accounting, Organizations and Society* (which was started in 1976) was where much of the social and more politically oriented research was published during the 1980s (and subsequently). This followed the seminal paper of Burchell et al. (1980), which called on researchers to study (management) accounting in its organizational and social contexts. This prompted a significant number of UK management accounting researchers to start using a variety of social theories, and to question the neutrality of accounting numbers. Such research challenged the assumption that accounting reports can provide an accurate reflection of some underlying economic reality. This was an assumption of many accounting researchers (including myself) in the 1970s. As a result, in the 1970s we were seeking the techniques that would provide the clearest reflection of that reality so that decision-makers could make optimal decisions. But by the 1980s, the alternative perspectives had led a quite substantial body of researchers to argue that rather than providing a neutral reflection of the underlying economic reality, (management) accounting was implicated in the construction of that reality.

As a result of the emergence of these alternative perspectives there is now a considerable diversity of methodological approaches in UK management accounting research, with some researchers continuing to use the traditional economic approaches and a positivist research methodology. In such research, the researcher is assumed to be a neutral and objective observer of the phenomena being studied, and attempts to measure associations between relevant variables in order to make predictions about these phenomena. But there are also researchers who adopt interpretive and critical perspectives. Such researchers reject the position of positivist researchers; instead they acknowledge that they themselves construct the phenomena being studied and that research is neither objective nor value-free. But whereas interpretive researchers seek to understand the world, critical researchers add an element of social critique to their research agenda. The three-way distinction between positive (or mainstream) accounting research, interpretive accounting research, and critical accounting research has been used by several writers over the years to classify the various strands of management accounting research (see Chua 1986; Roslender 1992; Baker and Bettner 1997; and also Baxter and Chua, Chapter 3, this volume).

This remains quite a good classification of the methodological perspectives of current UK management accounting research. There continues to be a group of researchers doing the traditional economic-oriented research, another group doing interpretive research, and a third group who undertake critical research. Whereas in the USA, for instance, the vast majority of researchers are in the first group, doing traditional economic-oriented research, and the other two groups are both very small, in the UK there are substantial numbers of researchers in all three groups.

15.3 **Relevance lost?**

Before completing this historical background and discussing the more recent management accounting research, it will be helpful to outline some of the responses in the UK to the claims made by Johnson and Kaplan (1987), who were writing principally about management accounting in the USA. In their well-known book, *Relevance Lost: The Rise and Fall of Management Accounting*, Johnson and Kaplan argued that much of the development of management accounting practices took place in the early twentieth century, and there were few further developments over the following sixty years or more; and that by the 1980s, management accounting had lost its relevance, having become subservient to the needs of external financial reporting. Their book had important implications for management accounting research around the world, and it had an impact on both management accounting researchers in the UK and on the representatives of the UK management accounting profession—the Chartered Institute of Management Accountants (CIMA).

It is probably fair to say that UK accounting academics were largely sympathetic to the idea that there were problems with management accounting practices in the 1980s. Issues of short-termism and the lack of international competitiveness of British industry had been widely discussed both by academics and by financial commentators. Furthermore, as mentioned above, UK management accounting researchers had already recognized the need to research management accounting practice and quite a number of studies were in progress (see Scapens et al. 1987[3]). These studies were exploring issues and problems in management accounting practice that were similar to those noted by Johnson and Kaplan. Thus, the notion that management accounting practices were not entirely relevant to the needs of business decision-makers was not completely new to UK management accounting researchers. But the reasons advanced by Johnson and Kaplan for this lack of relevance and their analysis of how management accounting could be made more relevant were greeted with some scepticism by management accounting researchers in the UK. An interesting early response to Johnson and Kaplan was written by Bromwich and Bhimani, whose book, *Management Accounting: Evolution, not Revolution*, was published by CIMA in 1989.

Professional management accounting bodies around the world, such as CIMA, had a vested interest in responding to the claims of Johnson and Kaplan, who were being very critical of their members as a professional group. CIMA funded a number of research projects, which attempted to assess the validity of the *Relevance Lost* thesis (Johnson and Kaplan 1987). The Bromwich and Bhimani (1989) book, *Evolution, not Revolution*, was commissioned by CIMA in 1988, and built on Bromwich's CIMA-funded research project, 'Fixed Overhead Allocation in High-Tech Industries'. Later, I led a research team which undertook another study for CIMA, looking at the interrelationship between external reporting and management decisions (see Scapens et al. 1996). Contrary to the arguments of Johnson and Kaplan, our research suggested that management accounting was not dominated by the requirements of financial reporting. We showed, through case studies, that in the age of modern database technologies, information systems can accommodate both the demands of external reporting and the needs of managers for financial information.

This alliance of CIMA and management accounting researchers provided practically relevant and academically informed responses to Johnson and Kaplan. In their book, *Evolution, not Revolution*, Bromwich and Bhimani argued that although there were clearly problems in management accounting practice at that time, there was a need for evolution and not revolution: 'No general crisis has been identified within the management accounting profession vis-à-vis a changing manufacturing environment and therefore no radical reforms are recommended at this stage' (1989: 3). In the revised edition of this book, now entitled *Management Accounting: Pathways to Progress* (also published by CIMA), Bromwich and Bhimani (1994) went on to outline a number of ways in which management accounting could be developed. As well as considering new approaches to cost management, such as activity-based costing (ABC), target costing, and throughput accounting, companies were encouraged to recognize that organizational and managerial factors need to be considered in redesigning accounting information systems. They also emphasized the importance of strategic management accounting (SMA) and the need to extend the boundaries of the management accounting system (MAS) to encompass supply chains and the like. Thus, although the basic arguments of Johnson and Kaplan were sympathetically received, their prescriptions, which focused largely on cost management in general, and ABC in particular, were questioned.

There were also a number of critiques by UK researchers of Johnson and Kaplan's historical analysis of management accounting's *Rise and Fall*. Johnson and Kaplan had based much of their historical analysis on the work of Chandler (1962, 1977), who used transaction cost economics to explain the development of the modern US corporation in terms of management's search for economic efficiency. A number of papers critiqued Johnson and Kaplan's historical analysis (1987: 7), which sought to portray the early development of management accounting as the outcome of innovative managers looking for efficient economic solutions to the problems faced by their growing businesses. For example, Ezzamel et al. (1990) argued that the genesis of management control systems could be traced to the knowledge-based disciplinary power of modern managerialism. Their work drew on the ideas of the French social theorist, Michel Foucault, and explored the development of management accounting in terms of the micro processes of power, and was part of the wider research in the UK, which used Foucault's ideas of disciplinary power to study the development of management accounting practices (see e.g. Miller and O'Leary 1993).

Other UK management accounting researchers contrasted Johnson and Kaplan's analysis of the evolution of management accounting with a labour process theory perspective, which characterized the development of management accounting in terms of capitalists, and their representatives (namely the managers of large corporations), seeking to control labour. By developing systems such as standard costing, it became possible to break down the activities of labour into elements that could be commodified and thereby more easily controlled (see Hopper and Armstrong 1991).

So to summarize the reactions to Johnson and Kaplan's *Relevance Lost* thesis: their essential ideas about the relevance of management accounting were received with some sympathy in the UK, but both their historical analysis of the problems and their prescriptions were questioned. Also, it is worth emphasizing that in the USA, Johnson and Kaplan—and particularly Kaplan—subsequently encouraged case study-based research and called for researchers to study management accounting practices. But in the UK, such research was already being undertaken. It had started at the beginning of the 1980s with the awareness of the gap between theory and practice. Furthermore, the case studies undertaken by UK management accounting researchers have tended to be much more detailed than the Harvard-type cases favoured by Kaplan. Before taking a look at more recent management accounting research, I will describe the changing nature of management accounting practices in the UK over the last 10–15 years.

15.4 The changing nature of management accounting practices in the UK

Although at times some writers have disagreed (see e.g. Lyne and Friedman 1997), it can be argued that there has been a change in management accounting practices in the years since Johnson and Kaplan wrote their book. Whereas the management accountants whom Johnson and Kaplan where describing could be characterized as working in the back-office and monitoring at a distance the performance of other managers—as scorekeepers or bean-counters—more recently, management accountants have come to be portrayed as providing business support, i.e. as business analysts working alongside other managers and providing direct inputs into management decisions, as members of the management team.

As mentioned above, CIMA commissioned a number of research studies following the claims of Johnson and Kaplan, and I participated in two such studies. The first (which was mentioned earlier), External Reporting and Management Decisions (1993–5),[4] examined the relationship between external reporting and management decisions. This study focused on Johnson and Kaplan's argument that management accounting is dominated by the requirements of financial reporting. The second, Management Accounting Change (1996–2000),[5] explored the reasons why MASs have appeared relatively slow to change, and focused on resistance to change.

Together these studies support the view that there have been changes in management accounting practices in the UK, but not necessarily extensive changes in the techniques being used. Using a questionnaire (sent to CIMA members in 1997), we examined the use of the so-called modern management accounting techniques. The left-hand column in Table 15.1 shows that according to the responses some of the modern techniques are used, but not (with the exception of non-financial measures) to any substantial extent. Our findings regarding ABC are probably in line with (or even slightly higher than) similar studies in other countries—23 per cent in the USA: Cagwin and Bouwman (2002); and 20 per cent in New Zealand: Cotton et al. (2003). The number of companies that have adopted non-financial measures (60 per cent of our sample) contrasts somewhat with the number claiming to use the balanced scorecard (BSC). This may be because the technique of the BSC, which has been promoted by Kaplan and Norton (1996, 2001), was probably not widely known at that time (the survey was conducted in 1997). Nevertheless, at that time there were quite a lot of respondents using non-financial measures, although they were not calling them a BSC. Today, many people who continue to use non-financial measures may label them a BSC, even if they are not necessarily adopting the approach advocated by Kaplan and Norton—although it is Kaplan and Norton who have popularized non-financial measures in recent years.

A further dimension to our survey was added in 2000 when Burns and Yazdifar (2001) undertook another questionnaire survey,[6] which asked CIMA members which techniques

Table 15.1 Management accounting techniques being adopted

	1997 (%)	Past* (%)	Future* (%)
Activity-based costing	31	11	39
Strategic management accounting	27	37	65
Non-financial measures	60	58	41
Quality measures	42	19	33
Balanced scorecard	20	13	31

* Past = five years prior to 2000
* Future = five years after 2000

had been important in the previous five years (1995–2000) and which techniques they expected to be important in the next five years (2000–5). Some of the findings from their survey are shown in the two right-hand columns of Table 15.1. As we can see, more CIMA members expected ABC and SMA to be more important in the next five years, than in the previous five years. The relatively low percentage (11 per cent) for ABC in the previous five years, as compared to the earlier survey (31 per cent), may have been due to the small sample size and the predominance of larger companies in the earlier survey. However, the importance of non-financial measures in the last five years (58 per cent) is almost identical to the findings of the earlier study (60 per cent). The somewhat lesser importance expected to be attached to such measures in the next five years is probably due to the expected increase in the importance of BSC. However, some CIMA members expected non-financial measures to be important, even though they did not expect Kaplan and Norton-type BSC to be important. Finally, it is notable that there was expected to be an increasing interest in SMA in the next five years.

Thus, there is interest in new management accounting techniques, and some management accountants consider them to be important, but not everybody is adopting ABC and BSCs, for instance. But in addition to these questionnaire survey findings about the new techniques, a number of case studies were undertaken that identified changes in the use of *traditional* management accounting practices (see Scapens et al. 2003). In particular, there is an emphasis on forward-looking information for management decision-making, rather than backward-looking information for management control. This new focus is reflected in the importance attached to rolling forecasts and forecasts to the year-end. Such forecasts seemed to be much more important than comparisons against the original budget. However, despite the proposals of the Consortium for Advanced Manufacturing—International (CAM-I) Beyond Budgeting (BB) project, that companies should go 'beyond budgets' (see Hope and Fraser 1997, 1999), few companies seem to have abandoned budgeting (see Prendergast 2000). Most companies continue to use budgets, but in a more forward-looking fashion, alongside rolling forecasts, forecasts to the end of the year, and so on. This is particularly important because, whereas budgets are usually associated with the accountants, forecasts are more closely identified with the managers. It is the individual managers who are expected to make these forecasts, and as a result they are likely to be more committed to them.

The case studies also identified an increasing integration of financial and non-financial information, with performance measurement, in the form of scorecards, dashboards, etc., becoming the focus of much management interest. As we found in our questionnaire surveys most people in all types of organizations (in both the private and the public sectors) are familiar with non-financial performance measures—although the terms used may differ—e.g. performance targets and league tables. The increasing competition and more global economic pressures on UK businesses have led to a more strategic or customer-oriented focus, i.e. a focus on external market factors, rather than an internal focus on the control of costs. This is not to say that cost control is unimportant—it remains crucially important. But costs have to be controlled with due regard to the strategic direction of the business, rather than independently and/or focused exclusively on cost reduction. This has led many companies to identify key performance indicators (KPIs), which measure aspects of the business that are crucial for its long-term success, and many of these KPIs are essentially non-financial in nature. As a result, monthly management reports now normally contain a mixture of financial and non-financial information, and management accountants are frequently responsible for collating this information and for the preparation of the management reports.

Another relevant finding of the case studies reinforced what we described in our earlier CIMA research project as the *decentring of accounting knowledge* (see Scapens et al. 1996). Up to some 15–20 years ago accounting information was usually entirely within a self-contained accounting system, located and controlled from within the accounting function, and accessed only by the people who actually worked in the accountant's offices. Thus, accounting knowledge resided in the accounting function, sometimes also called the finance function. It was the accountants who were the custodians of accounting knowledge. But with the development of integrated information systems, the accounting information is now much more widely accessible. Managers can now access accounting information on their desks or remotely via their laptops, provided they have the knowledge and skills required to do so. One of the changes that has taken place is that management accountants have 'moved out' of the accounting function and now work alongside managers, enabling them to access and understand the significance of the accounting information.

I give a very brief example. One of companies studied in the second CIMA project was a major multinational pharmaceuticals company. This company had traditionally had a very sound market position, but in the early 1990s, it started to experience severe market pressures. In common with other major pharmaceuticals companies, it was finding governments increasingly resistant to the high prices charged for both patented and generic drugs and medicines. Furthermore, in the early 1990s this particular pharmaceutical company was in a position where a number of its major, and highly lucrative, patents were about to expire. As a response to these market pressures it implemented a substantial change programme over the years 1994–8. This programme included various initiatives to reduce costs and to reorganize productive operations more efficiently. One of these initiatives was termed 'process ways of working' (PWW), which involved restructuring the business around the major business processes. Consequently, all its activities, with the exception of finance, information technology, and quality, were organized by processes rather than by functions. Although accounting (or finance as they termed it) remained a separate function, day by day most of the management accountants worked in the process streams, alongside the process managers.

During this period there was a substantial reduction in numbers of accountants—the number working in UK operations halved over a period of about six years in the mid-1990s. Nevertheless, the management accountants who remained worked principally in the process streams and were seen to be very important in the new structure, as they worked very closely with process managers. Some managers in the company described these accountants as 'hybrid accountants', as they were perceived as people who combined the skills of business managers and with those of accountants. Although many in the company freely admitted that their accounting systems were old-fashioned ('antiquated' they called them) and that they continued to use very traditional accounting systems, the information was clearly being used in quite different ways by these hybrid accountants. The following are some of the qualities that were perceived as being important in the hybrid accountants:

- Willingness and ability to be team member
- Extensive business knowledge
- Broad performance and interpretation skills
- Ability to integrate different understandings of the business
- Proactiveness in strategic matters
- Rigorous analytical skills
- Good communication skills

As such, the hybrid accountants were expected to be an integral part of the team that was responsible for managing the process stream. As might be expected, they needed the rigorous analytical skills normally associated with accountants, but coupled with extensive knowledge of the business, a focus on strategic issues, and the ability to communicate, i.e. to be able to interact with a wide range of people in the different parts of the business. The management accountants occupying these roles undertook a wide range of tasks within their process streams, including some of the following:

- Assessing the financial implications of operational decisions
- Short-term tax considerations
- Short-term currency dealings
- Establishing new (e.g. supplier) contracts
- Supporting R&D
- Assisting with licence/regulation issues

The primary task of these hybrid accountants was clearly to analyse the financial implications of operational decisions. But as the above list indicates, there were lots of other tasks that they undertook—these were not necessarily planned as a formal part of the management accountants' duties; rather, they were tasks that emerged in the individual process streams and the management accountants working in those streams were the people who took responsibility for them. They assisted the process managers and used their skills as needed to help the managers to manage the process. As such, they were perceived as accountants 'working out in the field' and their role was to contribute to the efficiency of the process by supporting process managers, and generally being cross-functional team players, who were able to work with different people from different functional and discipline backgrounds. Their main task was to integrate the operational performance, the accounting information, and the strategic context of the business, and to enable their process managers to take an informed view of the decisions that confronted them. Thus, the 'hybrid accountant' is somewhat of an all-rounder, and very different to the traditional view of the management accountant as the bean-counter.

This case study illustrates the way in which the role of the management accountant has changed in recent years. Over the last fifteen years or so, management accountants have changed from bean-counters to business analysts. Such changes in the nature of management accounting are not only seen in the UK. For example, Jablonsky et al. (1993), noting similar changes in the USA, distinguished between corporate policemen and business advocates. Furthermore, the International Federation of Accountants (IFAC) described the evolution of management accounting after 1995 as a period of ongoing transformation, in which attention 'shifted to the generation or creation of value through the effective use of resources, through the use of technologies that examine the drivers of customer value, shareholder value, and organizational innovation' (IFAC 1998: para. 7). Today, management accountants fulfil broad business roles, assisting managers to interpret the financial and non-financial information that is available to them, and also to evaluate both the operating and strategic consequences of alternative courses of action, and in particular their impact on value creation. The accountants' analytical skills, supplemented by extensive knowledge of the business, can put the management accountant in a position to recognize the more strategic impacts and value creation potential of decisions taken in the individual areas of the business. Such a role for the management accountant is crucial for the organization as it helps to integrate the various activities and functions of the business.

15.5 **Trends in management accounting research**

Against this background of *the changing nature of management accounting*, this section will begin to look more specifically at the recent trends in management accounting research. In parallel with the broadening role of the management accountant in practice, the scope of management accounting research has also moved beyond the traditional textbook notions, which portrayed management accounting as part of the formal hierarchical planning and control system of the organization. More recent management accounting research has begun to explore the much broader role of management accounting and management accountants in the organization. I will start with a brief review of the developments in management accounting research, drawing on papers published in *Management Accounting Research*, which I edit together with Michael Bromwich. Although this is an international research journal, during its first decade (1990–9) about 50 per cent of the papers came from the UK. However, the proportion was higher in the first five years (56 per cent) and somewhat less in the second five years (47 per cent).[7] In the most recent five years (2000–4) the proportion has been even lower (at just over 30 per cent). Nevertheless, the journal provides a good indication of the trends in both international management accounting research and the research being done in the UK. Based on a review of papers in *Management Accounting*

Research, it is clear that UK management accounting research is contributing to, and is an important part of, the broad international trends. But as I will discuss later, management accounting research in the USA has a somewhat different and rather narrower focus.

In an editorial that Michael Bromwich and I published in 2001 (see Scapens and Bromwich 2001), reflecting on the first decade of papers in *Management Accounting Research*, we concluded that management accounting researchers were beginning to build up good insights into management accounting practice. In that first decade there were various papers reporting questionnaire and field surveys of management accounting practice, as well as case studies of management accounting change and other studies of the broader organizational context in which management accounting is practised. These studies widened the traditional boundaries of management accounting research. In the papers that looked within the firm, there was increasing interest in issues of strategy formulation and control, as well as a continuing interest in more operational matters. As such, management accounting could be seen to be emerging as the link between broader strategic issues and the day-to-day operations of the business. But in addition to studies looking within the firm, there were also papers that were going beyond the boundaries of the firm, and showing an increasing interest in 'new' organizational forms, such as networks, joint ventures, and strategic alliances.

These papers published in the first decade of *Management Accounting Research* provided rich and varied insights into the intricacies and complexities of management accounting practice in its organizational settings. They explored the nature and role of management accounting in a variety of industries and in a range of different countries. However, although differences were seen to exist, the essential nature of management accounting practice did not seem to vary substantially across industries or countries. But the papers clearly demonstrated that the complexities of management accounting practice transcended the simple economic decision-making approaches portrayed in most textbooks. They also emphasized that management accounting and, to a lesser extent, management accountants were increasingly becoming involved, either directly or indirectly, in other functional areas, and that this involvement was, to some extent at least, context-dependent.

They also suggested that the traditional boundaries of the firm were being challenged—both internally with new organizational structures (e.g. business process-oriented structures and much flatter organizations) and externally with new organizational forms (e.g. supply chains, strategic alliances, and networks). The papers argued that such changes have potentially very important implications for the nature and role of management accounting. Furthermore, the papers also identified new forms of performance evaluation and the way in which non-financial measures have extended the boundaries of management accounting and, in particular, prompted interest in SMA. These papers published in *Management Accounting Research* illustrate the extent to which research in management accounting in the 1990s went far beyond the traditional areas of cost management and management control, and in many ways paralleled the changing nature of management accounting practices described earlier.

More recently, in the papers published in *Management Accounting Research* since 2000, I have discerned a continuing broadening of the scope of management accounting, with an emerging interest in issues of trust, discussions of information sharing and knowledge management, and continuing research on interorganizational management control. In addition, there have been various studies on management accounting change and the diffusion of new practices. These papers have mostly comprised fieldwork and case studies, but there have also been some surveys, and the focus has been more on performance measurement and BSCs, rather than on cost management and ABC (which was the focus of much research in the 1990s). The theoretical basis of such research has tended to be in institutional theory, including both new and old institutional economics, and institutional sociology, but there have also been some papers drawing on more conventional economic modelling. In addition, there have been papers exploring new management accounting techniques: BSCs, and to a lesser extent ABC, but also SMA. A continuing feature of the research published in *Management Accounting Research*, which as indicated earlier is undertaken by international management accounting researchers, as well as researchers based in the UK, is the diversity and eclecticism of the work. There is a broad range of topics, a wide variety of theoretical perspective, and a diversity of methodological approaches.

This broad scope of management accounting research in the UK contrasts with research in the USA, where management accounting research seems to be dominated by analytic and contingency studies, which either seek to identify the specific factors that influence the implementation, success, and applicability of new techniques or to find equilibrium solutions to problems of information, incentives, and performance measurement. Both types of research involve either economic modelling or large-scale questionnaire studies and statistical analyses to locate the individual factors that explain a particular phenomenon—such as the use of ABC, or more recently BSCs—or to explore the linkages between strategy, compensation schemes, and performance measures. Whereas management accounting research in the UK tends to be longitudinal, looking at the evolution of management accounting practices over time, Shields' review of research by North American management accounting researchers in the 1990s pointed out that 'the most popular theories and research methods...are more suited to static, cross-sectional analysis' (1997: 22). He went on to describe a large number of contingency and analytical studies, and concluded that the major problem with the approaches used in North American management accounting research is that they have difficulty in dealing with what are probably the most important elements of management accounting at the present—change, organizational learning, and strategic management. As indicated above, these are issues that have become features of the research undertaken by UK and other international researchers, and published in *Management Accounting Research* in recent years.

One particular feature of management accounting research in the UK, which is worthy of special comment, is that UK researchers tend to be very critical and often quite suspicious of new management accounting techniques. There are various papers by UK researchers that seek to question such new techniques (see e.g. the papers by Armstrong (2002) and Jones and Dugdale (2002) in a special section of *Accounting, Organizations and Society* on 'Debating ABC'). UK management accounting researchers frequently look for the negative aspects of new developments and the drawbacks of proposed new techniques. This is quite typical of the attitude of UK academics more generally. For example, if a researcher presents a case study that purports to show a successful accounting change to an audience in the UK, there will be very detailed questioning, and it will be difficult to convince the audience that it was a success. The general feeling is often that nothing is ever totally successful, and there must be at least some problems that the researcher has either ignored or just missed. Such attitudes can lead to important critiques of new techniques, but also explain why there have been no major new techniques developed by UK management accounting researchers.

This is not to say, however, that management accounting research in the UK has not been innovative. I believe it has been very innovative in terms of the theories and methodologies that have been used. In particular, it has provided rich understandings of management accounting practice, explaining why practices are the way they are, what the consequences of these practices can be, and how they can change or be resistant to change. In general, the focus of management accounting research in the UK has been on providing explanations of *what is going on in practice*. As mentioned earlier, this focus dates back to the 1980s, when UK management accounting researchers realized that they had little real understanding of the nature of practice—beyond the assumptions of economic models.

Since the 1980s, management accounting researchers have been studying in detail the nature of management accounting practice. These researchers have used a wide range of methodologies, disciplines, and theoretical constructs. Along with the methodological diversity, there have, at times, been methodological debates, some of which have been intensely sterile. For example, some of the research grounded in social theory, sociology, and political theory in the late 1980s and early 1990s led to debates about who is the 'best' social theorist to use in accounting research.[8] Such debates failed to make any real contribution to understanding management accounting practice. The debate was conducted at the level of social theory, sociology, or politics, rather than exploring the implications for management accounting. Such debates probably delayed real developments in the study of management accounting.

There have been such methodological debates over the years in most areas of science, and accounting is no different. Some methodological debates can be very productive, but others can impede developments. Incidentally, I think one of the latter types of methodological debates surfaced recently when Zimmerman (2001: 412) criticized management accounting research (in the USA), arguing that it had failed to produce a substantive cumulative body of knowledge. His contention was that the development of management accounting research had been hampered by the lack of economic-based research hypotheses (p. 425). For a very good rebuttal of Zimmerman's arguments, see the series of papers that appeared in the *European Accounting Review* in late 2002. Whilst I have some sympathy with the basic criticism of management accounting research advanced by Zimmerman (as will become clearer later), for me the fact that management accounting research has moved away from the exclusive focus on economic models, which it had in the 1970s, has been the major advance in management accounting research over the last forty years.

Rather than trying to privilege one particular methodological and/or theoretical approach (as Zimmerman is seeking to do), I believe we should exploit the pluralist nature of management accounting research; but I do recognize that this may not be easy. Nevertheless, provided we can avoid getting bogged down in unnecessary methodological debates, I have some optimism about the prospects for pluralism in management accounting research, especially in the UK. It does appear that management accounting researchers in the UK are willing to accept a large measure of theoretical and methodological diversity. And importantly, this diversity is recognized and rewarded in the research assessment exercises that are periodically undertaken in the UK. But in some other countries, it can be difficult for a researcher to step outside the prevailing methodological and/or theoretical perspective. In such countries there can be pressure to conform to the methodological mainstream and to publish papers in certain journals: journals that tend to publish only research that adopts a particular research perspective. Such pressures can undoubtedly restrict the development of the subject. This can be seen in the USA (and other countries that seek to follow the US model), where the overwhelming majority of management accounting papers appears in journals that publish only quantitative research, underpinned largely by economic theorizing.[9] Furthermore, in the USA there is a declining number of these papers, as it is perceived to be difficult to get management accounting papers published in these journals and young researchers tend to look to other (safer) areas for their research. But in the UK in recent years, a significant number of management accounting papers have been published, and there is a tolerance of different methodological approaches. But UK management accounting research is subject to other potential pressures to which I will return later.

This methodological diversity in UK management accounting research has included interpretive and critical research, alongside more traditional functionalist and positive research. There has also been a variety of research methods that have been used, including surveys, fieldwork, and case studies, as well as studies that have adopted a more conventional quantitative approach, e.g. contingency-type studies. There has also been some analytical work in what might be termed financial management, being at the interface between finance and management accounting. In terms of the discipline base of UK management accounting research, there has also been considerable diversity—with researchers drawing on organization theory, sociology, social theory, politics, social anthropology, and even economics (see Hopper et al. 2001 for a review). As well as economic theory and contingency theory, there has been a wide range of theories that have been used in UK management accounting research, including institutional theory, structuration theory, actor network theory, labour process theory, political economy, Foucault's genealogy and Derrida's deconstructionism.

In relation to the use of theory, Michael Bromwich and I, as editors of *Management Accounting Research*, are concerned that quite a lot of the research, especially the surveys and descriptive case studies, which was published in the first ten years of the journal, tended to be somewhat under-theorized. These papers provided an informed picture of management accounting practices, but often failed to theorize them. This might be seen in contrast to papers in *Accounting, Organizations and Society*, which particularly in the 1980s and early 1990s described various social theories and how they could be used to study management accounting.[10] Possibly, such papers had too much social theory and too little theorizing about management accounting per se, as well as inadequate discussion of the implications for management accounting in practice and the problems faced by management account-ants. At that time, developments in research tended to be the introduction of a new social theorist, rather than a deeper understanding of management accounting practice.

I now believe that we need to be somewhere between these two extremes. What is needed are theorized case studies of management accounting; with theory used to analyse the case, rather than cases used to illustrate the theory. I will return to this issue later, when I comment on the future directions of management accounting research. But first I will outline some of the current issues that I believe are important in management accounting research. Section 15.6 will set out a *personal reflection* on some current issues in management accounting—issues that I am currently finding particularly interesting.

15.6 **Current issues in management accounting**

Management accounting change is a continuing interest of UK management accounting researchers. Such research is focusing on the processes of change, i.e. how accounting change takes place in practice. Explaining resistance and the paradox of stability and change are issues of current interest for management accounting researchers. Much of this research has drawn on institutional theories and several studies of management accounting change have used the change framework grounded in old institutional economics developed by Burns and Scapens (2000). However, although this framework has been quite useful in explaining resistance to change (in other words, why some desired change has not been achieved), it has not provided real insights into the *processes* through which change is actually achieved. It explains how institutions, i.e. taken-for-granted assumptions, can shape the way in which individuals and groups react to proposed changes, and that there is likely to be resistance to change which is not in line with existing institutions. However, this leaves an interesting question unresolved: how can members of an organization bring about institutional change, when their actions and thoughts are constrained by these existing institutions? To answer this question much closer attention needs to be paid to the processes of change and the role of change agents within organizations. As such, it requires a focus on organizations that have changed, and not just on resistance to change. In other words, it needs research on 'successful' change—something that can be difficult for UK management accounting re-searchers, as mentioned earlier.

Furthermore, as the Burns and Scapens framework focuses on micro issues (i.e. within the organization), it needs to be supplemented with insights from institutional sociology in order to explain how more macro pressures from outside the organization can impinge on the processes of institutional change. As a result there is considerable scope for exploring the processes of institutional change through a combination of ideas from both old institutional economics and institutional sociology.

In recent years, performance measurement, or more broadly *performance management*, has become a particular interest of management accounting researchers—in some ways this is the modern expression of the notion of management control, which was a major feature of management accounting research in earlier years. CIMA has recently commissioned research in this area, seeking to link performance management systems with issues of strategy at one level, and operations at the other. However, there have been some suggestions recently that the trend outlined earlier for management accountants to 'work out in the field'—i.e. as members of the management team—raises issues of governance. For example, if accountants become too close to the business, there could be a loss of the traditional governance aspect of accounting. In this sense, governance is seen in terms of conformance to both external and internal rules and standards of accountability. But the solution may not be to separate the dual roles of accounting, i.e. conformance to rules and performance management. Rather it may be to integrate them into a broader system of 'enterprise governance' (see CIMA/IFAC 2004).

Figure 15.1 illustrates a governance framework developed by CIMA and IFAC. This framework links together the notions of corporate governance (i.e. conformance) and business governance (which is concerned with managing the performance of the organization). As can be seen from Figure 15.1, this framework draws a connection between accountability/assurance and value creation/resource utilization. In my recent work with colleagues in Italy and the USA we have gone further and argued for an integrated governance framework, which combines conformance, performance, and knowledge management—see Figure 15.2 (Busco 2005). Using case studies of global organizations, this project studied the role of performance measurement systems within the processes of managing such organizations, and in particular the way in which financial and non-financial information are integrated in a common 'global' measurement language. We concluded that there is a need for an integrated framework that broadens governance beyond compliance, and encompasses both measurement-based and knowledge-based governance. This research highlights the interconnection between the controllership aspects and the performance management aspects of management accounting, and their relationship with issues of knowledge management. As such, this further broadens the scope of management

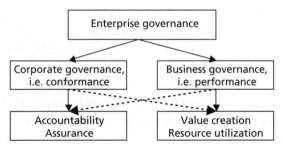

Figure 15.1 The enterprise governance framework
(*Source*: CIMA/IFAC 2004)

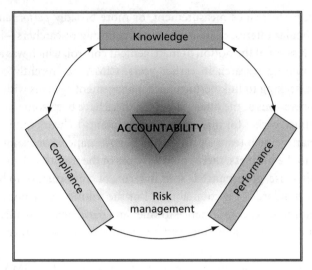

Figure 15.2 The three sides of accountability
(*Source:* Busco 2005)

accounting, but at the same time emphasizes the need to combine the various aspects in an integrated framework around the notion of accountability.

As mentioned above, in recent years there have been a number of papers addressing issues surrounding new organizational forms; i.e. going beyond the traditional boundaries of the firm, and focusing on supply chains, network organizations, joint ventures, strategic alliances, and so on. This research emphasizes horizontal relationships (or lateral relations), in contrast to the vertical relationships that characterize traditional hierarchical organizations. Lateral relations are relationships between autonomous and relatively equal parties—in other words, there are not subordinate and superior parties in such relationships, as is normally assumed in the traditional management control literature. In new organizational forms and also in modern organizations (e.g. those organized around business processes), lateral relations are becoming increasingly important. In a current paper with one of my Dutch colleagues we have illustrated lateral relations both between and within organizations (Meer-Kooistra and Scapens 2004). These illustrations identified some common themes and issues in lateral relations: specifically, information sharing and the exchange of knowledge, cooperation and competition, flexibility and standardization, and shared and shifting leadership roles. To manage such issues requires a form of relationship governance, rather than the more traditional form of management control.

Although lateral relations involve autonomous parties, their autonomy cannot be completely unrestrained and some minimal structures are needed to provide for the governance of the relationship. But these minimal structures have to leave sufficient room for manoeuvre to enable the parties in lateral relations to act flexibly, share information, exchange knowledge, create new knowledge, and react to new situations. This requires a governance structure that combines *firmness and flexibility*; in other words, structure and autonomy have to be balanced. As lateral relationships involve autonomous parties, without strong hierarchical ties, there needs to be some degree of trust between them, if they are to cooperate with each other. Trust can be built when the governance of the relationship provides sufficient structure to mitigate the risks involved in cooperation between autonomous parties who may have different interests and motives, while at the same time facilitating the sharing of information and the exchange of knowledge. This research emphasizes the importance of recognizing the interconnection of trust and control, in accounting research. Whereas in the past management accounting has tended to focus on control, there is now an emerging interest in how management accounting can promote and maintain trust.

The three issues identified in this section are a personal choice; they are what interest me at the present time. But they reflect the diversity of management accounting research and the extent to which it has changed over the years. As indicated in the brief history outlined above, when I began my research career, at the beginning of the 1970s, management accounting research was about developing sophisticated mathematical decision models, which were grounded in a largely neoclassical economic view of the organization and managerial decision-making. As the current issues outlined above testify, there has been very substantial change in management accounting research over the intervening years.

15.7 UK management accounting research

In the preceding sections I have been rather cavalier in my descriptions of UK management accounting research. I used papers published in *Management Accounting Research*, which is an international journal, to illustrate the trends in management accounting research. However, I believe that management accounting research in the UK is making an important contribution to these trends. Furthermore, as I have been offering my views of management accounting research and practice, it is inevitably a UK perspective. But to finish, I would like to focus specifically on the UK and ask: is there something called UK management accounting research?

There is certainly quite a lot of management accounting research done in the UK, but can it be called UK management accounting research? Currently, in the UK, there are relatively few young management accounting researchers. In my opinion there could be a potential problem for UK management accounting research in the future. Like Michael Bromwich and I, there are quite a few management accounting researchers who joined the research community in the late 1960s and early to mid-1970s, when universities in the UK were expanding and when accounting as a field of study was being introduced in many of these universities. However, this cohort of management accounting researchers will be retiring over the next few years. It seems to me that there is not a sufficient number of young management accounting academics in the UK to replace the people who will be retiring in the near future.

There are many Ph.D. students at UK universities, but few of them are from the UK. This is not a problem of national identity, but a more practical problem. Most of these Ph.D.

students will return to their home countries when they receive their degrees. Some of them may be tempted to stay in the UK. But even some of those who initially remain after completing their Ph.D. may only stay for a few years before returning home. Thus, we are not training the next generation of management accounting researchers for UK universities, and I can foresee a problem in the future—such a problem has already hit the USA, where, as I mentioned earlier, there are relatively few people doing management accounting research.

Nevertheless, there can be significant benefits of a large number of overseas Ph.D. students researching management accounting in the UK. Such people receive their research training and theoretical ideas in the UK, and then they export them around the world. Currently, I have two Ph.D. students from China, one each from Italy, Greece, and Thailand, and one from the UK—the latter is one of the few Ph.D. students from the UK that I have supervised over the years. In the past few years I have successfully supervised Ph.D. students from Italy, Portugal, Egypt, Malaysia, and Ireland. As already indicated, there are very few from the UK. This raises an interesting question about the nature of UK management accounting research. Recently, I published a paper with a former Ph.D. student from Malaysia (see Siti-Nabiha and Scapens 2005). This appeared in *Accounting, Auditing and Accountability Journal*, which is published by a publisher based in the UK, but edited by two Australians (Lee Parker and James Guthrie). Furthermore, although the paper was the output of Ph.D. research at a UK university, it was based on a case study of a Malaysian company: can this be described as UK management accounting research? I am not sure, but it does not matter.

What is important is that the ideas of UK management accounting researchers are being spread around the world. In addition to Ph.D. students who come to the UK for a period of research training and/or to complete a Ph.D., there are UK management accounting researchers who have gone to live and research abroad, and now are leading academics in other countries, many of whom may no longer be thought of as UK management accounting researchers. One notable example is David Solomons,[11] whom most people would consider to be one of the leading US management accounting researchers in the second half of the twentieth century. But not everyone recognizes that he spent some of his formative years at the London School of Economics (LSE) during the 1950s. He joined the LSE in 1946 and remained there until 1955, when he became the inaugural professor of accounting at the University of Bristol, only the third full-time professor of accounting in Britain. So I am not at all sure how I would define UK management accounting research. Consequently, in this chapter I have just tried to give my own UK perspective on management accounting research and, in particular, how it has changed over the years.

Thirty-five years ago, when I started my academic career, management accounting researchers were largely ignored by practitioners. They were regarded as being remote and not interested in the problems of practitioners. In the 1980s the researchers came down from their 'ivory towers' and began to recognize that what actually happens inside organizations is important. Initially, they undertook questionnaire studies—generally using mailed surveys—to describe the current practices. But by the 1990s more detailed field and case studies had become quite common, and management accounting researchers were seeking to understand and to explain management accounting practices. Today, it is probably fair to say that management accounting researchers are tolerated by practitioners in the UK; although practitioners frequently do not recognize the relevance of much of the research that is being published. For me, the future challenge for management accounting researchers is to work more closely with practitioners—as I will discuss in Section 15.8.

15.8 **Future directions**

It is likely that management accounting researchers will continue to undertake case studies that seek to refine explanations of management accounting practice. But what is needed are attempts to consolidate what we have learnt and to bring together the quite diverse understandings that have been produced using the various theoretical perspectives mentioned earlier. We now have a variety of explanations of practice, coming from different theoretical angles, and using a range of methodological approaches. I believe we are now at a stage where researchers need to pull these diverse understandings together to provide a more comprehensive understanding of management accounting practice. But much thought and care is needed in such research. As editor of *Management Accounting Research*, I see papers that list three or four different theories in a literature review, which is then followed by a case study. The authors then select observations from the case, pointing out that one observation can be related to, say, theory A, another observation to theory B, and so on. But there is no attempt to show how the theories can be integrated. What is needed, in my opinion, is an integration of the different theoretical perspectives into a framework, which can then be used to analyse the case. However, this may not be easy. The challenge for such pluralistic work is how to combine diverse theoretical and methodological approaches. This is likely to be very difficult if approached from a purely theoretical or methodological stance. What is needed is a focus on specific problems and/or issues; then the different theories and/or methodologies can be combined to address these problems and/or issues. Some of the current research, which is seeking to broaden the boundaries of management accounting, both within the organization and beyond, offers real opportunities for this type of work. Such research can draw on diverse theoretical perspectives, economic, organizational, institutional, and so on, to address specific issues. Furthermore, this research can explore the concerns of the practitioners who have to cope with the broadening scope of management accounting practices.

The future challenge for management accounting researchers, in the UK in particular, is to start working alongside practitioners. Together they could use the theoretical insights, which have undoubtedly been obtained through recent research, to focus on issues that are relevant to practitioners. In other words, the challenge is to explore the implications for management accounting practice and practitioners of the recent theoretical advances. This may not be such a challenge in some other countries; for instance, in Scandinavia there seems to be a very close working relationship between academics and practitioners. But this is still not the case in the UK. It seems clear to me that management accounting researchers in the UK have not had a significant impact on practice; rather, they have tended to follow practice.[12] I am not necessarily suggesting that UK management accounting researchers should be developing new fashionable techniques to compete with ABC, BSCs, and the like. I am arguing that UK management accounting researchers should give more attention to exploring the practical implications of their theoretical explanations. In recent years, management accounting researchers have provided a wide variety of explanations of management accounting practice, informed by diverse theoretical perspectives derived from economics, sociology, organization theory, psychology, and so on. What is needed now is to move from those theoretical explanations of practice to new ideas that are relevant for practitioners.

However, there can be constraints on such practically oriented research in the UK, reinforced to some extent by the Research Assessment Exercises (RAEs), which are conducted every few years to assess the quality of the output of the various subject areas within UK universities. Although, in principle, applied research is to be considered (and indeed encouraged) by the RAEs, it is the research papers in international journals that tend to receive the highest ratings. As a result, the appraisal systems within UK universities are focused on doing theoretical research, rather than developing practical implications. The challenge for researchers is to be able to do sound and innovative theoretical research, but in so doing to develop practical applications and to provide insights that are useful for practitioners.

Another problem in the UK is that there are now relatively few management accounting researchers who are professionally trained—or professionally trained accounting academics in any area. When I began my academic career, and subsequently throughout the 1970s, almost all my colleagues, and this was the case in most UK universities, had professional accounting training before, or at sometime during, their academic career. So we had university accounting departments with researchers who had practical as well as academic training. Today, there are few such people. Most accounting researchers now follow a very conventional path—an undergraduate degree, a master's degree, then a Ph.D., and subsequently an academic appointment doing both teaching and research. As a result, there is little in-depth personal knowledge of management accounting practice and, in many cases, little empathy with practitioners. I think this is a fundamental structural problem, which is going to be impossible to rectify, at least in the short term. Nevertheless, I think that in these changing times, the challenge for management accounting researchers is to find ways of increasing the practical relevance of theoretically informed management accounting research. UK researchers have been very successful over the years in developing new theories and using diverse methodologies in their management accounting research, but there have been problems in applying this research to assist the development of practice. This is the challenge for the future.

□ NOTES

1 Three surveys were commissioned and eventually published in Scapens et al. (1984). The surveys were of management accounting (Scapens); organization theory (Otley); and financial management (Lister).

2 Michael Bromwich was instrumental in setting up this conference and securing the necessary funding. The conference itself was organized by John Arnold, David Cooper, and me. Since that first conference there have been many others and they have evolved into what is now known as the Management Accounting Research Group, which meets twice a year—in London at the London School of Economics (LSE) in April and in Birmingham at the Aston Business School in September.

3 This book published by CIMA contains twelve papers based on 'British Case Studies', which had been presented at meetings of the Management Accounting Research Group during the early 1980s. A companion volume (Arnold et al. 1987) contained another twelve papers also presented at these conferences, but these papers were more theoretically oriented—hence the subtitle of the book: 'Expanding the Horizons'. Many of the papers in both volumes represented research in progress and the final results subsequently appeared in the form of journal articles and research monographs.

4 For the report of this study see Scapens et al. (1996).

5 For the reports of this study see Scapens et al. (2003) and Burns et al. (2003).

6 This second survey was undertaken because the response to the first survey had been disappointing—generating a sample of only ninety-one UK companies. The second survey produced 279 responses. But both surveys give a similar picture regarding the use of 'advanced' management accounting techniques.

7 The average for the ten-year period is not a simple average of the two numbers, as the journal had significantly more papers in the second five-year period.

8 Unfortunately, such debates resurface even today: see the paper by Tinker (2005), together with the commentaries and reply, which appeared in *Accounting, Auditing and Accountability* early in 2005.

9 There are some important exceptions, however, with a small number of US researchers publishing their research in *Management Accounting Research.*

10 I was one of the contributors to such research—describing the work of the UK social theorist Anthony Giddens and his structuration theory.

11 The annual prize for the best paper in *Management Accounting Research* is named after David Solomons.

12 It is here that I have some sympathy with the criticisms that Zimmerman made of management accounting research in the USA. But as I mentioned earlier, I do not agree with either his analysis of the problem or his prescriptions for improvement—both of which rely exclusively on traditional economic reasoning.

☐ REFERENCES

Armstrong, P. (2002). 'The Costs of Activity-based Management', *Accounting, Organizations and Society*, 27(1/2): 99–120.

Arnold, R. A. and Scapens, R. W. (1986). 'Economics and Management Accounting Research' in M. Bromwich and A. Hopwood, *Research and Current issues in Management Accounting*. London: Pitman, pp. 78–100.

Arnold, J. A., Cooper, D. J., and Scapens, R. W. (1987). *Management Accounting: Expanding the Horizons.* London: CIMA.

Baker, C. R. and Bettner, M. S. (1997). 'Interpretive and Critical Research in Accounting: A Commentary on Its Absence from Mainstream Accounting Research', *Critical Perspectives in Accounting*, 8: 293–310.

Bromwich, M. and Bhimani, A. (1989). *Management Accounting: Evolution, not Revolution.* London: CIMA.

—— —— (1994). *Management Accounting: Pathways to Progress.* London: CIMA.

—— and Hopwood, A. (1981). *British Accounting Theory: A Comparative Study.* London: Pitman.

Burchell, S., Clubb, C., Hopwood, A. G., and Hughes. J. (1980). 'The Roles of Accounting in Organizations and Society', *Accounting, Organizations and Society*, 5(1): 5–27.

Burns, J. and Scapens, R. W. (2000). 'Conceptualizing Management Accounting Change: An Institutional Framework', *Management Accounting Research*, 11(1): 3–25.

—— and Yazdifar, H. (2001). 'Tricks or Treats? The Role of Management Accounting is Changing', *Financial Management* (March): 33–5.

—— Ezzamel, M., and Scapens, R. (2003). *The Challenge of Management Accounting Change: Behavioural and Cultural Aspects of Change Management.* Oxford: Elsevier/CIMA.

Busco, C., Frigo, M., Giovannoni, E., Riccaboni, A., and Scapens, R. (2005). *Beyond Compliance: An Integrated Governance Framework.* London: Institute of Chartered Accountants in England and Wales.

Cagwin, D. and Bouwman, M. J. (2002). 'The Association Between Activity-Based Costing and Improvement in Financial Performance', *Management Accounting Research*, 13(1): 1–39.

Chandler, A. D., Jr. (1962). *Strategy and Structure: Chapters in the History of the American Industrial Enterprise.* Garden City, NY: Doubleday.

—— (1977). *The Visible Hand: The Managerial Revolution in American Business.* Cambridge, MA: Harvard University Press.

Chua, W. F. (1986). 'Radical Developments in Accounting Thought', *Accounting Review*, 61(4): 601–32.

CIMA/IFAC (2004). *Enterprise Governance: Getting the Balance Right.* New York: International Federation of Accountants.

Cooper, D. J., Arnold, J. A., and Scapens, R. W. (1983). *Management Accounting Research and Practice.* London: Institute of Cost and Management Accountants.

Cotton, W. D. J., Jackman, S. M., and Brown, R. A. (2003). 'Note on a New Zealand Replication of the Innes et al. UK Activity-based Costing Survey', *Management Accounting Research*, 14(1): 67–72.

Ezzamel, M., Hoskin, K., and Macve, R. (1990). 'Managing It All by Numbers: A Review of Johnson and Kaplan's *Relevance Lost*', *Accounting and Business Research*, 20(78): 153–66.

Ferrara, W. L. and Hayya, J. C. (1970). 'Towards Probabilistic Profit Budgets', *Management Accounting* (US) (October): 23–8.

Hope, J. and Fraser, R. (1997). 'Beyond Budgeting: Breaking Through the Barrier to the Third Wave', *Management Accounting* (UK) (December): 20–3.

—— —— (1999). 'Beyond Budgeting: Building a New Management Model for the Information Age', *Management Accounting* (UK) (January): 16–21.

Hopper, T. and Armstrong, P. (1991). 'Cost Accounting, Controlling Labour and the Rise of Conglomerate', *Accounting, Organizations and Society*, 16(5/6): 405–38.

—— Otley, D., and Scapens, R. (2001). 'British Management Accounting Research: Whence and Wither—Opinions and Reflections', *British Accounting Review*, 33(3): 262–91.

IFAC (1998). *Management Accounting Concepts*. First issued 1989. New York: International Federation of Accountants.

Jablonsky, F. S., Keating, P. J., and Heian, J. B. (1993). *Business Advocate or Corporate Policeman*. New York: Financial Research Foundation.

Johnson, H. T. and Kaplan, R. S. (1987). *Relevance Lost: The Rise and Fall of Management Accounting*. Cambridge, MA: Harvard University Press.

Jones, T. C. and Dugdale, D. (2002). 'The ABC Bandwagon and the Juggernaut of Modernity', *Accounting, Organizations and Society*, 27(1/2): 121–63.

Kaplan, R. S. (1975). 'The Significance and Investigation of Cost Variances: Survey and Extensions', *Journal of Accounting Research*, 13(2): 311–37.

—— and Norton, D. (1996). *The Balanced Scorecard: Translating Strategy into Action*. Boston: Harvard Business School Press.

—— —— (2001). *The Strategy-Focused Organization: How Balanced Scorecard Companies Thrive in the New Business Environment*. Boston, MA: Harvard Business School Press.

Lyne, S. R. and Friedman, A. L. (1997). 'Activity-based Techniques and the Death of the Beancounter', *European Accounting Review*, 6(1): 19–44.

Magee, R. P. (1975). 'Cost-Volume-Profit, Uncertainty and Capital Market Equilibrium', *Journal of Accounting Research*, 13(2): 257–66.

Meer-Kooistra, J. van der and Scapens, R. W. (2004), 'The Governance of Lateral Relations *Between* and *Within* Organisations'. Paper presented at the Annual Congress of the European Accounting Association, Prague.

Miller, P. and O'Leary, T. (1993). 'Accounting Expertise and the Politics of the Product: Economic Citizenship and Modes of Corporate Governance', *Accounting, Organizations and Society*, 18(2/3): 187–206.

Prendergast, P. (2000). 'Budgets Hit Back', *Management Accountant* (UK) (January): 14–16.

Roslender, R. (1992). *Sociological Perspectives in Modern Accountancy*. London: Routledge.

Scapens, R. W. and Bromwich, M. (2001). 'Management Accounting Research: The First Decade', *Management Accounting Research*, 12(2): 245–54.

—— Otley, D. T., and Lister R. J. (1984). *Management Accounting, Organisation Theory and Capital Budgeting: Three Surveys*. London: Macmillan/ESRC.

—— Cooper, D. J., and Arnold, J. A. (1987). *Management Accounting: British Case Studies*. London: CIMA.

—— Turley, S., Burns, J., Joseph, N., Lewis, L., and Southworth, A. (1996). *External Reporting and Management Decisions*. London: CIMA.

—— Burns, J., Ezzamel, M., and Baldvinsdottir, G. (2003). *The Future Direction of UK Management Accounting Practice*. Oxford: Elsevier/CIMA.

Shields, M. D. (1997). 'Research in Management Accounting by North Americans in the 1990s', *Journal of Management Accounting Research*, 9: 3–61.

Siti-Nabiha, A. K. and Scapens, R. W. (2005). 'Stability and Change: An Institutionalist Study of Management Accounting Change', *Accounting, Auditing and Accountability Journal*, 18(1): 44–73.

Tinker, T. (2005). 'The Withering of Criticism: A Review of Professional, Foucauldian, Enthnographic, and Epistemic Studies in Accounting', *Accounting, Auditing and Accountability Journal*, 18(1): 100–35.

Zimmerman, J. L. (2001). 'Some Conjectures Regarding Empirical Management Accounting Research', *Journal of Accounting and Economics*, 32(1/3): 411–27.

16 Strategic cost management: upsizing, downsizing, and right(?) sizing

John K. Shank

16.1 Strategic cost management

16.1.1 THE ORIGINS

I first encountered the term 'strategic accounting' in 1981 in the scholarly publications of Kenneth Simmonds (1981) of London Business School. His work is clearly among the seminal contributions. His linking of strategic concepts with cost analysis concepts in connection with pricing policy struck me as insightful, useful, and generalizable. That Ken's chosen academic discipline was marketing, rather than accounting, did not seem to me strange or problematic. I saw no reason why those of us in accounting or marketing could not reach out to other business faculties in creating a multidisciplinary approach to management accounting. In fact, most of the leading figures in management accounting at that time had grounding in 'business' as they came to the 'accounting' arena. Accounting was clearly seen then as the 'language of business'.

I remember discussions in the early 1980s with Michael Bromwich (1990), Anthony Hopwood, Robert Anthony, Gordon Shillinglaw, Charles Horngren, Robert Kaplan, and Sidney Davidson, among many other distinguished accounting scholars, about the 'evolution' of cost analysis towards broader linkages to business management. The field had been 'cost accounting' through the first four decades of the twentieth century. The focus then was heavily on product costing, standard costing, overhead allocation, and inventory valuation.

In the 1950s, the focus in the USA and UK began to shift towards 'managerial accounting'. Three seminal US textbooks by Anthony (1960), Horngren (1962), and Shillinglaw (1959) led the change in emphasis towards decision analysis in fields such as marketing (pricing), operations (make vs. buy), finance (capital budgeting), and organizational behaviour (responsibility accounting). The rise of 'MBA education' at that same time gave legitimacy in our universities to the idea that accounting should be a key part of the education of business managers.

Accounting fitted well as the source of the information that was the 'grist' for the 'mill' of 'M^4' (mathematical manipulation masquerading as management!). MBA programmes were already full of 'optimization' and 'simulation' and 'regression' and 'analysis of variance', all drawing heavily on accounting information. Management accounting had almost completely replaced cost accounting in graduate management education by the mid-1960s.

But, at that time, 'strategy' was still seen largely as just adding the 'general management' policy dimension to business. It was not yet a separate field of inquiry or analysis. That was to come later with the paradigm-shifting work of Professor Michael Porter (1980) at Harvard, which was popularized in such leading textbooks as Oster (1990) and Hax and Majluf (1984). Their work was reinforced by such organizations as the Marketing Science Institute at Harvard and the early 'strategic' consulting firms such as Boston Consulting Group, Bain and Company, and McKinsey.

Strategy emerged as an identifiable subject area in the 1970s and early 1980s. It came to be seen as the 'glue' that holds business management together. It became 'de rigeur' for most business disciplines to add the term strategy to their names, as in operations strategy, organization strategy, or marketing strategy. Well, why not 'strategic accounting' as well?

It seemed to me, then, that the rise of the belief that strategic considerations are central to our understanding of the role of accounting information in business decision-making was as 'natural' a transformation, for the 1980s and beyond, as was the transformation from cost accounting to management accounting between about 1945 and 1965. Strategic accounting would gradually supplant management accounting, just as the latter had gradually supplanted cost accounting.

Management accounting had brought new dimensions to the subject by emphasizing the role of financial information in decision-making across a wide spectrum of business problems. Cost accounting was too narrowly focused on the accounting, per se, rather than the business decisions accounting information is intended to facilitate. Cost accounting could never pretend to be the 'language of business' in that sense.

But, management accounting, c.1975, was, in its own way, equally emasculated. It did not consider, explicitly, the business context in which the functional decisions are embedded. In fact, it usually did not even *implicitly* consider the business context. Each functional discipline stood as a separate 'stove pipe', dominated by its own logic for its own set of topics.

Moving beyond this discipline-focused perspective on business to a strategy-focused perspective seemed to me to be the 'wave of the future' in about 1985. The functional disciplines would be integrated much more closely. Problems would come to be seen as 'business' problems, rather than 'marketing' problems, 'manufacturing' problems, or 'logistics' problems. In that context, 'strategic accounting' would become 'strategic cost management'(SCM). The role of financial information in business management would be to facilitate strategy formulation and strategy implementation. That sure sounded good to me at the time.

When I wrote the essay 'Strategic Cost Management: New Wine or Just New Bottles?' for the first issue of the *Journal of Management Accounting Research* (Shank 1989), I thought I was charting the future for management accounting researchers, teachers, and practitioners. In that issue of *JMAR*, Anthony, Horngren, and Shillinglaw wrote articulately about the past and present of our discipline, but I thought I was speaking for the future. That seemed particularly likely to me because it dovetailed so well with two other themes that were prominent then.

On one hand was the popularization across the USA and UK of the notion that internally focused corporate accounting, dominated by cost determination and cost reporting, was outmoded and outdated and had outlived its usefulness. Kaplan and Johnson (1987) published *Relevance Lost* to wide popular appeal. Johnson (1992) followed it up with *Relevance Regained*, emphasizing the strategic aspects of accounting analysis.

Between 1982 and 1990, internal accounting staff was cut by 40–80 per cent in a long list of major US corporations, including Ford Motor, General Electric, Motorola, American Express, Digital Equipment Corp, General Motors, and Honeywell. Finance expense dropped from an average of about 4 per cent of corporate revenue in the USA in 1965 to an average of about 2 per cent by 1985. It was 'decreed' that internal accounting departments were no longer to be so consumed by closing the books each month, continually updating the earnings forecasts, calculating and recalculating standard costs, and analysing budget variances. What, then, were the accountants to do instead? How about SCM?!

The second theme of the late 1980s that seemed to me to dovetail so nicely with SCM was the rise of activity-based costing (ABC) and its Siamese twin, activity-based management (ABM). ABC created a virtual revolution in our best thinking about how fixed manufacturing overhead should be assigned to products, customers, channels, or whatever. ABC was so appealing, initially, that it spawned an army of advocates who swarmed over the corporate landscape, revamping overhead allocation schemes hither and yon. By 1990, each of the 'big six' accounting firms had a division of its consulting arm specializing in ABC and/or ABM. This was clearly seen as a way to make managerial accounting more strategically relevant.

A 'big' issue of that era was whether ABC was a component of SCM, or vice versa. I remember lively exchanges at scholarly and professional meetings in which Robin Cooper would argue that ABC and/or ABM was 'really' the capstone concept for strategic accounting. I would rebut that SCM was 'really' the umbrella under which ABC was one very important component, along with other SCM themes such as value chain analysis, competitor costing, target costing, total cost of ownership, or cost of quality. Neither of us doubted that there was a bright future for strategically focused management accounting. The attention that strategic topics were receiving was music to our ears. The only question was which theme would lead the orchestra.

16.1.2 THE GLORY DECADE (1990–2000)

Heady times, indeed. Examples of pilot applications of ABC abounded in companies in the USA, UK, and Europe. Management accounting professionals saw great promise in the idea of retooling personal skill sets and corporate tool kits around the notion of the accounting function as central in the evolution of ever more strategically aware and strategically astute managers. There were also many examples of pilot applications of other SCM tools across a wide set of companies. Many of the examples found their way into case studies, which then found their way into the MBA classroom. My first collection of such cases, *The Evolution From Managerial to Strategic Accounting* (Shank and Govindarajan 1989), was well received and was even translated into Italian. The cases worked their way into dozens of MBA programmes over the next few years. Many other authors were also developing new teaching materials, including Robin Cooper, C. J. McNair, and Bill Rotch in the USA, Anthony Atkinson and Murray Bryant in Canada, Michael Bromwich and Al Bhimani in the UK, and Deigan Morris in France.

The book, *Strategic Cost Management* (Shank and Govindarajan 1993), went to ten printings in four years, was translated into seven other languages, and won business book awards in the USA, Brazil, and Japan. It has sold over 100,000 copies, which never ceases to amaze me. It is just 'accounting', after all.

Professional organizations in North America, Europe, and the UK picked up on the SCM themes in their publications and professional development programmes. As demand for conventionally trained management accountants continued to wane, organizations such as the Institute of Management Accountants (IMA) in the USA, the Chartered Institute of Management Accountants (CIMA) in Canada, the Chartered Institute of Management Accountants (CIMA) in Britain, and the 'Register Controllers' in the Netherlands pushed for a more strategic orientation and skill set in their members. The Financial Executives Institute (FEI) and the American Institute of Certified Public Accountants (AICPA) in the USA sponsored research monographs and continuing education seminars. In 1994, the AICPA crated a new Executive Committee for Management Accounting, which I chaired. This evolved into an AICPA Center for Excellence in Financial Management in 1997.

By 1995, most of the major consulting firms also had an active practice area in the topics of SCM. I was not alone among academics working in major corporations, often alongside the strategic consultants, on projects involving quality costing, supply chain costing, competitor costing, target costing, life cycle costing (LCC), or economic value analysis. SCM had become a billion-dollar-a-year industry. Some consulting firms, such as Stern, Stewart (Stern 1996), Marikon (McTaggart et al. 1994), or Mitchell-Madison, even specialized in 'strategic accounting' applications.

This was certainly an era of 'great expectations'. Great 'beginnings' abounded. I continued to publish case collections and professional articles over those years, highlighting SCM themes. It was troubling, however, that the subject was not working its way into mainstream academic accounting journals or mainstream management education programmes. Most examples in business were 'pilot projects'.

Most examples in the classroom were 'cameo appearances' inside pretty traditional management accounting courses. The topics were not working their way into mainstream accounting textbooks in a big way. Leading textbooks, including those of Drury (2004) in the UK and Horngren et al. (2004) in the USA, mentioned some of the topics, but not very prominently. I saw this general problem at that time as just a time-lag issue that would eventually correct itself.

The annual Management Accounting Conferences at the London School of Economics (LSE), under the leadership of Bromwich and Bhimani, showcased some SCM-type projects in the late 1990s. I saw this as affirmation of the trend. In 1999, I presented a paper at the LSE Conference jointly with the Controller of a major Division of Lucent Technologies, a $40-billion global telecommunications equipment firm. The topic was transforming Lucent's internal accounting system to 'materials only costing' (MOC), to de-emphasize 'fully loaded' costing in favour of 'throughput accounting' to support more strategic financial analysis. That year, several other SCM-type papers were also on the LSE Conference agenda.

In 1994, both the gold and silver medal prizes from the IMA were for SCM papers. I co-authored the silver medal paper (Shank and Constantinedes 1994), which described the efforts in Champion International, a $10-billion global forest products company, to eliminate standard costing with full manufacturing overhead allocation in favour of 'throughput accounting' with a 'balanced scorecard' (BSC) emphasis in one of its major North American divisions. That work expanded to several other divisions in Champion and several other major corporations over the next five years, including the work at Lucent.

One troubling aspect of many of these SCM projects was the lack of involvement of the internal management accountants in the companies. A project at Levi Strauss, for example, on supply chain reconfiguration for women's jeans involved representation from manufacturing, design engineering, logistics and distribution, and marketing, but not accounting. A major project on target costing at Lucent involved design engineers, manufacturing engineers, customer support, and Bell Labs, but not accounting. I would joke at the time that the accountants were too busy closing the books, updating the forecasts, and analysing the variances to have any time to actually help manage the company. I always assumed that management accountants would come around to the new emphasis, over time.

As the decade of the 1990s was ending, I was still very optimistic that SCM was going to emerge as the 'umbrella' theme for management accounting in the next decade. My friend, Robin Cooper, regularly chided me that I was overstating the abilities of accountants to 'learn new tricks'. He believed the SCM themes were evolving *outside* the purview of the accounting profession, which he saw as intellectually and emotionally unequipped for the transformation. I regularly chided him back that he and I were both accountants and we were making the transition! Why could our colleagues not do so, as well? Bromwich (1990) had raised similar concerns a decade earlier. Unfortunately, I have come to believe that Cooper and Bromwich were much more right than I was.

16.1.3 THE UNRAVELLING OF THE PIECES (2000–5)

By 2000, there was a fifteen-year history of great 'beginnings', 'pilot' projects, and 'cameo' appearances for SCM, but not much more. It has been a great topic on the lecture circuit and in cost management symposia. In military parlance, 'it briefs well'! But, the topics had not been gaining traction in mainstream academe or in the corporate world. When I presented the keynote address for the Annual Meeting of the Irish Association of Accounting and

Finance Professors at the University of Cork in 1999, the tone of the reception was guardedly quizzical. Where were the examples, I was asked, of real transformation after fifteen years? It was finally dawning on me that my 'pilot/cameo' examples were wearing a little thin.

Also, by 2002, the professional associations for management accountants in the USA were withering on the vine, not prospering. The IMA was shrinking in active high-level members. It was not able to convince its membership that high-end continuing education in broad-gauged general management is required. Its attempts to match the very successful 'Professional Fellows' programme of the Canadian CIMA were floundering. And, the CIMA programme was itself in decline as it dropped the publication of its very innovative Management Accounting Guidelines (MAG). The FEI drastically downscaled its long-standing research programme, the Financial Executives Research Foundation, because member firms were not supporting it. The AICPA initiative to build an SCM-oriented programme of outreach to its 150,000 members in private industry was never funded sufficiently to get it off the ground. It is staffed by only three professionals, out of a total in New York of more than 100 persons.

The professional magazines of all three of these formerly much more prominent organizations are not publishing SCM articles or stories. The AICPA's *Journal of Accountancy* rarely even publishes on management topics at all, even though more of its members are in private industry than in public practice. The IMA's *Strategic Finance* is much more 'strategic' in name than in content. The FEI's *Financial Executive* has become much more a trade news journal for chief financing officers (CFOs) than an outlet for innovative articles describing strategic accounting initiatives, if indeed there are any.

The management accounting curriculum is in decline in the leading American business schools. Management accounting has been dropped as a required MBA course at Dartmouth, Southern California, Chicago, Rochester, and Stanford among many schools. The senior accounting professor at Rochester, Jerry Zimmerman, argues very strongly that the role of managerial accounting in companies lies almost exclusively in management control rather than decision support. The leading management accounting academic journal in the USA, *Journal of Management Accounting Research*, has shrunk to only one issue per year, and seldom publishes on decision support topics, such as SCM themes.

Horngren has said, publicly, that he considers the 'balanced scorecard' term to be vacuous, at best, and dangerous, at worst. He argues that all the factors are certainly not of equal importance (balance) and that the causal links to performance are tenuously established, at best. In the UK, two researchers, Jeremy Hope and Robin Fraser, have gained substantial prominence arguing that budgeting systems should not be 'improved', but rather should be totally abandoned. Their counterpart in the USA is the Beyond Budgeting Roundtable, which also advocates eliminating basic budgeting systems, rather than trying to give them a more strategic focus.

The remaining 'big four' accounting firms no longer have large management accounting consulting practices. The Arthur Andersen spin-off, Accenture, has also largely dropped its management accounting practice, in favour of an emphasis on computer-based information systems and regulatory support systems.

In 2002, Professors Joseph San Miguel, Lawrence Carr, and I attempted a major research project for the FEI on strategic uses of the management information generated by the enterprise resource planning (ERP) systems, which became almost ubiquitous in large US companies between 1995 and 2001. The FEI was not able to identify even one large company willing to showcase strategic uses of its ERP. Virtually *all* ERP installations achieved a common data architecture for recording accounting transactions. Customer-accounting systems, vendor-accounting systems, human resource systems, and general ledger systems can now all communicate with each other in a common language. In *most* companies, internal transaction systems can also be linked with customers' and suppliers' ERP systems to provide open communication along the business supply chain. In *many* companies, the transaction information from all along the supply chain also can be stored for future use in off-line data warehouses. In *some* companies, the data warehouses also include non-transaction business information. And, in *some* companies the data warehouses are supported by relational database inquiry and analysis software to facilitate business use of the information. But, in *very few* companies in 2005 is that information from the data warehouse readily accessible at the desktop to managers across business functions for use in strategic planning and day-to-day strategic decision-making.

ERP was 'sold' as a decision-making tool, but it turned out to be only a transaction-processing tool. Like the promise of Management Information Systems (MIS) in the mainframe-dominated computer world of the 1960s, or Computer-Based Information Systems (CBIS) in the time-shared central processors of the 1970s, or Executive Information Systems (EIS) in the desktop computer environment of the 1980s, ERP in the 1990s delivered far less management support than it promised.

Of all the firms with which I worked on SCM ventures between 1985 and 2000, none now stand out as major success stories. Lucent, now a much smaller and weaker firm, has dropped all its SCM transformation efforts. Champion International was taken over by International Paper, whose accounting function is still firmly wed to traditional management accounting themes. Motorola barely survived bankruptcy and now focuses more on surviving than on accounting transformation. Digital Equipment Corporation was taken over by Compaq Computer, which merged into Hewlett Packard, where concern for survival has also driven out most of the SCM transformation work. Citicorp dropped its transformation agenda when it was 'acquired' by the Sandy Weil management team. Gulf Oil was merged into Chevron in an unfriendly 'takeover'. Chevron's financial management systems are still very traditional.

The accounting scandals in the USA since 2000 involving firms such as Enron, WorldCom, Cendant, Waste Management, and Tyco Industries, among many others, have redirected internal management accounting systems (MASs) and attention towards basic internal controls and fraud detection and/or prevention, rather than strategic information. The Sarbanes–Oxley legislation mandates this focus. The 'strategic support' role of accounting is now seen as part of the prior era in which basic internal controls were eliminated or ignored in the interest of financial reporting flim-flammery. There is very little emotional energy left for strategic accounting transformation after all the 'Sarbox' requirements are met.

Even the companies that still seem willing to consider the strategic transformation agenda appear to see it more as an add-on to traditional systems, rather than as a replacement. I have recently worked on projects in two large publicly traded American firms, Coca-Cola and HJ Heinz, and a multibillion-dollar privately owned supermarket chain. All three are willing to invest resources in management education programmes and 'pilot' projects. But none seems committed to really challenging the old mentality—the monthly 'hard close', the elaborate 'rear view mirror' reporting system, the 'financially focused' planning and budgeting systems, and the decision support models tied to 'variable contribution' and conventional return on assets and/or return on equity (ROA/ROE) metrics.

I am not aware of any professor in the USA or UK who is currently involved in real transformative SCM work in any corporation.

In a nutshell, I believe the SCM 'experiment' has largely failed. Cooper and Slagmulder still write regularly on the SCM theme for the journal, *Cost Management*. But, the audience has dwindled as that journal has declined substantially in stature and circulation from the days when it was edited by Barry Brinker or Larry Maisel. I take some pleasure in the fact that Professor Cooper now uses SCM much more regularly as his umbrella theme, rather than ABC and/or ABM. I consider him to be a convert to the language of SCM! However, the audience for the message is now limited pretty much to a smattering of mid-level accounting staff managers in a handful of companies where 'pilot' programmes are still the order of the day.

16.1.4 PROGNOSIS?

I really wish that I could find more in the management accounting milieu today that was supportive of the SCM agenda. It is still the major thrust of my writing, my teaching, and my consulting. I stay busy and am still excited by the intellectual challenges of linking management accounting explicitly to strategy and to a cross-functional view of the firm. But I now think Cooper was right ten years ago when he wrote off the management accounting establishment as ever being able to lead an SCM transformation.

The 1990s saw a further dramatic reduction in staffing levels in management accounting across the mainstream of US industry. The norm is now much closer to 1 per cent of employment in accounting than 4 per cent, which was typical in the 1960s, or 2 per cent in the 1980s. Accounting was almost always the largest staff function in large US companies through the 1970s. Now it has fallen to third place behind human resources and information technology.

The 1990s saw the transformation of information technology to common data architectures, client–server-based transaction processing systems, and relational databases for information management. Accounting information has become almost a 'by-product' of the ERP system in many companies. That further reduces the need for large numbers of accounting personnel.

And, Sarbox, resulting from the aftermath of the accounting scandals at the turn of the century, has absorbed a large proportion of the energy of the remaining accounting professionals. They are now caught up in 'make-work' regarding internal control and fraud. That work will not really stop the crooks from being crooked, but it will assuage the regulatory overseers until the first scandal happens in spite of Sarbox! Such a scandal is bound to happen, sooner or later, because Sarbox is still preoccupied with *internal accounting* controls, rather than broad-gauged *business* controls that would speak to the real strategic risks firms face in globally competitive markets.

MBA students are less and less likely to get a good, required, business-based foundation in management accounting because there seems to be no time for it in the curriculum and no inclination to push for it. More and more managerial accounting courses are taught by professors whose doctoral training and research interests lie in financial accounting. More and more accountants in industry in the USA are the products of an education system that sees accounting as an end in itself (Schools of Accounting!), rather than a business tool. The US university education system is oriented far more towards financial accountants than management accountants, and the balance shifts even further, year by year.

I have come to conclude that there is no energy in most corporations for moving management accounting beyond the comfortable boundaries than were set in the 'glory days' of the 1960s and 1970s. There is also no big push from senior-line managers, the users of accounting information. Whatever strategic information support they need is provided by analysts who work in functions other than accounting. They are part of the 'shadow' accounting staff and do not report to the CFO.

The few management accountants who are left are dedicated to keeping the ERP working smoothly (but not as a strategic management tool). They also manage the budgetary control systems that support financial planning and corporate compensation programmes. And, they actively pretend that 'accounting controls' can protect the firm from fraud on the part of managers who are smart enough to envision and undertake transactions whose deviousness totally eludes the hapless gatekeepers.

There is no professional association in the USA today with effective programmes directed at education, training, or peer support on the SCM themes; not the AICPA, not the FEI, and not the IMA.

Also, strategic transformation of internal accounting systems does not seem to be a high priority for very many corporate CFOs in 2005. They are consumed with the internal control issues in the Sarbox legislation and the public reporting issues related to ever-changing and ever more technical Financial Accounting Standards Board (FASB) standards and proposed standards.

When CFOs change companies, as they frequently do, they seem to be more concerned about their lack of familiarity with technical industry accounting standards than their lack of familiarity with basic business issues. *CFO Magazine* (a division of London's *Economist*) noted in a 2004 feature article (O'Sullivan 2004) that 'financial skills' are among the most readily transferred from company to company. 'Product and industry knowledge is important', they note, 'but far less so than for a sales executive who needs deep industry expertise.'

Are there not far-reaching implications of the 'fact'(?) that CFOs *do not* need industry expertise?!

CFOs come and go frequently. The same *CFO Magazine* story cited one survey in which 50 per cent of those polled were considering a change in industries and a second survey in which the figure was 75 per cent. With that much turnover, there is necessarily a resulting low level of industry knowledge among CFOs across a broad cross-section of US firms. It is thus perhaps not surprising that very few firms exhibit financial management leadership at the top with sufficient grounding in the strategic business issues facing the firm to even attempt to mount a strategically based transformation of the internal decision support systems. Like the universities, and the surviving public accounting firms, corporate USA is dominated in the accounting sphere by persons with no real interest or expertise in SCM.

In recent years, I have even encountered more than a few CFOs who are openly hostile to SCM concepts. In my view, they prefer a system in which they maintain full control over financial analysis and internal business reporting, no matter how strategically irrelevant that domain has become, versus a system that dethrones the 'gospel of traditional finance' in favour of a multifunctional approach, which empowers line managers to take the lead in strategic financial analysis.

In one egregious example, the president of a multibillion-dollar start-up venture in consumer telecommunications hired a consulting team to prepare a multiyear, net present value analysis of the full supply chain profitability of three of his core business units. We concluded, in contrast to the story reported in the company's highly aggregated historical cost financial statements, that the company's basic business model was not viable. We predicted, based on our SCM analysis, that the business would run out of cash in about thirty-six months. The CFO and his staff did not participate in the study or cooperate with it.

The CFO refused to acknowledge our conclusions and continued to report, internally and externally, that the company was 'on track' with its five-year growth plan. By the time our prediction of unavoidable bankruptcy and insolvency proved accurate, in thirty-four months, the CFO had moved on to a new job in a different industry, leaving the line organization holding the 'empty bag'. When bankruptcy was finally declared in May 2004, the stock price was $0.21 per share, versus $29 per share in the summer of 2001. This situation is explored in more depth in the case study, which is part of the chapter.

The above is not an isolated example of CFO attitudes towards relinquishing control over financial analysis and internal financial reporting. Although less blatant in their ramifications, I have experienced situations involving a similar mindset in the Discover Card Division of Morgan Stanley, in NOVA Chemicals, in Alcan Aluminum, in the Personal Investments Division of Fidelity Management, and in the American Automobile Association.

I now see the transformation from 'cost accounting' to 'management accounting' to 'strategic accounting' in a different light. Management accounting is much more decision-focused than cost accounting, but only in a superficial way. It forces the accountant to consider the decision-setting in which the accounting information is used, but it does not force the accountant to consider the business context for the decision or the strategic context for the business. The 'management accountant' can still focus largely on the accounting information itself. A 'strategic accountant' must really understand the business in which he (or she) works and the linkages in that business across functional silos and across business boundaries with customers and suppliers.

It is true that a management accountant must adopt a broader perspective than a cost accountant. But the jump is manageable for a person of reasonable intellect, modest training in the MBA disciplines, and well-developed quantitative skills. The jump to being a strategic accountant is a quantum leap in breadth of business perspective and depth of commitment to real strategic analysis, across functions, along the supply chain, and among competing firms. Management accounting pretends to be about business while it really is about decision models that masquerade as management problems. Strategic accounting really is about business in its full subtlety and complexity.

Too many accounting professors and corporate accountants have extreme difficulty in making the intellectual transition from accountant to real, multidisciplinary, strategic business analyst. Students in business schools are not often enough forced to confront this integrative dimension, which distinguishes purely 'managerial' accounting from truly 'strategic' accounting. Future accounting professors are also too seldom forced to confront this quantum leap in problem analysis in their graduate studies. Unless they have a solid grounding in 'general management' somewhere in their background, they probably will not develop it in an MBA or doctoral programme.

If accounting students do not get exposure to the strategic mindset, they will not develop an appreciation for it as they move on to the corporate world. If financial managers do not enter their business career with a solid awareness of this broader dimension of management information, they are unlikely to develop it 'on the job'. This is particularly true when they are immediately loaded down with Sarbox sophistry and are expected to worship at the altar of quarterly earnings forecasts and reports, as do their superiors.

Following this is a complex and politically rich case study and commentary describing a situation in which SCM concepts are applied to a business in which conventional financial analysis tools are inadequate for strategic analysis. For me, the case illustrates, simultaneously, the power of SCM tools, the relatively high level of 'general management acumen' necessary to use the tools effectively, and the possibility that the CFO organization may not want to acknowledge either the efficacy of the tools or the salience of the story they tell.

16.1.5 CONCLUSION

The famous physicist, Max Planck, is reported to have begun his graduate studies in economics. He is said to have switched from economics to physics because he found the 'softness' of economics to be too 'hard'. He preferred a discipline in which regularity, consistency, and closed-form solutions dominate. In a parallel vein, I now believe that most management accounting professors and most management accountants in the business world prefer the often complicated, but not very conceptually complex, world of 'management accounting' versus the really complex and conceptually challenging world of 'strategic accounting'. SCM's 'softness' is too 'hard' for them. It forces them towards a world view that is much more multidisciplinary and integrative than they are trained for or comfortable with.

I see very few champions for SCM in the corporate world or in academe. And I see a large array of forces working against the development of such champions, either in our universities, in the accounting firms, or in lower-level corporate training programmes. I still believe the ideas are sound and that SCM represents a conceptually superior framework for management accounting. But the arguments have had their chance and have not carried the day. And so it goes.

16.2 Comprehensive Home Communications: a case study

The 1996 Telecommunications Act opened the local telecommunications marketplace in the USA to unregulated competition. From 1996 to 2000, hundreds of Competitive Local Exchange Carriers (CLECs) emerged, all across the country. The ebullient US capital markets of the late 1990s provided billions in funding for these new telecommunications companies, which came in all shapes and sizes. This case considers the business model of one of the best capitalized CLECs—Comprehensive Home Communications (CHC) of Atlanta, Georgia.

16.2.1 THE VISION

In 1997, Miles Johnson, CEO of CHC, took to Wall Street his vision of a company that could effectively compete with incumbent telephone, cable, and Internet access providers in densely populated south-eastern cities. At the time, CHC operated very successful cable television franchises in Jackson, Mississippi, and Charleston, South Carolina. The economics of the Jackson franchise are summarized in Exhibit 1.

Johnson's plan was to 'overbuild' a comprehensive new fibre-optic network across the south-east. Since earnings before interest, taxes, depreciation, and amortization (EBITDA) were 40 per cent for telephone systems and 30 per cent for cable systems, the financial rationale for combining telephone, television, and Web access in one network seemed very strong. Combining all three services for customers through just one network and one management structure promised lucrative returns, as shown in Exhibit 2.

In the very heady investment climate of 1997, this simple capsule business proposition was sufficient to gain Johnson, a well-established telecommunications executive, a serious

Exhibit 1 The Jackson Market (as of 2000)

107,000 homes passed, at a capital cost of $46.3 million (10-year life)
Penetration is 82,600 homes (77%). Capital cost is $560/customer
Monthly revenue for a 'typical' customer:
  Regular cable (50 channels)
  Extra channels $49.50
  Set-top box rental
Customer equipment costs $250 per home connection (10-year life)

	10-year annual operating cash flow ($) summary (2000) for the average customer	
	Year 0	**Years 1–10**
Revenue		594
Programming cost		(263)
Customer acquisition	(73)	
Selling	(53)	
Marketing	(11)	
Sales commissions	(9)	
Installation	(91)	
Customer care		(36)
Billing		(12)
Repair and maintenance		(17)
Customer service		(7)
Network maintenance		(24)
Administration		(26)
Local market		(16)
Allocated corporate		(10)
Net	(164)	245
After tax	(98.4)	147

hearing with major venture capital funds, investment banks, and private investors. Johnson coupled the financial proposition with a strong story about the benefits for CHC's new customers. The company would offer very attractive prices well below competing individual services, state-of-the-art technology for very clear high-speed signals, and truly responsive customer service (in contrast to the telephone and cable monopolies), all combined in one easy monthly bill with no connection fees and no extra charges.

16.2.2 HIGH TIMES IN DIXIE

Over the three years from 1997 through 1999, CHC raised $3.8 billion in the US capital markets ($1 billion in convertible preferred from a single very prominent private investor, $2 billion in equity, $0.3 billion in convertible debt, and $0.5 billion in mortgage debt).

Exhibit 2 Overview of the CHC Business Plan

Invest $667 in the basic network for each home passed (20-year life)
Connect 67% of the homes ($1,000 per home connected)
Invest $500 in household equipment and activation costs for each home connected to the network (10-year life)
Charge $125/month for cable, high-speed Internet access, and unlimited local and long-distance telephone service, with no hook-up fees and no extra charges
Direct cost of services provided is 1/3 of revenue
Operating cost is 1/3 of revenue
The EBITDA margin is thus 1/3 of revenue, which is $500 before taxes, or $300 after taxes
With a 40% tax rate, the cash flow return for the project is as follows:

	Investment	Tax shield	Operations	Net cash flow
Year 0	(1,500)	40 (1)		(1,460)
Years 1–10	—	40	300	340

10-year 10% NPV = $629
10-year IRR = 19+%(real)

1) $1,000/20 = 50 \times 0.4 = 20$
   $500/10 = 50 \times 0.4 = 20 = 40$

Each time the company 'broke ground' in a new city, the public markets rewarded it with an ever-higher equity valuation. A 'de facto' strategy quickly emerged—break ground, watch the share price rise, raise more new money, break ground, and so on. With solid revenue growth, CHC was deemed to be a 'new economy' success by investors, the financial media, management, and employees alike, in spite of huge and steadily rising operating losses. Johnson ran television advertisements on local cable channels thanking his thousands of employees for 'building the empire'. He threw lavish and gala parties to celebrate each new self-proclaimed success.

At its peak in the fall of 1999, the CHC stock price at $52 a share was already rapidly closing in on the $60 conversion price in the convertible preferred issue. With 77 million shares outstanding, the equity valuation reached $4 billion. Adding the preferred issue and $800 million in debt, CHC's enterprise value was $5.8 billion with 1.4 million homes passed. The plan was to pass 8 million homes by 2002 and connect 3 million of them. Operations showed a $100 million cash loss in 1998, a $200 million cash loss in 1999, and a $300 million cash loss in 2000.

16.2.3 A SUDDEN DOSE OF REALITY

When the US stock market collapsed in February 2000, financing options that had recently appeared unlimited disappeared within a few weeks, leaving many CLECs in desperate straits. Fortunately, CHC had already raised enough money to finance fully its construction activities and operations to date with $1.6 billion cash still on hand. Many observers saw the drying up of capital sources as a big advantage for CHC over its competitors who were still seeking major new cash infusions.

However, with the capital markets now closed, CHC needed to change its focus very quickly from rapid infrastructure build-out to operating cash sufficiency. The strategy changed to building a profitable and cash-positive business around the 1.4 million homes the network already passed across in eight cities.

Johnson and his senior management team believed in the viability of the smaller-scale plan, but they had never really developed an explicit business model as a framework for management programmes and control systems. After two rounds of management turnover, Andy Davis, a well-regarded telecommunications turnaround expert, took over day-to-day operations as president and chief operating officer (COO) in January 2001.

16.2.4 ANDY DAVIS' CHALLENGE

Each of CHC's eight markets used different optical conversion and transmission technology, depending on the latest developments available at the time of the build-out. The two markets that were 'legacy' cable franchises used traditional coaxial cable technology. The company also had heavy capital investment in switches, cable head-ends, and routers—the traditional signal creation equipment required for telephone, cable, and Internet access service.

In addition to technology differences, each market was also at a different stage of development. Some markets, such as Charlotte, North Carolina, had been in operation since 1998 and were near the completion of their build-out, with well-established local sales, installation, and customer service departments. Other markets, such as Birmingham, Alabama, were in the early stage of development that required significant infrastructure investment. Exhibit 3 is a summary of capital investment, homes passed, and customer connections by market and service category as of April 2001.

Since the eight markets varied substantially in their technology and business profiles, Davis knew he would have to create separate business planning and control frameworks for each of them. There was no comprehensive management control system in place. He decided to start with Charlotte, the most mature market. His first challenge was to create a fully absorbed income statement for the market. The financial statements available to him combined all eight locations, with only selected statistics for individual markets. Except for corporate marketing, corporate administration, and the centralized call centre, all revenue and expense accounting was decentralized to the local markets. All network investment and network maintenance were also *managed* locally even though they were *reported* on a combined basis.

With help from local employees and managers, Davis was able to create the Charlotte income statement shown in Exhibit 4. This format follows the supply chain in that market. A more detailed breakdown on expenses is shown in Exhibit 5.

Charlotte was a critical market for CHC because Johnson had promised his key investors that this region would move 'into the black' (on a 'local EBITDA' basis) by September 2001.

Exhibit 3 CHC network statistics

Markets	Total	Charlotte	Atlanta	Birmingham	Little Rock	Jackson	Charleston	Memphis	Jacksonville
Network investment	$2.1 bn.*	$450 m.	$500 m.	$100 m.	$200 m	$70 m.	$100 m.	$400 m.	$280 m.
Homes passed (000s)	1,419	245	332	65	174	107	160	253	83
Connections (000s)									
Telephone	162.4	49.8	30.9	7.4	33.1	—	—	34.1	7.1
Cable	389.2	47.5	77.1	6.1	74.4	82.6	27.6	67.9	6.0
Internet	73.7	27.7	16.2	3.5	5.3	—	—	17.2	3.8
Total	625.3	125.0	124.2	17.0	112.8	82.6	27.6	119.2	16.9
% 'Bundled'	N/A	69	21	92	14	0	0	4	89

*Network $1,840 m.
Customer equipment 156 m. (625.3 × $250)
Deferred activation 106 m. (625.3 × $170)
$2,102 m.

Exhibit 4 Charlotte, March 2001 ($000)

Revenues		5,412
Telephone	2,854	
Cable	1,727	
Internet	831	
Direct product costs		(2,473)
Telephone	947	
Cable	1,205	
Internet	321	
Direct product margin (54%)		2,939
Telephone (64%)	1,907	
Cable (30%)	522	
Internet (61%)	510	
Operating costs		(6,709)
Customer acquisition	1,502	
Customer activation	517	
Customer care	1,054	
Operations support	2,223	
General and administrative	1,413	
Profit before taxes		(3,770)
'Local EBITDA' loss		(277)*

*Total loss	(3770)	
Add back:		
Depreciation—network	1,250	
Depreciation—customer support	438	
Corporate marketing allocation	557	
Call centre allocation(1)	538	
Corporate overhead allocation	710	
Local EBITDA loss	(277)	

(1) Call centre cost (March) was $2.69 m. for 253,000 calls.
    Total connections are 625,000, of which Charlotte is 20% (125/625).
    Charlotte's March allocation is $538,000 (0.20 × $2.69 m.).

CHC needed to demonstrate the ability successfully to operate the network it was creating. There was still $1 billion in cash on hand in April 2001, but operations in the preceding year had consumed $300 million and new network investments, another $300 million. Operations in the first quarter of 2001 generated another $100 million cash loss. Turning around the cash drain soon was a very high priority.

Charlotte was the test case to show that astute and aggressive 'supply chain management' could turn red ink into solid profit and return on investment (ROI). Davis saw no reason why Charlotte could not aspire to match or even exceed the returns the cable franchises regularly earned in Jackson and Charleston. He focused his analysis for Charlotte on the month of March 2001, which was typical of the current scope of operations.

Exhibit 5 Charlotte, March 2001 ($000)

Customer acquisition (one-time)		1,502
Selling	577	
Allocated corporate marketing	557	
Advertising	63	
Sales commissions ($50/connect)	305	
Customer activation (one-time)		517
Order processing	294	
Installation expense	223	
Dispatch	16	
Install	207	
Customer care (recurring)		1,054
Billing	215	
Allocated call centre operations	538	
Customer support	78	
Installation follow-up expense	223	
Dispatch	15	
Install	208	
Operations support (recurring)		2,223
Network maintenance	418	
Network operations	117	
Network depreciation*	1,250	
Customer support depreciation*	438	
General and Administrative (recurring)		1,413
Local administration	703	
Allocated corporate overhead	710	
Total operating costs		6,709

*See Exhibit 6C.

Although Charlotte was still showing almost a $4 million loss each month, the annualized loss was shrinking from $50 million in 2000 to a projected $30 million in 2001. The 'local EBITDA' loss, as shown in Exhibit 4, was less than $300,000 in March. At a cash margin of $23.50 per connection per month, this loss could be eliminated with 12,000 new connections. Since 6,100 connections were added and 2,200 lost in March (as shown in Exhibit 6A), 12,000 new connections represented only three months' net growth.

16.2.5 THE 'LIFETIME NPV' OF A 'GOLD' ACCOUNT

Because one-time expenses and recurring expenses are mixed in Exhibit 4, Davis could not easily project the lifetime profitability of the new accounts CHC was adding each month. Since local operations in Charlotte seemed to be rapidly approaching break-even cash flow, including substantial one-time expenses for all new accounts, Davis believed lifetime profitability for each new account should already be well 'in the black'.

Exhibit 6 Additional information for the Charlotte Market (March 2001)

Part A—Connections

	Total in service	% Bundled*	New	Disconnects
Telephone	49,800	80	2,600	1,100
Cable	47,500	67.5	2,000	700
Internet	27,700	100	1,500	400
Total	125,000	69	6,100	2,200

*2 or more services to the household (86,250 connections)

New network capital expenditures	$1,440,000
New investment in customer equipment	$1,525,000 (6,100 × $250)
New investment in deferred customer activation	$1,037,000 (6,100 × $ 170)
Dispatch	$ 73,000
Install	$964,000

Part B—Investment per Gold customer

Total network investment in Charlotte	$400 million
Homes passed	245,000
Maximum connections (× 3)	735,000
Reasonable maximum penetration (40%)	294,000
Investment per connection	$1,360 ($400 m. ÷ 294,000)
One *Gold customer* = 3 connections = 3 × $1,360 = $4,080	

Part C—Depreciation

Network depreciation:

$300m. of 30-year life basic infrastructure	= $10 m./year
$100m. of 20-year life technology enhancements	= $ 5 m./year
($15 m ÷ $400 m = 3.75%)	= $15 m./year
$15 m. ÷ 12 months	= $1,250,000/month

Customer support depreciation:

125,000 customer connections (125,000 × $420 = $ 52.5 m. with 10-year life)

Customer equipment	= $250 each
Deferred activation expense	= $170 each
Total	= $420 each

(Per month = $52.5 m. ÷ 10 years ÷ 12 months) = $438,000/month

Part D—Additional Gold account information

Monthly revenue = $125.
Monthly direct product cost = $55.
One-time sales commission at acquisition: $50 per connection, for a total of $150.
For all operating expenses, use averages based on dollars in Exhibit 5 and physical measures in Exhibit 6A.

Davis thought that a multiyear net present value (NPV) analysis of the lifetime profitability for one new account, as in Exhibit 2, would be a good way to show Johnson and the major investors that CHC had really 'turned the corner' towards future profitability. He chose 'one Gold customer' as the 'unit of analysis' to demonstrate the economic viability of the CHC business plan.

The best new customers were those who subscribed to the 'Gold Plan'—unlimited local and long distance telephone service, fifty cable channels including HBO, and full Internet access, all for $125 per month. This three-way 'bundled' service plan gave CHC the best chance to amortize its substantial investment against substantial monthly revenue.

Davis asked his top financial analyst to pull together a ten-year NPV for one Gold customer in Charlotte to proxy for the future profitability of the overall network, after start-up was completed. The information in Exhibits 4, 5, and 6 provides the basis for the Gold customer NPV analysis.

16.2.6 AN SCM ANALYSIS OF THE CHC CASE

This case is an excellent vehicle to show how fast-changing and complex businesses can lose sight of basic economic realities when they are forced to rely on aggregated historical cost financial statements. The CHC case is based on a real company, RCN, and its strategic dilemma in 2001. Many issues were interacting to create the confusion in the company about the economic viability of its business model:

- A mix of eight business locations, each with different technology in place and each at a different stage of development
- Combined corporate financial statements versus separate statements for each business location
- Cash flow versus accrual-based profit
- Single-year financial statements versus multiyear NPV analysis
- The relevance of EBITDA as an indication of business performance
- A mix of many different product or service offerings, each with differing revenue, cost, and operating characteristics
- A strong desire by top management to project an image of 'profitability', coupled with no real understanding of how to assess 'profitability':

'Let's choose to emphasize the measure on which we look the best!—annual EBITDA.'

- An interacting mix of one-time and recurring expenditures in each business market
- A serious question of historical cost versus replacement cost valuation for capital investments with indeterminate lives and rapid technological change
- A CFO whose focus was almost exclusively on Wall Street rather than SCM

The job of the consulting team brought in by the president was to clarify the strategic context, in SCM terms, to enable him to formulate a meaningful business plan to save the company. This task involved the use of several SCM themes:

- ABC
- Supply chain analysis
- LCC
- NPV-based multiyear product profitability analysis

A 'unit of analysis' that could proxy for the business in general had to be chosen. This was 'One Gold customer in an Established Market'. Choosing an appropriate unit of analysis is a much more important topic than is usually realized.

The following is an analysis of the multiyear NPV perspective on the business.

1. What would be the lifetime NPV (10 years at 10%) for one customer in the Jackson cable franchise?

Jackson, Cable TV Franchise

Net after tax cash flow summary

	Year 0	Years 1–10
Capital investment ($)	(560)	
	(250)	
Operations ($)	(98.4)[1]	147[2]
Depreciation tax shelter ($)	32.4	32.4[3]
	$(876)	$179.4

Notes:
1 $(164) × 0.6 = $(98.4)
2 $245 × 0.6 = $147
3 $560 + $250 = $810 ÷ 10 = $81 × 0.4 = $32.4

10-year NPV (10%) = $226
10-year IRR = 15.7% (real)

2. What is the lifetime NPV at 10% for one Gold customer in Charlotte?

(B) NPV/IRR analysis

10-year cash flow summary (after tax @ 40% rate)

Year 0	Capital	= $(5,340)
	One-time expense	= $(578) [$(964 × 0.6]
Years 1–10	Cash margin	$840
	Customer care	(303)
	Operations support cash	(65)
	General and administrative	(173)
		$299 × 0.6 = $179
	Depreciation tax shelter	$279 × 0.4 = $112
	Total (per year)	$291

Year 0 = $(5,918)   **10% NPV = $(4,130)**
Years 1–10 = $291   **10-year IRR is *negative***

Details for these calculations:

one Gold customer (Charlotte)—cash flows ($)

Capital investment	5,340	
Average share of network	4,080	(Exhibit 6B)
Customer equipment	750	(250 × 3)
Customer activation	510	(170 × 3)

One-time expense		964	
Customer acquisition		739	
Commission		150	(50×3)
Sell/Mkt/Adv		589	$(1{,}197 \div 6{,}100 \times 3)$
Customer activation		255	
Order processing		145	$(294 \div 6{,}100 \times 3)$
Dispatch/Install		110	$(223 \div 6{,}100 \times 3)$
Annual cash margin		840	
Revenue		1,500	(125×12)
Direct Cost		(660)	(55×12)
Recurring expenses (annual)		1,054	
Customer care		303	
Billing	62		$(215 \div 125K \times 3 \times 12)$
Call centre	155		$(538 \div 125K \times 3 \times 12)$
Customer support	22		$(78 \div 125K \times 3 \times 12)$
Installation service	64		$(223 \div 125K \times 3 \times 12)$
Operations support		344	
Network maintenance	51		$(418 \div 294K \times 3 \times 12)$
Network operations	14		$(117 \div 294K \times 3 \times 12)$
Network depreciation	153		$(4{,}080 \times 3.75\%)$
Customer support depreciation	126		
Equipment	75		$(250 \times 3 \div 10 \text{ years})$
Capitalized acquisition	51		$(170 \times 3 \div 10 \text{ years})$
General and administrative		173	$(1{,}413 \div 294 \times 3 \times 12)$

Lifetime NPV at each stage, cumulatively, along the full supply chain:

10-year NPV at 10% (assume taxes are relevant @ 40%)

	$	PV (A/T)	Cumulative NPV
Capital investment			
Network (4080)	(4080)	(4080)	(4080)
Customer Hook-up (1260)	(1260)	(1260)	(5340)
Tax shelter	279/year	688	(4652)
Start-up expense	964	(578)	(5230)
Cash margin*	840/year	3097	(2133)
Customer care*	303/year	(1117)	(3250)
Operations support*	65/year	(240)	(3490)
Administration*	173/year	(640)	(4130)

- 10-year PV of a $1 annual annuity payment is $6.14 at 10%. So, for example, $840 × 60% × 6.14 = $3,097

The Gold customer shows negative NPV before considering *any* operating expenses.

Given the actual costs to build the network, and hook up and activate the customer, total cash margin per customer would need to be $1420 per year for CHC to earn a 10 per cent return [$n = 10$, $i = 10$, PV = $5,230, FV = 0, PMT = ? = $852 = $1420 before taxes]. That is, $1420, versus current actual of $299!

With cash expenses of $541, cash margin must be $1961 per year (561 + 1,420). At a 56 per cent margin rate, revenue must be $3502 per year. This is $292 per month, versus $125 in the business plan!

Comparing three business models

	Per customer		
	Jackson Cable franchise	CHC Model	Charlotte Gold
Network investment	(560)	(1000)	(4080)
Hook-up investment	(250)	} (500)	(1260)
Start-up cost	(164)		(964)
Annual revenue	594	1500	1500
Cash margin (%)	56%	67%	56%
Cash margin ($)	331	1000	840
Annual cash operating expenses	(86)	(500)	(541)
10-Year IRR (real)	**15.7%**	**19+%**	**(Negative)**

What does CHC need to do to generate positive lifetime NPV for one Gold customer in the Charlotte market? At the actual investment level ($5,230 PV—see above), the monthly price must be raised from $125 to $292, which totally destroys the 'customer value proposition'. CHC cannot possibly cut operating expenses enough, since the ten-year NPV is negative with even *zero* operating expenses.

What is the significance of the distinction between 'local EBITDA' and 'full, accrual profit' as a performance measure for CHC? The distinction between 'local EBITDA' and 'operating profit' is useful only if the income statement contains significant allocated corporate expense items that have no relevance to the local markets. If Charlotte could stand alone, without corporate 'support', the full local income statement overstates the local operating loss. For Charlotte, corporate-level marketing and the corporate call centre are very real expenses. Corporate overhead is probably not.

Another issue that might be raised here is 'cash flow' versus 'profit'. In general, cash flow is only meaningful as a measure of business performance when property assets do not depreciate (real estate investments). If depreciation is a reasonable proxy for annual re-placement expenditures, 'free cash flow' is approximately equal to profit.

So, at best, 'local EBITDA' is an incomplete measure of local cash flow, not profit, and thus is not very meaningful. Local cash flow 'in the black' does mean that the cash drain has been stopped. But positive cash flow is far short of reasonable profit in relation to investment.

Based on this analysis, what is the best advice to Miles Johnson?

The analysis pretty clearly demonstrates that, looking forward, CHC is not a viable business. If the 'flagship' product (Gold Service) in the 'flagship' market (Charlotte) shows negative ten-year NPV, even with zero operating expenses, how can the business survive? In this 'real-world' parallel to the simple business model in Exhibit 2, all the variables have moved dramatically against profitability—investment, start-up costs, cash margins, and operating costs.

Can the business be 'turned around'? The 'good news' is that CHC has $1 billion in the bank to finance the 'turnaround'. The 'bad news' is that there is no real business here to 'save'!

EBITDA is a very misleading performance indicator when interest is a very real business expense (because of heavy leverage in financing the investment base), and depreciation and amortization are also very real, in a replacement cost sense. The deferred customer activation costs and depreciation expense are *cash items* as the business moves forward to continually replenish the customer base and replace the equipment as it becomes obsolete and/or worn out.

Is it worth trying to 'fix' the business model, or should the company 'declare failure' and return the remaining $1 billion to the debt holders? 'Hope springs eternal' in the breast of the budding entrepreneur, particularly if he or she is not hobbled by any awareness of how big a mess has been generated already!

The analysis shown here was replicated for two other key product offerings in two other key markets. All three of the analyses show the same conclusion—looming economic disaster in a few years. The impending disasters were not 'visible' because the financial measurement and analysis system in place was seriously inadequate, given the complexity of the strategic context.

When the lifetime NPV of your best customers is negative, even before considering operating expenses, the business is in trouble. Fortunately, for current management, $1 billion in the bank provides significant protection from the harsh business realities, if one does not want to face them.

We estimated that the $1 billion cash cushion could be stretched out for about three years before it would be exhausted, assuming no more major capital investments in any of the eight markets. That means walking away from the start-up investment ($380 million) in the two markets (Birmingham and Jacksonville), which are not yet fully configured. This is a painful object lesson in 'sunk cost' psychology.

16.2.7 A CONCLUDING NOTE ON CHC

The reader may be sceptical that real managers in real companies could be so oblivious to the basic multiyear NPV economics of the business they are operating. It may also be surprising that the person who put $1 billion into the CHC venture (actually, $1.65 billion in the real RCN situation) was the highly regarded investor, Paul Allen, who made billions in the Microsoft start-up. Allen's highly regarded Vulcan Management Company acquired the rights to 25 per cent of RCN for $1.65 billion in 1999. He sold 40 per cent of his interest in 2003 for $2 million.

I have seen this same phenomenon elsewhere on an even bigger scale, both before and after 2001. In 1994, work I did for McCaw Cellular (the largest cell phone company in the USA, which was acquired by AT&T in 1995 for $20 billion) indicated pretty clearly that the lifetime NPV of McCaw's average customer was *negative*. I doubt that AT&T had done this analysis. In 2004, work I did in the Discover Card Division of Morgan Stanley indicated very clearly that the $2.4 billion a year spent by the credit card industry on new customer acquisition between 2000 and 2004 ($12 billion, in total) yielded a grand total of about 10 million new accounts, virtually all of which showed *negative* lifetime NPV at the industry's 14 per cent cost of capital. This is part of the reason Morgan Stanley has been so publicly ambivalent in 2005 about retaining or selling its charge card business.

☐ REFERENCES

Anthony, R. (1960). *Management Accounting: Text and Cases.* Homewood, IL: Richard D. Irwin.

Bromwich, M. (1990). 'The Case for Strategic Management Accounting: The Role of Accounting Information for Strategy in Competitive Markets', *Accounting, Organizations, and Society*, 15: 27–46.

Drury, C. (2004). *Management and Cost Accounting.* London: Thomson Learning EMEA.

Hax, A. and Majluf, N. (1984). *Strategic Management: An Integrative Perspective.* Englewood Cliffs, NJ: Prentice Hall.

Horngren, C. (1962). *Cost Accounting: A Managerial Emphasis.* Englewood Cliffs, NJ: Prentice-Hall.

—— Sundem, G., and Stratton, W. (2004). *Introduction to Management Accounting.* Englewood Cliffs, NJ: Prentice Hall.

Johnson, H. T. (1992). *Relevance Regained.* New York: Free Press.

Kaplan, R. and Johnson, H. T. (1987). *Relevance Lost: The Rise and Fall of Management Accounting.* Cambridge, MA: Harvard Business School Press.

McTaggart, J., Kontes, P., and Mankins, M. (1994). *The Value Imperative.* New York: Free Press.

Oster, S. (1990). *Modern Competitive Analysis.* New York: Oxford University Press.

O'Sullivan, K. (2004). 'Job Search: Switching Industries', *CFO Magazine*, August.

Porter, M. (1980). *Competitive Strategy.* New York: Free Press.

Shank, J. (1989). 'Strategic Cost Management: New Wine, or Just New Bottles?', *Journal of Management Accounting Research*, Fall.

—— and Constantinedes, K. (1994). 'A New Reporting Emphasis on Thruput and the "Balanced Scorecard"', *Management Accounting*, September.

—— and Govindarjan, V. (1989). *The Evolution From Managerial to Strategic Accounting.* Homewood, IL: Richard D. Irwin.

—— —— (1993). *Strategic Cost Management.* New York: Free Press.

Shillinglaw, G. (1959). *Accounting: A Management Approach.* Homewood, IL: Richard D. Irwin.

Simmonds, K. (1981). 'Strategic Management Accounting', *Management Accounting* (UK), 59(4): 26–9.

Stern, J. (1996). *EVA and Strategic Performance Measurement.* New York: The Conference Board.

17 Environmental management accounting

Kazbi Soonawalla

Many companies consider productivity to be a cost-saving operational issue. We at DuPont have elevated productivity to the strategic level because we believe that it is central to our efforts in sustainability.

(Chad Holliday, Chairman and CEO of DuPont[1])

17.1 Introduction

Environmental accounting and management has had a growing public profile over the last three decades. Its cause has been helped along by disastrous industrial accidents, such as the lethal gas leak at Bhopal in 1984 and the Exxon Valdez oil spill in Alaska in 1989. Other events such as Shell's dilemma on disposing the oil rig Brent Spar mid-ocean received a lot of media attention. Public awareness of the harmful effects of industrial accidents, as well as the routine pollutants entering our water, air, and soil, coupled with increasing media coverage of these issues, has forced corporations to address calls for environmental prudence. Climate change, nuclear waste, and deforestation are commonplace concerns, especially as they begin to affect the health of those in the vicinity. The increased awareness of environmental factors is coupled with a growing acknowledgement of the paucity of clean resources. Demand for better business practice from shareholders, non-governmental organizations (NGOs), and other public interest groups is shaping a body of practices referred to as 'environmental management accounting' (EMA), which is of particular interest to not just large but small corporations also. Media and public opinion influence and inform government policy as well. Countries that are perceived as failing to take the threat of global warming and environmental pollution seriously are increasingly criticized and condemned (see e.g. *Economist*, 5 April 2001).

Through the 1970s and 1980s, the environment became an important stakeholder, influencing and being influenced by corporate action; the other stakeholders being people and interests that businesses might affect, such as employees, consumers, and suppliers. During this time, the environment began to see a powerful and influential lobby group acting on its behalf. With these issues firmly entrenched in the public consciousness, environmental issues acquired a new strategic importance. This strategic importance coupled with increasing regulatory requirements ensured that management acknowledged the power and force of the environmental movement.

This chapter provides a general discussion of the emergence of the environmental movement within the context of corporate responsibility and sustainability management, and presents the development of EMA in particular. It illustrates how media coverage on the harmful aspects of environmental problems played a defining role in management's desire to be considered ecologically sound and environmentally friendly. It describes in some detail how mainstream management accounting practices such as activity-based costing (ABC), life cycle costing (LCC), and the balanced scorecard (BSC) have been modified to incorporate environmental aspects. The chapter also discusses the role of government agencies and financial reporting, and the impact these have on managerial decisions.

17.1.1 THE ARRIVAL OF THE ENVIRONMENTAL MOVEMENT AND THE RISE OF EMA

Pressure for corporate environmental responsibility goes back several decades. Since before the Second World War well-publicized industrial accidents ensured that environmental concern was influencing public policy and corporate action (Bennett and James 1999*a*). The birthplace of the modern environmental movement may be regarded as the original Earth Day in April 1970, when millions of Americans participated in Earth Day celebrations, ensuring that the environmental issue came of age in American political life. The purpose of Earth Day was to demonstrate public concern about the environment and dissipation of natural resources to the political leadership (www.earthday.net). The creation of national environmental agencies, such as the Environmental Protection Agency (EPA) in the USA in 1970, formalized environmental policy into a national framework.

The European Environmental Agency was founded to support sustainable development in Europe, by providing timely and relevant environmental information to policy-making agents and the public. European environmental policies are formulated by the European Commission and various member states. As developing countries such as India and China rapidly industrialize, they too are being forced to acknowledge mounting environmental problems (see e.g. *Economist*, 19 August 2004).

The impact of NGOs on sustainability management has been profound and on occasion brought large corporations to their knees. Often acting as the intermediary between consumers and corporations, NGOs have gained the political and organizational clout to force change in government policy and corporate culture. The clash of cultures between NGOs and businesses has resulted in companies engaging in dialogue on environmental issues (Murphy and Bendell 2001). NGOs such as Greenpeace, formed in 1971, sought media attention to the environmental damage being done by large corporations. Greenpeace's maiden protest was against the underground nuclear tests the US government was conducting in Alaska (www.greenpeace.org). Since then its campaigns have encompassed saving the oceans, protecting forests, preventing climate change, eliminating nuclear waste, and encouraging sustainable trade amongst other things (see Box 17.1 for an example).

Box 17.1 Shell and Brent Spar

In 1995 Shell faced the issue of how to dispose of the Brent Spar offshore oil installation. It was decided that this huge, heavily contaminated oil installation would be dumped into the North Atlantic despite it being loaded with toxic and radioactive sludge. Greenpeace and other NGOs began a campaign of fierce criticism and confrontation, with environmentalists from Greenpeace occupying Brent Spar to prevent Shell going through with the original plan.

Eventually, Shell was forced to engage the Environment Council, a British NGO, to facilitate a series of discussions on alternative disposal options. Finally, Brent Spar was dragged to Norway, where it was dismantled and recycled as the foundation of a new ferry terminal building, in what was hailed as a 'unique reuse solution' by the company. Despite costing Shell £43 million to reuse the rig as opposed to a £4.5 million cost of dumping the structure under the sea, the reuse option allowed Shell to emerge relatively unscathed. The Brent Spar incident brought about a change in corporate mindset, whereby senior management realized the strategic importance of sound environmental policy and practice that involved dialogue, as opposed to conventional inward-looking decision-making. In response to the publicity accorded by the Brent Spar incident, Shell began releasing a series of annual reports covering its ethical, social, and environmental activities. As a company Shell began seeking a balance between various interests and tried to integrate sometimes competing principles in the complex and fractious years following Brent Spar (Mirvis 2000).

As more activist groups entered a public spirited smear campaign against large industrial groups, the pressure on management to accept responsibility or at least acknowledge these issues increased. Further, the rise of corporate citizenship initiatives such as sustainable business and corporate social responsibility (CSR) made individual consumers aware of alternative management approaches for profit-seeking enterprises. Their demand for ethical and environmentally responsible business practices, coupled with the availability of voluntary certification programmes such as those of the International Organization for Standardization (ISO), urged management to take environmental concerns seriously. The ideologies and principles promoted by Earth Day and Greenpeace were embodied in a more business and corporate context through the ideals of CSR and corporate citizenship.

For many, the case for CSR and corporate citizenship is firmly entrenched in sustainable business theorist John Elkington's famous triple bottom line of sustainable development: economic prosperity, environmental quality, and social justice (Elkington 1997). Advocates of this notion have pushed for businesses to improve their positive impact on society. The environmental programme created through the triple bottom line and CSR movement has over time evolved into a broader agenda based around sustainable development (Elkington 2001). Whereas the sustainability agenda began as a relatively straightforward attempt to harmonize financial and environmental results, it has, not surprisingly, evolved into something much more complicated.

The last two decades witnessed a proliferation of organizations, initiatives, and forums focused on raising awareness and facilitating dialogue on ethical and best practice issues. Examples of these are SustainAbility, the Institute of Business Ethics, and the Global Corporate Citizenship Initiative of the World Economic Forum, Business for Social Responsibility, World Business Council for Sustainable Development, and the Institute of Social and Ethical Accountability. These offer a range of services, case studies, educational and training forums, and awareness programmes. Interestingly, on occasion these and other centres for environmental research are funded or supported by large corporations that have been criticized for poor environmental practices. In part, involvement with these better practice organizations is corporate effort at being perceived in a more sensitive and positive social and environmental light.

In addition to pressure from consumers and NGOs, the EMA cause has been helped by progress in management accounting. The 1990s witnessed a proliferation of management accounting tools that went beyond traditional cost accounting, and no longer relied exclusively on backward-looking financial indicators (Kaplan and Norton 1992). Other inadequacies in traditional reporting practices had begun being reported in the 1960s with a growing number of managers showing concern that their accounting systems were not adequate (Brummet et al. 1968). It was increasingly felt that accounting failed to incorporate notions of business ethics, social responsibility, and human relations.

In arguing for the use of non-financial indicators in management accounting, Kaplan and Norton (1992) developed the BSC as a new approach to performance measurement. The BSC changed existing notions of management accounting, and provided an approach to think of the organization as strategy-focused (Kaplan and Norton 1996). Once viewed as a financial burden, environmental management is often perceived as an economic opportunity (Schaltegger and Figge 2000). As environmental concerns become issues of strategy and opportunity, not just compliance, it seems natural that they should find their place in strategic management accounting tools such as a modified BSC (Figge et al. 2002).

Similarly, other management accounting areas, such as LCC and ABC, also witnessed innovations to incorporate EMA issues (Todd 1992; Schaltegger and Muller 1998; Schaltegger and Burritt 2000). Through increasing discussion amongst academics and businesses, and by means of iterative feedback and usage, these tools were modified and tailored to specific situations and contexts. In addition to improving internal costing and allocation mechanisms, these approaches permitted management accounting to be used within a strategic and decision-making context.

While EMA continues to remain primarily the concern of regulatory compliance, merely satisfying statutory requirements is no longer considered adequate. Companies often need to do more than comply with regulatory requirements, or at least need to be perceived as doing more. Pinpointing the value consumers attach to environmental issues, and implementing corporate action commensurate with this value, continues to present a new arena of strategic decision-making and management.

Despite concerns about sustainable business practices over the past few decades, this is still a relatively new and developing field, in that there are few standardized definitions and equally few accepted practices and concepts. EMA, though the topic of discussion and academic debate for a number of years, has no formal definition (IFAC 2004). This is partly because no one group or professional body takes responsibility for EMA practices or sets a single code of conduct or ethics with respect to EMA. Despite attempts to define it, at best EMA remains a loosely held together collection of management and accounting practices, often subject to diverse interpretation. Environmental accounting itself is a loose and ambiguous term (Bartolomeo et al. 2000), with EMA being an application or extension of environmental accounting that involves best management accounting practices on environmental and sustainability issues.

17.1.2 THE ROLE OF EXTERNAL REPORTING

In the development of management accounting, there has been a conscious disparity between financial reporting and management accounting issues (Johnson and Kaplan 1987; Eccles 1991). This has permeated environmental management issues. Whilst financial reporting standards exist in most national generally accepted accounting practices (GAAP), there is no real link between internal EMA issues and external reporting. Perhaps it was this wedge that prompted EMA to develop into a formal discipline, whereas previously it was more likely to be incorporated within financial reporting.

Recent efforts to encourage the International Accounting Standards Board (IASB) to review environmental accounting coincide with efforts towards standardization and development of environmental management practices. There is also considerable interest in formalizing and establishing non-traditional reporting methods such as the Global Reporting Initiative (GRI) for CSR and sustainability reporting, and there are attempts to promote further consistency between internal and external reporting issues. In fact, by its very nature, EMA lies at the cusp of combining management, financial, and social accounting.

17.1.3 TOWARDS A FRAMEWORK FOR EMA

Formalizing coherent, unified EMA practice is a formidable challenge, not least because of a lack of uniform national and international policy, and due to the varying strategic and business incentives of corporations. Possibly, given the diversity of industrial practice, product range, and environmental implications, one may argue that a unified approach is impractical if at all necessary. Whereas environmental liabilities may be condensed into single-line items for financial reporting issues, it is hard to distil the complex and often contrary issues of internal management and environmental performance into a single set of rules.

Figure 17.1 presents the broad social, economic, and political forces that interact to create EMA as a strategic, decision-making, and accounting approach, which goes beyond the scope achieved by traditional cost accounting. It shows how NGOs, the public, and governments, spurred by industrial accidents and incidents, interact to force corporate reaction and awareness. Simultaneous developments in management accounting provide industry with sophisticated tools to respond appropriately. Coupled with these is the rising demand for better financial reporting and disclosure of environmental liabilities and costs, and for information on how these are linked with internal decision processes. Also influencing both management accounting and financial reporting, and the corporate world in general, are enhanced corporate governance mechanisms and ethical guidelines. In addition, the emergence of voluntary CSR reporting guidelines and management systems, such as the ISO series, permits management to go beyond compliance with government regulations and

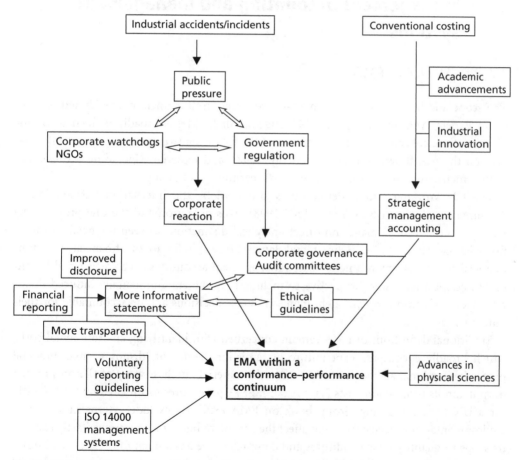

Figure 17.1 A framework for understanding the social, economic, political, and scientific forces influencing EMA

accounting rules. Finally, advances in the sciences have driven the evolution of eco-efficient production processes, better measurement mechanisms, and the use of renewable energy sources. All these together create a setting for EMA to evolve a distinct identity and to function as a compliance, performance, and enhancement frame of operation.

The rest of the chapter is structured as follows. Section 17.2 presents some alternative ways of conducting EMA within the scope of management accounting. The roles of government regulators like the EPA and their impact are then discussed in Section 17.3. Section 17.4 summarizes the role of financial reporting for environmental issues and also presents the importance of ethical guidelines and voluntary CSR initiatives like the GRI. Section 17.5 concludes the chapter and leaves open the challenge of further developing EMA beyond its role in accounting, into a complex and sophisticated performance-enhancing concept.

17.2 Management accounting and management systems

17.2.1 WHAT IS EMA?

The scope and breadth of environmental accounting itself is unclear. The United Nations (UN) Expert Working Group on EMA suggests that EMA is broadly defined to be the identification, collection, analysis, and use of the following two metrics: physical information on the use, flows, and fates of energy, water, and materials (including wastes), and money metrics on environment-related costs, earnings, and savings.

The UN Working Group definition is also used by the International Federation of Accountants (IFAC) in New York (IFAC 1998). This definition and the one proposed by Horngren et al. (2005) makes no direct analytical distinction between financial and non-financial aspects of EMA. Bennett and James (1998a) refer to the financial and non-financial aspects as 'environment-related management accounting'. Schaltegger and Burritt (2000) adopt a narrower perspective to include only the environmentally induced financial aspects of accounting that help managers make decisions and be accountable for their outcome.

Traditional definitions of EMA remain concerned with identifying environmental costs, which broadly encompass expenditure on emission treatment, disposal, environmental protection, and management, in addition to the material purchase value of all non-product output and its production costs (Jasch 2003). EMA procedures formulated by Jasch (2001) for a UN Expert Working Group book on EMA explicitly exclude externalities such as environmental and social effects that affect the general public. This group steadfastly restricts its scope to quantifying expenditures and comprehensive assessment of these expenditures. This commonly accepted definition of EMA is somewhat deficient in its exclusion of social costs to the general public, as well as costs and/or benefits associated with value to consumers

Table 17.1 Input and output types

Material inputs	Product outputs
Raw materials	Products
Intermediate product inputs	By-products
Packaging materials	*Non-product outputs (wastes and emissions)*
Merchandise	Solid waste
Operating materials	Hazardous waste
Water	Waste water
Energy	Atmospheric pollutants

Source: Adapted from IFAC (2004).

of corporate environmental policy. However, the UN focus is not to develop alternative managerial systems, but to make environmental costs transparent and visible.

In a push towards standardization of EMA concepts and definitions, IFAC issued an exposure draft on International Guidelines on EMA in 2004 (IFAC 2004). The purpose of this document is to bring together some of the existing information on EMA, and update and append it as necessary. Based on comment letters and responses to their exposure draft, IFAC issued new guidelines on EMA in August 2005 (IFAC 2005). The final document though intended for guidance is not meant to be a methodology or implementation manual. It deliberately excludes details on the various available EMA practices and methods.

Despite advances in EMA and environmental accounting, there are difficulties in incorporating sound environmental practices within a usable business framework. Amongst other problems, identifying environmental costs and how these are distinct from other operating costs, and using these to strategic ends, remains a challenge. Critical in the identification of these costs is the accurate measurement and itemization of environment-related costs and earnings. In their 2005 EMA guidelines, IFAC propose the input and output types similar to those summarized in Table 17.1.

17.2.2 THE USE OF MANAGEMENT ACCOUNTING

The need for new and innovative accounting systems has been suggested since the 1960s (Brummet et al. 1968). The need to understand sources of current management accounting practice and reflect on new demands for planning and control and to develop new strategy continued to be echoed in the 1980s (Kaplan 1984). Kaplan (1984) summarizes the historical development of cost accounting in US corporations through the demand for information on internal planning and control, citing evolving new organizational forms such as the development of vertically integrated, multi-activity organizations for mass production and distribution, as breakthroughs in efficiency. It is these breakthroughs that continue to influence modern management accounting and control systems.

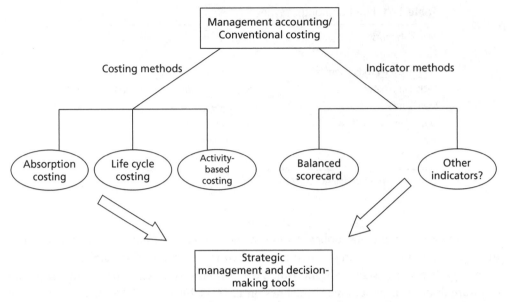

Figure 17.2   Selected approaches in modern management accounting systems

Major changes in the organization and technology of firms suggested new directions for cost accounting and production control systems research in the 1970s. Kaplan (1984) refers to the 'expanded role for management accounting information in complex settings', and it is possible to incorporate the widening scope of corporate citizenship in these expanded managerial settings. Figure 17.2 shows a limited set of costing and indicator-based practices, which have progressed from conventional costing and management accounting tools. The costing approaches rely mainly on the sophisticated identification and allocation of costs, whether over a product's lifetime or over a particular activity. The indicator methods are based on the usage of a critical mix of financial and non-financial indicators on a range of factors. Whilst work has been done on developing both sets of indicators in an EMA context, there is still scope further to integrate these methodologies for better strategic and decision-making purposes. This section will discuss at some length LCC, ABC, and the BSC modified for EMA. This discussion is not intended as an exhaustive review of EMA practices, but rather as an indication of the potential for environmental accounting to be incorporated in management accounting systems (MASs).

17.2.3 CONVENTIONAL COSTING

Prior to the development of sophisticated costing methods, a more conventional absorption costing approach was taken (Todd 1992). For this, internal environmental costs are assumed to be negligible and therefore treated as general overhead costs to be divided between all cost objects by using a predetermined cost allocation base. The example in Figure 17.3 adapted

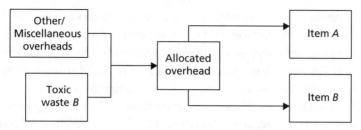

Figure 17.3 Conventional cost accounting approach
(*Source*: Adapted from Todd 1992)

from Todd (1992) illustrates a common situation where the costs of treating item *B*'s toxic waste are included in general overhead costs, which are then allocated to both products (items *A* and *B*) on the basis of an accepted cost allocation base.

This method is unsatisfactory if items *A* and *B* have different environmental impacts. Equal allocation of environmental costs to items *A* and *B* may lead to sub-optimal management decisions. For instance, suppose product *B* is the 'polluting' product and product *A* the 'clean' product. In this case, environment-related costs of toxic wastes of item *B* should be directly tracked and traced to that product. This is illustrated in Figure 17.4.

17.2.4 LIFE CYCLE COSTING

Several management accounting approaches are promoted by environmentalists and have been further developed by academic researchers. One such method is LCC, where costs relating to the whole life cycle of a product are identified, tracked, and accounted for. With LCC, the narrow-entity focus is abandoned in favour of a broader view, which allows inclusion of the whole life cycle of a product. There is a whole range of terminology associated with the life cycle perspective, and advocates suggest that this perspective can foster a thorough accounting of private costs (and potential cost savings) in addition to facilitating a more systematic and complete assessment of societal impacts and costs due to a firm's activities (EPA 1998). Some of the terms used in connection with LCC are life cycle design (LCD), life cycle assessment (LCA), and life cycle cost assessment (LCCA). LCD is an approach for designing more ecologically and economically sustainable product systems, by

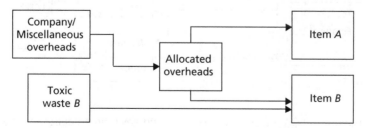

Figure 17.4 Direct allocation of environmentally induced costs
(*Source*: Adapted from Todd 1992)

integrating environmental requirements into the earliest stages of design. LCA is a holistic approach to identifying the environmental consequences of a product, process, or activity through its entire life cycle, and to identifying opportunities for achieving environmental improvements. LCCA emphasizes the costing aspect of LCA and is regarded as a systematic process for evaluating the life cycle costs of the activity by identifying environmental consequences and assigning measures of monetary value to those consequences (EPA 1998).

Despite discussion in the academic literature, LCC has not received extensive attention from the corporate sector. There are several practical problems with this method, including noisy estimation of external costs, low quality, inconsistent data, and high costs of data collection (Schaltegger and Burritt 2000). Despite these drawbacks, examining all the environmental costs of a product life cycle can be useful for strategic management (Schaltegger and Burritt 2000), and there is evidence of its use in industry (Bennett and James 1998b; Aye et al. 2000; Sterner 2000).

As with other methods of costing there is no prescribed standard on LCC. Reich (2005) uses a combination of LCA and LCC to assess the economics of a municipal waste management system. The study discusses financial and environmental LCCs, where a financial LCC is a tool for analysing the economic effects of an LCA system. Financial costs here are defined as the present value of all monetary costs for the system studies, negative or positive. Investment costs, operating costs, decommissioning costs, and sales revenues (a negative cost) discounted to present value are examples of such costs. Environmental LCC is the weighting of environmental impacts on an LCA system in monetary terms. The object of an environmental LCC is to reduce the number of decision variables into a manageable amount and better to communicate results from environmental studies.

Reich (2005) uses these definitions so that financial LCC becomes a parallel analysis tool at an LCA, whereby the same problem is analysed from different perspectives. Furthermore, LCA and environmental LCC become consecutive tools, where the environmental LCC can

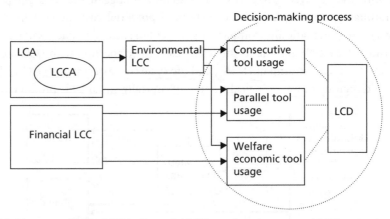

Figure 17.5 The use of LCA, LCCA, financial LCC, and environmental LCC as tools supporting the decision-making process.

(*Source*: Adapted from Reich 2005)

be applied to the results of an LCA, aggregating the results. Figure 17.5 is an extension of Reich's (2005) tool where LCCA is included within the LCA, and LCD is part of the decision-making process. It provides an illustration of how the combination of the LCCs suggested by Reich (2005) can be used for welfare impact analysis, if the relevant aspects of the system can be narrowed down to environmental and economic impacts.

17.2.5 ACTIVITY-BASED COSTING

ABC in the context of corporate environmental concerns is sometimes referred to as the 'environmentally friendly cost accounting' (Todd 1992). ABC is an analytical approach to link activities to costs via the detailed analysis of cost drivers. Some researchers suggest that ABC might help management make more informed decisions, especially in the context of environmental decisions (Emblamsvåg and Bras 2000), because it enhances the understanding of business processes and activities with each product.

For ABC to be effective in obtaining correct information, adequate allocation is necessary (Schaltegger and Muller 1998). ABC applied to environmental costs distinguishes between environment-related costs and environment-driven costs. The former are attributed to joint environmental cost centres, such as waste-disposal systems. The latter are hidden in the general overheads and do not relate directly to a joint environmental cost centre, e.g. increased depreciation or higher cost of staff (UNDSD 2003). A major advantage of ABC is that it permits the integration of environmental cost accounting into strategic management, and links these with management's objectives and activities (Schaltegger and Burritt 2000). Schaltegger and Burritt (2000) illustrate ABC's links with material flows, where relevant factors affecting corporate eco-efficiency and accountability of divisional managers are operationalized by allocating overhead costs such that they focus on the identification of activities causing the environmental impacts of material flows and the person or group within the organization responsible for such impacts.

Schaltegger and Muller (1998) and Schaltegger and Burritt (2000) present an example of the main steps in material flow-oriented ABC allocation (see Figure 17.6). The example is of a waste-disposal system (the joint environmental cost centre) that provides common environmental services to production centres (i.e. the responsible cost centres). There are two final cost objects, X and Y. After tracking and tracing, the costs of joint environmental cost centres have to be allocated to the responsible cost centres and cost objects. Allocation 1 (A1) involves the costs of the waste disposal being allocated to the two cost centres. For allocation 2 (A2), cost centres are to be allocated to the cost objects (X and Y). A second cost allocation key needs to be chosen for this allocation, one that reflects the separate costs of waste disposal that have been caused by each product within each cost centre (e.g. 100 per cent for the 'polluting' product X and 0 per cent for the 'clean' product Y).

Despite the two allocation steps A1 and A2, Schaltegger and Burritt (2000) suggest that some environment-related costs might have been excluded in the previous costing allocation. They also suggest that waste is avoidable and that wasted inputs could have been used

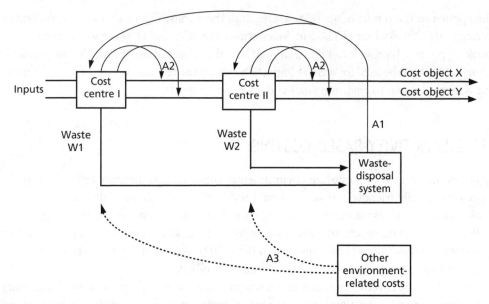

Figure 17.6 An example of the allocation of costs related to waste incineration
(*Source*: Adapted from Schaltegger and Burritt 2000)

to create economic value. The forgone value of these inputs represents an opportunity cost. Therefore, management needs to track, label, and account for these other environment-related costs. These costs may not be directly traceable to joint environmental costs centres but may vary with production activity. These environment-related costs are taken into consideration in the third allocation step (A3) (Schaltegger and Burritt 2000).

17.2.6 BALANCED SCORECARD

In the design of a BSC, Kaplan and Norton (1992) argue for the inclusion of non-financial measures and variables. They suggest that business needs to pay attention to measuring and improving its non-financial performance in order to meet its long-term financial objectives. The BSC is regarded by some commentators as a dramatic break from traditional cost accounting and managerial control systems in that it redefines a new performance measurement approach. It suggests that the efficient use of investment capital cannot be the sole determinant of competitive advantage. Instead, management increasingly needs to use soft factors such as intellectual capital, knowledge creation, and customer orientation in seeking value.

The incorporation of the customer perspective as one of the four indicators on the BSC heralded the arrival of including outside issues such as consumer concerns. The use of these other measures is especially pertinent when companies grapple with environmental issues, because alongside government regulations, consumers can wield influence over the direction corporations take in this regard. Traditional control and performance measurement systems strive to keep business units in compliance with an existing plan, not unlike environmental initiatives that seek to comply with legislation. The BSC permits executives to articulate a strategy, to communicate this, and accordingly to align individual and organizational initiatives into a common goal. Correspondingly, environmental issues acquired strategic importance, whereby they could be used to enhance a corporation's image and appeal to consumer instincts and preferences.

While the early premise of the BSC remained to motivate and measure performance, Kaplan and Norton (1996) suggest ways whereby it can be used to translate strategy into operational measures. In doing so, they suggest measures of consumer value propositions such as 'image' and 'reputation' that go beyond the previous core customer attributes. It is in precisely such measures that the full impact of environmental issues can be incorporated. As savvy environmental management becomes strategically necessary, these systems afford companies the opportunities to implement strategy, while allowing the strategy to evolve in response to changing corporate environments.

Figge et al. (2002) provide the rationale and steps for formulating a sustainability balanced scorecard (SBSC) to integrate environmental and social management within the general management of a firm. They posit that for companies to contribute to sustainable development, it is desirable that corporate performance improves in all three dimensions of sustainability—economic, environmental, and social—simultaneously. They suggest that the hierarchical structure of the BSC that guarantees that all business activities are linked to the successful implementation of the business strategy can also be used for the management of environmental and social aspects. The ability of the BSC to integrate the three dimensions of sustainability offers the possibility to integrate management of environmental and social aspects into mainstream business activities. Figge et al. (2002) propose that the integration of environmental and social aspects by subsuming them under the four standard perspectives is particularly important for strategically relevant environmental and social aspects that are already integrated in the market system. They also argue that an SBSC meets exactly the specific characteristics and requirements of the strategy. They suggest that the environmental and social aspects of a business unit must not be generic, but rather should be business unit-specific. Finally, environmental and social aspects must be integrated according to their strategic relevance, including additional non-market perspectives. The process of formulating an SBSC is described in Figure 17.7. Whereas the model described by Figge et al. (2002) incorporates five main perspectives, the one proposed here has seven, with employee and community perspectives being added.

17.2.7 OTHER INDICATORS AND THE ISO 14000 SERIES

As the drive to enhance the scope and role of MASs increases into sustainability management, so does the need to identify concise, yet comprehensive, indicators. In providing a framework for sustainability measurement and reporting, Ranganathan (1999) suggests

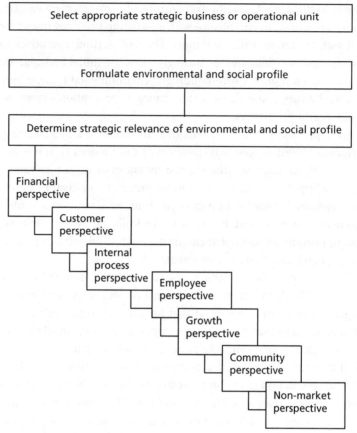

Figure 17.7 Process for formulating an SBSC
(*Source*: Adapted from Figge et al. 2002)

three main indicators to map the focus of current sustainability measurement and reporting efforts and to identify critical elements and interconnections. Examples of these are socio-environmental, socio-economic, and environmental-economic. These are derived from the overlap of more straightforward indicators of social performance, environmental performance, and economic performance. It is these broad pillars that permit existing measurement and reporting activities to be extended to encompass all elements of sustainable development, and the interactions between them. However, to create effective performance measurement, comparability between the key elements is needed. Given that measuring economic performance is well developed with a mature methodology, work on developing environmental and social indicators is necessary for a unified measurement and performance system. The impact of these indicators on an enterprise's decision-making may be regarded as a step towards integration of sustainability management into traditional management.

New management accounting practices, coupled with increasing consumer demand for accountability and corporate citizenship, see these disparate fields being blurred into one.

The popularity and widespread usage of the ISO 14000 certification schemes is testimony to the integration of environmental management into the corporate mindset. The ISO 14000 group of standards addresses various aspects of environmental management, including establishment of environmental management systems, procedures for conducting environmental audits, guidance and selection on use of indicators, and guidance on environmental communication. ISO helps companies devise management systems that confirm with certain environmental standards and is viewed as a means by which companies can achieve more environmental efficiency than required by regulation (Welch 1997).

Environmental indicators are central to several ISO standards and are critical in ascertaining the effectiveness of a firm's environmental management system in generating genuine improvements in environmental performance (Bennett and James 1999*b*). These indicators cover a range of environmental, operational, and management performance issues. The use of indicators for performance measurement and internal decision-making are broadly consistent with other areas of management accounting. However, Bennett and James (1998*a*) find that firms tend to focus on the relatively narrow and straightforward aspects of environmental performance evaluation, and at the cost of management performance indicators, thereby illustrating a gap between intention and practice. Nevertheless, as innovations in management accounting continue, the scope for integrating environmental management systems and EMA grows. Further developments could easily result in EMA practices that are complementary to ISO and other management systems.

17.3 Environmental regulators and the impact of regulation

In July 1970, the White House and United States Congress worked together to establish the EPA in response to the growing public demand for cleaner water, air, and land. Prior to the establishment of the EPA, the federal government was not structured to make a coordinated attack on the pollutants that harm human health and degrade the environment. The EPA was assigned the daunting task of repairing the damage already done to the natural environment and to establish new criteria to guide Americans in making a cleaner environment a reality (www.epa.gov). In creating the EPA, Congress was responding to public pressure and thereby ensuring that corporations by virtue of compliance with EPA statutes were also responding to public pressure. Before 1970, many persons and companies throughout the USA believed that pollution was the inevitable price of progress, and this view was often presented in political debate (Rogers 1990).

Through the years, the EPA has expanded its role from rule-maker to educator. In placing increased emphasis on good environmental management, the EPA began providing resources on environmental management, such as guidance documents, case studies, and benchmarking studies. It also created the Environmental Accounting Project 'to encourage and motivate businesses to understand the full spectrum of environmental costs and incorporate these costs into decision-making'. In 2002, the EPA funded the start-up of an Environmental Management Accounting Research & Information Center to take over and expand upon the activities of the Environmental Accounting Project.

Prior to the formation of the EPA, the Air Quality Act of 1967 was passed in the USA. However, it remained scattered and regional in focus, clearly demonstrating a lack of national agendum. Inaction after the 1967 Act led Congress to impose statutory deadlines for compliance with the emissions standards authorized under the 1970 statute, in the hope that those deadlines would spur action.

Probably one of the most documented and cited EPA legislations was the Comprehensive Environmental Response, Compensation, and Liability Act of 1980 and its 1986 amendments (SARA), collectively known as Superfund. Superfund is the US government's programme to locate, investigate, and clean up uncontrolled hazardous waste sites. The 1986 amendment is particularly interesting in that it has nothing to do with clearing up the environmental sites. Instead it grants the public a 'right to know' about emissions from individual industrial plants across the USA. Initiatives such as the 1986 amendments and other measures in emergency response training and establishment of community advisory panels were in part a response to the Bhopal gas leak (Terry and Yandle 1997).

The right to know as stipulated by the 1986 SARA amendment is addressed by an annual report called the Toxics Release Inventory (TRI). In investigating the TRI as a pollution control instrument, Terry and Yandle (1997) suggest that TRI is termed as effective because industrial plants already in compliance with EPA rules increased their efforts further to reduce the volume of emissions shown on the TRI. Reputation preservation was also an important motivation and firms would not want to be branded as a 'polluting company' (Konar and Cohen 1996).

Despite claims of better business practice and corporate responsibility, compliance remains one of the biggest motivators for corporate environmental action. Verschoor and Reijnders (2000) investigate how and why ten large, well-known corporations reduce toxics. Nine out of ten companies cite compliance as a primary reason. The only company that did not cite compliance as the primary reason was The Body Shop, and this company remains distinct in that its entire corporate ethos is grounded in sustainability. Most companies integrate environmental policy into the department of environment, risk, health, and safety, even though these are often subjected to different government legislation and rules. Often incorporation of these departments is a result of government requirements of the existence of environmental departments. In striving to comply with regulations, focus seems to be on the reduction of release of toxics rather than reduction in their use, thereby demonstrating reactive management rather than proactive decision-making. In formulating policies and decisions on the use and emission of toxics, management is also motivated by the cost of producer liability of post-consumer waste and anticipation of increased future legislation. In fact, none of these companies studied even mentioned that CSR was a reason for toxics reduction. In a similar vein, Morrison (1991) finds that the necessity to comply with legal requirements was more than twice (69 per cent) as important as social responsibility

(32 per cent). What actually makes a difference on environmental reporting remains unclear and controversial (Terry and Yandle 1997). However, it appears that a public reporting medium on environmental issues might prove more influential than mandatory clean-up and compliance activities.

In claiming that monitoring is critical for environmental management, Verschoor and Reijnders (2001) investigate environmental monitoring of large international companies. They suggest that in the last decade many firms have implemented environmental monitoring for broadly the same reasons that environmental management has grown: legislation, external criticisms, and growth of environmental costs and investments. Their study suggests that environmental monitoring and audit are closely tied in with environmental management, especially those systems that focus on the environment, management system, and operating results (Welch 1997). Because legislation is the main reason for most monitoring, companies stop short of performing comprehensive monitoring. Verschoor and Reijnders (2001) find that none of the companies they investigate use the extensive monitoring systems needed for all-round integrated environmental management, and that most available information is related to physical information. Some of the difficulties companies face are non-uniform definitions and non-uniform executions, and lack of comparable information. Their study reiterates the call for good quality information to be available to both managers and society before further advances can be made.

17.4 Environmental issues and external reporting

Having a wedge between EMA and financial reporting practices could potentially lead to discrepancy in management and reporting objectives. Not only do both disciplines stand to benefit from each other, but they may also shape and inform mutual decision-making. To date, environmental financial reporting is highly variable across accounting regimes, especially on the estimation and reporting methods of environmental expenses and liabilities. National efforts at improving environmental reporting and tracking have been ongoing and are entwined with public policy. Standard-setting agencies such as the IASB, US Financial Accounting Standards Board (FASB), and UK Accounting Standards Board (ASB) wield substantial power over the direction environmental reporting takes, and the extent to which it is globally harmonized.

Government regulatory bodies such as the US Securities and Exchange Commission (SEC) also issue rules and regulations to provide protection for investors and ensure that the securities markets are fair and honest. In some cases the SEC has required that environmental liabilities be disclosed even when not recognized under GAAP (Williams and Phillips 1994). Ethical guidelines issued by professional organizations and voluntary reporting regimes such as the GRI also stand to play a large role in environmental management, accounting, and disclosures. These issues are briefly discussed in turn in the following subsections.

17.4.1 FINANCIAL REPORTING FOR ENVIRONMENTAL ISSUES

The urgency for uniform and reliable financial accounting standards is felt in reporting for environmental issues, as much as for other accounting issues. When financial accounting standards and regulatory requirement vary across jurisdictions, they can significantly affect reported results. Financial reporting for environmental liabilities and costs is to some extent hampered by the unclear nature of estimating these items and remains a controversial issue. Their impact on management decision-making has been studied in the case of individual businesses, but large sample studies have not been, or cannot be, undertaken because of the lack of readily usable data.

Extant empirical research on financial reporting broadly falls into the following categories—market valuation of environmental liabilities and costs (Barth and McNichols 1994), effects of potential environmental liabilities on earnings response coefficients (Bae and Sami 2005), market reactions to environmental legislation (Blacconiere and Northcut 1997), investors' assessment of implicit environmental liabilities (Cormier and Magnan 1997), consequences of environmental liabilities disclosures (Kennedy and Mitchell 1998), and factors influencing environmental disclosures (Barth et al. 1997).

One of the main concerns with financial reporting standards is the depiction of environmental outlays (Johnson 1993). Specifically, often asked is whether costs incurred for environmental purposes are expensed or capitalized? In the USA, certain environmental outlays are permitted to be capitalized. From an environmental viewpoint capitalization should be the preferred method if pollution prevention creates future environmental benefits (Schaltegger and Burritt 2000). Furthermore, by facilitating amortization over a number of years, capitalization encourages long-term planning (Williams and Phillips 1994). The main environmental issues in financial reporting can be briefly summarized as follows:

- Environmental costs: to expense or capitalize?
- Classification of environmental costs
- Disclosure on details and/or breakdowns about environmental costs
- Treatment of environment-related financial impacts on assets
- Treatment of liabilities and contingent liabilities and how to recognize these?
- Measurement of liabilities and contingent liabilities
- Environmental reserves, provisions, and charges to income
- Impact of accounting rules (GAAP) on corporate behaviour
- Which of the above to disclose in greater detail?

As with standardization efforts for EMA, there are also attempts to harmonize financial reporting for environmental issues. The IASB has recently come under pressure from the Fédération des Experts Comptables Européens, an umbrella organization for the accounting profession in Europe, to examine international accounting standards as they relate to reporting for environmental issues (see, for example, *Insight Magazine*, February/March 2003, www.insight-mag.com).

Before the corporate orientation towards management accounting as a distinct and independent function, environmental issues were more likely to be addressed through financial reporting items such as profitability, sales, return on investment (ROI), etc., and these items were likely to be used for environmental and other decision-making. However, as financial accounting and management accounting developed into separate and independent fields of practice, EMA began to develop on its own. The development of sophisticated costing and strategic management tools as part of the attempt to break away from 'backward-looking' financial reporting opened up opportunities for EMA. The recent demand for better environmental information and management along with more transparent and comparable financial statements suggests an interesting triangulation of consumer or investor demands, management accounting, and financial reporting.

The merits of the integration of corporate financial reporting and shareholder value creation concepts alongside corporate governance and CSR are increasingly discussed, and EMA again finds a role along a notional conformance–performance continuum (Bhimani and Soonawalla 2005). This continuum is a frame of reference that connects issues of corporate requirements and stakeholder responsibility. By finding a nesting point on this integrative framework, EMA as a discipline can interlink with better financial reporting, stronger management practices, and sound corporate governance.

17.4.2 GOVERNMENT REGULATION FOR ENVIRONMENTAL DISCLOSURE

Evidence of government involvement in reporting and compliance issues are apparent in the SEC's operations to enhance disclosure of US companies' environmental assets and liabilities. The SEC already has S-K disclosure regulations in place that are likely to elicit environmental disclosure. These require companies to disclose the material effects of compliance with federal, state, and local environmental provisions, and to describe legal proceedings arising from environmental provisions. The SEC also expects companies to detail information on any environmental matters that could materially affect company operations or finances.

Their future planned activities are documented in a Governmental Accountability Office (GAO) report (GAO 2004), a report that was produced in response to a request by US senators to determine stakeholders' views, company disclosure, adequacy of SEC efforts, and future actions on environmental disclosure. In response to the senators' questions, the GAO was unable to formulate a response on stakeholders' views, due to the complexity of the issues at stake. The GAO, however, did make suggestions on improving transparency and better utilizing EPA data. According to prior agreements, the EPA agreed to supply corporate environmental information to the SEC. These data are aimed particularly at companies that have been designated as potential responsible parties for the clean-up of Superfund sites but have not recognized or disclosed information about environmental liabilities in their annual reports (Schaltegger and Burritt 2000).

Outside the USA, disclosure of environmental liabilities is less well developed. The European Union (EU) Directive on Civil Liability for Damage Caused by Waste, introduced in 1993, is similar to the Superfund law, and its financial implications are expected to be considerable (Schaltegger and Burritt 2000). However, expected to come into force in 2007 is the new EU Environmental Liability Directive. This directive specifically implements the 'polluter pays principle'. Its fundamental aim is to hold operators whose activities have caused environmental damage financially liable for remedying this damage. The directive also holds those whose activities have caused an imminent threat of environmental damage liable to taking preventive actions (http://europa.eu.int).

Government requirements such as those of the SEC and EU, coupled with more stringent GAAP, are likely to impact EMA, especially when management is called upon to explain and defend reported and disclosed numbers. The impact is also felt when reported numbers are used for strategic and decision-making purposes.

17.4.3 THE ROLE OF PROFESSIONAL BODIES AND ETHICAL GUIDELINES

In addition to national regulations and accounting standards, accountants are also bound to abide by the ethical guidelines instituted by their professional bodies. Professional bodies, nationally and internationally, such as the Institute of Chartered Accountants in England and Wales (ICAEW), the Institute of Management Accountants (IMA) in the US, Certified Management Accountants (CMA) Canada, the Association of Chartered Certified Accountants (ACCA), the Chartered Institute of Management Accountants (CIMA) in the UK, and the Fédération des Experts Comptables Européens, provide codes of ethics and conduct. Members of these bodies are obligated to adhere to these or risk disciplinary action or losing their professional membership. Ethical guidelines and the assurance of ethical behaviour by accountants are seen as fundamental to ensuring public trust in financial reporting and business practices.

Central to business ethics is the conflict of interest that often arises between businesses and the public. Ethical guidelines exist to guide a variety of financial accountants, management accountants, auditors, and other professionals in the face of such conflicts. Despite appearing to be somewhat general in cases, ethical guidelines can have an impact on a wide range of issues and practices. They serve to protect employees who might make disclosures that are inconsistent with the corporate interest, but that are in the public interest. Most ethical guidelines have strong rules about violating confidentiality without proper authorization. However, keeping in mind that conflicts of interest do arise and that 'whistle blowers' may be caught between confidentiality to employer and larger public interest on some issues, the guidelines may draw on the relevant laws to protect the employee. For example:

The Public Interest Disclosure Act 1998: The Act protects not only employees but most consultants from dismissal or some other detriment as a result of making a 'protected disclosure'. Such disclosures include the disclosure of information relating to criminal offences, any failure to comply with a legal obligation, health and safety matters and damage to the environment, as well as deliberate concealment of any of these issues. (Chartered Institute of Public Finance and Accountancy's Standard of Professional Practice on Ethics 2000: Appendix C)

Most professional bodies have similar guidelines for professionals faced with information that they believe to be substantially true, and that may be relevant to public health and safety. These guidelines can inform and influence management accountants to disclose information if their company is a polluter but is not making this publicly known.

17.4.4 GLOBAL REPORTING INITIATIVE

Reporting on environmental issues is not restricted to national and international GAAP. Closely aligned with management accounting aspects is the voluntary GRI (www.globalreporting.org). The aim of this initiative is to widen the scope of financial accounting beyond its traditional boundaries of reporting to shareholders, by developing a globally applicable framework for reporting an organization's sustainability performance on a voluntary basis. The framework describes reporting principles and specific content indicators to guide the preparation of organization-level sustainability reports. Proponents of this broader reporting framework envisage reporting practices that incorporate a wider array of stakeholders, including consumers, suppliers, communities, and the environment. They argue that reporting on these aspects would go hand in hand with better business practices.

GRI provides a framework that incorporates sustainability reporting guidelines, technical protocols, guidance documents, and sector supplements to produce a sustainability report. The core of these is the sustainability reporting guidelines issued in 2002, and currently being revised following an extensive feedback process, for release in 2006. With respect to the environmental measures in the report, organizations are encouraged to relate their individual performance to the broader ecological systems within which they operate. For example, organizations could seek to report their pollution output in terms of the ability of the environment (local, regional, or global) to absorb the pollutants. GRI provides the following core and additional environmental indicators:

- Materials
- Energy
- Water
- Biodiversity
- Emissions, effluents, and waste
- Suppliers
- Products and services
- Compliance
- Transport
- Overall

In reporting on environmental indicators, reporting organizations are also encouraged to keep in mind the broader notion of sustainability.

Adoption of GRI is purely voluntary, but as public pressure for sustainability reporting increases, so does acceptance and adoption of GRI reports. In a further step to influence sustainability management and reporting, GRI recently joined the ISO 26000 working group. In this initiative, it is the ISO that has embarked on its first ever multi-stakeholder standard-setting process, by seeking GRI's participation in this effort. In adding 'responsibility' to the current collection of GRI tools and standards in this field, ISO is deliberately attempting to enhance and expand existing initiatives, not duplicate them.

Financial reporting, government disclosure guidelines, ethical guidelines, sustainability reporting, and responsibility reporting, all influence the transference of environmental information from businesses to the general public. While each work in a variety of ways, whether mandatory or voluntary, whether regulated through the public or the private sector, they have one thing in common. They influence and inform corporate decision-making. In the case of mandatory regulations or standards, failure to inform can be very severe, resulting in heavy fines, legal action, risk of disciplinary action, and loss of professional membership. In the case of voluntary action, the implications may be less severe. Comprehensible and transparent reporting, whether financial reporting or sustainability reporting, signal better and more accountable management practices, and these are rewarded or penalized accordingly.

17.5 **Conclusion**

EMA issues have covered a spectrum from conformance to performance initiatives. From its nascent days of compliance with regional and national environmental statutes, it has evolved into a powerful tool used by management as a strategic and decision-making device. Its incorporation into the complex world of corporate management bears evidence of the changing forces, both governmental and market.

Already, great progress has been made in incorporating sustainability management issues within the domain of management accounting (Schaltegger and Muller 1998; Schaltegger and Burritt 2000; Figge et al. 2002; Reich 2005). Simultaneous development of management accounting from a measurement to a strategic and decision-making perspective enabled EMA to shift from a costing and compliance discipline to a performance and value enhancement mechanism (Kaplan and Norton 1996). Further developments in financial reporting and voluntary reporting initiatives stand to strengthen the links between internal management and decision-making, and external reporting. These changes, compounded with increasingly stringent corporate governance and ethical guidelines, and government regulations, create space for EMA within a notional continuum of conformance, performance, and value creation (Bhimani and Soonawalla 2005). Indeed, these changes redefine the depth of the continuum further.

There is a continuing need for research on qualitative and quantitative methodologies to address ethical, social, and environmental concerns, and internal and external accounting issues. The impact of these on corporate and managerial action needs to be understood as further advances in management accounting are made. The possibilities are extensive and the scope for integration of the complex and disparate environmental issues influencing organizational reporting and management continues to evolve.

☐ NOTE

1 'Sustainable Growth, the DuPont Way', *Harvard Business Review* (September 2001): 129–34.

☐ REFERENCES

Aye, L., Bamford, N., Charters, B., and Robinson, J. (2000). 'Environmentally Sustainable Development: A Life-Cycle Costing Approach for a Commercial Office Building in Melbourne, Australia', *Construction Management & Economics*, 18(8): 927–34.

Bae, B. and Sami, H. (2005). 'The Effect of Potential Environmental Liabilities on Earnings Response Coefficients', *Journal of Accounting, Auditing & Finance*, Winter, 20(1): 43–70.

Barth, M. E. and McNichols, M. F. (1994) 'Estimation and Market Valuation of Environmental Liabilities Relating to Superfund Sites', *Journal of Accounting Research*, 32(3) (Suppl.): 177–209.

—— —— and Wilson, G. P. (1997). 'Factors Influencing Firms' Disclosures about Environmental Liabilities', *Review of Accounting Studies*, 2: 35–64.

Bartolomeo, M., Bennett, M., Bouma, J., Heydkamp, P., James, P., and Wolters, T. (2000). 'Environmental Management Accounting in Europe: Current Practice and Future Potential', *European Accounting Review*, 9(1): 31–52.

Bennett, M. and James, P. (1998a). 'The Green Bottom Line', in M. Bennett and P. James (eds.), *The Green Bottom Line. Environmental Accounting for Management: Current Practice and Future Trends*. Sheffield: Greenleaf, pp. 30–60.

—— —— (1998b). 'Life-Cycle Costing and Packaging at Xerox Ltd', in M. Bennett and P. James (eds.), *The Green Bottom Line. Environmental Accounting for Management: Current Practice and Future Trends*. Sheffield: Greenleaf, pp. 347–61.

—— —— (1999a). 'Key Themes in Environmental, Social and Sustainability Performance Evaluation and Reporting', in M. Bennett and P. James (eds.), *Sustainable Measures: Evaluation and Reporting of Environmental and Social Performance*. Sheffield: Greenleaf, pp. 29–75.

—— —— (1999b). 'ISO 14031 and the Future of Environmental Performance Evaluation', in M. Bennett and P. James (eds.), *Sustainable Measures: Evaluation and Reporting of Environmental and Social Performance*. Sheffield: Greenleaf, pp. 475–95.

Bhimani, A. and Soonawalla, K. (2005). 'From Conformance to Performance: The Corporate Responsibilities Continuum', *Journal of Accounting and Public Policy*, 24(3): 165–254.

Blacconiere, W. G. and Northcut, D. W. (1997). 'Environmental Information and Market Reactions to Environmental Legislation', *Journal of Accounting, Auditing & Finance*, Spring, 12(2): 149–278.

Brummet, R. L., Flamholtz, E. G., and Pyle, W. C. (1968). 'Human Resource Measurement—A Challenge for Accountants', *Accounting Review*, 43(2): 212–24.

Cormier, D. and Magnan, M. (1997). 'Investors' Assessment of Implicit Environmental Liabilities: An Empirical Investigation', *Journal of Accounting & Public Policy*, 16(2): 215–41.

Eccles, R. G. (1991). 'The Performance Measurement Manifesto', *Harvard Business Review* (January/ February): 131–7.

Elkington, J. (1997). *Cannibals with Forks: The Triple Bottom Line of 21st Century Business*. Oxford: Capstone.

—— (2001). 'The "Triple Bottom Line" for the 21st Century Business', in R. Starkey and R. Welford (eds.), *The Earthscan Reader in Business and Sustainable Development*. London: Earthscan, pp. 20–43.

Emblemsvåg, J. and Bras, B. (2000). *Activity-Based Cost and Environmental Management: A Different Approach to the ISO 14000 Compliance*. Boston: Kluwer Academic.

EPA (Environmental Protection Agency) (1998). 'An Introduction to Environmental Accounting as a Business Management Tool', in M. Bennett and P. James (eds.), *The Green Bottom Line. Environmental Accounting for Management: Current Practice and Future Trends*. Sheffield: Greenleaf, pp. 61–85.

Figge, F., Hahn, T., Schaltegger, S., and Wagner, M. (2002). 'The Sustainability Balanced Scorecard— Linking Sustainability Management to Business Strategy', *Business Strategy and the Environment*, 11: 269–84.

GAO (Government Accountability Office) (2004). 'Environmental Disclosure: SEC Should Explore Ways to Improve Tracking and Transparency of Information'. GAO, Washington, DC, July.

Horngren, C., Foster, G., and Datar, S. M. (2005). *Cost Accounting: A Managerial Emphasis*. Englewood Cliffs, NJ: Prentice Hall.

IFAC (International Federation of Accountants) (1998). 'Environmental Management in Organisations: The Role of Management Accounting'. Study 6, New York: Financial and Management Accounting Committee, IFAC.

—— (2004). *Exposure Draft on International Guidelines on Environmental Management Accounting*. New York: IFAC.

—— (2005). *International Guidance Document on Environmental Management Accounting*. New York: IFAC.

Jasch, C. (2001). *Environmental Management Accounting—Procedures and Principles*. New York: United Nations.

—— (2003). 'The Use of Environmental Management Accounting (EMA) for Identifying Environmental Costs', *Journal of Cleaner Production*, 11: 667–76.

Johnson, H. and Kaplan, R. (1987). *Relevance Lost: The Rise and Fall of Management Accounting*. Cambridge, MA: Harvard Business School Press.

Johnson, L. T. (1993). 'Research on Environmental Reporting', *Accounting Horizons*, 7(3): 118–23.

Kaplan, R. S. (1984). 'The Evolution of Management Accounting', *Accounting Review*, 59(3): 390–418.

Kaplan, R. S. and Norton, D. (1992). 'The Balanced Scorecard: Measures that Drive Performance', *Harvard Business Review* (January/February): 71–9.

—— —— (1996). 'Using the Balanced Scorecard as a Strategic Management System', *Harvard Business Review* (January/February): 75–85.

Kennedy, J. and Mitchell, T. (1998). 'Disclosure of Contingent Environmental Liabilities: Some Unintended Consequences?', *Journal of Accounting Research*, 36(2): 257–77.

Konar, S. and Cohen, M. A. (1996). 'Information as Regulation: The Effect of Community Right-to-Know Laws on Toxic Emissions', *Journal of Environmental Economics and Management* (March): 109–24.

Mirvis, P. H. (2000). 'Transformation at Shell: Commerce and Citizenship', *Business and Society Review*, 105(1): 63–84.

Morrison, C. (1991). *Managing Environmental Affairs: Corporate Practices in the US, Canada and Europe*. New York: The Conference Board.

Murphy, D. and Bendell, J. (2001). 'The "Triple Bottom Line" for the 21st Century Business', in R. Starkey and R. Welford (eds.), *The Earthscan Reader in Business and Sustainable Development*. London: Earthscan, pp. 20–43.

Ranganathan, J. (1999). 'Signs of Sustainability: Measuring Corporate Environmental and Social Performance', in M. Bennett and P. James (eds.), *Sustainable Measures: Evaluation and Reporting of Environmental and Social Performance*. Sheffield: Greenleaf, pp. 475–95.

Reich, M. C. (2005). 'Economic Assessment of Municipal Waste Management Systems—Case Studies Using a Combination of Life Cycle Assessment (LCA) and Life Cycle Costing (LCC)', *Journal of Cleaner Production*, 13: 253–63.

Rogers, P. G. (1990). 'The Clean Air Act of 1970', *EPA Journal* (January/February): 21–3.

Schaltegger, S. and Burritt, R. (2000). *Contemporary Environmental Accounting Issues, Concepts and Practice*. Sheffield: Greenleaf.

—— and Figge, F. (2000). 'Environmental Shareholder Value: Economic Success with Corporate Environmental Management', *Eco-Management and Auditing*, 7: 29–42.

—— and Muller, K. (1998). 'Calculating the True Profitability of Pollution Prevention', in M. Bennett and P. James (eds.), *The Green Bottom Line. Environmental Accounting for Management: Current Practice and Future Trends*. Sheffield: Greenleaf, pp. 86–99.

Sterner, E. (2000). 'Life-Cycle Costing and Its Use in the Swedish Building Sector', *Building Research & Information*, 28(5/6): 387–93.

Terry, J. C. and Yandle, B. (1997). 'EPA's Toxic Release Inventory: Stimulus and Response', *Managerial and Decision Economics*, 18: 433–41.

Todd, R. (1992). 'Zero Loss Environmental Accounting Systems', in B. R. Allenby and D. J. Richards (eds.), *The Greening of Industrial Ecosystems*. Washington, DC: National Academy Press, pp. 191–200.

UNDSD (United Nations Division for Sustainable Development) (2003). *Environmental Management Accounting Procedures and Principles*. New York: EMARIC Environmental Management Accounting Research and Information Center.

Verschoor, A. H. and Reijnders, L. (2000). 'Toxics Reduction in Ten Large Companies, Why and How', *Journal of Cleaner Production*, 8: 69–78.

Verschoor, A. H. and Reijnders, L. (2001). 'The Environmental Monitoring of Large International Companies: How and What is Monitored and Why', *Journal of Cleaner Production*, 9: 43–55.

Welch, T. E. (1997). *Moving Beyond Environmental Compliance: A Handbook for Integrating Pollution Prevention with ISO 14000*. London: Lewis.

Williams, G. and Phillips, T. (1994). 'Cleaning Up Our Act: Accounting for Environmental Liabilities: Current Financial Reporting Doesn't Do the Job', *Management Accounting* (February): 30–3.

18 Organization control and management accounting in context: a case study of the US motion picture industry

S. Mark Young
Wim A. Van der Stede
James J. Gong

18.1 Introduction

The value chain as developed by Porter (1980, 1985) is one of the most widely acknowledged frameworks for understanding how industries and firms are organized and operate. The value chain develops the key activities that contribute to the ultimate value of the products or services that firms deliver. For each step in the value chain, management accounting and control system designers establish standards of performance to motivate behaviour, develop mechanisms by which performance can be monitored, and design appropriate systems to reward value-creating behaviours (Atkinson et al. 2004). In this chapter, we use the value chain framework to provide a detailed overview of the motion picture industry and to discuss several management accounting and control issues associated with each stage of motion picture development and commercialization both within and across firms in this industry.

Research on the effects of management accounting and control systems has been conducted in a wide variety of contexts most notably in manufacturing (Anderson et al. 2002; Bhimani 2003), hospitals (Abernethy et al. 2005), and the public sector (Covaleski et al. 2003); however, very little research has been undertaken in the creative industries. The creative industries include the arts, music, television, games, and motion pictures (see Young, forthcoming, for an overview). Studying the creative industries is particularly challenging from a management accounting and control perspective given the complex interplay between art and commerce. This interplay involves the selection of intellectual properties such as music or a screenplay, a myriad of contractual relations (Caves 2000), specific performances of many types of individuals (artists, director, producers), the backing of distributors, and the fickle tastes of the public. Moreover, since virtually none of the outputs of the creative industries are commodity products, each product becomes a project with very few elements that can be easily repeated or replicated. Finally, and perhaps of most interest, the lack of predictability of outcomes, such as the commercial success of a film, tends to create short-term behaviours and control problems among executive decision-makers and 'the talent' that help create the product (e.g. Ravid and Basuroy 2004).

In many ways, however, the creative industries and its management and organization are like any other. Participants in these industries develop a product and then sell it to a consumer. They are involved with some level of production, marketing, and sales through which they seek to create or satisfy an ongoing consumer demand that allows them to stay in business. But there is one significant difference. Each product they sell must always be 'new' in some way if the creative industries are to retain and grow their customer base. In other words, in the areas of production, marketing, and sales, the creative industries perhaps parallel the patterns and procedures of traditional industries. Where it differs, however, is in the very product it seeks to sell. Each aesthetic product, while it may reflect or incorporate familiar or similar aesthetic elements, is a unique creation and is marketed and sold with that in mind. In other words, a film may be a sequel to another popular film, using the same actors, situations, and tone, but it is not the same film. The lack of repeatability leads to a project-based system of organization that is quite different from commodity production businesses. Balancing traditional business practices with a demand for 'the new' is the pivotal characteristic, and challenge, of the management and organization of the creative industries (Jones 1996; DeFillippi and Arthur 1998; Jones et al. 1998).

The goals of this chapter are to expand the domain of management accounting and organizational control research into the creative industries and develop a framework for studying perhaps the best known of these industries—motion pictures. The chapter discusses both traditional and emerging issues in-context that managerial accountants ordinarily address in most organizations across a diversity of industries. These include issues of performance evaluation, incentives, contracting, strategic assessment, value chain analysis, budgetary systems, cost control, cost behaviour, and profit analyses among others. The framework for achieving this focuses on the US motion picture industry, which has the longest history and is the most developed film industry globally. Studying the US motion picture industry (Hollywood) is of significance for a number of reasons. Entertainment, and specifically motion pictures, is one of the most significant exports of the USA, accounting for over $100 billion in revenues and approximately 75 per cent of worldwide motion picture exports (MPAA 2005). The motion picture industry attracts over a billion cinema patrons to theatres a year in the USA alone. Global media conglomerates rely on US motion picture studios to supply a stream of products for their international subsidiaries. Besides, media conglomerates rely on the motion picture industry for their home video arms, television channels, consumer products divisions, theme parks, and video games. Many of these have had a profound effect on worldwide popular culture. The development of the industry is also tied to many significant technological developments such as celluloid film, and more recently, digital technology.

From an academic standpoint, however, perhaps most intriguing is the paucity of research in management accounting and control that has been conducted directly in the motion picture industry despite a wealth of topics that are directly relevant for our field, including product development and its payoffs and a myriad of contracting and incentive issues among actors, agents, and managers, directors, producers and other production talent, writers, marketeers, and the all-important financial backers. Hollywood has a reputation for being impenetrable and a 'closed society' not amenable to research. In other literatures (e.g. cultural economics and marketing), one major stream of research has relied on public data to determine motion picture box office success (e.g. Litman 1983; Smith and Smith 1986; Litman and Kohl 1989; Wyatt 1991; Sochay 1994; De Vany and Walls 1997, 1999, 2002; Ravid 1999; Ravid and Basuroy 2004; Gong et al. 2005). It appears that this line of research has been sparked by Goldman's famous quote (1989) in *Adventures in the Screen Trade*, that when it comes to predicting success, 'no one knows anything'. Other research in psychology has attempted to understand the role that celebrity plays in the entertainment industry (Young and Pinsky 2005). There is also much to study within the motion picture industry that is of interest to management accounting and control. A critical step in this direction is to develop a framework to illustrate how this industry is organized.

We begin the development of the framework by looking first at the organization of the global market for motion pictures. We then turn to specifics of the value chain as applied to the US motion picture industry. For each stage of this value chain, we identify several research opportunities.

18.2 Organization of the US motion picture industry

To place the US motion picture market in perspective, global annual film production is in excess of 3,000 films (Screen Digest 2005). Currently, India produces the largest number of films per year. In 2004, for instance, approximately 800 films were distributed in that country. Historically, Indian films have had very little distribution outside of India; however, they are beginning to develop a following, particularly in Europe. The USA is the second largest producer of motion pictures and released 475 films from about thirty distributors including the six major studios in 2002. About half of these films are distributed by the major studios and half by the independents, or *indies*. The third largest film producer is China with 212 films released in 2004.

Annual global box office revenues amount to $21.4 billion, across 205,000 theatres, with a total seating capacity of 13.6 million seats. Global annual revenues (including video/DVD, cable, and television revenues) are forecast to increase at a rate of 20 per cent per year to an estimated $450 billion by the end of 2005. Hollywood films currently account for about 35 per cent of total industry revenues by value (almost $63 billion) (Screen Digest 2005).

At the core of the motion picture industry in the USA are six major studios, all of which are owned by very large media corporations. These vertically integrated conglomerates,

Table 18.1 Major studios and their corporate owners

Major studios	Distribution arm	Parent corp	Revenue (%)*	Operating income (%)*
Paramount Pictures	Paramount Pictures Corporation	Viacom, Inc.	13.5	8.9
Universal Pictures	Universal International Films, Inc.	General Electric	6.0†	10.0†
Columbia Pictures	Columbia TriStar Film Distributors International, Inc.	Sony Corporation	7.7	1.8
Warner Brothers Pictures	Warner Brothers International Theatrical Distribution	Time Warner Entertainment Company, L.P.	21.7	9.1
Twentieth Century Fox	Twentieth Century Fox International Corporation	News Corporation	27.0	15.5
Walt Disney Pictures	Buena Vista International, Inc.	Walt Disney Company	23.6	2.7

*All percentage data represent not only the motion picture distribution but also the video and television segments, given the limited corporation disclosure.
†Data are for the year 2001 except for Universal, as Universal was acquired by GE in 2004. Universal data are for the year 2004 and the revenue and operating profit data reflect NBC Universal instead of Universal only.
Source: PBS (2001), 'The Monster that Ate Hollywood'; Hoover's Business Information; and company websites.

shown in Table 18.1, also include many other forms of media including major radio, cable, and network television stations, and book publishing. For instance, Viacom, Inc. owns Paramount Pictures, CBS, MTV, Showtime, Infinity Broadcasting, Simon and Schuster, The Free Press, and Blockbuster Video.

The corporate parents of the major studios also own some speciality studios that produce and distribute certain genres of films. For instance, Time Warner also owns Castle Rock Entertainment, and Walt Disney owns Touchstone Pictures. Both the major studios and their speciality studios are organized under an entertainment group within the conglomerate. For instance, as the motion picture arm of the Walt Disney Company, Walt Disney Studio Entertainment owns both Walt Disney Pictures and Touchstone Pictures. Within Sony Corporation of America, Sony Pictures Entertainment owns Columbia Pictures, Sony Pictures Classics, Screen Gems, and TriStar Pictures. Other well-known independent distributors include DreamWorks, SKG, Focus Features, Imagine Entertainment, and Lion's Gate. The industry provides over 360,000 wage and salary positions (Bureau of Labor Statistics 2005).

Researchers have examined the industry using theories such as transaction cost economics and industrial organization. The topics that they have examined include the emergence of the studio system, industry competition, barriers to entry, mergers and acquisitions, and strategic dynamics among major studios (e.g. Collette 1998; Litman and Hoag 1998; Chisholm 1993, 1997, 2004; Borcherding and Filson 2000). An interesting question relates to the debate concerning how high levels of media concentration and the influence of Hollywood films, in particular, affect what the general public consumes. For example, if the public's choices are so narrowly defined by a small number of studios and executives, how does it affect the homogenization of worldwide culture? Very little research has been conducted on this topic.

18.3 **The value chain**

Compared to economics research, business research in the motion picture sector is scattered. Two well-studied areas in business are advertising effectiveness and the prediction and modelling of the financial success of films. This chapter proposes a value chain framework to guide future research. Value chain analysis as developed by Porter (1980, 1985) describes the activities within and around an organization, relates those activities to an analysis of the competitive strength of the organization, and evaluates which value each particular activity adds to the organization's products or services. We apply and develop the value chain framework to the US motion picture industry (Figure 18.1). We discuss each of its stages and identify several research opportunities.

Figure 18.1 shows the value chain for motion pictures from pre-production through all retail distribution channels. Pre-production, the first part of the chain, involves four main groups of participants: property owners, talent and intermediaries, producers, and financiers. Surrounding these are several regulatory and organizational forces such as the guilds, unions, and federal regulatory agencies that also play a central role in monitoring and regulating the industry.

Following pre-production are production, marketing, and theatrical release. Following initial distribution—theatrical release at the box office—there are numerous other steps in the value chain. The right-hand side of Figure 18.1 shows how a motion picture moves into other markets. In today's film-making environment, it is these steps in the value chain where the vast majority of revenues are generated. It is no longer the case that ticket sales pay for

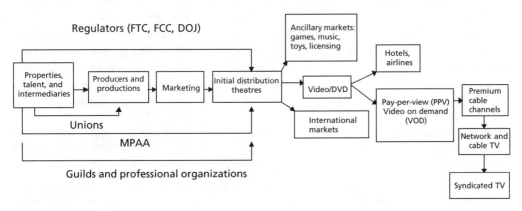

Figure 18.1 Motion picture value chain

the cost of films. However, box office sales are still important because box office receipts brand a film as a hit or flop, influencing the general public and determining a film's revenue potential in other channels (Ravid 1999; Lehmann and Weinberg 2000).

Film revenues come not only from the box office—which has been the most frequent, even almost exclusive, source of revenue studied in prior academic research—but also from video and DVD sales and/or rentals, network and cable television rights (including syndication), independent television rights, pay-per-view and pay television rights, airline screening rights, college campus screening rights, international distribution rights, music sales for soundtracks from films, merchandise related to the film, book publishing rights (if the book comes out after the film release), and product placement (products strategically shown in a film). As such, films often continue to generate revenues for their production studios across all of these sources, known as 'windows of exhibition', for years after their theatrical release. Table 18.2 shows the major sources of these revenue streams and their windows.

The chain of value created by motion pictures is consistent with one of the underlying assumptions behind the wave of mergers and acquisitions in the entertainment and media industry in the 1990s. Conglomerates realize synergies between different branches of the entertainment business by exploiting a film, film 'brand', or 'franchise' across a number of different sectors in a coordinated manner. For example, conglomerates provide the means for creating lucrative films and television franchises. In other words, major studios owned by the big conglomerates are producing not so much blockbuster films per se, but brands or franchises. Or, as noted in the *Economist* (19 November 1998: S5):

Some character or idea can be marketed in a thousand different ways. A brand is often launched with an 'event' film, as with Disney's *Lion King* or Sony's *Godzilla*, but brands can start a life in all sorts of ways. Viacom's *Rugrats*, which has just been turned into a film, came from a children's cable channel, Nickelodeon; Time Warner's *Batman* is an old and revered comic book character that happened to translate nicely into a live action film and much, much more.

Table 18.2 Major sources of motion picture revenues and their windows

Channels	Window	Beginning
Theatrical	6 months	Initial theatrical release
Home video (VHS/DVD)	7–10 years	6 months after initial theatrical release
Pay-per-view	2 months	8 months after initial theatrical release
Pay television	18 months	12 months after initial theatrical release
Network television	30 months	30 months after initial theatrical release
Pay television second window	12 months	60 months after initial theatrical release (30 months if no network television sale)
Syndication or basic cable	60 months	72 months after initial theatrical release (42 months if no network television sale)
Syndication or basic cable second window	60 months	132 months after initial theatrical release

Note: Omitted from the distribution channels and windows are foreign sales, the video game sector, consumer products merchandising, and theme parks. Foreign sales usually begin after the initial theatrical release in the USA. Each territory has different windows for different channels. Video games based on blockbuster films such as *Lord of Rings* and *Terminator 3* sometimes earn equivalent revenues to theatrical releases.

18.3.1 PRE-PRODUCTION

18.3.1.1 Properties

The first step in the value chain is the acquisition of a property. In the motion picture industry this property is a treatment (an overview of the film with a discussion of the characters and brief plot synopsis) or a completed screenplay. A property may be an adaptation of an existing book or an original piece of work. Acquiring promising properties is a highly contested part of the value chain. All participants in the motion picture industry, actors, directors, producers, and distributors (studios), can buy a copyright on a property and then seek partners to finish the project.

The dream of literally thousands of screenwriters worldwide is to have their screenplays made into a motion picture; however, the chances are slim. A small number of highly successful screenwriters are often asked to submit screenplays based on a property that a studio wants to produce; however, literally thousands of individuals would like to see their own screenplay made into a film. Those individuals lucky enough to see their screenplay come to life in the form of a film (often produced by small independent filmmakers) would still like to have their film distributed by a major or independent studio. Unless the film is picked up directly, the most common approach is to show the film at a major film festival. So what are the odds of this happening?

Leipzig (2005) presents a dismal picture of the odds. As an example, he cites statistics related to perhaps the most famous venue for hopeful independent filmmakers, the Sundance Film Festival. In 2004, 2,613 films were submitted. Of these, only 120 were screened. In a good year, perhaps ten (0.3 per cent) of these films will be distributed in the USA. There are 2,500 film festivals worldwide, all hoping that some very small percentage of their top films will be produced and distributed. So, the odds are indeed very small.

What is largely unknown is the control process that leads to the selection of films to produce at any of the studios. In some cases, such as sequels, the outcome is believed to be largely determined by the success of the original property. But who actually decides on what screenplays should be produced and what films should be green-lighted? Ultimately, a studio head has the last say in signing off on a film, but the process of selecting screenplays often comes down to the tastes and preferences of a few executives. Because of the unpredictability of what films will be successful, it is believed that studio executives choose less risky films in order to keep their jobs. Such films often appeal to the lowest common denominator regarding the film-going public. These contentions, however, must be carefully researched as virtually no systematic evidence exists.

18.3.1.2 Talent

What sets the creative industries apart from, let us say, companies producing commodities is the ongoing nature of the creative process. That process initially begins as an aesthetic endeavor pursued in some isolation from the marketplace, usually by an individual artist or group. While the artist may seek financial returns for his or her efforts, it is initially usually not the only or overriding motivation. The artist seeks to express something or create an experience to be shared with a larger audience.

Historically, people who are considered 'creative' come up the ranks from at least two very different pathways. Some go to film or theatre schools to hone their craft and expand their skills. They may leave school as accomplished or promising artists. They may seek further experience by going into the theatre or audition through casting calls. Others try to succeed without formal training by moving to Hollywood and hoping to be discovered. However, the odds of even securing an agent are minuscule. Thus, one reason for the popularity of the 'Idol' music competitions worldwide is that it gives people without formal training hope that they might be able to obtain a record contract. It is rare, however, that any of these individuals receive much of a business education on how to sell what they produce or deal with the realities of the marketplace. In fact, artists tend not to think about art as an industry or market until they decide that it is time to sell their creation, whether it is a musical composition or their acting talent.

While other industries employ skilled individuals who work, say, on assembly lines or in laboratories, the creative industries employ people many of whom are thought to have different mindsets or hard-wiring. Talent in the motion picture industry includes actors, directors, producers, costume and set designers, lighting and electrical specialists, and so on, employed in approximately sixty types of unions and guilds. The term 'union' in the creative industries describes labour organizations that represent technical personnel, and are referred to as 'below-the-line' unions. The term 'guild' describes labour organizations that represent creative people, and are referred to as 'above-the-line' unions. These designations result from their actual position on the pages of production budgets in which 'creative' and 'technical' costs are divided by a line. In a typical motion picture production budget, for example, below-the-line costs are fixed, whereas above-the-line costs are flexible.

There are unions or guilds for actors (Screen Actors Guild, American Federation of Television and Radio Artists), producers (Producers Guild of America), directors (Directors Guild of America), and unions for every type of worker including the International Alliance of Theatrical Stage Employees, and Communication Workers of America.

While buying a property is a simple transaction, contracting with talent is a complex process. Writers, directors, and actors receive upfront payments, but most of them also demand either profit or revenue-sharing contracts.

One of the more intriguing areas of study is the nature of celebrity. Braudy (1997) has noted that all societies have singled out individuals and lavished them with fame. Huge marketing campaigns, often as expensive as the motion pictures themselves, tout the stars of films—the celebrities—as never before (Grigoriadis 2005). In the USA, five shows in primetime focus on celebrities: *Entertainment Tonight, The Insider, Inside Edition, Access Hollywood*, and *Extra*, and together they attract more than 100 million American viewers each week (ABC News.com, 18 April 2005). However, Young and Pinsky (2005) point out that celebrities are simultaneously the most widely exposed, yet most understudied and least understood, group in our society.

Understanding the nature of celebrity is a critical issue for the study of the entertainment industry. For instance, there is a difference between those celebrities with true talent and those who have garnered their reputation through contrived media campaigns. Studios have to evaluate carefully the star power of a celebrity before engaging in contracts with them. This is not to say that truly talented actors will necessarily generate huge box office receipts. It goes without saying that, here again, contracting issues are difficult and worthy of extensive study.

18.3.1.3 Intermediaries

As part of the first stage of the value chain, artists turn to intermediaries who play critical roles in managing their careers. The people who provide artists with opportunities are business managers, agents, publicists, and attorneys (some agents and business managers are attorneys). Many intermediaries are independent or work in small firms, but others are employed by large companies such as Creative Artists Agency or William Morris Agency. The existence of intermediaries provides a layer of complexity in the creative industries that does not exist in most other industries. While there are thousands of people who would like to become wealthy and famous based on their talent, many never have the opportunity. Intermediaries have a notorious reputation in Hollywood. Who they choose to represent, and how they represent them, provides yet another interesting set of contracting issues.

Managers play the role of chief operating officer (COO) in managing an individual. They advise their clients on every aspect of their career such as who to sign with and what projects to take. They also coordinate the activities of the agents, attorneys, and publicists. Agents must be licensed by the state to procure employment or make engagements for their clients. There are two types of agents: literary agents who handle writers and authors; and talent agents who handle actors, musicians, and directors. Their job involves discovering talent, matching talent to each other, and locating employment opportunities. Publicists find opportunities for their clients to make personal appearances, engage in interviews, and promote themselves. Attorneys represent their clients' interests by protecting their intellectual property; they oversee contracts and litigate disputes. In today's business environment, it is almost impossible for artists to succeed without a team of people working on their behalf. But stories abound in Hollywood about how the contractual process among these parties can break down, even though having the right representation is critical for success.

Since agents, publicists, and managers work as a team, research on how they manage their clients' careers would be most intriguing. A large part of the entertainment industry and those on the outside see the interaction of these individuals as one of the key black boxes that need to be unravelled.

18.3.1.4 Producers

Intermediaries also match properties and artists with producers. (Producers can also obtain material to be developed into products such as films and music directly from studios or labels.) In the motion picture industry, producers hire screenwriters and directors and find project financing. Producers can be independent or tied directly to a studio. The independent producer's job is to interest distributors in their products and obtain financing. If the producer is tied to a studio, finding financing is significantly easier as the studio will often foot all, or a significant part, of the production costs. Financing in today's environment can be complex. Apart from relying on studios, finding financing from other sources such as using equity and foreign investors, bank loans, and making judicious use of intricate tax shelters are some of the methods used.

18.3.1.5 Financiers

Financing for films produced by studios and independent producers go through different procedures. For studio-produced films, a studio head has the last say in giving the green light for a film. Since financing decisions need to be made on the basis of little more than an idea, studio executives make decisions in an environment in which they are unable to forecast. Little is known about the process that leads to the selection of films to produce at any of the studios.

A recent phenomenon, however, is the decline in the number of films produced by the major studios. Only a relatively small proportion of releases consist of in-house productions, while the majority result from co-production and co-financing deals with smaller, semi-independent production companies. In such deals, the large studios typically buy a substantial equity stake in these semi-independent production companies, which is expected to initiate and develop film projects that are then co-financed by both parties as part of long-term agreement.

Independent producers, on the other hand, often have to sell distribution rights to different channels (e.g. theatrical, television, and video distribution) in different territories (domestic, international) in order to get financing. Because there are more financing partners involved, these deals tend to involve complex arrangements for the division of costs and revenues, distribution territories, and rights to theatrical, television, and video distribution. As an example, consider the case of *Terminator 3: Rise of the Machines*. An independent production company, C-2 Pictures, sold rights to Warner Brothers, Sony Pictures, and other foreign distributors. Warner Brothers contributed $55 million to production and marketing to obtain the rights for domestic theatrical distribution and video sales and rentals of the film, yet was entitled to only 50 per cent of the revenues from these distributions (Hayes and Bing 2004).

18.3.2 PRODUCTION

Producers are responsible for preparing production budgets. The actual production (shooting) and post-production budgets are implemented by the director. A film's production costs (also called 'negative costs') have several components. They are the costs of manufacturing the master print. The costs include any upfront payments to talent and other employees, costs of sets, and other costs incurred during the production process. If it is a studio film, the studio also charges a fee for use of its facilities. The studio also charges interest on the negative cost and overheads.

The budgeting process for motion pictures is a very fertile area for research. Very little is known about it, but the process is said to require a great deal of judgement. When a budget is being prepared, every page of the actual screenplay itself is scrutinized and budgeted according to the experience of the producers. For example, in the film remake of *The Italian Job*, the chase scene down Hollywood Boulevard in Los Angeles required careful attention to the cost of closing down that well-travelled road for three days, bringing the entire crew to location, paying for insurance for all surrounding shops, and also paying the storeowners to close down during the shooting of the scene. Neale and Allerston's survey (2005) on the role of 'production accountants' in the motion picture industry, however, reveals that very few certified management accountants work in film production. These so-called 'production accountants' assist the producer of the film in preparing the budget and assessing the commercial viability of the project.

18.3.3 MARKETING

In more than half of cases, a film is marketed and distributed by a major studio's distribution arm. Almost the same number of films is distributed by speciality distributors within conglomerates. Very few films are distributed by completely independent distributors. Studios need a regular supply of films to fuel their domestic and international distribution operations and earn distribution fees. Distributors are responsible for the design and implementation of the marketing campaigns for the channels and territories for which they have the distribution rights.

At every stage of the process of developing a film, marketing research is conducted. Film screenings, telephone surveys, and trailer tests all play a role in assessing the reaction of targeted audiences which, in turn, influences and directs the positioning of the overall marketing campaign. Nielson NRG is a company that specializes in screening tests. The company recruits potential audiences, shows them the film, asks them to complete questionnaires, and holds focus group discussions on the film's weaknesses and strengths. Several rounds of screening tests results provide useful information for editing the film and designing advertising campaigns before the film is released. In addition to traditional marketing channels, such as in theatres, print advertisements, and television, the Internet also recently has played an increasingly significant role in providing information, such as streaming video of upcoming films.

In the case of large blockbuster releases, such as *Independence Day*, there is an attempt to turn the initial launch of the film into a major event. Studio distributors now spend much more on advertising (and prints) in promoting their films than a decade ago, recognizing that such efforts can substantially boost a film's revenues. Studios will even spend a great deal of money on premiere events. For *Pirates of the Caribbean: The Curse of the Black Pearl*, starring Johnny Depp, Disney spent $2 million on the lavish affair. The premiere was held at Disneyland and the park was closed down in the early evening for the first time since it opened in 1955. Disney received a huge amount of press on this event and the film went on to gross $653 million at the worldwide box office and over $320 million in domestic video/DVD sales and rentals (www.the-numbers.com). As such, marketing budgets have increased proportionally much faster than production costs. However, it is not well understood how much a studio should spend on marketing a film. Is there an optimal level? Can a studio salvage a poor film with additional marketing, or should it invest in, or redirect resources to, a large(r) DVD campaign? Another question is whether upstream advertising efforts for the film affect downstream sales of the film in ancillary markets and/or its offshoots (e.g. video games)? This question can only be examined by adopting a product life cycle perspective to advertising effectiveness. In the words of King (2002: 73):

Release in the cinema remains the biggest stage on which to display Hollywood's wares. It is the most prestigious part of the life cycle of Hollywood entertainment ... [and] translates into the greatest levels of success further down the chain. This is why so much is often invested in initial advertising and promotional campaigns that can act as loss leaders. Their costs can be a sound investment in the longer-term value of the product. . . . Big hits at the box office are usually the titles that fill the walls in video rental and retail outlets and earn the biggest fees for release to cable, satellite, and terrestrial television.

18.3.4 THEATRICAL RELEASE

As discussed earlier (Table 18.2), distribution takes place domestically and internationally and includes not only primary (initial) distribution to exhibitors such as theatres (in the case of films) but also ancillary distribution in the form of video/DVD sales, cable and satellite television, pay television, and network television. A relatively new and promising channel for distribution is mobile entertainment, whereby consumers will be able to use the device of their choice to download film clips no matter where they are.

A film will stay exclusively in theatres from two weeks to four months. Some films continue to run in theatres after the period of initial exclusivity is over. Of the revenues generated at the box office, the studio usually gets 50–55 per cent, leaving the balance to exhibitors (theatre owners). During the early weeks of a film's release, the studios receive as much as 90 per cent of the box office; at the end of a long run, this ratio can be inverted, with 90 per cent for the exhibitors and 10 per cent for the studios. This creates an incentive for the exhibitor to stay with a particular studio's product and serves to keep the competition out.

Theatrical release is the most important stage in the life cycle of a film given its impact on all other ancillary markets. Nevertheless, global box office revenues (domestic and international) typically account for only about 20 per cent of the total revenues for a film over its entire life cycle. Hollywood films still dominate the theatres and are released internationally anywhere from within a couple of days to as long as six months following the US release.

US studios control three-quarters of the distribution market outside the USA. And in dollar terms, filmgoers in the USA still account for about 44 per cent of global box office (Dyson 2004).

With the coming of megaplex theatres, a big-budget blockbuster film can be exhibited on as many as 3,000 screens at any point in time. Studios pre-announce a desirable release date for a major film a year in advance or more. Big-budget blockbuster films tend to be concentrated into particular periods, such as the spring holidays, the summer months, and the Christmas season.

There is an obsession in Hollywood with opening box office performance. New technology makes box office numbers quickly available as a measure of a film's success. As such, it is perhaps not surprising that most industry and academic research to date in the motion picture industry has been concerned with predicting motion pictures' success at the box office, particularly opening box office performance (Hayes and Bing 2004).

18.3.5 VIDEO SALES AND RENTAL

The home video market is the booming business. About 200 million films and music videos were shipped in 2004, a 100 per cent increase over 2002. Consumer spending on videos in 2002 was approximately $25 billion, while film ticket sales were $7.5 billion (Standard & Poor's 2005). Consumer demand for most rentals historically peaks in the first three weeks of availability and then drops off precipitously, which could be why video renters rely on an unorthodox revenue stream—late fees—to help increase revenues. Late fees are the largest profit generator for rental stores.

DVDs in some cases account for 30 per cent of a studio's retail revenue from sales and rentals. DVDs can be found in wholesale for only $10–15 each (compared to $45–65 apiece for video cassettes) and are sold to consumers at $18–30. Simply put, the DVD market provides the film industry with a large new source of revenues at minimum cost, and allows them to exploit their film libraries more than ever before. As a result, studios have been investing heavily in upgrading their film libraries. Sony's acquisition of MGM was fuelled in part by MGM's film library of 4,000 titles. Two of the biggest emerging markets are the 'made-for-video' and 'new-to-video' categories. Made-for-video are films typically with low budgets that studios believe will garner sizeable revenues. Some of these films are ones that were initially set to have a theatrical release but the studios changed their mind. New-to-video are films that currently exist in a studio library but have never been released on video or DVD.

Home video has a protected window of six weeks to six months, meaning that the only place consumers can rent or buy the film is on video or DVD. Now that pay-per-view has become more popular, and video-on-demand has become a reality, some in the home video industry have argued that this window of exclusivity is too short and does not give stores enough time to turn a profit.

18.3.6 TELEVISION MARKET

When the exclusive home video window closes, studio films are then made available on pay-per-view venues, on both cable and satellite television systems. At this stage, the film is available exclusively for 2–6 weeks on pay-per-view. (Note that the film will always be available on video after its initial availability, so subsequent discussions of 'exclusivity' do not include the home video window.) Generally, studios will get anywhere from 45–55 per cent of the revenues generated from pay-per-view, depending on the individual film and the number of pay-per-view channels on which it can be exhibited. If News Corp.; had been able to purchase DirecTV, the leading satellite operator would have been paired with one of the six major studios under one roof (Twentieth Century Fox is owned by News Corp.; see Table 18.2). As it is, however, AOL Time Warner is the only media conglomerate that owns both a studio and a cable operator.

After the exclusive pay-per-view window expires, the film can then be shown on premium cable channels such as Showtime, HBO, and Starz. The film is shown concurrently on both the premium cable channels and pay-per-view for approximately six weeks. Then the pay-per-view window closes, leaving an exclusive window for the premium cable channels that lasts for approximately eighteen months. HBO, Showtime, and Starz each have exclusive deals with the individual studios in which they agree to pay the studio for all of the films it produces in a given year. The amount that the premium channel pays per film is based on domestic box office revenues, and can go as high as $20–25 million for a blockbuster film. The average is approximately $6–8 million per film.

After premium cable (pay) television, the film appears on network (free) television for one or two runs; this interval lasts for 12–18 months. Top-rated cable channels (USA Network, TBS, TNT) have been able to outbid traditional networks (ABC, CBS, NBC) to obtain rights to broadcast films. For a very popular film, the network or cable channel may even buy future runs at five- or ten-year intervals. The network or cable channel negotiates with the studio for each film. Generally, the network will pay the studio a fixed amount ranging from $3 to $15 million, depending on the film and the number of runs.

Following the broadcast premiere and second run, the film goes into syndication, again either on network television or a cable network, or both. This can go on for five years. Films are licensed to the highest bidder on a title-by-title basis. Studios can exhibit the films for as long as they own the copyright or the right to distribute the film. The price that a network pays for each film is negotiated on a case-by-case basis; however, there is no formula for the studios' share. As the size of the market increases, so does the studios' share of the profit. In the largest television markets, studios may charge up to $5 million.

18.3.7 CONTRACTING ISSUES

A distinctive feature of the creative industries is the interplay among the various parties and the complexities of the contracting process, which often take place long before the production of the film (Caves 2000). It is the management and organization of the creative industries that determine how to negotiate and secure the artistic product that they will then present, market, and sell to the public. In the first instance—the relationship between the creative industries and the individual artist(s)—management and organization deal primarily with rights, royalties, agents, contracts, and commissions. In the second instance—between the creative industries and the audience or consumer—the focus shifts to production and production costs, marketing and promotional plans, audience-building and fund-raising, and consumer testing and polling.

There have been quite a few high-profile legal cases involving profit-sharing plans between distributors and the talent side of the business (Weinstein 1998). After subtracting production, distribution, advertising, and other costs including studio 'overheads', any profits (or losses) are divided accordingly. The studios remain powerful players in the motion picture marketplace through their expertise in marketing and through their distribution networks, taking a large slice of any profits.

18.4 Other forces in the motion picture industry

Aside form the unions and guilds there are other key organizations that help regulate the motion picture industry. These organizations support artists and play a significant role in promoting their products and protecting their rights. One of the best known is the Academy of Motion Picture Arts and Sciences (AMPAS). This organization bestows the Oscars. Among its many roles, the Motion Picture Association of America (MPAA) develops ratings for each motion picture, approves trailers, and combats copyright infringements. There are also several federal agencies such as the Federal Commerce Commission (FCC), Federal Trade Commission (FTC), and the Department of Justice (DOJ) that play critical roles in monitoring content, addressing issues of industry concentration, and anti-trust violations. Censorship will be one of the most hotly contested issues over the next few years as new standards for content will undoubtedly be derived.

18.5 Summary

Our goal in this chapter has been to provide a broad analysis of aspects of management accounting and organizational control issues by engaging in an overview of the US motion picture industry. We hope to have provided practitioners interested in this industry with a structured framework with which to consider such issues. The motion picture industry certainly is not the only one such unexplored sector in the management accounting literature, but it is an important one in terms of its size (sales and employment) and worldwide economic and cultural impact. We thus hope that we have also piqued the interest of researchers with diverse backgrounds and expertise in various management accounting areas (e.g. in cost accounting, budgeting, performance measurement, incentives) and various theoretical perspectives to generate their own ideas about the many potential researchable questions in this particular industry that have remained largely unexplored and for which we as management accounting researchers may have a comparative advantage. We realize, however, our limitations in being able to provide an exhaustive set of management accounting research opportunities.

One of the key difficulties in studying this industry is access to the major studios and to databases. Hollywood, as mentioned earlier, is considered a relatively closed society. That said, our initial forays into this industry have been met with some success. The industry is complex enough that it is often difficult for those in the 'eye of the storm' to make sense of what is going on around them. We believe that expanding management accounting investigations into all areas of the entertainment industry worldwide will provide a great deal of insights useful to students, practitioners, and scholars with an interest in this specific area. Such studies will also continue to inform those concerned with general aspects of organizational control and management accounting.

☐ REFERENCES

Abernethy, M., Horne, M., Lillis, A., Malina, M., and Selto, F. (2005). 'A Multi-Method Approach to Building Causal Performance Maps from Expert Knowledge', *Management Accounting Research*, 16: 135–56.

Anderson, S., Hesford, J., and Young, S. M. (2002). 'Factors Influencing the Performance of Activity-Based Costing Teams: A Field Study of ABC Model Development in the Automobile Industry', *Accounting, Organizations and Society*, 27: 195–221.

Atkinson, A. A., Kaplan, R. S., and Young, S. M. (2004). *Management Accounting*. Upper Saddle River, NJ: Prentice Hall.

Bhimani, A. (2003). 'A Study of the Emergence of Management Accounting System Ethos and Its Influence on Perceived System Success', *Accounting, Organizations and Society*, 28: 523–48.

Borcherding, T. and Filson, D. (2000). 'Conflicts of Interest in the Hollywood Film Industry: Coming to America—Tales from the Casting Couch, Gross and Net, in a Risky Business', *Claremont Colleges Working Papers in Economics*.

Braudy, L. (1997). *The Frenzy of Renown: Fame and Its History*. New York: Oxford University Press.

Bureau of Labor Statistics (2005). *Career Guide to Industries 2004–05 Edition*. Available at: http://www.bls.gov/oco/cg/pdf/cgs038.pdf. Accessed on 31 July 2005.

Caves, R. (2000). *Creative Industries: Contracts between Art and Commerce*. Cambridge, MA: Harvard University Press.

Chisholm, D. (1993). 'Asset Specificity and Long-Term Contracts: The Case of the Motion Picture Industry', *Eastern Economic Journal*, 19: 143–55.

Chisholm, D. (1997). 'Profit Sharing Versus Fixed-Payment Contracts: Evidence from the Motion Pictures Industry', *Journal of Law, Economics and Organization*, 13: 169–201.

—— (2004). 'Two-Part Share Contracts, Risk, and the Life Cycle of Stars: Some Empirical Results from Motion-Pictures Contracts', *Journal of Cultural Economics*, 28: 37–56.

Collette, L. (1998). 'The Wages of Synergy: Integration into Broadcast Networking by Warner Brothers, Disney, and Paramount', in B. Litman (ed.), *The Motion Picture Mega-Industry*. Boston: Allyn & Bacon, pp. 122–43.

Covaleski, M., Dirsmith, M., and Samuel, S. (2003). 'Changes in the Institutional Environment and the Institutions of Governance: Extending the Contributions of Transaction Cost Economics within the Management Control Literature', *Accounting, Organizations and Society*, 28: 417–42.

DeFillippi, R. J. and Arthur, M. B. (1998). 'Paradox in Project-Based Enterprise: The Case of Film Making', *California Management Review*, 40: 125–39.

De Vany, A. and Walls, W. D. (1997). 'The Market for Motion Pictures: Rank, Revenues, and Survival', *Economic Inquiry*, 35: 783–97.

—— —— (1999). 'Uncertainty in the Movies: Does Star Power Reduce the Terror of the Box Office?', *Journal of Cultural Economics*, 23: 285–318.

—— —— (2002). 'Does Hollywood Make Too Many R-Rated Movies? Risk, Stochastic Dominance, and the Illusion of Expectation', *Journal of Business*, 75: 425–51.

Dyson, S. (2004). *Global Film: Exhibition and Distribution*, 7th edn. London: Informa Telecoms & Media.

Economist (1998). 'A Brand New Strategy: The Industry Used to Produce Films, TV Programs, Books, and Music; Now It Makes Brands', 19 November: S5–8.

Goldman, W. (1989). *Adventures in the Screen Trade*. New York: Warner Books.

Gong, J., Van der Stede, W., and Young, S. M. (2005). 'Intangible Investments in the Creative Industries: A Study of the Motion Picture Industry', Working paper, University of Southern California.

Grigoriadis, V. (2005). 'Celebrity and Its Discontents: A Diagnosis'. Available at: www.newyorkmetro.com. Accessed on 21 July 2005.

Hayes, D. and Bing, J. (2004). *Open Wide: How Hollywood Box Office Became a National Obsession*. New York: Hyperion.

Jones, C. (1996). 'Careers in Project Networks: The Case of the Film Industry' , in M. B. Arthur and D. M. Rousseau (eds.), *The Boundaryless Career: A New Employment Principle for a New Organizational Era*. New York: Oxford University Press, pp. 58–75.

—— Lichtenstein, B., Hesterly, W., Borgatti, S., and Tallman, S. (1998). 'How Component Knowledge, Architectural Knowledge, and Social Capital Influence Project Performance: An Empirical Test from the Film Industry', *Organization Science*, 9: 396–410.

King, G. (2002). *New Hollywood Cinema: An Introduction*. New York: Columbia University Press.

Lehmann, D. R. and Weinberg, C. B. (2000). 'Sales via Sequential Distribution Channels: An Application to Movie Audiences', *Journal of Marketing*, 64: 13–33.

Leipzig, A. (2005). 'The Sundance Odds Get Even Longer'. Available at: www.nytimes.com. Accessed on 16 January 2005.

Litman, B. (1983). 'Predicting Success of Theatrical Movies: An Empirical Study', *Journal of Popular Culture*, 16: 159–75.

Litman, B. and Hoag, A. (1998). 'Merger Madness', in B. Litman (ed.), *The Motion Picture Mega-Industry*. Boston: Allyn & Bacon, pp. 97–121.

—— and Kohl, L. (1989). 'Predicting Financial Success of Motion Pictures: The '80s Experience', *Journal of Media Economics*, 2: 35–50.

MPAA (Motion Picture Association of America) (2005). *U.S. Entertainment Industry: 2004 MPAA Market Statistics*. Available at: www.mpaa.org.

Neale, B. and Allerston, A. (2005). 'Financial Control in the Film Production and Broadcasting Sector', *CIMA Research Bulletin*.

Porter, M. (1980). *Competitive Strategy*. New York: Free Press.

—— (1985). *Competitive Advantage*. New York: Free Press.

Ravid, S. A. (1999). 'Information, Blockbuster, and Stars: A Study of the Film Industry', *Journal of Business*, 72: 463–92.

—— and Basuroy, S. (2004). 'Managerial Objectives, the R-Rating Puzzle, and the Production of Violent Films', *Journal of Business*, 77: 155–92.

Screen Digest (2005). *Global Film Production and Distribution 2004*. London: Lynehense Studios.

Smith, S. P. and Smith, V. K. (1986). 'Successful Movies: A Preliminary Empirical Analysis', *Applied Economics*, 18: 501–7.

Sochay, S. (1994). 'Predicting the Performance of Motion Pictures', *Journal of Media Economics*, 7: 1–20.

Standard & Poor's (2005). *S&P Industry Surveys: Movies & Home Entertainment* (March).

Weinstein, M. (1998). 'Profit Sharing Contracts in Hollywood: Evolution and Analysis', *Journal of Legal Studies*, 27: 67–112.

Wyatt, J. (1991). 'High Concept, Product Differentiation, and the Contemporary U.S. Film Industry', in B. Austin (ed.), *Current Research in Film: Audiences, Economics, and Law*, 5. Norwood, NJ: Ablex.

Young, S. M. (forthcoming). *Entertainment Management: Understanding the Business of Motion Pictures, Television, Music and Games*. Upper Saddle River, NJ: Prentice Hall.

—— and Pinsky, D. (2005). 'Narcissism, Childhood Trauma and Substance Abuse Among Celebrities', Working paper, University of Southern California.

☐ INDEX